A HISTORY OF THE
UNITED STATES OF AMERICA

Volume Two

A HISTORY OF THE
UNITED STATES OF AMERICA

VOLUME ONE
The Search for Liberty
From Origins to Independence

VOLUME TWO
An Empire for Liberty
From Washington to Lincoln

VOLUME THREE
The American Dream
From Reconstruction to Reagan

An Empire for Liberty

From Washington to Lincoln

ESMOND WRIGHT

BLACKWELL
Oxford UK & Cambridge USA

First published 1995

Blackwell Publishers, the publishing imprint of
Basil Blackwell Ltd
238 Main Street
Cambridge, Massachusetts 02142
USA

108 Cowley Road
Oxford OX4 1JF
UK

Library of Congress Cataloging-in-Publication Data

Wright, Esmond.
An empire for liberty : from Washington to Lincoln / Esmond Wright.
   p.   cm. — (A History of the United States of America; v. 2)
Includes bibliographical references and index.
ISBN 1–55786–260–5
1. United States — History — 1783–1865.   I. Title.   II. Series:
Wright, Esmond. History of the United States of America; v. 2.
E301.W75   1995
973–dc20   93–42377
CIP

British Library Cataloguing in Publication Data

A CIP catalogue record for this book is available from the British Library.

Typeset in 11 on 13 pt Sabon Symposia by Apex Products, Singapore
Printed in Great Britain by T. J. Press Ltd, Padstow, Cornwall

This book is printed on acid-free paper

Contents

Maps

Plates

Chronologies

Foreword

This is the middle volume of what is becoming a three-volume saga: from Christopher Columbus to Ronald Reagan. It is the result of a lifetime of reading, teaching and research – with interruptions that were the consequence of World War II, of visits to the US to lecture or for research, and of political activity that led to a three-year spell as a Member of the House of Commons. The American story has, however, been my central interest, hobby, and pastime. I have been immensely aided in writing by Enid MacDonald, who has typed every word at least once, by Sarah McKean's skill as selector of illustrations, and by the care and zeal of Sue Martin as copy editor.

General Chronology

1785	Ordinance passed for sale of western lands.
1787	Constitutional Convention meets in Philadelphia; Northwest Ordinance provides for government of national domain.
1787–8	Alexander Hamilton *et al.* published *The Federalist Papers*, highly influential essays in support of the Constitution.
1788	Constitution ratified.
1789	George Washington elected first US President.
1790	First US Census shows population of 3.9 million.
1791–6	Hamilton–Jefferson feud leads to emergence of the first American party system (Federalists vs. Democratic-Republicans).
1793	Eli Whitney invents the cotton gin.
1794	General Anthony Wayne defeats Maumee River Indians at the battle of Fallen Timbers, and secures American control of Ohio; John Jay negotiates treaty with Britain (signed in 1795).
1795	Treaty of San Lorenzo with Spain secures 31st parallel as northern boundary of Florida.
1796	John Adams elected second US President.
1798	Alien and Sedition Acts; Kentucky and Virginia Resolutions.
1800	Thomas Jefferson (Democratic-Republican) elected third US President.
1803	Louisiana Purchase extends US border to Rocky Mountains.

1807	African slave trade to US abolished.
1808	James Madison elected fourth US President.
1812–14	War of 1812 against Britain.
1815–17	Collapse of Federalist party.
1820	Missouri Compromise excludes slavery from Louisiana Purchase Lands north of 36° 30'.
1823	Monroe Doctrine; James Fenimore Cooper, *The Pioneers.*
1824	Election of John Quincy Adams as sixth US President heralds break-up of Republican party.
1825	Erie Canal links Hudson River and Great Lakes.
1826	James Fenimore Cooper, *The Last of the Mohicans.*
1828	Noah Webster, *An American Dictionary of the English Language*; Andrew Jackson elected seventh US President.
1830	US population reaches c.13 million.
1831	Nat Turner uprising in Virginia; Edgar Allan Poe, *Poems.*
1832–3	Nullification Crisis leads to scaling-down of tariffs on imported goods.
1833	American Antislavery Society founded.
1835–40	Alexis de Tocqueville, *Democracy in America.*
1836	Colt pistol patented; Texas achieves independence from Mexico and becomes a sovereign republic.
1837	Ralph Waldo Emerson, 'The American Scholar'.
1840	Abolitionists launch Liberty party; William Henry Harrison (Whig) defeats Martin Van Buren (Democrat) in contest for US presidency.
1841	Horace Greeley launches *New York Tribune.*
1843	W. H. Prescott, *History of the Conquest of Mexico.*
1845	Annexation of Texas.
1846	Introduction of McCormick mechanical reaper; by agreement with Britain, US acquires control of Pacific Northwest up to the 49th parallel (Oregon Treaty).
1846–8	War with Mexico leads to acquisition of California and Pacific Southwest.
1849	California gold rush; Francis Parkman, *The Oregon Trail.*
1850	Nathaniel Hawthorne, *The Scarlet Letter*; Compromise of 1850; seventh US Census shows a population of 23 million.
1850–3	Collapse of Whig party.
1851	Herman Melville, *Moby-Dick*; *New York Times* launched.
1852	Harriet Beecher Stowe, *Uncle Tom's Cabin.*

1854	Kansas-Nebraska Act repeals Missouri Compromise; emergence of Republican party; Henry David Thoreau, *Walden*.
1855	First edition of Walt Whitman's *Leaves of Grass*.
1857	Supreme Court's Dred Scott decision denies citizenship to US blacks and right of Congress to exclude slavery from territories.
1859	John Brown's raid on arsenal at Harper's Ferry, Virginia.
1860	Abraham Lincoln (Republican) elected sixteenth US President.
1861	Secession of Southern states leads to outbreak of Civil War; Morrill Tariff inaugurates new high-tariff policy.
1862	Homestead Act.
1863	Emancipation Proclamation frees slaves in areas under rebel control.
1865	Surrender of Confederate forces; slavery abolished by Thirteenth Amendment; assassination of President Lincoln.

Introduction:
The New Nation,
Unique and Peculiar

In 1783, when Independence was won, the colonists were over-whelmingly English and Scots, with a few pockets of 'Scotch-Irish' (to use the American style) Dutch and Germans (or, to use the idiom again, Pennsylvanian Dutch); one in four of the settlers was a slave. English of a fashion was the language of the colonial frontier. That frontier, after 150 years of settlement, reached only some 150 miles inland, roughly along the line of the Green Mountains, the southern Great Lakes, the lands beyond the Blue Ridge in Virginia, the Great Smokies, with the long hunters probing the approaches to the Mississippi, the Father of Waters. But three frontier territories were soon to reach statehood; Kentucky in 1792, Tennessee in 1796, and Ohio in 1802. In 1825, when Chief Justice John Marshall was being entertained at a banquet in Kentucky, he was challenged to give a toast in rhyme containing the word *paradox*. He responded:

> In the Blue Grass region
> A paradox was born:
> The corn was full of kernels
> And the colonels full of corn.

The new nation was governed by gentlemen. They likened them-selves to the patricians who had ruled in Rome. All the early pres-idents, from Washington through John Quincy Adams, came from the eastern seaboard, and all except the first had a college education or its equivalent. Besides their preference for education, breeding, and simplicity, the statesmen of the early republic were like the Romans in another way. The old Romans were not the most artistic nor the cleverest people that history has seen, but they were strong in character, and part of their strength derived from a sense of mission. Likewise, the Americans of the early republic were crude and insensitive in some ways, but they too were strong and believed deeply in a God-given mission. This was no less than to launch, nourish, and make secure the world's greatest experiment in self-government. On the day he retired from the presidency in 1809, Thomas Jefferson reminded his fellow citizens:

... the station which we occupy among the nations of the earth is honorable, but awful. Trusted with the destinies of this solitary republic of the world, the only monument of human rights, and the sole depository of the sacred fire of freedom and self-government, from hence it is to be lighted up in other regions of the earth, if other regions of the earth shall ever become susceptible of its benign influence. All mankind ought then, with us, to rejoice in its prosperous, and sympathize in its adverse fortunes, as involving everything dear to man. And to what sacrifices of interest, or convenience, ought not these considerations to animate us? To what compromises of opinion and inclination to maintain harmony and union among ourselves and to preserve from all danger this hallowed ark of human hope and happiness.[1]

In language that was to be matched by no successor until Abraham Lincoln, Jefferson was proclaiming the mission of his country; and with greater solemnity than in his first Inaugural he was invoking the spirit of national unity in the face of greater danger than then existed.

1 THE NEW NATION

When the first census was taken in 1790, the population of the United States was found to be just over 3,900,000, of whom some 750,000 were slaves. Virginia was the largest of the states, its population some 750,000, of whom 40 percent were slaves.

The pattern of life was rural; compared with France, said Volney, the French traveler, in 1796, "the entire country is one vast wood." Land, however, was too fertile and too abundant to call yet for

[1] Jefferson's remarks of March 4, 1809, are in Saul Padover, *The Complete Jefferson* (New York, Duell, Sloane and Pearce, 1943), pp. 552–3.

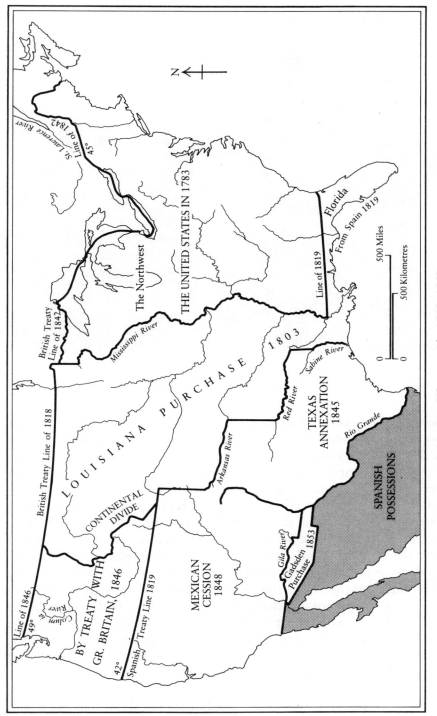

Map 1 US expansion 1783–1853.

Plate 1   John Whetton-Ehninger, *The Yankee Peddler* (1853).
(Collection of The Newark Museum. Gift of William F. Laport, 1925.)

scientific agriculture; there was no general rotation of crops, the plow
was crude, reaping and threshing were done by hand, the land was
quickly overworked. But there was, if small scientific knowledge,
a growing scientific interest. There were pioneer agricultural societies; new plants and fertilizers were discussed; the need for diversification and rotation of crops was accepted; there was growing
correspondence among the larger farmers. In the South, the production of cotton was hindered by the need to separate the fibers
from the seed by hand, and it was some time after Eli Whitney's
ingenious invention of the cotton gin to remove the seeds from the
short-staple cotton, that the door of opportunity was seen to be
open. In 1791 the total cotton production of the whole United States
was 400 bales. In 1810, it had become 178,000 bales. Not for the
first or last time, the south's resource was developed by a Yankee.
Although manufacturing was coming to be important – a number of
towns were already distinguished for special products: Danbury, Connecticut, for hats; Waterbury, Connecticut, for clocks and watches;
Lynn, Massachusetts, for shoes; Pittsburgh, for glass; and the towns

of western Pennsylvania and Virginia for iron manufacture – yet the merchant still stood above the manufacturer. The Yankee peddler still walked the rural roads.

In Washington's America, life was more than rural, it was rustic. The cloth used was mainly homespun: the North liked its "linsey-woolsey," a mixture of wool and flax, and the South "fustian" (flax and cotton) or "jean" (cotton and wool mixed.) Sugar too was home-made, from maple sap; and soap too. Most articles were home-made as much for reasons of defense as for reasons of lack of opulence, to use Adam Smith's distinction. William Cobbett noted that the appearance of the farm was neither so "neat" nor so "tight" as in England. Farther west, log cabins were the characteristic dwelling, standing in newly cleared fields that were full of stumps, or in the midst of dead and girdled trees. [2]

Cities were still few, and Philadelphia, with its paved streets and the beginnings of a water supply, was still the most important. Its population in 1790 stood at close to 40,000. It was, said John Adams, "the pineal gland" of the continent. The traveler Moreau de St Mery, who visited the United States in the 1790s, found it a fascinating place:

An inhabitant of Philadelphia, who in the beginning saw perhaps three carriages in the entire town, with only two or three vessels arriving from London in the course of a year and only a few small craft sailing to the colonies, has in the course of a lifetime seen the three carriages grow to three hundred, and twelve or fifteen vessels sailing daily for every port of the globe, even for the Antipodes.

There was small sign in 1790 of the future importance of New York, badly affected by the Revolution. Only 3 percent of the population lived in the six towns of more than 8,000 people (Philadelphia, New York, Boston, Charleston, Baltimore, and Salem). Although the wealthier citizens might live in brick houses of Georgian style, houses were mainly of wood, and lighted by candles. Glass for windows was rare: oiled paper was generally used. When the streets were lighted, it was by oil lamps, and they were not used in moonlight or rain. Sanitation was primitive. And town life was scarred each summer by the recurrent epidemics of yellow fever; the outbreak of 1793 led to the mass evacuation of Philadelphia and 10

---

[2] William Cobbett, "Energy and prosperity of American farmers," in Allan Nevins (ed.), *America Through British Eyes* (New York, Oxford University Press, 1968), p. 9.

percent of the population died. Again in 1797 there was a mood of panic in Philadelphia, and it was repeated in the epidemics in New York in 1798 and 1803. The "fevers" of high summer, not yet traced to the mosquito, seemed more menacing to the new republic than an army of Redcoats. Dr Benjamin Rush's remedies, although they included sanitary reforms, were almost as menacing as the fever itself: he favored bleeding and purging.

Except in the vicinity of Philadelphia and in Connecticut, communications were still poor. There were, of course, as yet no railways, and few good highways, and not until the 1790s did the first steamboat appear – John Fitch's far from successful operation on the Delaware. (The Founding Fathers had been privileged to see its trials in 1787.) Water communication was easier than that by land, and there were many canal projects, some of them fantastic. Until 1812 the shortage of capital was as much an obstacle to these developments as nature herself. Along the coast, travel by sea and river was favored. As a result, the roads that were built headed west. In the South, where capital went almost automatically into land and slaves, what roadbuilding there was was done by the states; to federal action for internal improvements there were constitutional objections. And progress over the mountains was slow. In the North, however, private turnpike companies appeared, levying tolls; by 1800 there were 72 of them. There were even some private bridge companies. But it was ferries and fords that the Virginia presidents had to use on their regular journeys to the North.

The lack of roads and scarcity of bridges had many consequences. It cost $30 and took at least four days to travel from Boston to New York. It took President Adams three days to reach the new federal city from Philadelphia in 1800. Postal services were haphazard; postal rates were high and were paid by the recipient. Even President Jefferson was apt to act as postman when he travelled north to Philadelphia. It was not until 1800 that a regular mail route was in use from Maine to Georgia, taking 20 days. In this isolation, political issues stayed stubbornly local.

The trans-Allegheny country suffered most. It was little explored as yet. Here nature, in Henry Adams's words, was still "Man's master rather than his servant." The Western farmer was cut off, remote from Eastern cities, from political centers, and from markets. Three major wagon roads crossed the Alleghenies in Pennsylvania, one to Pittsburgh, one from the Potomac River on to the upper reaches of the Monongahela, and the third which passed through Southwest Virginia on to Knoxville in Tennessee and through the Cumberland Gap into Kentucky. The obvious trade route was the

Mississippi. This raised social and political issues. Until steamboat days the route was long and costly, the profits slight. Meat and grain went down river on flatboats, with small but tough crews addicted to such sports as rough-and-tumble fighting and gouging. The boats were broken up and sold as lumber in New Orleans and the crews returned home on horseback or on foot through hostile country where they had need of all their fighting spirit. Until the Pinckney Treaty of 1795 Spain had a stranglehold on this trade and used it to tempt from their American allegiance the colorful but utterly untrustworthy men living on the Western waters.

The other expedient open to Westerners was to transform their grain into whiskey and to transport this by packhorse to Eastern markets. When Hamilton's excise tax, designed as a fiscal rather than a Puritan measure, imposed financial prohibition the corn was fed to hogs, and hogs on the hoof were driven from Ohio and Kentucky to their destination back East. It is not for nothing that the highway, and the mobility it brought with it, is the central feature of American life, the keystone of its economy and of its capacity to survive as a federal society. Equally it is no accident that the isolation and remoteness that were nature's gift to the Westerners made them independent and sturdy-minded, gregarious and unaddicted to privacy, rough and loud in manner, but warm and egalitarian.

This society, scattered and diverse though it was, lived a common and largely agricultural life. They lived by farming, fishing and hunting – and they were excellent marksmen, because they had to be, at the expense of squirrels and deer, wolves and beers, turkeys and wild pigeons. Manufacturing – except for iron – was on a small scale, short of capital and short of skilled craftsmen. It was as yet a primitive life, and European travellers, even as they saw America in the van of progress, noted the dirt, the lack of sanitation, and the poor roads. They noted too the monotonous if cheap and abundant food, and the high infant mortality, five or six times as high as it is today. The principal crop was Indian corn or rye, needed by the Germans for bread, by the Scotch-Irish for whiskey; the diet was based almost uniformly on rye or Indian bread, corn pone or hoecake, hasty pudding or hominy, and cod or salt pork. "Give me the children that's raised on good sound pork after all the game in the country," wrote Fenimore Cooper in *The Chainbearer*, describing America in 1784. "Game's good as a relish, and so's bread, but pork is the staff of life."

The uniformity of the beverages that went down with it was even more marked. The water was often undrinkable. Chastellux noted

Plate 2 Unknown artist, *Return from Town.*
(New York State Historical Association, Cooperstown. © New York State Historical Association, Cooperstown, NY.)

in 1780 the popularity of coffee But other beverages were more popular, and more native. The first temperance movement, some ten years later, was said to have been due to the disgust caused by the regular intoxication of ministers in their pulpits. Travellers in the South, such as John Bernard, described with zest the "diurnal potations," the mysteries of mint sling and bumbo, apple toddy or pumpkin flip. James Madison, by no means a sociable figure and not reckoned a toper, regularly drank a pint of whiskey a day, a goodly share of it before breakfast. Cobbett thought drinking the national disease: at all hours young men and "even little boys at or under twelve years of age go into stores and tip off their drams." Henry Adams, in commenting on this, notes that the mere comparison with Britain proves how great was the evil, for the English and the Scots were notoriously the largest consumers of beer and alcohol on the globe. Perhaps for this reason, few Americans lived long lives, and 50 was thought of as old. Those like Jefferson who reached 83, or like Adams who reached 91, were indeed men of parts.

If art was not yet much in evidence, there was a growing interest in nature. The first generation of artists were imitators rather than creators; Feke and Smibert were mannered and clumsy;

Peale, Copley, and Stuart were shaped more by London than by America. The architecture, too, was imitative, even if the South made Georgian and Palladian styles as gracious in their new settings as ever they were in the old. The models remained for a while stubbornly English, and there were as yet few of the graces. But there were many signs of promise and an irrepressible optimism. "After the first Cares for the Necessaries of Life are over, we shall come to think of the Embellishments," wrote Franklin. "Already some of our Young Geniuses begin to lisp Attempts at Painting, Poetry and Musick." For Jefferson himself, Philadelphia was never as attractive as Monticello. But the American Philosophical Society created by Benjamin Franklin had been refounded in 1769, and he found William Bartram, the naturalist and geologist, David Rittenhouse, the astronomer, Benjamin Rush, the doctor, and the Peale family, the artists, a highly congenial and like-minded group. They were interested in discovery and exploration; they were practically all of them deists in religion; and they had about their new nation in its unexplored continent an infinite curiosity; and there was among many of them a readiness to go out and explore it for themselves. St Mery makes the point that

Americans, indifferent · in love and friendship, cling to nothing, attach themselves to nothing. There is plenty of evidence of this among country dwellers. Four times running they will break land for a new home, abandoning without a thought the house in which they were born, the church where they learned about God, the tombs of their fathers, the friends of their childhood, the companions of their youth, and all the pleasures of their first society. They emigrate, especially from north to south, or toward the outermost western boundary of the United States on the Ohio. Everywhere, even in Philadelphia, which is America's outstanding city, everything is for sale, provided the owner is offered a tempting price. He will part with his house, his carriage, his horse, his dog — anything at all.

The embellishments were likely to be increasingly native. "Had I come to Europe sooner in Life I should have known nothing but the Receipts of Masters," said Benjamin West. Americans were beginning to pioneer and to take pride in the pioneering. Linnaeus drew on the work of John Bartram of Philadelphia, whose research won him a European reputation. Jared Eliot of Connecticut found English treatises on agriculture unsuitable to New England and wrote his own. Jefferson showed his questing mind in his *Notes on Virginia* and challenged Buffon. It has long been fashionable to trace the origins of Jeffersonian republicanism – inaccurately, it now seems – to a famous "botanical expedition" up the Hudson

River conducted by Jefferson and Madison in 1791. Cadwallader Colden also combined a taste for politics with an interest in natural history. John Winthrop set up a physics laboratory at Harvard. Benjamin Waterhouse pioneered in treating smallpox by inoculation. William Shippen and John Morgan had already established the first American medical school at Philadelphia in 1762.

The note was critical: it was also practical. Franklin's interests were in stoves for homes and cures for smoky chimneys, in fire companies and colleges, courants and almanacs. Reflecting the Enlightenment as expressed through the philosophical societies that sprang up on both sides of the Atlantic, Franklin and Jefferson shared an interest in flora and fauna, and in harnessing as well as discovering natural resources. By 1787 there were 15 colleges in being, and Harvard was already 140 years old; there were some 80 newspapers, and almost every village had a school of some sort.

The American people in 1790 lived close to nature. They had a strong sense of equality and small sense of class. Their measuring rod was not tradition but utility, not status but worth. They were better informed by newspapers than were Europeans; and from their pulpits, their town meetings, and their county courthouses they were addicted to talk and debate. They were democratic-minded and argumentative, articulate, and contentious.[3]

2   IN DIXIELAND

In the New World, the most striking, indeed unique, feature was not the utopia of the West or New England's literati, but the cotton kingdom of the South. The term was used of the 15 slave-holding states south of the Mason-Dixon Line, but it implied a unity that did not exist. Southerners produced a wide range of crops, the most important of which, both in value and acreage employed, was corn.

Easy to produce, corn fed the farmer and his livestock, and was the major item in the diet of slaves. Unlike the North, where the range of food produced was more diverse, the failure of the corn crop in the South was viewed as a catastrophe. The Deep South simply did not produce enough corn for its needs; the result was an importation of the grain that tightened the economic interdependence of the South and West.

[3] Thomas L. Purvis, "The European ancestry of the United States population 1790;" Symposium, *William & Mary Quarterly*, 41.1 (Jan. 1984), and Forum, "The standard of living in North America," ibid., 45.1 (Jan. 1988).

In South Carolina and Georgia, extensive attention was given to rice production, while lower Louisiana focused its energy on sugar. In the upper South, particularly in Virginia, Maryland, and North Carolina, tobacco, although plagued with problems, remained a major crop; but in Virginia its value was exceeded several times by that of the wheat crop. Hemp played a significant role in Kentucky, where it was grown to provide bagging and rope for baling cotton. In addition, large herds of cattle and other livestock roamed the southern pines and the grasslands of Texas. The preoccupation with staple crops had one consequence that all visitors to the antebellum South noted: wealth and poverty existed in an uneasy tandem.

Of all Southern production, cotton had the largest impact on the world's economy, and as a money earner it was king. In 1860, as in years before, about 75 percent of the cotton crop was exported. The return on the sale of raw cotton constituted well over half of American foreign earnings.

Cotton was greedy for ever fresh land, and when the soil showed signs of exhaustion, the Southern farmer shifted his attention to yet more new land. It was a ruthless form of soil mining that gave to Southern agriculture a nomadic quality; planters took it for granted that they would decamp and push westward to richer lands. The pressure for a quick return on their effort, particularly in frontier regions, tended to encourage planters to exploit the soil, an asset that was both cheap and seemingly limitless. Misuse of the soil further accentuated the dominance of a few large planters who could afford to rotate their crops or rest their fields.

No single aspect of antebellum Southern life impressed itself more upon history than the plantation. The great manor houses of the James River, or of South Carolina's Ashley and Cooper Rivers, are generally recalled as the visible symbols of the quality of antebellum life. To dwell in one of these houses was the aspiration of untold numbers of Southern planters, who regarded it as the final mark of achievement. Equally impressive were the vast buildings that housed cotton presses and provided storage space for the products that underscored the plantation's existence. The twofold symbols of plantation life were the many-columned mansion and the mill smokestack; in fact the former existed because of the latter.

Throughout the decades leading up to the Civil War, landholdings throughout the United States tended to decline in acreage, but in the cotton-producing South the process was reversed. This was especially true in the fertile regions such as the Black Belt of Alabama. In the lush delta country of Louisiana, Mississippi, and Arkansas, holdings of as much as 25,000 acres were recorded. Similar holdings of great value were characteristic of the rice regions. An investment of from \$50,000 to \$500,000 was usual for rice plantations, and estates of from 300 to more than 1,000 slaves were commonplace. But the rice country, particularly that of South Carolina, was suffering a decline before the Civil War, a development which encouraged planters to sell their slaves to cotton plantations or to switch part of their investment to cotton culture.

The self-assured great planters, although but a tiny proportion of the total southern population, dominated politics, society, the Church, and the means of information. Increasingly inbred, they made small effort to ingratiate themselves with their less fortunate neighbors. Only the antipathy of the yeomanry to the slave prevented an extreme conflict; on one point Southern whites were in general agreement: the black had to be kept in subjugation.

Remote from his market and often preoccupied with the details of administering his plantations, the Southern planter was obliged to rely on an outside agent, the factor, to manage his sales, finances, and purchases. These agents, working out of interior cotton markets, were willing to buy cotton on the spot, relieving the planter of shipping costs. The larger planters tended to ship their bales to the great cotton ports of New Orleans, Charleston, Savannah, and Mobile. There prices were more competitive. The credit obtained from sales was then used to cover the cost of supplies, household goods, and luxuries that the planter might require.

The dependence of the planter upon his factor was accentuated by his inability normally to obtain direct credit. To meet his need for funds he had to work through the factor, who in turn was dependent upon credit sources located in New York and Liverpool. Not infrequently disputes broke out between planter and factor. The factor frequently had to meet his own obligations, and his pressures upon planters to deliver a specific crop were aimed at assuring him steady access to credit in the North or abroad. The relationship was further complicated by the tendency of most planters to run into debt in expectation of good crops and high prices. But most damaging to the stability of the southern economy was the preoccupation of the planter with expanding his slave force.

Equally striking was the peculiar institution of slavery. It was a system that perplexed most Southerners, who recognized that they were hard pressed to reconcile enslavement and the principles of equality and Christianity upon which the nation was based. But whatever the misgiving of Southerners, in the decades before the Civil War, and particularly after 1830, open criticism of the institution was scarce. Nonetheless, slavery affected every aspect of Southern life. It gave the region a social stratification which legitimates the description of Southern antebellum society as a caste system. For as slavery defined the scope of a man's property, slave ownership, which was confined to a small minority of Southerners, accentuated the wide divergence in property holdings throughout the South. Of the more than 8 million Southern whites in 1850, only 384,884 owned slaves, and 88 percent of the total slaveholders owned fewer than 20 slaves; of this number, more than 200,000 owned 5 slaves or less. But these figures are deceptive. Some 300 slaveholders owned more than 200 slaves, and 2,300 were masters of 100 or more. This group probably owned in excess of 500,000 slaves, a property valued in 1850 at more than $250 million. This meant a *per capita* holding in slave property alone of about $100,000.

In the whole South approximately a quarter of all whites belonged to families that held slave property, but the proportion varied from state to state. Generally in the Deep South, holdings involved from one-third to a half of all whites, while in the upper South, the proportion ranged from 1 in 30 to a quarter. Similarly, the distribution of slaves was uneven within the states; invariably the heaviest concentrations were in counties that produced huge staple crops.

Criticisms about slavery came from within the system. These ranged from the charge that the existence of slavery degraded white labor to the argument that slave labor was inefficient. Critiques emphasized that the heavy investment in slaves diverted capital from more productive commercial and industrial enterprises. Most treated slavery as a social system designed to regulate the relations between the races.

Obviously, for the large holders, the return would be handsome, but emphasis upon bookkeeping profits does not come to grips with the question of whether slavery adversely affected the whole South. If nothing else, the distribution of slave ownership indicates that the returns benefited only a minority of the whites, and since the institution confined the development of alternative economic options, it reduced a substantial part of the white population to a subsistence-level livelihood.

The cost of maintaining a slave rarely exceeded $35 annually, and much of this expenditure was a payment in kind. The slave diet was rude and unvaried but adequate, a description which also applied to the shelter provided. The annual clothing ration ordinarily consisted of two cotton shirts, a pair of woolen pants and jacket, and heavy work shoes for a man; a woman received 12 yards of material, thread and needle, and work shoes. Provision was also made for their medical care. In providing care for their slaves, the planter was not acting from philanthropic impulse; his motive was economic: each slave was an entry in the credit side of the plantation ledger. Rather than risk the life of his slaves in performing dangerous work, planters frequently hired white labor, often Irish and German immigrants.

There were slave revolts — but few and erratic. In 1822 Denmark Vesey led a rebellion in Charleston, South Carolina which was rapidly crushed; in 1831 the more serious riot in Southampton County, Virginia, led by Nat Turner, killed 55 whites before it was suppressed — stimulating the major debate in the Virginia legislature over the rights and wrongs of slavery.

3   JEFFERSON: WHITE AND BLACK?

As with the patricians in Rome, slavery was a fact of life. It has been thoroughly analysed by recent scholars, as part of the fashion of our own times. The study of Thomas Jefferson reveals the slavery problem at its most intimate level. Jefferson's views were not only analyzed but psychoanalyzed by Winthrop D. Jordan in *White Over Black: American attitudes toward the Negro, 1550–1812*,[4] an exhaustive and brilliant examination of source materials of great bulk and variety. According to its author, whites on both sides of the Atlantic regarded the Negro as sexually aggressive, intellectually inferior, and physically dangerous. Although these attitudes had many origins, color was a main ingredient. In sixteenth-century England, "black was an emotionally partisan color, the handmaid and symbol of baseness and evil, a sign of danger and repulsion." Jordan argues that such notions persisted to the period of the American Enlightenment, and in a section on Jefferson he brings out the sexual implications in white attitudes. The white man's professed repulsion at Negro sexuality was, he argues, really a projection of his own suppressed desires. It was the white who committed aggression, but instead of recognizing his own guilt he blamed the Negro's libidinous nature. Jordan's analysis is based primarily on *Notes on the State of Virginia* written by Jefferson in 1781–2, in reply to questions from François Barbe-Marbois, secretary of the French legation in Philadelphia. This compendium — sometimes called Jefferson's only

[4] Winthrop Jordan, *White Over Black: American attitudes to the Negro, 1550–1812* (Chapel Hill, NC, University of North Carolina Press for Institute of Early American History and Culture [hereafter IEAHC] 1968), p. 477.

"book" – discusses the geology, geography, history, and resources of Virginia. Such a wide-ranging inquiry inevitably included a discussion of slavery and its effects on both whites and blacks.

Much attention has recently been paid to Jefferson's private life, and he has been frequently charged with having a slave as his concubine. This accusation owed its origin not to British commentators or to Mrs Trollope, but to the Federalist journalist writing in the *Richmond Recorder* newspaper, James Thomson Callender, whom Jefferson had at first befriended, but who was later jailed. When Jefferson became President – and before – Callender and a bunch of highly partisan journalists blackened his reputation, and charged, *inter aliis*, that he kept "as his concubine, one of his own slaves." In 1803, the popular Irish poet Thomas Moore used the story in a book he wrote after a tour of the fledgling America, using it to illustrate hypocrisy, with Jefferson "dreaming of freedom in his slave's embrace." The theme was taken up by, among others, Mrs Frances Trollope, mother of novelist Anthony Trollope, in her book *Domestic Manners of the Americans (1832)*, which was a sensation on both sides of the Atlantic. Mrs Trollope wrote that Jefferson was a "most heartless libertine," who was "the father of children by almost all his numerous gang of female slaves." It is good juicy stuff – and the viciousness of the attacks on the Man in the White House has continued ever since (it was in fact the intensity of the heat in the kitchen that led Washington to give up the presidency four years before, and thus, inadvertently, establish "the two-term tradition".) What are the facts?

Sally Hemings was one of a family of ten slaves, whose mother Betty was herself the daughter of an English sea-captain and an African Negress. Jefferson acquired them all in 1774, on the settlement of the estate of his father-in-law, John Wayles. Many of them were strikingly light in color, and all were skilled – some of them as craftsmen, masons, or carpenters, others as domestics. Two of Betty's daughters, Gritta and Sally, worked permanently at Jefferson's Virginia mansion, Monticello. There is every likelihood that Sally, and some of her siblings, were the children of John Wayles, and that Sally was thus the half-sister of Jefferson's wife, to whom he was devoted, for whom he built Monticello, and whose death in 1782 left him shattered (he was then 39). Sally had been a house-slave at Monticello since 1774, when she was 14. It was natural that when his wife died, Jefferson should ask Sally to look after his two young children, to whom she was thus related. She accompanied them to Paris as companion in 1784, when Jefferson succeeded Benjamin Franklin as ambassador.

Jefferson ignored Callender's charges as coming from the "vengeful pen of an unscrupulous man;"[5] and Callender in fact committed suicide a year after publishing his rumors. The reason that led the President to ignore the charges was not only that he deemed them unworthy of notice, and that his public reputation for fastidiousness and for devotion to his dead wife's memory was well established; but that to respond would have given attention to what he saw as obvious calumnies. The most likely "guilty man," if one can rely on the oral traditions among the slaves themselves, was not the President but Peter Carr, Jefferson's favourite nephew whom he treated as a son. In his will, the President freed all the Hemings whom he thought had the necessary skills as artisans and craftsmen to allow them to survive in the free and competitive world outside; for the plight of the free blacks — much more than of the field- or the house-slaves — was the most difficult and most complex aspect of the slave system.

What light does the writing throw on this one personality involved in the most complex issue of his times? In 1974 the late Fawn Brodie's *Thomas Jefferson: An intimate history* revived the unprovable charge that Jefferson kept a slave mistress at Monticello and fathered her five children. Despite the fact that Mrs Brodie produced no new evidence, her biographical account gained wide popular acceptance. By 1979, when Barbara Chase-Riboud published her novel, *Sally Hemings*, the sexual liaison between Jefferson and his slave mistress was widely taken as based on historical fact. In *The Jefferson Scandals: A Rebuttal*, Virginius Dabney has gathered the evidence surrounding the charge against Jefferson.[6] He pointed

[5] In the words of the best Jefferson scholar to date, the late Dumas Malone, *Jefferson and His Times*, vol. IV, *Jefferson the President, the First Term* (Boston, Little, Brown, 1970), p. 214.
[6] Fawn Brodie, *Thomas Jefferson: An intimate history* (New York, Menton Books, 1974; Edmund S. Morgan, *American Slavery, American Freedom: The ordeal of colonial Virginia* (New York, Norton, 1975); Scot French and Edward L. Ayers, "The strange career of Thomas Jefferson: race and slavery in American memory, 1943–1993," in Peter Onuf (ed.), *Jeffersonian Legacies* (Charlottesville, University of Virginia Press, 1993), pp. 418–56. The most powerful indictments of Jefferson's record on slavery include Robert McColley, *Slavery and Jeffersonian Virginia* (Urbana, University of Illinois Press, 1964; 2nd edn, 1973); William Cohen, "Thomas Jefferson and the problem of slavery," *Journal of American History*, 56 (1969), pp. 503–26; John Chester Miller, *The Wolf by the Ears: Thomas Jefferson and Slavery* (New York, Free Press, 1977); David Grimstead, "Anglo-American racism and Phillis Wheatley's 'Sable Veil,' 'Lengthen'd Chain,' and 'Knitted Heart,'" in Ronald Hoffman and Peter J. Albert (eds), *Women in the Age of the American Revolution* (Charlottesville, 1989), pp. 338–444, esp.

out that it was perpetuated first in *Clotel, Or the President's Daughter*, a novelization published in 1853 by the former slave, William Wells Brown, and then in belated, possibly doctored, interviews given in old age by two former Monticello slaves, one of them a son of Sally Hemings who claimed Jefferson as his father. Counter-evidence comes from Jefferson's descendants as well as from a former manager of Monticello (from 1804 to 1820), who asserted that the father of Sally Hemings's children was one of Jefferson's nephews. Dabney includes in his account the scholarly reviews of Fawn Brodie's book, most of which, unlike the favorable press notices, pronounced her case unprovable. Finally, he adds his own "rebuttal," or, more accurately, dismissal, of Brodie's suppositions.

Despite Dabney's tendency to substitute a tone of incredulous sarcasm for a careful exposition of the flaws in Brodie's presentation, he is obviously in the right. Henceforth it is hardly conceivable that the slave-mistress charge will be regarded as anything more than a conjecture, albeit a fascinating one. And yet, by approaching the subject as an apologist rather than as a disinterested historian, Dabney has unintentionally raised other questions about Jefferson's life and the manner in which it has been treated by historians.

In the first place, concerned as he is exclusively with the defense of Jefferson, Dabney ignores the role played by historians in the popular acceptance of Brodie's thesis. Thus, in an article published in 1976 and quoted but not commented on by Dabney, a scholar looking over the reception of Brodie's *Jefferson* by historians, observed: "What is striking is that professional reviews were so gentle; the book suffers from serious flaws, defects noted by remarkably few reviewers."

"Gentle" is the right word, for the historians were obviously clear in their own minds about the factitiousness of Brodie's account. But they also knew that she had made something of a feminist issue out of her case. She had represented herself as entering the male bastion of Jefferson studies and bringing to it a specifically feminine appreciation of "feeling" and "nuance." By 1979, when Chase-Riboud's novelization appeared, this notion of woman's intuition had become anathema among feminists. But at that point, to attack a novel that was at once a cry of outrage against male oppression and an apotheosis of Sally Hemings as Jefferson's most

---

pp. 414–36; and Paul Finkelman, "Jefferson and slavery: Treason Against the Hopes of the World,' " in Onuf, *Jeffersonian Legacies*, pp. 181–221.

intimate companion, hardly made for a more attractive prospect. Nevertheless, unpleasant as the task of criticism undeniably was, historians had a responsibility to speak out, which they once again shirked.

Nor is Dabney interested, any more than were Brodie or Chase-Riboud, in the broader implications of Sally Hemings' presence at Monticello – a matter of far greater import than the titillating question of her relationship to Jefferson. Although Dumas Malone was right to dismiss the rumors about Sally Hemings, the issue could hardly be dropped there, for it pointed up the deeply problematic circumstances of Jefferson's life at Monticello. For, whatever his relationship with Sally Hemings, Jefferson in his day-to-day life was closely involved with her three brothers and sister, whom he acquired together with her when he married. Two of the boys became his personal servants, travelling with him when he went to Philadelphia to write about the meaning of freedom (in the Declaration of Independence), and to Europe where he championed the same cause as a diplomat. Sally Hemings, her brothers, and her sister were by all accounts fathered by Jefferson's father-in-law; and thus Jefferson's wife, whether she knew it or not, brought with her to Monticello three boys who were her half-brothers and two girls who were her half-sisters. All were her slaves.

Mrs Jefferson brought other relatives with her to Monticello as well: a half-brother and two half-sisters of Sally Hemings. Where the others were light-skinned, these two girls were black. Eventually both the mulatto and black slaves had children – nieces and nephews of Mrs Jefferson – who grew up as slaves. They all apparently acted as house servants or skilled workers on the plantation rather than being sent to labor in the fields. Jefferson's personal servant in his last years was one of his wife's (black) nephews. Finally there were the nearly white children of Sally Hemings and her sister, probably fathered by Jefferson's two nephews from nearby plantations.

It seems evident that Jefferson did his best to resolve the moral contradictions in which he was enmeshed. Certainly he pursued the most humane policies that the circumstances permitted. He allowed his nearly white slave relatives to run away, set others free after they had served apprenticeships calculated to prepare them for the world, and set still others free in his will. After all, he could not afford to grant freedom for too many, lest he go bankrupt and put the others in danger of being sold into a worse condition of slavery. Yet the more enlightened his policies, the more vivid grew the contradictions. Thus when Jefferson returned home after nearly five years in Europe, the slaves from his three plantations voluntarily gathered at Monticello to greet him. They rushed forward, unhitched the horses of the carriage bearing him and his two daughters, and dragged it to the entrance. Then, kissing his hands and feet, they bore him in their arms into the house. These acts of self-abasement were being performed by blood cousins of Jefferson's own daughters.

It is in the lights of such contradictions between Jefferson's ideas and his practical behavior that his putative affair with Sally Hemings must be viewed. Dabney, in allowing the issues to become narrowed to the question of Sally Hemings alone, has in effect adopted the perspective of Brodie, Chase-Riboud, and the popular press. The true Jefferson scandals concern the abrogation of scholarly responsibilities, first on the part of those who failed to speak out forthrightly about Brodie's thesis, and then by those who, though narrowly correct in their dismissals, have failed to deal with its implications.

Jefferson hated slavery, it is true, but he never freed the majority of his slaves. Moreover, as historians in the 1960s pointed out, he bought, sold, bred, and flogged his slaves, and hunted for fugitives in much the same way his fellow Virginia planters did. These may seem like small trivial matters, but they are not – not where Jefferson is involved; for the nature of American society itself is at stake. The shame and guilt that Jefferson presumably suffered because of his secret love, Brodie suggested, were the same shame and guilt white Americans have always felt in their tortured relations with blacks. History seems to support her.

People see America in Jefferson. When Garry Wills in his *Inventing America*[7] argued that Jefferson's Declaration of Independence owed less to the possessive individualism of Locke and more to the communitarian sentiments of Francis Hutcheson, one critic accused Wills of aiming "to supply the history of the Republic with as pink as dawn as possible." The Jefferson that emerges out of much recent scholarship thus resembles the America that many have visualized in recent years – self-righteous, guilt-ridden, racist, doctrinaire, and filled with liberal pieties that under stress are easily sacrificed. This is not the America or the Jefferson that Dumas Malone has evoked in his study. His Jefferson is a very different symbol – designed not to provoke passions but to calm them. His is the Jefferson that Jefferson would have liked: temperate, rational, and balanced, a man who was "one of the most notable champions of freedom and enlightenment in recorded history."

---

[7] Garry Wills, *Inventing America: Jefferson's Declaration of Independence* (New York, Doubleday, 1978).

If Jefferson failed to solve his personal problems, all he could do was to live with them — is it not usually so? At least in his balance sheet, it can be added that he contrived to double the extent of American territory by the purchase of Louisiana. It was a remarkable, if lucky, *coup.* In 1803, Napoleon Bonaparte, the First Consul of France, sold to the US a vast and ill-defined region between the Mississippi River and the Rocky Mountains for — territory that had been returned to France by Spain in 1800 — for the sum of $15 million. With good reason, the treaty has been called the greatest real estate bargain in history; but at the time the only part of the area important to the United States was New Orleans; control of this city gave farmers in the American West the unrestricted right to float their produce down the Mississippi on rafts and small boats, and to store it until it could be transferred to ocean-going ships. Of the former Spanish West, the maps were few and sketchy: but it was recognized as vast in extent and resources.

On November 7, 1805, Captain William Clark wrote in his journal: "Great joy in camp we are in view of the Ocian, this great Pacific Ocean which we been so long anxious to See." In the face of fantastic difficulties, the party led by Meriwether Lewis and Clark had made the first overland journey to the mouth of the Columbia River and by this, as Bernard DeVoto points out, "gave not only Oregon but the entire West to the American people as something with which the mind could deal." The territory they had crossed, taking 18 months on the way, was "a blank, not only on the map but in human thought ... an area of rumor, guess and fantasy." They camped on high ground on the shore of the state that ought to be named Jefferson, but is, alas, called Washington.[8]

Jefferson, understanding that the West must become American, had long dreamed of despatching such an expedition as he had earlier told the American Philosophical Society; the purchase of Louisiana from Napoleon made the mission more urgent, though Congress had already given its approval to the project in secret six months before the French foreign minister Talleyrand staggered James Monroe, whom Jefferson had sent to France with a plan to buy New Orleans, by offering him an area twice the size of the United States at a price of roughly 3 cents an acre. Jefferson's detailed directive to Lewis shows remarkable vision and imagination. The main purpose of the mission was "to explore the Missouri river,

[8] *The Journals of Lewis and Clark*, ed. Bernard DeVoto (Cambridge, MA, Houghton Mifflin, 1953), p. 279.

and such principal stream of it, as, by it's course and communication with the waters of the Pacific Ocean, may offer the most direct and practicable water communication across this continent, for the purposes of commerce." In short, Lewis was to find a route which would break the Canadian monopoly of the fur trade, and perhaps provide a short cut to China which would eliminate the long beats round the Capes Horn or Good Hope. In addition, he was to define the new boundaries of the United States, make contact with the Indians, and collect data on the geography, climate, vegetation, and animal life of this vast acquisition.

This expedition is undoubtedly one of the most fascinating and important chapters in human exploration, and its success was primarily due to the cool confidence, competence and courage of its leaders. As the party poled and dragged its boats up the Missouri from Fort Mandan, where it had spent the first winter, it had to learn the techniques of survival or perish: how to deal with different Indian tribes, to live on roots, to build crude carts to portage the canoes round the Great Falls. Their difficulties at this point are calmly described in this entry by Clark:

... those not employed in repairing the course, are asleep in a moment, maney limping from the soreness of their feet some become faint for a few moment, but no man complains all go chearfully on. To state the fatigues of this party would take up more of the journal than other notes which I scarcely find time to set down.

Wet, hungry, ill, exhausted; these were the normal rigors. Supplies ran very low, Lewis had to give away his uniform coat in barter for a canoe the party needed desperately, and his men cut off their buttons to trade for dried fish. The Indians stole from them; they were misled about the route ahead; they were constantly anxious about their food, their powder, their instruments, journals, charts, and the specimens Lewis was collecting for the President.

Yet, sharing these difficulties, was a young Indian girl — married to Charbonneau, one of the interpreters — and her baby boy, only two months old when they left the Mandan villages. Sacajawea, who was a Snake Indian, proved an invaluable asset when the party began the crossing of the Rockies, because horses were needed, and these could only be obtained from the Snakes, who were so suspicious of an ambush that they evaded every effort Lewis made to get in touch with them. Then came a fantastic coincidence. Lewis persuaded a young Snake chief to go back with him to the main group so that he could talk to him through an interpreter; he turned out to be the brother of Sacajawea, who had been seized several years before by a raiding party of Minnetarees. The party got its horses.

In 20 months they had traveled 4,000 miles, mostly by water, from St Louis. They had traced the Missouri to its source, crossed the Rockies, and picked up the Columbia River and followed it to the ocean. They had thus confirmed Jefferson's theory, comfortably maintained at home in Virginia, that at the peak of a watershed the headwaters of the main rivers that run east and west are more or less linked. It was intelligent of Jefferson to guess it, and heroic of Lewis and Clark to endure it. In so doing the party had become the first men known to have crossed the continent by its waterways. They mapped and opened the whole mainland of America to commerce and assured that the young United States should hold it.

Jefferson worried over the constitutional legitimacy of his act in authorizing the expedition, but not over its fascination or its potential. "An empire of liberty," he called it; certainly it was extensive, and only inhabitable by industrious and fortunate men, who would do more, and enjoy life more, if they were free men.

4 AN EMPIRE OF LIBERTY

When Jefferson retired from the presidency he returned to Virginia and never again left it. In fact, he virtually never again lost sight of his beloved Blue Ridge. He became more narrow-minded and localist than he had ever been in his life.

Decay was everywhere in early nineteenth-century Virginia and Jefferson felt it at Monticello. His debts kept mounting and he kept borrowing, taking out new loans to meet old ones. He tried to sell his land, and when he could not he sold slaves instead. He was, as Malone says, "a mass of contradictions." He complained continually of his debts, but refused to cut back on his lavish hospitality and expensive wine purchases. Unable to comprehend the economic forces that were transforming the country and destroying the upper South, Jefferson blamed the banks and the speculative spirit of the day for both his and Virginia's miseries.

These were only cracks in his optimism, only tinges of doubt in his democratic faith, but for an innocent like him these were enough. Jefferson went further in his state-rights principles and in his fears of federal consolidation than did his friend James Madison, because he had so much higher expectations of the Revolution and the people. He had always invested so much more of himself intellectually and emotionally in the future and in popular democracy than Madison had. Madison never lost his dark foreboding about the America yet to come, and he never shed his skepticism about the people and popular majorities. But Jefferson had nothing but the people and the future to fall back on; they were really all he ever believed in. That is perhaps why we remember Jefferson far more than Madison. Or perhaps it was that Madison, less the grand seigneur and more the egalitarian, was also more realistic. His experiences both in Orange County among the Presbyterians and as secretary of state bred a cynicism missing in Jefferson.

Jefferson was a patrician dressed as democrat, a scholar, a geologist and naturalist, a gardener, an architect, an estate-owning and self-managing aristo. Like many of his companions, he had a small army of slaves. Jefferson's "canine appetite for reading," as he called it, was insatiable. Works of classical antiquity "in the beauties of their originals" seemed to have priority, and he never lost his taste for Homer and Virgil. He was equally at home in French, Italian, and Spanish, however, and not only read the classics in those languages and English, but kept up remarkably well with writers of his own era. He had promised to forgo newspapers for Tacitus and Thucydides, but it is obvious that he followed current events as avidly in retirement as ever. His correspondence through the war and peace of this turbulent period is an illuminating commentary on the history of the times at home and abroad. The historian Gilbert Chinard called Jefferson's literary legacy "the richest treasure house of information ever left by a single man."

With Andrew Jackson, the seventh President, we enter another world; still more so, with Lincoln and the threat of secession. But one feature of our times is the respect paid by the scholarly foundations and the federal government to the preservation of the papers of the presidents and the Founding Fathers, and the editorial skills such generosity has supported. It has been the legacy of the New Deal, and it has altered public attitudes outside libraries and universities as well as inside them. For it was not until the advent of the New Deal that Jefferson – with Adams and Wilson, the only intellectuals among America's great statesmen – became a secular saint to his predominantly activist nation. In 1937, when the New Deal was at its height, American hagiography underwent certain changes. The traditional buffalo and Indian head disappeared from the five-cent piece and in their place nickels bore on one side a portrait of Thomas Jefferson and on the other a picture of his house, Monticello. At about the same time the method of American stamp issue was rearranged, the first president's portrait appeared on the one-cent issue, Adams on the two-cent, while Jefferson took the place of Washington on the ubiquitous three-cent stamp. And, in America's capital, a pompous marble temple was hurried to completion: the Jefferson Memorial, equal and complementary to the Lincoln and Washington memorials.

In the New Deal years Jefferson was seen as in many ways the outstanding exemplar of America's greatness, and, at the same time, the symbol of America's tragedy. In Malone's *Life*, Jefferson's failure is as obvious as his success. In his thought as in his life there were weaknesses – he was, for example, inclined to accept *laissez-faire* policies; but if Jeffersonian doctrine had been accepted by Americans, utility could not have become the aim of American education, American politics, and American social life. The New Deal Administration was naturally disinclined to accentuate Jefferson's failings, and over-eager to equate Jeffersonian ideals with Rooseveltian achievement; but, as Jefferson more than any other Revolutionary leader created Americanism, so did the New Deal more than any previous administration attempt to revive Jefferson's standards, and to pay heed to the warnings that he had given 150 years earlier. Other American regimes, Lincoln's among them, had contrived to muster Jefferson as a ghostly supporter (and ultimately every political and social philosophy thought out by Americans for America must measure itself against a Jeffersonian yardstick), but none with such skill or with such success as did the New Deal.

The first president – for his own selfish reasons – had his capital city built in its swamp, which was not far from his own home and his plantation. For the new nation it was a brave project, and constructed by a Frenchman in a fashion to curb the tumults and riots that were then endemic in his native land. Nowadays, when Congressmen have time to take the air and stroll amid the endless traffic outside their debating halls, they run the risk of physical assault if they take the wrong direction, and particularly if they walk; for Washington like most big cities across the world, is now an unsafe place to stroll. Jefferson never did like cities – though he can never have foreseen the riots to which they now are prone (but it should be added that, he held, if blacks were to be free, they should live in a separate community). But if Congressmen find that walking is permissible, they can enjoy sights which vividly enshrine their country's own history, short though it has been: the Monument in its stark majesty that recalls a reticent, courageous, if ill-educated, founder-president; the square that surrounds the White House and testifies to the foreign volunteers who fought for

American independence – Lafayette, Kosciusko, Pulaski; and the two monuments to two of the greatest and most philosophic of the immortals, Jefferson and Lincoln.

Visitors from England in the early nineteenth century, however, came up with barbed impressions. For them, it seemed, American government was not by gentlemen but by King Mob – although De Tocqueville recognized that, in all its novelty, it held a pattern for the future everywhere. The vast trans-Mississippi west – unmapped as yet, and unexplored – was *terra incognita* and "an empire of liberty." But not quite so: it was terrain for trusted scouts to map and explore, to whom the President could be part Ralegh, part Maecenas; and those who were first there were rarely themselves free; captive Indians, black slaves, restless scouts, those nominally free who, too often, found it hard to verify their status, and were treated as runaways. But it was empty land, and much of it treeless, inviting free men to settle and to exploit; and it was cheap, even free, for the comer. It was an empire for such, if not yet of them.

The "empire of liberty" that Jefferson envisaged was one with that described in the second number of *The Federalist*:

a people descended from the same ancestors, speaking the same language, professing the same religion, attached to the same principles of government, very similar in their manners and customs, and who, by their joint counsels, arms, and efforts, fighting side by side throughout a long and bloody war, have nobly established general liberty and independence.

But the Jeffersonian Empire of Liberty was more than this. Language, religion, customs, and traditions shared in common indubitably provided the sense of commonalty essential to nationhood, but an insistence upon uniformity might also be equated with tyranny. Toward tyranny in any form Jefferson had vowed eternal hostility, and in his Empire of Liberty, therefore, tolerance of diversity was implicit. Nowhere did he express this better than in a letter to Dr Joseph Priestley, the clergyman-scientist whom he recognized as a kindred spirit:

As the storm is now subsiding, and the horizon becoming serene, it is pleasant to consider the phenomenon with attention. We can no longer say there is nothing new under the sun. For this whole chapter in the history of man is new. The great experiment of our Republic is new. Its sparse habitation is new. The mighty wave of public opinion which has rolled over it is new. But the most pleasing novelty is its so quickly subsiding over such an extent of surface to its true level again. The order & good sense displayed in this recovery from delusion, and in the momentous crisis which lately arose, really bespeak a strength of character in our nation which augurs well for the duration of our Republic; & I am much better satisfied now of its stability than I was before it was tried.[9]

Liberty, and almost-free land, also spelt utopia. More than a hundred "utopias" were founded in the United States before 1861. Because the country was large and sparsely populated, land was cheap. As a result, much of this experimentation was centered in self-contained communities whose members could put unconventional ideas into practice. Among the most interesting of the early nineteenth-century settlements were the Shaker communities, the first founded by "Mother" Ann Lee near Albany, New York, in the 1770s. Mother Ann, who had had four stillborn children and who almost died in childbirth, became convinced that "cohabitation of the sexes" was bad business; she and her followers practiced celibacy. (She also believed that the millennium was at hand and that Christ had returned to earth and quite literally resided in her person). After her death the Shaker movement expanded, becoming a joyful and profoundly emotional religion whose celibate practitioners lived together in harmony and produced the remarkable furniture, simple and beautiful, which is so highly prized today.

Another community, Harmony, was founded in western Pennsylvania in 1804 by a German immigrant, George Rapp. The Rappites were also celibate and hardworking. They pooled their wealth and prospered greatly. But "Father" Rapp ruled Harmony with an iron hand – anyone who committed a sin during the day was required to confess to Rapp before going to bed – and he moved the entire community, more or less on a whim, first to Indiana, then back to Pennsylvania. After he died in 1847 the community began to shrink, but it did not finally disappear until 1905. In 1824 Rapp sold the Indiana property for $150,000 to Robert Owen, an English industrialist, who founded New Harmony, a socialist community of some 900 persons, which was, according to Owen's son, "a heterogeneous collection of radicals ... honest latitudinarians, and lazy theorists, with a sprinkling of unprincipled sharpers thrown in." Owen's socialist experiment did not work. There was much "grumbling, carping, and murmuring" about members suffering from the "disease of laziness." Owen soon abandoned the community, selling the land to the settlers at bargain prices.

[9] Jefferson to Joseph Priestley, March 21, 1801: Julian Boyd (ed.) *The Papers of Thomas Jefferson* (Princeton, NJ, Princeton University Press, 1950) vol. VIII, p. 22.

Nashoba was established by Frances Wright, a friend of the Owens, who was much influenced by the elder Owen's ideas. In 1825 Wright purchased Nashoba, a plantation in Tennessee. She installed there a small group of slaves, her idea being that by living in a friendly, supervised atmosphere they could learn skills and pay off their cost by their labor. They were then to be freed and set up on their own somewhere outside the United States. The community was a failure, both financially and in its plan for helping the slaves to earn their freedom. Wright freed the slaves anyway and shipped them off to a new life in Haiti. She then settled for a time in New Harmony, where she advocated doing away with the legal institution ·of marriage, and indeed of monogamy.

Brook Farm was another "Owenite" community, but the antithesis of Wright's Nashoba. It was founded in 1841 by well-known Boston transcendentalists led by George Ripley, a Unitarian minister. The residents of Brook Farm sought a "union between intellectual and manual labor." They created a cross between a cooperative and a joint-stock company, a community in which all work was paid for at the same rate and (in theory) members were to earn 5 percent a year on their investments. Things did not work out as planned, but most Brook Farmers appeared to enjoy themselves. Nathaniel Hawthorne, who owned stock in Brook Farm and lived there briefly, called it "a day-dream, and yet a fact."

Hopedale, another experiment in socialism-cum-religion, was founded in Massachusetts by Universalist minister Adin Ballou, at about the same time as Brook Farm. Ballou believed it was literally possible to create the kingdom of heaven on earth. Members of his community, who purchased shares for 50 dollars, were guaranteed work, and all shared equally in what was produced. All members – irrespective of sex, color, occupation, wealth, rank, or any other natural or adventitious peculiarity – were treated the same, and all were pledged to oppose "all things known to be sinful against God or human nature." Hopedale grew slowly and by 1853 was a going concern. But by that time two of its members had bought up nearly all the stock. They decided to liquidate the organization and devote its assets to a conventional Hopedale Manufacturing Company, and without capital the community gradually withered away.

Oneida was founded by John Humphrey Noyes in 1848 in New York. Noyes was a "Perfectionist," one who believed that when once "converted," a person could be free of sin and totally happy. At Oneida he hoped to combine perfectionism with socialism. He invented and practiced "complex marriage," a system where all the men were married to all the women, but he combined it with "male continence" – sexual relations between individuals were supposed to be regulated by the group. Children were raised in community nurseries. Competition of any kind was frowned upon, and stress was placed on all sorts of community activities. Wrongdoers were subjected to "mutual criticism" by a committee headed by Noyes. Oneida prospered, manufacturing high quality silverware, and eventually Noyes dropped both socialism and complex marriage. In 1880, Oneida became a corporation.

Nauvoo was the Illinois community created by the Mormons, the followers of Joseph Smith, in 1839. Smith, who claimed to have discovered and translated a sacred text (the Book of Mormon), was a handsome, outgoing man whose religious ideas encouraged people to enjoy life to the full, but he ruled Nauvoo with an iron hand. The community prospered, but ran into opposition from nearby nonbelievers when Smith instituted "celestial marriage," the practice of polygamy, himself accumulating a very large number of wives. He also created a private army, the Nauvoo Legion, and announced his intention of running for President of the United States. Smith made many enemies in and out of his community, and in 1844 he was arrested and lynched before he could be brought to trial. The Mormons then entered upon their epic march westward under a new leader, Brigham Young. He led 16,000 Mormons from Illinois to Utah in 1846–52, founding Salt Lake City and establishing the Perpetual Emigrating Fund Company, which during the years from 1852 to 1877 assisted approximately 80,000 converts to migrate to Utah from Great Britain, Scandinavia, and Europe. He also established 350 daughter settlements in Utah, Idaho, Wyoming, Nevada, Arizona and California, all connected by the 1,200-mile-long Desert Telegraph Line.

The Union Pacific Railway, which Mormon builders completed in the late 1860s, brought cash – and also the gentile energy of traders and tourists, some of whom came out of idle curiosity, to see one whom Phineas Barnum considered "the greatest show in America." It was the presence and the scorn of those who laughed at polygamy that finally in 1890 ended that strange chapter in the Mormon tale. Brigham Young's biographer, Stanley P. Hirshson, makes much of Young's own polygamy: 70 wives, 56 known children; but if a despot, he was also benevolent: Utah gave women the vote in 1870. Young built the Mormon Tabernacle in Salt Lake City, the Salt Lake Temple, and the university named for him. His 500 sermons, delivered over 30 years, stressed practical religion, improving living conditions, and good relations with the Native Americans. It is difficult to believe that today's impressive state and magnificently planned city should have descended from such a founder.[10]

Icaria, the brainchild of French socialist Etienne Cabet, a man far different from Joseph Smith, took over much of the property of the Mormons in Nauvoo. Cabet, who was influenced by the Owenites, had written a widely read utopian tale, *Voyage en Icarie*, which won him a wide following in France. He obtained a huge tract of land in Texas, intending to found a community there. However, upon reaching New Orleans with several hundred followers, he discovered that the land was too remote for development. He therefore took his group to Nauvoo in 1849. Settling in an already established community, the hard-working Icarians prospered, farming and running various small businesses including a distillery, though they did not themselves drink. Eventually, however, the group split in two and their communal way of life was abandoned.

The utopias testified to the amount of land that was available; and those few that flourished did so only when they abandoned their original communist or socialist dreams. The US by 1861 had become a land of opportunity for free men; – and for some men only; one in four of its people were slaves. It faced race problems from the start and continues to live with them. The Civil War was but one test.

As a nation, the US was not quite totally free in 1861. Despite the oceans that isolated it and the peace that they should have bestowed, the US has always been involved in Europe's and Asia's wars. It was rich in communal and utopian experiments from 1620 onwards, but they have flourished only as their capitalist and frontier characteristics have prospered. Thanks to good luck, and Jefferson's foresight, the new Americans had shattered Napoleon's dream of an American colonial empire, and had become possessors themselves of a vast, uninhabited, indifferently mapped land. A state that is secular – and by decree – it has been rich in churches and sects of the most varied and exotic styles. In its salad-bowl culture, its vast resources, and its immense variety of climate, in being at once both empire and republic, it is a unique society.

---

[10] Stanley P. Hirshson, *The Lion of the Lord: a biography of the Mormon leader Brigham Young* (Dent, 1971); Fawn Brodie, *No Man Knows My History* (London, Eyre and Spottiswoode, 1975); Mark Holloway, *Heavens on Earth: Utopian communities in America 1680–1880* (New York, Library Publishers, 1951); Leonard Arrington, *Brigham Young, American Moses* (New York, Knopf, 1985).

1

Who Should Rule at Home?
The Arguments Then and Now

1 THE RESULTS OF INDEPENDENCE

A new nation had thus proclaimed itself, under the impact of a history of repeated injuries and usurpations, real or imagined, and had won its independence. Protests against Britain before 1775, like the War itself, had produced passionate appeals to nationalism. At the Stamp Act Congress of 1765, Christopher Gadsden had declared: "There ought to be no New England man; no New Yorker, known on the continent, but all of us Americans." Nine years later, Patrick Henry orated: "The distinctions between Virginians, Pennsylvanians, New Yorkers and New Englanders are no more. I am not a Virginian, but an American ... All distinctions are thrown down. All America is thrown into one mass." "When the honest man of Boston who has broke no law, has his property wrested from him, the hunter on the Allegany must take the alarm," said the freemen of Botetourt County, Virginia, in October 1775. "Unite or die," pleaded Franklin.

The most distinguished of the early national historians, Dr David Ramsay, in his *History of the American Revolution*, published in 1789, noted the impact of the war as a nationalizing experience. Before 1775, he wrote,

Americans knew but little of one another. ... Trade and business had made the inhabitants of their seaports acquainted with each other, but the bulk of the people in the interior country were unacquainted with their fellow citizens. A continental army, and Congress composed of men from all the States, by freely mixing together, were assimilated into one mass. Individuals ... disseminated principles of union among them. Local prejudices abated. By frequent collision asperities were worn off, and a foundation was laid for the establishment of a nation.[1]

By the end of the war, as Ramsay predicted, there was an awareness of national identity.

Pennsylvania-born and Princeton-educated David Ramsay practiced medicine in Charleston (and married three times, each time more profitably than the last), and became politically active as a Southern Federalist. His *History of the American Revolution* was heavily plagiarized at the time, and has been raided since. For him there were no dubieties and no European intellectual and near-theological arguments. For Ramsay, the new republic was unique in its founding and in its institutions, and it had a special origin: enough to give it a sense of nationhood. As Arthur Shaffer puts it, "A strong independent and republican American character arose from the distinctive conditions of the New World, was articulated and reinforced by the Revolution, and was rationalized by the federal Constitution." For all his pride in Princeton, Ramsay was, first and last, a dedicated nationalist who became also an active Federalist defender of the Constitution. Shaffer calculates that there were over 40 likeminded with him. They included Jedidiah Morse, Jeremy Belknap, Noah Webster, George Minot, John Leeds Bozman, the Episcopalian and former Loyalist, Hugh Williamson of North Carolina, and the Irishman-turned-Virginian John Daly Burk. They were clergymen and lawyers – and New Englanders – for the most part: George Bancroft had his predecessors. They were aware that they were a part of a European Enlightenment, sharing a citizenship in the republic of European letters, but equally proud of the distinct culture and environment of their New World. Indeed, one of David Ramsay's works was entitled *Universal History Americanised*. They were not yet free from theological overtones, didactic by nature and prophets by function, and they saw the Revolution as part of a Grand Design. "God sifted a whole nation," proclaimed William

---

[1] David Ramsay, *The History of the American Revolution* (1789), ed. and annotated by Lester H. Cohen, 2 vols (Indianapolis, Liberty Fund, 1990). See also L. Cohen, *The Revolutionary Histories* (Ithaca, NY, Cornell University Press, 1980); and cf. John Shy, *A People Numerous and Armed: Reflections on the military struggle for American Independence* (London, Oxford University Press, 1976), and his essay, 'The American Revolution: the military conflict considered as a revolutionary war,' in Stephen G. Kurtz and James H. Hutson, *Essays on the American Revolution* (Chapel Hill, NC, IEAHC, University of North Carolina Press, 1973).

Stoughton, "that he might send choice grain over into the wilderness." "Next to the introduction of Christianity," declared Richard Price, an English Nonconformist minister whose writings were greatly admired in the New World "The American Revolution may prove the most important step in the progressive course of human improvement. It is an event which may produce a general diffusion of the principles of humanity and become the means of setting free mankind from the shackles of superstition and tyranny."

Despite their intense local loyalties, the contemporary historians of the Revolution all believed to a quite remarkable degree that there was a new nation in being in the New World, and indeed their writings helped to make it so. They all agreed that armed rebellion was an honorable last resort; and that now constitutional issues were at stake. The new nation in being, product in part of their own writing, was the product of the united efforts of a united people, and not just the work of "designing men." At a time when archives were non-existent, these writers corresponded with each other; they exchanged notes and sources — and critical comment; they were determined and they were productive: 43 writers produced some 60 books. Although most of them were involved in the bitter and contentious issues of their day, as historians they contrived to avoid partisanship — although Mercy Otis Warren and John Marshall have to be described as conspicuous and brilliant exceptions to this rule. But of the group as a whole it is not too much to say that these historians constructed their own national past; it was in large measure their creation.[2]

Moreover, of ten non-New England histories published between 1785 and 1812, five were by men who had neither been born, raised in, nor educated in the states whose history they had written: David Ramsay of South Carolina, Robert Proud of Pennsylvania, John Daly Burk of Virginia, and Hugh Williamson of North Carolina. Moreover, Ramsay and Williamson had strong links with New England, Ramsay by correspondence and Williamson through years of residence in Boston and as a student of theology in Connecticut.

Not all were Federalists: least of all one of the most striking, Mercy Otis Warren. She struck a more critical, even satiric note,

---

[2] Arthur H. Shaffer, *The Politics of History: Writing the history of the American Revolution 1783–1815* (Precedent Publishing, Chicago, 1975), and his intellectual biography of Ramsay, *To Be An American: David Ramsay and the making of the American Consciousness* (Columbia, University of South Carolina Press, 1991). Mercy Otis Warren, *History of the Rise, Progress and Termination of the American Revolution* (1805), 2 vols, ed. and annotated by Lester H. Cohen (Indianapolis, Liberty Fund, 1989).

and was especially afraid of the commercial republic that she saw enshrined in the Constitution. There were still Old Whigs around, and feminists also – but many more of the former than the latter. Indeed, Mercy Otis has a claim to be unique.

The Thirteen Colonies were, however, very precariously united against Britain. They were, as Professor Van Tyne observed, 13 independent states "temporarily acting together in the business of acquiring their individual independence." The struggle against Britain by the continental army was accompanied by a struggle for power, for influence, and for land between each state and section – a struggle, that is, over who should rule at home. Alongside the rebellion against Britain there were several conflicts less obvious but quite as significant: Tidewater versus frontier, planter versus merchant, and everywhere, in greater or smaller degree, Loyalist versus patriot. Some of these tensions took explosive form. The Revolution was not the smooth, ordered, gradual transition that American nationalists or British liberals have, for different reasons, made it. There are in American history so many examples of tension, violence, and war that it is hard to maintain the great American myth that they are an unbelligerent people.

There were many border and sectional problems that threatened conflict. There was the 20-year-old dispute over Fort Pitt between Pennsylvania and Virginia. Connecticut had claims on the Wyoming valley along the Susquehanna River, and was attempting to settle it with armed men. New York and New Hampshire were wrangling over the possession of the Green Mountains. The seizure of Ticonderoga and the wartime rivalry of Ethan Allen and Benedict Arnold were part of a local as well, as of an international war. There was no certainty over the future of what was to be Vermont. There was suspicion, still a reality in Maryland until 1781, over the sea-to-sea claims of the Old Dominion. Many besides Otis, Galloway, and Braxton believed that only British power prevented the outbreak of a number of civil wars between the colonies.

There were before and during the War sectional clashes along the frontier: the march of the Paxton Boys on Philadelphia in 1764, the tenant riots in Westchester and Dutchess Counties in New York in 1776, the anti-Eastern wars in the North Carolina frontier, in which Regulators became reluctant Loyalists when the Tidewater failed to provide lawcourts, magistrates – and clergy. In South Carolina, the gracious planter-merchant aristos of Charleston were Janus-like, liberal and Whig when they looked across the Atlantic, hard-faced and Tory when they looked west across the pine barrens. They did in the end make some provision for circuit courts, and these helped avert the civil war that affected North Carolina.

Behind these examples there were forces in the West that were to be at work throughout the Revolutionary period and were to erupt again in Shays' Rebellion in Massachusetts in 1786, and in the Whiskey Rebellion of 1794. Courts of law were too few and justice remote, unpredictable, and expensive; the one court of law in South Carolina was seated, in the diarist Woodmason's words, "not central but in a nook by the seaside."[3] In Pennsylvania there was fear of Indians, and in the Carolinas still more fear of other whites. "We live not as under a British government ... but as if we were in Hungary, or Germany, and in a state of war, continually exposed to the incursions of hussars and pandours." Prophetic demands were being voiced: for a paper currency; for more adequate roads; for the replacement of a poll tax by a tax levied in accordance with capacity to pay, and to pay in kind; for election by ballot; for a curbing of the speculators, who had acquired their vast and empty estates through their influence "back East;" and for a fairer representation of the West in eastern assemblies, the common cry from the Mohawk to the Smokies.

If Woodmason's diatribes against "vexatious pettifoggers or litigious miscreants, Rogues and Whores," have been thought fevered by later historians, there can be no querying the less eloquent but more moving petition of the 260 inhabitants of Anson County, North Carolina, in October 1769, ending with the request "that Doctr Benjamin Franklin or some other known patriot be appointed Agent, to represent the unhappy state of this Province to his Majesty, and to solicit the several boards in England." They did not once mention the Proclamation Line or the wickedness of Britain; they wanted justice, good order, religious freedom, and democracy; their enemies were mercenary attorneys and little bureaucrats in the Tidewater, doing the harm there that Britain's agents were doing at the ports. This was the country for which the Virginian Patrick Henry spoke; and it was in Waxhaws on the South Carolina frontier that Andrew Jackson spent his formative years. South of Virginia, the frontier tended to loyalism throughout the Revolution. In Pennsylvania, in New England, and not least in Vermont, it was avidly patriot.

---

[3] Charles Woodmason, *The Carolina Backcountry on the Eve of the Revolution*, ed. Richard Hooker (Chapel Hill, NC, IEAHC, University of North Carolina Press 1953), *passim*.

There were almost everywhere basic differences between Piedmont and Tidewater. They were separated by distance, and in the Carolinas by barrens and by empty land. One was a country of small farms, few slaves, and fewer aristocrats, and with a marked mixture of races – Scotch-Irish, German, Welsh, and English – and of religions – Presbyterians, Baptists, and various pietist groups. The other was characterized by small towns or plantations, with slaves in considerable numbers in the South, and with a church and a society that reflected in its tone and uniformity a new colonial establishment. If there were not 13 revolutions, there were certainly at least two distinct societies in America in 1776. They were at times at war not only with Britain but with each other, and to keep them in gear was a major political achievement. On March 23, 1776, John Adams wrote to General Gates, Washington's colleague:

all of our misfortunes arise from a single source – the reluctance of the southern colonies to republican government. The success of this war depends on a skilful steerage of the political vessel. The difficulty lies in forming constitutions for the whole. Each colony should establish its own government, and then a league should be formed between them all. This can be done only on popular principles and maxims which are so abhorrent to the inclinations of the barons of the south and the proprietary interests in the middle colonies as well as to that avarice of land which has made upon this continent so many votaries to Mammon that I sometimes dread the consequences. However, patience, fortitude and perseverance with the help of time will get us over these obstructions.

The middle way and the skillful steerage were evident in the political and social reforms of the war years. Despite the fears of the aristos, while there was some violence there was no anarchy, except perhaps in North Carolina, where it was hardly a novelty. There was no widespread destruction. No royal governor lost his life, not even Governor Dunmore of Virginia, who most deserved to.

Congress declared in May 1776 that all royal government was to be suppressed and that new state governments should be set up. This was smoothly done. Each state produced a constitution – sometimes, as in Connecticut and Rhode Island, by altering existing charters. Except in Massachusetts, they were all drafted within a few months. They were normally drawn up by the provincial congresses, but Pennsylvania summoned (and needed) a special convention. Massachusetts submitted its draft to a referendum of the voters, and many features of the undemocratic result – the work of John Adams – long survived. All were soundly based on colonial experience and in this sense were evolutionary, not revolutionary.

All were written documents and the work of lawyers; all contained declarations of rights; all emphasized separation of powers and the primacy of the elected legislature, elected by those people with some — although now a smaller — stake in the community (from the payment of a small poll tax in New Hampshire, North Carolina, and Pennsylvania to Virginia's requirements of 25 acres of settled or 50 acres of unsettled land).

In Georgia and in the Carolinas, in Massachusetts and New Jersey, only Protestants could hold office. There were normally property qualifications imposed on members of legislatures or state officials. In Massachusetts the governor had to own £1,000's worth of free-hold property; in South Carolina he was worth ten times that amount. The legislature usually elected the governor, who held office for only one year and who lost his veto power in practically all states. In Pennsylvania, where the franchise was unusually wide and all taxpayers had the suffrage, and in Georgia's first constitu-tion, there was only one House; elsewhere there were two — the second, sometimes chosen by an electoral college, designed to act as a check on the "mobility" that James Allen and John Adams and many other revolutionaries feared. The western areas in Pennsylvania and the states south of the Potomac were given increased representa-tion; they gained some seats, but not usually their fair share, least of all in South Carolina. Only in Pennsylvania, North Carolina, and Georgia could the new constitutions be said to be really democratic documents. Pennsylvania's was so democratic, with a denial of veto to the executive, a referendum, and a council of "censors," that it survived only for 14 years.

Nor was the social revolution much more pronounced than the political. There was the striking disappearance of the Loyalists, and there was confiscation of crown and proprietary lands by decision of Congress in 1777. The estates of Sir John Wentworth in New Hampshire, of Sir William Pepperrell in Maine, of Sir John Johnson in the Mohawk valley, of the Phillipses in New York, Lord Fairfax in Virginia, Henry McCulloch in North Carolina, and Sir James Wright in Georgia were taken over. But when Loyalist land was sold the motive was punitive or fiscal rather than egalitarian: Tories must pay for the war. Except in New York, where there was unusual breakup of the 59 confiscated estates, the land was usually sold as a unit to wealthy men or to speculators; practically all the state governors were interested in real estate. Revolutionary leaders like the Livingstons and the Van Rensselaers added to their holdings. So did Washington — not only the first, but also one of the wealthiest of all the presidents. The prices and terms of sale were, in fact, much less favorable to "little men" than the British had been; but in the end, some land did percolate down to smaller holders and carried voting rights with it as it came.

The right to acquire and possess property without restriction was indeed as important a civil right as free speech, and to most people in the eighteenth century it meant more. Property was largely real estate and was widely dispersed; it was esteemed in America as the reward of effort and success rather than of inheritance. The disappearance of its feudal aspects was strength rather than weakness. Quit-rents were abolished in every state between 1775 and 1789; they prevented the easy acquisition of land, and they were resented as remnants of feudalism. Entail and primogeniture disappeared also from New York and the South: but entail had not been a universal custom, even in the Tidewater; docking had been a common practice and primogeniture had applied only in cases of intestacy. Their removal, egalitarian though it seemed, hardly weakened the plantation economy or the long-tailed families; rather did it indicate a right to do what one liked with one's own in an ever-expanding society in which there was more than enough for all. It seems not to have had the importance that Jefferson foresaw; it would, he thought, open the Republic to "the aristocracy of talent and virtue which nature has wisely provided for the direction of the interests of society;" nor did it have the significance attributed to it by Tocqueville, who thought it the major factor in the growth of American democracy. But superficially there was a note of social equality. Republicanism was naturally associated with the campaign against royalty and loyalism. Titles were unpopular, including "Excellency" and "Honorable." A number of state constitutions sought to forbid hereditary office-holding and any development of a privileged class. Two forbade the creation of titles of nobility. Jefferson looked forward to the time when the "plebeian interest" would prevail over "the old aristocratical interest." And Royall Tyler, a veteran of the Revolution, rhapsodized in the prolog to his play *The Contrast*, produced in New York in 1787:

> Exult each patriot heart! this night is shewn
> A piece, which we may fairly call our own;
> Where the proud titles of "My Lord!" "Your Grace!"
> To humble Mr and plain Sir give place.

Religious freedom was strengthened, partly by the separation from parent churches, partly by the disestablishment of the Anglican (but not of the Congregational) Church, partly by the spread of rationalism and deism as the philosophical accompaniment to revolution, partly by the growth of militant dissenting sects, and partly by the steady secularization of American life. At the time of the Revolution there were some 3,100 churches in the colonies, the majority Congregational, Presbyterian, or Baptist. Congregationalism reigned in Massachusetts, New Hampshire, and Connecticut. In six other colonies, the Church of England was the established religion – although the majority of none of these colonies were Anglicans. In Virginia, where the Anglicans claimed no more than half of the population, the other half – including Presbyterians, Baptists, Methodists, and Lutherans – were nevertheless taxed for support of the Anglican Church. In Maryland, there were more dissenters than members of the Established Church. The number and variety helped the separation of church from state and weakened authoritarian religion. Jefferson thought the Statute of Virginia for Religious Freedom, which he drew up and which became law in 1786, one of his three most important achievements – the others being the writing of the Declaration of Independence and the founding of the University of Virginia: "All men shall be free to profess, and by argument to maintain, their opinion in matters of religion;" "Truth is great and will prevail if left to herself." The radicals of the Revolution honored Milton as well as Locke. In each state, establishments were overthrown – though not necessarily immediately: in New Hampshire, Connecticut, and Massachusetts not until the next century. The spirit of localism and of what became states' rights was strong, and continuous. Thus, the Massachusetts constitution of 1780 insisted that religion was the foundation of morality and of the state; it required that public funds be used to maintain the churches, and that a man be a Christian before he could hold public office. Deism, curiously, made its biggest inroads in "feudal" Virginia, always in fact a more liberal society than its social system revealed. And as the state debates on ratification of the Constitution would reveal, it was this variety of opinions, state by state, that led in the end to the enactment of the Bill of Rights.

There were some trends that can be described without qualification as liberal. The colonial criminal codes were always much less harsh than Britain's – in part because of necessity, since it was easier to provide rules than to provide prisons – and now they were made even more liberal. In the Pennsylvania constitution of 1776, capital punishment was restricted to four offenses. Jefferson's code for Virginia would have limited it to murder and treason; defeated by one vote, it was not enacted until the 1790s. Congress similarly limited capital punishment in the Northwest Territory in 1788.

Again, at the time the War broke out, there were about half a million slaves in the Thirteen colonies; most of them in the South, but a fair number elsewhere – some 25,000 in New York, perhaps 55,000 in the whole of the North. The first anti-slavery society in the United States (or anywhere else for that matter) was founded in Philadelphia in April 1775, composed mainly of Quakers. Other such societies soon followed. The Continental Congress in 1774 had decreed an agreement not to import slaves, and the prohibition on slave-trading seems to have held throughout the War. Legislatures began to act. In July 1774 Rhode Island passed a law declaring that all slaves brought into the colony thenceforth should be free. The law's preamble is instructive:

Whereas the inhabitants of America are generally engaged in the preservation of their own rights and liberties, among which that of personal freedom must be considered as the greatest, and as those who are desirous of enjoying all the advantages of liberty themselves should be willing to extend personal liberty to others ...

By the end of the century the majority of states had forbidden the importation of slaves, and all New England, New York, and Pennsylvania had provided for abolition or gradual emancipation. Many Southerners thought it an evil, and manumitted slaves by deed or will, as did Robert Carter and George Washington. Only South Carolina and Georgia, still in need of slaves, stood out against a complete ban on the institution. It was, over-optimistically, expected that slavery would die a natural death. The War was a struggle for political independence, but it was accompanied by a social and institutional revolution in each of the 13 states. Moreover, the seeds of abolitionism were first planted as a result of the Revolution – in Britain as in North America. Although – since there is always a codicil – Benjamin Franklin, who brought two slaves as his personal servants with him when he came to London in 1755, acquired his first interest in educating the slaves from his friends in the Society of Dr Bray; but he insisted – as in London they did not – that the schools for blacks should be segregated.

Especially in the Jeffersonian circle there was a concern with "causes;" Benjamin Rush had advanced ideas on the treatment of the insane, whom he insisted on describing as the "mentally ill," and he wanted a Peace Department in the federal government; and Anthony Benezet crusaded not only for these but for temperance and for the fair treatment of the Indian as well.

Freedom for the person was a real thing. It was, however, tightly confined to one sex. Despite the role of Mercy Otis Warren as poet, historian, and participant in the Revolution, and of the active Abigail Adams, women were not held – even by Jefferson – to be the equal of men. If married, they could not hold property or will it. They could not sue in the courts, nor could they easily contrive to be publicly educated. Yet Charles Brockden Brown, America's first professional man of letters, reflected the *Aufklarung* of Europe by publishing in 1797 his *Alcuyn: A dialogue on the rights of women.* One of his female characters complained that "lawmakers thought as little of comprehending us in their code of liberty as if we were pigs or sheep." The first American novel to gain popularity, *Charlotte Temple, a Tale of Truth* (1791) by Susanna Rowson, was a highly sentimental but strong plea for women's rights.

On this theme there is now a considerable literature. It too has its heroines, and one of them has been frequently quoted: Abigail Adams. She was sufficiently stirred (or irritated?) by her husband John's crusading for political causes among the delegates of the Continental Congress in Philadelphia that she penned a rebuke to him:

In the new code of laws which I suppose it will be necessary for you to make I desire you would remember the ladies, and be more generous and favourable to them than your ancestors. If particular care and attention is not paid [us], we are determined to foment a rebellion, and will not hold ourselves bound by any laws in which we have no voice.[4]

He responded to his mutinous wife's "saucy" request with characteristic firmness: "As to your extraordinary code of laws, I cannot but laugh." The delegates, he added, "know better than to repeal our masculine systems" and would fight the "despotism of the petticoat." But it was not literacy nor social claims that altered women's role, but the War itself. A survey of local newspapers revealed advertisements by women blacksmiths, gunsmiths, shoemakers, shipwrights, tinworkers, barbers, and butchers. The *Virginia Gazette* carried a notice of an arrest of a runaway slave signed by "Mary Lindsey, gaoler" of Henrico County. In these years of crisis at least ten American newspapers were published by women. From 1767 until her death at age 55 in 1775, Anne Catherine Green, widow of printer Jonas Green, by whom she bore 14 children, served as printer to the province of Maryland and publisher of its first newspaper, the *Maryland Gazette.* The province's second newspaper, the

---

[4] L. H. Butterfield, Marc Friedlaender and Mary-Jo Kline (eds), *The Book of Abigail and John* (Cambridge, MA, Harvard University Press, 1975), p. 125.

Maryland Journal, was also published by a woman: Mary Katherine Goddard. In addition to her editorial work, the indefatigable Miss Goddard managed Baltimore's busiest printing firm, owned a bookstore, and became city postmaster. In her career, Miss Goddard followed the example of her mother, Sarah Updike Goddard, former publisher of the Providence *Gazette*. Publishing was by no means the only field in which American women made significant contributions. Agriculture, for example, profited immensely by women's innovations. Elinor Laurens of Ansonborough, South Carolina became the first colonist to cultivate a wide variety of exotic fruits and vegetables – including olives, capers, limes, ginger, guinea grass, and Alpine strawberries. The most exceptional female planter, however, was Mrs Eliza Lucas Pinckney, also of South Carolina. When only a girl, managing her absent father's large plantation with what one friend called "a fertile brain for scheming," Eliza decided to start cultivating West Indian indigo. At first she suffered setbacks from frost and insect blight, but within seven years she was able to produce an indigo dye of sufficient quality to export to England. Thanks to Eliza's pioneering, indigo was one of the southern colonies' greatest exports; in 1775, South Carolina alone produced a crop worth about £260,000.

Not even the pulpit remained a male preserve. Mother Ann Lee, "Anne the Word," left England with a small band of followers in 1774 and established a religious community at Nistegaone, New York. The American Shakers – so named because of the tumultuous singing, dancing, shaking, and shouting at their services – regarded Mother Ann, who reportedly could be inspired to speak in as many as 72 tongues, as the female manifestation of God. But despite all the evidence, and despite (or because of ?) Abigail's persuasion, John Adams was not convinced that women should have the vote: "Their delicacy renders them unfit for practice and experience in the great businesses of life."[5]

---

[5] For the place of women in the Revolutionary years see Mary Beth Norton, *Liberty's Daughters: The Revolutionary experience of American women 1750–1800* (Boston, Little, Brown, 1980); her article, "The evolution of white women's experience in early America," *America Historial Review*, 89 (June 1984), pp. 593–619; and also Linda Kerber, *Women of the Republic: Intellect and ideology in Revolutionary America* (Chapel Hill, NC, IEAHC, 1980); Robert Hoffman and Peter J. Albert (eds), *Women in the Age of the American Revolution* (Charlottesville, University Press of Virginia, 1989). See also Jan Lewis, "The Republican wife: virtue and seduction in the early republic," *William & Mary Quarterly*, 44.4 (Oct. 1987), pp. 689-721.

Freedom for the person brought little immediate native blossoming of the fine arts. For the most part, Gilbert Stuart's portraits were stilted, and his confreres were even more derivative than he. Higher learning was savaged by the war. College buildings were commandeered to serve either as barracks and stables or as military hospitals. Only Yale and Dartmouth, of the nine colleges functioning in the country before the Revolution, were able to carry on their educational work, and in 1800 the Harvard faculty consisted of a president, three professors, and four tutors. The vandalism of the troops quartered in the colleges resulted in great loss of libraries (Charleston, burned in 1778), paintings, and scientific equipment. Many endowment funds were wiped out by the ravages of inflation. Some advances in educational principles were made during the war period. The idea of a more democratically organized school system came into favor with educators (Thomas Jefferson was already planning for public schools for Virginia), and the need for a more utilitarian learning was recognized at institutions such as Franklin's College in Philadelphia and William and Mary College in Williamsburg, where chairs of modern languages and law were substituted for those of classics and divinity. In 1762, Dr William Shippen began a series of lectures in Philadelphia on midwifery, and with the cooperation of Dr John Morgan he established the first American medical school at the University of Pennsylvania. This school languished in the general wartime decay of colleges, but was revived after the War. In 1782, John Warren opened the Harvard Medical School.

Yet there were emerging a new nationalism and a new cosmopolitanism, both in part the result of the presence of French and Hessian troops. Noah Webster's notion of a uniform American speech and Jedediah Morse's geography expressed the first. Webster's *Blue-Backed Speller* sold over 100 million copies, and was used throughout the United States even as late as the Civil War. This textbook illustrated Webster's credo that America should be as independent in literature as in government, and it incorporated moral maxims on the virtues of thrift, temperance, and hard work — though his attempts to propagate some advanced ideas on spelling and grammar in his writing met with less immediate success. So with John Trumbull and Benjamin West, Philip Freneau and Timothy Dwight. So, too, with the Order of the Cincinnati, the society of officer veterans of the Revolution of which Washington and Henry Knox were leaders, and of which the American eagle became the emblem — even Jefferson took great pride in American flora and fauna. The French language and style became fashionable; the new city on the Potomac was planned by Major Pierre Charles L'Enfant, although with little result in his own lifetime; dueling became a gentlemanly response to insult, with permanent effect on the code of chivalry in the South; neoclassical architecture, already heralded in Jefferson's Monticello, appeared on a small scale; chairs in modern languages and law were established at William and Mary College. In 1794, Dr David Hosack imported an imposing collection of plants from Europe, and with them established a botanical garden in New York City. Benjamin Silliman, the first proficient American geologist, made a formal and edifying comparison of European and American minerals. Even the Iroquois had a French dancing master.

The War itself inevitably stimulated interest and enhanced skills in medicine and dentistry. Some able doctors — some of them Edinburgh-trained — served both armies: William Shippen and John Morgan of Philadelphia, the brothers Warren, John and Joseph, Benjamin Rush, and David Ramsay on the American side; Samuel Bard and Peter Middleton of New York and Alexander Garden of Charleston serving the Tory cause. Their methods were in general crude and their resources limited; the first American medical book and the first pharmacopeia were published for their guidance.

Perhaps the most striking of their number was Benjamin Rush. Born near Philadelphia in 1745, Rush studied medicine in Edinburgh and London and then returned to Philadelphia to take up his practice. In 1772 he published his first book, *Sermons to Gentlemen on Temperance and Hygiene* which was followed shortly after by an anti-slavery pamphlet. Rush was a signer of the Declaration of Independence, and was surgeon-general of the continental army until his opinionated mind and lack of practical prudence got him into trouble in military politics. He resigned his army appointment and returned to civilian practice continuing to publish tracts on temperance, education, capital punishment, and a host of other social questions. As a physician, Rush was an enthusiastic champion of the virtues of phlebotomy (bleeding), believing that all diseases proceeded from a single source — spasms in the blood vessels. But despite his adherence to such an unscientific notion as this, Rush was a notably enlightened man, and his treatise called *Medical Inquiries and Observations upon the Diseases of the Mind* was a pioneer work in psychiatry. He was instrumental in making Philadelphia the center of American medical learning, an eminence held by that city until the foundation of the Johns Hopkins University in Baltimore in 1867.

The War stimulated interest, too, in the theater. Congress voted in 1774 to discourage plays, horse-racing, and such diversions, but in fact each side used the stage as propaganda. Wherever the British army moved, such was the leisurely pace of war, it carried acting with it. Philadelphia remembered that fantastic pageant, the *Meschiana*, long after Howe had beat a retreat; and in some of the productions the feminine roles were played, remarkably for the age, by women – women, as one author put it, "such as follow the drum." But in society as on the stage, scandal has always been the twin sister of sophistication.

Liberation brought few signs as yet of America's great practical genius, but the war years produced some remarkable people. Jefferson was experimental in method and catholic in range. His *Notes on the State of Virginia* were a noble attempt to set down a complete catalogue of all significant information about the state. In this work Jefferson included a great deal of natural history, describing the flora, fauna, landscape, and geography of Virginia. His strong partisan preference for the New World and his dislike of England are abundantly clear from the *Notes*. Prominent among a wide sweep of considerations are Jefferson's views on slavery and local government; his advocacy of popular education as the keystone of democracy; his plea for religious toleration and the separation of church and state; his belief in free trade; and his apprehensions over the letdown in political idealism that he foresaw as an aftermath of the Revolution.

Jefferson's friends were gifted; Eli Whitney with his cotton gin, and Oliver Evans and John Fitch with their steamboat experiments, showed specialized skills. David Rittenhouse (1732–1796) was second only to Benjamin Franklin among American scientists of the eighteenth century. Of Quaker background, Rittenhouse began his scientific career as a clockmaker and technological artisan, studying so hard in his spare hours as to wreak considerable damage to his health. Optics was his first great interest; he fitted George Washington with glasses and constructed the first telescope in America. In astronomy, he made exceptionally precise observations on the 1769 transit of Venus, and in 1793 he discovered a new comet. Rittenhouse conducted experiments in magnetism, electricity, and other fields of practical scientific inquiry, devoting himself also to research in higher mathematics. During the Revolution he made munitions for the continental army, and after the war he served as the first director of the United States Mint. Rittenhouse represents the self-made genius typical of the eighteenth century, the scientist who progressed from master of mechanics to a study of theoretical principles.

Benjamin Thompson – better known under his later title of Count Rumford – was born in Massachusetts in 1753. His family was

poor, and from his early youth he resorted to living by his wits —
a practice at which he was always eminently (and unconscionably)
successful. During his early apprenticeship to a Salem importer,
Thompson studied mathematics and other sciences in his spare time.
In 1770 he was heard of in Boston, studying French (then the
lingua franca of science). In 1771 he began to study medicine. For a
time he taught school, and soon married a wealthy widow. Through
her social connections, he met and so impressed the governor of
New Hampshire that he was promptly made a major in a New
Hampshire cavalry regiment. Throughout this period, he was carrying on important experiments with gunpowder. In the early years
of the Revolution, Thompson mingled with the Whigs and even
sought to obtain a commission under Washington. Rejected because
of the clearly unstable character of his loyalties, he turned to the
Tory side. He went to London, made many friends in high official
circles, and was taken into the Royal Society, which he incidentally
helped organize. After fighting briefly in America as an officer in
the British army, Thompson was in 1791 made a count of the Holy
Roman Empire. (The name "Rumford" which he chose for his title
was that of a town in New Hampshire.)

Crop rotation and fertilization were introduced under French stimulus. Societies for the promotion of agriculture, industry, and "the
useful arts" came into being, most of them short-lived. So did small-
scale industrial establishments for the manufacture of cloth and gunpowder and the production of iron. The shipping industry survived
the war and was stimulated by it, for privateering could pass as
patriotism, but whaling and the West Indian trade that went with it
were badly hit. Trade, like taste, began to feel its way, slowly, into
new channels — to Dutch ports, to Portugal, and to China; but the
export trade in tobacco, rice, and indigo slumped. America was now,
for good or ill, without the protection or control of the imperial
system.

If each region now suffered from the exclusion from Britain's
mercantilist protections and guarantees, New England suffered particularly. It had before 1775 depended heavily on the export of fish
to the British West Indies. Britain now kept this market firmly
closed; New England's cod exports fell over 40 percent in the late
1780s from what they had been pre-War. Exports of American meat
and dairy products met the same fate. American ships — usually
Yankee — were barred from West Indian ports; American whale-oil
imports into Britain now met prohibitive duties. Britain cut down
on its iron imports from the Middle Atlantic states. Southern indigo
planters no longer had a British subsidy and could not compete

with West Indian producers. If tobacco still found its traditional market in Britain, the price fell. Nor did Americans ride this readjustment with the same Puritan zeal in 1784 that they had displayed a decade earlier. The country imported heavily from Britain once the War was over; it found it hard to repay in exports and drew heavily on gold and silver, which further aggravated the shortage of money. During the War, gold and silver had poured in from army expenditure and foreign loans. These sources of largesse were now cut. Continental paper money had depreciated steadily in value; as all money supplies dried up, prices fell – between 1784 and 1788, wholesale commodity prices in Philadelphia and Charleston fell by 25 percent. Farmers suffered most: they were unable to meet fixed mortgages or to buy imports or to pay taxes. Speculators were glad to use the worthless paper to pay off debts or buy up land. And Rhode Island and North Carolina, by making paper money legal tender, allowed this to happen even where the payment was refused by the creditor. There was great pressure to print money, or to issue notes on the security of land mortgages. Virginia, Connecticut, and Delaware had no paper money. But when the Senate in Maryland defeated a paper-money bill, riots followed.

In Massachusetts, similarly, the legislature refused to issue any more paper money. And it also decided to redeem wartime paper money at the value it had when issued, even though it had depreciated greatly. This action more than doubled the state debt. It decided also to repay the state debt quickly. To do so, it relied on a poll tax – on all males over 16. Failure to pay could lead to seizure of property – or to jail sentences if estates were insufficient. These seizures brought in little; men with dependent families went to jail for inability to pay small amounts. Some towns were unable to send delegations to the state legislature, in which, in any case, the wealthy communities were over-represented – and which was indifferent to appeals for paper money and stay laws. The poor thus saw the courts and the legislatures as the instruments of their oppression. Hence the protest by almost a thousand farmers in Springfield against foreclosure for debt known as Shays' Rebellion in 1786. It is worth noting the comment of the one-time radical Samuel Adams on Shays: "The man who dares to rebel against the laws of a republic ought to suffer death." Once it was over, all Shaysites were pardoned. The legislature still held out against paper money and stay laws, but it lowered taxes and exempted both household goods and tools of trade from seizure. The general improvement in economic conditions helped.

As yet there was little impetus to manufacturing. Inflation badly hit the army and all the fixed-income groups. Town workers sought both higher wages and the fixing of prices as a check on profiteers and speculators. Capital was short; so were the skills and the labor. One reason was an unusual one: lack of immigrants; in the years from 1776 to 1800, only some 4,000 immigrants per year were entering the United States. This allowed the mold of the country to become fixed; western land was acquired before the human flood poured in. Yet by natural increase the population grew rapidly, and by 1790 it was almost 4 million.

Nevertheless, this was in economic terms an age of unusual stability behind the political and social tensions. The Republic was, in fact, in happy equipoise. Liberal forces were at work, but they were of a traditional and largely an inherited kind. North America had, even in colonial days, enjoyed a far more striking degree of both freedom and equality than contemporary Europe — without always being ready to appreciate the good fortune. It had destroyed its aristocracy, and its society and its interests were middle-class. Despite the Old South, they remained stubbornly so. In almost all the new states, Frontier and Tidewater, by 1787 the men of substance were in control, and the idealists sometimes proved themselves incompetent executives. Not the least striking feature of the years of construction from 1776 to 1787 was the minor role played by the propagandists and pamphleteers of the decade of agitation. If there was a contest over who should rule at home, there was no social revolution. It was, in fact, not needed. "I say again," said John Adams, "that resistance to innovation and to unlimited claims of Parliament, and not any new form of government, was the object of the Revolution."

The transformation of the rights of Englishmen living in America into those of Americans was a smooth one and was decisively confined to the years from 1774 to 1776, or even, perhaps, from April 1775 to July 4, 1776. Only in 1775 — though Franklin began to suggest it two years earlier — did the argument shift its ground from the follies of Parliament to those of the king. And the argument, only at the very end becoming an argument for separation, included no suggestions for basic social or economic change. There was no Thermidor in 1787 because there were no Jacobins in 1776. If the franchise was widely held, it was exercised openly and orally — and usually on market day; not surprisingly, it was in general use to elect an existing elite. At least in the Tidewater, those elected before 1776 were usually elected again afterwards. If the Establishment, from being foreign (i.e. English or even Scottish), became native, and if it was far easier to get into than in the Old Country, it remained, after 1787 as before, an elite and never a *demos* that ruled. There being no feudal system, once entail and primogeniture and proprietorial estates had gone, there was no need for the establishment of a centralized power rooted in popular emotion to overthrow or to transform it. This was, after all, a reluctant, a pragmatic, and, as its course and results were to confirm, an unmessianic revolution. The richest irony of it is that, once independent, the new society introduced the bishops and vice-admiralty courts that it had so much feared, and then proceeded with equal reluctance but more efficiency to levy taxes on itself.[6] The revolution from the bottom up was not the revolution intended – is it ever, in *any* revolution? In fact the cause was led by a self-conscious elite, born on native soil, local aristos defending their local privileges and extensive acres against what they saw as centralization and were prompt to label "tyranny." It was not so in effect, and could never be, given the 3,000 miles of ocean that divided Mother from enterprising Daughter. But declarations of purple prose are not meant to be provable at law.

The leaders were ambitious men, many of them classically educated, somewhat ashamed of their humble origins where they had them (witness John Adams), and quick to detect them in those imposed on them as "royal" governors. They were a natural aristocracy; equality meant equality of opportunity not of condition; the word "equality" usually indicated a claim for equal treatment for Americans as such as against British in a political and constitutional context, not a pretence that any one man was the equal of another, which patently defied the many varying talents and skills of manysided men. Industry, certainly hard physical labor, was not for this *aristoi* – unless on horseback. They sought to destroy an aristocracy based on patronage and dispensed mainly from London or by London's minions, and replace it by a native aristocracy of talent. By their frequent reflections on "virtue" and the "moral republic" they saw public service as important, in part as being the mark of the likeminded, rooted in decorum, deference, and disinterestedness; only men with land and property were truly independent, only the autonomous could be free. They saw themselves, as Edmund Randolph

---

[6] In recent years there have been some sophisticated studies of Anglo-American relations, in addition to those of the Loyalists. Among them are Alison Gilbert Olson and Richard Maxwell Brown (eds), *Anglo-American Political Relations 1675–1775* (New York, Rutgers University Press, 1970); Michael G. Kammen's superb *People of Paradox* (New York, Vintage Books, 1973); and Kammen (ed.), *Politics and Society in Colonial America* (New York, Holt, Rinehart and Winston, 1967); see also the studies of Jack Sosin, notably *Whitehall and the Wilderness* (Lincoln, University of Nebraska Press, 1961).

said, not on new ground but "on the Republican ground of Greece and Rome." When crises came, back they went to their "own vine and fig tree." Without this personal security, they were at risk: witness Robert Morris as merchant, Silas Deane in his confusion between the private and the public purse, the failure of the gifted immigrant lawyer James Wilson. When Aaron Burr and Alexander Hamilton retired from public office, they went to New York to make money; when things went wrong and they were without estate and status to fall back on, they could abscond and go West, witness again Burr, William Augustus Bowles and General James Wilkinson. Revolutions are not static, and men came forward with novel experiences alongside their classical learning, and aware of living in a new nation. Natural leaders did emerge: and there was a vacuum to fill.

2 IDEOLOGIES

What have historians made of these events? In the decade before the nation's bicentennial celebration in 1976, three classic studies appeared. In 1967 came Bernard Bailyn's *Ideological Origins of the American Revolution*,[7] an elaboration in book-length form of his 200-page introduction to a collection of reprints of contemporary pamphlets, which revealed the extent to which the American revolutionary writers drew on parallels with the English Civil War of the seventeenth century, and saw themselves engaged, like the Puritans and the Levelers, like Milton, Harrington and Sidney, in what they saw as a struggle for liberty, and fighting a conspiracy to impose a tyranny upon them. The Revolution of 1776 was a highly literate revolution, with, as its tool, no less than 38 newspapers, and with tracts and pamphlets, broadsheets and almanacs universally popular. The American Revolution owed its intellectual coherence to its inheritance of the ideas of the English Civil War and Commonwealth; they looked back to 1649 rather than 1688.

Bailyn shows the importance of that group of seventeenth-century and early eighteenth-century men such as Milton and Algernon Sidney, the journalists Trenchard and Gordon, authors of *Cato's Letters*, and the good Bishop Hoadly, who, to others, was "the best hated clergyman of the century." And the ideas that ran through this "opposition" and "country" writing were secular. Their advocates

---

[7] Cambridge, MA, Harvard University Press.

wanted adult manhood suffrage; the elimination of the rotten borough system; the substitution of regular units of representation systematically related to the distribution of population; the binding of representatives to their constituencies by residential requirements, and of "Instructions" to them; alterations in the definition of seditious libel, so as to permit full freedom of the press to criticize government; and the total withdrawal of government control over the practice of religion. The vocabulary of the 1640s became that of the 1770s also. And in this integrated group of arguments, beliefs, and fears, there was a conviction that what had happened before could happen again, that the conspiracy of government that had needed a rebellion and the execution of a tyrant to halt it in 1649 could need it again, and that, as Andrew Elliot wrote in 1765, when tyranny is abroad, "submission is a crime." In early eighteenth century Britain, Viscount Bolingbroke's contribution was important. As author of *The Idea of a Patriot King*, he was seen as the source of George III's ideas; and the venom of his attack on prime minister Robert Walpole left behind a smear on all government and on London politicians.

The ROBINARCH, or chief ruler, is nominally a MINISTER only and creature of the prince; but in reality he is a sovereign, as despotic, arbitrary a sovereign as this part of the world affords. ... The ROBINARCH ... hath unjustly engrossed the whole power of a nation into his own hands ... [and] admits no person to any considerable post of trust and power under him who is not either a RELATION, a CREATURE, or a THOROUGH-PACED TOOL whom he can lead at pleasure into any dirty work without being able to discover his designs or the consequences of them.[8]

These notions of conspiracy and corruption recur half a century before 1776; and they made it possible for American leaders to see in events in Britain, in the Wilkes case, or in the language used by the party of Pitt and Burke in attacking successive London ministries, evidence to support their view, however far-fetched in fact the models might be. And by 1769 each side was living by imagery, imprisoned in its own assumptions. "The Americans," Burke said that year, "have made a discovery, or think they have made one, that we mean to oppress them: we have made a discovery, or think we have made one, that they intend to rise in rebellion against us; we know not how to advance; they know not how to retreat. ... Some party must give way."

---

[8] *A Dissertation upon Parties* (1735), originally published in *The Craftsman*.

When all this is said, however, the "Commonwealth" inheritance took root in an alien and freer land. To some, like Jefferson, the foreign and exotic character of the New World was not only its fascination but its salvation. There was, of course, the problem of size of territory; all the ancient and modern republics had been small in size. It was here, in his plans for the Northwest, that Jefferson in fact was at his boldest and most dreamy-eyed; the Ordinances he drew up for the Northwest Territories are perhaps, of all the achievements of these years, the most truly far-sighted and original. The availability of land made it an empire for liberty. Moreover, the Americans were fully aware that some aspects of the Commonwealthmen were worrying indeed. A republic sounded, and was, a splendid, a rational, an Enlightened, achievement. A "democracy" was something else. To few was a democracy attractive: not even to Jefferson or Adams. "I was always," wrote John Adams, "I was always for a free republic, not a democracy, which is as arbitrary, tyrannical, bloody, cruel, and intolerable a government as that of Phalaris with his bull is represented to have been." Andrew Elliot pointed out the "many inconveniences which would attend frequent popular elections;" John Dickinson believed that "a people does not reform with moderation;" and William Drayton stated forthrightly that he was as desirous of checking "the exuberances of popular liberty" as he was the excesses of prerogative. The men of 1776 were radicals in politics, not economics, and their vision was of a political transformation. And though it would be easier to remove an absentee tyrant than it had been in 1649, had there not been a Restoration in 1660?

None of this is to argue that the pamphleteers were historians or classicists. They were concerned with current affairs: with British interference with their trade with the French colonies, the raising of the price of molasses, the loss (so it was asserted) inflicted on the old colonies by the annexation of Canada and Florida, the dangers of admiralty jurisdiction and of episcopal aggression, the exorbitant claims of the Virginia clergy, the underestimated sacrifices made by the colonies for what were essentially British interests in "the French and Indian War;" these were the common themes of discussion. Did they, however, genuinely connote tyranny? Could the England of George III, the mad, bad, and despised king, be represented in terms worthy of Juvenal, with Lord Bute, the king's choice as prime minister, as Sejanus?

Bailyn and his Harvard school write persuasively, and are steeped in the pamphlet literature. Not all historians, however, accept Bailyn's "conspiracy theory." James Hutson wittily demonstrates that if the conspiracy theory is pushed to the ultimate, it implies that the

American Revolution was due to mass paranoia and to a massive delusion, that the United States was conceived, not in liberty, but in madness. This is an idea, he says, which strikes most Americans as being "more or less blasphemous." Richard Bushman, examining the literature of political conflict in Massachusetts in the early eighteenth century, points out that, although the opposition writers were well known, in Massachusetts at least political issues were parochial rather than ideological. Similarly, Jack Greene questions whether the "oppositionist" ideology had the effect on the American mind that Bernard Bailyn believes. And Isaac Kramnick has queried whether a single ideology held sway: a free implies a competitive world, and there was constant controversy in the many public prints. What was striking about the radicals was the diversity of their political ideology and of their social composition.

Moreover, why limit the idea of conspiracy to those who sought to undermine American liberties? Is there not equal validity in the view that there was, in the Sons of Liberty and the committees of correspondence, in the Boston Tea Party and the extra-legal conventions in the Raleigh Tavern in Williamsburg or the Green Dragon in Boston, abundant evidence of another conspiracy?

The origins of Revolutionary political culture were further explored by J. G. A. Pocock in *The Machiavellian Moment: Florentine political thought and the Atlantic republican tradition*. And in 1969 Gordon Wood published *The Creation of the American Revolution 1776–1787*. All these studies recalled not only the Founding Fathers' interest in the previous century, but their own thorough grounding in the classics, and the classical languages; Roman institutions became the models, and Latin provided the vocabulary of political virtue. They all paid tribute to the study of an earlier decade, Caroline Robbins' *The Eighteenth-Century Commonwealthman*, which traced the survival into the mid-eighteenth century of the ideas of Milton and Harrington, Sidney and the Puritans. The notion grew of a great conspiracy against liberty in which English church and state, courts, City and colonial governors, were all engaged.[9]

---

[9] Caroline H. Robbins, *The Eighteenth-Century Commonwealthman* (Cambridge, MA, Harvard University Press, 1959); R. A. Humphreys, "The rule of law and the American Revolution," *Law Quarterly Review*, 53 (1937), pp. 80–98; Bernard Bailyn, "The transforming radicalism of the American Revolution," introduction to *The Pamphlets of the American Revolution 1750–1776*, vol. I (Cambridge, MA, Harvard University Press, 1965); Gordon S. Wood, *The Creation of the American Republic 1776–1787* (Chapel Hill, NC, University of North Carolina Press, 1969); and J. G. Pocock, *The Machiavellian Moment: Florentine political thought and the Atlantic republican tradition* (Princeton, NJ, Princeton University Press, 1975).

Moreover, the influence of the Levelers and of the men of 1649 – whatever its strength in shaping the opinion of some of the leaders of 1776 – was curiously non-pervasive. On 1787 and on Jeffersonian republicanism they had little impact. What drove the Jeffersonian republicans of the first decades after Independence was the writing of Tom Paine, of Adam Smith, and not least of Paine's 20 or more immigrant and radical apostles who edited Republican journals in New York and Philadelphia, Richmond, Baltimore, and Charleston. These radical English exiles spoke the language not of Milton, Sidney, and Harrington, but of Locke, Smith, and Paine: egalitarianism, advocacy of commercial development and a vision of unlimited progress. Little wonder that in their correspondence in retirement Jefferson and Adams often wondered how successful "their" Revolution had been.[10]

Isaac Kramnick is wise to argue that there were several and simultaneous bodies of thought on which Americans were drawing during and after the War of Independence. It was not simply the second round of the English Civil War.[11] And there is yet another doctrine that should be added to the kaleidoscope of views on Independence/Republicanism. Throughout the 1760s and 1770s a number of American revolutionaries were primarily concerned with law and their constitutional rights as Englishmen. The claims they made were often better rooted in constitutional history and practice than those on which Parliament rested its case. Across the divide the reliance on law – and lawyers – would continue.[12]

3   THE GOOD AMERICANS

The research of the last two decades, however, has altered the history of these years in two major – and somewhat antithetical – ways:

[10] Michael Durey, "Tom Paine's apostles: radical emigrés and the triumph of Jeffersonian republicanism," *William & Mary Quarterly*, 44.4 (Oct. 1987).
[11] Isaac Kramnick, notably in "The great national discussion: the discourse of politics in 1787," *William & Mary Quarterly*, 45 (1988), pp. 3–32, and *Republicanism and Bourgeois Radicalism* (Ithaca, NY, Cornell University Press, 1990); and J. G. A. Pocock's reply stressing that, in 1787 and before, many varieties of Whiggism were in circulation.
[12] John Phillip Reid, *Constitutional History of the American Revolution: The authority of rights* (Madison, University of Wisconsin Press, 1986), and idem, *Constitutional History of the American Revolution: The authority to tax* (Madison, University of Wisconsin Press, 1987); Jack P. Greene, *Peripheries and Center: Constitutional development in the extended politics of the British Empire and the United States 1607–1788* (Athens, University of Georgia Press, 1987).

in its stress on the role of the radicals and of the crowd, and on the part played (or, more accurately, promised but not performed) by the Loyalists.

On the outbreak of war, most Americans, of course, were loyal if not Loyalist. The war began at Lexington, Concord, and Bunker Hill, and was clearly in origins the result of a Boston-Virginia alliance. John Adams' view was that one-third of the American people were Patriot, one-third Tory, and one-third neutral. But this was a superficial view. It now seems more likely that the proportion was one-fifth rather than one-third Loyalist. New York City was, as the British headquarters throughout the war, a Loyalist center, but it extended only a little way farther north than what is now the financial district – the Hudson valley was no man's land. There were strong pockets of loyalism in Pennsylvania, Georgia, and in the Carolinas. When Governor Dunmore in Virginia responded to the crisis by taking refuge on the British man-of-war *Fowey* off Norfolk, and put out an offer of freedom to all slaves who would join him, 300 runaways enlisted in the Ethiopian Regiment; their uniforms carried the slogan, "Liberty to Slaves." When Dunmore's force of 600 men, including the freedmen, was defeated at Great Bridge, those blacks who survived fell victim not to the Patriots but to a smallpox epidemic. Clearly, wherever the British Army appeared, there were waves of Loyalist sentiment, though these were as often out of self-interest as from conviction, and they could ebb as the British withdrew – in the Hudson valley as General Burgoyne failed to reach it, in New Jersey and Philadelphia, as General Howe's forces fell back, and in the Southwestern valleys of Virginia after General Cornwallis surrendered.

One group of Loyalists could be disturbingly and clearly identified from the outset: the Iroquois. The Mohawk valley had been administered for the previous 20 years by Sir William Johnson, the Northern Superintendent, whose skill had kept at least four of the six nations at peace, and firmly on the British side, until his death in 1774. His son Sir John and his nephew Guy continued the tradition, and throughout the war Joseph Brant and his Mohawks were active on the British side. In the War Brant led the Indians on St Leger's expedition, and with 400 savages, supported by a number of whites, set up the effective ambush at Oriskany in August 1777. With Butler's Rangers he struck along the New York frontier; he was falsely accused of being involved in the Wyoming valley massacre of 1778, but was, along with Walter Butler, responsible for the devastation and massacres in Cherry Valley.

The Indians were troublesome allies. Their use of the tomahawk and the scalping knife was savage; and they were hard to control.

There was a great loss of goodwill towards the British along the frontier after Indian raids, and notably when the Indians scalped Jane McCrea in the course of Burgoyne's invasion down the Hudson valley in 1777. The account of the episode varies in the telling: some accounts speak of her as a beauty with long raven tresses, and others that she had "clustering curls of soft blonde hair." Whatever her coloring, she was attacked and killed by Burgoyne's Indian allies; and she was engaged at the time to David Jones, a Tory with Burgoyne's army. The story of her murder played a considerable part in spreading the legends of Indian atrocities in the wake of the Redcoats. Similarly, the annual "Liberty Day" or "Massacre Day" addresses in Boston, exaggerating and elaborating, kept tempers high. Revolutions owe as much to rumor as to reality.

It has nevertheless to be said that the Mohawks in their barbarous way were active fighters on the Frontier, and that they stood by Britain throughout the war. And to them Britain, after the war, was generous in turn. Brant obtained from General Haldimand a grant of land six miles wide on each side of the Grant River in Ontario, and, after a visit to London in 1785 when he was presented at Court, and was superbly portrayed by Romney, he obtained funds for the Iroquois to indemnify them for their losses and to buy more land. Brantford, Ontario, is named in his honor; his son John fought in the War of 1812 and was in 1832 a Member of the Canadian Parliament. [13]

The white Loyalists tended to be drawn from the upper and middle classes in the colonies. Most Anglican ministers, some but not all doctors of medicine (Edinburgh University Medical School, the major training ground for colonial doctors, produced as many radicals as it did patriots), many government officials, and customs and admiralty officers were of course Tories. So were almost all the Scottish factors at the tobacco ports, who usually served only a spell of years before returning home – as did John Cumming, though he left behind his colony of Strathspey Scots who were soon acclimatized and accepted in Catskill, NY. So were many Quakers, and many followers of John Wesley. And so, in a curious way, were the Germans in Pennsylvania, in part because they were the most recent emigrants and had not yet fully rooted themselves in the land. Indeed, it could be argued, as by Professor William Nelson of Toronto in *The American Tory*, [14] that the Loyalists represented a

[13] Isabel Thompson Kelsay, *Joseph Brant 1743–1807: Man of the two worlds* (New York, Syracuse University Press, 1983).
[14] New York, Oxford University Press, 1961.

collection of cultural minorities in the new society. And among them were those Scots and Scotch-Irish immigrants who had reached the valley of Virginia and the pine barrens of the Carolinas, many of them as refugees and ex-Jacobites from Scotland. Paradoxically, many of the militia who fought at Moore's Creek Bridge in 1776 fought under Loyalist banners, though they were Highlanders or the sons of Highlanders who, 30 years before, had fought for Bonnie Prince Charlie at Culloden.

The Loyalists, in other words, represented a wide cross-section of American society and were by no means exclusively drawn from the Establishment. When in June 1776 a number of people were arrested in New York on suspicion of plotting to kill George Washington, they included the mayor of New York and some officials but also farmers, tavern-keepers, two gunsmiths, two tanners, two doctors, one saddler, one silversmith, one shoemaker, "a pensioner with one arm" and an unfortunate described only as a "damned rascal." When an Act of Banishment was passed against 300 Loyalists in Massachusetts in 1778, one-third were farmers, and the rest artisans, laborers, and small shopkeepers. In June 1778 Delaware listed 46 Tories to whom it refused to give a general pardon. They included 2 captains, 3 physicians, 1 lawyer, and 7 described as assembly-men, office-holders and wealthy citizens. But the list also included 9 husbandmen, 2 yeomen, 2 innkeepers, 3 pilots, 3 shallop men, 2 mariners, 2 laborers, 3 coopers, and 1 weaver, 1 saddler, 1 tailor, 1 coppersmith, 1 bricklayer, 1 hatter, and 1 cordwainer. Most of those who settled in Canada were poor and signed their name with a cross.

Some Loyalist themes are recurrent: some colonial leaders held that certain fundamental legal and constitutional principles governed the Empire and forbade revolution. Among them were governors like James Wright and Thomas Hutchinson, and Cadwallader Colden and Jonathan Sewall. Some sought to reach some form of accommodation between Britain and the colonies – including William Smith Jr, governors Franklin, Bull, and Wentworth, accommodating clergymen such as Andrew Elliot, and those, like Samuel Quincy and Robert Beverley, who in the end sought no part in political action at all. Then there were those who might be called the Revolutionary *Ultras*, those who saw colonial resistance as "morally wrong and esthetically abhorrent." Among these were Samuel Peters and Jonathan Boucher, Peter Oliver, Samuel Seabury, and Myles Cooper. Myles Cooper and Peter Oliver proved less accommodating than Governor Wright or Governor Franklin. For Loyalism affected some half-million people, 80,000 of whom in the end went into exile.

They cannot easily be reduced to any category, and if the attempt to reduce them fails, that failure reflects only the variety and bewildered nature of Loyalism itself. The Revolution was certainly less bloody and cruel than some other American crises, internal or external, from Bull Run to Saigon. But it was less a Revolution than a War of Independence; it was for many Loyalists bloody and cruel enough; and it left most of them with nowhere to call home.

Many important families were split: the Fairfaxes, the Randolphs, the Bulls, the Curwens, the Ruggles, and the Dulanys. So were recent immigrants as James Hogg in Transylvania from his brother Robert in New York. For this was not only a guerrilla war but a war inside families. Divided, Tory in sentiment and upper-class in tone, the Loyalists produced few natural leaders and no outstanding military figures, unless one counts Benedict Arnold, the traitor who plotted to sell West Point to the British in 1780. Traitor or not, he was an able battle commander.

William Franklin, Benjamin Franklin's illegitimate son, the royal governor of New Jersey and a firm Loyalist to the end, lacked his father's political finesse and capacity for leadership. The Board of Associated Loyalists did not come into being until 1779 with Sir William Pepperrell, the grandson of the hero of Louisburg, as its chairman. But it was little more than a body with which to pursue claims for losses against the British government in London. Perhaps the most prominent Loyalist family was that of Beverley Robinson, born in Virginia but identifying with New York, where he had married the wealthy Susanna Phillipse. He raised the Royal American Regiment and served with General Clinton in 1777.

The Loyalist role in the war has been studied by Paul Smith of the Library of Congress in *Loyalists and Redcoats*, and from his analysis of the War Office papers in the Public Record Office in London he lists 41 Loyalist regiments; he concludes that 19,000 men fought on the Loyalist side. Other estimates go higher, to as many as 50,000, but this is unlikely; it has to be remembered that some enrolled more than once to obtain bounty money, or served in different places. There were in all some 300 companies – at one time or another – in some 50 provincial corps. Alongside the familiar regiments – the Royal Americans, Butler's Rangers, the Royal Greens and the King's Royal Regiment – are the more exotic titles: the Roman Catholic Volunteers (who had a number of Irish volunteers among them), Skinner's Greens, the Royal American Reformers, the Black Pioneers, and, not least, the Ethiopian Regiment. Two Loyalist regiments became regular units of British infantry – the Royal Highland Emigrants and the Volunteers of Ireland; and in the last two years of the War in the South they at last came into their own. Though their major role in battle was slight, they played a key part in the underground world of the spy and the informer. Thus James Rivington, who edited the Loyalist *Gazette* in New York throughout the War, was able to survive in New York for a time without molestation, presumably because he had throughout been a double agent. But his paper was silenced forever on December 30, 1783, after he was called on by the New York mob led by Isaac Sears and Alexander McDougall. Rivington tried unsuccessfully to stay in business as a bookseller, but he failed, to die a pauper in 1802.

During the War, however, many Loyalists became exiles. In the end some 8,000 settled in Britain and 5,000 (1,300 from Canada) claimed for compensation from the British government. By 1790, when the final report of their claims was published, the government had distributed over £3 million in doles as well as offering government posts and appointments of ministers to parishes, against a total claim of over £10 million. This was, of course, the saddest part of the American story. Thomas Hutchinson, American-born, businessman, colonial historian and good servant of Massachusetts went into exile in 1775 and died in London in 1780, with his heart still aching for Boston. He lived for most of these years in Brompton Row, and in the houses alongside him were some 25 fellow Bostonians, a lost and broken colony of exiles. Nor were he and his colleagues adequately consulted by the home government; after meeting the king on his first night in London, he never had a close personal conversation with him again. The British government, during the war as before it, neglected its friends. But it did reward those who removed to the bleak wastes of Nova Scotia with government land to the extent of 3 million acres and, given the conditions there, treated them well. Nine million dollars was spent on resettling them.

Robert Calhoon writes of "A Special Kind of Civil War." It was not at all like those of France, Russia, and China. All revolutions are not the same thing in different costumes. The people of New England and the Seaboard were the most politically literate community since classical Greece, but their political philosophy could not be separated from a religious imperative which was intensely individualistic and ethical. These people were concerned not only with taxes, but with how far a community can rightly go to silence criticism. Testimony before justices and committees of correspondence shows clearly a general effort to avoid confrontation, to look for compromise, and to inflict no more than token punishment. Even if the managed Boston mob was for a moment at the center of events, its long-run effect was trivial.[15]

The treatment of the Loyalists who stayed behind varied from state to state. The great majority stayed as quiet as they could. But some were exotics. One of these was Philip Skene. He owned 34,000 acres south of Lake Champlain at Skenesborough, now Whitehall. He had fought for Bonnie Prince Charlie in 1745, and in the French and Indian War in America. In 1775 he was appointed Lieutenant Governor of Fort Ticonderoga and Crown Point. As an avowed Loyalist, his person and his estates were an obvious target for the Green Mountain Boys. But when in May 1775 John Barnes's Company seized his estate and took off his sister and daughters to Connecticut, they discovered that Skene himself was still *en route* from England; he was in fact seized on shipboard as he landed in Philadelphia in June 1775. What they found in his home came as a surprise. They found the corpse of his wife in a small apartment partitioned off in the cellar. It was laid in a very nice wooden coffin, superior to anything which the carpenters of the country could make. And this was enclosed in a lead coffin, which was sealed and soldered up so as to render it quite air tight. His wife had a legacy left her of a certain sum per day whilst she was above ground and Skene had placed her here to receive this legacy.

Major Skene was a larger-than-life figure. In person he was big and heavily set. When under arrest in 1775 in Philadelphia, he was lodged, perhaps unwisely, in the city tavern. Here the innkeeper, an Irishman, entertained him too generously. He was apt after a meal to address the passers-by in a stentorian voice, shouting "God save great George, our King." This attracted crowds and drew loud applause.[16]

But lesser figures than Skene fared less comfortably. Some were made prisoner in Simsbury Mine in Connecticut. Some 40,000 were driven from home, and by 1783 100,000 in all (1 in 30 of all white families) had chosen to go, many of whom lost their property for ever. The majority, having no place to go, took the oath of

[15] Robert M. Calhoon, "The reintegration of the Loyalists and the disaffected," in Jack P. Greene (ed.), *The American Revolution: Its character and limits* (New York, New York University Press, 1978), pp. 51–74; and *The Loyalists in Revolutionary America, 1760–1781* (New York, Harcourt Brace Jovanovich, 1973).

[16] For Skene and the Loyalists see Robert M. Calhoon, *The Loyalists in Revolutionary America 1760–1781* (New York, Harcourt Brace Jovanovich, 1974), and Gregory Palmer (ed.), *Biographical Sketches of the Loyalists of the American Revolution* (Westport, Conn., Meckler Books, 1984).

allegiance to the US, and accepted their exclusion from public office and from the professions. New York made $3,600,000 from the sale of confiscated Loyalist property, Maryland $2,000,000. The peace treaty stipulated that the states return the property, but little was in fact done by way of restitution. But in a personal sense, they were rarely met with violence. Of Pennsylvania's Loyalist "blacklist" of 490 names, only a few were punished, and only two were hanged.

Finally, investigation of the sale of confiscated estates reveals that no sweeping generalization can be made regarding the redistribution of Loyalist property. It is clear that in some states a more equitable land system did result; in other states, the opposite can be said. And, finally, in other areas, no conclusion at all can be drawn. As John Alden has said:

Had there been as a result of the American Revolution a vast economic leveling, it would be entirely appropriate to use the label of Internal Revolution. No such leveling occurred. There was neither general expropriation nor general partition of land. The patriots, including many men of wealth, largely retained their property, with some profiting from the conflict and others losing. Redistribution did come, as the result of the seizure and sale of the lands of the Tories, in Southern as well as in Northern states. Tenants, farmers, and artisans bought them, often with depreciated currency, and in consequence moved upward in terms of wealth, social status, and political power, while Tory aristocrats were reduced and exiled. The effects were doubtless substantial, but should not be overstressed. Most loyalists were not aristocrats; many of them did not lose their property; and the purchasers of that which was seized included rich as well as poor patriots. Ownership of land shifted, but only moderately, and without far-reaching consequences. [17]

Perhaps two final points should be made. First, if the story of the Loyalists is seen first and last as the record of a failure, the failure was only in the North American colonies south of what is now the state of Maine. If they failed in the United States, they succeeded overseas: 35,000 of them settled in Canada, and they are essentially its Founding Fathers. They were important in Nova Scotia, New Brunswick, and Prince Edward Island, and they created Ontario. Without them Canada would hardly have been strong enough to survive ultimate American annexation. And under their leadership it did not, or at least not until recently, become the melting pot

[17] John R. Alden, *The South in the Revolution, 1763–1789*, vol. III of *A History of the South*, ed. W. H. Stephenson and E. M. Coulter (Baton Rouge, Louisiana State University Press, 1957), pp. 337–8.

that happened south of the 49th Parallel. The promise of the Quebec Act was made real by the fact of this Loyalist influx, and Canadian nationalism was built on Loyalist foundations. Similarly in the Bahamas: all the names on Bay Street, Nassau, are of Loyalist descendants. And Loyalists are, of course, the founders of Sierra Leone; its elite of doctors and lawyers for long were called the Nova Scotians because they came *via* Nova Scotia.

The second point that needs emphasis is their loyalty to Britain itself, and its consequences. The 7,000–8,000 people who exiled themselves between 1776 and 1782 made a real contribution to British and European history. Some of them, indeed, became notorious in different ways: Dr Jefferies was one of the first trans-Channel balloonists; Benjamin Thompson became a count of the Holy Roman Empire; William Cunningham was executed as a criminal; Lloyd Delany was killed in a duel in Hyde Park; at least one became a prostitute, and at least one had a spell in Newgate jail for debts. But the major legacy of the exiled Loyalists was to the British services. Of those who came to Britain, or their sons, at least 3 held senior rank in the Royal Navy, one of them being a son of Mary Phillipse; 8 held the rank of colonel; at least 2 were army surgeons; and no less than 4 were full generals. Sir David Ochterlony became a major-general in the army of the East India Company and died at Meerin in 1825. Sir John Stuart, a major-general in the British Army, was the son of the John Stuart who served as Superintendent of Indian Affairs to the Southern Department after coming to Georgia with Oglethorpe, the founder of the state. And three of Beverley Robinson's sons had careers of distinction: Morris a lieutenant-colonel; Sir Frederick a lieutenant-general; and Sir William as head of the British Army's Commissariat. It was not a mean legacy.

4 THE RADICALS: THE VIEW FROM THE BOTTOM UP

The Bicentennial of 1776 marked a divide between one "school" of interpretation and its successor; the transition from a concern with the intellectual and Whig view of the causes of the Revolution, or with the protest of the Loyalists, to a more realistic and social emphasis. Three studies marked the transition: Jack Greene's Inaugural Lecture as the Harmsworth Professor at Oxford – *All Men Are Created Equal: Some reflections on the character of the American Revolution*; Jackson Turner Main, *The Social Structure of Revolutionary America*, which, like the writings of Merrill Jensen, stayed loyal to Charles Beard, concerned with class and hierarchy, and with who owned what; and, third, Margaret and James Jacob's *The Origins of Anglo-American Radicalism.*[18] Alfred Young's (ed.) *The American Revolution: Explorations in the history of the American Revolution*[19] is a collection of studies by the members of the emerging radical school. The language now was no longer that of classical and republican virtue but of urban and rural, sectionalism and poverty, interests, as the future President, James Madison, would see them, that shaped that elaborate balance of power, the American Constitution, of which he was the major architect. Every unit of government, he held, must have a partial interest in the operation of others. Or, in his phrase, ambition must counter ambition. Madison was less a philosopher than an operator and a realist. Like the radicals, Madison recalled the words of Publius: "If every Athenian citizen was a Socrates, the whole would still have been a mob." The language and rhetoric of virtue and justice was the language of war; after the victory was won came the plotting, and the style and attitudes of *realpolitik*; from Cato to Machiavelli. Or, as Bailyn put it in the title to his introduction to his collection of *Pamphlets of the American Revolution*, "The transforming radicalism of the American Revolution." If the war experience made for national sentiment, the arguments to justify it pushed towards revolution.

The radicals' standpoint, however, is social and economic more than intellectual/political. Their work includes analyses of communities and states, and of urban politics, especially of Philadelphia's artisans.[20] Eric Foner's study of Tom Paine places its subject firmly

[18] Jack P. Greene, *All Men Are Created Equal: Some reflections on the character of the American Revolution* (Oxford, Clarendon Press, 1976); Jackson Turner Main, *The Social Structure of Revolutionary America* (Princeton, NJ, Princeton University Press, 1965); Margaret and James Jacobs, *The Origins of Anglo-American Radicalism* (London, Allen and Unwin, 1984).

[19] De Kalb, IL, Northern Illinois University Press, 1976. See also for a new and radical view, Edward Countryman, *The American Revolution* (London, Taurus, 1986), and for the earlier Becker–Beard studies, see n. 44 below.

[20] For studies of New York, see Patricia U. Bonomi, *A Factious People: Politics and society in colonial New York* (New York, Columbia University Press, 1971); Sung Bok Kim, *Landlord and Tenant in Colonial New York: Manorial society 1664–1775* (Chapel Hill, NC, IEAHC, University of North Carolina Press, 1978); and Edward Countryman, *The American Revolution* (New York, Hill and Wang, 1985), and *The Development of a Revolutionary Mentality* (Library of Congress Symposium on the American Revolution, Library of Congress, 1972). For North Carolina, see A. Roger Ekirch, *"Poor Carolina:" Politics and society in colonial North Carolina 1729–1776* (Chapel Hill, NC, University of North Carolina Press, 1981); for Virginia, Rhys Isaacs, *The Transformation of Virginia 1740–1790* (Chapel Hill, NC, University of North Carolina Press, 1982). For urban politics,

in a social context.[21] The Revolutionary committees are considered, in different ways, by Gordon Wood and Edward Countryman, and also by Richard D. Brown and Richard Alan Ryerson.[22] Crowd action is one theme of the studies by Maier, Foner, Nash, Countryman, Ekirch, Bonomi, and Kim; but for Dirk Hoerder it is the major topic.[23]

The writers since the mid-1960s have, of course, been writing in an age marked by rediscovery at home of poverty and of racism, by commitment to civil right for blacks, by American intervention planned or attempted in Cuba, Vietnam, and the Gulf, by urban crime and instability, and by the evidence via television of tyranny, mass murder, and all but endless civil wars abroad. From this perspective, what is now the scale of the Stamp Act (which was repealed anyway) and of the Boston Tea Party? Or is our world, abroad as at home, a continuous revolution, as the eighteenth century was not? Certainly in the world outside, so in a study of the past, it is difficult to hold to the view of history as consensus, as an easy straightforward survey, as evidence of any doctrine of automatic progress being the American birthright. The radicals have taken upon themselves to write history "from the bottom up," from a "New Left," a neo-Beardian or Marxist viewpoint; Eugene Genovese, Herbert Aptheker, Jesse Lemisch, Michael Lebowitz, write as avowed Marxists. It is the fashion nowadays to scorn elite-history and hero-worship, to be less interested in Washington and Jefferson than in their balance sheets and their slaves. Alfred Young's anthology on *The American Revolution* is subtitled 'Explorations in the history of American radicalism.' Young also traces the Revolutionary experience of one Boston shoemaker in his prize-winning essay, "George Robert

---

see Gary B. Nash, *The Urban Crucible* (Cambridge, MA, Harvard University Press, 1979). See also Pauline Maier, *From Resistance to Revolution: Colonial radicals and the opposition to Britain 1765–76* (New York, Knopf, 1972), which she supplements with *The Old Revolutionaries: Political lives in the age of Samuel Adams* (New York, Knopf, 1980).

[21] Eric Foner, *Tom Paine and Revolutionary America* (New York, Oxford University Press, 1976).

[22] Wood, Creation of the American Republic; Countryman, *The American Revolution* and *Development of a Revolutionary Mentality*; Richard D. Brown, *Revolutionary Politics in Massachusetts: The Boston Committee of Correspondence and the towns 1772–1774* (Cambridge, MA, Harvard University Press, 1970); Richard Alan Ryerson, *The Revolution is Now Begun: The radical committees of Philadelphia 1765–1776* (Philadelphia, University of Pennsylvania Press, 1978).

[23] Dirk Hoerder, *Crowd Action in Revolutionary Massachusetts, 1765–1800* (New York, Academic Press, 1977).

Twelves Hewes: A Boston shoemaker and the memory of the American Revolution."[24] Hewes's career, comments Edward Countryman, led him through so many of the Revolution's transformations that he comes close to becoming Mr Everyman. Or, to quote Bertolt Brecht, "In the evening when the Chinese wall was finished, Where did the masons go?"

These detailed studies are facilitated by the use of statistics, population studies, graphs, and charts. But tracing the story of Everyman is a little like that of the Unknown Soldier: given the paucity of hard facts, it is easier to treat him anonymously and call him a Representative Man. The radicals labor under the difficulty of peopling the past. How do you portray the faceless and the nameless? And, given that problem, how do you then account for the quirks and oddities of personality? When spokesmen of the underdog are able to reveal themselves – Samuel Adams, say, or Paul Revere, or Tom Paine – they rarely fit any determinist pattern.

Much of this history is monographic, and there has been a striking development of edited collections of essays, alongside or sometimes replacing the historian's individual volume. Like almost all the symposia I have cited, they are often the legacies of Festschriften, or of endowed conferences. Such symposia are immensely varied in content and often uneven in quality. In all cases, however, the quest for synthesis and moral judgment is abandoned; discordance, the ironic, and the episodic are now the fashion.

Two questions remain unanswered. Given the scale of the poverty in the late eighteenth century that radicals believe, was it worse than in Europe, and how does this argument affect the general praise of European visitors for the American standard of living? Tom Paine, held up as model by many of the New Left, considered that "the generality of the people" lived in "a style of plenty unknown in monarchical countries." A constant theme in Franklin's writing is of the superior living conditions in America, compared to the hovels he saw in France and Ireland. Why, then, a revolution? And, a related question, if there was an element of class war here, why is there so little sign of it in Washington's army – despite his severe strictures on the levies of which he took command at Cambridge in 1775? If a social divide held in North Carolina, a colony/state devoid of the large-scale planters of its neighbors to north and south, and if the North Carolina Regulation on the frontier was a class rather than a sectional conflict, why did the poor and oppressed of the East

[24] *William & Mary Quarterly*, 38 (1981), pp. 561–623.

not join their western brethren against their oppressors? Had they done so, on whose side would they have been at Moore's Creek Bridge?

What marked the decade between the Stamp Act and Lexington Green was the militant participation in politics by ordinary people on the streets, with headquarters in pubs and rooms above pubs and market halls. Even elected assemblymen, when dismissed by loyal governors, re-convened without any legality and plotted over a tankard, as in Williamsburg in 1775. Crowds nullified the Stamp Act before it was repealed by Parliament, and frustrated the activities of customs commissioners; they broke open jails and pillaged the property of a lieutenant governor or of a stamp distributor. When troops were sent over as providers of law and order, they were attacked, and their presence was seen as little more than a provocation, not least when they acted as cheap labor. Crowds bred leaders of their own, such as Isaac Sears, the son of an oyster-catcher, Alexander McDougall, the son of a milkman in New York, and Ebenezer Mackintosh, a cobbler in Boston. Neither in colonial America nor in Britain were mobs novel, and they were easily aroused by cries of anti-popery, before and after 1776. But in the years before the War they played an avowed political and inter-colonial role, and moved almost with self-discipline. The Sons of Liberty were a valuable intelligence corps: "Bent on militant opposition to British policy, they provided both geographical links between widely separated places, and social links between the Whig elite and the plebs."[25]

Moreover, the Sons of Liberty spread the message beyond Boston. It was not as easy a task to stir a rural countryside, where the vast majority of the people lived, as it was to storm the Boston water-front or New York City markets. In New York City, in riots in the theater area and in attacks on troops, and in the tenant riots in the Hudson valley, there was much of a flavour of class war about it (as again in the draft riots of the Civil War a century later). In Pennsylvania, the Paxton Boys marched on Philadelphia – though their victims were Indians; the Regulator Movement in South Carolina was a demand for law courts, in North Carolina it was part of that long tension between the wealthy East and the poor, under-represented and Indian-threatened West; there were land riots in New Jersey. Each of these was specific, but they all gave expression to

[25] Edward Countryman, *The People's American Revolution* (British Association for American Studies pamphlet No. 13, 1983), p. 19.

unrest. And in political terms, in urban and county committees, and in province-wide conventions, protests were being organized, however illegal they might be. Many "new men" took political action for the first time.

To this evidence of riot and rebellion, add the marches and demonstrations of artisans and smiths, notably in Worcester and in Philadelphia, and there is abundant evidence of protest. What remains unproven is that it was part and parcel of the struggle for political independence from Britain, and that its violence had the political purposes that marked, for instance, the crowds on the streets during the Revolution in Paris in 1789 – or of the capitals of eastern Europe in 1990–1. Indeed, the mob alarmed many good citizens. Gouverneur Morris of New York was cynical but disturbed; the movement was the work of "the Jack Cades of the day, the leaders in all the riots, the bellwethers of the flock." "A great metamorphosis" was taking place, the work of "the god of Ambition and the goddess of Faction." He saw a sharp distinction between a powerful group of "tribunes" and a powerless group of "patricians." If the dispute with Britain continued, "we shall be under the worst of all possible dominions; we shall be under the domination of a riotous mob." It was in the interest of all men to seek for reunion with Britain. And at the least it was essential that, if there were to be mobs, they should be provided with leaders from those with a stake in society. In April 1776, Carter Braxton of Virginia foresaw all too clearly the clashes of colony with colony; if independence were asserted, he thought that "the continent would be torn in pieces by intestine wars and convulsion." John Dickinson in Pennsylvania predicted in 30 years' time a separate commonwealth to the north of the Hudson River. Two of the leading proponents of the colonial debate – the two most concerned to distinguish between internal and external taxes – had ceased by 1776 to lead the cause: Dulany became a Tory; Dickinson, though he stayed a Patriot, was highly cautious. In October 1775 James Allen of Philadelphia joined a battalion to defend the city against Britain, but in a mood of distrust: "a man is suspected who does not ... I believe discreet people mixing with them may keep them in order." In March, with "the Mobility triumphant," he thought, "The madness of the multitude is but one degree better than submission to the Tea Act."[26]

---

[26] See Aubrey Land, *The Dulanys of Maryland, A Biographical Study of Daniel Dulany the Elder, 1685–1783 and Daniel Dulany the Younger (1722–1797)* (Baltimore, Johns Hopkins University Press, 1968); Milton Flower, *John Dickinson, Conservative Revolutionary* (Charlottesville, University Press of Virginia, 1983).

In the same month, John Adams, whose diary suggests a nervous and naive enjoyment of the danger and excitement of these months, wrote to Horatio Gates, now Washington's adjutant-general and chief of staff, that from fighting half a war they were now about to wage three-quarters of a war. But even this "is not Independency, you know, nothing like it ... Independency is a Hobgoblin of so frightful Mien that it would throw a delicate person into Fits to look it in the Face."[27] New York and Philadelphia in particular were reluctant converts to the idea of separation.

Add: the dog in the night. For the most striking feature of all in North America was that the real sufferers – the slaves – were promised nothing by the Patriots (at least Lord Dunmore, safe on his cruiser in Virginia, did hold out hopes to them of their freedom, whatever his purpose in doing so), and they did not erupt into violence at all. Whoever won, it could be assumed, made no difference to them.

Valuable and concerted as this research has been, it does need qualification. As Richard Maxwell Brown has demonstrated, violence in itself was not a cause of the American Revolution. "The colonial tradition of insurgency" was a century old, and the riot had been "a purposive weapon of protest and dissent" both in Britain and America for two centuries.

In the period from 1645 to 1760 there were eighteen insurgent movements directed by white Americans toward the overthrow of colonial governments. Among these eighteen insurrections were five major ones: Bacon's Rebellion in Virginia (1676–1677) and Leisler's Rebellion in New York (1689), the overthrow of Gov. Edmund Andros in Massachusetts (1689), Coode's Rebellion in Maryland (1689), and the overturn of the proprietary government in South Carolina (1719). Medium-grade uprisings were the Ingle-Claiborne insurrection in Maryland (1645–1646). Fendall's first rebellion in Maryland (1660), the New Jersey antiquitrent uprising (1672), Culpeper's Rebellion in North Carolina (1677–1678), the overthrow of Gov. Seth Sothel in North Carolina (1689), the ouster of Gov. John Colleton in South Carolina (1690), and Cary's rebellion in North Carolina (1709–1711). Finally, there were such minor insurgencies as the Davyes-Pate uprising in Maryland (1676), the second Fendall rebellion in Maryland (1680–1681), Gove's insurrection in New Hampshire (1682–1683), the Essex County uprising in Massachusetts (1687), the rebellion against Gov. Andrew Hamilton in New Jersey (1699), and Hambright's

[27] L. H. Butterfield et al. (eds), *The Diary and Autobiography of John Adams*, 4 vols (Cambridge, MA, Harvard University Press, 1961–), vol. I, p. 64.

march on the Pennsylvania government in 1755. Only six of these uprisings were violent, and only one — Bacon's Rebellion in Virginia — produced major violence. More typical of these eighteen colonial upheavals were the seven armed uprisings unaccompanied by violence and the five non-violent uprisings that employed neither force nor the explicit threat of force.

There were also six black insurrectionary plots or uprisings in colonial America before 1760. Slave uprising plots were uncovered and broken in New Jersey in 1734, in Maryland in the late 1730s, and in South Carolina in 1740. The three black uprisings that did occur were far more violent than most of the white uprisings. Violent black upheavals occurred in New York City in 1712 and 1741 and in South Carolina (the Stono insurrection) in 1739. All six of the black plots or uprisings came during a period, 1712 to 1741, when, with one exception, white insurrections had run their course. All of the black plots or uprisings failed, and none had the impact upon their colonies that Bacon's or Leisler's rebellions, for example, had on theirs. But the violence of the three black insurrections that actually occurred (along with the brutality with which they were suppressed) points to a significant degree of psychic tension between whites and blacks in colonial America. As in the case of the white rebellions it is possible to connect the black uprisings with a major trend in American colonial history. Winthrop D. Jordan has seen these black disturbances "which affected many colonies around 1740" as "suggestive of widespread heightening of diffuse social tensions throughout the colonies" and has noted that "the disturbances coincided with the Great Awakening of religious excitement". Although white people looked with horror and morbid fascination upon the idea of black rebellion, the black uprisings may have served to keep the idea of insurrection in the background of white consciousness long after the main period of colonial insurgency had come to an end.[28]

For, paradoxically, the evidence of mob action does not always point in a radical direction. Boston differed sharply from Philadelphia in character. The various "mechanics" were often patriots, and estimated that they would profit from the economic boycotts, as merchants would not. Some groups, however, like Philadelphia's "White Oaks" — fraternities of inarticulate ship's carpenters — were the very opposite of a radical revolutionary group. The research carried through by James H. Hutson shows them to be a law-and-order group that took a position close to that of Benjamin Franklin, in opposition to the Paxton Boys, to Germans and proprietors. Hutson disagrees with earlier historians of colonial Pennsylvania, who have assumed a tie between frontiersmen and urban working

[28] Richard Maxwell Brown, "Violence and the American Revolution" in Kurtz and Hutson, *Essays on the American Revolution*, pp. 85–8.

men in furthering democracy. The White Oaks were usually conservative, though they supported non-importation in opposition to the Townshend duties. They were from the lower class, but they were not alienated; nor did they seek goals through violence.

Nor was the Revolution a campaign for equality of status or condition. It excluded women and slaves, and all who were dependent on others. For the suffrage in the colonies, as in Britain, property was a prerequisite. As Jack Greene put it: "Equality of opportunity thus meant to the Revolutionary generation the preservation of the individual's equal right to acquire as much as he could, to achieve the best life possible within the limits of his ability, means and circumstances. Every man was to have an equal opportunity to become more unequal." [29]

Aspects neglected by previous "schools", and not least by Bernard Bailyn and his colleagues, have been stressed by the New Left. Thus, Gary Nash points out important distinctions between revolutionary Boston and unrevolutionary Philadelphia. Poverty was a major problem in urban eighteenth-century America. Nash says that while the Continental Congress was debating independence in their handsome building on Chestnut Street, eight blocks away the managers of almshouses were writing a doleful report on the care of the poor. They pointed out that of the 140 men, 78 women, and 85 children admitted to almshouses during the previous year, most of them were naked, helpless, and so emaciated with poverty and disease that a number of them died a few days after their admission. He argues that in a state with 6,373 taxable Americans, a quarter or more could be classified as poor or near poor by the standards of the time. [30]

A similar lesson has been drawn by James Henretta in his study of Boston. It is legitimate to conclude from this that there was considerable unrest in many urban communities, but its precise significance as a cause of the Revolution remains unmeasured. Pauline Maier stresses that the mob was a relatively common feature of colonial life, and indeed at a time when governments had only the most primitive methods of social control, mobs were in a sense an extra-legal expression of political concern. They were not usually very violent, and were limited to specific purposes. Jesse Lemisch, however, draws a different conclusion. He sees riots as spontaneous

---

[29] Greene, *All Men Are Created Equal*, pp. 8–9.
[30] Gary Nash, "Poverty and poor relief in pre-Revolutionary Philadelphia," *William & Mary Quarterly*, 30 (1976).

expressions of lower-class discontent and rioters as radicals playing a major part in precipitating the Revolution.[31]

The New Left has a totally different view of the Revolution from that of Bailyn's school, hard as Pauline Maier has tried to bridge the gap. They show that the revolutionary movement in Boston was very different from, and more extensive than, that in Philadelphia. There was a wide gap between literate ideologized leaders living primarily in urban centers and the mobs, and between both of them and the mass of rural farming people. Kenneth Lockridge has shown that literacy among white Americans outside New England was probably at or below two-thirds throughout the eighteenth century, as it was in Britain. In Virginia, though, it seems that no more than one in four of all adults could sign their name. This was, in other words, a society attuned rather to speech than to writing, and it is dangerous to assume that all American males were able to comprehend the gospel according to Trenchard and Gordon. Rhys Isaacs writes: "We have ... made only slow progress in the task of investigating the manner in which the literary-ideological formulations of the elite were communicated to the humbler ranks, to whom the pamphlets were rarely addressed, nor have we gone far in analyzing the ways in which ideological commitment was translated into a mass social movement."[32] Gordon Wood similarly stresses the "genteel" character of much of the pamphleteering literature.

One other phenomenon needs to be mentioned, if only to be weighed in the scales. Not only was there hesitation about separation, and extensive loyalism; there was also — as John Murrin and Jack Greene have recently demonstrated — a growing anglicization of American life in the years up to 1776. The Declaration of Independence was far from being the expression of a steadily growing national temper. Rather, there was widespread admiration for British culture, with steadily closer ties of trade and commerce and closer ties with the Inns of Court and with universities, notably the University of Edinburgh — though study there seems to have produced many more Patriots than Tories. Each colony had closer ties with London than with its neighbors. "It was London that

---

[31] James A. Henretta, *"Salutary Neglect:" Colonial administration under the Duke of Newcastle* (Princeton, NJ, Princeton University Press, 1972); Maier, *From Resistance to Revolution*; Jesse Lemisch, "The American Revolution seen from the bottom up," in Barton J. Bernstein (ed.), *Towards a New Past: Dissenting essays in American history* (New York, Pantheon Books for Random House, 1968).
[32] Rhys Isaacs, "Dramatizing the ideology of the Revolution: popular mobilization in Virginia 1774–1776," *William & Mary Quarterly*, 30 (1976).

commanded their attention," says Jack Rakove, "not Hartford or Annapolis, Trenton or Charles Town."[33] If there was a general criticism of Britain, it was that the mother-country was the aberration, corrupting the true spirit of English liberty that was now better evident abroad than at home. It would not, of course, be the first occasion, or the last, when what seemed a conservative call to honor the true faith and the Old Loyalty would prove to be radical and upsetting. A call to preserve the pristine past from the accretions of tradition is the usual herald of revolution.

Radicalism, like Revolution, is a many-sided word. Given that colonial America was trans-Atlantic, monarchical, patriarchal and hierarchical, the War years wrought another change. As Gordon Wood has argued, colonial society was "a truncated society," lacking both the top tiers of the English hierarchy and its sunken lower orders. Colonial elites found it impossible to replicate traditional forms of leadership and faced many challenges to their authority. Weaknesses in established religion and in royal authority further emphasized the tenuousness of hierarchy in the colonies. Wood sees the revolution, as did European observers at the time, as marking a deep rupture with the past. While eighteenth-century thinkers were intensely interested in republican government, they assumed it could be established only in small states, such as the Italian republic of Lucca or the Swiss canton of Zug. The world was astonished when the Americans set up a republic with a population of millions and a territory larger than any European kingdom. How was it accomplished? And, given that political theorists had always said it was more difficult to maintain a republic than to establish one, how could it be kept in being?[34]

Wood argues that a far-reaching change was the secret of the United States' enduring success. Pre-Revolutionary American society reflected the imperial design of the colonial regime, but although the colonists shared every Englishman's love of political liberty, American domestic and community life before 1775 was more authoritarian than those of England: wives and children were more submissive, servants more servile, parishioners more docile, and tradesmen more deferential. American society was also more stratified into patricians and plebeians. Artists and shopkeepers had patrons, not customers, and patronage characterized the relations between rich and poor.

---

[33] Jack N. Rakove, *The Beginnings of National Politics* (New York, Knopf, 1979).
[34] Gordon S. Wood, *The Radicalism of the American Revolution* (New York, Knopf Borzoi, 1991); the quotations that follow are all from this volume.

The financial innovations that had made England a commercial society by 1750 were slow to take hold in the New World. Moreover, there was a sharp distinction between the Roman civic sense of virtue entailing the sacrifice of the private to the public in all things, and the American. What they wanted was a republic that would respect their private rights and interests, a republic committed to *individual* life, liberty, and property. Their virtue, writes Wood, would be of a different kind:

Virtue became less the harsh self-sacrifice of antiquity and more the willingness to get along with others for the sake of peace and prosperity. Virtue became identified with decency. Where the ancient classical virtue was martial and masculine ... the new virtue was feminized and capable of being expressed by women as well as men; some, in fact, thought it even better expressed by women.

The new republicanism was built not on love, respect, and consent, as the Founding Fathers had hoped, but on social competitiveness and individualisms:

The revolution resembled the breaking of a dam, releasing thousands upon thousands of pent-up pressures. Nothing contributed more to this explosion of energy than did the idea of equality. ... Within decades following the Declaration of Independence, the United States became the most egalitarian nation in the history of the World.

The American conception was not simply one of equality of rights, or equality of opportunity, or equality in the eyes of God; it was, as Wood puts it, a "basic down-to-earth belief [that] no one was really better than anyone else."

The fusion of democracy and individualism was furthered by the merging of the old social classes into what was, in effect, a single middle class:

In America, in the North at least, already it seemed as if the so-called middle class was all there was. Middling sorts in America appropriated the principal virtues of the two extremes and drained the vitality from both the aristocracy and the working class. ... The aristocracy lost its monopoly of civility and politeness and the working class lost its exclusive claim to labor.

The disappearance of the Establishment and of class divisions clearly saved America from the instability of the new European republics, which were undermined by conflict between bourgeois and

proletarian interests. Even in Switzerland, social difference produced oligarchies behind the façade of popular sovereignty. And
the divisions in the American republic that were more or less identical to those in Switzerland led, as in Switzerland, to civil war –
namely, the political divisions inherent in any federal constitution
that fails to achieve equilibrium between central authority and local
autonomy.

This was a society distinct from the Old Country, and potentially
much different. Yet if no longer monarchical, aristocratic, or deferential, yet it retained some features that kept it distinctly still English:
a jealous concern to have free speech and free assembly, which it
would indeed set in marble in its Constitution, an unruliness that
marched uneasily with respect for law, trial by jury, no taxation
without representation, and a promptness to defend themselves,
which "right" again it would enshrine by inscribing in its Bill of
Rights the citizen's right to carry (and inevitably therefore occasionally the risk of using) arms.

5 A PEOPLE FECUND AND FREE – BUT WITH ECCENTRIC LEADERS

By frequent reference to the Declaration of Independence and to its
precursor, the writings of John Dickinson in *The Farmer's Letters*,
it is customary to see the winning of Independence as part of the
eighteenth-century Enlightenment, as a feature of the new society's
"progress," as the work of unusually rational men, dedicated to
the pursuit of great political truths. It was, in fact, more familiar
than this suggests. Not democratic, in any modern sense, but there
was a greater level of citizen participation in decision-making in
the British colonies than anywhere else – in Britain itself, in Latin
America or in Europe. The white man was not in chains, despite
Rousseau's rhetoric. This was, in John P. Roche's words, "an open
society with closed enclaves." And even its perversities were English
and familiar: when in 1661 the Restoration of Charles II heralded
a wholesale reorganization of colonial governments, the Great and
General Court of Massachusetts Bay rejected the British right to
reimpose the Navigation Acts, but then it passed in its own right
its own statutes enforcing the same measures – just as the home
government a century later, after repealing the Stamp Act, passed
a Declaratory Act stating that it nevertheless had the right to do
so if it chose. Washington, Jefferson, Hamilton, Madison – in
all their differences of background and attitude – were certainly
men of outstanding qualities. But is this the whole story? From

recent research, a major qualification needs to be added to the story: psychology.[35]

One aspect of this has been brilliantly outlined by James Hutson. Looking only at the two leading colonies in opinion-making, Massachusetts and Virginia, his view is:

The leaders of Massachusetts were anything but reasonable men. James Otis, considered mad by some as early as 1760 tottered on the edge of insanity throughout the decade. In 1771, a Massachusetts court declared him a "Lunatick" and sent him into confinement "bound hand and foot". A year earlier, drunk and distracted, he had bawled out to his former adversary, Thomas Hutchinson, that he was "cruelly persecuted". The whig leader of Western Massachusetts Joseph Hawley, was a victim of an hereditary mental disorder — apparently a manic-depressive psychosis with persecutory delusions — which "killed" his grandmother and caused his father to cut his throat with a razor in 1735. The malady overtook Hawley in 1760 — his biographer describes him as succumbing to a fit of "mild insanity" — recurred throughout the decade, and totally and permanently incapacitated him in 1776. The one biographer who has undertaken a psychological study of Samuel Adams had found him "non-rational", "not entirely normal", "probably ... a neurotic; in any case nervously unstable". Adams is represented as being afflicted with a massive "inferiority complex." During the conflict with Great Britain he is said to have created "an imaginary world," which he constructed "through the principle of projection", the defense mechanism operative in paranoia. The "inequalities" of John Adams' temper were conspicuous to his contemporaries. Benjamin Franklin, for example, believed that on occasion Adams was "absolutely out of his sense", while Jonathan Dayton claimed that he suffered from a "derangement of intellect" serious enough to disqualify him from public service. Recent historians have pronounced Adams a "neurotic personality," have found him burdened with a "handful of vigorous complexes, from hypochondria to mild paranoia". His latest biographer has revealed that he suffered three nervous "breakdowns" between 1771 and 1783. Professor Bailyn himself, in 1962, described how Adams "became paranoic" in the "intense heat of domestic politics".

The Lees of Virginia, to whose political alliance with the Adamses some historians only half facetiously attribute the Revolution, were hardly models of rationality. Arthur Lee, in fact, presents a textbook case of paranoid symptomatology. His suspicions were pathological: "He has confidence in no body. He believes all Men selfish — And, no Man honest or sincere". "His jealous dispositions", wrote a contemporary," led him to apprehend

---

[35] John P. Roche, "The strange case of the 'Revolutionary' establishment," in John Parker and Carol Urness (eds), *The American Revolution: A heritage of change* (Minneapolis, James Ford Bell Library, University of Minnesota, 1975).

designs injurious to him in every one he dealt with". He had "a Sick
Mind", wrote another contemporary, "which is forever tormenting itself,
with its Jealousies, Suspicions, and Fancies". A letter Lee wrote to Samuel
Adams of June 10, 1771 Professor Bailyn pronounced "perhaps the most
paranoid ... in the entire literature of the American Revolution". Like
Joseph Hawley, Lee seems to have been plagued by problems which ran
in his family. His sister, Alice Lee Shippen, her "imagination disorder'd",
was forced into confinement in the Pennsylvania countryside during the
Revolutionary period. A favorite nephew, Francis Lightfoot Lee, went mad
in the prime of life. And his brothers, Richard Henry Lee included, do
not appear to have entirely escaped the family affliction.

To reinforce his point, Hutson adds:

The superciliousness of the British toward the colonials, their refusal to
treat them as anything like equals, deeply wounded American self-esteem.
Then came the Stamp Act, which by depriving the colonists of the fundamental rights of Englishmen to taxation by their representatives and
trial by their peers, brutally announced that Americans were not authentic
Englishmen. The act, therefore, was more than a public law. It was also
an assault on the identities which the American elite had assumed, a
rejection of them personally, and a relegation of them to a status of inferiority. As a blow to America's self-esteem, the Stamp Act served the
psychological role of a precipitant and in its wake the paranoid delusions
that Britain was conspiring to enslave Americans began to flourish.[36]

   To Hutson's indictment of many of the Massachusetts and Virginian leaders, add Tom Paine, a recent immigrant to Philadelphia
thanks to his cultivation of his friendship with Franklin in London,
where he had made life unendurable for himself, his wife, and all
who crossed his path. Throughout his life – in England, North
America, Revolutionary France and the United States again – Paine
was always an irascible misfit, a citizen of the world because no
single place in it could stand him for long. But as a journalist he was
brilliant and could be devastating. With leaders and propagandists
like these, the coming of American Independence seems less the
Contagion of Liberty than a mass delusion, the work of "Fanaticks."
   Moreover, there was a considerable colonial elite on whom Britain
had drawn for governors' councils. Deferential political norms operated in the eighteenth-century Anglo-American world. There was
nothing new in Britain's desire that only the better sort of colonial –

[36] James Hutson, "The American Revolution: The triumph of a delusion," in Erich
Angermann, *New Wine in Old Skins* (Stuttgart, Klett, 1976), pp. 181–3.

"men of good life and well affected to our government and of good estates and abilities and not necessitous persons or much in debt" – ought to be tapped for service. James Kirby Martin shows that this norm operated and that the executive elite was drawn from the well-to-do and wealthy 10 percent of Americans. The wealthy expected to conclude life as honored councilors. And when the very wealth of an expanding colonial society "produced a glut of available candidates on the officeholding market," at the same time that Britain in the 1760s decided upon centralized rule, then crisis followed. When these "men of substance in their local communities" found themselves outside the "favored inner group," they declared that honors went to placemen, plural officeholders, and tyrants. In short, Martin holds that they resolved this structural conflict by "depersonalizing the problem and issuing statements to the effect that British appointees in the provinces were partakers in a ministerial conspiracy to destroy American liberties."[37]

This was not then a class struggle, but rather a "struggle within the ruling class," brought about by frustration and terminating in revolution. This was not the revolution of levelers, but rather of an upper class, localist in orientation, who believed that all men should be equal to compete for the inequality of office and honor. These men were perhaps a little younger than those who became Loyalists and were more likely to have been educated in America than in England. The Revolutionary governments now elected their governors and overwhelmingly called for the direct election of senators (read the old councilors); moreover, the new senators had to be both property-holders and residents of their election districts.

There is another viewpoint. Although there were increasingly close connections socially, politically, and in trade between the governing elites of the Tidewater and their agents and kin in London, Liverpool, Bristol, and Glasgow, more spells of residence in the Home Country by the privileged, such as the Lees, the Byrds, and the Morrises, and steadily growing numbers of American law students training at the Inns of Court and of American-born medical students in Edinburgh University, there was also, and perversely, a mounting pride in being American, and more awareness that American resources were part of Britain's strength. As early as 1751, in his *Observations concerning the Increase of Mankind, Peopling of Countries etc.*, published in America in 1754 and in London in 1755,

---

[37] James Kirby Martin, *Men in Rebellion: Higher governmental leaders and the coming of the American Revolution* (New Brunswick, NJ, Rutgers University Press, 1973), p. 173. Martin provides in effect a collective biography of some 487 leaders.

Benjamin Franklin had worked out that in each generation, the population of the continental colonies was doubling, and consumption of British goods increasing in proportion; the population of the West Indies, by contrast, stayed static; in the mainland colonies the population increase was ninefold between 1700 and 1775. By further contrast, the population of England and Wales increased by only 27 percent between 1701 and 1771 (from c.5 million to c.6.4 million). In 1760 Franklin wrote to Lord Kames, his Scottish lawyer friend, that "the foundations of the future Grandeur and Stability of the British Empire lie in America ... broad and strong enough to support the greatest Political Structure Human Wisdom ever yet erected." It followed that, within a century, there would be many more British in America than in the motherland, "a glorious market wholly in the power of Britain." There was no danger of incompatible interests. "So vast is the territory of North America that it will require many ages to settle it fully ... labor will never be cheap here, where no man continues long a journeyman to a trade, but goes among those new, and sets up for himself." The view was not special to Franklin. "The foundations of the Power and the Glory of Great Britain are based in America," wrote John Dickinson in 1765. America, said George Wythe in 1774, "is one of the Wings upon which the British Eagle has soared to the skies." The union of Britain with the American colonies had raised her, the Second Continental Congress affirmed, "to a power the most extraordinary the world had ever known." "The commercial advantages Britain had enjoyed with the Colonies," declared the Committee of Secret Correspondence on March 3, 1776, "had contributed greatly to her late wealth and importance." "The English," wrote John Adams on August 4, 1779, "by means of their commerce and extensive settlements abroad, arose to a degree of opulence and naval power" which had allowed them to tyrannize the world.[38]

It followed, logically, that in the connection with America lay Britain's real strength, and on it depended the European balance of power. "Our trade was rapidly increasing with our increase of people, and in greater proportion," a committee of Congress declared

---

[38] *The Papers of Benjamin Franklin*, ed. L. W. Labaree, (New Haven, Yale University Press, 1968), vol. IX, pp. 7–8; Milton E. Flower, *John Dickinson, Conservative Revolutionary* (Charlottesville, Friends of the John Dickinson Mansion, University of Virginia, 1983); Butterfield et al. (eds), *Diary and Autobiography of John Adams*. For what John Murrin has called "anglicization," see "Feudalism, communalism and the yeoman freeholder: the American Revolution as a social accident," in Kurtz and Hutson, *Essays on the American Revolution*.

in March 1776. With these facts in mind, John Adams concluded that in another war the power of a united British Empire would have destroyed France's existence as a maritime and commercial power, and would have been "fatal" to her. The kingdom, declared Richard Henry Lee at the First Continental Congress, "could not exist" without the commercial connection with America; the dissolution of this connection, the Second Continental Congress informed the inhabitants of Great Britain, would "deliver you, weak and defenceless, to your natural Enemies," and would reduce Great Britain, a correspondent of Franklin's predicted, "to a State of being a Province of France."

In 1751 Franklin had composed his essay on the Increase of Mankind, as an ardent expansionist, and as intense an imperialist as Pitt himself. Picturing the future in America, he exclaimed: "What an Accession of Power to the *British* Empire by Sea as well as Land! What Numbers of Ships and Seamen!" His imagination was fired, as was Pitt's, by the limitless prospect of power and grandeur that opened before the British empire in those years. In Albany in 1754 he took the lead in devising a scheme of intercolonial federation; in London he argued vigorously for westward expansion. He put it thus to Lord Kames in 1767:

I have lived so great a part of my life in Britain, and have formed so many friendships in it, that I love it, and sincerely wish its prosperity; and therefore wish to see that Union, on which alone I think it can be secured and established. As to America, the advantages of such a union to her are not so apparent. She may suffer at present under the arbitrary power of this country; she may suffer for a whole in a separation from it; but these are temporary evils that she will outgrow ... America, an immense territory, favored by Nature with all advantages of climate, soil, great navigable rivers, and lakes etc., must become a great country, populous and mighty; and will, in a less time than is generally conceived, be able to shake off any shackles that may be imposed on her, and perhaps place them on the imposers. In the mean time, every act of oppression will sour their tempers, lessen greatly, if not annihilate, the profits of your commerce with them, and hasten their final revolt; for the seeds of liberty are universally found there, and nothing can eradicate them. And yet, there remains among that people, so much respect, veneration and affection for Britain, that, if cultivated prudently, with kind usage, and tenderness for their privileges, they might be easily governed still for ages, without force, or any considerable expence. But I do not see here a sufficient quality of the wisdom that is necessary to produce such a conduct, and I lament the want of it.[39]

[39] *The Papers of Benjamin Franklin*, ed. Labaree et al., vol. XIV, pp. 69–70, 25 Feb. 1767.

Franklin had immense confidence in the future of an America turning and looking West. He believed that it would grow and flourish,
inside or outside the British connection – just as Washington, much
less reflective but with some knowledge too of the West, believed
that if war came, America could never be conquered by a British
army supplied from the ocean and dependent on its fragile grip on
the coast. Franklin had given his allegiance to an empire of Anglo-
American culture. In his London years (1757–62 and 1764–75), he
had been confirmed in his strong bent toward territorial imperialism.
They were the years when Pitt's leadership offered prospects of continuing expansion and optimism. He was, however, already drawing
strikingly different conclusions from those of Pitt.

There was here an imperialism of its own, land-based and expansionist, even if it did not – yet – expand across salt water. It
was agrarian and utopian, liberal and non-governmental. The faith
was in people, not bureaucrats or Navigation Acts, and in the
free farmer. Although always himself an urban figure, he shared
the physiocratic assumptions of Jefferson. Franklin was still an Old
England man, and rising remarkably through an open Atlantic society. He came from the New World to the Old as already a Fellow
of the Royal Society, scientist, and philosopher; his fame owed
nothing to caste or class: by origins he was a leather-apron man,
from the Boston waterfront. His faith was transatlantic and non-
elitist, and had a viability of its own if the winds came to blow.

This rich inheritance, however, would pass to younger men than
Benjamin Franklin, some young enough to be grandsons rather than
sons. For perhaps the most striking feature of the next generation
was not its fecundity but its youth. In the decade before 1775, half
the North American population was under 16, and three-quarters
under 25. In 1776, James Monroe was 18, Alexander Hamilton and
Rufus King 21, Madison 26 and Jefferson, a bookman and something
of a "loner" in Philadelphia, 33. George Washington at 44 was seen
as venerable, and as commander-in-chief was seen by his young
aides as a father of a family. In 1787 nearly half of the signers
of the Constitution were in their 20s and 30s. As young men, it
was natural for them to be rebellious against an older generation
at home, as well as in London's imperial administration, and to
identify themselves with the critics of the Establishment, whether
in 1776 – as in their reading of tracts and newspapers – with the
"Opposition" to Walpole; or – as in their reading of history – with
the radicals and Levelers of 1649. For the majority of younger
rebels, it was easier to find their heroes in Patrick Henry, Ethan
Allen, and Tom Paine, easier to identify with the restless misfits,

with the noise-making frontiersmen, with the loud mouths making a reputation. And, for paradox is recurrent in history, some of these young rebels in their quest for self-identity stayed loyal and thus Loyalist, even if "the old man" himself became a rebel. Thus young and handsome William Franklin, who accompanied his father Benjamin on his trip to London, became a dashing and fashionable colonial gentleman at Northumberland House, the town-house of the duke of Northumberland, and was rewarded with the governorship of the Jersies when he was only 32; he broke with his father, and stayed — an unhappy and exiled — Loyalist until the end. In this family, as in others, the generation gap was never bridged.

6 THE RELEVANCE OF "DEMOCRACY," 1776—1787

"Democracy," with all its emotional overtones, meant little to the Founding Fathers. Insofar as it could be grasped, it was unwelcome. "Give the votes to the people who have no property," said Gouverneur Morris, "and they will sell them to the rich." To James Otis democracy was "a government of all over all." "The most ignoble, unjust and detestable form of government," was John Adams' comment. Democracy was taken to mean rule by the will of the people; but one of the most radical Revolutionary leaders, George Mason of Virginia, said that "to entrust the selection of leaders to the people would be like giving the choice of colors to a blind man;" only those could hold office, he said, who were substantial property-holders. And by 1787, at the beginning of the Constitutional Convention, both Elbridge Gerry of Massachusetts and Edmund Randolph of Virginia agreed that "we have suffered from an excess of democracy."

Thus we will learn little from a study of eighteenth-century North America before or after Independence if we judge all societies by the measuring rod of the suffrage, and if we require all societies of which we approve to be based on equal suffrage for all citizens over the age of 18. The American states, in each of which the qualifications "requisite for electors of the most numerous branch" of the state legislature determined also who should vote in federal elections (Article I, Section 2 of the Constitution), all denied the vote to all women, all Indians, and all blacks. In 1776 it did not seem that voting was so very important, and all but three of the states retained some measure of tax-paying or property-owning in their qualifications for the suffrage. [40]

[40] J. R. Pole, *Political Representation in England and the Origins of the American Republic* (London and New York, Macmillan, 1966), p. 155. Compare Bernard

Nevertheless, the franchise, based generally on the 40-shilling free-hold with a minimum of religious restrictions on voting, was far broader than in Britain, if only because land-holding was so widely distributed. From 1776 in Massachusetts the towns were represented on a scale determined strictly by population. But those who voted and those for whom they voted – and they voted openly, not by secret ballot, and often "went merry to the Court House" – were still privileged. The magisterial tradition of officeholding still continued. And "Representation in Virginia was a process of social selection," says J. R. Pole. American society after 1787, as before 1776, was not "democratic" but elitist and deferential.

Widespread popular participation in politics began during 1774 with the various provincial congresses and other extra-legal organizations. Although the majority of these bodies seem to have been made up of men of standing, both artisans and farmers appeared in greater numbers than they had in the colonial legislatures. South Carolina's House of Commons contained 48 men in 1772, but almost twice that number attended the first Provincial Congress in December 1774 and four times as many were present in January 1775. By 1775 the western districts were sending about one third of the members. Similarly, nothing now prevented New Hampshire's country villages from choosing representatives, and they seized the opportunity. Since the "frontier," the "inland counties," had few that can truly be labeled "upper class", and those there were were mainly Loyalist, many new men came to fill the much larger number of civil offices and to sit in legislatures. In New Hampshire, merchants and lawyers, who had furnished about one-third of the members of the 1765 legislature, now comprised only one-tenth of the membership. Similarly men of wealth totaled one-third of the former legislature but less than one-tenth of the latter. The well-to-do element that

---

Bailyn: "Nowhere in eighteenth century America was there 'democracy' – middle-class or otherwise – as we use the term. The main reason for the wide franchise was that the traditional English laws limiting suffrage to freeholders of certain competences proved in the colonies, where freehold property was almost universal, to be not restrictive but widely permissive." Bernard Bailyn, "Political experience and Enlightenment ideas in 18th century America," *American Historical Review*, 67 (1962), pp. 346–7. John P. Roche speaks of "an open society with closed enclaves," in "The strange case of the Revolutionary Establishment," in Parker and Urness, *The American Revolution: A Heritage of Change*, p. 136. See also Wood, *Creation of the American Republic*, pp. 168–9; Richard Buel Jr, *Securing the Revolution: Ideology in American politics 1789–1815* (Ithaca, NY, Cornell University Press, 1972).

had dominated the pre-war Assembly with 70 percent of the seats was now reduced to a minority of about 30 percent. Thus a very large majority of the new legislature consisted of ordinary farmers who had only moderate properties. Ten members of the prominent families had seats in the 1765 house; by 1786 there were only four in a body two and one half times as large. New areas, moreover, were represented in legislatures, and new men came from them. In New Jersey, the economic upper class of well-to-do men that had held three-quarters of the seats before the war saw its control vanish. After 1785, fully two thirds of the representatives were ordinary farmers, presumably men of more than average ability and sometimes with military experience, but clearly part of the common people. Again, these changes occurred not just because new areas were represented but because the counties which had sent delegates in the prewar years now chose different sorts of men. In New Jersey, the counties of Cumberland, Salem, Hunterdon, Morris, and Sussex had previously been under-represented. If these are eliminated, we find that the proportion of men of moderate property rose from 20 percent to 73 percent and of farmers (exclusive of large landowners) from 23.5 percent to 60 percent.

In the south all of the six legislatures had been greatly changed as a result of the Revolution. The extent of that change varied from moderate in Virginia and Maryland to radical in New Hampshire and New Jersey, but everywhere the same process occurred. Voters were choosing many more representatives than before the war, and the newly settled areas gained considerably in representatives. The locus of power had shifted from the coast into the interior. Voters were ceasing to elect only men of wealth and family. The proportion of the wealthy in these legislatures dropped from 46 percent to 22 percent; members of the prominent old families declined from 40 percent to 16 percent. Most of these came from the long-established towns or commercial farm areas. Of course, many men who were well-to-do or better continued to gain office, but their share decreased from four-fifths to just one-half. Even in Massachusetts, the percentage of legislators who were wealthy or well-to-do dropped from 50 percent in 1765 to 21.5 percent in 1784.

Significantly, the people more and more often chose ordinary yeomen or artisans. Before the Revolution, fewer than one out of five legislators had been men of that sort; after Independence they more than doubled their strength, achieving in fact a majority in the northern houses and constituting over 40 percent generally. A writer in a Georgia newspaper rejoiced in 1789 that the state's representatives were "taken from a class of citizens who hitherto have thought

it more for their interest to be contented with a humbler walk in
life," and hoped that men of large property would not enter the
state, for Georgia had "perhaps the most *compleat* democracy in the
known world," which could be preserved only by economic equality.
To Jedidiah Morse, the government of Virginia still seemed to be
"oligarchical or aristocratical;" but to a Virginian, a revolution had
taken place. The newly chosen House of Burgesses, wrote Roger
Atkinson in 1776, was admirable. It was "composed of men not
quite so well dressed, nor so politely educated, nor so highly born
as some Assemblies I have formerly seen." But "they are the People's
men, and the People in general are right." Perhaps coming in a
Virginia setting they were welcome because of their scarcity.[41] These
six legislatures, from New Hampshire to South Carolina, shared the
same qualities. Although farmers and artisans comprised probably
between two-thirds and three-quarters of the voters in the six colonies, they seldom selected men from their own ranks to represent
them. Not more than 1 out of 5 representatives were of that class.

Nor is there any lesson for those to whom the democratic measuring rod is that of Parliament with a government directly and constantly under attack from a vigilant opposition – a government itself
chosen from and by the members of Parliament, and a Parliament
in frequent session. One of the issues of 1776 of course, was "no
taxation without representation." This did not for many mean representation at Westminster itself, however, and sometimes took the
form of "virtual representation" – the claim that Americans, and
many British for that matter, were "virtually" represented in Parliament and consented to its measures, even though unrepresented
in any direct sense. Even where it did mean representation at Westminster, the idea of constant parliamentary probing of legislation
and of a tight two-party system had not yet been born. In the 1787
Constitution, neither the president nor his cabinet were to sit in
Congress, nor were they to be directly answerable to it. Arguably,
in the light of Watergate, this separation of powers was to prove
too binding. Suffice it to say that there are few parliamentary lessons
to be learned from 1776 or 1787.

It is easy to cite the assumptions and the characteristics of twentieth century revolutions, and of democracy, twentieth-century style:
the equality in law and in status of all citizens regardless of sex,
origins, education, or attainment; the denial of the importance of

---

[41] Jackson Turner Main, "Government by the people: the American Revolution
and the Democratization of the state legislatures," *William & Mary Quarterly*,
23 (1966), pp. 391–407.

"deference", of "class", and of "privilege" – indeed, the assumption that these are inherently wicked; the absence of all restrictions on the suffrage; strong personal leadership and some "charisma" in he or she who leads; the belief, indeed, that *demos* can speak through an authoritative leader, evidenced in Hitler's view that he was the people made incarnate, and evident in men and women as varied as Joseph Stalin, Gamel Abdel Nasser, Indira Gandhi, Idi Amin, and John F. Kennedy; and the belief that on some complex and all-but-unsolvable constitutional or moral questions, only referenda will settle the question – if the question is so framed to make a clear answer possible; and finally, the assumption that democracy requires a measure of violent social transformation, and without revolution and bloodshed it has not been fully achieved. If these are the assumptions of democratic society as it has emerged, there is little to learn from eighteenth-century America. Whatever the implications of the Declaration of Independence or its ultimate Jacksonian consequences, Jefferson's and Adams' world was predemocratic and non-social-revolutionary. The word "democracy" does not occur in the Declaration of Independence, nor in the Constitution. Indeed, despite much of the recent debate on the proposed Equal Rights Amendment, on civil rights, and on the "right to privacy," it is worth stressing that nowhere does the Constitution make reference to the Declaration of Independence or to the idea of equality. Moreover, Madison's own notes of the Convention show that the framers had no intention to abolish slavery. Indeed, no less than nine of its clauses specifically protect the institution.

Nor is it possible to draw the lesson from 1776–87 that a revolution, to be total, requires a social leveling or the spilling of much blood. R. R. Palmer has made the point that in the French Revolution there were only 5 emigrés per 1,000 of the population, whereas in America there were 24 per 1,000: "The sense in which the Loyalists are forgotten."[42] The disappearance of the Loyalists did mark the end of a colonial aristocracy. There was, for a generation, room at the top, but it was not yet for poor men. Today's old families of Boston are, for the most part, derived from the *nouveaux riches* of the Revolution; Hancock and Cabot, like the Browns of Rhode Island, came up in the smuggling trade or in privateering. Staughton Lynd says of Dutchess County, New York, that the confiscation and sale of Loyalists' estates was "the first

---

[42] R. R. Palmer, *The Age of the Democratic Revolution* (Princeton, Princeton University Press, 1959), vol. I, p. 190.

major breakthrough of the independence struggle into social change."
But it did take a generation for the De Lancey estates to reach the
hands of more common men, and it was done very smoothly, where
it was done at all. In Pennsylvania, Chews and Shippens were as
prominent after as before 1776. The confiscation of the Loyalists'
estates in Bergen County, New Jersey, and in Georgia did little to
advance democracy. And in New York, where alone there seems
evidence for the view that confiscation led to widespread social
change, the law of 1779 allowed attainted persons as well as Patriots
to have the right to purchase the farms on which they were tenants.
Some four out of five of the new owners of land at Philipsburgh
Manor were small farmers, most of whom had been tenants. Patriot
lords of manors could keep their estates intact.[43]

Yet of how many revolutions since 1776 could such a story of
social tranquility be told? The view that the American Revolution was
a revolution less made than prevented is reinforced by the Beard-
Brown-Macdonald controversy. The Browns and Forrest McDonald
have not only proven that the franchise was considerably wider than
Charles Beard (and most of his generation) believed, but that the
argument from deference led to the upper classes gaining support
from the middling and lower orders anyway. Jackson Turner Main
similarly has shown the extent of vertical mobility and the openness
of the social system that resulted from economic abundance.[44]

[43] Staughton Lynd, "Who should rule at home?: Dutchess County, New York, in
the American Revolution," *William & Mary Quarterly*, 18.3 (July 1961), pp. 330–59;
Ruth M. Keesey, "Loyalism in Bergen County, New Jersey," ibid., 18.4
(Oct. 1961), pp. 558–76. Richard D. Brown, "The confiscation and disposition
of Loyalists' estates in Suffolk County, Massachusetts," ibid., 21.4 (Oct. 1964),
pp. 534–50; Robert, S. Lambert, "Confiscation of Loyalist property in Georgia
1782–1786," ibid., 20.1 (Jan. 1963), pp. 80–94; Michael P. Riccards, "Patriots
and plunderers: confiscation of Loyalist lands in New Jersey 1776–1786," *New
Jersey History*, 86.1 (1968), pp. 14–28; Beatrice G. Rubens, "Pre-emptive rights
in the disposition of a confiscated estate: Philipsburg Manor, New York," *William
& Mary Quarterly*, 22.3 (July 1965), pp. 435–56.
[44] The viewpoint of the early twentieth century is seen in Carl Lotus Becker, *The
History of Political Parties in the Province of New York, 1760–1776* (Madison, Univer-
sity of Wisconsin Press, 1909); Charles Beard, *An Economic Interpretation
of the Constitution of the United States* (New York, Macmillan, 1913); John
Franklin Jameson, *The American Revolution Considered as a Social Movement*
(Princeton, NJ, Princeton University Press, 1926); and Arthur M. Schlesinger's
"The American Revolution reconsidered," *Political Science Quarterly*, 34 (1919),
pp. 61–78. Jameson's views are re-evaluated in Frederick B. Tolles, "The American
Revolution considered as a social movement: a re-evaluation," *American Historical
Review*, 60 (1954–5), pp. 1–12. The Becker-Beard approach is currently carried
on in the work of Merrill Jensen, particularly in *The Articles of Confederation:*

Does it follow, then, that 1776–87 affords no "model" at all? If not, another paradox becomes clear: for so unrevolutionary a change, it has been curiously imitated and its phrases and creeds repeatedly invoked. It is easy to see why. R. R. Palmer put it succinctly when he wrote that the revolutionary ideas

were transferable; they had a "universal" appeal; persons of many kinds, classes, nationalities, and races, when faced by wholly different difficulties or problems, could find in them a message and application to themselves. ... The bad things were held to be special privilege, hereditary legal advantage, unjustified discrimination, group exclusiveness, unfair treatment, unnatural and unnecessary barriers, as they were thought to be, that stood in the way of individual merit, liberty and achievement. The actual practices or institutions charged with these forms of badness have varied with circumstance, time, and place.[45]

Are there any lessons then to be drawn for the world from a reassessment of the Revolutionary and the Constitution-making period? Clearly there was little change of mood between 1776 and 1787, neither a Terror nor a Thermidor. In neither decade was there a revolutionary drive. Indeed, recent scholars like Bernard Bailyn and Gordon Wood are not in fact far from the viewpoint of that early historian of the period, David Ramsay, to whom the debate over the Constitution was only incidentally a debate over principles.

During this period, a mode of government suitable to "the genius of the Americans, their republican habits and sentiments," had been institutionalized. These governments, Ramsay concluded,

are miniature pictures of the community, and from the mode of their election are likely to be influenced by the same interests and feelings with the people whom they represent. ... The assemblage of these circumstances gives as great a security that laws will be made, and governments administered for the good of the people, as can be expected from the imperfection of human institutions.[46]

An interpretation of the social constitution history of the American Revolution 1774–1781 (Madison, University of Wisconsin Press, 1948); see his article "Democracy and the American Revolution," *Huntington Library Quarterly*, 20 (1956–7), pp. 321–41. Compare also Elisha P. Douglass, *Rebels and Democrats: The struggle for equal political rights and majority rule during the American Revolution* (Chapel Hill, University of North Carolina Press, 1955).
[45] R. R. Palmer, "The Great Inversion: America and Europe in the eighteenth-century revolution," in Richard Herr and Harold T. Parker (eds), *Ideas in History: Essays presented to Louis Gottschalk by his former students* (Durham, Duke University Press, 1965), p. 19.
[46] Ramsay, *History of the American Revolution* vol. I, pp. 348–5.

The Constitution was neither a revolution in first principles, nor a break with the past: "The people of the United States gave no new powers to their rulers, but made a more judicious arrangement of what they had formerly ceded. They enlarged the powers of the general government, not by taking from the people, but from the State legislatures."[47]

Common to all the new North American constitutions were the seventeenth-century principles of annual elections and rotation in office for governors, representatives, and members of the general assemblies. This was seen as central to the notion of "virtue" in a republic. Unlike today, the objective was executive and legislative weakness; the fear was of the tyranny not only of kings but of elected "grandees." An elected magistrate was to be feared as much as one who was hereditary. James Burgh argued in his *Political Disquisitions* (1774) that if a republic is to guard against the "continual danger to liberty," representatives must be chosen for short terms and rotated frequently. Article IV of the Frame of Government of Pennsylvania, for example, stipulated that "after the first seven years, every one of the said third parts, that goeth yearly off, shall be uncapable of being chosen again for one whole year following: that so all may be fitted for government, and have experience of the care and burden of it." Not only would the principle of rotation make it possible for more people to serve in government, but, as Gordon Wood notes, it would also compel mobility in a deferential society "where men too often felt obliged to re-elect their rulers for fear of dishonoring them." Moreover, according to James Burgh, rotation acted as a check on tyranny and on the unbridled usurpation of political power. By 1777, 7 of the 10 new state constitutions – those of Pennsylvania, Delaware, Maryland, Virginia, North Carolina, South Carolina, and Georgia – had limited the number of years that an executive officer could serve. Typical of those constitutions is the statement made in Article XXXI of the Maryland constitution of 1776: "That a long continuance, in the first executive departments of power or trust, is dangerous to liberty; a rotation, therefore, in those departments, is one of the best securities of permanent freedom."[48]

One state went much further in adopting the principle of rotation. The new Pennsylvania constitution of 1776, considered the most radical constitution of the revolutionary era, required rotation in office for all elected officials – executive and legislative – to prohibit, as the constitution stated, "the danger of establishing an

[47] Ibid., vol. II, pp. 341–2.
[48] Wood, *Creation of the American Republic*, p. 140.

inconvenient aristocracy," or, as a radical pamphlet printed in Philadelphia put it, "to make room for others of equal, or perhaps superior, merit." An anonymous publicist in Pennsylvania called rotation "one of the life guards of liberty," and according to "Cato" (the British writers John Trenchard and Thomas Gordon), rotation was "essentially necessary to a free Government: It is indeed the Thing itself; and constitutes, animates, and informs it, as much as the Soul constitutes the Man."

Elections, especially of representatives and counsellors, should be annual, there not being in the whole circle of the sciences a maxim more infallible than this, "where annual elections end, there slavery begins". These great men ... be [chosen] once a year — like bubbles on the sea of matter borne. They rise, they break, and to that sea return. This will teach them the great political virtues of humility, patience, and moderation, without which every man in power becomes a ravenous beast of prey. [49]

In 1828 Andrew Jackson would return to rotation as a first principle of government: a safeguard against that corruption that arises from long familiarity with office, and which can make of public service a species of personal or family property. In turn, however, in the hands of his agents, it became again a vehicle for the empowerment and enriching of his own men, along the all-too-familiar lines of "to the faithful belong the spoils."

However, such was the wish to strengthen a weak executive in 1787 there is no inclusion in the Federal Constitution of a requirement for term limitation or for mandatory rotation of office. Presumably, it was taken for granted — as by Washington and Jefferson, in their emphasis on serving for only two terms as president. "Government is instituted for those who live under it," said Sherman of Connecticut. "It ought therefore to be so constituted as not to be dangerous to their liberties. The more permanency it has the worse if it be a bad government." The absence of rotation in office, of annual elections, of "instructions" to and of recall of elected officers became the major criticisms of the document by the Anti-Federalists in the state debates on ratification. [50]

The American political operators were familiar with charters and constitutions. In colonial days they had sent agents, or employed

[49] John Adams, "Thoughts on Government, 1776," in George J. Peek (ed.), *The Political Writings of John Adams* (New York, Macmillan, 1985), p. 89.
[50] Max Farrand (ed.), *The Records of the Federal Convention of 1787* (New Haven, Yale University Press, 1966 edn), vol. I, p. 423.

English lawyers, to defend their rights before the Board of Trade or in the Privy Council. Now they would do their complaining at home, in their own assemblies or in their own courts of law. For if a government of laws is preferable to a government of men – John Adams's antithesis – in practice government by laws means government by lawyers. That has been not a unique but a characteristic feature of the US since 1787.

One feature of the eighteenth-century debate – drawing on its own precursors in 1649 – may, however, be relevant today: when there is mounting awareness of the life tenure of judges, and of the dominance of the incumbency rule in Congress, where Senators and Representatives have small battalions of aides and abundant postage facilities to ensure their steady re-election.

A revolution, then? Yes and no. Government by remote but by liberal and lax control was defeated; and with it there went into exile many of its agents. Both it and they had gone without fanaticism and terror. The exiles were not an elite, but a cross-section of society. The great estates – those of the Pepperells in Maine, of the Fairfaxes in Virginia, of Sir George Wright in Georgia – were broken up, however; and slowly, over a generation or more, they and all the Tory estates came down to lesser men. Speculators did well: they often do. But the American Revolution, in all its liberal consequences, was not a class war. Liberty, not equality, was its code-word. Even more important, measures were taken that affected those unequal social institutions and customs inherited from European feudal society. Thus, within a decade of the signing of the Declaration of Independence, every state but two had abolished entails, and those were two states in which entails were rare. Within 15 years, every state without exception had abolished primogeniture, and in some form instituted equality of inheritance. If a revolution in content, it would be a slow, dispersed, and gradual one. There was no democracy here (since in form ownership of property was a prerequisite for the suffrage), and more concern with liberty than equality. It was a revolution with no Terror, no Thermidor, and no Caesar. Given indenture, and given slavery, it was not a society with equality of condition. Only those who owned property had the leisure and resources to engage in public affairs; in justifying property as a source of independence, there was still rule by an elite. But there was opportunity for many to invade this elite, and given that there was a new kind of property coming into being – venture capital, money borrowed, risk capital – there was also a new society, entrepreneurial, volatile and dynamic.

7 THE SIGNIFICANCE OF 1776–1787

The events of 1776 and 1787 and the years of war between have four distinct characteristics: (1) a war for independence; (2) the use of a "foreign" but inherited and opposition ideology; (3) Enlightenment thinking; (4) the setting up of a republic.

In the first place, *as a colonial war for independence*, as T. C. Barrow has said,[51] the American war was "generically different" from later revolutionary struggles. The struggle in North America was not between an aspiring native society or culture and an imposed alien foreign system, but between Englishmen. The first rights claimed were expressly those of Englishmen.

There are parallels between 1776 in North America and 1811 in Latin America. The revolutions in Latin America were "Algérien" in character, revolts of white settlers, the *criollos* against the mother-country. The *criollos* were the superiors of the *mestizos* or the *indios*. It was the *criollos* who fought the War of Independence, even if they borrowed the grand phrases; and they and their descendants treated their inferiors more harshly than Madrid (or London) had ever permitted. It can indeed still be argued that (Peru, perhaps, apart) the many subsequent revolutions in Latin America have been between and among competing groups of *criollos*; when they invoked the ideas of revolution, it was from France rather than the United States that they borrowed. France was the source of their culture; French was, until recently in Latin America, the required second language; and it was Napoleon who, by the invasion of Madre Patria, made the events of 1810 and 1811 possible. The party songs of the Liberals in Colombia and of the revolutionary movement APRA in Peru are both set to the tune of *La Marseillaise*. As J. Halcro Ferguson put it, "up till recently wellbred Argentine children believed that babies, like everything else Mama bought, came from Paris."[52]

The parallels of 1776 and 1810 are close only in that it was a struggle between whites. Simón Bolívar preached the equality of all born in the Americas, and the blacks were declared free, but in their landless and penniless state freedom meant little to them.

[51] T. C. Barrow, "The American Revolution as a colonial war for independence," *William & Mary Quarterly*, 25.3 (July 1968), pp. 452–64.
[52] J. Halcro Ferguson, *The Revolution of Latin America* (London, Thames and Hudson, 1963), pp. 17, 19.

Moreover, the people of the vast and geographically divided continent, underdeveloped and underpopulated, had none of the apprenticeship in self-government of the North American colonists. Although they borrowed the institutions of 1787, they found them unsuitable, and the imported presidential system, with its sharp divorce of executive from legislative, reinforced the social divide and the tendency to *caudillismo* that was to characterize Latin American history; 1776/1787 was not for imitation, nor for export.

Secondly, the *opposition ideology*. Bernard Bailyn and Caroline Robbins have demonstrated that the case made for separation from Britain in 1776 – for it was that, not for revolution – drew on that same inheritance by adopting the intellectual apparatus of the Commonwealthmen of a century earlier: "The configuration of ideas and attitudes which comprised the Revolutionary ideology could be found intact – completely formed – as far back as the 1730s." These ideas had their origin in the "transmission from England to America of the literature of political opposition that furnished the substance of the ideology of the Revolution. Almost, but not quite, all of the ideas and beliefs that shaped the American Revolutionary mind can be found in the voluminous writings of the Exclusion Crisis and in the literature of the 'Glorious Revolution.'" It was, in other words, the result of an easy inheritance inside a transatlantic society, the result not of Establishment but of anti-Establishment thinking; the ideas were those of 1688 or 1649, and George III could be seen as Charles I in new guise; it was fed and watered by the reading not only of Locke as mentor and of Bolingbroke as "enemy," but of John Trenchard and William Gordon, of Francis Alison of Glasgow, and of Tom Paine. As Carl Becker said of Jefferson and his ideas, it was hardly a question of where he got them, but of where he could have got away from them.[53]

Here the parallels go deeper. The colonial revolutions of our own day reflect a similar paradox: the ideas of Ho Chi Minh –

---

[53] Bailyn, *Ideological Origins of the American Revolution*, and *Pamphlets of the American Revolution*; Edmund S. Morgan, *The Birth of the Republic* (Chicago, University of Chicago Press, 1956), and "Colonial ideas of parliamentary power: 1764–1766", *William & Mary Quarterly*, 5 (1948), p. 311; "The American Revolution considered as an intellectual movement," in Arthur M. Schlesinger Jr and Morton White (eds), *Paths of American Thought* (Boston, Houghton Mifflin, 1963); "The Puritan ethic and the American Revolution," *William & Mary Quarterly*, 24.3 (1967). Compare Robbins, *The Eighteenth-Century Commonwealthman*, and H. Trevor Colbourn, *The Lamp of Experience: Whig history and the intellectual origins of the American Revolution* (Chapel Hill, NC, University of North Carolina Press, 1965).

even when he fought the French in the 1940s and early 1950s —
were as much derived from Paris and the Left Bank as from Peking;
the Philippines and the East Indies each reflect not so much indigenous cultures as the ideas and the language of their former
masters, whether American or Dutch, and their models draw heavily
on Washington and The Hague; the political system of British India,
however deviant now, is more a London than a native manufacture,
and the London School of Economics, Cambridge, and Sandhurst
have, like Paris, made their own special contributions to the course
of independence in India and Africa. It has been Paris and London
— or, more accurately, the Sorbonne, Sandhurst, and the LSE —
that have been the mentors, rather than the men and ideas of
Washington, DC.

In the third place, there was, however, an element minimized by
Bailyn, who has been preoccupied by the material in the sermon
and pamphlet literature which is heavily English and derivative: *an
Enlightenment ideology.* The new nation was conceived in a natural
framework that was awesome, challenging, and exciting. This was a
New World, and it would produce New Men. Much of the descriptive language used by visitors to the New World was like that
of Loyalist Edward Parry of New Hampshire, or Patriot Thomas
Jefferson in his *Notes on the State of Virginia*: it was to write of
America as "Elisium and the Wilds." It was the Mirage in the West,
the *novus ordo Saeculorum.* So it was with John Smith and Robert
Beverley in an earlier age; so with Crevecoeur and de Chastellux a
little later. To Bishop Berkeley or to the pre-1775 Benjamin Franklin
or to historian David Ramsay, it was clear that westward the course
of empire was set. "The Arts have always travelled Westward,"
wrote Franklin to Charles Willson Peale on July 4, 1771. Jefferson
sought to discover Nature, and Nature's Laws, in politics as in all
else. Temperature reading became a habit. Ezra Stiles of Yale filled
six volumes with weather and climatic reports. So with Jedidiah
Morse and William Bartram.

The new continent might or might not produce special flora or
fauna or new men; it certainly would, it was believed, produce a
new order of political society, something different in kind from the
anti-Establishment world of seventeenth-century England or even of
Enlightenment Paris.[54] In 1787 that new nation was only emerging,

[54] James H. Mcguire, " 'Elisium and the Wilds': a Loyalist's account of experiences
in America at the beginning of the American Revolution," *Historical New Hampshire*,
26.4 (1971), pp. 31–44; Jeremy Belknap, *History of New Hampshire*, 3 vols (Boston
and Philadelphia, R. Aitken, 1784–92), vol. I, p. 3.

but the threads to its character were already many and varied. It was providentially blessed both by God and Nature. The Lord had singled out New England, wrote William Stoughton, "above any nation or people in the world." It might lack army and church, ethnic unity and monarchy, but it was held together by a sense of common and manifest destiny. It would be a model for mankind. "Next to the introduction of Christianity," said Richard Price, "the American Revolution may prove the most important step in the progressive course of human improvement. It is an event which may produce a general diffusion of the principles of humanity and become the means of setting free mankind from the shackles of superstition and tyranny." "The free system of government we have established," wrote James Madison, "is so congenial with reason, with common sense and with a universal feeling that it must produce approbation and desire of imitation." In America even the state would respond to the laws of reason; here a "political experiment" – Madison's term – could take place in a new and strange laboratory and Newtonian political laws be revealed. Men would discover what John Adams called "the principles of political architecture." "It has ever been my hobby-horse," he wrote to Count Sarsfield in 1786, "to see rising in America an empire of liberty and a prospect of two or three hundred millions of freemen, without one noble or one king among them. You say it is impossible. If I should agree with you in this, I would say, let us try the experiment."[55]

This was Enlightenment thinking, but in a New World setting and therefore special and unique – more nationalistic than would have been welcome to the *philosophes*. Much of the language was familiar and universalist, that of Hume, Montesquieu, and William Robertson, emphasizing the constancy of human nature, the universality of human experience, the operation of binding general laws, history, as to Bolingbroke, serving as philosophy by example. It *was* unique. The Americans had permanently ended the We vs. They of the social contract. They were building a harmonious social order and had halted the cycle of historical inevitability. There was, in this sense, a touch of Marx in both Jefferson's and Adams' vision of tomorrow. This mixture of uniqueness-in-universality recurs in France in 1789,

[55] William Stoughton, *New England's True Interest* (Cambridge, MA, 1670), p. 4; Richard Price, *Observations on the Importance of the American Revolution* (Boston, 1784), p. 5; Adrienne Koch, *Power. Morals, and the Founding Fathers: Essays in the interpretation of the American Enlightenment* (Ithaca, NY, Cornell University Press, 1961), p. 128. Compare also Mercy Otis Warren, *History of the Rise, Progress and Termination of the American Revolution*.

in Russia in 1917, and in China in 1949. But in 1787, unlike its later "derivatives," it was unique because it was innocent, a Once-and-Only Place. Later revolutions had little of its innocence and none of its naivety. Robespierre, like Lenin and like Mao and like all their lesser imitators, was in the end corrupted by power.

And finally, *as a republic*, the model has held. No colonial revolts since 1776 have had kings as their legatees, but they have had emperors, declared or undeclared, and dictators galore. What saved the United States was not just Washington's restraint. Behind the Revolution of 1776 lay the bedrock of religious dissent, the Congregational Church, and those claims to freedom of thought and interpretation that were rooted in Protestantism. The cry of "No Bishop, no King" was very old and very much an inheritance from Stuart England.

The model was not just republican and Protestant, but also Dissenting. It bore the marks of the Dissenting academies and of a non-London world. This was less the South of England image of the "church on the hill" than of "the chapel in the valley" and the dales. The American image has always had not only an anti-Establishment overtone, but also a touch of the Dissent and of the unpretentiousness of the North of England and of Scotland. It is 40 years (*William & Mary Quarterly*, 1954) since Bernard Bailyn and the late John Clive pointed out the parallels, at mid-eighteenth century, between Scotland, Ireland, and North America as being in some measure three colonial associates of England; to which, add the spontaneous friendship of Benjamin Franklin with his Scottish friends in his London years (1755–75), the common emphasis on Dissent and on the importance of schools and colleges, and the hungering for equality of status – though not of condition.[56]

---

[56] "England's cultural provinces, Scotland and America," *William & Mary Quarterly*, 3rd ser., 11 (1954), pp. 200–13.

2

Making the Government

1 THE ARTICLES OF CONFEDERATION

The negotiations that led to the new constitution began when James
Madison of Orange County, Virginia, persuaded his state colleagues
to discuss with their Maryland neighbors the navigation problems
along the Potomac and in Chesapeake Bay. Each was taxing the
shipping of the other. The Maryland commissioners arrived at
Alexandria in March 1785, but found no Virginians to greet them;
they were invited to George Washington's home, Mount Vernon, a
few miles south. Washington offered his hospitality, as landowner
and ex-commander-in-chief: he was host, but not a participant.
However, he could not be described as disinterested. As a wealthy
planter and with land holdings in the West – he had wisely bought
up some of the land bounties given his troops on their disbandment,
and which they could not afford or work themselves – Washington
wanted to open up the West to settlement, to exploit his own location on the river, to bring the Potomac to the Shenandoah and
Ohio valleys by a series of locks, and to ensure that his own crops
reached the sea as easily and cheaply as possible.

Meantime, through the winter from October 1785 to April 1786,
the surviving Congress of the Articles had a quorum on only three
days. Delegates were ceasing to be interested in a central government that was powerless and without resources. At Mount Vernon,
the representatives of the two states had agreed to institute tariff
uniformity, to set up a joint committee to regulate commerce and
defense, and to submit future problems to an annual arbitration.

It became clear that it would be wise to bring further neighboring states into their discussions. Thus, at the Annapolis Convention in September 1786, five states were invited to discuss the commercial regulations on the river; New York, Pennsylvania, Delaware, New Jersey, and Virginia; the host state, Maryland, surprisingly failed to appoint delegates or to attend. Five states were thus represented, but in fact only 12 men were present. However, two of the men mattered: Alexander Hamilton, the young West Indian who had been Washington's aide-de-camp in the War, now a New York lawyer who had married into money; and James Madison. And from this meeting, on Hamilton's urging, came a resolution inviting all the states to attend a meeting in Philadelphia to revise totally the Articles of Confederation, the feeble central government under which the War of Independence had been fought, and to devise a government "adequate to the exigencies of the Union." The date set was May 1787. In effect, the Mount Vernon Conference made Annapolis inevitable, and the audacity of the nationalists turned that ill-attended convention into a summons for Philadelphia.

Such meetings were becoming regular events. In 1754 at Albany, Benjamin Franklin for Pennsylvania and Thomas Hutchinson for Massachusetts, had drafted a plan for an imperial federation, with an intercolonial governor, and even the prospect of a third, an American, parliament; but it won no support in any colony, nor in London. Similar proposals preceded and followed the discussions at the Stamp Act Congress in 1765. In 1774 Joseph Galloway brought forward his plan for imperial federation at the First Constitutional Convention. And the war-time constitution, the Articles of Confederation, certainly needed strengthening. They had not been agreed upon until November 1777, and were not accepted by all the states in rebellion until 1781, six months before Yorktown.

The War was thus fought and won by a government claiming independence that was effectively powerless; it had no king, tyrant or otherwise, in authority; there were no hereditary aristocratic lions around thrones; it had no power even to raise taxes, which was the prerogative of the states – their resources found by loans or by the emission of paper currency, rarely acceptable beyond individual state boundaries. Thirteen independent states, 13 various societies, 13 distinct currencies; and a Congress that had begun as a protest organization, reconstituted itself as an instrument for military coordination, but was devoid of regular revenue and of any coercive authority over the states. During the war about $378,000 was contributed by the states to the joint operations of the Confederation; by contrast, $44 million was issued in paper currency and about

$55 million was borrowed from European sources, mainly Dutch and French bankers. Each legislature, said Samuel Adams, "sought to be the sovereign and uncontrollable power within its own limits and territories;" and each was further restrained from becoming a "tyrant" by a bill of rights. The executive was formed by committees, rich in absentees. It was very weak, and was meant to be so.

The Articles no doubt provided as strong a union as the temper of the people would then sanction, since there was, as yet, no all-pervading feeling of American nationalism and patriotism – nor, after 1781, of crisis. Nevertheless, the central government during these years was totally inadequate for the task it had been assigned: directing the War, and then the post war economy. Being powerless, few were willing to serve in it, and business was repeatedly suspended for want of a quorum. Moreover, it was laid down that no one could be a Congressman for more than three years out of every six, nor its president for more than one year in three. The delegates were subject to recall by their state legislatures, to whom they were thus effectively subordinated. As a result, many of the best men preferred the wider scope offered by the state governments, as did Jefferson himself; and the states grudged the expense of sending delegates. Seven delegations were the minimum required for the transaction of business, and this was often hard to attain; and for important matters the votes of nine states were needed.

The principal weakness in the system of government devised in the Articles of Confederation, however, lay in the financial provisions: it depended totally upon the states, and the states could not be depended upon to pay up. The Congress had neither the power to tax nor the power to regulate commerce, for "Each state retains its sovereignty, freedom and independence." There were early proposals that Congress be granted the right to levy import duties, but interstate rivalries prevented these proposals coming to fruition. New York, as a major importer, especially resented its potential loss of revenue. From 1781, when the Articles came into effect, near-anarchy prevailed. Each state pressed its own special interests; it treated its neighbors as it would a foreign power. It was but "a firm league of friendship." The Pennsylvania and New Jersey army mutinied in 1781; only Washington's prestige averted a general mutiny in 1783. The Congress was driven from Philadelphia in that year by a band of unpaid soldiers, so that Washington as commander-in-chief said his farewell to it in 1783 in Annapolis, where it was hiding from a victorious but unpaid and therefore rebellious army. The army was discharged with difficulty, and the soldiers returned to their homes without their pay or land bounty warrants. The United States was left virtually without a force for defense after 1783.

To these weaknesses, add the effect and devastation of war. At one time or another, the British had occupied every major city from Boston to Savannah, and New York City from 1776 to the end of the fighting. Much of the South had been ravaged in the struggle; in Virginia some 30,000 slaves had melted away, in South Carolina some 25,000 had been carried off by the British. The old links of overseas trade, especially with the mother-country and with the other British colonies, were shattered. Exports of cotton and rice, tobacco and indigo, had fallen; warehouses were crammed with crates of furniture and fabrics for which there was no cash. Immigration seemed to be coming to a halt. And, with the British connection severed, shipbuilding was part of the slump. Victory spelled confusion. As David Ramsay put it in 1783, "This revolution has introduced so much anarchy that it will take half a century to eradicate the licentiousness of the people."

Spain added to the problems; it refused to permit western settlers to send their products to the Gulf by way of the Mississippi, barred American ships from its colonial possessions, quarreled with the United States over the southwestern boundary, intrigued with the Indians, and sought to entice Tennessee and Kentucky to come under its fiat. Efforts to settle these questions failed – in part, at least, because many easterners had no desire to weaken their states by encouraging their fellow citizens to move across the Alleghenies. The Congress had no authority to regulate interstate commerce or extra-state relations.

Both Britain and the United States violated the terms of the treaty of peace. Despite the peace settlement, Britain held on to the north-western posts, refused to compensate for slaves carried away during the war, declined to send a minister to the United States, and closed her West Indies possessions to American trade. The United States could not compel the states to restore lands confiscated from the Loyalists, or force citizens to pay their debts to Britain.

A similar story of power vacuums can be told for each member state. Americans' familiarity with their colonial charters made them draw up similar formal written constitutions for each state – the first to be created *de novo* in the English-speaking world since the Cromwellian interregnum. Connecticut and Rhode Island took the easy course, by simply turning their seventeenth-century charters into constitutions. In the other states constitutions were drawn up by conventions sitting as legislatures, and were not submitted for popular ratification. But after objections to this procedure in Massachusetts, a special constitutional convention met in 1779–80 and made some show of submitting the document to the people. New Hampshire's first convention actually had its work disapproved by the electorate, and a new constitution was produced in 1783 and ratified in 1784. Through these tentative essays there was worked out what became the typically American method of constitution-making: a special convention followed by a referendum. This procedure established the doctrine that constitutions preceded the laws and were the roots of them; so too for judicial review in its American form.

The new constitutions were similar to each other in many respects, and followed colonial models, with elected governors and upper houses replacing the nominees of the Crown or the Proprietors. They thus included provision for legislatures, normally of two houses (but unicameral in Pennsylvania and Georgia), a single executive head – the governor – elected by the legislature or by the voters directly, and a suffrage limited to property-owners or taxpayers.

At least five schemes of government for Virginia were proposed in press and pamphlet, including John Adams' *Thoughts on Government*. The main difference among them was in their ideas about the composition and appointment of the upper house by the lower – for life. The threat of "aristocratical" triumph in Virginia produced from the liberal conservative Adams a denunciation of "dons ... bashaws ... grandees ... patricians ... sachems and nabobs." The most important part of the Virginia constitution was its declaration of rights – George Mason's handiwork – and that became a model.

The constitution of Pennsylvania (1776 version) was to have no governor, weak or strong. Instead, the executive consisted of a council elected by the people every three years, with one member from each county. Its powers were severely limited, and all real authority rested with the unicameral legislature. Every seven years a Roman-style Council of Censors was to be elected by the freemen to review the constitution, and, if necessary, call a state convention to amend it. The legacy of this *bouleversement* was clear to Benjamin Franklin at the end of the decade: "We have been guarding against an evil that old states are most liable to, *excess of power* in the rulers. But our present danger seems to be *defect of obedience* in the subjects."[1]

The question of the suffrage was one of the issues fought over between conservatives and radicals in all the states, and they also

---

[1] *The Papers of Benjamin Franklin*, ed. L. W. Labaree et al. (New Haven, Yale University Press, 1968), vol. XXII, p. 218.

differed over the provisions regarding religion (in Georgia and the Carolinas, Massachusetts and New Jersey, only Protestants could hold office), over qualifications for office-holding, over legislative apportionment, and over the extent of the powers of the governor as against the legislature. The radicals stood for legislative supremacy, the conservatives for the principle of the separation of powers. On the whole the radicals achieved notable success both as regards a wider franchise and as regards a better representation of the interior. Again, authority was, on the whole, concentrated in the legislatures and especially in the lower house. Four states – Pennsylvania, Delaware, North Carolina, and Georgia – allowed all male, white taxpayers to vote, and Vermont had free manhood suffrage. The other states all retained some property requirements for voters. Most states, too, required much higher property qualifications for office-holders. Only in Massachusetts was the governor given a veto.

Indeed, in Massachusetts the governor had greater powers than in almost any other state. In other states his powers were often very restricted, but in Massachusetts his veto could only be overridden by a two-thirds vote of the legislature, and he had wide appointive functions. The judiciary was appointed "during good behavior," a synonym for life tenure. Property qualifications for office were high. The governor must be a rich man with property "worth" £1,000 (in South Carolina he had to be worth ten times that sum); a senator must be worth £600 and as a representative £100. The ordinary voter had to have a freehold estate of £3 income a year, or property worth £60. Thus property was in effect represented twice in the constitution: once, geographically, in the apportionment of senate seats, and again in the qualifications for office. Since wealth was a qualification for governor, and the governor had a strong veto, the popular will could be easily checked unless it was almost unanimous. Similarly, in New York, while the assembly, senate, and governor were all to be elected by the people, a property requirement of £20 was set for the suffrage for the lower house, and £100 freehold must be held to vote for senator or governor. The constitution attempted "balance," but its strong bias towards property bore out Jay's maxim that "those who own the country ought to govern it."

The radicals also distrusted the idea of an independent judiciary, and in several states the judges were to be chosen by the legislatures and for very short terms only. In contrast, however, to the more democratic provisions of the new constitutions in states such as Pennsylvania, Virginia, and North Carolina, some states such as Maryland which remained under conservative control showed less radical influence in their constitutional documents.

The return of peace brought one dramatic change. A Philadelphia newspaper recorded in the summer of 1784 the arrival of 1,400 immigrants in one week. By the end of 1786 it was estimated that, since the end of the war, 20,000 German, Irish, and Scottish immigrants had arrived. And, via Pennsylvania, they moved west and southwest. Kentucky's estimated white population (in June 1779) of 1,700 had by 1785 become 30,000; Tennessee's had risen from 8,000 in 1776 to 36,000 in 1790; in the same period the population of the back country of Virginia nearly doubled, from 400,000 to 750,000. Vermont, totaling 30,000 in 1784, had 85,000 in 1790. "A rage for emigrating to the western country prevails," wrote John Jay. "The Continental Land Office is opened, and the seeds of a great people are daily planting beyond the mountains."[2]

The War had been fought as – almost – 13 wars. Its legacy was diplomatic/frontier clashes of state with state. Pennsylvania and Connecticut were at odds over the title to the Wyoming valley, and though the federal court of arbitration reviewed the Pennsylvania-Connecticut question and decided in favor of Pennsylvania, this did not allay the hostility of the Pennsylvania legislature toward the "foreign"-born residents of the Wyoming valley. Vermont, while desiring admission as a state, was a bone of contention between Massachusetts, New Hampshire, and New York; it contemplated joining Canada or even remaining independent altogether.

A rapidly growing population pressed on the land that was available in New England. Many rural residents turned to household manufactures. The efforts of these women and men laid the foundation for American self-sufficiency and prosperity. In the small village of Hallowell, Maine, most young women learned to weave; and the surge in household cloth production dramatically reduced American dependence on British manufactures. During the Revolution, artisans in the town of Lynn, Massachusetts, had similarly raised their output of shoes. By 1789, the town was turning out 175,000 pairs of shoes each year, and by 1800, no fewer than 400,000 pairs. As Alexander Hamilton noted proudly in 1792, the countryside was "a vast scene of household manufacturing ... in many cases to an extent not only sufficient for the supply of the families in which they are made, but for sale, and even, in some cases, for exportation." Merchant entrepreneurs such as Ebenezer Breed of Lynn directed many of these rural enterprises. This new capitalist system of production for market, however, increased economic conflicts. Many

---

[2] Richard B. Morris, *John Jay: The nation and the court* (Boston, Boston University Press, 1967), p. 125.

back-country farmers went into debt to expand household production. As debts increased, so too did defaults and law suits. The courts directed sheriffs to sell the property of bankrupt farmers and artisans to pay merchant creditors and court costs. "Mark any Clerk, Lawyer, or Scotch merchant," warned North Carolina farmer Herman Husband; "We must make these men subject to the laws or they will enslave the whole community." Actually, merchants usually had the law on their side, so, during the 1760s, Husband and his followers intimidated judges, closed courts by force, and broke into jails to free their arrested leaders. Anti-merchant sentiment during the 1770s pushed forward the independence movement in Virginia, where Scottish traders had extended credit to more than 32,000 tobacco planters. And it appeared yet again in western Massachusetts in the 1780s. Between 1784 and 1786, the Hampshire County Court heard 2,977 debt cases. Angry Massachusetts farmers defended their property from seizure by closing the courts. Farmers – like women and slaves – now used the democratic-republican heritage of the American revolution to justify their actions. They met in extra-legal conventions and spoke of the "Suppressing of tyrannical government." Back-country unrest, anti-tax sentiment and resistance to the enforcement of court decisions and to foreclosure orders in Massachusetts, triggered off a rebellion in the spring of 1787 led by the war veteran Captain Daniel Shays. The central government could give little aid in restoring peace; in the end, the debtor farmers were dispersed by state militia, and Shays fled to Rhode Island, then Vermont. His name was frequently invoked, however, by the Founding Fathers in Philadelphia throughout their discussions: for he might have too many imitators. "The people have turned against their teachers the doctrines which were inculcated in the late revolution," was Fisher Ames's conclusion.

For lack of money, the payment of the interest and principal of the domestic and foreign debt also went largely by default. The current coin of the United States was a hodge-podge of foreign pieces, badly plugged and clipped. States fell far behind in paying the sums requisitioned by the central government. Seven of them met the postwar depression by currency inflation. Continuous efforts to amend the Articles so that the central government could collect duties on imports were fruitless. There was no power to enforce treaties, and individual states sought unilateral agreements with the Indians.

"We have reached almost the last stage of national humiliation," said Alexander Hamilton. He proposed that Congress be given undefined powers to coordinate interstate trade, commercial agreements, paper money, taxation to meet War costs and debts, and control of the army. He favored "one Supreme head," even a monarch; along with Henry Knox, Robert Morris (the "financier of the Revolution" who had opposed independence in the first place), and Gouverneur Morris, there was talk of a *coup*, and of Washington as king. "Affairs are rapidly drawing to a crisis," wrote Washington. "I do not conceive we can exist long as a nation without having lodged somewhere a power, which will pervade the whole Union." But he would have nothing to do with any plot. He would not respond to this call. Others like Noah Webster echoed these dismal views. Clearly it was necessary for Congress to call a general convention of the states "to take into consideration the situation of the United States, to devise such further provisions as shall appear to them necessary to render the constitution of the federal government adequate to the exigencies of the Union."[3]

2 DONE IN CONVENTION

The Convention that began to assemble in the Philadelphia State House in May 1787 was therefore not novel, and was meeting formally only to draft amendments to the Articles of Confederation, approved six years before, the wartime form of government. If a number of them were intent on devising a stronger form of government, they were not unmindful of Bolingbroke's cautions: "The Statesman who would reform the Constitution, must never declare his intention." In any case, since under the Articles any changes required the unanimous consent of the state legislatures, time and patience were required. And if boldness did prevail, would this not be yet another illegality, yet another change so early on in the Republic's very short four-year history?

Nor were the Convention's delegates punctual. Rhode Island, familiarly known to the rest as Rogues Island, since it flourished as much by smuggling as by legitimate trade and by regular emission of paper money of doubtful value, did not attend at all – to the relief of most. Only two of New Hampshire's four delegates appeared, and then only at the end of July – by which time two of New York's

---

[3] Gordon S. Wood, *The Creation of the American Revolution 1776–1787* (Chapel Hill, NC, University of North Carolina Press, 1969), pp. 87, 140, and esp. ch. 12, "The worthy against the licentious;" Richard L. Perry (ed.), *Sources of Our Liberties* (Chicago, American Bar Association, 1978), pp. 209–21; Jackson Turner Main, *The Anti-Federalists* (Chapel Hill, NC, University of North Carolina Press, IEAHC, 1961), p. 12.

three delegates had returned home. That the Virginians came early at least allowed their best-read and most shrewd member, James Madison, to draft the Virginia Plan, sometimes labeled the Randolph Plan since, with a politician's skill, he had it presented to those assembling by Virginia's governor, Edmund Randolph. In the eyes of fellow-delegate William Pierce of Georgia, Madison was "the best informed man on any point in debate ... a Gentleman of great modesty." He became the craftsman of the document. His plan became in essence the Convention agenda. He had worked tirelessly at drafts for months. He it was who persuaded Washington that it was essential for him to attend, and he assured him it would not fail, and that his precious reputation not to be put too much at risk. In the end most of his draft became the supreme law. Even more significantly, the Convention decided that the new frame of government would require the approval only of nine – but specially summoned – state conventions. It was in fact part of a long, vigorous, and great debate.

In all, 55 delegates were present in Philadelphia, of whom 32 were to become front-rank figures. Among them were 2 future presidents, 2 future chief justices, and 6 future state governors. At the time, 2 (William S. Johnson and Abraham Baldwin) were college presidents; indeed, Johnson was also the son of the first president of King's College, New York (now Columbia), and himself had degrees from Harvard, Yale, and Oxford (of which he was a Doctor of Civil Law). Three (George Wythe, James Wilson, and William C. Houston) were or had been professors; while 26 others were college graduates, at a time when there were only nine colleges in colonial America. No less than 9 were Princeton men. Over 20 had served in the army. Four delegates had read law at the Inns of Court in London – in all 33 were lawyers; 28 had served in Congress, and most of the others in colonial or state legislatures. Eight were merchants, 3 were doctors, and 15 shareholders. Ten of them were planters; 15 were slave-owners (not all from the South). But, for all their experience, many of them were young men: Madison 36, Hamilton 30, Charles Pinckney 29. The leading radicals of the decade before were absentees: Thomas Jefferson, Tom Paine, Patrick Henry, who was suspicious of the business, and Samuel Adams, who was not elected. One potential delegate, Erastus Wolcott of Connecticut, refused to attend because of the fear of yellow fever; one who did, Daniel Carroll of Maryland, insisted on staying at Germantown because it was "high, healthy and at a suitable distance" from the city. Of those attending, however, ten would be financially ruined, two would die in duels, one (at least one) was a dipsomaniac, one

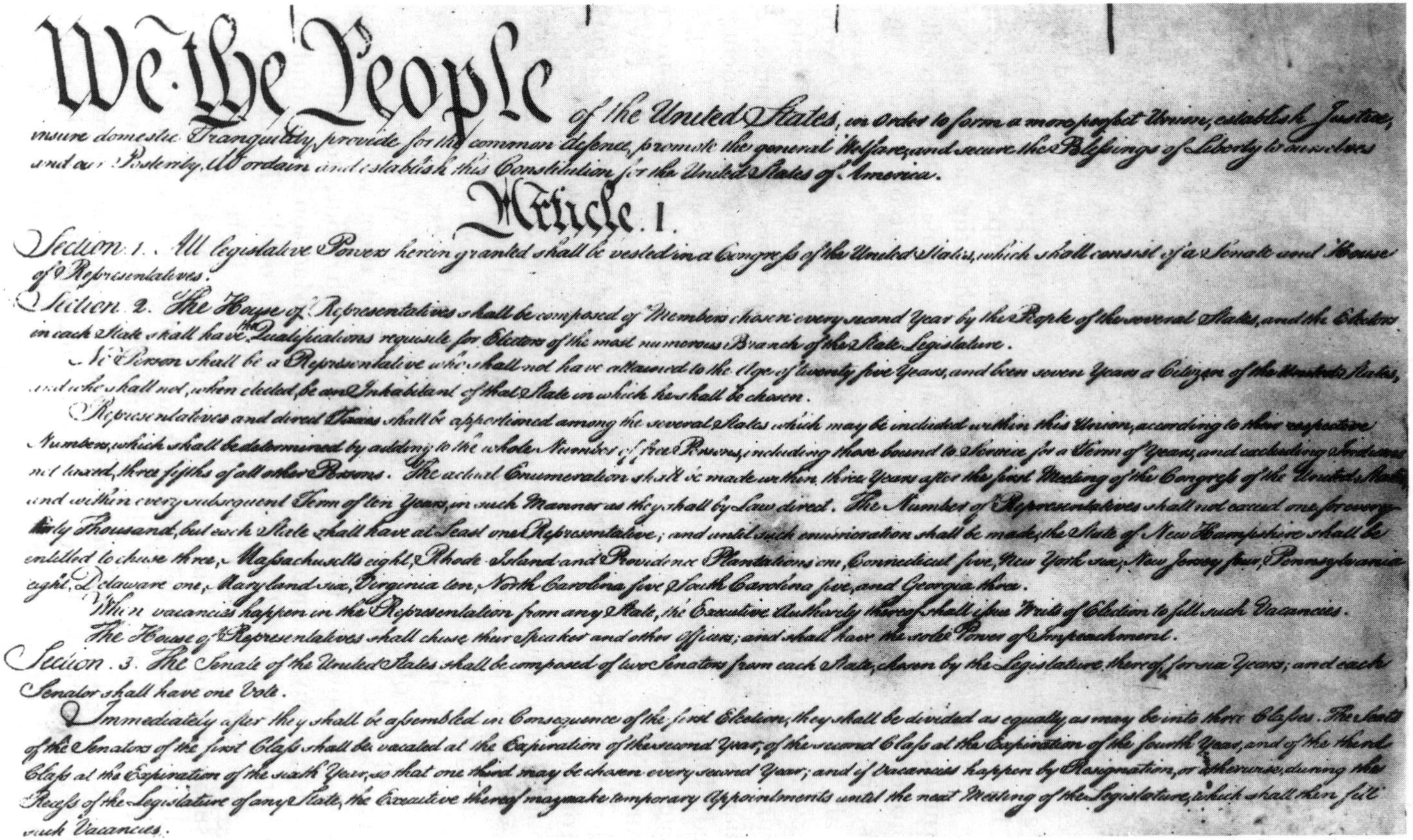

We the People of the United States, in Order to form a more perfect Union, establish Justice, insure domestic Tranquility, provide for the common defence, promote the general Welfare, and secure the Blessings of Liberty to ourselves and our Posterity, do ordain and establish this Constitution for the United States of America.

Article. I.

Section. 1. All legislative Powers herein granted shall be vested in a Congress of the United States, which shall consist of a Senate and House of Representatives.

Section. 2. The House of Representatives shall be composed of Members chosen every second Year by the People of the several States, and the Electors in each State shall have the Qualifications requisite for Electors of the most numerous Branch of the State Legislature.

No Person shall be a Representative who shall not have attained to the Age of twenty five Years, and been seven Years a Citizen of the United States, and who shall not, when elected, be an Inhabitant of that State in which he shall be chosen.

Representatives and direct Taxes shall be apportioned among the several States which may be included within this Union, according to their respective Numbers, which shall be determined by adding to the whole Number of free Persons, including those bound to Service for a Term of Years, and excluding Indians not taxed, three fifths of all other Persons. The actual Enumeration shall be made within three Years after the first Meeting of the Congress of the United States, and within every subsequent Term of ten Years, in such Manner as they shall by Law direct. The Number of Representatives shall not exceed one for every thirty Thousand, but each State shall have at Least one Representative; and until such enumeration shall be made, the State of New Hampshire shall be entitled to chuse three, Massachusetts eight, Rhode Island and Providence Plantations one, Connecticut five, New York six, New Jersey four, Pennsylvania eight, Delaware one, Maryland six, Virginia ten, North Carolina five South Carolina five, and Georgia three.

When vacancies happen in the Representation from any State, the Executive Authority thereof shall issue Writs of Election to fill such Vacancies.

The House of Representatives shall chuse their Speaker and other Officers; and shall have the sole Power of Impeachment.

Section. 3. The Senate of the United States shall be composed of two Senators from each State, chosen by the Legislature thereof, for six Years; and each Senator shall have one Vote.

Immediately after they shall be assembled in Consequence of the first Election, they shall be divided as equally as may be into three Classes. The Seats of the Senators of the first Class shall be vacated at the Expiration of the second Year, of the second Class at the Expiration of the fourth Year, and of the third Class at the Expiration of the sixth Year, so that one third may be chosen every second Year; and if Vacancies happen by Resignation, or otherwise, during the Recess of the Legislature of any State, the Executive thereof may make temporary Appointments until the next Meeting of the Legislature, which shall then fill such Vacancies.

Plate 3 The first few lines of the Constitution.
(National Archives, Washington, DC.)

would engage in treason, another be poisoned by a greedy heir; another became insane and yet another disappeared without trace. There is no record of Luther Martin ever being sober in Philadelphia. To Jefferson, however, writing in retrospect, they were a collection of "demi-gods." One who had come up the hardest way, Roger Sherman of Connecticut, by origins a shoemaker, had become mayor of New Haven, where he became treasurer of Yale University and keeper of its bookshop: he too was a lawyer, though self-taught. Written constitutions, and lawyers to interpret them for each generation, set the pattern of American politics. Many presidents have been lawyers, and almost every vice-president and every secretary of state except the occasional soldier has been a lawyer. Then, as now, a training in law usually suggested a future in politics.

The document framing the Constitution, 4,000 words long, was compiled over four months by those 55 men. Eighty-four delegates had been named to attend, but attendance was erratic. Of the 42 who stayed long enough, 39 signed the final draft on September 17, 1787; 3 of those who attended refused to sign. They were not empowered to draw it up at all: the War of Independence was four years past, but their 13 now-independent states charged them only to amend the Articles of Confederation, the loose alliance which had been the single-chamber and all-purpose government for the duration of the seven years of war and its aftermath. The delegates were thus exceeding their instructions in drawing up a new document.

Their achievement is familiar enough, and well chronicled. Yet it was chronicled only with difficulty. The official secretary, William Jackson, was far from efficient. His notes were not published until 1819, and when they appeared James Madison of Virginia proceeded to alter his own private notes, which had been much more fully kept, in accordance with them. These were themselves not issued until 1840, four years after his death, by which time fiction about the Founders bulked as large as fact. Madison's notes, now transformed, were far from reliable. Not until Max Farrand's *The Records of the Federal Convention* appeared in 1911 was it possible to see clearly just what had occurred in Philadelphia.[4]

The delegates were prompt in making four decisions. First, after little debate they agreed to draw up a new and stronger central

[4] Max Farrand, *The Records of the Federal Convention of 1787*, 4 vols (Yale University Press, 1911). For an analysis of the groups and interests, not least of those he describes as "hard-nosed and tough-minded," see *Notes of Debates in the Federal Convention of 1787*, reported by James Madison, with an introduction by Adrienne Koch (Akron, Ohio, Ohio University Press, 1966).

government – and thus disobey their instructions from the Confederate Congress only to consider amendments to the Articles. Thus
they became themselves an illegal body. Second, they decided to bypass the state legislatures – which they saw as too radical – when
they sought ratification: that would be the task of specially elected
ratifying conventions. Third, though it would clearly be necessary
for a secretary to keep a record of motions and votes, no formal
report was to be kept of the content of the debates, of who said
what, and when. Moreover, secrecy would obtain; no press releases,
no reporters to be present, not even wives. There would be no
leaks, not even when they dined afterwards at the Indian Queen. And
fourth, the document would not require unanimous ratification: it
would go into operation when nine states had ratified it.

A gathering, then, of unusually talented men, able to debate in
secret and keep secret what they said; a basic agreement on what
needed to be done to strengthen the government; and small concern,
in contrast with the men of 1774–6, with the "why" of political
action. The lawyers, Madison and Hamilton preeminently, were now
concerned with the mechanics of state-building. To Madison, as a
student of constitutions, and to Hamilton, with his taste for executive energy in government, this was a congenial task. The American
Constitution was, of course, in Farrand's phrase, "a bundle of compromises;" its political strength lay in the fact that controversy could
be resolved by compromise. Again and again recourse was had to
statements that sought to reconcile opposing viewpoints, or to a
deliberately evasive form of words; thus, the two-year term for congressmen was a compromise between one year and three.[5] Yet in
essence there was only one compromise: that on July 5. The Great,
the Connecticut, or the Sherman Compromise – since it was largely
his doing – was fundamental; it determined the shape of the central
government – the decision on federalism.

Only three people voted against strengthening the government;
two, Oliver Ellsworth and Roger Sherman, agreed later, when it
was decided that the states should have equal representation in the
Senate. The third, Robert Yates of New York, left the convention
after about six weeks and opposed ratification of the Constitution.

Arriving early, the Virginians had prepared, or had listened to
Madison's elaboration of, a plan whereby there was to be a legislature of two houses, the lower to be elected by the people, and the

[5] Forrest McDonald, *Novus Ordo Seclorum: The intellectual crisis of the constitution* (Lawrence, University Press of Kansas, 1985) ch. 6.

upper to be elected by the lower. There were also to be a single executive and judiciary, both chosen by the legislature. Both houses – one directly, the other indirectly – would thus reflect population rather than statehood; this Virginia Plan was, therefore, acceptable to the larger states. There was bitter feeling on this point, for the disparity of the states in size and composition was striking. Delaware had 60,000 people; Rhode Island 68,000; Virginia, excluding Kentucky, had 750,000, of whom 300,000 were slaves; and Massachusetts, excluding Maine, 380,000, very few of whom were slaves.

New Jersey countered Virginia's Plan with its own, one much closer to the Articles, presented by William Paterson: a legislature of one house, elected by the states regardless of population, and with a plural executive elected by Congress.

The compromise reached after a month's debate gave the states equal representation in the Senate (the upper house) while maintaining the national principle – representation by population – in the House of Representatives (the lower house). This was an important result, not merely because it became the basis of the American government, but also because it saved the Convention from dissolution. Yet it is possible to argue that, important though it was as a reconciliation of federal and national principles, it was designed to meet a dilemma – the rivalry of great and small states – that was largely illusory. Maryland, a small state, and Virginia, a large one, shared on the Chesapeake a common economy of tobacco plantations and slave labor. Similarly, Connecticut and Massachusetts were alike in their commercial interests. The rivalry of state against state has never been as important in American history as the clash of sections.[6]

The other compromises were at the time less important but were subsequently to become matters of controversy, largely because they reflected economic and sectional tensions. The first concerned the method whereby slaves were to be counted for both representation and taxation. The northern states wanted slaves excluded from representation, since they were neither citizens nor voters, but included

---

[6] For the secret origins of the Great Compromise – over a meal in the apartment of John Rutledge of South Carolina, which along with Roger Sherman of Connecticut in the end involved seven other delegates (to plot what? ask critics) – see Calvin C. Jillson, "Constitution-making: alignment and realignment in the Federal Convention of 1787," *American Philosophical Society Review* (1981), p. 610; Forrest McDonald, *E Pluribus Unum: The formation of the American Republic 1776–1790* (Boston, Houghton Mifflin, 1965), pp. 166, 173; Clinton Rossiter, *1787: The Grand Convention* (Macmillan, 1966), pp. 159–264.

for tax purposes, since they were property. This Yankee subtlety the South could not appreciate. The result was the adoption of the so-called "three-fifths compromise," whereby a slave was counted as three-fifths of a person for both purposes. But this solution was not the result of a compromise in the Convention. It had first been proposed as an amendment to the Articles in 1783 and had been ratified by 11 states before the Convention met. There was here material for future trouble, as there was, also, in the South's fear that Congress might use the power to regulate commerce to interfere with the importation of slaves or to levy export duties on her staple products.

That these problems did not arouse the excitement then that they were to do in 1828 or 1861 was due precisely to the legalism and practicality of the delegates. In legislatures, assemblies and dining clubs, they had wrestled with problems like these for a decade or more. Indeed, the coincidence of the publication of Madison's notes in 1840 with the rise of the slavery question gave an impression that it had been a major issue in 1787. It was not. As John Rutledge of South Carolina put it, "Religion and humanity have nothing to do with the question. Interest alone is the governing principle with nations. ... If the Northern States consult their interests, they will not oppose the increase of slaves, which will increase the commodities of which they will become the carriers." They did consult their interests and a series of agreements followed: no interference with slave importation until 1808; Congress to be granted the power to regulate foreign and interstate commerce; but to protect the South, all treaties to require for ratification a two-thirds vote of the Senate; Congress to be forbidden to levy export taxes. But none of these matters was very controversial. The most bitter attack on slavery at the Convention came in fact from a Virginian.

On the final problem, the shape and the power of the federal government and its popular base, there was less controversy and less need for compromise, for the Fathers spoke and thought with remarkable unanimity. They declared that the Constitution was the supreme law of the land. The Tenth Amendment, declaring that the powers not expressly delegated to the federal government stayed with the states, has received so much attention that one is apt to minimize that to the Founders the central feature was the creation of this supreme power, as expressed in Article VI, Section 2. The new government should be strong, unlike the Congress of the Articles, and should be clearly sovereign. It was to be national rather than federal; it was no mere confederation of sovereign states. It should act not on the states but on the people. It should legislate for all individuals in all the states. This was the real Revolution – and utterly unforeseeable back in 1776. This new government should be empowered to levy taxes and to coin money; to declare war and make peace, to raise an army and navy, and to suppress uprisings (like Shays' Rebellion); to regulate foreign commerce, and commerce between the states; it should be able to admit new states on terms of absolute equality with the old; and, not least, it should have authority to make all laws "which shall be necessary and proper" in order to execute its powers (Art. I, Sec. 8). The state issue of paper money and legislation impairing the obligation of contracts were prohibited. The new government was something far more than "a firm league of friendship" between the states. In many ways it was at once the apogee of the Revolution and its Thermidor.

The other compromises are very familiar: a House of Representatives to be elected directly, the suffrage being governed by the state suffrage; the Senate elected indirectly by the state legislature – as was so until the ratifying of the 17th Amendment in 1913; the President elected still more indirectly, by a cumbrously chosen electoral college. The last was the most academic device of all in an otherwise very practical document. It was hit upon in the closing stages of the Convention by a special committee set up to settle a number of questions on which agreement had not been reached. It survives now, emasculated by the growth of political parties, as a curious relic of eighteenth-century political mechanics. The judiciary was to be appointed by the President, subject to senatorial approval but quite beyond popular control.

Yet in all the rich variety of their processes of election, the three branches of government were nicely balanced one against the other. They were to be equal, coordinate, and, so far as could be contrived, harmoniously interlocked. None could for long be seized by either democrats or potential tyrants. The strong government so patiently manufactured was still made as weak and as divided as could safely be managed. The very first Article, like the Articles being "amended," took pains to list at length the powers that the federal government did not have. Least of all did the Fathers attempt, either explicitly or implicitly, to define the government; nor did they forbid amendments – though they were and are not easy to accomplish; it was in fact the amendment provision that reconciled Patrick Henry to the new constitution. Again, the omissions are significant; and wars and near-wars were to be needed to resolve the question of whether they were building a nation or a federation, and just what "We the people" implied.

A short document: yet it was the result of 400 hours of debate through a hot summer. Its ambiguities and vagueness it was left to the future to clarify. As Madison said, ambiguity was the price of unanimity. They wrought well, not primarily because they were constitutionalists – they were after all overturning one constitution with some casualness – but because they had supreme faith in their own handiwork, in the new country, in the revolution they had led to victory, and in the future they glimpsed of their own resources and fortune. They were politicians of whom some were scholars, like Madison; some creative thinkers, like Hamilton; some, and not least important, party managers and manipulators like John Beckley of Philadelphia; and like good politicians they had faith, most of all, in themselves. It was for the politicians that Franklin spoke on the last day of the Convention. There had been criticism of the omission of a Bill of Rights, defining the area in which an individual lived a life free from governmental constraint. There was criticism of the powers given to the central government. There was talk of summoning yet another and more representative Convention. Franklin met these challenges in a famous and characteristic plea:

I confess that there are several parts of the Constitution which I do not at present approve, but I am not sure I shall never approve them. For having lived long, I have experienced many instances of being obliged by better information or fuller consideration, to change opinions even on important subjects, which I once thought right but found to be otherwise. It is therefore that, the older I grow, the more apt I am to doubt my own judgment and to pay more respect to the judgment of others. ... Thus I consent, sir, to this Constitution because I expect no better, and because I am not sure that it is not the best. ... On the whole, sir, I cannot help expressing a wish that every member of the Convention who may still have objection to it, would with me, on this occasion, doubt a little of his own infallibility and to make manifest our unanimity, put his name to this instrument.[7]

3   RATIFICATION

The major problem, however, on which compromise would be all but impossible, was the ratification of the Constitution. This involved a public debate outside the State House in Philadelphia and the

---

[7] Benjamin Franklin, speech in the Convention, Sept. 17, 1787, in A. H. Smyth (ed.), *The Writings of Benjamin Franklin*, 10 vols (New York, Macmillan, 1905–7), vol. IX, p. 607. For the nationalism-forming role of the Congress of the Articles, see Jack Rakove, *The Beginnings of National Politics* (New York, Knopf, 1979).

approval of popularly-elected state conventions. As we have seen, the Convention was, although in name only, amending the Articles of Confederation. To do so required the unanimity of all 13 states. In the absence of Rhode Island, this was clearly unattainable. The Convention therefore took the highhanded view that the new document would become effective when ratified by nine states in specially summoned conventions.

The debate in the country was far more bitter than that in Philadelphia, and much less amenable to control. It was now that the "democratic" issue was most clearly raised, and in the course of the debate that faction and party first appeared. Yet the opposition to the new document did not challenge its main themes; the Republic and its balanced government were fully accepted. Nor could it provide a clear leadership: Randolph hesitated and became a Federalist; John Hancock in Massachusetts was won over by the expectation of rewards; Samuel Adams was impressed by the support for the Constitution he found among the shipwrights of Boston at a carefully arranged meeting at the Green Dragon, and by the final compromise to include in it a Bill of Rights. The central theme of the Anti-Federalists was the fear of an encroachment on the rights of the states and on "liberty." This fear was stronger in the larger and more "democratic" states than in the smaller. Between December 7, 1787, and January 9, 1788, five states ratified the Constitution. The Delaware convention ratified promptly and unanimously; New Jersey a little less promptly, but also unanimously. It took Pennsylvania a month of debate and some rather rough practices to come to accept it. It did so by 46 votes to 23; but the minority claimed that in the elections of delegates only 13,000 freemen voted out of 70,000 entitled to do so; here was still a sharp divergence between the interests of Federalist Philadelphia and Anti-Federalist western Pennsylvania. Connecticut and Georgia also ratified. In Massachusetts, in February 1788, the Federalist victory was narrow: 19 votes out of 355. Not until June 1788 did the ninth state, New Hampshire, give its approval. At that point it was not clear that the two key states, Virginia and New York, had agreed to support the Constitution. In fact, Virginia had approved it by a narrow majority of ten votes, 89 to 79, before learning of the action of New Hampshire. New York's majority was even smaller – 30 to 27 – when it came to its decision in July.

This result in New York was once again evidence of Alexander Hamilton's energy, political flair, and persuasive power. At Philadelphia he had been in a minority in his delegation; he attended only occasionally, and his theories of centralization made him suspect.

His colleagues Abraham Yates and John Lansing, who had finally withdrawn from the Convention on the grounds that it had exceeded its authority, were friends of George Clinton, governor of the state and a leading Anti-Federalist. Clinton expressed his fears in a series of articles under the pen name "Cato". New York's politics were personal and peculiar, and they were largely the mercantile politics of the City of New York. It commanded the trade of the whole country, and in 1787 – as in 1776 and earlier – it preferred neutrality or even independence to coming down on the wrong side. To these motives of fear, of cupidity, and of commercial risk and profit, as well as of public spirit, Hamilton appealed in the series of newspaper essays in support of the Constitution that became, along with essays by Madison and Jay, *The Federalist Papers*, published in book form in May 1788. They still remain the best analysis of the problems the new country faced, and of the reasons for adopting the Constitution. There was small hope, he believed, for the future of the country so long as the government was powerless and was scorned by foreign traders, so long as it was handicapped by varied and conflicting state laws and currencies, and so long as it was incapable of paying its own debts or compelling the states to meet theirs. He won the New York convention to his views by the sheer force of his arguments.

The victory in New York was narrow. The nation as a whole, had it been polled individually, might well have been opposed to the Constitution. Charles A. Beard's figures, suspect though they now are, showed that only one in four of the adult males voted for delegates to the state ratifying conventions; probably not more than one in six of them ratified it. Hamilton thought that four-sevenths of the people of New York were against the Constitution. Neither Rhode Island, which submitted it to its town meetings, nor North Carolina, adopted the Constitution until the new government was in operation, when they had little choice. The extent of the opposition led seven states to accompany acceptance by a series of amendments, and in the first session of the new Congress 12 of these were agreed upon and submitted to the states. Ten were ratified and became the Bill of Rights. This was a concession by the Federalist leaders to their critics.

The Constitution was drafted and enacted by a group of determined men, very much a minority among their fellows and acting without legality; so it had been with the Revolution, and so it is with most great developments in human history. Neither the document nor the methods whereby it was made the fundamental law were the work of a majority; nor were they tributes to democracy, still an ideal of the future. The Federalists were nationalists; in nothing were they so skillful as in the name they chose, for their intention was unitary rather than federal. They were led by two masterful politicians, Hamilton and Madison. If Hamilton appears, in print as in his subsequent legislation, an apologist for the economic royalists, it is impossible not to see in his handiwork, as in his consistent purpose, a policy that had about it, at this stage at least, courage, foresight, and idealism. If Madison supplied the scholarship and the draftsmanship, Hamilton provided the drive and combative power that were even more necessary.

4 THE INTERPRETERS

Of all aspects of the Revolutionary period, the motives that led to the drafting of the Constitution have become the most controversial. As the United States grew and prospered, it was natural that the Constitution as its basic law should become revered, and that its Founding Fathers should be seen as men of remarkable wisdom. This view was natural, but has not gone uncontested in American history. The crisis of 1814, the Civil War of 1861, and the controversies over the legality of the New Deal, were indications that the compromises of 1787 had not been final solutions for all problems. There has been in fact no "consensus," to use today's fashionable word, on the central theme of the American story – whether it is a *plures* or a *unum*, a federation or a centralized nation. Yet once the Civil War was won and nationalism was triumphant, Hamilton emerged as the patron saint of the American entrepreneur, and the Constitution was seen once more as a work of great prescience. It came to win approval abroad in the eloquent encomiums of Gladstone and of Bryce. Nationalist historians such as George Bancroft praised it still more lavishly. John Fiske, writing in 1888, accepted the Federalist arguments of a century before, to compose his study of *The Critical Period* and to portray the Founders as inspired and dedicated men who had brought order and security out of chaos.

It was natural that there should be a reaction from this patriotic view; and of it Charles Beard became the spokesman. Product of a Midwest that was then passing through the Populist and Progressive phase and of British politics in its Fabian heyday, Beard's *Economic Interpretation of the Constitution* (1913) was, as much as Fiske's book, a product of its time. To use a phrase employed six years before by one of Beard's mentors, J. Allen Smith, in his *The Spirit of American Government*, Beard saw the Constitution as "a reactionary document," or at least as one that was counterrevolutionary. It was the product, Smith had said, not of democracy but of men who feared democracy, a "scheme of government ... planned and set up to perpetuate the ascendancy of the property-holding class leavened with democratic ideas." Or, as Burke had said of 1688, it was a revolution not made but prevented.[8]

Beard argued, as did Merrill Jensen later, that the Federalists, the conservatives or nationalists of their day, had exaggerated the weakness of government in the decade before 1787, and that Fiske *et al.* had accepted their partisan indictments as statements of permanent truth. He pointed to the many fears the Federalists expressed of "democracy," their provisions guarding contracts debts, their concern with a strong judiciary and the separation of powers as checks on majority rule. And he substantiated his argument by a massive analysis of the economic interests of the Founders, drawing heavily on the Treasury Department on lines that anticipated the cumulative-biography approach of Sir Lewis Namier toward British eighteenth-century politics. Not one of the Founders, he argued, was a farmer or an artisan; and five-sixths of them stood to gain from the Constitution, since they owned securities or slaves or land for speculation. Far from being disinterested men, the patriots who came to the rescue of their country – Washington and Randolph, James Wilson and Rufus King, Oliver Ellsworth and Alexander Hamilton, Robert Morris and John Dickinson – had such a large stake in its property and society that the document they drafted was inevitably biased toward their own economic interest. Their motive was the safeguarding of property rights. The value of their bond holdings appreciated by some $40 million when supported by the credit of the new government. Moreover, they were not popularly chosen and were a small but highly influential group. By controlling elections and manipulating conventions they put through an undemocratic document to which the majority of Americans were in fact opposed.

If Beard's analysis represents a piece of historical debunking, an expression in fact of militant Jeffersonian populism, it was brilliantly done and has left a profound mark on all subsequent writing on this period. It stimulated many state-by-state analyses; it greatly influenced the attitude of all later writers, some of whom, like V. L. Parrington, made contributions to American historical writing quite

---

[8] Charles A. Beard, *An Economic Interpretation of the Constitution of the United States* (many editions; first published New York, Macmillan, 1913); J. Allen Smith, *The Spirit of American Government* (New York, Oxford University Press, 1907).

as significant as Beard's; it reinforced the trend toward the "new" and social emphasis in historical writing, evidenced in the work of Carl Becker, J. Franklin Jameson, and Arthur Schlesinger Sr; and, not least, many of the Founding Fathers at last emerged as explicable and human figures. They were not only human, they were capitalists and speculators. Beard was seeking to portray what he called the true "inwardness" of the Constitution. This was needed, he thought, expressly because the document gives no outward recognition of any economic groups in society, mentions no special privileges, and, as he puts it, "betrays no feelings;" "Its language is cold, formal and severe." It could hardly be said to be either cold or non-controversial after he had written about it.

The extent of Beard's impact is best evidenced by the scale on which his work has recently been attacked. For it was equally bitterly censured in his own time, not only for its economic determinism, but for its demonstration that a work believed to be of near-divine ordering had been in fact the product of a very mundane self-interest. And much of the criticism then made was as weighty as that of our own day. E. S. Corwin in 1914 criticized Beard's exaggerations and faulted his figures; and he pointed out that one of the biggest property-owners of the convention was Elbridge Gerry, who refused to sign the Constitution and opposed its adoption. R. L. Schuyler, in his excellently balanced study of the Constitution, while accepting that the two main groups were based principally on economic interests, stresses that there were many other motives; among the Federalists it was impossible to exclude patriotism, the wish to see the new country playing a dignified role in international affairs, the belief that only a strong and vigorous government would preserve the Union, experience in and respect for the army rather than the Continental Congress; among critics, there was fear for liberty, strong state-right sentiments, and much sectional jealousy. The leaders, it was pointed out, were as much lawyers as businessmen and speculators; they were politicians also playing for power. It was Franklin who spoke of the United States as a "Nation of Politicians," and none could speak of the profession with more authority. Yet they were also, in some measure, idealists. They were affected, says Charles Warren, "by pride in country, unselfish devotion to the public welfare, desire for independence, inherited sentiments and convictions of right and justice."[9]

---

[9] Robert L. Schuyler, *The Constitution of the United States* (1923); Charles Warren, *The Making of the Constitution* (Boston, Little, Brown, 1928).

Economic determinism is persistent and unfashionable in the United States. And in recent years a new political attack has been launched on Beard's interpretation of the Constitution. Robert E. Brown has examined Beard's thesis in great detail and denied not only its validity but the research on which it was based. The records that Beard used date, he has argued, from several years after the Constitutional Convention. The holdings of the Founding Fathers were in land far more than in securities. If their property was adversely affected by the situation before 1787, so were the property interests of the great majority of people, for the ownership of property was widespread. If they were selected by their state legislatures rather than popularly elected, such a method was the constitutional form under the Articles. If a man refrained from voting for delegates to the ratifying convention, this was more from indifference, and therefore presumably from contentment with the *status quo*, than from disfranchisement. And if both the Founders and the people acted as they did, it was as much for reasons of conviction as for reasons of economic self-interest.

The same author in his *Middle-Class Democracy and the Revolution in Massachusetts 1691–1780*, argues that there was no large working class denied the vote in Massachusetts and that the farmers in the western part of the state had as full representation in the legislature as the merchants of the east. Massachusetts, he believes, was already a democratic state. And, even more bravely, he holds that the same arguments can be sustained for Virginia. Not all the latest research accords with this interpretation, and it would indeed be revolutionary if similar views were to obtain of the Southern states. But the emphasis is clear. It has been driven home even more ruthlessly by Forrest McDonald in a name-by-name analysis of the Fathers and of the states, proving that they represented agriculture far more than commerce or securities, that many of them were lawyers with many varied clients to represent, and that their interests were far more diverse than Beard's categories revealed. Clearly, there was no sharp division between the interests of real and personal property. [10]

---

[10] Robert E. Brown Jr, *Charles Beard and the Constitution* (Princeton, NJ, Princeton University Press, 1956); Robert E. and B. Katherine Brown, *Virginia 1705–1786: Democracy or aristocracy?* (East Lansing, Michigan State University Press, 1964); Robert E. Brown, *Middle-Class Democracy and the Revolution in Massachusetts 1691–1780* (Ithaca, NY, Cornell University Press, 1955). Forrest McDonald, *We the People: The economic origins of the Constitution* (Chicago, University of Chicago Press, 1958).

At this point one is tempted to recall Louis Hartz's remark: "But after all is said and done Beard somehow stays alive, and the reason for this is that, as in the case of Marx, you merely demonstrate your subservience to a thinker when you spend your time attempting to disprove him."[11] What the critics are asserting, however, is partly the superiority of recent research to Beard's avowedly "fragmentary" methods, and still more the viewpoint of the mid-twentieth century. The Fathers, they remind us, were patriots after all, men with principles as well as pocketbooks. If they represented property, they spoke for many constituents, for there were many property-owners. They sought to create a strong government not only, and perhaps not mainly, to curb democracy but also to create a new nation and preserve the gains of the Revolution. For they had pride in both achievements. The fashion today is to revere the Constitution almost as did Bancroft and Fiske, and to see it as conserving a society that had already gone far toward becoming a property-owning democracy. The most remarkable characteristic of the political theory of the Revolution, says Clinton Rossiter, was "its deep-seated conservatism." "The American future was never to be contained in a theory," writes Daniel Boorstin. "The Revolution was...a prudential decision taken by men of principle rather than the affirmation of a theory." Beard, despite his errors, has it seems been legitimized; the Founders were not selfish; they were only wise.[12]

Indeed, Merrill Jensen and his acolytes at the University of Wisconsin continued to reflect the progressive views of Charles Beard; for them, too, the Constitution was an anti-democratic document written in secret by a group of self-interested men to secure their own property rights, against the opposition of small farmers and debtors, of personalty against realty. And these liberal, anti-statist views reflected the writers' views on the problems of their own day.

The nationalist leaders from the Declaration of Independence to the Philadelphia convention – men like Robert Morris, John Jay, Gouverneur Morris, James Wilson, Alexander Hamilton, Henry Knox, James Duane, George Washington, and James Madison – were bold, energetic, articulate; and they knew each other.

---

[11] Louis Hartz, *The Liberal Tradition in America* (San Diego, Harcourt Brace Jovanovich, 1955), p. 28.
[12] Clinton Rossiter (ed.), *The Federalist Papers* (New York, Mentor Books, 1981), Introduction; Daniel Boorstin, *The Americans: The colonial experience* (New York, Random House, 1958).

Most of these men were by temperament or economic interest believers in executive and judicial rather than legislative control of state and central governments, in the rigorous collection of taxes, and, as creditors, in strict payment of public and private debts. They declared that national honor and prestige could be maintained only by a powerful central government. Naturally, not all men who used such language used it sincerely, for some were as selfish and greedy as their opponents said they were. The nationalists frankly disliked the political heritage of the Revolution. They deplored the fact there was no check upon the action of majorities in state legislatures; that there was no central government to which minorities could appeal from the decisions of such majorities, as they had done before the Revolution. ...

From the outset of the Revolution there were two consistently opposed bodies of opinion as to the nature of the central government. There was, of course, a wide variation of belief among adherents of both points of view. There were extremists who wanted no central government at all and others who wanted to wipe out the states entirely. There were some who wanted a monarchy and others who would have welcomed dictatorship. But such extremists are not representative of the two great bodies of men whose conflict was the essence of the years both before and after 1789.[13]

Moreover, the nationalists (the contemporary word they used was Federalist, in part to hide their centralizing motif) were 10 to 12 years younger than those then called Anti-Federalists. At the beginning of the War, George Washington at 44 was the oldest of them all; six were under 33 and four were in their 20s. Of the cautious, doubting, and state-centered Anti-Federalists in 1776 only three were under 40, and one of these, Samuel Bryan, son of George Bryan, was a boy of 16. The Anti-Federalists were indeed older and men of little faith. Their rivals, despite their youth, had made their mark on the national stage, and had rendered the states considerable service.

The work of the Constitution-makers was marked, it is now clear, less by centralists vs. federalists, less by the class conflict of haves and have-nots that was basic to Beard's thinking, than by the tangled interplay of state, sectional, group, and individual interests that Namier would have understood more clearly than Beard.[14]

In more recent writing, three themes can be identified, and are all much more sophisticated: sectionalism; the nationalist politics

[13] Merrill Jensen, *The New Nation, a History of the United States during the Confederation 1781–1789* (New York, Knopf, 1950).
[14] For a survey, see James H. Hutson, "Country Court and Constitution," *William & Mary Quarterly*, 38.4, (July 1981), pp. 337–68.

and maneuvers of the Congress of the Articles; and ideologies; and one sub-theme – and all interlock. Thus, H. James Henderson stresses the importance of sectionalism as an element in Congressional politics: New England, the South, and the middle states. Subsequent American history can indeed be written around the interplay between these sections. [15]

Secondly, "the new age" of younger men drew on their previous experience as pragmatic republican politicians, either in the Congress of the Articles, or in the state legislatures. They were less theorists than practitioners, indeed devisers of a new science of politics – fixers, realists, arrangers, reconcilers of contradictions, and in the end initiators. Their interest was in stability more than liberty. Jack Rakove sees the parallels between the 1780s and the 1770s, between the nationalists of the 1780s – Madison and Hamilton – and the older radicalism of Richard Henry Lee and Samuel Adams. The outcome was a product of cautious tactics and canny calculators. The unity that emerged in 1787 was utterly unheralded; it was built not on heroism or on any special political finesse but on a laborious series of compromises, threats, and maneuvers; it was, like so much else in history, a damned near close-run thing. The Founding Fathers had no particular faith in the virtues of men – though they might talk of Man in suitably pious fashion. The Constitution in its complex system of compromise and balance assumed and took for granted and therefore was designed to offset the all-too-predictable workings of the deceits and deals, the log-rolling and lobbying, that mark in practice the ways not of rational Man but of irrational Men. Being sinful men, they took sin into their reckoning, and their work has survived treason and civil war. Or is it simply that, as Bismarck put it, a special Providence has always looked after fools, drunkards, and the United States of America? [16]

The third strand in recent writing is a legacy of the research of Bernard Bailyn and Gordon Wood, and of their aforementioned

[15] H. James Henderson, *Party Politics in the Continental Congress* (New York, McGraw Hill, 1974); Joseph L. Davis, *Sectionalism in American Politics 1774–1787* (Madison, University of Wisconsin Press, 1977).
[16] Rakove, *Beginnings of National Politics*; Wood, *Creation of the American Republic* and *The Radicalism of the American Revolution* (New York, Knopf, 1991); Jack P. Greene, *The Re-Interpretation of the American Revolution 1763–1787* (New York, Harper and Row, 1968); esp. the essays by Stanley Elkins and Eric McKitrick, "The Founding Fathers: young men of the Revolution" (originally in *Philosophical Society Quarterly*, 72 (1961); pp. 181–216, and John P. Roche, "The Founding Fathers: a reform caucus in action" (originally *American Philosophical Society Review*, 55 (1961), pp. 799–816.

studies of the intellectual origins of the Framers' political ideas. If Bailyn, Caroline Robbins and J. G. A. Pocock traced the origins of pre-Revolutionary thinking not to the liberal Lockean writings but to the English seventeenth-century republican tradition, it was Bailyn's student Gordon Wood who explained how similar notions were influential in the years leading up to the Constitutional Convention.[17]

The preoccupation of these writers is, in a word, with the republic – its origins, its form of government and ensuring its survival. For Garry Wills, it was a product of the Scottish Enlightenment as well as of the classics; for Henry May and Donald Meyer, it was European in origin. For some of these writers, trade and commerce (and "corruption") were the same threats that they had been to Country party men at home and abroad in Walpole's England. Garry Wills has also explored the image-making that went into Washington as Cincinnatus. And one of the most original and penetrating studies of the period has come from Joyce Appleby, emphasizing less the republican and nostalgic themes derivative from the seventeenth-century, but the liberal and forward-looking: the notion of a society of socially liberated, politically equal, and economically progressive individuals, who could welcome and not be suspicious of what would – later – be described as commercial capitalism. There were many contradictory notions to be reconciled: Southerners were firm that property was the guarantor of liberty, John Adams-style Yankees stressed virtue, by which he meant the subordination of private ambition to the collective good – ideas, and indeed bodies of doctrine (Scots, English, classical), rivalled and clashed with other bodies of doctrine. In this view, however, Jefferson's election as President in 1800 was the single most important change in the history of American political culture.[18]

[17] Wood, *Creation of the American Republic*, J. G. A. Pocock, *The Machiavellian Moment: Florentine political thought and the Atlantic tradition* (Princeton, NJ, Princeton University Press, 1975); and *idem* (ed.), *Three British Revolutions* (Princeton, NJ, Princeton University Press, 1980), particularly for J. M. Murrin's essay "The Great Inversion, or Court *versus* Country", pp. 368–453.

[18] Henry F. May, *The Enlightenment in America* (New York, Oxford University Press, 1976); Donald H. Meyer, *The Democratic Enlightenment* (New York, Putnam, 1976); Ralph Ketcham, *From Colony to Country: The Revolution in American thought* (New York, Macmillan, 1975); Pocock, *Three British Revolutions*; James H. Hutson, "Country, Court and Constitution: Antifederalism and the historians," *William & Mary Quarterly*, 38 (1981), pp. 337–68; Drew R. McCoy, *The Elusive Republic: Political economy in Jeffersonian America* (Chapel Hill, NC, University of North Carolina Press, IEAHC, 1980); Garry Wills, *Inventing America: Jefferson's Declaration of Independence* (New York, Doubleday, 1978), and Ronald Hemowy's critique of Wills in *William & Mary Quarterly*, 26 (1979),

And the sub-theme? Running through all this recent scholarship is the most constructive probing question. What did the Founding Fathers mean by the words they used; did they agree with each other in using them; and do the words still, 200 years on, mean the same? For at the heart of the debate, then and since, are the key words: *republic*, *property*, *liberty*, *natural* and *civil rights*. These words had been the vocabulary of the Levelers and Diggers of the seventeenth century too – and of Locke and Machiavelli, and if it comes to that, of Plato and Aristotle.[19]

5 PROBLEMS AND PARADOXES

Yet some of the major issues the Founding Fathers evaded, or fudged, or simply did not recognize as issues at all.

The presidential role

The Founders decided that they needed a one-man executive, not the Committee which in form had acted as executive under the Articles. They did so, however, because they had trust in George Washington, the 55-year-old Virginian planter who had been commander-in-chief through the War, and who had been persuaded – very reluctantly and after great hesitations since he had "a reputation to put at risk" – to serve as the chairman of the Constitutional Convention. No one but him could be seen as the first President, and the office was largely "designed" with him in mind.

Washington was gifted with neither eloquence nor literary skills: his hunger to remain at Mount Vernon was seen as natural and re-assuring; when he did become the first President he planned to retire after one term, and was vehement to do so after the second. This was a Cincinnatus unwilling to leave the plough except in response to his country's call. His experience was unmatched; he looked the part of "Leader;" and he was beyond reproach. The device for select-ing the President seemed almost unimportant, a matter of mechanics,

pp. 563–623; Garry Wills, *Explaining America: The Federalist* (New York, Doubleday, 1981); McDonald, *Novus Ordo Seclorum*; and Joyce Appleby, *Capitalism and a New Social Order: A republican vision of the 1790s* (New York, New York University Press, 1984).
[19] See Douglass Adair, *Fame and the Founding Fathers*, ed. T. Colbourn (New York, Norton, 1974), and the writings in particular of J. G. A. Pocock, Garry Wills, and Forrest McDonald.

but they came back to the problem again and again: should he be elected by the people, as was urged by James Wilson, "Jamie the Caledonian," but which few supported? Or by the Senate, as many favored? Each time they discussed it, and they did so on 12 occasions over four months, they settled on a different formula. In the end they left it to the Committee on Postponed Matters, charged essentially to settle a number of thorny problems, none of which seemed crucial; for whatever the device, they assumed that power would stay with themselves or with men like themselves, the power-barons of each state.

The President's duties were expected to be formal, to send and receive ambassadors, to act as a supreme magistrate. He "was simply charged with the superintendence of the employees." The words are those of doctoral candidate Woodrow Wilson, in his Ph.D. dissertation of 1885, later published as *Congressional Government*. "The inevitable tendency of every system of self-government," he went on, "is to exalt the representative body to a position of absolute supremacy." It was a natural enough view, 18 years after the impeachment of President Andrew Johnson. The doctoral candidate would see it very differently himself in 1913–20. But the line drawn between executive and legislature was sharp. No Cabinet officer can sit in or be answerable to Congress; the government was meant to be ineffective. "That government is best," said Thomas Jefferson, "which governs least." And when one branch did act, another was meant to thwart or at least to check it.

After the months of to-and-fro, the shape was clear; and it was given form by the Committee on Style. The President, expected to play a largely formal role as the supreme magistrate (a title once thought of for him), would be elected not directly but by a cumbrously devised electoral college, consisting of a group of men appointed, not elected, by each state, and meeting in each state on a fixed date and only for this purpose. The Senate, with two members from each state serving for six-year terms, was again chosen not directly by the people but by the state legislatures or as they directed – as it remained until 1913. A judiciary, members of which served for life, was chosen by the President, but with the advice and consent of the Senate. Only the House of Representatives, sitting for two-year terms, was elected by the people – or, more accurately, by the people as citizens of subdivisions of their states. Power, when it could be found, lay with the Congress, but the new federal republic would, it seemed, be run by the leading senators from the leading states, who alone got to know and to trust (or distrust) each other. The model in fact was parliamentary, not presidential, but a parliament built of checks and balances, and free from "corruption" by government, strong in civic virtue, and with no king.

Presidential power

Presidential power on its present scale was totally inconceivable. The objective was balanced government, stronger than had obtained since 1776, headed by one man, not a committee – but not by the awesome figure of today. When Jefferson went from the White House to Capitol Hill to deliver his inaugural address in 1800, he walked. Little was said, therefore, of presidential powers, except that the President was commander-in-chief of the army and navy, and of the militia of the several states; nothing was said of *where* or *why* troops would be located, nothing on his role as negotiator-in-chief. He had a modified and reviewable veto power; he had an appointive and treaty-making power, in collaboration with the Senate; and he was required to "take care that the laws be faithfully executed." In this sense, the United States has survived and prospered not because of the Constitution but in spite of it: in spite of a system of separate institutions permanently engaged in battle with each other, in spite of special interests dominating narrow segments of public policy, in spite of the development of "strong" demagogic party leaders chosen by national conventions, in spite of a presidential election that has now become a long television-oriented ordeal that is closer to a carnival than to a sustained and serious discussion. And, indeed, in spite of a President who is now enjoying a power unimagined and unwelcome in 1787, but who must reach his foreign and domestic objectives only by perennially struggling with, and carefully contriving treaties with, the two houses of Congress, and with a legion of interest groups. The presidential oath binds him to preserve, protect, and defend the Constitution of the United States. Despite the passage of a War Powers Act in 1973 (passed over President Nixon's veto) designed to secure Congressional approval to major moves in foreign policy, the President's authority today is all but unlimited – witness Grenada in 1983, Libya in 1986, "Irangate" in 1989, the Gulf in 1990–91, and the deposing of General Noriega in Panama in 1989. Even where these foreign interventions have had Congressional and popular approval, these exercises of presidential power would have horrified the Founders (as would Roosevelt's skill as radio communicator, and Ronald Reagan's ease and mastery on TV). So too would the corruption that has characterized some President's terms of office:

Mr Madison thought it indispensable that some provision should be made for defending the Community against the incapacity, negligence or perfidy of the chief Magistrate. The limitation of the period of his service, was not a sufficient security. He might lose his capacity after his appointment. He might pervert his administration into a scheme of peculation or oppression. He might betray his trust with foreign powers. ... In the case of the Executive Magistracy which was to be administered by a single man, loss of capacity or corruption was more within the compass of probable events, and either of them might be fatal to the Republic.[20]

The judiciary

In the Founding Fathers' discussions, the *federal courts* received the least attention. The Confederation had had no judiciary at all, except for a tribunal to try maritime cases. In 1787 a Supreme Court was agreed on, and while power was given to set up inferior courts, their number and character were left to Congress "to ordain and establish." The Constitution gave the Supreme Court no authority to negative Acts of Congress or those of the state legislatures. The major worry was, indeed, lest any federal court intrude in the affairs of the states. The Court did not become in essence a third branch of the federal government until the chief justiceship of John Marshall, 1801–36, who had had exactly one month of formal legal education, but who "reigned" over the Court for a third of a century. Marshall was an intense nationalist, and had served as secretary of state to President John Adams. He asserted the right of judicial review, and made it a doctrine of judicial supremacy. In *Marbury* vs. *Madison* (1803), the Court struck down the Judicature Act of 1789, and through the next half-century it pronounced regularly on the validity of Acts of Congress, though sustaining them all.

Cynics like Mr Dooley have said that the judges followed the election returns.[21] In fact, if they have been so influenced, they have followed them a generation late, since, though appointed by one President, as holders of appointments for life they have pronounced during the presidencies of his successors. In the first half of the nineteenth century, they upheld slavery, notably in the Dred Scott judgment of 1857. In this, by a 7–2 vote, they declared that Scott as a Negro could not be a citizen of the US, that as such he could

---

[20] *The Papers of James Madison*, ed. Robert Rutland (Chicago, University of Chicago Press, 1977), vol. X, p. 108, July 20, 1787.
[21] Martin Dooley, an Irish saloon-keeper, was the creation of the Chicago editor, Finley Peter Dunne. See his *Mr Dooley Says* (London, Heinemann, 1910).

not sue in the federal courts, and, further, that he could not become free by residence in territory made free by Act of Congress, because Congress had never had the constitutional power to exclude slavery from the territories. This in effect negatived the Missouri Compromise of 1820, which had forbidden slavery in the Wisconsin Territory. As such, it promised the expansion of the Southern way of life – and overturned, 37 years afterwards, the elaborate efforts of Congress in 1820 to compromise on slavery.

The Northern victory in arms ended slavery in law, and gave citizenship and the vote without regard to color or previous condition of servitude. But it was business enterprise, not blacks, that was "liberated." The Court's support for enterprise and big business, indeed, permitted the Jim Crow system of segregation to continue on railways and public transport, just as the judgment in *Plessy* vs. *Ferguson* (1896), in ruling that segregation did not constitute discrimination, in effect condoned it. The Court threw out a host of measures from civil rights to the horrendous proposition of a federal income tax, which in the end required an amendment to the Constitution (1913). Roosevelt's criticism of the Supreme Court is familiar, as are the chief judgeships of Earl Warren and of Warren Burger, which have swung the Court down a liberal path: invalidating the anti-abortion laws in no less than 44 of the states, ruling against compulsory prayers in public schools, pronouncing separate schooling in itself unequal, approving bussing, decreeing preference for minority applicants in jobs, and (until in California in the Bakke case) decreeing preference for minority applicants in entry into graduate schools. As one bitter Southerner put it, the Court has driven God from the classroom and put the Negro in. President Reagan recalled Thomas Jefferson's warning that the Constitution must not be made a blank slate through "construction."

Clearly, from being envisaged as playing a minor jurisdictional role (the "least dangerous branch of government," in Alexander Hamilton's words), the Supreme Court has in fact developed two major functions. The American people have come to see it on the one hand as, in Lord Bryce's words, "the living voice of the Constitution," the conscience of the nation, deliberate not eccentric, unhurried and responsible, as in essence what, in constitutional textbooks, second chambers are said to be. Not for it "the pressure of public hysteria, public panic and public greed," in Justice Learned Hand's phrase, or the pressures of constituents and the popularity contest of elections. But, alongside this, the judges have also been judicial activists, legislators under another name, learned men and women enjoying lifetime security and prestige, but the ultimate arbiters on

every matter of acute and bitter controversy. Far beyond the planning
of 1787, the Constitution has become what the Supreme Court says
it is. The words are those of Charles Evans Hughes, but he was
speaking before he became chief justice. American political and
social advance has not been calendared by parliamentary enactments, but by the pronouncements of the judges. In this it has had
no imitators. The whole system of judicial interpretation of (and in a
measure control over) legislation is indigenous to the United States.

Indeed, the only truly basic changes made in the direction of
the US internal economy or of its society have been made by the
judges' interpretation of the Constitution or of its relatively few
amendments. The Thirteenth, Fourteenth, and Fifteenth Amendments,
designed to emancipate the blacks, who were, though a century later,
the ultimate beneficiary of them, proved to be the essential vehicles
for the transfer of power from the states to the federal government
and, within that government, to the Supreme Court. The Court has
been, through the generations, the guardian of the covenant, but
also its interpreter and adapter. It has exercised a veto power over
the subordinate courts, and over the actions of the states and of
the federal government. In the late nineteenth century it steered the
federal government toward a policy of *laissez-faire*, and thus fostered
American entrepreneurial growth – and the monopoly powers of a
few; those whom President Theodore Roosevelt called the "male-
factors of great wealth." (It was Congress, not the Court, that was
liberal on slavery in the nineteenth century, and worried over social
and working conditions.) In the late twentieth century, it seems
set on a contrary line, enhancing federal power in order to ensure
freedom of opportunity to the hitherto disfranchised and minority
groups in society. This evolution, and the doctrine of judicial review (so strikingly missing from other constitutions, notably that
of the USSR), have made the formal amendment process all but
unnecessary. (There has never been a national convention to initiate
an amendment, and only once – for the Twenty-first Amendment –
has a state convention process been used.) The Constitution has
4,000 words; but the Supreme Court reports on it and on its meaning number over 450 volumes. The Court is, in fact, a "continuing
constitutional convention," and it is through the courts that there
has been what Carl Swisher has called "the infusion into American
government of new conceptions of righteousness as they developed
in the national community;"[22] to use Earl Warren's phrase, "The

---

[22] Carl Swisher, *The Supreme Court in Modern Role* (rev. edn, 1965).

Law floats in a sea of ethics." This development, as unforeseeable in 1787 as was the matching growth in the authority of the executive, has had – and perhaps can have – few imitators abroad. Strong dictatorial prime ministers and presidents and life-presidents – the new words for tyranny in much of the developing world – are legion, from Paris to Peking, from Nairobi to Delhi, from Malawi to Korea; but, outside the United States, strong, wise, and powerful judges without personal political ambition are rare. Would that it were otherwise.

Slavery

The Founding Fathers evaded the issue of slavery; the slave trade worried them, but the fact of slavery as such in 1787 was a "given," and to the South was seen as a necessity. It worried many Southerners, but however "liberal" they might be, few gave up their slave "property," not even on death, since slave labor was needed to work a plantation. Even Thomas Jefferson, however troubled by the institution, only liberated a few slaves on his death, though he may even have had a slave mistress (though the lady sometimes so identified, Sally Hemings, was in fact, as we have seen, the illegitimate half-sister of his dead wife and "acting mother" to his two surviving daughters.) The 80-year-old Chief Justice Taney, in defining Dred Scott as a slave in 1857, ruled that "under the Fifth Amendment no person could be deprived of life, liberty and property, without the due process of law," and that slaves were property. It required a four-year Civil War, costing more lives than all other American wars combined, before the blacks were, in law though not in fact, given their "freedom." (Though that war should more accurately be described as the War Between the States, since the Constitution did not mention, nor therefore deny, the right of secession to a state or states, and the country could thus be seen by five New England states, which discussed secession in 1814, and by Southerners, who did secede in 1861, as a confederation rather than a nation.) Those powers not specifically allocated to the federal government remained, the Constitution expressly said, with the states – including, presumably, the right to withdraw.

Blacks were, of course, readily identifiable, and – until the Civil War Amendments to the Constitution – they could assume that their color determined their status; the prewar "free blacks" had never had an easy life, as Abraham Lincoln recognized in his Peoria speech in 1854. Until the 1840s, moreover, American free society was not only white, but overwhelmingly British. After 1865 the presence of a conspicuous minority that was "free" only in name was a new problem for the US. The Founding Fathers could not have been expected to discern the many problems of contemporary America, consequent on its becoming a polyglot and multicultural country. Yet, even today, despite its variety, it stays free from threats of secession, except among the more eccentric followers of Islam; virtually all of its people want to remain American.

Given its importance, given its explosive mixture of ethics, religion, economic survival, and property rights, the Founders spent surprisingly little time in formal debate on slavery, because they lived with the problem and knew how central a fact it was to the South. In 1787, no fewer than 750,000 blacks (20 percent of the entire population of the United States) were held in hereditary bondage. However, democratic republican theory and Christian idealism alike threatened the institution of slavery, the American legal order, and the Southern economy. In 1784, Virginia Methodists condemned slavery, using both religious and republican arguments. They declared that slavery was "contrary to the Golden Law of God on which hang all the Law and Prophets, and the unalienable Rights of Mankind, as well as every Principle of Revolution." These arguments laid the intellectual basis for black emancipation in the Northern states, where there were relatively few slaves. By 1784, Massachusetts, Pennsylvania, Connecticut, and Rhode Island had either abolished slavery or provided for its gradual end. Two decades later, all states north of Delaware had adopted similar legislation.

The abolition of slavery in the North exposed additional contradictions within republican ideology. American Patriots had fought the British not only for their lives and liberty, but also for the rights of private property. Indeed, the three values were closely linked in republican theory. The Massachusetts Constitution of 1780 protected every citizen "in the enjoyment of his life, liberty, and property, according to the standing laws." The Virginia Bill of Rights went further; it asserted that the "means of acquiring and possessing property" was an inherent right. Like John Adams, the authors of most state constitutions believed that only property-owners could act independently, and they restricted voting rights to those with freehold estates. For them, republicanism was synonymous with property rights.

The root of the dilemma was that slaves were property. As James Winthrop pointed out, the abolition of slavery in Massachusetts in 1784 meant that "a number of citizens have been deprived of property formerly acquired under the protection of law." To protect white property rights, the Pennsylvania Emancipation Act of 1780 did not free slaves already in bondage. The Act awarded freedom only to slaves born after 1780 – and then only after they had served their mothers' masters for 28 years. In fact, American republican ideology was ultimately derived from ancient Greece and Rome, and was fully compatible with slavery. "As free men," the poet Euripides had written of his fellow citizens in the ancient Greek republics, "we live off slaves."

This aristocratic-republican ideology combined with economic self-interest to prevent the emancipation of slaves in the South. Slaves accounted for 30–60 percent of the Southern population and represented a huge financial investment. Most Southern political leaders were slave-owners, and they actively resisted emancipation. In 1776, the North Carolina legislature condemned the actions of Quakers who freed their slaves as "highly criminal and reprehensible."

Understandably, Southern blacks sought freedom on their own. Two white neighbors of Richard Henry Lee, a signer of the Declaration of Independence, lost "every slave they had in the world," as did nearly "all of those who were near the enemy." More than 5,000 blacks left Charleston, South Carolina, with the departing British army. Other American slaves bargained wartime loyalty to their Patriot masters for a promise of liberty. Using a Manumission Act passed in 1782, Virginia planters granted freedom to more than 10,000 slaves.

Yet black emancipation in the South was doomed even before the expansion of cotton production gave slavery a new economic rationale. The rice planters of Georgia and South Carolina strongly opposed emancipation throughout the Revolutionary era. Their demands at the Philadelphia Convention resulted in a clause (Article I, Section 9) that prevented Congress from prohibiting the trans-atlantic slave trade until 1808. By that time, Southern whites had imported an additional 250,000 Africans – as many slaves as had been brought into all the mainland colonies between 1619 and 1776.

Female suffrage

So, of course, with female suffrage in 1787: it was totally unconsidered. (Female suffrage was first introduced in the Territory of Wyoming in 1869 and nationally by the Nineteenth Amendment in 1920; the recently debated Equal Rights Amendment did not secure enough support from the state legislatures to become constitutional.) The suffrage in any case was a matter for the states, and in almost all of them only white property-holders voted.

In the new country, as in the old, those who chose the law-makers should be men "freed from dependence upon others" – the words of Cromwell's commissary-general, Henry Ireton. This did not necessarily mean ownership of property in land, but, in the words of the Pennsylvania constitution, it did require possession of property in the form of some "profession, calling, trade or farm," and thus excluded servants, paupers, women, and those on poor relief. The only people actually to gain citizenship as a result of Independence were Catholics and Jews, who, in most places, were granted the suffrage through the abolition in individual states of religious tests for voting.

Territorial acquisitions

Again, there is nothing here concerning the problems of territorial acquisitions – of the provision of money for territorial improvements, of roads West – and nothing of political parties. Part of the document's strength lies, paradoxically, in precisely what it does not say. One can debate endlessly whether matters are constitutional or unconstitutional. But much of America's political and economic development has simply been extra-constitutional.

6 THE UNIQUE DOCUMENT

Yet, behind the omissions, the tortuousness and the artificiality, what the Founders devised was a very different structure from Old England's limited monarchy. It was to be a republic, and a federal republic, and on a continental scale. There was to be a government at the center stronger than that of 1776; and if only half of one of its branches was to be popularly elected, those chosen would come from all the member states and be responsible to those who sent them; they would control money, and would be enabled to raise it directly from each American, no longer via the goodwill or otherwise of the member states; given the extent of territory and the slowness of communication, the political animals among them would be a minority selected by a minority, and powerful. Indeed, given the availability of land, and the novel absence – for a whole generation as it happened – of any major enemy on its frontiers, those who did get to the center through all the checks and hurdles were offered a rare opportunity to secure life and liberty, and to indulge in the pursuit of property on a scale never available before.

In contrast with the states of contemporary Europe, American society 1787 was small in numbers, reasonably unified, and strongly democratic. If there were classes, they were much closer to each other than in Europe, and careers in America had long been open to talents, before the phrase became a slogan of European revolution. There was, as the French troops saw, a much greater degree of economic equality than in Europe. There prevailed in America what Franklin called a "happy mediocrity." If there were conservatives and radicals, they were not yet completely aligned, and not recruited from the same groups in every state. As Oscar and Mary Handlin have shown, the Federalists and Anti-Federalists of 1788 in Massachusetts do not correspond either politically or socially with the conservatives and radicals of a decade earlier.[23] Opinion was in flux. The revolutionary Patrick Henry ended up a conservative. Wealthy landowner George Mason was a radical who feared aristocracy, yet he opposed the suggestion that the President be directly elected, on the un-radical grounds that "it would be as unnatural to refer the choice of a proper character for chief magistrate to the people, as it would to refer a trial of colors to a blind man"; the people, he said, had not "the requisite capacity to judge." And the proposal that the chief executive should be directly elected was made by the conservative jurist James Wilson. Edmund Randolph, who helped to draft the Constitution, refused to sign it, then campaigned for its ratification on his return to Virginia. Individuals can rarely be reduced to a pattern either of economic or of any other determinism. Nor indeed can states. The wealthy states like New York and Virginia hesitated longest over adoption. As Washington noted, the opposition to the Constitution came from "the men of large property in the South," not from "the genuine democratical people of the East."

The West was at once a political threat and an economic opportunity. Would a vast empire not be impossible to marry with the concept of a republic, given the classical view, on which all the Founders had been reared, that a republic necessitated a small homogeneous community of virtuous citizens? Would the West, in producing many pressure groups and rival commercial forces, breed many factions, or would their numbers in fact offset each other, and ambition counter ambition? Whatever the result, this too was

[23] "Radicals and conservatives in Massachusetts after Independence," *New England Quarterly*, 17 (1944), p. 343. Robert Thomas has shown in similar fashion that the line between Federalist and Anti-Federalist in Virginia follows no clear pattern of property-holding: 'The Virginia Convention of 1788: a criticism of Beard's *An Economic Interpretation of the Constitution*,' *Journal of Southern History*, 19 (1953), p. 63.

unique: an empire of settlement by freemen. For, in the memorable words of J. G. A. Pocock, "Pitt had not conquered the St Lawrence and the Ohio to open the way to Daniel Boone and George Rogers Clark."

The American Constitution remains unique, not least in its capacity to survive. No other written Constitution has lasted so long. The independent state is historically if not geologically young, only 200 years old. By contrast, two-thirds of the world's 160 constitutions have been adopted or revised since 1970, and only 14 predate World War II. Two states, Syria and Thailand, have each had 9 constitutions in the past 40 years, and one of them, Syria, had 2 within one year. And, by my reckoning, since 1787 Germany has had at least 4 and France at least 8. Moreover, in no other country's case, however prosperous or successful its history, has a constitution in itself ensured stability, continuity, prosperity, or security against *coups*. Nor are national institutions naturally transferable, whether British or American. Governmental systems are not, in Sir Stafford Cripps's phrase, "commodities of commerce, readily exportable." Even when other ex-British colonies reached independence, and leaders appeared with training and experience (sometime graduates of British jails as well as of the London School of Economics or Sandhurst), and British parliamentary delegations formally conferred on them a mace as a symbol of parliamentary government, the parliaments so blessed have usually had a short life. At least 21 of the 44 African republics created since 1945 are in fact run by military regimes, and in almost all of them, except (on my scorecard) Malawi, Mali, Tanzania, and the Ivory Coast, there has been at least one *coup*. Here, as in the nineteenth-century Balkans, governments labeled republican and democratic emerge as in fact tribal; at the top they are autocracies tempered only by assassination. Hardly a single one has emerged smoothly from its colonial tutelage; in almost every case it has been the result of civil and sometimes of international war, of boycotts, of bloodshed, of barbarism, and of many reigns of terror. In each a Great Fear prevails – and lingers on. No bill of rights availed critics or suspected critics behind the Iron Curtain, or in most of Asia or Africa. Where it exists at all, it is usually a piece of rhetoric, devoid of sanctions. Parliamentary leaders in Africa make themselves presidents, then presidents for life – even once an emperor, allegedly practising cannibalism – and there no checks and balances obtain. Opposition is seen as treason, as in seventeenth-century Britain, and freedom of speech, assembly and worship are denied. Constitutions today abound and flourish; but constitutionalism is a rarity.

Nor has the American "model" itself been any more successful abroad than the British. The struggling nationalisms of Hungary and Bohemia, Italy and Norway, in the nineteenth century drew heavily on the symbolism of 1776–87. In 1919, Thomas Garrigue Masaryk stood on the steps of the White House to proclaim the independence of the new Czechoslovakia, but, sadly, no "charisma" became evident. The Rhodesian manifesto of independence of November 11, 1965, used the incantatory phrases of Jefferson's Declaration, but no equality, no guarantees of life, liberty, and the pursuit of happiness came to Zimbabwe by magic; Vietnam in its 1945 declaration did the same, and reaped a whirlwind. Behind the phrases, and the currying of Western approval, all the imitators have been and are centralizers, not liberals, authoritarians in a hurry, and certainly not believers in divided powers. The failure of transferability of institutions, even in their own hemisphere from North America to the Caribbean and the South, was especially striking. Indeed, when the South American states invoked the ideas of revolution, it was from France rather than the US that they borrowed. It was Napoleon who, by his invasion of Madre Patria, made possible the events of 1810–11 in Latin America. In 1787, by contrast, the new US saw itself as *Novus Ordo Seclorum*, "an Elysium in the Wilds." The Founding Fathers saw themselves as architects of an harmonious social order, men who had halted the cycle of historical inevitability. Robespierre and Napoleon, like Lenin and Stalin, Mao and Ho, and all their lesser imitators, were in the end corrupted by power. Washington and Jefferson were not. Hamilton, who just might have been, was shot in a duel – and his murderer, Aaron Burr, by acting so, thus ended his own special threat to the republic.

In this same 200 years, the Constitution has been amended on only 26 occasions, the first 10 being added in 1791 as the Bill of Rights. In that time the state has grown from 13 constituent states to 50, from $3\frac{1}{2}$ million people to 240 million. A Congressional District was to have 30,000 voters in 1787. In 1980 the quota was approximately half a million per Congressman.[24] Yet when George Bush took his oath of office in 1989, he swore to uphold the same government and system that George Washington swore to uphold in 1789. During that time a bitter, bloody, and four-year-long Civil War had been fought, as had seven international wars; and a scientific and technological revolution had transformed the world into something which George Washington and his contemporaries would not have recognized, and which would probably

[24] The average constituency in Britain has approximately 70,000 electors.

have horrified them. What began as a loose confederation is now continental in extent, with one state in mid-Pacific, another in the Arctic, and with a largely Hispanic commonwealth in the Caribbean. With no king or castles (except those imported, like San Simeon), it has no aristocracy of title, no Eton, no Ascot — to use Henry James's criterion of those institutions whose absence drove him to become a British citizen and to live in Rye. Thus, devoid of all those excuses for pageantry and myth, the US has invented its own, and made of July 4 each year, and of September 1987, the country's bicentennial birthday, an occasion for special rejoicing. For there is much to celebrate, whatever the omissions in the founding document, whatever the paradoxes.

7   THE ARCHITECT OF THE EXTENDED REPUBLIC: JAMES MADISON

Just as the British failure to master a continent from their tiny toe-holds on the Atlantic coast, which was the real reason for the survival of the American army, owed more to Washington's patience and endurance than to any other man, just as the preliminary peace treaty of 1782 in Paris, which became the final treaty of 1783, owed more to Franklin's patience and blarney than to anyone else, so James Madison of Orange County, Virginia, was in essence the architect of the Constitution. This diminutive and untypical Virginian squire, one of 12 children who himself married late and had no children of his own, who never traveled farther from his home in Orange County in the foothills of the Blue Ridge than he could help (the Mohawk valley in New York was in fact the farthest he did go, and that as companion to an applause-hungry General Lafayette in 1824), who never weighed more than 100 pounds and was so much victim to bilious attacks, so timid, and with so weak a voice that he could neither become the preacher nor the lawyer for which he was trained; this was a reluctant and unusual Great Man. The school Madison attended in King and Queen County, Virginia, when he was 11, was that run by Donald Robertson, who had arrived from Scotland only ten years before. Madison discovered later that the Latin and Greek he learnt there he pronounced with a Scottish burr; Robertson was a graduate of Aberdeen and Edinburgh. Madison went on to Princeton, then the college of New Jersey, because it was feared that the malarial climate of Williamsburg's William and Mary College might kill him. This least revolutionary of men, addicted to books, bookbuying, and melancholia, was a delegate at the Constitutional Convention; he drafted in advance a model constitution, and drew up the agenda. He was, in Clinton Rossiter's phrase, a "single-minded political monk." With very few close friends, and almost all of them male and Virginians, with little emotion showing in his vast correspondence, this intensely private man's energies nevertheless went into public life: politics became his métier. He was meticulous in attendance at the Convention, a note-taker, a source of ideas, an authority on other constitutions, on which he had prepared a 41-page notebook and precis, and not least a debater; despite his timidity, he intervened on no less than 161 occasions in the four months of debate, and gave ground only when he saw the force of the contrary arguments.

In the debate on ratification in Virginia, Madison led the Federalist cause, and out argued the best popular orator in North America, Patrick Henry. Henry did not believe that the new "empire for liberty" would survive without a dictator. But thanks to Madison's detailed and quietly-voiced rebuttals, point by point, Virginia approved the document.

Throughout the months of the ratification debates in the states in 1788, as Anti-Federalist criticisms mounted to a call for a second constitutional convention, Madison made a digest of their demands. In all, five states wanted a Bill of Rights added; nine states had asked for some changes; in all 210 amendments had been proposed. A Bill of Rights would offset this challenge, and might even induce North Carolina and Rhode Island to ratify the Constitution and make the Union complete — even though neither had a Bill of Rights in its own state constitution. After the first federal House of Representatives had assembled in 1789 (though on the date set, March 4, it lacked a quorum), Madison, present as an elected representative of his own section of Virginia and playing a role not unlike that of a prime minister, announced on May 4, 1789, that he would introduce a number of amendments to the Constitution. He had reduced the 210 to 80 major proposals, but even if each of these had run only to 50 words, they would together have been longer than the Constitution. So he edited, and re-edited. In nine states, three basic proposals seemed to be recurrent: Congress should be prohibited from interfering with the right of the states to set the time and place of elections; there should be some limitation on the power of Congress to collect taxes; and it should be stated clearly that all powers not given by the Constitution to the national government were reserved to the states. Seven states asked for a guarantee of trial by jury, and six asked for a guarantee of freedom of religion; for an increase in the number of Congressmen; and for a prohibition against maintaining armies in time of peace. The most popular proposals, however, were not the most important. Only in five states were the rights mentioned that had been the cause of much furore on the eve of the Revolution: protection against search of private homes without a search warrant; the right of the states to control their militias; and the rights of freedom of speech and freedom of the press. And some of the most important rights of all – the right of freedom of assembly; guarantees of speedy and public trials; and assurance that no person could be deprived of his life, liberty, or property without due process of law – were mentioned by delegates from less than one-third of the states.

In the end Madison introduced 19 amendments into the House of Representatives. Off and on during the summer of 1789, as the House worked out its other major laws, these amendments were discussed. Many argued that such a bill was unnecessary, in part because most of the state constitutions already provided for such rights (the Virginian Bill of Rights had been drafted by George Mason of Gunston Hall, a wealthy planter and neighbor of Washington, as early as 1776), and in part, as Hamilton argued in essay No. 84 of *The Federalist Papers*, "The Constitution is itself ... a Bill of Rights." In fact, by 1701 all the colonies, as heirs of the English common law tradition, had at least some written guarantees in effect. But these contentions were not convincing to Madison: some states did not have such guarantees, and "I think we should obtain the confidence of our fellow citizens as we fortify the rights of the people against the encroachments of the government." The House made one minor and one major change before passing the proposals on August 24. The minor change was a rewording that made it possible to consolidate them into 17 amendments. The major change was that amendments were to be tacked on to the end of the Constitution rather than inserted at various places in the body of the document.

The proposed amendments were then sent to the Senate, where they were taken up for discussion on September 2. Madison's Bill of Rights, as passed by the House, would have restricted the power of state and local governments, as well as that of the national government. For example, the states were left free to maintain tax-supported churches if they were so disposed, as Connecticut did until 1818 and Massachusetts until 1833; states also could hold criminal trials without juries, as Kentucky did until the 1850s. Otherwise, however, the Senate approved the House proposals, consolidating them still further into 12 amendments.

At the end of September the proposed amendments were sent out to the individual states for their approval. The first results were that North Carolina and Rhode Island ratified the Constitution, the first in November, 1789, the second in May, 1790. Then, one by one, the various states voted on the 12 amendments. The first two amendments, which would have increased the number of Congressmen and prevented Congressmen from raising their own salaries, were never ratified. The other ten, which became the Bill of Rights as we know it, officially became part of the Constitution on December 15, 1791. Madison had been at work for four and a half years on the Constitution and the Bill of Rights. It was as well that he had trained himself at Princeton to survive with only five hours of sleep each night.

The list of individual freedoms – of religion, of speech, and of the press; freedom of assembly; the right to keep and to bear arms; security in persons and homes; the right not to incriminate oneself; the right to speedy and impartial trial, and to trial by jury – is still seen by many as the most important achievement of all in these years, and most worthy of emulation across the world. In fact, at the Constitutional Convention itself, hardly a word had been said about a Bill of Rights. George Mason's proposal of it came late and as an afterthought. It did not seem necessary, because the federal government had only the powers expressly granted to it, and it did not seem possible that it would misuse powers it did not have. Moreover, political enactment in some of the states weakened any danger of tyranny. Several of the state constitutions made it mandatory for senatorial candidates to live, not just own property, in election districts. Actual inhabitants were to represent constituents, and thus families with extensive kinship connections, even if present in several communities, were unlikely to have relatives with residences in enough districts to permit continuing domination of executive offices. The importance of family ties declined with the invocation of new governments. Diffusion of the appointive power, and fixed election districts along with residency requirements, broke the hold that many eastern families of distinction exercised over high offices; and there were tenure restrictions upon executive offices. But a Bill of Rights, nevertheless, would help to "sell" the document in the course of the struggle over ratification. And it was, said Jefferson, "what the people are entitled to against every government on earth ... and what no just government should refuse." If the Constitution set up a central government, however federal and weak, the Bill of Rights protected that spirit of nonconformity of individual difference and dissent that had led to the peopling of the undiscovered wilderness in the first place. And it was Madison who did the work.

Again, it hardly needs saying that this is the feature of the Revolutionary years that has proved most difficult to emulate. Few
governments in the developing world, much as they mouth the great
memorable phrases (usually, however, only drawn from the second
paragraph of the Declaration of Independence, and from little else),
have been able to ensure to their citizens genuine freedom.

What in essence was Madison trying to say through these four
years, and what was it in his speeches, his note-taking and his writing, that was for the US prophetic? At Princeton he squeezed his
four-year course, modeled on a Scottish MA, to two, but spent a
third year as a graduate on Moral Philosophy and Hebrew, directly
with College President John Witherspoon. Witherspoon had got
the job in 1768, partly because of his combative quality, but also
because he brought with him from Paisley in Scotland his library of
5,000 books, a library of the Scottish Enlightenment including the
works of David Hume, Adam Ferguson, Thomas Reid, and Adam
Smith. Witherspoon and his two assistants, then Nassau Hall's total
strength, taught that human nature, like the universe, moved according to laws, and that if these could be grasped, political, social,
and economic institutions could be brought into a social order that
would guarantee liberty and even happiness (and perhaps even
equality?) for all. As Fisher Ames said of him in 1789, politics for
Madison was "rather a science than a business." He studied the real
world, and his mentor, Witherspoon, was himself active in that
world. Witherspoon had arrived from Paisley (where many were glad
to see him go) only in 1768, but he became well enough known to
be a delegate at the Second Continental Congress in 1775, to sign
the Declaration of Independence in 1776, and, with his college
empty, to serve in the Congress and on 100 of its committees.
Witherspoon's pupils included not only a future president, and a
vice-president of the new state, but 21 US senators, 29 members of
the House of Representatives 12 state governors, and 33 judges.
And his students were everywhere in the Revolutionary Army. In
the words of his most eminent successor as president of Princeton,
Woodrow Wilson, Witherspoon made of Princeton a "seminary of
statesmen." Like Witherspoon, Madison knew the wealth and potential of the New World, and believed that its people might indeed
escape Old World corruptions and stay more innocent and virtuous
than any other people. But he did not believe that that could be
assumed; he did not want to depend on virtue for success. One
of the themes of *The Federalist Papers* is that of the intrusion of
sin into the garden, the threat of self-interest, delusion, and irra-
tionality. In the index to Clinton Rossiter's edition of *The Federalist*

Papers[25] are no less than 14 references to this black side of human nature. Despite the Utopia that lay around them, Americans were not angels, and therefore needed government; and they needed to discuss the document itself in secret, and they did so. Unlike his Princeton successor, Woodrow Wilson, with his naive call for "open covenants openly arrived at," Madison said that "No constitution would have been adopted by the Convention if the debates had been public."

When Madison read his history, read the books of the intellectuals of contemporary Europe, notably David Hume, or reflected on his own Christian heritage and the idea of original sin, he found ample confirmation of the notion that man, though capable of virtue, is by instinct a rebel who has in practice to be controlled. Although his college saw itself as part of an Enlightenment culture, Madison – and Hamilton – were realists, not optimists. Human beings are generally governed, they held, by base and selfish motives, by suspicion and prejudice, by jealousy and vanity, by passion, greed, and ambition. In *Federalist* essay No. 55, he said: "As there is a degree of depravity in mankind which requires a certain degree of circumspection and distrust, so there are other qualities in human nature which justify a certain portion of esteem and confidence." He was more realistic and cynical than Jefferson, as whose lieutenant he saw himself, and whom he would serve as secretary of state in 1801, and – though less successfully – succeed as President in 1809. There is little talk in Madison of the infinite perfectibility of man: "The purest of human blessings must have a portion of alloy in them; the choice must always be made, if not of the lesser evil, at least of the greater, not the perfect good" (*Federalist* essay No. 41). "What is government itself but the greatest of all reflections of human nature? If men were angels, no government would be necessary. If angels were to govern men, neither external nor internal controls on government would be necessary" (*Federalist* essay No. 51).

This was thus Whig theory but of a skeptical and conservative kind. Madison would not assume, as did Hobbes, that the absolutism of Leviathan was the price to pay for self-preservation. But Hobbes mattered as much as Locke, and Machiavelli almost as much as Plato. And if it was Locke, it was not Locke as amended by Jefferson: it was life, liberty, and *not* the pursuit of happiness, but property. He stressed the importance of the protection of property interests against the attack of popular majorities, rather than the

[25] See n. 12 above.

protection of "the people" from the tyranny of the executive (as indeed did Jefferson in his first draft of his Declaration of Independence): "Wherever the real power in a Government lies, there is the danger of oppression. In our Government the real power lies in the majority of the community." Popular government, yes, but he might almost have used Burke's phrase, "The tyranny of the multitude can be a multiplied tyranny." The tyranny of the majority could be avoided, first, by a system of federalism and the clear separation of powers, but, equally important, by so multiplying interests and passions in society that no one group or combinations of groups could form a stable dominating force. Parties were not foreseen, but "faction" was much feared; when parties came they would form subordinate unifying forces across the nation, but they would exercise their pressures erratically. Parties in nineteenth-century America were never more than creaky coalitions of changing sectional interests, and, until Roosevelt's Democratic Party was built, were never consistently or federally ideological forces.

Because of his unusually wide reading, Madison was Enlightenment Man *par excellence*. He believed that the strength of the new republic, free from monarchy, from aristocracy, and from all claims based on heredity, must rest on the public spirit of its citizens, on what then was called "public virtue." In *Federalist* essay No. 10, he translated it as "patriotism and love of justice." Good government could be guaranteed only if good men would spend their talents in the service of the *res publica*. It required the best men, and the best in men. This was the "given" in all contemporary political argument, and had been so from Aristotle's day. Indeed, this was why, to Madison, Washington's presence at the Constitutional Convention was essential. But, given his reading and his profound Christian code, he was also a realist. He abandoned the language of natural law. He believed in controlling passions and greeds with countervailing passions and greeds.

Ambition must be made to counteract ambition ... what is government itself but the greatest of all reflections on human nature? If men were angels, no government would be necessary ... In forming a government which is to be administered by men over men, the great difficulty then is this: you must first enable the government to control the governed, and in the next place oblige it to control itself. (*Federalist* essay No. 51)

The real world was not based only on reason and virtue, but even more on self-interest. As Adam Smith recognized in economics, public good could arise from the individual's own pursuit of his own interests. The art of politics therefore lay less in the preachment of virtue, in exhortation to good works or social needs, or in the nurture of men as gods, but in the management of conflict, in recognizing the passions and greed that nature gives, and deliberately balancing them off. Madison made no assumptions of public spiritedness or "good citizenship" in those who came to rule, by whatever slippery slope they rose. The growth of factions in any and every society was as constant as human greed. Man cannot be improved; he can only be controlled; and Madison ensured that in his document there were enough checks and safeguards to do just that. He respected and sought to cultivate republican "virtue," but recognized its rarity and its unreliability as a firm basis for the new state. He was remarkably shrewd and farsighted. Only the passions aroused by human slavery in an increasingly white and free society, three generations later, strained his achievement; but his country – by 1865 far-stronger than in 1787 – withstood that awful test.

Despite his collaboration with Hamilton in writing The *Federalist Papers*, Madison would not move towards the aristocratic, plutocratic, and centralizing policies of Hamiltonian federalism when they ran counter to what he considered to be the interests of the people and their republican rights. He was certainly far from "democratic" theorists like Rousseau. Just as he refused to look to the notion of a disinterested monarch or of an aristocracy, since neither could in practice be above the battle, just as his realism led him to reject the idea of the "General Will," so he poured an equal scorn on concepts of a "Legislator" or a "Dictator" who would magically resolve the people's problems and then, equally magically, ride away into the sunset – though this is one of America's and certainly Hollywoods great myths. Even a Cromwell, he might have said (but did not), acquired ambitions of his own, if not for himself, then for his posterity.

The foundation of the "American science of politics," then, was a hard-headed and, we would now say, "realistic" view of human nature. Rejecting the belief of a few of the more radical thinkers of the European Enlightenment in the perfectibility of man, the Founding Fathers were virtually unanimous in their distrust of the human animal. Indeed, to John Adams, the first vice-president and second president, democracy was "the most ignoble, unjust and detestable form of government," to James Otis it was "the government of all over all." "When the pot boils," he said, "the scum will rise." "Give the votes to the people who have no property," said Gouvernor Morris, "and they will sell them to the rich." "To entrust the selection of leaders to the people would be like giving the choice of colours to a blind man." "Effrontery and arrogance...are giving rank and importance to men whom wisdom would have left in obscurity," said John Jay.

The men who drew up the Constitution in Philadelphia during the summer of 1787 had a vivid sense of human evil and damnation; they read Hobbes as well as Locke and Bolingbroke, and they believed with Hobbes that men are selfish and contentious, and that the natural state of mankind is a state of war. They were men of affairs, merchants, lawyers, farmers, planter-businessmen, speculators, investors. Having seen human nature on display in the marketplace, the courtroom, the legislative chamber, and wherever wealth and power are sought, they felt they knew it in all its range – and its vulnerability. To them, a human being was an atom of self-interest. They did not believe in man, but they did believe in the power of a good political constitution to control him.

The document alone, however designed, would not in itself be enough. When in his confrontation with Patrick Henry in Richmond in Virginia's ratifying convention, Henry argued that in a republican government in a large state such as the United States, congressmen would live far away from, and out of touch with, their constituents, and become gradually as corrupt and self-seeking as members of the contemporary House of Commons, Madison countered:

I go on on this great republican principle, that the people will have virtue and intelligence enough to select men of virtue and wisdom. Is there no virtue among us? If there be not, we are indeed in a wretched situation. No theoretical checks, no form of government can render us secure. To suppose that any form of government will secure liberty or happiness without any virtue in the people is a chimerical idea.

Virtue was, thus, still an important word. Every one of Madison's teachers was either a clergyman or a devout Christian layman. The concept of the worth of the individual soul, like the faith in the republic itself, came out of a Christian and a classical tradition.

The government to be set up, however, was republican. In *Federalist* essay No. 43 Madison defended the provision of the Constitution which authorizes Congress "to guarantee to every State in the Union a republican form of government." Nor should it casually be overthrown, or changed with frequency. Stability was as important as liberty itself. As a realistic interpreter of human behavior, as the practical builder of a constitution, he had to dissent from Jefferson's conceit of a political change every generation, whether that meant 19 years or 34. "Stability in governments is essential to national character ... as well as to that repose and confidence in the minds of the people, which are among the chief blessings of civil society," (*Federalist* essay No. 37), and, as events would show, he would oppose rights of nullification or secession. The centralist, the nationalist, and the conservative in him was dominant.

If he was both contractarian and conservative, he was also the pragmatist, the problem-solver. Government is set up to curb faction and to curb man's capacity for error and for sin, and this means that it must (1) be balanced; (2) have its powers separate, though overlapping; (3) be extensive; (4) be representative; and (5) be strong. In his letters of 1786 and 1787 to Jefferson, Washington, and Randolph, proposing his draft for a Constitution, Madison developed his practical ideas on constitutional reform: he wanted a stronger national government than that of the Articles of Confederation – and he called it "national" – with the right to regulate trade, and with a negative on the legislative acts of the states, "in all cases whatsoever." He wanted it to have the right to raise money, by an impost on trade. He wanted a national judiciary with supremacy over state courts; he wanted a bicameral legislature, with a seven-year term for senators, a council of revision, and an executive, about which, in 1787, he admitted that he had "scarcely ventured" to think in detail. He sought "tranquility" within each state, the right of coercion against delinquent or fractious states, and, "to give a new system its proper validity and energy," he wanted the new charter ratified by the people and not merely by the legislatures of the states. It was no accident that the document begins with 'We, the people," not "We, the states ...."

Almost all Madison's dreams came true in 1787. Federalism, however, was no mere matter of reflection on a wide reading. It reflected also his observations in Philadelphia of the diverse interests of all the states, diversity enhanced by distance and poor roads. Jefferson as President, on his regular 120-mile rides between Monticello and the New Federal City on the Potomac – nowadays a two-hour car run but then requiring three days – had some eight creeks or rivers to ford, floods and storms permitting, and usually acted as mailman for those on his path. When, as from 1789 until 1913, senators were elected by state legislatures, they acted more and more conspicuously as senators less for political units than for oil or timber, for cotton, for tobacco or for corn. States' rights would become a battle cry in the nineteenth century. As the US spread farther and farther west and southwest, so the diversity increased. It still does, as today's Los Angeles bears witness. And as new states came into being, the interests diversified still more. But the formula held and endures. *Annuit coeptis, novus ordo seclorum*, as the Great Seal testifies.

The verdict? A modest man, with no presence and little money who by studying and by reason constructed – in all its omissions – the most intricate and longest-surviving Constitution in human history. Its very restraint and its brevity may have helped to allow it to be the acceptable form of government for three million farmers on the Atlantic coast in 1787, and today for 260 million people of every race and color from coast to coast. Madison knew what was important: separation of powers, property rights, federalism – and the ability to reconcile and live with tensions; but there were, he said, "no models." He came to his conclusions from his own re-flection and experience. His reading could do little for him here. Past revolutionary and republican theory had guided the Founding Fathers when it came to the defense of the Revolution, the estab-lishment of Independence, and the temporary ordering of their own state and national affairs. But once it was believed that the Articles of Confederation were not adequate to the task of establishing re-publican government in a large state, previous republican thinkers were either silent or pessimistic.

Indeed, there was almost absolute unanimity on the impossibility of organizing a republic for a vast territory or for a heterogeneous population All the pundits, and every contemporary student of con-stitutions, ancient and modern, and notably Montesquieu – all were unanimous that republics could survive only in small territories or in city-states. Both John Adams and Alexander Hamilton believed that sooner later the American people would have to return to a limited monarchy: so great was the size of the country, so diverse were the interests to be reconciled, that no other system could secure both justice and liberty. Even Patrick Henry of Virginia, whose de-fiance of Governor Dunmore in Williamsburg in 1775 had triggered the outbreak of war there, predicted (on June 9, 1788, in the Virginia Ratifying Convention) that "one government cannot reign over so ex-tensive a country as this is, without absolute despotism." Hamilton's hero was Caesar. When the call came (in Pennsylvania in 1794), he was prepared to act the part. None of this is surprising. All the Founding Fathers' reading of history confirmed their thesis. There had been stable and prosperous empires, but all had been held together from above, and by a king – views that both Patrick Henry and Hamilton would echo in the debates of 1787. From totally different viewpoints, they yet concurred on the need for "absolute despotism." All their reading endorsed it: Hobbes, Grotius, Pufendorf, were all advocates of the absolutist state. The men of the Enlightenment in

Europe had all sought their reforms through despots, as do twentieth-century Asia and Africa. In Madison's own memoranda, "Notes of Ancient and Modern Confederacies," or his fascinating "Vices of the political system of the U. S." he confessed that even the Lycian League and the Dutch Republic were less useful as models than as warnings.

Even the great classical models were silent. Aristotle had little or nothing to say about a republican federal state, and Madison mentions him only once. He could derive from his reading of the classics a healthy respect for the farming class as the backbone of a polity, but he could have found little or nothing about a federal polity comparable to the actual political situation he faced in America. He may have found in Cicero a conception of natural law which had become so deeply embedded in Western thought that it had become a basic premise of constitutional theorists in the sixteenth, seventeenth, and eighteenth centuries. Cicero spoke eloquently of a true law which men might know by reason, an eternal law which "summons men to the performance of their duties," an unchangeable law which "restrains them from doing wrong," a law which cannot morally be invalidated by human legislation, a higher law to which the state and its rulers are subject. But again, there was, in Cicero and in most other advocates of natural law, nothing about the problems of a large federal commonwealth. And Cicero – like Plato, Machiavelli, and Rousseau – in any case gets no mention at all. Moreover, Madison was empiricist, not dogmatist. If he was sometimes zealously committed to key ideas, he never insisted that a theory for democratic Greece or republican Rome or constitutional England could be transferred automatically to popular government in America. Aristotle, Machiavelli, Calvin, Harrington, Locke, Montesquieu might suggest "lessons," but they did not have solutions. Madison had to devise a theory that would take into account a large expanse of land and its diversity of resources, the prevalence of local self-government and of local and regional ambitions, the widespread distribution of property, an enterprising economic spirit, a deeply rooted constitutional ethos – what Jefferson called "the unquestionable republicanism of the American mind" – and some kind of federal division of powers. He made it durable not because of the arguments of *Federalist* essay No. 10, or new states having parity with the original 13, but because he rested a strong central government on acceptance by the people in the states; by making it national and federal. And the way of life it secured was prosperous enough to give the people – in all their greed and ambition, and their proneness to faction, which he fully recognized – the will to make it work. This is more than can be said for any *philosophe*. Madison was the rarest of beings, a very successful and creative politician, a risk-taker, or, more accurately, a political mechanic in what he himself called "a workshop of liberty."

Societies, and successful constitutions with them, adapt as they grow. The natural state is not Hobbesian and brutal, not Lockian and contractual, not Rousseauist and idyllic, but a state of development, of constant and organic change. This being so, Law is not "made" but discovered; and human beings do not construct society, it is society that fashions human kind. The Constitution is a living document, constantly reinterpreted by the courts, and made responsive to social and political needs. Burke, who was otherwise so critical of "abstractions" and "universals" and "theory," could have been more critical in 1776 and more understanding in 1787. The Constitution, of course, was a strange piece of eighteenth-century political mechanics, and the Electoral College still shows its contrived character. But it worked, and it was Madison, its planner, who saw that it would. It would grow, and change naturally as it grew. The President, cumbrously selected in 1789, was meant to be a chairman; he grew into a leader. The court was seen as a minor department, until strong chief justices like John Marshall made it more than this. Within three generations, the Upper House, with its longer tenure and its diversity of sectional strength, became a more powerful and wiser (and smaller) chamber than the febrile House of Representatives, though such again was not the intention in 1787. The Constitution was a form of words, but capable of transformation through reinterpretation. It was not, and was not meant to be a democratic government. It was devised by intelligent magistrates to ensure continuity and peace for men like themselves. But all its critical provisions were sufficiently flexible to be adaptable to the rise of political democracy. Its flexibility was its strength.

The great achievement of the New Nation was neither republicanism, independence, the Bill of Rights, nor the widening of opportunities. The distinct achievement was federalism itself. The attempt to combine federalism and republicanism in so vast and unknown an area seemed to eighteenth-century Europeans an invitation to catastrophe. It reached 1,000 miles from the St Lawrence to northern Florida, and a 1,000 miles to the Mississippi. The vast unoccupied and unmapped interior was 1 million square miles in extent – larger than any European country except despotic Russia, but rich in timber, minerals, and farm land that had never known a plough. The West was little explored and the fortunes of the men of the western waters seemed to lie with Spain. British and French agents were busy for the next 20 years in the Northwest and in

Canada, as the papers of Robert Liston, Britain's first minister to the US, testify. Vermont, dominated by the Allen clan, talked of independence from both Canada and the United States. The careers of John Sevier and William Blount in Tennessee, of General Wilkinson in New Orleans, and the later years of Aaron Burr in New York, prove that there were many plans to divide and destroy the new republic. That it survived was thus remarkable; and the major legacies were not the Constitution alone, but also the Northwest Ordinances of 1785 and 1787, ensuring the equality of the new states with the old "in all respects whatsoever."

Britain – then and since – found little to admire in the American system. When Grenville, the foreign secretary, introduced the Canada Act in 1791, he declared that "we are now about to communicate the blessing of the English constitution to the subjects of Canada, because we are fully convinced that it is the best in the world." Prime Minister William Pitt the Younger hoped that "they were all agreed to give to Canada a free constitution in the English sense of the word." There was here no indication that liberty included a right to self-government, nor any willingness to refrain from imposing the imperial will on colonial societies. There was no indication that any lesson had been learned, from 1776 or from 1787.

Behind this political contrast lay the economic realities: the United States was still economically dependent on Britain, which took most of its exports and provided most of its imports, its immigrants, and its credit. By 1815, Britain was infinitely stronger than in 1783; it looked east now rather than west; it was to be another half-century before Britain tried federalism of a sort in Canada, and before British travelers to the United States began to say generous things about American democracy. Gladstone might be eloquent about the US Constitution, but that did not prevent his expressions of sympathy for the South, nor his apparent hopes for the permanent separation of South from North. Nor has there ever been in Britain – except for a passing interest recently in the role and power of congressional investigating committees – any real assumption that the parliamentary system has anything to learn from the presidential.

One overarching achievement of the years of Articles-making and Constitution-making, years of war though they were also, was to provide a forum for intelligent and thorough debate on fundamental issues of government, with a positive achievement at the end. Although set in motion by a denial of the authority of king and of Parliament, and fearing party as faction, the efforts at constitution-making did provide an assembly in which sections would argue with sections, and – in the end – parties with parties. The President was

an elected Cincinnatus; Congress was a law-making parliament at
the center of a novel federal and ever-extending continental system
of state legislatures and courts of law. Yet it was set up against a
panorama of continuous tensions: urban upheavals, border conflicts,
the Newburgh Conspiracy, separatist movements in Vermont and
in the state of Franklin (Tennessee); Spanish, Canadian, and British
threats; and despite an almost annual popular outburst defying the
laws – Shays' Rebellion, the whiskey insurrection, Fries' Revolt,
Gabriel's slave uprising, the war with the Barbary corsairs, the Baltimore riots of 1812, and the Hartford Convention threatening secession. Yet the Constitution endured and survived its tests ... and
would again in 1861. Inside its debating hall on Capitol Hill, it
made controversy pacific and legitimate, and by legitimating it, it
weakened the destructive and violent threats to the stability of an
ever-extending, expansionist, rapidly increasing, febrile, and ever-
optimistic society. It gave a chance, if not for reason, at least for
verbal argument to counter the threat of violence in a still-frontier
environment – even if, as Dickinson reminded the Framers, "reason
may mislead us." Once established, it grew. So we witness today not
only frequent invocation of the Constitution as the unifying symbol
of American nationhood and citizenship, and as the "Ark of the
Covenant," but more than that, what A. E. Dick Howard of the
University of Virginia Law School has called "the constitutional-
ization of American life, a growing American tendency to discover
in the Constitution an answer to problems."[26]

8   THE FOUNDATIONS

There were three reasons, other than Madison's hard-headed practicality and his wisdom, for the success and survival of the Fathers'
handiwork. First, their geographic and social inheritance was in
fact an inheritance not of tyranny and persecution but of freedom.
Behind all the rhetoric of 1776 and of the War years, American
society was of necessity freer from governmental control than it had
ever been willing to admit. In 1776, the Americans were not an
oppressed people. Land-holding, and with it the suffrage which, as
in contemporary Britain, was a legacy of it, had always been more

---

[26] Robert S. Peck and Ralph S. Pollock (eds), *The Blessings of Liberty* (Washington,
DC, American Bar Association, 1987), p. 4. For a more critical view of Madison
(in order the better to "boost" Hamilton?), see McDonald, *Novus Ordo Seclorum*,
pp. 205–9.

widespread than in Britain. Fifty to sixty percent of all white adult males could vote in America; in Britain about 4–5 percent. Many white immigrants had made their way over the seas under indenture, as, in essence, slaves to the master who bought them, and whom they served, usually for five or seven years. Their number included John Harrower from the Orkneys, tutor to Washington's step-children; William Buckland who built Gunston Hall; Matthews Thornton of New Hampshire; at least one signer of the Declaration of Independence; and Charles Thomson, secretary to the Continental Congress. America was a land of opportunity before 1776 as well as after it — and might have been so without political independence. The population of each colony/state was doubling every generation. In Britain, by contrast, half of all babies died within five years of their birth.

The colonial experience, moreover, was heavily encrusted with "the privileges, franchises, and immunities" of English law, as was that of those still living in England. This is the language of the charters by which each colony was governed. They had guarantees quite distinct when contrasted with the colonists who emigrated from Seville, Cádiz or Lisbon, Nantes or Bordeaux. The form of government, by inheritance and in the plans for 1787, was also parliamentary. Each colonial assembly had acted as a miniature parliament, seeing its governor as a king's man and treating him therefore with much respect and some abuse, as was the form; and arguing constantly over his salary, which they paid only annually — but reluctantly, and usually after argument, and sometimes in arrears. They resented their governors' avarice, but still more that they were rarely eminent enough. And, although Madison said that of the affairs of Georgia he knew as little as those of Kamchatka, and although the interests of tobacco, rice, and sugar planters did not chime automatically with the cod and whale fishermen of Marblehead and Nantucket, yet the language, the ideology, and the political conventions of elected assemblies were common to all the states; and, as we have seen, the majority of their leaders were steeped in Whiggism. By 1787, moreover, they had come to know other state leaders all too well.

The Loyalist exodus of some one in five of the population left many estates in the hands of new men and removed what there was of local aristocracies — private property was sacrosanct, but not for Tories. Contrast France in 1815, Russia in 1917, and China from 1911. If an Established Church existed in 1770 in almost all the colonies, disestablishment took place during the War, or afterwards and smoothly: for Thomas Jefferson, the Virginian Statute for

Religious Freedom, the founding of the University of Virginia, and the revision and codification of the laws, were as important as the Declaration of political Independence. But the right to religious freedom in the First Amendment was a restriction only on the federal government. Variety of religious worship remained untouched in each state. But only three established churches – all in New England – survived beyond 1785, and died out in the next 40 years. Local and, in large measure, state self-government were far more the legacy of a colonial past than of victory on the battlefield, as were the items in the Bill of Rights: trial by jury, *habeas corpus*, fear of standing armies, the right to bear arms in self-defense – all were English before they were American. The Founding Fathers assumed social freedom, and that a right to vote was theirs already. Many Loyalists found the demands for independence simply incomprehensible. As the Loyalist Peter Oliver put it, it was "the most wanton and un-natural rebellion that ever existed."

Geography reinforced history. In economic terms, the wide tidal rivers, the rocky coast and the sandbars of the South had from col-onial beginnings made smuggling as easy as it made British wartime operations difficult; the Hancocks of Boston, the Browns of Rhode Island, and many lesser men had long flourished as much by illicit as by open trade. The Paxton Boys in Pennsylvania made frontier tension a problem for Franklin to solve in 1764; the Regulators in the Carolinas in the 1770s protested against the comfortable folk back East because they had too little government, no justices, no courts of law, and no guarantees of personal security. It was this, more than questions of patriotism – which in 1776 posed the issue of patriotism for whom – that moved the Scottish Highlanders to fight in 1776 at Moore's Creek Bridge, as Loyalists; in general, however, the Scotch-Irish were part of the core of the Continental Line; to "Light-Horse" Harry Lee, the Pennsylvania Line might well be called the Line of Ireland. Even then, and over a waste of seas, Ulster Scots went one awkward and dissenting way, High-landers another. Despite Shays' Rebellion in 1786, which so worried the Founders, this was not a society with a clear social or a per-manent class division. The Americans did not need to fight for social or economic freedom; they inherited it. Only in the South, especially the Carolinas with their slave majority, could one detect cultural differences within the mainland states similar to the Protestant–Catholic split in Ireland, or to the English-French divide in Canada. Indeed, much of the social distinctions that existed were far beyond the power of legislators to influence. The magisterial tradition still held. The Marquis de Chastellux noted how deferential the Virginians continued to be to the older "long-tailed" families and to the familiar names; and John Adams was aware that even in leveling New England, townsmen usually elected and re-elected the well-known names; and even in the West, in the Connecticut River valley, the great farmers were known as the "River Gods."

In the second place, by 1787, this fund of shared political experience had been reinforced by the shared experience of seven years of war. Those who served with Washington in the Continental Line, many of them Scots-Irish, were shaped by their own common military experiences and hardships. They had endured cold, hunger, repeated retreats and defeats, for a cause that certainly crossed state lines. In the end, from the Kennebec to the Santee, at Saratoga, Valley Forge, and at Yorktown, they had met and overcome a well-disciplined professional army. Some in the South, whose plantation economy had been thoroughly tied to Britain, had learnt to fight and win guerrilla wars. In the Carolina lowlands, Andrew Pickens, Thomas Sumter, and Francis Marion ("the swamp fox"), in the West John Sevier and Isaac Shelby, are in their distinct ways revolutionary heroes almost worthy to stand alongside Washington. All, whether Southerners, Northerner, or Westerners, became aware of a continent beyond the Alleghenies that could be theirs; and out of the comradeship of war a new nation was born. And with it were also enshrined the right of the civilian to bear arms for his own defense, and the suspicion of a standing army; as the Virginia Bill of Rights puts it, the militia was seen as "a noble Palladium of Liberty" and "the proper natural and safe defense of a free state." But, more than this, all veterans were due arrears of pay, and even more than civilian creditors and the many speculative purchasers of federal and state bonds, they believed that only a strong government would meet its obligations. There was a mutiny among Pennsylvania troops in 1781, and only Washington's personal appeal held the soldiers of the continental army in line in 1783. Most went home unpaid, except for promissory notes, hopes of western land grants if the states with western lands would surrender them, and with their muskets, which they were allowed to keep, since they would need them to hunt for food; but for most of them, to return home was enough, with or without pay.

But to the Continentals, the Congress had always shown gratitude and support. In 1776 officers and men got half pay if disabled. In 1778 officers agreeing to remain in service for the duration of the War and for seven years afterward were to receive half-pay – an offer changed in 1783 to full pay; and from 1780 pensions were provided for widows and orphans of Continental army officers. When a new federal government was instituted in 1789, it took over the states' commitments to invalid pensions. Thereafter, the provisions were extended. It was not, though, until 50 years after the War was over, in 1832, that the US Congress passed its first comprehensive pension grant: a yearly grant to every still-surviving veteran, whether officer or other rank. Although a number of officers did organize the society of the Cincinnati, of which Washington became president, and 27 of the 55 Founders were members of it, its limitation to officers and its hereditary character thwarted whatever threats it might have presented to the new republic. When the veterans went home, the army was left with 46 officers and 840 men to defend a territory stretching 1,500 miles from the Kennebec to Savannah, and across the Alleghenies to the Mississippi. There could be no serious pretense here of the threat of a standing army to the civil order.

For the Continental Line, however, the War had been an exciting, a unifying, and a national experience; and for them to get their land grants, they needed a national government strong enough to bring weight to bear on the large and land-owning states such as Virginia, Pennsylvania, and New York. The Continental Line, the veterans, and even the state militia, all buttressed support for the new constitution.

Thirdly, behind the geographic and military buttressing of federalism was an ideological buttress: a republican mood. It was especially clear in the Northwest. The Confederation, in all its executive weakness, constituting only a firm league of friendship, and allowing the long war to be directed by some 80 committees (and John Adams served on as many as he could), yet gave one enduring legacy to the new government: the Northwest Ordinances of 1787. Using an earlier proposal of Jefferson's, this provided that new states be created out of the land owned by the Confederation; and in the Northwest, now the old Northwest (i.e. north of the Ohio and west of Pennsylvania) slavery was banned. A territory wishing to become a member of the Union had to go through a series of steps before being admitted. When statehood was granted, however, the new member was to stand on an equal footing with the old states. When hesitant Rhode Island at last joined, and Vermont followed in 1791, Kentucky in 1792, Tennessee in 1796 and Ohio in 1802, they all joined on equal terms to Virginia – the old dominion – or Massachusetts – the Bay Colony of the Puritans' foundation. This extension of the revolutionary doctrine of equality was the most important contribution of the Confederation period. It meant that America's own colonial policy was to be based on the principle that all colonies of the United States would ultimately become equal –

and free – states. By the twentieth century it held true of Alaska, Hawaii, and Puerto Rico. The United States was, in other words, destined to be one of the great colonial powers of the nineteenth century, despite its horror of the name – but colonialism with a difference. For, rightly, it never saw itself as such, and constitutionally was not. The Northwest, and the entire trans-Mississippi region, however, were as much colonies of the United States as India, Canada, and Australia were of Britain. But they were largely empty and rich lands, to which people chose to move of their own free will, and where they could reap their own rewards. In Gertrude Stein's words, the United States is a country where there is more space where nobody is than where anybody is. The American plan of admission to the Union, as first set down by Jefferson in 1784, made it possible for the United States to be an imperial, without ever being an imperialist, power. Recognition of this phenomenon occurred in the early twentieth century, when the United States, as a result of the Spanish-American War, gained territories which apparently were not destined to become states. Only then did the nation have to reconsider the significance of the Northwest Ordinances of 1787. But not even Jefferson had foreseen the problems of American citizenship for Puerto Ricans, nor of the legacy of the freeing of Cuba from Spain, or of the role of the marines in ensuring stability in the Caribbean. But he had – perhaps as portent – refused to pay blackmail to the Barbary corsairs, and as President he founded the Military Academy at West Point. It is remarkable how the broad responsibility that lies on presidents, like kings, alters a man's faith that his fellows are endowed with ideals like his own. For Jefferson, as for Madison much earlier, the truth did come through.

The American mood, however, and the strategy in 1784 and 1785, as in 1787, were non-imperial. They stood in sharp contrast to those of contemporary British governors-general and administrators in India, who protected British-held Bengal by ringing it with buffer states, in client relationships which were unambiguously called simply "subsidiary treaties." There was no pretense there about the rights of men, or of freedom for all men regardless of color or status. But the popular language in America was not only Whig, but radical and dissenting. Madison was not alone in absorbing "Scotch" ideas; in his country, dissent was worth votes. The parallels are not with the New but with the Old Dominions. The Australian, New Zealand, and Canadian peopling, and much of their folk memory, was largely drawn from the lands north of a line drawn from Bristol to the Wash, even if the England of their dreams is of the South Downs. Why else did the brilliant Canadian O. D. Skelton turn against the

Old Country and towards Canadian nationalism in the 1920s and 1930s? The Canadian ties have been not with the "Raj" or the "Anglo," but with the lone shieling on the misty island; and all the Scots from Cape Breton to Vancouver recall, however mistily, the Hebrides – or the Gorbals, or Ulster. "British we were," said Skelton, "but British in the sense of southern English we never were." Why else did John Buchan of Perth and the Borders write so engagingly of South Africans, or of Canadians, whose hearts like his were in the Highlands or the Borderlands?

The main buttress, however, of what Madison called this "political experiment," was luck, and luck twice over. Not even Madison could have sensed the scale of the ultimate resources that would be opened up in a unique land. Nor could he predict that within two decades of the debates of 1787, his neighbor and friend the third President would double the extent of the US without firing a shot, by the purchase of the Louisiana Territory for 15 million dollars – approximately 3 cents an acre; and do it without consulting either Congress or the Supreme Court. No nation since then has had this fortunate combination of resources, and the freedom to exploit and develop them without foreign intervention. For a second piece of luck, and America's greatest good fortune, was not the document of 1787, in which neither the development of a strong President nor of an activist Supreme Court were foreseen or sought, but that, in the very year 1789 that its first, unambitious, President, George Washington, took office, the French Revolution broke out. Washington was inaugurated President, and took his oath of office on the balcony of Federal Hall, Wall Street, New York, on April 30, 1789. On 5 May the States-General assembled in Paris; the Bastille fell on 14 July. For the 25 years that followed, the European Powers and their overseas colonies were embroiled in war. The 13 states of North America, now happily independent, were left alone for a full generation, and by 1815 there were 17. The United States was, for the first time in its 200-year history, secure from foreign invasions – which was just as well, since in 1800 it had neither army nor navy. If there had been a "revolution" in 1776, by 1789 it stopped at its own frontiers. Washington said "No" when Francisco de Miranda asked for help to free Venezuela; he did nothing to help Tom Paine, in prison in France under the Terror. Indeed, the US's only war during the years from Yorktown to the "War of 1812" was in Africa; its first – and for long its only – foreign entanglement was on the shores of Tripoli, against the Barbary corsairs as the marching song of the Marine Corps testifies. Whatever its constitutional fragility in 1787, it was blessed immediately after by 25 years of freedom from European interference; during that benevolent truce, it looked west, doubled its territory by the Louisiana Purchase, moved the Indians west and began to destroy the basis of their way of life, the buffalo, and began to build the canals, the turnpikes, the wagon roads and the highways, out of which came its own distinct national identity. As Rufus Miles of Princeton has put it: "The extraordinary affluence of the US has been produced by a set of fortuitous, non-repetitive and non-sustainable factors." The Jeffersonian era in the US outlasted the Napoleonic in Europe.

By contrast, the emerging nations of today are overwhelmingly one- or two-crop economies tied, inevitably, to one or another foreign market and dependent upon it, and lacking in native capital, credit, and sometimes skills. They are thus involved in one or other power bloc, however "free" in form they may wish their political systems to be, however anti-imperial their political vocabulary. For the poor and hungry there can be little freedom. "First feed the people, then ask of them virtue," wrote Dostoevski. Add to this tribal and clan loyalties, and the role of armies as training schools of elites offering quick access to power, and it is hard to see parallels with 1776 or 1787 in Africa, Asia, or Latin America. If there are any American parallels at all, they are with the First rather than the Third World.

9 FINALE

In his final speech in the Convention in September 1787 — a speech read for him by James Wilson, for he was physically frail by then — Benjamin Franklin said:

Sir, I cannot help expressing a wish that every member of the Convention who may still have objection to it, would with me, on this occasion, doubt a little of his own infallibility, and to make manifest our unanimity, put his name to this instrument.

After the end of the Philadelphia Convention in 1787, a lady said to Franklin; "Well, Dr Franklin, what have you given us — a monarchy, an aristocracy, or a republic?" Franklin thought for a moment and then replied; "A republic, madam — if you can keep it."

It may well be that few of the Founders looked as far ahead as we now assume. Their expedient of an electoral college as the device to elect the President has an academic and tortuous ring to it — did they expect it to be used long, or would Congress not itself in fact gradually do the choosing? But what they had done was novel as well as creative: a new government was set up, federal and republican, with, at its center, a quite short document. Until then, by "constitution" the English language had understood an "assemblage of laws, institutions and customs;" Bolingbroke's words still hold of the United Kingdom, and range thus from institutions like parliaments and lawcourts to laws and traditions, habits and ways of doing things. Now, to Americans the Constitution became the fundamental covenant, a bible to be read and re-read, and interpreted in every generation – "a thing antecedent to a government," as Paine said in 1791; "a government is only the creature of a constitution."

The interpretation was done openly, frequently, in a daily press keen to make news. Alongside the three branches of government – executive, legislative, and judicial – set up in 1787, there has grown a fourth, the "fourth estate," the Press – totally unforeseen by and, in so far as it could have been foreseen, one would judge very unwelcome to the Founding Fathers. In their four months of deliberation, during a hot sticky summer in 1787, the 55 men insisted on, and honored, a pledge to absolute secrecy, even when they adjourned to the Indian Queen or local boarding houses for a rum flip or a mint sling. In 1787 there would have been total scorn for Woodrow Wilson's academic gestures of "open covenants openly arrived at", and for Senator Muskie's remark, that there can be an "over-obsession with secrecy;" the Fathers first and last were realists, and knew "open" and "diplomacy" to be contradictory terms. The advice of Benjamin Franklin, in the words of *Poor Richard*, is still the essence of intelligence "operations;" Franklin, who lived by journalism and probing and by being endlessly curious, could still say: "If you want to keep a secret, keep it secret."

The role of the fourth estate, the lax libel laws, the freedom of information legislation of recent years, the vigilance of the Court in protecting the Bill of Rights, all are now heightened in the US by the impact of television – Speaker O'Neill once said that President Reagan's secret weapon, one that no congressman could rival, was "the daily six o'clock TV news." And the peculiarities of Washington DC offer rich material to the probing reporter. It is a totally artificial creation, a federal district set down in a swamp, planned to honor the first President and his home five miles away at Mount Vernon. It is, in contrast to many American cities, largely devoid of industry (except newsprint) and of trade (except two airports); Washington is a Southern city in ethos, with 75 percent of the population black; with lawyers, with 435 congressmen, 100 senators and their staffs, many of them themselves lawyers. Ten thousand official lobbyists have offices on Capitol Hill, and there is a further bureaucracy of at least 10,000 on the Hill, and a matching number in or near the White House, in the National Security Council and the departments of state and Treasury, not to mention the staffs, across the line in Virginia, of the Pentagon and the CIA.

There is another conclusion to be drawn. The Declaration of Independence of 1776 was written by a Virginian planter-farmer, Thomas Jefferson, a bookish lawyer-trained architect, naturalist, and botanist, who, as President, doubled the size of the US by the purchase of Louisiana, and did it without consulting Congress, and was aware (and tortured by the fact) that he had acted unconstitutionally. Independence, however, was won not by words but by seven years of war, and by an army commanded by another Virginian, George Washington, also a planter-farmer but on a bigger scale, who by the extent of his lands and by the marriage that enabled him to enlarge them, became probably the richest man of his time, but had begun from near-poverty; and whose estate at Mount Vernon was to become a national shrine, just as he became first in war and first in peace.

The Constitution was the work of a third Virginian, much less affluent than the other two, and more scholarly by nature even than Jefferson, James Madison; a shy man and a hypochondriac, yet much wiser and shrewder about the ways of men (though probably not of women) than the others. His handiwork, the Constitution, was given dynamic by yet another Virginian, a distant cousin as well as a political enemy of Jefferson, with a log-cabin childhood on Virginia's frontier, and a meager schooling, but with great physical strength, and a persistence and willpower on a par with that of Washington, with whom, after all, he had suffered at Valley Forge. John Marshall's experience in Congress taught him mistrust of legislatures; and as an envoy to Revolutionary France he learnt contempt for democracy. But, like Washington, he had intense national pride in the country he fought for, and shaped; and like Washington again, he allied transparent integrity and a commanding presence to dedication. In his 35 years as chief justice, his Supreme Court dealt with 1,106 cases, and in 519 of them he himself wrote the opinion. Of the 1,106 cases, no less than 62 dealt with the "meaning" of the Constitution; and of those 1,106, he dissented from the decisions on 9 occasions only. He dominated the Court and gave it permanent status. The debt of the US to these four men of the Old Dominion beggars all description.

There was truth in Washington's comment:

It appears to me, then, little short of a miracle, that the Delegates from so many different States (which States you know are also different from each other), in their manners, circumstances, and prejudices, should unite in forming a system of national Government, so little liable to well founed objections ... We are an independent nation, and act for ourselves ...[27]

[27] Washington to Alexander Hamilton, April 14, 1796, cited in Douglas Southall Freeman, *Washington*, abridged in one volume by Richard Harwell (London, Eyre and Spottiswoode, 1970), p. 695.

3

First in War, First in Peace

1 CINCINNATUS

The Constitution was ratified with the adherence of New Hampshire on June 21, 1788. There was a general expectation that Washington would be the first President, and the celebration of his 56th birthday in July became the occasion for the call to be launched. A toast was drunk at Wilmington, Delaware, to "Farmer Washington – May he like a second Cincinnatus, be called from the plow to rule a great people." Washington had his customary doubts; the electors had not. The electors were chosen in the different states on the first Wednesday in January 1789, and they met and cast their ballots on the first Wednesday in February. Some were chosen by voters, others by the state legislatures, those of New Jersey by the governor and council. Washington was unanimously chosen as President by all the electors, with John Adams his Vice-President. On April 16, 1789, once again he left Mount Vernon at his country's call. He told Henry Knox that he felt like "a culprit who is going to his place of execution." In New York he would be a gentleman-planter in a den of lawyers.

His journey to New York was like a royal (or should it be a Roman?) progress, through Philadelphia and Trenton. It was a carnival too. As he sailed up the Hudson, he was met by sloops on which choirs sang odes in his honor – one of them ironically set to the tune of "God Save the King." ("Joy to our native land ... For Washington's at hand ... With glory crowned.") Ribbons of rhetoric entwined him all the way. The peals of bells in the New York churches were drowned by the noise of 13-gun salutes from ship and shore batteries. At his inaugural on April 30, although he behaved nervously – his gestures awkward, his voice low, and his hands restless – he became the part, with his dress sword and his shoe buckles of silver; his canary-colored coach, imported from England, was decorated with gilded nymphs and cupids and with his own coat of arms, and drawn by six horses. The manners became the man, if not yet the office. If Fisher Ames thought his modesty "an allegory in which virtue was personified," he brought his own natural dignity to the presidency and the new nation.

The formality became an ex-general. Fourteen white servants and seven slaves were brought from Mount Vernon to work in the house on Cherry Street, and then to the larger Macomb House on Broadway, to which he moved in February 1790. Each Friday evening he would attend his wife's levées: no handshakes, formal bows, and few brief remarks, and the President withdrew at 9 p.m. It suited him: he was partly deaf and all but toothless. He had the tastes and the style of a wealthy planter, one of the wealthiest – if not the wealthiest – man of his time.

The Vice-President, by contrast, appeared to suffer from a case of "the fidgets." The portly envoy who for ten years had impressed kings and foreign ministers with his plain talk and studiedly plain air was president of the Senate:

My country in its wisdom has contrived for me the most insignificant office that ever the invention of man contrived or his imagination conceived ... It is, to be sure, a punishment to hear other men talk five hours every day and not be at liberty to talk at all myself, especially as more than half I hear appears to me very young, inconsiderate and inexperienced.

Bostonian Adams well knew that the vice-presidency was a kind of afterthought of the Constitution's makers. They feared that the states' electors might vote for local heroes for President, so they decreed that each elector must vote for two candidates from two different states. Nobody ever doubted that the first winner would be Washington, but that left the vice-president a mere straw man, representing little, and with nothing much to do. He also worried about the proper form of address for Washington. He observed that to call him simply "Mr President" would put him "on a level with the Governor of Bermuda." A Senate committee took thought and proposed "His Highness, the President of the United States of America and Protector of their Liberties." This was too much even for many senators to accept, but Adams insisted on the need for some such title. Said he: "The President must be something that includes all the dignities of the diplomatic corps, and something greater still.

Religion and government have both been used as pageantry. Signs do not necessarily imply abuse." The only result was that some senators mocked Adams as "His Rotundity."

2 THE PRESIDENCY OF GEORGE WASHINGTON: THE MAN

The presidency of George Washington remains, surprisingly, among the most controversial of all the presidencies. Surprisingly, because it has been abundantly chronicled; indeed, overabundantly. The hagiography that began with the itinerant book-peddler and ex-parson Mason Weems, whom Senator Beveridge was later to describe as "part Whitefield, part Villon," and who invented the hatchet and the cherry-tree story, has continued ever since, and no later writers have ever quite managed to shake themselves free from it. They have, happily, rarely been as naive as he was.[1]

But successive biographers have in their own ways been quite as careless with the facts. Jared Sparks, in publishing the first edition of Washington's writings in 1837, did so only after a careful vetting and doctoring of his style. The most gifted of his nineteenth-century biographers, Washington Irving, writing in 1855–9, portrayed him as a good churchgoer, which he was not, and denied that he married for money, which he did. The Washington portrait has been carved in marbled prose, lost to flesh and blood and temper.

It is only recently that Washington's biographers have had the temerity to point out his all-too-human sensitiveness, and his all-too-natural leaning to the cause of order and of nationalism, to which, largely at others' command, he had dedicated his life. The heavily magisterial tone of D. S. Freeman's volumes, while rich in detail, contrives to leave the man interred in the achievement; in places his sixth volume suggests that Washington never fully understood the broad intent of the Hamiltonian program. The final volume of Freeman's collaborators leaves many questions unasked and unanswered. Irving Brant's comprehensive biography of Madison reveals how misled Washington was in 1795 in his view of Randolph, and how easy it was to mislead him. Some studies, like those of Alexander DeConde in foreign policy and the studies of party growth of the late Joseph Charles, reveal the limitations, the perplexities, and the human traits of this very noble, if not highly

[1] Mason Weems, *George Washington* (1800).

articulate or intellectual, figure.[2] Forrest McDonald is brave enough to say:

Admittedly, he was far from being an ordinary man, but he was a long way from being a saint. As a soldier he had been capable of blundering, rashness and poor judgment. He was addicted to gambling, apparently indulged in a good deal of wenching, was avid in the pursuit of wealth, and was a "most horrid swearer and blasphemer". He was vain, pompous, pretentious, and hot-tempered in the extreme.[3]

To criticize the first President has always been akin to heresy; one might almost call it *lèse-majesté*. The assessment of the man has been made more difficult by his own lack of facility with words, both in speech and with pen; he was heavily dependent on others, his "writing aides" as he called them, when he wrote dispatches or messages. His letters are conspicuously lacking in those statements of general ideas to which his contemporaries were so addicted. They are confined to specific matters; they are brief; and they are apt to be stilted in style. There is little in the way of analysis or of personal reflection and less still of gossip. His collected writings throw little light on the man himself.

The process of glorification was a quite deliberate, indeed an inevitable, one. It was even more the work of artists than of writers. The Washington we know is the image popularized by Gilbert Stuart, who painted him at least 124 times. At three sittings the President gave in Philadelphia in 1795, four Peales set up easels around him: Charles, brother James, and sons Rembrandt and Raphaelle. In sculpture, Jean Antoine Houdon, his finest portrayer, Horatio Greenough and others made the image still more Roman and heroic. He was seen either as the Virginia colonel in buff and blue, or as the Roman *imperator* with sword and toga, or, at least with some concession to reality, as Cincinnatus at the plow. The creation of this public image was noted quite clearly by contemporary outsiders such as the British minister, Robert Liston, and his

---

[2] Douglas Southall Freeman, *George Washington: A biography* 6 vols (New York, Scribner's, 1948–53); vol. VII by John A. Carroll and Mary Wells Ashworth (New York, Scribner's, 1957); Irving Brant, *James Madison*, 6 vols (Indianapolis, Bobbs-Merrill, 1941–61); Alexander DeConde, *Entangling Alliance* (Durham, NC, Duke University Press, 1958); Joseph Charles, *Origins of the American Party System* (New York, Harper Torchbooks, 1956).

[3] Forrest McDonald, *Novus Ordo Seclorum: The intellectual origins of the Constitution* (Lawrence, University of Kansas Press, 1985), p. 192.

Plate 4 George Washington: bust by David d'Angers.
(Henry E. Huntington Library and Art Gallery, San Marino, CA.)

wife. Within five days of Washington's death, Henrietta Liston wrote
to her uncle in Glasgow that the first President "stood the barrier
betwixt the Northernmost and Southernmost States. He was the
Unenvied Head of the Army, and such was the magic of his name
that his opinion was a sanction equal to law." Her husband viewed
the first birthday celebrations after Washington's death with more
detachment:

... these ceremonies tend to elevate the spirit of the people, and contribute to the formation of a national character, which they consider as much wanting in this country. And ... Americans will be gainers by the periodical recital of the features of their Revolutionary war and repetition of the praises of Washington — The hyperbolical amplifications of the Panegyricks in question have an evident effect, especially among the younger part of the community, in fomenting the growth of that Vanity which to the feelings of a stranger had already arrived at a sufficient height.[4]

The apotheosis of Washington is the more surprising in that it took place in an Age of Reason, dedicated to a strictly rationalist view of mankind; an age, too, of pamphlet wars and pamphleteering, when men like Cobbett and Callender and William Duane were prompt to blacken reputations. It is true that the attacks on Washington in the last year of his presidency greatly disturbed him, but they were never quite as vicious as those on Jefferson and Burr, Adams and Hamilton. How, in any event, did the popular opinion of him, the affection and trust, emerge through the barriers of distance and etiquette that surrounded him, and which he in some measure encouraged? How far was the popular legend accepted by his closest associates, how far used by them for their own purposes? How far did Washington as a person come to be politically exploited before his death as well as after it? And was he ever aware that he was being exploited? These are the questions that still challenge the modern historian of the Revolutionary period.

Despite all that is in print, we still need to know much about the man, not least his presidency. It seems clear that the man had faults. To sum up, Washington seemed to have been in love with Sally Fairfax, the wife of his best friend. He married for money — and for land. He was not a teetotaller, he swore, he was not notably religious and makes few references to religion in his letters, and he was not a very dutiful son to an admittedly tiresome mother. He found in marriage not excitement (of which he had plenty elsewhere) but tranquility. To use James Flexner's description of the Weems volume, the man who comes out from his pages is not "a repellent, goody-goody, Sunday-school-inspired-prig," but a warm and strong character who curbed his sexual with his other passions, and always had a half-hunger for children of his own. He was not at ease with words, in speech or on paper. He needed his writing aides, as

---

[4] Papers of Robert and Henrietta Liston, Scottish Record Office, Edinburgh, MSS. Cf. Bradford Perkins (ed.), "Henrietta Liston, a diplomat's wife in Philadelphia 1796–1800," *William & Mary Quarterly*, 11 (1954), pp. 592–632.

commander-in-chief, and again as President. His Inaugural Address
of 1793 (mainly Madison's writing), ran to no less than 73 pages,
so it is perhaps just as well that it was never delivered at all. We
know, of course, of Washington's ultra-sensitiveness to criticism and
of his own concern with his reputation. What becomes clearer in
Flexner's study, however, than elsewhere, is his vigor and authority.
As Flexner puts it:

Washington had to have the fierceness necessary to a successful soldier,
the self-will necessary for a leader of men, the self-interest essential to the
amassing of a large estate. He exploded sometimes into actions of which
his best judgment disapproved. He could be very overbearing to his sub-
ordinates, even to fellow statesmen of such stature as Jefferson and Hamilton.
In his private life, as in his public, he was not always understanding, not
always kind. Yet Washington wished to be wise and good ... Washington's
character comprised that pull of opposites which give color and depth. [5]

It was the war – for which he had little preparation but an
immense presence and even more immense patience – that gave him
the images: the crossing of the icy Delaware, the victory at Princeton,
the bold but unsuccessful battles at Brandywine and Germantown,
and, not least, the cold, hunger, nakedness, and the camaraderie,
of Valley Forge. It was here that a legend was born. Being human,
he made mistakes – but humanity helped to put life into the legend.
He had enemies – could an army commander avoid them? The
Conway Cabal almost succeeded in 1777 in replacing him. Burgoyne,
after all, surrendered at Saratoga to Horatio Gates, not to Washington. He was guilty of indiscretions – notably his comments on
the lack of discipline in his New England troops (for a commander,
whatever Weems might say of him, should not always speak the
truth). He had affection notably for his staff lieutenants, his writing
aides, and for John Laurens and the rich young Lafayette most of
all; and those not admired by him could be envious and bitter men.

He led a cause that objective observers would have called hopeless. He was devoid of military experience except on the frontier,
yet he outlasted three British commanders, and by outlasting them,
defeated them and their cause. A Virginian landowner, he led a
force mainly of Yankee farmers. And, though he led a revolutionary
army, he argued steadily for tolerance, and always saw his men as
citizens as well as soldiers. Fortune – and geography – certainly

[5] James Flexner, *George Washington, A Biography*, 4 vols (Boston, Little Brown,
1965–72), vol. II, p. 540.

shone on the American cause, but in no aspect was this so true as in the character and dedication of the obstinate, steady, and un-ambitious man who came to lead it. From each re-telling of the War he emerges with ever greater credit and stature.

He was not made for politics – for its small talk, its intrigue, its chicanery. At dissembling, he was especially unagile. The Jefferson who returned from Paris at his summons was from the beginning of his secretaryship of state always aglow with distrust, less than chivalrous in his relations with the President, and apt in his letters and memoranda to be addicted to asperity of language towards him. It was never an easy relationship. What comes out with equal freshness in recent studies are Washington's dependence in the early days of his presidency on James Madison, and his own deep affection for Gouverneur Morris. He was no prisoner of Hamilton's magic, or of his ideas; it is clear he was always his own master, however much he might protest his intellectual limitations.

But the major discovery of Flexner's study, and one which is highly contentious, is the claim that Washington's views of slavery have never before been thoroughly analysed. One point is fresh; in Flexner's volumes he argues that Washington started from the con-ventional Southern position on slavery, but found that, as he grew older, slavery became more and more repugnant to him, whereas the Jeffersonians increasingly stilled their doubts on this embarrass-ing moral issue. Flexner claims that Washington saw advantages in Northern institutions precisely because they offered an alternative economic system to the slavery of his own South, and that his support of Hamilton's financial measures owed something to this recognition. A paragraph in a hitherto unnoticed letter, of which Washington kept a copy on his files, reveals what has remained unknown for almost two centuries, that before returning to Mount Vernon from the Presidency, Washington secretly freed some of his own house slaves. Nor has there been adequate recognition of the political significance of his doing what the Jeffersonians con-spicuously did not do – freeing his own slaves in his will. Flexner contends, and substantiates that claim, that Washington's own convictions were strongly on the side of emancipation. The final chapter in Flexner's fourth volume is a quite superb essay on the man and his temperament, which was a remarkable blend of vigor and restraint. The fundamental *gravitas* in Washington came, he says, from "a wide streak of darkness." Flexner establishes that the Father of his Country was no simple and marmoreal figure, but a complex, tightly disciplined, and immensely strong, personality. The debt of his country to him is beyond calculation. It has tried to repay it by giving his name to one state, 7 mountains, 8 streams, 10 lakes, 33 counties, 9 colleges and 121 towns and villages. The federal district named after him has a Roman flavor – but he remains, as he always did in spirit, on the Potomac, near which he was born, and where he inherited from his beloved half-brother the home and the acres he cherished.

3 THE TURBULENT WEST

From his youth as surveyor and through the years of French Indian and British wars, the West was always problem number one for Washington the Virginian. It remained so after 1783: whoever commanded the Mississippi was threat to the new country's security and survival. Equally to the wary heirs of the Spanish conquistadors, the increasing flow of American settlers toward the southwest was seen as an increasing threat – a threat to Spain's control of the Mississippi valley and ultimately to its rich Mexican mines. As the Count of Aranda, Spain's ambassador to France, once said: "A day will come when the United States will be a giant, even a colossus. We shall watch with grief the tyrannical existence of this same colossus."

To block that supposed threat in 1787 was the mission of Estaban Miro, aged 45, the pudgy Spanish governor at New Orleans. In the disputed area north of Florida, he armed the Creek Indians and encouraged their raids against frontier villages. Along the Mississippi itself, which Spain kept tightly closed, he exacted as much as 25 percent in tariffs on all non-Spanish traffic. To any American who would swear allegiance to King Charles IV of Spain, Miro offered 240 acres of land, a tacit tolerance of Protestantism, and an exemption from the river tax.

The man who did most to help Miro in this effort to divide and dominate the American settlers was not a Spaniard at all. He was James Wilkinson, a onetime American brigadier-general who in the past five years had made a big name and a fortune for himself in the troubled Kentucky territory. Wilkinson was a Marylander with bottomless pockets and a considerable capacity for drink and rabble-rousing. His war record was little short of scandalous. He had served in the War as aide to Benedict Arnold and General Gates, was tainted in the plot to displace Washington as commander, then resigned as the continental army's clothier-general when grave irregularities were found in his accounts. But he left his reputation behind when he moved West.

In 1787 he journeyed down the river with a small fleet of flatboats filled with tobacco, flour, and bacon, and wormed his way into Miro's counsels. He stayed three months and sold his goods at a high price. In return, it was rumored, Wilkinson secretly swore allegiance to the King of Spain and was put on a salary of $6,000 per year as the sole American trading agent for the river. In any case, he had certainly done his best since then to encourage his fellow Kentuckians to secede from the United States and form a separate state under Spanish protection. Wilkinson even started a potential capital for such an inland empire, the city of Frankfort. He laid out a set of streets there to encourage customers for his real estate speculations.

The idea of independence held considerable appeal in Kentucky and its adjacent territories. Most of the controversial land belonged to Virginia and North Carolina. But once over the mountains, the settlers then found themselves largely on their own, with few easy trade outlets to the east and no protection at all. Being independent in spirit, they often took matters into their own hands, and in the 1780s no fewer than four separate groups set themselves up as independent governments, because of what one of them called "necessity and self-preservation." Among them were: Westsylvania, at the forks of the Ohio; Transylvania, around Boonesborough in the Kentucky territory; Watauga, the oldest, near the Holston River; and, finally, the sovereign commonwealth of Frankland, south of the Cumberland. Starting in 1785, Frankland managed to run itself very well. It levied its own taxes, appointed its officials, organized riflemen to fight off the Cherokees, made treaties, and even applied to Congress for admission as the 14th state. Only in 1788 did North Carolina finally suppress Frankland by force, while the Franklanders complained that neither the eastern states nor Congress could "protect their property or favor their commerce."

The Kentucky district had for some years wanted to become an independent state within the Union. But after eight local conventions on the subject, back-and-forth negotiations with both Virginia and the new national government remained stalled. There was considerable ill will involved, partly because over-the-mountain trade was unwieldy, while the way down the Mississippi lay clear — except for Spain. Kentuckians were deeply angered, therefore, when they learned that, in a proposed treaty with Spain, secretary for foreign affairs John Jay had tentatively offered to "forbear" insisting on free trade down the Mississippi for 25 years in return for fishing concessions useful to New England merchants.

Though the treaty was shelved because of Southern resistance, Wilkinson thoroughly whipped up his neighbor's resentment. To improve its offer to American settlers, he offered better terms on river trade, and an increase in land grants to as much as 3,000 acres per person. The Kentucky district grew so fast that Wilkinson prospered whether his foray into subversion succeeded or failed. Local experts believed that Kentucky would soon come to terms with the new government and be admitted into the Union as a separate state. President Washington himself, in fact, was far less worried about its secession than about the "ambitious and turbulent spirits" of the Kentuckians, who just might load up their flatboats with long rifles and cannon, float down on Miro's largely unprotected city, and take it — lock, stock, tax rights and all.

4 WASHINGTON'S SERVICES

Washington's services are striking enough. There was, first his contribution as an organizer of the government. He inherited from the Confederation only a handful of unpaid clerks and a large number of debts; the outstanding paper money was worthless, and there were only three banks functioning in the country. North Carolina and Rhode Island were not yet in the Union; Vermont was still intriguing with Canada and Wilkinson intriguing with Spain; Britain held on to the western posts and was dangerously friendly with the Indians. The American army had 840 officers and men; there was no navy at all. Hamilton's view of the Constitution as "frail and worthless" seemed nearer reality than Washington's talk of "a hopeful experiment." Washington was on, he knew, "untrodden ground;" everything he did would set a precedent. What distinguished his work in creating the administrative system was his sense of order, his discretion and his freedom from advocacy. What he wrote to his favourite nephew, Bushrod Washington, in refusing his application for appointment as United States District Attorney for Virginia, held of his attitude generally: "My political conduct in nominations, even if I was uninfluenced by principle, must be exceedingly circumspect and proof against just criticism, for the eyes of Argus are upon me." He regarded the executive branch as distinct from but equal to the legislature; the choice and form of legislation was a matter for Congress, but the President had the right to remove and, subject to congressional endorsement, to appoint officials. This was not an easy task; there were some 3,000 applications for federal employment even before a single job was created. The effect was that control of administrative and diplomatic officials fell to the executive, not Congress.

The First Federal Congress was the most important congress in American history: it adopted the Bill of Rights, erected the executive and judicial branches of government, organized the collection of the first federal revenues, decided on the location of the capital city, and funded the federal and state Revolutionary war debt. As part of these achievements, it organized its own removal for the next decade to Philadelphia, where, in a sense it had all begun nearly 20 years before. The Congress was dotted by striking personalities: Madison, acting in effect as floor leader and/or prime minister, Senator William Maclay of Pennsylvania as a would-be Opposition critic, and distinguished Yankees like Fisher Ames and Rufus King.[6]

The Judiciary Act of 1789 set up the legal system that is basically still in operation: district courts, circuit courts of appeal, and a Supreme Court of one chief justice and five (now eight) associates. To ensure uniform legal interpretations throughout the nation, the Supreme Court was to rule on the constitutionality of state-court decisions. John Jay was appointed chief justice, and the Court sat for the first time in February 1790, resplendent in judicial robes, but without the white wigs of their English counterparts.

Treaty-making was a more difficult matter. Washington took quite literally the constitutional provisions that treaties be made with "the advice and consent" of the Senate. He thought that on some occasions it should be possible for the President to appear before the Senate to explain the purpose of a treaty, and to obtain forthwith a "yes" or "no" on the points he raised. He thought of the Senate, that is, as a council of state. In order to settle the long-standing boundary dispute between the Creek Indians and the state of Georgia, Washington proposed negotiations with the Creeks, to attempt to wean them from the temptations of an alliance with the Spanish in Louisiana. In August 1789 with this in mind, he appeared before the Senate in person with a series of proposals; the most vigorous dissenter to them among the senators, William Maclay, asked that the treaty be deferred to a committee. According to Maclay, whose portraits were often etched with acid, Washington stalked out with a "discontented air," declaring that deferment "defeats every purpose of my coming here." He got the Senate's approval two days later, but the incident had important consequences: it became the rule for treaties to be presented to the Senate for approval after, and not before, they were negotiated; in the Senate the committee system

[6] Margaret C. S. Christman, *The First Federal Congress 1789–91* (Washington, DC, Smithsonian Institution Press, 1989).

began to develop; and the Senate made it clear that in its own esti-
mation it was not a council of state but an elected and a legislative
body, in no way subordinate to the President.

Increasingly, therefore, Washington turned for advice to his "Cabinet," the officers at the head of his three executive departments:
State, Treasury, and War. They were not mentioned in the Constitution and they were responsible only to the President, not to
Congress; they were denied the right to sit in Congress, to Hamilton's
chagrin; they came, however, to be the originators of policy; they
were all consulted on all matters, not merely on their specialisms.
The Cabinet, unmentioned in the Constitution, thus became a privy
council, which the Founding Fathers had clearly meant the Senate
to be. And to the first two offices Washington appointed men of unusual capacity. Thomas Jefferson, the 46-year-old Virginian architect,
naturalist, and lawyer, patrician, America's *uomo universale*, who
had been serving as minister in France since 1784, became secretary
of state; 32-year-old Alexander Hamilton, Washington's aide in the
war, and now a lawyer, a son-in-law of rich General Philip Schuyler
of New York, became secretary of the Treasury and Washington's
major adviser. Henry Knox, the secretary of war, continued in the
office he had held under the Confederation – a more corpulent and
genial, but a much less able, man than his colleagues. Edmund
Randolph, former Governor of Virginia, became attorney general.

The creation of the working administration, therefore, was Washington's achievement. But it was Hamilton rather than the President
who gave what he himself called "executive impulse" to the administration. Hamilton was in 1790 and 1791, as in Philadelphia in
1787, the exponent of high federalism, of authority in government,
and of a sound system of public credit. His three great state papers
were his report on *Publick Credit* (January 1790), on *The Bank*
(December 1790), and on *Manufactures* (December 1791). He pre-
faced each with a persuasive prologue, justifying his proposals,
cogent, well-argued, and indicating a clear philosophy that in a
new nation the government must provide not only the ideas but the
capital to back them. Brought up in a store on the fringe of the
British Empire, a mercantilist and an admirer of Pitt the Elder, he
easily became an American nationalist and a centralist, and proud
to be so. He urged that all outstanding debts, foreign and domestic,
whether of Congress or of the states, should be assumed at face
value and paid by the federal government. The purpose was political
as much as economic; not merely would creditors (and many speculators) be bound to the national cause, but that cause would be
greatly strengthened both at home and abroad. "A public debt," he

argued, "is a public blessing." The interests of the propertied classes would be tied up with the government; government stock would rise abroad and trade would be encouraged. The assumption of the debts of the states by the federal government would allow it to dominate the revenue sources of the country and consolidate national – and central – authority. A Bank of the United States should also be set up, modeled on the Bank of England, to act as the fiscal agent of the government; and a system of tariff duties on imports and excises on home-produced liquor should be used to provide revenue. Hamilton emerged in fact as the first champion of protection in American history. He gave his reasons clearly in his *Report on Manufactures*: to encourage industries essential to the national defense, to diversify American economic life, and to develop a home market for agriculture. But even here it was less protection from foreign competition than incentive and energy at home that he sought. Bounties mattered far more than excises. Government had, in an infant state, to promote immigration and reward invention. "The public purse must supply the deficiency of private resource." He proposed taxes on general property – lands, houses, and luxury possessions, excises on salt and tobacco; tavern licenses; polls of servants; stamps for legal documents; and import duties in addition to those granted to Congress. All taxes, where possible, were graduated with respect to presumed ability to pay. Property owners were to declare their lands, on oath, and to give information concerning their carriages and servants. Houses were minutely classified as to size and quality, and collectors were to visit them annually for the levy.

Hamilton had indeed a very modern view of economics and of the capacity of a people to bear burdens.

The truth is, the ability of a country to pay taxes depends on infinite combinations of physical and moral causes which can never be accommodated to any general rule – climate, soil, productions, advantages for navigation, government, genius of the people, progress of arts and industry, and an endless variety of circumstances. The diversities are sufficiently great in these States to make an infinite difference in their relative wealth, the proportion of which can never be found by any common measure whatever.

Hamilton's purposes were clear and persuasively expressed. He was as much concerned with "energy in government" as with "order in the finances." His own creative zest and overpowering capacity for work made him impatient and autocratic. He had little sympathy for democracy:

All communities divide themselves into the few and the many. The first are rich and well-born, the other the mass of the people. The voice of the people has been said to be the voice of God; and however generally this maxim has been quoted and believed, it is not true in fact. The people are turbulent and changing; they seldom judge or determine right.

Government was a matter for the rich, the well-born and the able; to him they were apt to be synonymous categories. At first glance, the sentiments are surprising, coming from him: of illegitimate birth in the British West Indies, son of a wandering Scottish trader, he became the great American protagonist of government and connection; a poor boy in origins, he had come up the hard way, and was convinced that men were the slaves of their own ambitions and interests. They were not, he said, rational beings, but "ambitious, vindictive and rapacious." He was so himself, and was courageous not just in admitting it, but in making energy and enterprise the bedrock of his policies. *Poor Richard* and Father Abraham would have been proud of him. He was first and last a realist; he understood economic forces – as Washington did not – and understood how to unleash them and harness them to the new state; and, more than any of his contemporaries, he had consuming energy and ambition. His proposals became the core of that Federalist economic program that, later, Whigs and, later still, Republicans, have made their own.

Hamilton's highly partisan financial proposals were strongly opposed by crotchety senators like William Maclay of Pennsylvania and suspicious congressmen like Madison; they disliked the rewarding of bondholders who were often merely speculators, the penalizing of states which had already tried to honor their obligations to their creditors, and the dangerously wide implied powers suggested by the setting up of the Bank. His *Report on Manufactures* fell on deaf ears in Congress and produced no legislation. Patrick Henry gave voice to an issue that would gradually become a battle cry; he denied that the Constitution gave any authority to the federal government to assume the obligations of the states or to charter a Bank. There was coming here to be a significant alignment of the South versus New England, of agrarian interests versus commercial and financial. In the end, by Jefferson's complaisance (which he later claimed to regret), a deal was made. The Hamiltonian program for the assumption of state debts would go through on condition that the Potomac should ultimately become the seat of the federal government. After a decade in Philadelphia (1790–1800), the capital was to be sited closer to the South and more amenable to its influence. Ten years later the federal city, as it was then called, came into being near Georgetown.

In Washington's first term, therefore, if his services are obvious enough, the creative energy was Hamilton's. This very energy produced partisanship and factional strife.

From August 1790 onward the differences between Hamilton and Jefferson became sharper, on the excise and Bank proposals, on Federalism versus state rights, and increasingly on the issues raised by the French Revolution. By 1792 the tone of the public debate was reminiscent of 1775. Paine's *Rights of Man*, written in France, was dedicated to Washington; it was welcomed by Jefferson, reviled by Hamilton. A bitter press campaign of principles and personalities was unleashed; John Fenno's *Gazette of the United States* was countered by Philip Freneau's *National Gazette*. And the latter was again talking of social conflict: "Another revolution must and will be brought about in favor of the people." The campaign began to train its guns not only on the Cabinet but also on its Head, to sneer at "the drawing Room," "those apparent trifles, birthday odes," and the Friday-evening levées. Senator Maclay, never an unprejudiced observer, accused Washington of "pushing the Potomac." "The President," he said, "has become, in the hands of Hamilton, the dishclout of every dirty speculation, as his name goes to wipe away blame and silence all murmuring."

> Each day a fresh report he broaches,
>   That Spies and Jews may ride in coaches
> Soldiers and farmers, don't despair,
>   Untaxed as yet are Earth and Air.

Nor were foreign affairs easier to master. France was in revolution, and faced a slave rebellion in her richest West Indian province, Santo Domingo; this might involve a request by France that the US fulfill the terms of the French-American alliance of 1778 and embroil the new republic in European affairs. On its own frontier, the US was at war anyway. The Miami and Wabash tribes had raided in Ohio and Kentucky, and General Harmar's punitive column, based on Fort Washington in Ohio (the present Cincinnati), had failed to curb them. "I expected little," said Washington, "from the moment I heard he was a drunkard." In 1790 General St Clair had been instructed to establish a strong military post in the Northwest, at Miami Village (the present Fort Wayne). Treaties were to be attempted with the tribes that seemed well-disposed, but St Clair was to "seek the enemy." Jefferson agreed: the Indians must be given "a thorough drubbing." The event was a repetition of Braddock's disaster on the Monongahela: 15 miles from his goal, St Clair was attacked and overwhelmed, and nearly 1,000 of his force were casualties. A wave of alarm ran along the frontier – as in 1756, as in 1763, as in 1777–9.

5 WASHINGTON'S SECOND TERM

As a result, Washington welcomed the prospect of retirement at the end of his first term. In the spring of 1792 he had a number of discussions with Madison on the shape of a farewell address. He found him a convinced opponent of the idea: the rise of party spirit, Madison urged, was a reason rather for staying on than for withdrawing; another four years would save the country from the risks of a new regime or the dangers of monarchy, and would give "tone and firmness." Hamilton, Knox, and Randolph endorsed this advice. In the summer of 1792, Jefferson, too, was urging Washington to consent to serve again, and used an argument that had influence: "North and South will hang together if they have you to hang on." The Farewell Address that Hamilton and Madison prepared was not used for another four years.

On March 4, 1793, Washington was inaugurated President for a second time, with John Adams again Vice-President. Washington's re-election had been unanimous; not so that of Adams. The Senate remained Federalist; but there was an Anti Federalist, Republican or "Democratic" majority – the terms were synonymous and pejorative – in the "Lower House." Already the European scene was darker; Louis XVI was guillotined in January; on February 1, France declared war on Britain, and a great European coalition was formed to resist the Revolution. In his handling of this, as in foreign policy in general, Washington was a more assured figure.

The French Revolution was a decisive event in American history. It has been seen, naturally enough, as important in exacerbating the partisan conflicts of Federalists and democratic Republicans. This it did. There were – for a time – outbursts of "Bastille fever;" Royal Exchange Alley in Boston became Equality Lane; for a time even honorific titles like "Judge," to which later democratic America was to show itself curiously prone, went out of fashion. Even "Mr" gave way to "Citizen"; one critic, angered by the excesses, suggested that "Biped" was preferable as it would suit men and women alike and thus be more fully democratic. And the *Pittsburgh Gazette* rejoiced that Louis Capet had lost his *caput*.

But the real importance for the United States of the French Revolution was far more significant than this passing excess of emotion.
For within five years France was seen more as enemy than ally. What
did not change were the facts of geopolitics. For more than 20 years
Europe was convulsed by war, and the war was both international
and civil, a war engaging the peoples of Europe as never before, a
war of ideas. For the 20 crucial years of its own adolescence as a
nation the United States was left in freedom and allowed to consolidate itself. Immigrants were strikingly few – some 4,000 per
year. They were no longer aristocratic adventurers like Lafayette, or,
advocates of revolution like Tom Paine, but refugees like Dupont de
Nemours. The value of foreign travel was now seen as less important
and all agreed on the need for education at home. The Atlantic
became for a generation less a bridge than a barrier, a shield of the
new Republic.

The situation of 1793 made explicit what had hitherto been implicit in Washington's attitude. When the Revolution broke out in
1789, the fact on which he had seized was American remoteness.
"We, at this great distance ... hear of wars and rumors of wars,
as if they were the events or reports of another planet." At times,
particularly in his letters to Lafayette, he expressed sympathy with
the Revolution, but from the first he saw the threats that a war in
Europe presented to America. He wanted, he had written in 1790,
to be "unentangled in the crooked policies of Europe" and sought
only the free navigation of the Mississippi. He sensed the tumult and
the paroxysms of France, the "more haste than good speed in their
innovations," and wanted no part in the attendant political disputes
of Europe. These views were reinforced by the events of 1790–3,
domestic as well as foreign, and by the alarms in Florida and New
Orleans, in the Caribbean and in the Ohio country.

In April 1793, with the outbreak of war in Europe, the United
States issued a proclamation declaring its intention to pursue "a
conduct friendly and impartial toward the belligerent powers." It
was drawn up by Edmund Randolph, the attorney general, and it
did not contain the word neutrality – indeed, to Jefferson it was not
a declaration of neutrality at all. The proclamation marks the real
beginning of the break between President and secretary of state. For
Washington it was an expression of neutrality, in fact if not in
word. Jefferson's view was more devious. Publicly, he argued that
by holding back a declaration of neutrality the United States might
induce the European powers to bid for it, and thus secure "the
broadest privileges of neutral nations." Privately, however, he thought
it pusillanimous, a "milk and water" instrument, which disregarded

American obligations both to the cause of France under the alliance of 1778 and to the larger cause of liberty. His five years in Paris when the turmoil was unfolding had left him with strong French sympathies, and the conviction that the French were trying to do what the Americans had done in 1776. When "Pacificus" Hamilton came out in support of the proclamation, Jefferson encouraged "Helvidius" Madison to attack him: "For God's sake, my dear Sir, take up your pen, select the most striking heresies and cut him to pieces in the face of the public." However much idealism lay behind Jefferson's methods, they appear less noble and infinitely less discreet than Washington's. His academic turn of mind led him to dot his writing with juicy extremist phrases: "The tree of liberty must be refreshed from time to time with the blood of patriots and tyrants, and is its natural manure." It also gave him a deviousness that was dangerous: he found a post as translator in the State Department for Philip Freneau, as a cover for his editing the *National Gazette*, and in it being critical of Federalist and neutral policies.

Washington was convinced of the wisdom of neutrality. His purpose, he later declared to Patrick Henry, was

to keep the United States free from political connexions with every other country, to see them independent of all and under the influence of none. In a word, I want an American character, that the powers of Europe may be convinced we act for ourselves and not for others.[7]

He admitted a friendship for, even some obligation toward, Lafayette. Gouverneur Morris, the American minister in Paris – himself as indiscreet on the other side as Jefferson – was instructed to convey informally to the French the regard of America for Lafayette, and to Madame de Lafayette to convey "all the consolation I can with propriety give." When Henry Lee informed Washington that he was considering enlistment in the French army and requested advice, the reply was impeccable and magisterial:

As a public character, I can say nothing on the subject ... As a private man, I am unwilling to say much. Give advice I shall not. All I can do, then ... is to declare that if the case which you have suggested was mine, I should ponder well before I resolved, not only for private consideration, but on public grounds.[8]

[7] Flexner, *George Washington*, vol. IV, p. 248.
[8] idem, p. 180.

And then, just to be sure, he advised Lee to burn the letter. If Lee failed to act on one piece of advice, he saw the point, however guarded, of the other.

The problems posed by the war in Europe were not just matters of personal alignment and personal sympathy. Some three-quarters of America's trade was with Britain, and 90 percent of her imports came from there. But it was still hard for the friends of Britain in America to raise their voices; Britain on the seas and in the western posts was still an arrogant power.

The first real challenge to the Federalist quest for neutrality was presented, however, by the arrival of Edmond Charles Genet as the French Girondin minister to the United States. France could hardly have selected a more tactless ambassador. As luck would have it, his ship was blown out of its course, and he landed, in April 1793, at Charleston, in "Democratick" territory. His 28-day journey, by easy stages, to Philadelphia, was a procession which evoked an enthusiasm reminiscent of the President's own, four years before. It gave him a quite false notion of his popularity and of his role. Genet was deterred neither by the announcement of neutrality nor by a chilly reception from Washington in Philadelphia. With the support of Jeffersonians, he proceeded to act in most undiplomatic fashion. As he lyrically reported to his changing masters in Paris, "I provision the Antilles, I excite the Canadians to free themselves from the yoke of England, I arm the Kentuckians." He organized expeditions against Florida and Louisiana; George Rogers Clark found himself "commander-in-chief of the French Revolutionary Legion on the Mississippi River." He sent out privateers and he sponsored Jacobin clubs.

By June, even Jefferson was alarmed at this – "indefensible" ... never "was so calamitous an appointment made ... Hotheaded, all imagination, no judgment, passionate." By August he was, thought Jefferson, "absolutely incorrigible," and the Cabinet unanimously demanded his recall. The responsibility, however, was not Genet's alone; it was also Jefferson's, who had at first abetted his schemes. For by 1793 Madison and Jefferson were becoming afraid that behind the mask of neutrality lay "a secret Anglomanny." Jefferson's years in Paris had left him with no love of the English – "those rich, proud, hectoring, swearing, squibbling, carnivorous animals who live on the other side of the Channel" – or of those in America who admired their institutions or imitated their ways. And he thus for a time encouraged Genet in his rashness.

Washington was kind to Genet but resolute in his neutrality. He believed that "the defensive alliance" with France had come to an end when the treaty of peace with Britain was signed in 1783. His first obligation was to the United States, and to the facts of a revolution in Europe from which, if possible, the United States must be protected. This, he told Congress in December 1793, necessitated firmness and strength as well as subtlety:

There is a rank due to the United States among nations, which will be withheld, if not absolutely lost, by the reputation of weakness. If we desire to avoid insult, we must be able to repel it; if we desire to secure peace, one of the most powerful instruments of our rising prosperity, it must be known that we are at all times ready for war.[9]

The Genet affair added zest to the domestic party battle. Years later, in correspondence with Jefferson and with memory blurred, Adams wrote of the "thousands" in the Philadelphia mobs who threatened to drag Washington from his house and to bring the government down. He was convinced that revolution was averted only by the coming to Philadelphia in the late summer of a still more deadly scourge: yellow fever. After it had passed, the political temperature stayed high. The "Marseillaise" and "Ça Ira" were now the marching songs of Anti-Federalism. To the Jeffersonians, the Federalists were "British boot-lickers" or worse. To Fenno, to British exile William Cobbett, and to the Federalist *Gazette of the United States* the Republicans were "Democraticks," "filthy Jacobins," "frog-eating, man-eating, blood-drinking cannibals."

The Democratic Societies or Jacobin Clubs, the *National Gazette* and the Philadelphia *Aurora* (edited by William Duane) were now the instruments of a party of which Jefferson was the obvious leader. It was coming to be based on an alliance of Virginia with New York; its chief figures, after Jefferson, were Madison and William Giles of Virginia, William Maclay and Albert Gallatin in Pennsylvania, Samuel Adams and John Hancock in Massachusetts, George Clinton in New York, and stormy Matthew Lyon in Vermont. Now even foreign policy fed the flames of faction.

The pattern of the future was becoming clear. By 1794, Washington's idea of good government was almost identical with Hamilton's. The identity was never complete. Hamilton was bolder and brasher than Washington, with a gift of words and a grasp of finance — and of intrigue — far surpassing the President's. Washington though less intellectual, was infinitely superior to Hamilton in judgment. Jefferson's range was wider than that of either of them, his cast

[9] Flexner, *George Washington*, vol. IV, p. 326.

of mind more contemplative and contradictory. But Washington could have little sympathy with Jeffersonian ideas, and the man of affairs found himself much more attuned to the administrative emphasis and to the concrete program of the Hamiltonians. From 1789 to 1794 he was above party, an enemy of what he called "faction," a Federalist. By 1794 he went further and became a Hamiltonian. The partisanship spread; Madison went the other way, and Jefferson resigned the secretaryship of state on December 31, 1793 (to be replaced by Edmund Randolph) in order, quite openly, to take up partisan politics.

The Hamiltonian influence was now clearly visible. When in July 1794 open rebellion against the excise tax on home-produced liquor – the whisky Rebellion – broke out among the farmers of western Pennsylvania, federal Treasury officials, like state officials before them, were driven back. Under Hamilton's persuasions, Washington saw in the rebellion "the first formidable fruit" of the Democratic Societies, and of "their diabolical leader, Genet." Unless it was broken, "we may bid adieu to all government in this country, except mob and club government." There were no federal police to enforce the law, but the Constitution empowered the federal government to call out the state militia when necessary. Would the states acknowledge this authority? Washington put the matter to the test, called out the militia, and talked of leading it in person over the mountains. Hamilton accompanied the troops as a kind of political commissar. By the time the militia appeared – 15,000 turned out at the call – the rebellion had come to an end. Having displayed the power of the federal government and satisfied conservative opinion as much as he alarmed Jeffersonian, the President pardoned the insurgents. For him, firmness again was allied to clemency.

The same Hamiltonian policy led Washington to attempt a settlement of the dispute, with Britain. General Anthony Wayne's victory over the Maumee River Indians at Fallen Timbers in 1794 opened up the Ohio country and weakened British influence over her forest allies. Britain still held the fur posts, drawing from them a trade estimated at £100,000 a year, still excluded American ships from her West Indian ports, and still dickered over the boundary with Maine. It was countering the revived and lucrative American trade with the French West Indies by invoking the Rule of 1756 (that trade closed in time of peace could not be opened in time of war), and, under its cloak, seizing American ships. Britain also claimed the right to search American ships for British deserters at a time of lax naturalization laws and inadequate proof of citizenship. This interference was particularly resented in New England, the Federalist stronghold;

and in the debates in the House of Representatives in 1794, New England and the middle states seemed in process of aligning on this issue with the South. Despite the unpopularity of any suggestion of rapprochement with Britain, Washington felt that an effort should be made to settle these outstanding problems, and that it should be done by a special mission and a treaty requiring only Cabinet and Senate approval. Accordingly, in April 1794 he dispatched John Jay as special envoy to London.

When the news of the treaty signed by Jay in November 1794 reached the United States the following March, Washington's popularity at home was given its severest test. Jay knew that his work would meet with opposition, but thought that the terms were the best that could be obtained: Britain agreed to evacuate the fur posts by 1796 and to open her East Indian ports to American ships; she agreed to open her West Indian ports also, but only to vessels under 70 tons; the United States agreed not to export sugar, molasses, coffee, cotton, or cocoa; joint commissions were to settle the Maine boundary dispute and claims for damages arising from seizures, but nothing was said about impressment, the trade of neutrals with France, or Indians. Washington did not pretend to like these terms and kept the treaty for four months before submitting it to the Senate. The Senate ratified the treaty after long discussions in June 1795, by the minimum number of votes necessary, but rejected the West Indian clauses and the ban on exports.

When the terms of the treaty leaked to the press, they met a wave of popular protest. "The cry against the Treaty," Washington wrote to Hamilton, "is like that against a mad-dog; and every one, in a manner, seems engaged on running it down." There was worse than this waiting for Hamilton, whose support for the treaty led to his being stoned in the streets. For a time the House refused to appropriate the money called for by the treaty and requested a copy of Jay's instructions. Washington refused: "The nature of foreign negotiations requires caution, and their success must often depend upon secrecy." This was, he claimed, the reason for vesting the treaty-making power in the President, acting with the advice and consent of the Senate. Washington saw the dispute as one not on the merits of the treaty alone but on the treaty-making-power and the Constitution itself. It was only "the Colossus of the President's merits with the people," wrote Jefferson, that had allowed the "Anglo-men" to get their handiwork enacted, after months of wrangling. The President signed the treaty in August 1795.[10]

[10] Flexner, *George Washington*, vol. IV, p. 290.

Though the Treaty of 1795 failed to make clear what were the rights of neutrals, and he had his reservations about it, Washington was right in thinking that it was the best treaty that could be won at the time. It represented, on however small a scale, the beginnings of arbitration in Anglo-American disputes. Spain became so alarmed at the prospect of an even closer Anglo-American accord that it proceeded to negotiate a settlement of its own disputes with the United States in the Godoy-Pinckney Treaty, the Treaty of San Lorenzo. This treaty got little attention and less applause, but it was a complete diplomatic success for Charles Pinckney: Spain granted to the United States the rights of navigation on the Mississippi and the right of deposit at New Orleans free of duty for ocean-going American goods; it recognized the 31st parallel as the northern boundary of Florida and agreed to try to restrain the Indians from border raids. The treaty helped the United States retain the fluctuating loyalty of the Kentucky and Tennessee area, which became states in 1792 and in 1796 respectively; it pointed the way south and west; and for a generation it made the nation Mississippi-minded.

By 1795 the domestic scene, however, like so much in the handling of foreign policy, had become completely partisan. Randolph, who had succeeded Jefferson as secretary of state in 1793, was dismissed in 1795 on the doubtful grounds of receiving bribes from France. Hamilton returned to the practice of law in order to maintain his steadily increasing family. Henry Knox, too, resigned: a good general, he had become "a furious Federalist," but an administrator of only modest capacity. By 1796 the government was completely recast; conscientious and combative Timothy Pickering at the State Department, the efficient and self-effacing Oliver Wolcott at the Treasury, and the inefficient Irishman James McHenry as secretary of war. New men — and by now an avowed principle: "I shall not," Washington wrote to Pickering, "whilst I have the honor to administer the government, bring a man into any office of consequence knowingly, whose political tenets are adverse to the measures, which the general government are pursuing; for this, in my opinion, would be a sort of political suicide." Washington had come to a position he disliked, and for which the Constitution gave no warrant; the pattern of party rivalry in the United States, like the pattern of government itself, stems from the years of his administration.

The partisanship of the press made Washington's last year in Philadelphia one of acute misery. He was particularly hurt by a reference of Jefferson's to the "men who were Samsons in the field and Solomons in the council, but who have had their heads shorn by the harlot England." He was being compared, he said, to a

Nero, or even to a common pickpocket; after 45 years of public service, he was tired of being "buffeted in the public prints by a set of infamous scribblers." He now looked forward eagerly to his retirement.[11]

The decision was not one of principle. Washington was physically and mentally a tired man. And no one so sensitive to his reputation could long continue in a post now vulnerable to partisan attack, to innuendo, and to public censure.

Over the authorship of his Farewell Address of September 1796 there has been much debate. Washington had always sought secretaries who, as he put it, would "possess the soul of the General;" if he left the writing of the Address to others, and especially to Hamilton, it incorporated – as he insisted it should – much of Madison's draft of 1792, and he went over it carefully himself. It is a Federalist document, the nearest approach in his writings to a declaration of the Washington credo – that unity of government is primary; sectionalism and partisanship open the door "to foreign influence and corruption." More than anything else, Washington in his Farewell Address counseled against "the insidious wiles of foreign influence." It was not so much a policy of isolation from Europe that he advocated as the exclusion of Europe from America, and the maintenance thereby of an American national character. The "primary interests" of Europe and America were quite distinct. There should be no independent "permanent inveterate antipathies against particular nations, and passionate attachments for others," but constant vigilance, preparedness, and, if necessary, temporary alliances on extraordinary occasions.

Washington, though bequeathing a legacy and no doubt fully conscious of it, was also speaking in a particular situation – deploring the meddling of Genet and his successors Fauchet and Adet in American affairs, the intrigues of Jefferson and Freneau, and advocating that the United States have the strength to resist insults, whether from the Barbary pirates or the French revolutionaries or the captains of British frigates. He was speaking as a realist out of long experience, and concluded that nations, like men, must depend in the end on themselves alone; this was the lesson of all revolutions, the goal of all national movements: "There can be no greater error then to expect, or calculate upon real favors from Nation to Nation." Not isolation for all time, then, but independence; not sectionalism or partisanship, though it appeared to be "inseparable from our nature," but loyalty to the national cause; not party controversy,

---

[11] Flexner, *George Washington*, vol. IV, p. 382.

but "strength and consistency" to give the country "the command of its own fortunes;" this was the legacy of 1776 as well as of 1796. Like all else, it set a precedent, and one of the wisest. The passing of the years has made Washington's Farewell Address almost as important a bequest of the first President as the drafting of the Constitution itself. It is read in both the Senate and the House of Representatives at noon on each February 22, as a tribute and as a reminder.

Washington's last speech to Congress was delivered on December 7, 1796. In it he pressed the case for a naval force, for a military academy, and for a national university. It was dangerous, when revolution ran through Europe, to send young Americans abroad at their most impressionable age. In a republic they should be taught "the science of government," and taught it at home. On this, as on many other points, Washington's view was shared by Jefferson. The latter thought French a useful language, but Canada the best place to learn it. "While learning the language in France, a young man's morals, health and fortune are more irresistibly endangered than in any country of the universe." The French, Jefferson was now stressing, lacked patience and experience. He had from the first seen the risks if man was studied only in books and not in the real world. Even the ideologue was a realist at heart. And by 1796, despite all the bitterness of party spirit, Monticello was not so far away from Mount Vernon.

6   THE ACHIEVEMENT

The role of Washington as President remains difficult to assess. It is clear that he began with a belief (shared by John Adams) in an independent executive, but that he moved steadily toward the Hamiltonians in his sympathies, especially after 1793; on financial matters he was completely dependent on Hamilton's guidance. Yet to the end Washington deplored the growth of parties: one reason he cited for refusing to consider a third term was that by 1796 party bitterness prevented universal acceptance of the President. He sought to remain a chief of state and to exalt the authority of government only to find that the country would be no more united by him than by anyone else.

It is clear that for Washington this was a bitter blow. To be above the battle – if above it he was – was not, he found, to escape public censure. Washington was both hurt and baffled by the attacks of the rascally Freneau and by the savagery of Tom Paine's open letter from Paris in 1796. He had learned the hard way the truth of Fisher Ames's analogy: "A monarchy is like a merchantman. You get on board and ride the wind and tide in safety and elation but, by and by, you strike a reef and go down. But democracy is like a raft. You never sink, but, dammit, your feet are always in the water." A much later President had a still more vigorous comparison. "If you can't take the heat," reflected President Truman, "you should get out of the kitchen."

In the domestic field, Washington was not a forceful leader in his own administration, once he had managed to set it up. He provided few ideas; the problems that aroused him were those in which he had direct personal experience – relations with the Indians, military affairs, defense of the frontier, the maintenance of national unity. His Farewell Address says nothing about "the rights of man" and nothing about slavery, the basic threat to those rights in the next two generations. Its theme is Washington's own, even if the language is Hamilton's: the need for union and the danger of foreign entanglements. Washington moved away steadily from a Virginian to a national, at times a nationalist, position: the break was not only with Jefferson but with Madison as well, with James Monroe and with Patrick Henry, despite the talk of nominating the latter for secretary of state in 1795. The break with his near-neighbor George Mason had taken place long before. His system, he said, was to overlook all personal, local, and partial considerations, and "to contemplate the United States as one great whole."

It now appears surprising that Washington did not foresee the likelihood of the rise of party spirit. But John Adams did not see it either or, if he did, refused to face the consequences. He, too, tried to act as though the executive were above party, representing the national interest; and he paid the price with defeat in 1800. In Washington's case, the attitude is explicable enough: he was no theorist; his concern was with sound administration – of his estates, of the army, or of the nation. He could hardly be expected to know how bitter and irresponsible the press charges would be, or how savagely they would treat his concern with "respectability." "I was no party man myself," he wrote to Jefferson in 1796, "and the first wish of my heart was, if parties did exist, to reconcile them."

What he did understand was the threat of sectionalism, and of states' rights, to the unity won in 1783, and the threat of international revolution to the institutions of 1787. In this he was remarkably far-sighted. He was in modern history the first leader of a successful national revolt against imperialism, but for him, unlike Jefferson and Monroe and Paine, America's national revolt was not part of an international revolution. It was not part of a crusade to be launched across the world, but the product of a particular situation in America in 1776. By 1797 the new and free country had to be protected against revolution, as the Constitution protected it against democracy. The America that became the guide to Latin America in the 1820s, to Greece and Hungary, Italy and Ireland, was Jefferson's – not Washington's – America. There was no response from Washington to the adventurer Francisco de Miranda's appeal to lead a second liberation movement in Latin America.

Yet the decision to cut the country free from Europe's entanglements was of profound importance. Sheltered by 3,000 miles of ocean, the United States was left free to settle its frontier disputes with Britain and Spain far more smoothly than would otherwise have been possible. It was able to declare itself neutral toward Europe and to erect neutrality into a "Great Rule." It was able by 1798 to end the entangling alliance of 1778. It was able, without commitment by itself, to have new republics growing up in the Americas to the south in place of the old Spanish Empire. And it was able, at a lucky moment in 1803, to buy out the French holdings in the trans-Mississippi West without firing a shot. The French Revolution was as pregnant a development for the United States as the fact of its own independence, for more than anything else it made that independence permanent. It permitted the United States to develop along its own natural, distinct, non-European lines. It was in the fact of America's isolation that American nationalism at last began to grow.

It grew too from the Hamiltonian program of 1791–4. It has been for the most part praised as inspired and percipient; as giving prestige to American currency; as assuring national stability and the supremacy of the propertied classes; as stimulating trade and capitalist enterprise; as making for close relations with Britain; and as providing a base for the steady expansion of the role of the federal government. The program has been assessed less on financial than on political grounds, as Hamilton intended it should be. For his intentions were primarily political, even imperial. At a time when few dared to tackle the economic problems of a bankrupt and agrarian society, a clear direction was given to the new nation and distinct "energy to government," in Hamilton's own phrase, as well as "order to the finances." And they were imposed from above. Hamilton, in 1791 as in 1787, advocated republicanism but not democracy. His views have always brought refreshment and support to the right in American politics, as Jefferson's to the left. Jefferson stood for the limitation and control of the powers of government. That government is best, he said, which governs least. He believed in men and in their capacity for rational decisions. But his men were assumed to be educated and reflective, property-owning and rural-minded. These two men have become the permanent symbols of the two main camps in American politics.

At home, the legacy of Washington's two terms was administrative rather than political. He was a gifted and experienced administrator – and the federal government after all, had fewer employees in 1790 than did Mount Vernon; on his and his wife's six great plantations he had over 300 slaves. As discipline was the soul of an army, so, he said, "system to all things was the soul of business," System involved industry, integrity, impartiality, and firmness. "No man" said John Adams, "has influence with the President. He seeks information from all quarters, and judges more independently than any man I ever knew." His standards for appointments were very high – higher than those in contemporary Britain or France, higher than those of most of his successors. He sought, and found, men who "would give dignity and lustre to our National Character."

He was helped by a rising standard of living. Though not an era of good feelings, his presidency was an era of good times. One reason for the popularity of the Constitution was the fact that it coincided with an upswing of prosperity. All sections of the nation and all ranks of society shared in it, and the federal government, regardless of the party group in control, was the beneficiary.

In foreign affairs, too, Europe's agony was America's advantage; the situation in Europe facilitated the settlements with Britain and Spain, it eased the tension on the western border, and it made closer the ties between the Tidewater and the trans-Allegheny country. There were associated problems: the French Revolution gave further impetus to American democracy, and foreign refugees and foreign ideas brought the risk of dangerous involvement in Europe. But in its prosperity at home and its policy of peace abroad, the Washington administration laid a sound foundation for the new republic. Never before had a republican government attempted to organize so vast an area on a federal pattern. Rarely before had an executive been so directly responsive to the popular assemblies. Rarely has an office, one that was to grow into the most important executive office in the world, been so clearly given the stamp of one man's character.

Washington sensed that Europe's distress could be for America destiny as well as advantage. "Sure I am," he wrote, if this country is preserved in tranquality twenty years longer, it may bid defiance in a just cause to any power whatsoever; such in that time will be its population, wealth and resources. ... Why quit our own to stand upon foreign ground? Europe has a set of primary interests which to us have none or a very remote relation."[12]

[12] Farewell Address, Sept. 17, 1796, cited in H. S. Commager (ed.), *Documents of American History* (New York, Appleton, Century Crofts, 5th edn, 1949).

4

Federalism, High, Low, and Devious

---

1 THE FIRST PARTY SYSTEM

Jefferson had a fresh, and essentially democratic, view of the function of political parties. Others, including Washington, looked upon political parties with distaste, considering them as breeding grounds of factionalism and cradles of strife. Jefferson, however, was one of the first great political leaders to realize that political parties were essential to self-government. Opposition parties were necessary not only as vehicles for the expression of political aims and passions, but also as checks upon the party in power. Without political parties there could be no self-government:

... in every free and deliberating society, there must, from the nature of man, be opposite parties, and violent dissensions and discords; and one of these, for the most part, must prevail over the other for a longer or a shorter time. Perhaps this party division is necessary to induce each to watch and to relate to the people the proceedings of the other.[1]

He was, of course, no common partisan. He told Francis Hopkinson:

... I never submitted the whole system of my opinions to the creed of any party of men whatever, in religion, in philosophy, in politics or in anything else where I was capable of thinking for myself. Such an addiction

---

[1] P. L. Ford (ed.), *The Writings of Thomas Jefferson*, 10 vols (New York, G. P. Putnam's Sons, 1891–9), vol. VII, p. 264.

is the last degradation of a free and moral agent. If I could not go to
heaven but with a party, I would not go there at all.[2]

To Jefferson a political party was a democratic instrument to be
used, not an ecclesiastical institution to be revered. For him, there
were many good men in both parties. His description of the two
parties that were struggling for power has an air of pleasant and
almost amused objectivity:

... the former of these [political parties] are called Federalists, sometimes
Aristocrats or monocrats & sometimes Tories ... (the latter are republicans, whigs, Jacobins, Anarchists, disorganisers, &tc. these terms are in
familiar use with most persons. ... The most upright and conscientious
characters are on both Sides [of] the question, and as to myself I can say
with truth that political tenets have never taken away my esteem for a moral
and good man.[3]

The first hint of the division into parties in the American system
came with the struggle for the ratification of the Constitution. The
temporary cooperation of the War of Independence and the four
months of debate in Philadelphia had stimulated rather than abated
the disputes between the colonies. Frontier and land disputes, the different life styles of the small farmers, of the merchants of the North
and the slave-holding plantation owners of the South, persisted.
Sectionalism bred rivalry, envy, bitterness, and personal conflicts.
Federalists and Anti-Federalist positions were strongly voiced in the
state ratifying conventions. It needed all Madison's skills in devising
a Bill of Rights to counter criticism and to manufacture agreements.
The Federalist Papers, written by Alexander Hamilton (who composed 51 of them), James Madison (who wrote 25), and John Jay
(who wrote 5), under the pen name of Publius, were published in
New York as part of the Federalist campaign. They were widely
circulated. The Anti-Federalists came from the older generation: men
like George Clinton, Samuel Adams, and John Hancock were suspicious that the tyranny they had overthrown might return in a
different shape. They thought the new Constitution, in the words of
Patrick Henry, "squinted towards monarchy." To Elbridge Gerry it
was "a many-headed monster ... nor have its friends the courage to
denominate it a Monarchy, an Aristocracy or an Oligarchy."[4] To

---

[2] ibid., vol. V, p. 175.
[3] ibid., vol. VIII, p. 274.
[4] Robert A. Rutland, *The Ordeal of the Constitution: The Anti-Federalist and the
ratification struggle of 1787–1788* (Norman, University of Oklahoma, 1966).

George Mason, it would move from "a moderate aristocracy" to a monarchy or "a corrupt oppressive aristocracy" or "vibrate some years between the two." There were bitter arguments over protocol and title. They wanted annual elections and rotation of office as in the Roman Republic. Only the enactment of the Bill of Rights seemed to stem opposition.[5]

Alongside party alignment went intrigue. Born and bred to it in his West Indies origin, Hamilton intrigued to ensure that in 1789 John Adams should have fewer votes than Washington, lest in the undifferentiated two-vote system the wrong man won. The memory of wartime cabals was still sharp. In later years Adams would recall "the dark and insidious manner" in which Hamilton worked, "like the worm at the root of the peach." But Hamilton as schemer was not alone. Madison thought Hancock "weak, ambitious, a courtier of popularity," and was critical of John Adams's "extravagant self-importance;" he too wanted to ensure that Washington was the first president. Patrick Henry of Virginia was pushing Governor George Clinton of New York for vice-president. Intrigue was as rife as party spirit.

In 1789, every one of the 69 electors had voted for Washington. John Adams secured 34 votes (treatment, he thought, "scurvey ... an indelible stain on our Country, Countrymen and Constitution.") John Rutledge of South Carolina collected 6 of his state's 7, John Jay 9 votes, and Hancock only 4. Of these, if the first two had done no "politicking," much had certainly been done by lesser men. And as it was in the beginning, so would it recur ... politics from the start, one might say, was as American as apple pie.

The origin of the two parties, Federalist versus Anti-Federalist, Hamiltonian versus Jeffersonian, lay firmly in the debates of 1787 and 1788. They surfaced early in the first Congress, notably in the testy politics of William Maclay, the junior senator for Pennsylvania. Not only did he differ with the Father of his Country – and most others – but he kept a journal recording his dissents. Maclay's record is valuable not just because of his caustic comments about political leaders, ranging from his presiding officer, the dithering John Adams,

---

[5] *Documentary History of the First Federal Congress of the United States of America, 4 March 1789–3 March 1791*, ed. Kenneth R. Bowling and Helen E. Veit (Baltimore and London, The Johns Hopkins University Press, 1988); Jack R. Pole (ed.), *The American Constitution, For and Against* (New York, Hill and Wang, 1987); *The Federalist Papers*, many editions; Herbert J. Storing, *What the Anti-Federalists were for* (Chicago, University of Chicago Press, 1981); Ralph Ketcham (ed.), *The Federalist Papers and the Constitutional Convention Debates* (New York, Mentor Books, 1986).

through the icy and usually inarticulate George Washington, to the erratic Princetonian William Branch Giles. The diary was not discovered until 1880, and is the only continuous surviving report of the early debates, when all that was said took place behind closed doors and no official record was kept. Maclay emerges as a critic of the Hamiltonian program, a defender of the small farming class and — in the months before Jefferson returned from Paris — a democratic leader pushing his state in what would later be called a Jeffersonian direction. In fact he was later distressed by Jefferson's attitude as secretary of state, particularly by his building a navy for an attack on the Algerian pirates. Through Maclay's eyes, it is possible to notice the shift from support of the new Constitution and the Federalists in 1788 and 1789 to a more critical appraisal of the Washington administration by early 1791. Though a "westerner" and a democrat, and an ally of Robert Morris, the senior senator, in Pennsylvania politics, Maclay began to suspect the motives of the administration early in the Congress's first session. He feared that Adams's taste for titles might indicate a taste for anti-republican monarchism, and he suspected the motivation of the lawyers busy pushing their Judiciary Act through Congress. Despite these suspicions, he did not break with the Administration. Instead, he pushed for rapid consideration of the impost, and remained unimpressed by the Anti-Federalist antics of Richard Henry Lee and Elbridge Gerry. Only when confronted with Alexander Hamilton's assumption and funding programs did he move into solid opposition. He believed that the nation had the right to implement the new funding system, but he feared that funding and assumption were designed to enrich speculators, who would become corrupt supporters of the new monarchists. He came to suspect Hamilton, Washington, and even Jefferson, of wishing to create a pale copy of the British system, resting on an army, navy, national bureaucracy, bank, and funding system. To Maclay's suspicious mind, the new Administration seemed set to follow the patterns of eighteenth-century British politics, and for him Hamilton became the American equivalent of Sir Robert Walpole; it became easy to label the Washington administration by a familiar word: "corruption."

A further indication of the split between Federalist and Anti-Federalist positions emerged in 1790 with Hamilton's first report, on *Publick Credit*. Until then both Hamilton as secretary to the Treasury and Madison as leader of the House of Representatives had agreed on the necessity for energetic central government, as *The Federalist Papers* had indicated. The two men had worked together since 1782 to strengthen the Articles of Confederation, and then in 1787 to devise a wholly new form of government for the United States.

But Madison could not forget his allegiance to his own "country," Virginia, and its agrarian economy. In 1790 Hamilton proposed that the federal government assume the state debts. This would bring within the orbit of government all the state creditors, the most influential part of the community, and would put the onus and power of collecting taxes on the federal government. As Hamilton visualised it, such an assumption would serve as a double-edged sword with which to strike at the roots of state sovereignty. Thus seen, the national debt was a national blessing.

In order to pay the cost of underwriting these debts and of the extra $21 million owed by separate states as a result of the war, Hamilton decided that he had to levy excises on goods such as whiskey manufactured inside the United States. Virginia, which had already conscientiously paid off most of her state debt, objected to being taxed a second time to pay the debts of other less conscientious states, and to line the pockets of speculators, most of them – it seemed – located on the northeastern seaboard. Jefferson felt that for a largely agricultural country like the US to indulge in protective tariffs was to tax the majority on behalf of the minority, "to prostrate agriculture at the feet of commerce." Madison, as a Virginian, wanted to distinguish between original holders of government securities and speculators who had purchased them. Four-fifths of the national debt was owing to citizens living north of the Mason-Dixon line, and Madison did not see why farmers in the South should subsidize speculators in the North.

In the end, thanks to considerable behind-the-scenes maneuvers between Hamilton, Madison, and Jefferson, including the choice of the federal city as capital, all Hamilton's measures were approved, including the creation of a national bank and the establishment of a sinking fund. The measures did much to increase the power of the federal government. Although this created a great deal of opposition at home, which crystalized into the opposition Republican party, the measures also gave the US government credibility abroad which enabled it to borrow again. By 1792, largely as a result of Hamilton's persuasions and zeal, the heavy war debt was beginning to be paid off, the price of government securities had been stabilized close to their face value, hoarded wealth had been brought out of hiding, a federal revenue system had been brought into being, and foreign capital began to be invested in the United States. But Jefferson, whose support of the main objectives of the Washington administration had seemed assured (in 1788 he had pronounced *The Federalist Papers* to be one of the greatest treatises on government ever written), now feared the entrenched government of the Hamiltonians. The two men differed in personality and experience, in temperament and tastes. To these can be added the division on issues – part cause, part effect.

The immediate precursor of and catalyst to party growth was Hamilton's financial program of 1790–1. On each issue, a sharp and rancorous sectional division in congressional voting occurred and recurred. For example, in the second ballot on assumption, members from the Northern states voted 24 to 9 in approval, while congressmen from the South opposed it 18 to 10. However, 4 of the latter 10 represent changed votes, the result of Jefferson's and Madison's arrangement with Hamilton. The division on excise resulted in a vote of Northern delegations 28 to 6 in favor (4 of the latter from Pennsylvania), and Southerners opposed 15 to 7. Finally, on the bill to create a national bank, Northern representatives voted affirmatively 33 to 1, and Southern representatives voted negatively 19 to 6.

The two parties which developed over the next decade were not, however, completely sectional. If the Republicans came to rely for most of their support in the South and West, yet they also attempted with marked success to win adherents in the middle-Atlantic and New England states. The Virginia–New York intra-party alliance crystalized in the 1790s, and soon came to dominate Republican inner councils – and in fact much of American politics for more than a century. Aaron Burr's superbly coordinated political machine in New York City, victorious over the Hamiltonians in 1800, provided the foundation for Jefferson's election to the presidency in that year. Even in solidly Federalist areas the steady growth of Republican minorities was impressive. In 1796 Jefferson had little strength in New England, but by 1800 Republicans won half of the Massachusetts congressional delegation.

Jefferson became the champion of minimal government and *laissez-faire*. Although he had been a supporter of the Constitution, he had disliked the indefinite re-eligibility of the President, and the absence of a Bill of Rights. He urged that all holders of government securities and bank stock be excluded from holding seats in Congress, though he did not wish to exclude slaveholders or land speculators. For him, the farmers trying to preserve farming from the hand of big business were the chosen people of God – if ever, he characteristically added, "He had a Chosen People." Hamilton wanted to subvert republicanism and replace it with a monarchy; and Hamilton's monarch might not be Washington but himself.[6]

[6] *Notes on the State of Virginia in 1785*, Query XIX, in Saul Padover (ed.), *The Complete Jefferson* (New York, Duell, Sloane and Pearce, 1943).

By 1792 these quarrels were being aired in public. Overt party propaganda began early. The *Gazette of the United States* had been founded in 1789 to "endear the General Government to the people." John Fenno, the editor, was helped financially by receiving printing contracts from the Treasury Department, and in return he was generous in his praise of Hamilton, who contributed to his paper. So – not quite wisely – did John Adams, printing his *Discourses on Davila*, a follow up to *Defence of the Constitutions*, written in 1786–7, in which he constantly stressed that the executive branch must be separate and powerful, and that there was much to be said for an hereditary rather than an elective head of state, with semi-regal titles like "His Highness." Jefferson countered by clandestinely funding the *National Gazette*, giving its editor Philip Freneau a salary for a nominal job in the State Department. In the pages of his *Philadelphia Aurora*, Benjamin Franklin Bache, grandson of the bearer of a distinguished name ("Lightning Rod Junior"), was savage in his attack on Washington. When the time came for Washington's "Valedictory," he greeted it, in March 1797, thus: "If ever there was a period for rejoicing, this is the moment." Adams was welcomed – but soon the spleen returned. And, drawing on his youth, spent with his grandfather in France, sounded a strong pro-French note.

Jefferson and Hamilton were alike anxious over the succession to Washington in the presidency, and before long each was appealing to him in their campaigns; but the President did not enjoy the political dirt. To some, Jefferson was a gullible visionary; to others Hamilton was seen as a monarchical serpent in an idyllic republican paradise supported by evil speculators. Jefferson was prompt – too prompt? – to voice disgust at politics, a fear of a strong central government dominated by bankers and brokers, and of a large national debt. That blood – always, of course, other people's blood – was the manure of liberty was a literary turn of phrase that came smoothly to one at ease with words. In fact Jefferson was more timid than bold, more the *philosophe* than the warrior. He believed in the good sense of the people, or said he did, and in local rights rather than bureaucratic central government. But the Republicans' pride in their liberalism did not prevent their support for slavery. Paradoxically, support for slavery was the one factor which cemented the unnatural alliance in the Republican party of small farmers and wealthy planters, 'long-tailed' and interlinked.

By 1795 with the ratification of the Jay treaty with Britain and the controversy over relations with the Republican government in France, the party alignments reflected international as well as purely national issues. It was natural for Jefferson, given his contacts with the French Revolutionary leaders in his years as diplomat, to be enthusiastic about the new Republic, although even he (and they) were embarrassed by the tactless exploits of the French emissary to the US, Citizen Genet. Similarly the Federalists, with their commercial interests and their muted respect for the tradition of monarchy, leaned towards Britain. John Adams once compared the American and French Revolutions in one line: "Ours was resistance to innovation; theirs was innovation itself." Neither life nor property seemed safe in a revolution that, to Federalists, bred not liberty, equality, and fraternity, but atheism, despotism, and imperialism. The virtues of the English system, on the other hand, could be viewed more dispassionately by Federalists who were no longer rebels. The mother-country, after all, was the birthplace of Anglo-Saxon laws and institutions – stable, orderly, well-balanced between aristocratic rule and democratic privileges.

By 1795, and with a presidential election ahead, the issues of Federalism and Republicanism had been firmly established, and could be cast in national, even universal, terms: the Republicans supported states' rights against excessive central government; they believed in democracy and the rights of the common man; but as a Southern-based party they also believed in slavery, and internationally their allegiance was to France rather than to Britain. In contrast, the Federalists were in favor of strong central government; they were suspicious of democracy; and although they preferred a policy of neutrality in foreign affairs, they leaned towards Britain rather than France. The ratification controversy of 1787–9 had been played out on a state-by-state basis. The Jay treaty battle, by contrast, was national in character and in its impact. Lines of political communication went out from the capital to every state, and to town after town. Every state had its representatives in the Congress. Members of Congress brought the issue home to their constituents, from New Hampshire and Vermont to the far-off, new frontier states of Kentucky (1792) and Tennessee (1796). And a burgeoning, highly partisan newspaper and pamphlet press kept the issue at white heat. More and more members of Congress took to writing open letters to their constituents, often through the press. In the end the Jay treaty battle marked the final establishment of the Federalist and Republican parties.

Two treaties ratified during Washington's second administration helped to gain the support of Westerners. Jay's treaty, by removing the British from the frontier posts, signified the cessation of Indian raids, and the opening of the Northwest to farmer and land speculator; Pinckney's treaty with Spain, by opening navigation of the Mississippi River through Spanish territory, was a vital economic boon to trans-Appalachian frontiersmen. The West remained an unruly region, generally Republican at election time, and with strong separatist tendencies. Nevertheless, the effect of the Jay and Pinckney treaties was to win over a small but steadfast minority of Western conservatives to the cause of Federalism. In the South also, Federalism was far from dead, and on occasion displayed vigorous recuperative abilities. Hamilton enjoyed powerful connections with influential South Carolina leaders. Virginia Federalists looked to George Washington and John Marshall, and even Madison's apostasy was later offset by Patrick Henry's conversion to the Federalist cause.

Although by 1796 the issues and the leadership had become clear, the membership of the two parties was still formed by shifting allegiances, often based on local issues and personal interests. The Republican party was very much a coalition of interests: farmers and planters who feared the commercial exploitation of the agrarian states by Federalist merchants and financiers; southerners, westerners, and veterans who hated the tariff and the internal taxes that the Federalist regime used to pay off eastern bondholders; "mechanics" and artisans in eastern towns, organized in the Democratic Societies modeled on the Jacobin Clubs of 1793, who wished to seize the political and economic power promised them by the democratic ideals of two Revolutions; advocates of states' rights who were struggling against the consolidating tendencies of the Hamiltonians; advocates of civil liberty, and those who simply opposed the establishment in their localities; new men of the rising middle and lower classes who saw their best hope for advancement in the success of the Republican party. It was broadly an economic kaleidoscope – but never quite binding. The port of Wilmington, Delaware, was a Jeffersonian stronghold; the two southern counties of that state, in small-scale and self-sufficient agricultural units, were, and remained for long, a Federalist camp. Religion threw its own shadows: Congregationalists, strong in Connecticut, were the most rabid Federalists; Baptists in Rhode Island were Republicans; older Catholic families in Maryland were Federalist, more recent Catholic immigrants in urban centers were Republican. Some voted, not on the basis of issues at all, but rather for well-known local figures. The same South Carolina district continued to support Robert Goodloe Harper even though he switched from Republican to staunch Federalist. To some, local problems were of paramount significance: the fact that Federalists insisted on the efficacy of a standing army struck a responsive chord in certain western Carolina and Georgia areas where Indian raids were common. The factors affecting voting behavior and party allegiances in the 1790s are complex. Increasingly the central factor in the preservation of party unity was the presence of Jefferson himself.

The backbone of the Federalist party was dominated by the mercantile, shipping, and financial interest. At one end of the party were the upper-class landowners who were raised in the code that they had a right to rule those they saw below them in the social and economic scale. They argued that national security had been threatened under the weak government of the Articles of Confederation. But among them were also lawyers, merchants, farmers, and clergymen, the functionaries of the system. Had not Federalism also attracted the votes of the farmers and town artisans, it would never have attained power in the United States. The party also appealed to the more prosperous farmers living near the cities and growing cash crops. The Federalists believed that government must be rendered capable of resisting the passions of the people. Democracy was a delusion to be tempered by firm government. Already, mourned Noah Webster, "the preposterous doctrine of equality has stripped old men of dignity and wise men of their influence." Government of the people and for them, they could accept; but not government by the people. Government was still the preserve of sober and discreet men, seasoned by wealth and education and dedicated to keeping passion, their own and other people's, within bounds. There was a genuine fear of the mob as democracy's chief weapon; the sanctity of property rather than freedom was the purpose of constitutional government. To save them from the mob-addicted working men of the cities, the Federalists looked to the farmers – as well they might, for the American electorate consisted at this time of about half a million citizens, the overwhelming majority of whom were farmers. Like Jefferson, they regarded farmers as "cautious and reflecting men" whose passions were moderated by the fact that they had a substantial stake in the country. As the 1790s progressed, the Federalists became increasingly insistent on property qualifications for voting, whilst Jefferson believed in universal suffrage but thought that it ought to wait upon universal education.

In the struggle for power between the Federalist and Republican parties, the Federalists claimed that they had saved the country from chaos in 1787–8 and that they represented the forces of law and order against democratic Levelers. But they could also claim the support of the man who saw himself as being above party politics – George Washington. Washington, however, was a Federalist of a very special kind: his nationalism did not prevent him from trusting the people. In words reminiscent of Thomas Jefferson, he declared that: "the mass of our Citizens require no more than to understand a question to decide it properly."

In the early stages of the party contest, the Federalists enjoyed the advantage of better organization and more administrative experience, but even so, as early as 1792, the Republicans were able to register a significant measure of support for their candidate for the vice-presidency, George Clinton. During most of the period of Federalist ascendancy, the House of Representatives was almost evenly divided between the two parties. In 1796 there were 50 Republicans and 49 Federalists in the House. Two years later the Federalists had a majority of 5. In the Senate, on the other hand, the Federalists consistently had a majority. Nevertheless, especially in the House of Representatives, many members refused to wear the livery of either party; instead they made a point of voting as the interests of their state and section determined. Even as late as the Third Continental Congress (1795–6), almost half the members of the House prided themselves upon being free of party ties and obligations.

By 1795 Washington had abandoned his efforts to keep a balance of North and South, Federalist and Republican, in his cabinet. "I shall not," he said in September of that year, "bring any man into any office of consequence whose political tenets are adverse to the measures which the general government are pursuing." By this time, Virginia had become predominantly anti-Federalist. In the South, South Carolina was the main outpost of Federalism. But the majority of American people were little more than spectators of the struggle being waged in Congress. In the early 1790s only about 3 percent of the population voted and it was not until the appearance of political parties that those Americans who were qualified took advantage of their right to vote – hence a great increase in the percentage vote of 1800 over that of 1788.

In structure, the first parties were loose collections of provincial interests. Highly localized, and without heredity as bedrock, they had to be organized and sustained. The New York-Virginia axis was the coalition that formed the backbone of Republican party development. It emerged from a series of personal affiliations dating in some respects from the Revolution, and it was established by 1796 when Jefferson became the agreed presidential candidate for the New York and Virginian Republicans. Near the center of the Republican web was John Beckley, the clerk of the House of Representatives, and that busy medico-politician Benjamin Rush; they had contacts with Aaron Burr in New York, already plowing his own way in the devious intrigues that marked Manhattan. New York politics was characterized by a whirl of shifting alliances among the great landowning families. The Livingstons and Clintons were sometimes in alliance, but more often in opposition. Aaron Burr, Morgan Lewis, and Daniel D. Tompkins at one time or another commanded the allegiance of important segments of party opinion. Indeed, for a time after 1800, Burr constituted a third force all his own in the state.

In New England more than in other regions, party rivalry represented a struggle between an established political, economic, and social elite and a rising body of diverse individuals and groups dissatisfied with the power structure. But the struggle was not just along class lines. Some of the wealthiest men in New England were Republicans, while the Federalist strength in some areas rested on the sure foundation of yeomen farmers. Religion was an important factor dividing New England across class lines. In Connecticut, Orthodox Congregationalist leadership dominated political life, while the separation of Church and State became an especially strong issue for Republicans in Massachusetts, as Dissent grew after the Revolution.

In the South, the Republican voting strength of artisans, farmers, mechanics, and small manufacturers was topped by a solid social, cultural, and political elite of planters, small town lawyers, and rural opinion leaders, which gave the Republican movement a respectability and prestige missing in the New England states. As the population grew and the political climate changed, so allegiances shifted. Rhode Island, the state most adamantly opposed to the Federal Constitution, became for a time a Federalist state, and Massachusetts, almost evenly divided in 1788, won distinction in the 1790s for its solid Federalism. Everywhere religion, local issues, personal interest, along with issues regarding national security or individual freedom and rights, contradicted the general pattern of a Federalist North and a Republican South and West.

The two emerging political parties showed similar basic characteristics — but with important differences. First of all, there was the matter of structure. Hamilton and the Federalists forged links from the center at the capital to the states, counties, and towns. Personal friends, business associates, shared interests, the partisan press, the many citizens Hamilton had been able to oblige when he was secretary of the Treasury — all helped to advance the Federalist cause. Former military officers, the Congregational clergy and their flocks, local notables, mercantile magnates in New York, Boston, and Philadelphia, and even many wealthy planters in the South — these and others joined to form the inner structure of the Federalist party. The Federalists appealed to a wide range of persuasions, from shipbuilders and shipping magnates to ideological conservatives crying out for stability. By temperament and ideology, as well as interest,

most Americans who admired Britain were Federalists. National and
local political leaders collaborated to advance the Federalist cause.
These activities ranged from forging connections between the executive and legislative branches of government – indeed, Hamilton was
a past master at it – to nominating candidates, mobilizing voters,
"electioneering," and shaping public opinion. Many of these activities,
of course, could be carried forward only in the states, counties, and
towns. But coordination from the center was also essential. Further,
the Federalists over the years had developed a distinctive point of
view, or partisan ideology. They could at the outset draw on the
prestige and charisma of George Washington. The stress on stability,
an elitist tone, respectability, and English norms were also part
of their ideological and emotional baggage – along with capitalist
development and social stability, and a concern for a strong national
government.

In party structure and development, the rival Jeffersonian Republicans followed much the same pattern of development as the
Federalists, but with some crucial differences. They were slower in
shaping a coordinated national structure; but when they did move
in this area, they quickly outstripped the Federalists. As the early
underdogs, the Republican forces also had to work harder than the
Federalists if they were ever to win power in the national arena.
Finally, of course, the developing liberal ideology of the Republican
forces was almost the mirror image of the Federalist view. Indeed,
there are few instances in the history of American politics that exhibit the degree of ideological combat that marked the contentions
of Federalists and Republicans. In the end the Republicans would
win out, in considerable part because they were not tinged with the
condescension the Federalists showed in an increasingly democratic
republic.

Politics in the states themselves played a major role in party
growth. Thus, in the Empire State of New York, the organization
George Clinton had forged in the 1780s virtually became the Republican party of New York in the 1790s; and similar lines of local
party development were manifest in Massachusetts, New Jersey, and
Pennsylvania In some other states such as Delaware, Maryland (in
part), Virginia, and South Carolina, local politics was marked by
patterns of social and political deference. The sway of deference was
inherited from eighteenth-century England and had become ingrained
in the political culture of the American colonies. In a deferential
society, "lesser" men looked up to their social and economic superiors
and bowed to their judgment, in local affairs and in the larger range
of politics. Thus wealth – especially in land – superior social status,

learning, "fine manners," and dress marked certain men as "natural" leaders. In Delaware, for example, the dominance of Federalist, high-toned family connections was so great that Jefferson described the state as virtually "a county of England." At the same time, a Delaware Federalist complained that there was more than "one d..n democrat" in the state – although they were mostly in the northern, industrial part of the state. But, ironically, Jefferson's own state of Virginia was also a virtual showcase of deference. Great planters with their wide acres and legions of slaves set themselves above the ordinary freeholders, who usually followed the neighborhood nabobs in politics and in local affairs.

Recent writing has re-shaped the pattern of interpretation of the origins of party spirit. The Progressive historians of the first three decades of the twentieth century – Charles Beard, Claude G. Bowers, and Vernon L. Parrington – were on the whole pro-Jeffersonian. Hamilton's reputation sank to its lowest point during the depression of the 1930s as the Republican party fell into disfavor. The New Deal enshrined Jefferson and saw the Jefferson Memorial as a rival temple to that of Lincoln. The booming American economy during the wartime and postwar period no doubt helped to revive Hamilton's reputation. With the mounting postwar affluence of American society, there was less tendency by historians to read an economic class conflict back into the American past. In fact, the positive achievements of Hamilton's economic program in stabilizing and reviving the nation's economy in the 1790s and early 1800s received much praise in the post-World War II period.

The most important new tendency in the 1940s was not the presentation of Hamilton in a more favorable light, but rather a more evenly balanced evaluation of the Hamilton-Jeffersonian tension. Richard Hofstadter, in his book of essays, *The American Political Tradition and the Men Who Made It*, published in 1948, de-emphasized the differences between the two men and stressed instead the continuance of Hamilton's system under Jefferson as President. The beliefs that Hamiltonians and Jeffersonians had in common, said Hofstadter, proved to be a more powerful bond in uniting them than the specific political issues that were dividing the two groups. The tendency of earlier historians to place political conflict in the foreground of American history, he claimed, had obscured the common areas of agreement among political leaders who were often pictured as antagonists. "However much at odds on specific issues," Hofstadter wrote, "the major political traditions have shared a belief in the rights of property, the philosophy of economic individualism, the value of competition; they have accepted the economic virtues of capitalist culture as necessary qualities of man."[7] Indeed, he could have gone further. There were many Federalist hues: older men like Timothy Pickering, who had led the movement for independence, believed in "deference," and who "stood for" office, were not to be seen, except in their own terms, as "ultras;" younger Federalists envied, then copied, the Republican party organization. They "ran for" office, and openly courted mass electorates. More recent writing, as by Noble E. Cunningham Jr and by David Hackett Fischer, was rooted in Namier-like study of individuals in their locales, in eighteenth-century not twentieth-century style.

Marcus Cunliffe, covering the years 1789 to 1837, warned readers not to view the period solely in terms of a struggle between Hamiltonianism and Jeffersonianism, and stressed instead a number of other forces in conflict — urban vs. rural areas, nationalism vs. sectionalism, and conservatism vs. experimentalism — that had given rise to national tensions. A second general study by John C. Miller, dealing only with the period when the Federalist party was in power from 1789 to 1801, argued that out of the two extreme positions held by Hamiltonians and Jeffersonians there had emerged a middle-of-the-road approach that served the nation well in future years.[8]

One thing that has intrigued scholars was the seeming paradox between the thought and practice of the Founding Fathers over political parties. On the one hand, Federalists and Jeffersonians took a public stance in the 1790s opposing the formation of any parties. On the other, both set to work furiously to establish party organizations almost as soon as the new national government was founded.

2   WASHINGTON LEAVES OFFICE

With John Adams it was no longer possible to maintain the theory of a President above partisanship, for by 1796 it was obvious that the contest for the presidency had become the most important aspect of the now-virulent party battle. In that year the Democratic Republicans had high hopes; their candidate for President was Jefferson, and Aaron Burr of New York was put forward for the

[7] Richard Hofstadter, *The American Political Tradition and the Men Who Made It* (New York, Knopf, 1948), p. viii.
[8] Marcus F. Cunliffe, *The Nation Takes Shape 1789–1837* (Chicago, University of Chicago Press, 1959); John C. Miller, *The Federalist Era 1789–1801* (New York, Harper, 1960).

vice-presidency; their case was strong, thanks to the financial measures of Hamilton and the forceful suppression of the Whiskey Rebellion. Federalism was out of favor in the West and in the South. It was possible to use Jay's treaty to present the Federalists as pro-British; and they could equally appear as a party of overriding centralization and of high finance, behind whom were the insidious wiles of a hated foreign influence. Republicans proclaimed that "Thomas Jefferson is a firm Republican – John Adams is an avowed monarchist," and, moreover, "the declared advocate of ranks and orders in society." On the other side, according to the Federalists, Jefferson was at once a feckless vacillator and the iron-handed director of the "French faction", which would subvert the American form of government. Not merely Hamilton in his nationalism, but the Supreme Court in *Chisholm* vs. *Georgia*, in upholding the right of the citizen of one state to sue another, seemed to be riding rough-shod over the rights of the sovereign and still self-conscious states.

If the clash of parties and issues was clear enough, the choice was not. Washington did not publish his Farewell Address until September 19, and it did not appear in many newspapers until October. A number of Federalist electors had been still thinking of Washington rather than of Adams until the late summer. This handicapped Adams, but it hurt Jefferson still more, particularly in New England, where he was less well known and very much less well liked. Until the Twelfth Amendment was passed, the rule was simply that the candidate with the most votes in the electoral college became President, and the runner-up Vice-President, whatever their party allegiance might be. The Constitution, in its innocence, had not recognized parties. The actual "Spirit of '96" was to be intensely partisan. "At last!" John Beckley of Philadelphia exclaimed. With "the name of WASHINGTON" out of the way, the *Aurora* rejoiced, "a new era is now opening ... public measures must now stand on their own merits."

Hamilton, who was aware of Washington's decision to retire at least a month before it was public knowledge, exerted his own influence on the electors. Despite their Federalist ties, another element was injected into the contest: for the imperious Hamilton had never been at ease with Adams, despised his moderation, feared his personal friendship with Jefferson, and questioned Adams's allegiance to the Federalist cause. Partly to undermine Adams, but also in the hope of winning Southern votes for the Federalists, Hamilton proposed that the popular Thomas Pinckney of South Carolina, fresh from his diplomatic triumph in Spain, be put forward in the presidential scramble. Under the constitution at the time, each presidential elector was to vote for two persons, and the Constitution did not require the candidates to be named specifically for each office. The man who had the most electoral votes would become President — if he had a majority; and the runner-up Vice-President. Thus Hamilton might make Pinckney President, while Adams would be left in the limbo of the vice-presidency. The voters or legislatures in each state who would select the electors, meanwhile, were left to assume that Adams would be the Federalist favorite for the presidency, with Pinckney as his running mate.

Hamilton miscalculated the extent of the support for Adams in New England. The electoral voters there voted solidly for Adams, their "native son," but gave a scattering of votes to others, instead of giving equal support to Pinckney — intending thus to ensure that Adams would become President, and Pinckney, as also-ran, Vice-President. Sixteen states participated in the election, with Vermont, Kentucky, and Tennessee added to the original 13. In 7 states presidential electors were chosen by popular vote, with the other 9 choosing electors by the state legislatures or by mixed procedures. The result was that while Adams secured 71 votes, Pinckney got only 59; and Jefferson, with 68, became not only leader of the opposition but Vice-President, although no one had voted for him as anything but President. What Adams had seen as a remote possibility but "a dangerous crisis" in January, had now come to pass. President and Vice-President were in opposite boxes — for the first, and the last, time in American history. And for this the major responsibility rests with Hamilton. There were now Federalists, High and Low: Hamilton men versus Adams's Moderates. The split was never healed, and the Federalist party as a national force was greatly weakened.

After leaving office in 1795 in order to earn money to maintain his eight children — and he left office a poor man — Hamilton developed a lucrative private practice at the New York Bar, earning much more than his $3,500 salary as secretary of the Treasury; he built a vast house, "The Grange," at what is now Amsterdam Avenue and 141–5 Street, New York. Life should have been as contented as it was rich. But in Hamilton the fire of ambition, fueled by addiction to clever strategies that often went wrong, was still a searing and a naked flame. He was fully aware that the hostility of the South stood in the way of his own road to the presidency; so did his brilliance, his arrogance, and his foreign birth. Adams was hard to like, and Hamilton did not try very hard. In fact, he intrigued steadily against him in 1796, and until he died. Moreover, there was a party alignment here that would stay — more or less — solid. Adams's 71 electoral votes came from 9 of the 16 states (all of New England, plus victories in New York, New Jersey, Delaware, and Maryland, with one vote each from Virginia and North Carolina). Jefferson swept the South and Southwest, won the lion's share of Pennsylvania's electors, and 4 of Maryland's to Adams's 7.

3 HONEST JOHN

Of all the Founding Fathers, honest John Adams has waited longest for recognition. There is no monument to him in Washington DC, not slow to salute its citizens, or even in Massachusetts, for which he drafted a state constitution that is still in force. He himself sensed and predicted the neglect. Writing to Benjamin Rush in 1809, he said "Mausoleums, statues, monuments will never be erected to me ... Panegyrical romances will never be written, nor flattering orations spoken to transmit me to posterity in brilliant colors." The neglect is the more surprising in that Adams was the one prominent New Englander in high federal office, and that few of the Founding Fathers, many of whom appreciated their role in history and faithfully kept their records to prove it, were quite so zealous in preserving their papers, keeping their diaries, or caring for their books. The tide has now turned. His correspondence with Jefferson has been carefully edited and published; several biographies have appeared; and there was launched in 1955 an impressive scholarly project, the *Adams Papers*, in which the complete correspondence of John Adams and of the family are being published in definitive form.

The tribute so long overdue has already shown Adams to be far more significant than previous histories have implied. As a political thinker, he was perhaps the most original and, with Madison, the best read in constitutional history and law of all the Founders. He was remarkably self-contained and, if neither objective nor unemotional, he had a marked capacity for forming an independent and dispassionate judgment on events; and he had, we can now see, political courage of an unusually high order. His own prickly and unmalleable Yankee personality, however, made him hard to harness to a party. Like Robert Peel, he was "a difficult horse to go up to in the stable" – as were his son, grandson, and great-grandson after him. He never had a party or a personal following, and until the end he made it plain how superior a lack he thought this was. "I am determined to support every administration whenever I think them in the right," he wrote in 1808. "I care not whether they call me Federalist, Jacobin or Quid." In a political society one pays a high price so to indulge one's own integrity. J. Truslow Adams, the historian of the family, called him simply "bull-headed." He carried his rectitude like a banner; and he stopped now and then to salute it. "Amicus Plato, sed major veritas."

In 1797 John Adams was 62, bald and rotund. It is ironic to reflect that he had, 30 years before, been offered by Britain the post of advocate-general in the Court of Admiralty − a post he promptly rejected; that he had successfully defended the British troops involved in the Boston Massacre; and that in 1771 he had given up his legal practice in Boston because of what he thought was failing health. In 1774 he had begun a second career on a larger stage. He had been an enthusiastic, almost naive, member of the Continental Congress; "the Atlas of Independence," he had served with grim conscientiousness during the war on at least 80 committees and presided over 25 of them; he had represented the new Republic in Paris, London, and The Hague; he had helped to draw up the Treaty of Paris, and he had then, from 1785 to 1788, schooled himself to the difficult task of being the first minister to Britain,

He had thus a rich experience of domestic, and a rare knowledge of foreign, affairs. He was able and scholarly; he was highly critical of himself, as of others; and he was all too conspicuously honest. But despite his experience he was in many ways a political innocent, incapable of dissembling. Almost from the start, the Vice-President was not one of the President's closest team; and Franklin had always thought the office "His Superfluous Excellency." Moreover, Adams's candor and transparency left him, in fact, without defenses, and easily hurt. Outspoken and indiscreet, engrossed in himself, jealous and suspicious, he was without finesse in the handling of men. Senator Maclay has left a savage portrait of him as president of the Senate:

He takes on him to school the members from the chair. His grasping after titles has been observed by everybody. Mr Izard, after describing his air, manner, deportment, and personal figure in the chair, concluded with applying the title of ROTUNDITY to him. I have really often looked at him with surprise mingled with contempt when he is in the chair and no business before the Senate. Instead of that sedate, easy air which I would have him possess, he will look on one side, then on the other, then down on the knees of his breeches, then dimple his visage with the most silly kind of half smile which I can not well express in English. The Scotch-Irish have a word that hits it exactly − smudging. God forgive me for the vile thought, but I can not help thinking of a monkey just put into breeches when I saw him betray such evident marks of self-conceit.[9]

[9] William Maclay, *Journal*, ed. Edgar S. Maclay (New York, Appleton, 1890).

But Jefferson's verdict on him in 1787 is probably closer to truth:

He is vain, irritable and a bad calculator of the force and probable effects of the motives which govern men This is all the ill which can possibly be said of him. He is as disinterested as the being who made him; he is profound in his views and accurate in his judgment, except where knowledge of the world is necessary to form a judgment. He is so amiable, that I pronounce you will love him if ever you become acquainted with him. He would be, as he was, a great man in Congress. [10]

Adams's presidency was ill-starred. His Cabinet was inherited from Washington; of its members, Timothy Pickering as secretary of state, Oliver Wolcott at the Treasury, and James McHenry as secretary of war, were far more loyal to Hamilton than to the new president; Jefferson saw them as only a "little less hostile" to Adams than to himself. Nor were any of them, including Charles Lee (the attorney general), men of stature. Washington had found it a difficult, indeed a humiliating, task to recruit to the administration after Jefferson's and Hamilton's resignations. Adams was aware of this; he had written in 1795 to Abigail bemoaning it:

The expenses of living at the seat of government are so exhorbitant, so far beyond all proportion to the salaries, and the sure regard of integrity ... is such obloquy, contempt and insult, that no man of any feeling is willing to renounce his home, forsake his property for the sake of removing to Philadelphia, where he is almost sure of disgrace and ruin. [11]

The circumstances of his election did not make it likely that Adams would be any more successful a recruiting sergeant than Washington. There was in 1796 no precedent for a change of officials with a new administration. Nor did Adams favor the principle of rotation in office. He wanted a strong and disinterested executive and the good will of his aides. He got neither.

From Adams's inaugural until the summer of 1798, the differences smouldered; Cabinet comments were those of Hamilton at second hand. But much as he disliked Hamilton, he was not yet aware of treachery; so long as Adams breathed firmness in foreign policy, the differences did not come to the surface.

Adams's dilemma lay in France. Under Washington, relations with Spain and with Britain had improved. This was not only the result

---

[10] Ford (ed.) *Writings of Jefferson*, vol. VII, p. 264.
[11] Lynne Withey, *Dearest Friend: A life of Abigail Adams* (New York, Free Press, 1981).

of the Pinckney and the Jay treaties; it was due also to shrewd diplomacy. In private correspondence with Foreign Secretary Grenville, Jay sought to persuade him to discontinue impressment of American seamen; Robert Liston, the urbane British minister, reinforced the pleas. But with France relations had deteriorated. Genet, Fauchet, and Adet were singularly indiscreet in their behavior in America; Gouverneur Morris's haughtiness had made him *non grata* to the French; James Monroe's Republican zeal made him *non grata* to the Federalists; his over-optimistic assurances to the French made the Jay treaty inexplicable to them, and they were naturally surprised and indignant. They regarded it as proof of a deep Anglo-American understanding; and indeed, having accepted the British view of neutral rights, the United States was now ordering French privateers to leave her ports. In Paris, said Monroe, the United States was seen as "a perfidious friend." The Directory announced the termination of the 1778 alliance; by June 1797, 300 American merchant ships had been seized and their cargoes confiscated; Monroe's successor, Charles C. Pinckney, brother of Thomas Pinckney, was refused recognition and told to leave the country.

Adams sought particularly to avoid a clash by sending three commissioners – Charles Pinckney, John Marshall, and Elbridge Gerry – to Paris; the news of the efforts of the Directory – or of Talleyrand's underlings – to extort *pourboires* before beginning discussions produced a fierce reaction in the United States. Pinckney's rebuke – "It is no; no, not a sixpence" – was inflated into the legendary "Millions for defense but not one cent for tribute." The XYZ affair – the initials given to the euphonious but unpronounceable names of the French agents – still reads like a piece of fiction. Even if bribery was usual in eighteenth-century European diplomacy, the contempt for the United States implied by the dubious approaches of Hottingeur, Bellamy, and Hautevel was hard for sensitive Republicans to stomach.

The Directory, of course, was in aggressive mood; reasserting a traditional rather than a revolutionary view of the dominance of France in Europe, it was surrounding itself with vassal states; only Britain and the United States remained aloof from its influence. It was bringing pressure on Spain to cede the Floridas and Lousiana to France; there were French agents in the Mississippi country and along the Canadian line; Milfort, the half-breed leader of the Creeks, was commissioned a brigadier in the armies of France. During the negotiations, there were hints at the existence of a French "party" in the United States. Bribes apart, it was quite impossible for the Federalists to consider the French request for an American loan without running the real risk of war with Britain. And in fact Hamilton was himself pressing hard throughout 1797 and early 1798 for steadily closer relations with Britain. In March 1798 Adams announced to Congress the failure of his peace mission. On June 21, he went further:

I will never send another minister to France, without assurances that he will be received, respected and honored as the representative of a great, free, powerful and independent nation.

Behind these patriotic banners the Federalists could rally. Many Republicans rallied, too: "'Trimmers dropt off from the party," wrote Fisher Ames of the Republicans, "like windfalls from an apple tree in September." War fever increased. Congress declared all treaties with France null and void, ordered the construction or purchase of new ships, and created a Navy Department. And as no unimportant dividend of national unity and belligerence, the Federalists triumphed in the congressional election of 1798 — their very last triumph.

Adams endorsed these steps as necessary measures for defense and for diplomatic maneuver. Led by Hamilton, the Federalists urged President Adams to declare war on France. The President refused to do so, his aim being to extort respect for the American flag rather than to shed American blood. But a considerable defense program was inaugurated. Men-of-war were built, armed merchant vessels were put to sea, the regular army was greatly increased, a marine corps was raised, $7,000,000 was borrowed, and the treaty with France was abrogated. Vice-President Jefferson signed a contract with Eli Whitney, the Yankee inventor, for 10,000 muskets. The country was in a state of undeclared war with France.

Adams hoped to avoid war, although he would accept it if it were declared by France. To Hamilton, however, 1798 was like the Whiskey Rebellion of 1794; an opportunity to be used. War could destroy the Republicans, unite the country behind the Federalists, and — not least — strengthen the government. Adams did not share these extravagant enthusiasms. He disapproved particularly of the extent of congressional plans for enlarging the army. The civilian President suspected one who had, four years earlier, so obviously played the role of the man on horseback leading an expeditionary force. The army was to be increased to 20,000 men, but Hamilton hoped to raise these figures much higher; it was — and remains — proper to ask for what so large a force was intended in 1798; coastal defense against an invasion which then seemed unlikely, or adventure against New Orleans, the Floridas, or the Louisiana country? It seems clear now that Hamilton had not forgotten earlier approaches to Washington to act the part of liberator; and it was rumored that the Venezuelan patriot-adventurer Miranda hoped, in collusion with the British fleet, to free the Spanish Main.

Adams's suspicions of Hamilton came to a head when Washington, whom he asked to act as commander-in-chief, requested that Hamilton be appointed second-in-command and be the actual chief of operations in the field. Adams believed in seniority; Lincoln, Morgan, and Knox came before Hamilton. On Washington's threat of resignation, however, Adams yielded; but his suspicions of his Cabinet were now no longer dormant. He preferred to trust to a navy for defense; he became worried by Hamilton's enthusiasm in his role of inspector-general in recruiting officers and men; Pickering's opposition to the appointment to the army of Adams's son-in-law, William S. Smith, added to the tension.

The year 1798 saw the emergence of a group of High Federalists, of which Hamilton was the undisputed leader and policymaker. They included not only his aides in the Cabinet such as Timothy Pickering and Oliver Wolcott, but also Fisher Ames and Theodore Sedgwick of Massachusetts, Uriah Tracy of Connecticut, Robert Goodloe Harper of South Carolina, Rufus King and George Cabot, both in London. The essence of High Federalist policy was war with France; partly because, like Ames, they shuddered at the prospect of anarchy on the frontier; partly because, like old General Schuyler or Senator Sedgwick, they wanted to destroy the Jeffersonians; partly because, like Hamilton himself, they believed that order and stability in government were essential and that they could only be guaranteed by a standing army.

The martial spirit of 1798 and 1799 had three aspects, and in each the rift between the High Federalists and the Low was clear. The first aspect was domestic and party-political, and its authors were the Federalists in Congress, the party of the black cockade. The French ally of 1778 was forgotten; Jacobin and Democrat became terms synonymous with traitor, and America suffered its first wave of political hysteria. Although immigrants were not numerous, many of them were French or Irish and they were often radicals; French agents were at work in the West; some of the newcomers were conspicuous recruits to Republicanism as editors and pamphleteers, and it was easy to brand them unpatriotic, or worse.

Three major laws were enacted in June–July 1798. The Naturalization Act, designed to halt the recruitment of new voters by the Republicans, raised the residence requirement for citizenship from 5 to 14 years. The Alien Act empowered the President to deport or imprison "dangerous' aliens. The Sedition Act made it a crime to publish false or malicious writings against the government or its officers. The effect of these measures was not as ugly as might have been feared, partly, because many leading Federalists, including Adams, deplored them. The only Act to be seriously invoked was the last, under which ten Republican editors and one member of Congress, Matthew Lyon, were convicted, and a number of individuals were prosecuted for over-indulgence in free speech. As Adams had foreseen, they promptly became martyrs. Later in the year, the Kentucky and Virginia Resolutions, drafted respectively by Jefferson and Madison, declared that these Acts were unconstitutional, that they violated the Bill of Rights, and that states were the proper judges of constitutionality and could, if they chose, act to nullify such laws. If the protests were as much propagandist as were the laws themselves, they at least raised a major issue. And if Adams and Hamilton differed on many matters, they were both as alarmed as Jackson was to be by the dangerous talk of nullification, or as Lincoln was to be by the more dangerous fact of secession.

Paradoxically, it was the Republicans who stood for localism and for federalism; the High Federalists, in fact, were centralists and nationalists. At this stage Adams was of their company. While making no direct recommendation to Congress on these measures, he made his contribution to the high spirit of the times by his intemperate replies to the addresses that poured in upon him. Only the Republicans gained by the unwisdom and unpopularity of this legislation: if the Fries rebellion in western Pennsylvania against the federal property tax levied in 1798 was suppressed, one consequence was that this area became thereafter solidly Republican in character.

The second aspect of 1798–9 was the fact of an undeclared war with France. In two years, French commerce in the West Indies was in large measure destroyed. Privateering had a rebirth. Jingoist sentiment now inclined to the idea of a standing army, an alliance with Britain, and dominion over the South American states. There were here, thought Adams, dreams of conquest scarcely less grandiose than those of the Pizarros. Rufus King reported from London in February 1798 that the Spanish colonial empire would disintegrate when France invaded Spain; Miranda, backed by Britain, would lead an expeditionary force; the United States must aid Britain lest France re-establish her American empire. The new Republic's best defense, it seemed, was not only offense, but an empire of her own in the West, and, in the Caribbean, protection for the newer republics of whom she might be mentor. Guns captured from French ships were donated by Britain to the United States for the defense of Charleston

— an act of such gratuitous international kindness as to be diplomatically highly suspect. Anglophile sentiment ran high, particularly in Rufus King and Robert Goodloe Harper, and it was discreetly abetted by Robert Liston, the British minister. If the High Federalists had had their way, the Great Rule of Washington would have been abandoned before it had been fully established, and a foreign policy of adventure abroad might have permanently replaced the principle of isolation.

Finally, through this crisis, Adams, unlike Hamilton, sought to hold off the dogs of war in the Cabinet and Congress. He deplored the warlike mood the Hamiltonians induced. He disliked the idea of a standing army and the political ammunition it provided for the Republicans. In this he was far more shrewd than Hamilton. He was unable to curb Congress, however. Dr Logan of Pennsylvania had already gone to Paris in his solitary but highly suspect efforts to keep the peace with France; Congress, by passing the Logan Act, promptly made his peaceful crusade a misdemeanor — a charge that still holds if an American citizen is rash enough to seek to intervene in a dispute between the United States and a foreign government. The same ugliness attended even the President's own efforts, and it was on this fundamental note that the final break with the High Federalists came.

Through Elbridge Gerry, and William Vans Murray at The Hague, Adams was informed that Talleyrand wished to renew diplomatic intercourse. Reports from John Quincy and from Rufus King confirmed this. The French put out soothing statements about "XYZ"; alleging that the American commissioners had innocently allowed themselves to be imposed upon by charlatans. Although preparations for war went ahead, the president sought with dogged courage to keep the doors open to negotiation. By his influence in his party, in Congress, and indirectly in the cabinet, Hamilton pressed as hard for war. To the horror of the senate, Adams recommended, first, in February 1799, the appointment of Murray as minister to the French Republic, and then, when the Senate showed violent objection, the appointment of a three-man peace commission — with advice that it should not sail until there was evidence of real French good will.

This step, taken entirely on his own initiative, rallied opinion to him. Diplomatically, it was wise; economically, it was sound, for as many were profiteering from trade with the French West Indies as were likely to profit from war, and the federal military program had doubled the cost of government; and, as political tactics, it was not only shrewd but necessary. To have permitted war with France in 1799 would have been tantamount to permitting the risk of civil war at home and to the acceptance of government by militarism. For Adams, peace was a necessity. Such was the Federalist split, however, that, also of necessity, it brought a widening of the gulf between the High Federalists and the President. Adams's refusal to dismiss his cabinet ministers Timothy Pickering and James McHenry, even though he was aware of their intrigues against him, and his long absence at Quincy in the summer of 1799, like his similar absence in the previous year, were acts of unwisdom. On his return in October – his Cabinet met at Trenton because of the fever in Philadelphia – he acted once more on his own authority and ordered the mission to sail. At this point the two groups broke apart. As in 1792 and 1796, the High Federalists began their now customary intrigues to deny office to the man who, almost unaided, had kept his country out of war.

For one with a sharp sense of his own importance, and who, on the broad question of peace or war, was remarkably mature, John Adams was curiously long-suffering. In the end McHenry resigned, after a stormy interview, and not even his friends mourned his departure. Pickering was, in May 1800, at last dismissed from office. The Federalist leaders, at odds with each other, now openly campaigned against the President, and Hamilton produced his Letter Concerning the Public Conduct and Character of John Adams. He described Adams as unfit for the Presidency, and revealed Cabinet secrets. It appeared in the last week of October, too late to permit of a reply before the elections.

The legacy of this rivalry and dissension was twofold. On September 30, 1800, peace with France was concluded at Morfontaine; it was Adams's own achievement. In October, as his thanks, he was defeated in the electoral college, gaining 65 votes to Jefferson's and Burr's tied 73. The last months of office were months of gloom and petulance; the midnight judges were appointed, and in the cold dawn of March 4, 1801, a few hours before Jefferson's inaugural, Adams made an angry, unforgiving, and ungracious exit from the still uncompleted presidential mansion in the far from completed federal city.

4   THE CREOLE BASTARD

It is, however, much too simple to explain these four years in terms of a personal vendetta. Certainly Adams and Hamilton were utterly different in temperament and attitude, and there was personal dislike and mistrust. Adams was much older than Hamilton and lacked his flamboyant and mercurial driving force. He saw Hamilton as one who attached himself to the great, linked by service to Washington and by marriage to Schuyler; he saw him as clever, arrogant, and a libertine; he saw him, to Hamilton's particular disgust, as an outsider, "the Creole adventurer," "the Creole bastard," isolated by origins and by birth; he was one, he thought, who would almost inevitably be passed over for posts of real responsibility. In 1809 Adams excused Hamilton's errors on the grounds that he was "not a native of America," "he never acquired the feelings and principles of the American people." Hamilton was by 1797 aware of this himself, and his gloom and frustration grew with the years: "Everyday proves to me more and more that the American world was not made for me."

It was due to Hamilton, Adams believed, that he had obtained less than half the electoral votes for Vice-President in 1792; it was Hamilton who conspired against him with his own Cabinet; it was Hamilton who thwarted what chances he had of a second term, by publishing a pamphlet condemning the negotiations with the French as "capricious and undignified," and attacking the President's "extreme egotism." Adams later wrote:

In this dark and insidious manner did this intriguer lay schemes in secret against me, and like the worm at the root of the peach, did he labor for twelve years, underground and in darkness, to girdle the root, while all the axes of the Anti-federalists, Democrats, Jacobins, Virginia debtors to English merchants, and French hirelings, chopping as they were for the whole time at the trunk, could not fell the tree.[12]

If Adams cannot be thought impartial, Noah Webster, a staunch Federalist, equally deplored Hamilton's wrecking of the party. In his open Letter to General Hamilton, in 1800, he said; "your ambition, pride and overbearing temper have destined you to be the evil genius of this country." Abigail Adams saw the trend even more sharply "That man," she said, "would become a second Bonaparty if he was possessed of equal power!" The charge was valid; Hamilton's hero was Julius Caesar. To this rivalry Aaron Burr added his quota. Burr, like Hamilton, was brilliant, ambitious and erratic. Adams in fact polled as well in 1800 as he had done in 1796, except in one state, New York, where Burr, Jefferson's ally, had turned the state to Jefferson. Because the votes for Burr and Jefferson were tied, the

---

[12] *The Diary and Autobiography of John Adams*, ed. L. H. Butterfield, 4 vols (Cambridge, MA, Harvard University Press, 1961), vol. II, p. 64.

still-Federalist House of Representatives had to decide between them, with each state casting a single vote. By 1800, there were 16 states (Vermont in 1791, Kentucky in 1792, and Tennessee in 1796 had joined the original 13), so 9 were needed to win. For 35 agonizing ballots, 8 states voted for Jefferson, 6 for Burr, and 2 stayed undecided. But, much as Hamilton distrusted Jefferson, he feared Burr more; Burr lacked "moral scruple," he thought: "Adieu to the Federal Troy, if they once introduce this Grecian horse into their midst." On the 36th, thanks to Hamilton's persuasions, Jefferson was elected.

Hamilton now had two enemies: Burr and Adams. And Burr never forgave Hamilton. In 1804 they fought a duel, in which Burr killed Hamilton, and went into exile himself — thus ending two threats to the republic.

The death of Hamilton and the Vice President's flight, with their accessories of summer-morning sunlight on rocky and wooded heights, tranquil river and distant city, and behind all, their dark background of moral gloom, double treason and political despair, still stand as the most dramatic moment in the early politics of the Union. [13]

Behind the long clash between dour, crusty, and family-rooted Yankee and versatile, illegitimate and ambitious West Indian lay a deeper clash of principle. Hamilton was the true monarchist, and of all the Revolutionary leaders the man who qualified best for the title of man of "Little Faith." For him the Constitution was always a second best, and his doubts about its durability continued until the day he died. He described it in 1802 as "a frail and worthless fabric which I have been endeavouring to prop up," "a shilly shally thing of mere milk and water." What he admired were discipline and authority in government; what he preached was mercantilism. He subsidized those who invested in manufactures and public securities; he taxed the landed interest. He favored a "hereditary" chief magistrate, representing the "permanent will" of society and capable of curbing the "turbulent and uncontrouling [*sic*] disposition" of democracy. He wanted the "Officers of the General Government" protected by the courts. He wanted a permanent army. He wanted to increase the legal power of the federal government over the states, and the larger states to be reduced in size. He wanted federal roads and canals built throughout the nation. He wanted an upper house chosen for life on a property basis. "Our real disease," he wrote on the night before he was shot, "is democracy."

[13] Henry Adams, *History of the United States of America* (New York, Scribner's 1890), vol. II, p. 19.

His economic-cum-political views were shaped, in fact, less by America than by his youth in the store in the lush sugar islands, where prosperity depended – hurricanes permitting – on an elaborate trading system, and where society was hierarchic. He had no sympathy with Jefferson's farmer-democrats. The rich, the well-born, and the able were to be given every encouragement, and the fluidity of a free society would allow them to be creative, not destructive.

This was not Adams's view of Federalism. For one thing, he was a farmer's son and, if a lawyer by vocation, he remained an agrarian in background. He was far more a physiocrat than a mercantilist. There was a simplicity and frugality in Adams's code, a taste for "a frock and trowsers, a hoe and a spade." If he shared the belief in order and status and leaned for a time to monarchism, the emphasis was very different. To him the federal Constitution was "the greatest single effort of national deliberation that the world has ever seen." He did not in fact share Hamilton's view that the executive should be exalted above faction, a constitutional monarch. While to Hamilton the "rich" were the capitalists, to Adams land was the most desirable form of property. He accepted the trading systems and the assumption of state debts as necessary, but he disliked the use of assumption in order to reward speculators. He was, thus far, more typical of the conservative farmers and small traders than was Hamilton. He accepted the need for a national bank of deposit, but he had a Jeffersonian horror of local banks issuing paper far beyond the amount of their own capital – "the madness of the many for the profit of the few." He had no taste for the speculators in land or in paper. When the High Federalists spoke with awe of "the wise, the good and the rich," Adams respected only the first two categories. He deplored plutocracy. He deplored also the sense of adventure on which the Hamiltonian system, like the Hamiltonian career, was based. His standpoint was unblushingly civilian; there was no taste for military glory in Adams.

As the years passed, Adams's virulence increased. "The trading system and the banking system which are the works of the Federalists," he wrote in 1809, "have introduced more corruption and injustice ... than any other cause." By this time he was moving away from a now wrecked Federalism and, perhaps because he was in part the architect of the disaster, his language had a pungency unusual to 74-year-olds:

As Hamilton was the Sovereign Pontiff of Federalism, all his Cardinals no doubt will endeavour to excite the whole Church to excommunicate and anathematize me. Content. It was time for a Protestant Separation.

Neither Adams nor Hamilton was consistent. The former moved from revolutionary causes through realism to conservatism; a not unfamiliar transition. Hamilton's inconsistencies were more heinous. In *The Federalist Papers* (Nos. 12 and 21) he recognized that "the genius of the people" hated excises, yet he made them an essential part of his revenue system in 1791, and in 1794 he was employing force to crush the resistance to them of the Whiskey Rebels in Pennsylvania; the advocate of isolation (in *Federalist*, 11) became in 1794 the notorious anglophile of the Jay treaty; the supporter of free elections and free choice in 1787 threatened in 1800 to use force to nullify the people's will. In 1787, and in 1791–4, he claimed to "think continentally," yet by 1800 he was the now fully avowed leader of the High Federalists, at odds with President Adams and wrecking both Adams's administration and his own party.

Increasingly Hamilton advocated the use of armies: in 1794 to crush the Pennsylvania farmers; in 1798, when he became inspector-general, to go to war with France, or perhaps to embark on a great crusade as a liberator in Spanish America; in 1800 to preserve Federalist power in New York. "In times like these," he told John Jay, "it will not do to be over-scrupulous." He split with Adams because the President kept peace with France. He thought Jefferson ought to go to war to gain Louisiana, but when Jefferson achieved its purchase in a staggering diplomatic triumph, Hamilton wrote:

the advantage of the acquisition appears too distant and remote to strike the mind of a sober politician with much force. ... It ... must hasten the dismemberment of a large portion of our country, or a dissolution of the Government.

The passionate nationalist could become the most bitter and irrational of partisans. He was brilliant and far-sighted, driven by great qualities, perhaps the most creative personality in the age of the American Revolution; but he was not made for politics, or for the tact and the compromises that politics demands. His own life, which held out so much promise, was tragic. His ideas triumphed a century later.

As always when a governing party splits into two, the opposition inherits power by default. The decline of the Federalists was paralleled in these years by the rise of the Democratic Republicans. They profited from the errors of the Federalists. They were strong in the South and in the West. They became the exponents of states' rights, and in the Virginia and Kentucky Revolutions of 1798 they expressed their own political philosophy almost as clearly as did

Hamilton and the early Madison in *The Federalist Papers*. They were by 1799 well organized in particular states, with Madison, it is now clear, even more their mastermind than Jefferson. They, too, had a personal rivalry to settle — that between Jefferson and Burr; it was Hamilton's role in settling it, by swinging the votes of the states in the House of Representatives against Burr, that put Jefferson in the White House, and earned Hamilton Burr's dangerous enmity.

The presidency of John Adams, like that of Jefferson after him, revealed the strength and the weakness of the scholar as politician. Despite all his travel, his reading, his pessimistic Puritan strain, and his shrewdness, he who was a skeptic in the study could not make himself a cynic in the Cabinet, and it is from this dichotomy that he often appears in action as naive. A big man on the big issues, like peace with France, he found it hard to be forceful or creative or even at ease in his dealings with individuals. What he lacked were not so much the human qualities of warmth and comradeship, though these were not conspicuous, but cynicism about the motives and knowledge of the ways of the men around him. These might have allowed him to guess at the perfidy of some of his associates and thus have averted the ruin of his party. As it was, his virtues as a man proved to be a source of weakness to him as a politician. He has been described as an angry man in the presidency, but he was not so much angry as unlucky, constantly set to play difficult, unpopular, and lonely roles. Thus, he notably and successfully defended British soldiers in the Boston Massacre. He was a member of the committee to draw up the Declaration of Independence, but he deferred to Jefferson as its major author. As a minister in France, he took orders from Franklin, of whose morals he profoundly disapproved. He was Vice-President to Washington in his new presidency, but in the election of 1800 he had to watch Jefferson and Burr intrigue for the job he held himself. He reached giddy heights, but he never enjoyed them; in the last analysis, he was not made for politics, or for luck — and they are related commodities.

As Jefferson had said, Adams was a "bad calculator." While he had no illusions about Hamilton and saw himself as a very wise student of affairs, in practice he treated Hamilton's lieutenants with quite unmerited charity and with unusual patience. In his closing months of office — when, to Jefferson's chagrin, he filled the judicial places with his own appointees — he rewarded not only John Marshall, who had replaced Pickering for a few months as secretary of state, but also Wolcott. Even in the years of bitter harvest that followed, it was only to Hamilton and "Tim Pick" — Hamilton's supporter Timothy Pickering — that he refused forgiveness, although by 1818 he was telling Jefferson that in a future world he might overcome his objections to meeting even them, "if I could see a symptom of penitence in either."

What must, however, be stressed here is that the story is not merely a personal one. Party spirit was the real novelty. Adams felt as alien to it and as disturbed by it as had Washington. In their view, there was no place for it, and they saw its existence as evidence of human wickedness, or of foreign intrigue, rather than as the expression of a different point of view. Federalists saw in Republicans men opposed not merely to the administration but to the Constitution, and dupes of France. To Republicans the Federalists were "Anglomen." It was still the springtime of party history, and if such charges were later the small change of party controversy, in 1798 and 1799 they were, to many, matters of belief and bitter hatred, convictions and not yet conventions. There was an unusual acrimony in debate, as politicians learned to accept the paradox that a healthy democracy necessitates keen, and often violent, partisanship. Adams suffered acutely: from the charge that the executive was head of a party, which in his eyes degraded the office; from the immoderates in both groups, none of whom respected the middle way; and from the fact that his own partiality was not only for Low Federalists but for Old Whigs, his comrades of 1776 like Eldridge Gerry and Benjamin Rush. He suffered for his faith — a curiously unrealistic one — in the possibility of an independent executive.

Even if one concedes, however, that the fault did not lie in himself, it is incontrovertible that he contributed to his own debacle: by inheriting Washington's Cabinet and not forcing the issue with it, or its gray eminence, much earlier; by losing goodwill over his failure to oppose the Alien and Sedition Acts, hard though he tried later to deny responsibility for them; by failing to match intrigue with firmness; and by failing to build up a following of his own. For one who favored a strong executive, he was a surprisingly weak president. And he had — always — too many scruples. By 1800 the most conspicuous feature of American politics was the extent and virulence of partisan spirit. It made Washington's last year, and Adams's whole term, miserable and unproductive.

Yet the services of John Adams cannot be minimized. If his distrust of democracy, a distrust he shared with the High Federalists, was as substantial as his distrust of faction, out of it emerged his decision to use the interval between November 1800 and March 1801 to make the judiciary staunchly Federalist. If the motives were partisan and suspect, the long-term results were to prove beneficial;

the powers not only of the courts but of the federal government as well were enhanced; loose construction and judicial review were part of the Adams legacy. Not the least of his services was that he gave John Marshall to the Supreme Court.

More than this, he could claim with justice to have kept the peace with France, to have curbed the foreign policy of adventure abroad advocated by Hamilton, and to have strengthened the Great Rule of Washington. He had been, in 1774, one of the first to see that isolation was a logical consequence of the Revolution. He held to it through all the tensions of 1798 and 1799, and, by keeping the peace with France, he unknowingly made it possible for his successor to acquire the Louisiana Territory and the West by simple purchase. Although as much a man of impulse as Hamilton, he had a basic understanding of the value to the new country of peace and stability. And on this he was more consistent than Hamilton. Isolation from Europe was not only a political advantage for America, it was a moral distinction; he shared the faith of 1776 in New World values. Hamilton was a High Tory; John Adams, in all his changing moods, was an Old Whig.

5

The Virginia Dynasty

1 THE SAGE OF MONTICELLO

Mr Jefferson was a tall strait-bodied man as ever you see, right square-shouldered: nary man in this town walked so straight as my old master: neat a built man as ever was seen in Vaginny, I reckon or any place — a straight-up man: long face, high nose ...

Old master was never seen to come out before breakfast — about 8 o'clock. If it was warm he wouldn't ride out till evening: studied upstairs till bell rang for dinner. When writing he had a copyin machine: while he was a-writin he wouldn't suffer nobody to come in his room; he had a dumb-waiter: When he wanted anything he had nothing to do but turn a crank and the dumb-waiter would bring him water or fruit on a plate or anything he wanted. Old master had abundance of books: sometimes would have twenty of 'em down on the floor at once: read first one, then tother. Isaac has often wondered how old master came to have such a mighty head: read so many of them books: and when they go to him to ax him anything, he go right straight to the book and tell you all about it. He talked French and Italian ...

Mr Jefferson always singing when ridin or walkin: hardly see him anywhar out doors but what he was a-singin: had a fine clear voice, sung minnits [minuets] and sich: fiddled in the parlor. Old master very kind to servants ...[1]

---

[1] From *Memoirs of a Monticello Slave: As dictated to Charles Campbell in the 1840s by Isaac, one of Thomas Jefferson's slaves*, ed. Rayford Logan (Charlottesville, The Tracy W. McGregor Library, 1951), quoted by Francis Coleman Rosenberger, *The Jefferson Reader* (New York, Dutton, 1955), p. 74.

Such was the portrait left by Isaac, one of his slaves, of Thomas
Jefferson, key figure of the first generation of Americans, the man
of reason and the man of paradoxes. Even in his own day, Jefferson
was everything to all men: seen with condescension by British diplomat Sir Augustus Foster; with panic by Timothy Dwight of Yale.
("Shall our sons become the disciples of Voltaire, and the dragoons
of Marat; or our daughters the concubines of the Illuminati?");
with a flutter of excitement by Margaret Bayard Smith ("And is
this," said I, "the violent democrat, the vulgar demagogue, the bold
atheist and profligate man I have so often heard denounced by the
federalists? ... I felt my cheeks burn and my heart throb, and not
a word more could I speak while he remained.") The coolest-minded
of the Revolutionary generation seemed to generate controversy then,
as he has done since; the least heroic of leaders has proved the most
seminal of minds, the most contradictory of Founding Fathers has
been the most invoked. [2]

By birth, Jefferson was both aristocrat and frontiersman. His
mother was a Randolph – one of the oldest and most important
families in a state where kinship counted. Through her, Jefferson
was cousin to the Randolphs of Tuckahoe, one of whom presided
over the Revolutionary Congress, another of whom stayed – and
died – loyal to his king. His father, Peter Jefferson, less well-born
but with literary tastes, was a land surveyor with substantial property
in Albemarle County, in the foothills of the Blue Ridge – and with
greater impact than had the mother on the son. Thomas was given
a good education: not the best, the education at schools in England
that was the preserve of the wealthiest in Virginia, but a good
training in philosophy and law at the little College of William and
Mary in Williamsburg, the second oldest in the Thirteen Colonies.
Williamsburg, the colonial capital, was a social as well as a political center, and Jefferson was taught not only by William Small
of Aberdeen (in philosophy) and George Wythe (in law), but also
learned the social graces from Governor Fauquier. It was his introduction to the world of the Enlightenment, and to habits of study
that he never lost.

The habits he acquired were scholarly. He became a linguist,
familiar with French, Italian, Dutch, Spanish, and German; he was
interested later in Anglo-Saxon and in the vocabulary of the Indians,
as he came to see in philology an index to the problem of the origin

[2] Margaret Bayard Smith, *The First Forty Years of Washington Society*, quoted
in Rosenberger, *Jefferson Reader*, p. 57.

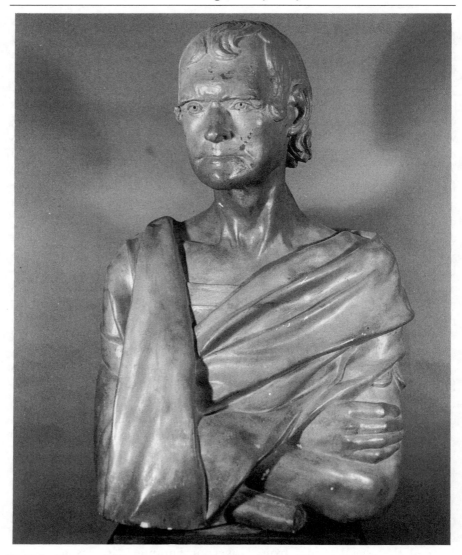

Plate 5 Thomas Jefferson: bust by John Henri Isaac Browere (1825).
(New York State Historical Association, Cooperstown. © New York State Historical Association, Cooperstown, NY.)

of man. The advice on reading that he gave to his young friend Bernard Moore indicates something of his power of concentration. The student, he argued, should divide his time: from rising until eight in the morning, physical studies; from eight to twelve, read law; from twelve to one, read politics; in the afternoon, read history; from dark to bedtime, *belles lettres*, criticism, rhetoric, and oratory.

A visit to Monticello, with its music stand and architect's table, its library, its dumb-waiter, and its carefully designed clock and many gadgets, its stables and polygraph machine, confirms the versatility and the Leonardo-like range of interests of the third President, who was architect and classicist, educator and philosopher, naturalist and musician.

> The big hands clever
>   With pen and fiddle
> And ready, ever,
>   For every riddle.
>
> From buying empires
>   To planting 'taters,
> From Declarations
>   To dumb-waiters.

Or as Henry Adams put it more grandiloquently, Jefferson was "martyr to the disease of omniscience."

Yet even when he was studying and practicing law – in the years before the Revolution – his interests were catholic, and in the best sense amateur. When he married the widow Mrs Martha Wayles Skelton on New Year's Day 1772, the home to which he took her was one he was building himself, to his own design atop his little mountain in Albemarle. In its grace and proportion, Monticello remains a lovely example of Palladian Georgian. Jefferson's interest in architecture – awakened, apparently, by Dr John Morgan on a visit to Philadelphia in 1766 to secure inoculation against smallpox – remained with him for life. During his ambassadorship to France from 1784 to 1789, he filled his travel notebooks with observations and measurements of houses and public buildings in France, Italy, Germany, and Holland – and with designs for home decoration, with the details of landscape gardening, and even with recipes for macaroni. The great interest of his last years was the building of the University of Virginia, and he could follow the progress of the erection of its serpentine walls and its beautiful pavilions by telescope from his mountain top. He filled his home with books, as Isaac testifies; and his library was sold to become the nucleus of the Library of Congress after the capital was burnt by the British in 1814. Equally impressive were his notebooks, immaculately filed and cataloged. From 1785 until his death 41 years later he kept an "Epistolary Record" in which he recorded in parallel columns virtually every letter that he wrote or received. It runs to 656 pages. His correspondence is estimated to include more than 50,000 separate items.

Nor was Jefferson a man of books only; he was an ingenious inventor of gadgets, and they still abound at Monticello: a swivel chair, a bed that could be hoisted to the ceiling, a polygraph device for copying his letters; there were designs for a moldboard plow, for a leather buggy top, for a hemp-beater. The target, as to Franklin, was not pedantry but useful knowledge. And there was taste too; a taste for music, for color and texture, and a palate for wine – a cellar that astonished Daniel Webster, and a French chef who persuaded him to feed his guests on something other than his "native victuals," as Patrick Henry called them, of hog, hoe-cake and hominy grits.

In many ways the least striking of Jefferson's practical achievements was his work as President. This was due, in part, as we have already seen, to his character, which, said Hamilton, "warrants the expectation of a temporizing rather than a violent system." The universal man was as always suspect. Certainly he was repeatedly attacked. His interest in fossils and plants – so well brought out in his *Notes on Virginia* – was in his own day associated with a scientific questioning of religious fundamentals and even with atheism, and it met with ridicule. As the youthful William Cullen Bryant expressed it:

> Go, wretch, resign thy presidential chair
> Disclose thy secret measures, foul or fair,
> Go, search with curious eyes, for horned frogs
> Mid the wild Wastes of Louisianian bogs;
> Or, where the Ohio rolls his turbid stream,
> Dig for huge bones, thy glory and thy theme.[3]

To his Federalist opponents, especially their editors, he was the first of their foes: they put them in descending order as Tom Jefferson, Tom Paine, and Tom the Devil. Even in 1804, when he was re-elected by every state in the Union except Connecticut and Delaware, the majority of the newspapers, controlled by the "monied corps," "this mass of anti-civism" as he called it, were opposed to him even then. To them he was not a Leonardo but a Devil: Tom the Magician, Tom Conondrum, were the phrases used to smear his reputation.

---

[3] William Cullen Bryant, *The Embargo, or Sketches of the Times* (2nd edn Boston, 1809).

His many-sidedness, however impressive, carried political liabilities, as it always does. With all his gifts for words and style – and his most decisive contribution to the beginnings of the Revolution was his "pen-manship" – he was shy in speech and averse from oratory. He discontinued the practice followed by his two predecessors of delivering his messages to Congress in person. He said it was to save time, but it was in fact because he disliked speaking in public. At his Inaugural in 1801 he walked from Conrad's boarding house to the still unfinished capitol to take the oath, whereas in 1789 Washington had used a coach and six; he abolished the presidential levée and the rule of precedence at receptions – to the discomfort of British and Spanish ambassadors, and the greater discomfort of their wives. Part of the explanation was that as he lacked a hostess, he had little choice; but there was little physical magnetism, little of that surging, almost tangible, vitality that marked Hamilton. There was a sensitiveness that some called womanish, and others feline – as emerged in the wild despair when his wife died, and the timidity he showed as governor of Virginia during the Revolutionary war. And some problems defied all his reasoning, because they were perhaps in large measure insoluble.

For Jefferson, himself an owner of some 200 slaves, slavery presented an agonizing problem: "The whole commerce between master and slave is a perpetual exercise of the most boisterous passions." Blacks he saw as, at least, intolerably "different" from whites; despite his later welcome for the evidence of their intellectual capacity, and despite his views on government for the Western territories that "there shall be neither slavery nor servitude in any of the said states" after 1800, he did not want free blacks in America, lest they "stain the blood" of the whites. "The slave, when made free ... is to be removed beyond the reach of mixture." He favored freeing the children of slaves after a certain date, but he did not believe – and in this he shared the general assumptions of his day – that the two races, if both were free, could coexist in the same country. There would have to be mass black emigration. The white was, he believed, superior to the Negro, except in memory, in musical ability, and in courage – and the last was due only to his inadequate reasoning. Nor was Jefferson any more liberal towards the Indian. As long as the Indian was a hunter, he and the white man could not, he thought, be neighbors. He pushed the Creeks and Chickasaws from their land in Georgia and Alabama into the land west of the Mississippi, and when Louisiana became American by purchase he sought to induce the Indians to exchange their lands east of the Mississippi for others in the new West.[4]

The cast of mind was speculative – but it was not unambitious. There is preserved in the University of Virginia Library Jefferson's personal scrap-book, indicating a human preoccupation with his own success. Monticello was remote and on the frontier: in 1801, in the hundred miles that lay between it and Washington, eight rivers had to be crossed, and five of them had neither bridges nor boats. Philadelphia was still more distant, a journey of some seven to ten days. Yet Monticello was no ivory tower. The diffident man among his books and gadgets was a skilled party organizer, as gifted in intrigue as any more orthodox politician, and he was thought of by his Federalist opponents with a certain uneasy fear. He rarely intervened in controversy himself, and when attacked he remained maddeningly aloof – but not unhurt. His main instrument was correspondence. Even in the campaign of 1800, he stayed quietly at Monticello, and expressed his views by letter which his friends could quote. But he could hide his political maneuvers equally dextrously behind botanical expeditions up the Hudson, or by doing deals with Hamilton himself, or by acting as adviser to Lafayette and his group of would-be liberal reformers in Paris in 1789. The fascination of Jefferson recalls that of Milton and of Michelangelo, of Locke and Burke, of Lamartine and Hugo, the mixture of artist and man of affairs, the tension between political philosopher and political tactician.

This does not exhaust the catalog: experimental farmer, student of the classics and of the Bible, naturalist, horticulturist and palaeontologist, surveyor and builder, lawyer and administrator, Jefferson in fact was one of the last of the universal men, in the last century that could produce them. There is a Renaissance quality, an emphasis on the complete man, on the need for physical as well as mental development, on the value of literary learning and of the practical wisdom of the classics. His was not only a pre-industrial, but also a pre-specialist age.

Jefferson owed his election in 1800 to Alexander Hamilton. He owed his victory also to his own skill as organizer of a party. Yet to partisanship – and to power – he came, unlike Hamilton, late, and with reluctance.

On his return from France in 1790, Jefferson had described himself as neither Federalist nor anti-Federalist, "of neither party,

[4] P. L. Ford (ed.), *The Writings of Thomas Jefferson*, 10 vols (New York, G. P. Putnam's Sons, 1891–9), vol. III, pp. 266–7, and vol. V, pp. 66–7.

nor yet a trimmer between parties." He wanted, he told Francis Hopkinson, to avoid attracting notice: "I find the pain of a little censure, even when it is unfounded, is more acute than the pleasure of much praise."[5] Yet by 1792 while serving as secretary of state he was, in effect, with Madison and with John Beckley, clerk of the House of Representatives, organizing a political party and directing a pamphlet and press war. Concerned as he was with freedom of opinion – he said he would prefer a society without government but with newspapers to one with government but without newspapers – it was a natural step to make of newspapers the instrument of protest and of policy. By nature Jefferson was an intellectual. His introduction to state and national politics was as pamphleteer. He has been called the Scholar Boss, if not the Philosopher King. Even so, he did not seek the limelight.

There was ample material for party controversy: the Genet episode and the "Anglo-manny" of Washington's Administration, the excise tax and the whiskey rebels, the Jay and Pinckney treaties. But it was not until 1798 that the division between the two wings of the federal government and the Federalist party became clearcut, with the passing of the Alien and Sedition Acts. These Federalist measures were intended to curb the growing Republican party, but they had in fact the opposite effect. The three Acts which dealt with aliens – providing for deportation and stiffer requirements for naturalization – aimed to curb the political activities of new immigrants, who were, for the most part, supporters of the Republican party, many of them labeled (and libeled) as Jacobins. Worse than these, however, was the Sedition Act, which provided for the punishment of "those who wrote, printed, or uttered any false, scandalous, and malicious statements against the government of the United States or either House of Congress of the United States." This, of course, was a flagrant interference with the rights of freedom of speech and freedom of the press. Ten Republican editors and printers were tried and convicted under the Sedition Act. Irish-born Matthew Lyon of Vermont accused President Adams of "unbounded thirst for ridiculous pomp, foolish adulation, and a selfish avarice." For his loose pen he paid a fine of $1,000 and served four months in jail.

The Sedition Act was passed by an alarmed and leaderless Congress; its chief result was to alarm the country as to the insecurity of personal liberty under a Federalist government. Hamilton, as an anti-Adams Federalist, protested against the Sedition Act with the

[5] ibid., vol. V, p. 78.

appeal: "Let us not establish tyranny. Energy is a very different thing from violence." The divided leadership of the Federalists was fast becoming a discredited leadership.

It was to counter this legislation that, anonymously for reasons of personal safety, Jefferson and Madison drafted the Resolutions that the Kentucky and Virginia legislatures were persuaded to approve and sponsor and which were then circulated among the states. Government, said Madison, is a compact "to which the states are parties." When the federal government exercised unconstitutional powers it was the right and duty of the state to object. The states, wrote Jefferson for the Kentucky legislature, could decide what measures were "void and of no force." In 1799 these states passed a second set of Resolutions to the effect that "the rightful remedy for a state was nullification." It is doubtful that the authors intended to formulate the compact theory of the Constitution or develop the theory of nullification. Indeed, both Jefferson and Madison denied that the Resolutions were intended to advocate disunion. In later years Madison declared that the Virginia and Kentucky Resolutions were written purely as campaign documents, which later Americans in 1832 and again in 1860 would cite.

The mood of the years 1798–1800 would in itself have ensured a change of government in 1800s: it was helped by the split between Adams and Hamilton, and by the skill with which for a decade Jefferson had manufactured a national party from a number of sectional groups, and given it a liberal and republican character. There was much to feed on: the free-speech curbs of the Alien and Sedition legislation, the burden of taxes the Federalists had levied to pay for the undeclared war with France, the continuing impressment by Britain of American seamen, the rising national debt, and indeed Hamilton's whole program for capitalist development, from the national debt to the Bank of the United States. Behind all of these particular issues, there was the ideological issue: pro-British or pro-French; a strong national government or a limited government; "consolidation" or states' rights. There were also "mottos" or slogans in plenty, some of them scurrilous. The hapless Adams was a pro-British "Monocrat", "King John the First." In turn, Federalists asked the voters whether they would prefer "GOD – AND A RELIGIOUS PRESIDENT;" or impiously declare for "JEFFERSON – AND NO GOD!!!" – Jefferson, an "intellectual voluptuary," whose serene home at Monticello ought to be called "Dog's Misery," because Jefferson practiced vivisection there.

While the Federalists were busy with rhetoric, the Republicans were busy with organization. Marache's boarding house in Philadelphia, where Republicans had tended to stay when Congress was in session, became a virtual national headquarters. At Marache's in May 1800 some 40 congressmen and other Republicans held a caucus to select the nominees for President and Vice-President. Jefferson was the obvious choice for President; and most of the group favored Aaron Burr for the vice-presidential entry. In the tough school of New York, Burr had proved his extraordinary ability as a political organizer, particularly among the masses of New York City. Moreover, his nomination would confirm the New York-Virginia axis that the Republicans had relied on in the past. Republican party organization was impressive from Massachusetts in the North to John Beckley's Pennsylvania, as well as in Maryland, where the able merchant-politician Samuel Smith took the lead. Most of the Southern and Southwestern states looked "safe," and at least the beginnings of Republican organization could be found as far as South Carolina — once firmly Federalist, but no longer so. In the end, adroit propaganda, the Republican press, and organization were to triumph.

As we have seen, 16 states participated in the election of 1800, as they had in 1796. But this time, ironically, only five states chose presidential electors by popular vote, as compared to seven in 1796; the rest were chosen by state legislatures. Despite Hamilton's continued intrigues against Adams, Adams was the Federalist champion, while Charles Pinckney was the Federalist choice for Vice-President. Both parties had learned to concentrate their electoral votes on one candidate for each office, in order to make the most of their strength. When the electoral votes were counted, Jefferson and Burr each had 73, while Adams had 65 and Pinckney 64. Once again, the Federalists swept the five New England states — and won in New Jersey and Delaware. The Republicans carried crucial New York and all of the six Southern and Southwestern states except North Carolina, which divided, 8 for Jefferson and 8 for Adams — as did Maryland, 5 to 5.

Nonetheless, the outcome was clear. The 12-year rule of the Federalists — of Washington, Hamilton, and Adams — was over. The fact was dramatically underscored by the congressional results. The Republicans had elected 66 members to the House of Representatives that would convene in 1801, to only 40 for the once invincible Federalists. The Senate, with only about a third of its members facing election in each two years, would also have a Republican majority — 18 seats to 14. Future elections would augment the Republican forces in Congress at Federalist expense, and the Federalists would never win the presidency again. Or so it seemed, and was in the end; but it took time. Jefferson and Burr each had 73 electoral votes. The Constitution stipulated that the "person having the greatest Number of [electoral] Votes shall be the President, if such Number be a Majority." But, in case of a tie, the House of Representatives would make the choice, with each state delegation having one vote. Although Jefferson was the choice of his party, technically Burr had the same number of electoral votes. The House would have to settle the matter. The House in turn had been elected in 1798; and the Federalists had a majority there. In this situation, a group of die-hard Federalists schemed to deny Jefferson his victory, and make Aaron Burr president. If this stratagem succeeded, they assumed, Burr would be pliant to their wishes. The Republicans, of course, protested against such "chicane" and corruption.

In the House – the first to meet in the new capital city of Washington – ballot after ballot was taken in February of 1801. As March 4 approached – the day the new president had to take office – there was no resolution. Rumors spread that irate Jeffersonians were planning to march on the Capitol and make Jefferson President by force of arms. The issue was a major constitutional and political crisis. But on the 36th ballot, on February 17, the deadlock was broken. Enough Federalists absented themselves from the House to give Jefferson the majority of states that was required – they could not bring themselves to vote for him, but they would abstain, many of them persuaded by Hamilton and his distrust of Burr.

On the last day of December 1800, Dr Nathaniel Ames of Dedham, Massachusetts, considered the American past, and what he thought the future would bring. Dr Ames was the brother of the arch-Federalist Fisher Ames, but the doctor was a strong Republican, as many physicians were at the time. "Here ends the 18th Century," Dr Ames wrote. "The 19th begins with a fine clear morning wind at S. W.; and the political horizon affords as fine a prospect under Jefferson's administration, with the irresistible propagation of the Rights of Man, the eradication of hierarchy, oppression, superstition and tyranny." But his brother's hatred for Jefferson and Madison, the leaders of the democratic forces, was apoplectic. He called them "those apostles of the race-track and the cock-pit."[6]

Thus the "Revolution of 1800:" not smooth – rancorous, and personally bitter. But at least, it was as the Constitution prescribed.

[6] Vernon L. Parrington, *The Connecticut Wits XXII*, quoted in Saul K. Padover, *Jefferson* (London, Jonathan Cape, 1942), p. 178.

The Constitution at least endured, and there was no blood on the streets.

2 THE REVOLUTION OF 1800

Jefferson was the first President to be inaugurated at Washington, to which the capital had been moved from Philadelphia in June, 1800. The new national capital was hardly more than a village, with 3,200 inhabitants. Only one wing of the Capitol building was ready for use. The White House was unfinished, part unplastered, and the principal staircase was not even begun. The streets were rough roads through the swamps and underbrush which covered most of the site of the future city. A few stone chips from some of the public buildings, thrown into the worst mud holes, were the only signs of sidewalks. Yet when he walked from his new home to the Capitol in March 1801, Jefferson saw his election victory as a pacific revolution – "as real a revolution in the principles of government as that of 1776 was in its form." For the first time in the Republic – indeed, the first time in modern history – a smooth and bloodless transfer of power took place.[7] "The Federalists wished," he wrote later, "for everything which would approach our new government to a monarchy; the Republicans to preserve it essentially republican." He moved cautiously. In his Inaugural Address in March 1801 – the first to be delivered in the new federal Capitol, but so softly spoken that few could hear it – he appealed for unity. There was to be friendship with all nations, "entangling alliances with none" – a clear indication that the alliance of 1778 with France was safely dead. "We are all Republicans," he said, "we are all Federalists." He appointed his two ablest lieutenants, Madison and the Swiss-born Albert Gallatin, to the secretaryships of state and of the Treasury, but he gave Cabinet posts to New Englanders – where Federalism was strong – and did not rush to dismiss Federalists from office: to the distress of his followers, who held that rotation in office was a high republican principle, which, when translated, meant that to the victors belonged all the spoils. The Federalists had increased the number of judges in their last moments of power. Jefferson resented the Federalists' "death clutch on the patronage," and ordered that those officials who had not received

---

[7] C. H. de Witt, *Jefferson and the American Democracy*, trans. R. S. Church (London, Longman's Green, 1862), p. 2.

their commissions before Adams's term expired should not be appointed to office. He prevailed upon Congress to repeal the Judiciary Act of 1801 and other Federalist Acts. Federalists holding office in the federal service were not discharged, although Jefferson complained that, disobligingly, they neither died nor resigned. But gradually and deftly the Republicans got their rewards. By July 1803, of 316 posts in the gift of the President, 186 were held by Republicans.

Jefferson's first term was one of remarkable success. The whiskey excise which hurt the Western farmers was repealed; it cost the government $1 million a year in revenue, but the repeal not only honored a party pledge, it also reduced the number of federal tax officials. The civil and armed services were reduced in number, and taxes and the national debt were reduced also. The Alien Act was allowed to lapse; all jailed under the Sedition Act were released. Jefferson favored a liberal naturalization policy: America was to be a haven for all who sought freedom. State after state abolished property qualifications for the suffrage and passed more humane laws for debtors and criminals. And an important constitutional amendment, the Twelfth, was enacted. In the presidential election of 1796 a Federalist, Adams, had been elected President and a Republican, Jefferson, Vice-President. Now in 1800 the electoral system had again failed. Its failure was clearly due to the fact that the framers of the Constitution had not provided for the rise of political parties. An amendment to the Constitution was needed to give constitutional recognition to the rise of the party system of government. The new Republican Congress proposed the Twelfth Amendment, which went into effect in 1804. By it, electors were to cast separate ballots for President and Vice-President. The Constitution was not again amended until after the Civil War.

Jefferson, both as a naturalist and as a piedmont Virginian, looked West. The Kentucky and Virginian Resolutions identified him clearly with the states. And the problems of the West appealed to him, even if he had to act against his first principles in order to help them. For the trans-Appalachian population, which rose in numbers from 100,000 in 1790 to 400,000 in 1801, needed federal help. New states, like Kentucky and Tennessee, and territories soon to become states like Ohio, could not raise enough money from taxes to build the roads and bridges and schools they needed.

In the older states, private companies were being chartered and were being given rights of way on liberal terms as well as the right to charge tolls for the use of the roads or turnpikes they constructed. The states governments aided the companies with grants from the proceeds of the sale of the state lands, or authorized lotteries by which money was raised, or made the privileges of the companies look so attractive that men with money were eager to lend the necessary capital. By 1811 New York had chartered 137 turnpike companies. Eight turnpikes radiated from Albany as from a hub. One of the most successful roads was the Philadelphia and Lancaster turnpike, 62 miles long, following almost a beeline between the two cities. Along these turnpikes taverns were built where travelers might stop for the night. Stagecoach lines announced regular services.

In the West, however, the communities were too small and scattered for it to be profitable for private companies to function. The federal government agreed to set aside one-twentieth of the income from the land sales within the state as a special fund for the construction of a road to extend from Cumberland, Maryland, on the Potomac to Wheeling on the Ohio. In 1806 Congress appropriated $30,000, but the work of construction was not started until 1811. Ultimately, this National Road (also called the Cumberland Road) was extended from Wheeling across Ohio and Indiana to Vandalia in Illinois (1838).

When Ohio became a state in 1802 its population was about 50,000. By 1811 it had reached 230,000. Kentucky, with 220,000 people in 1800, had 406,000 in 1810, and the population of Tennessee increased from 105,000 to 260,000 in the same 10-year period. Land companies put out pamphlets describing the value of their lands. So great was the rush of westward-bound settlers that the landowners of the East raised a protest against the "plots to drain the East of its best blood." But the lure of the West overcame every effort to stop the migration.

3 THE LOUISIANA PURCHASE

Around 1650, what is now the US was a vast unexplored wilderness – although Spanish explorers and adventurers had nibbled at the southern and southeastern regions. For instance, Alvar Nuñez Cabeza de Vaca had from 1728 to 1736 made his way from the ruins of an abortive expedition to Florida along the southern shore of what is now the US, recognizing the Mississippi River and making his landfall at what is now Galveston. He wandered through what are now Texas, New Mexico, and Arizona, at last reaching the Spanish settlements in Mexico. This expedition provided much information, but not about the heart of the continent. Further Spanish

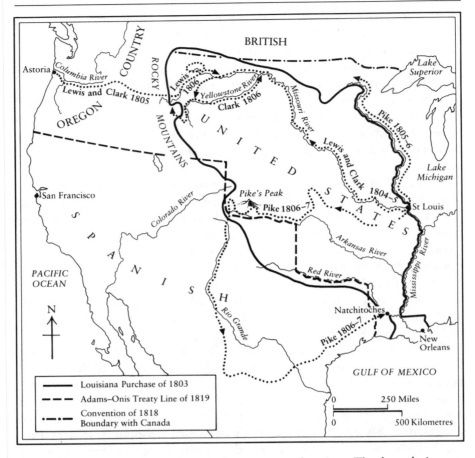

Map 2 The Louisiana Purchase and western exploration. The boundaries ran roughly along the continental divide or down the Mississippi River, but it was unclear whether the Purchase — which doubled the size of the US — included Texas and West Florida.

exploration was limited by climate, terrain, and the hostility of the Indians. In the seventeenth century the chief exploratory effort was French. La Salle descended the Mississippi and claimed for his king a vague area he called "Louisiana." He was murdered by mutineers in Texas in 1687, after a three-year expedition to establish a base at the mouth of the Mississippi. In 1698 a French naval expedition led by Pierre de Moyne, Sieur d'Iberville, established a fort at Biloxi. The first French permanent settlement in Louisiana was at Natchitoches in 1714. New Orleans was founded in 1718.

French colonists, in their traditional quest for furs and Spanish gold, moved into the area near the confluence of the Mississippi and Missouri rivers, but by 1762 only one settlement of consequence had been founded there: Ste Geneviève, 50 miles south of what is now St Louis. In 1762 Louisiana was transferred from France to Spain, her ally in the Seven Years' War (known in America as the French and Indian War), by a secret agreement, the treaty of Fontainebleau, and in 1764, under Spanish rule, St Louis was founded. In 1763, the Treaty of Paris ended the War. By its terms, France ceded to Britain all of Canada and all land east of the Mississippi except New Orleans. Thus France lost out to all; and, with in the end miserable consequences, for Britain and for Spain territorial imperialism replaced commercial mercantilism.

In 1800, Napoleon compelled Spain to cede Louisiana to France by a secret treaty. Napoleon kept the matter secret and delayed taking possession because the news might well provoke a Spanish, British, or American invasion. He had his own dreams of a vast Empire in the Americas, West, Central and Caribbean. The food and lumber of Louisiana would complement the products of France's West Indian plantations. The prospect alarmed Jefferson who, like all Westerners, feared a strong power at the mouth of the Mississippi, down which Western products moved and from which as exports they went to foreign markets. "There is on the globe one single spot, the possession of which is our natural and habitual enemy ... The day that France takes possession of New Orleans" Jefferson said: "We must marry ourselves to the British fleet and nation."[8] In August 1802 he instructed Robert Livingston, the American minister in Paris, to open negotiations with France for the purchase of a sufficient area at the mouth of the river to guarantee freedom of navigation and transshipment of cargoes. He sent his young lieutenant James Monroe to help Livingston effectively to obtain New Orleans.[9]

By the time of Monroe's arrival, events had moved in his favor. The truce agreed at Amiens in 1802 was over, and Europe was again at war. For Napoleon, Europe came first. Moreover, Napoleon was being compelled to abandon his great dreams of a western empire because of the opposition French troops were meeting in the island of Santo Domingo, where the great black leader, Toussaint l'Ouverture, – in origin a coachman, fed on Revolutionary ideas – was putting up a furious opposition and tying down 30,000 men.

---

[8] Ford, *Writings of Jefferson*, vol. VIII, pp. 145–6.
[9] For the negotiations of the purchase of Louisiana see Henry Adams, *History of the United States of America during the First Administration of Thomas Jefferson* (New York, Scribner's, 1889–90), vol. I, chs 14–17, vol. II, chs 1–6.

They were decimated by guerrilla war and even more by yellow fever. By the time Monroe arrived, Napoleon had offered the sale of Louisiana for 80 million francs ($15 million), and the offer was accepted, almost with alarm at its boldness and the prospects it opened up. The American commissioners had gone to bargain for the security of, perhaps the purchase of, New Orleans. Without time to await instructions, they paid more than they were authorized to do – but they doubled the size of the republic, and acquired territory from which in the end 13 new states would be carved.

Hamilton would have enjoyed conquering Louisiana by force of arms (and in the characteristic fashion of politicians criticized Jefferson for doing peacefully what he would have liked to do himself and at far greater expense). Other Federalists feared that it would alter the character of the Union by increasing the slave power, and wanted the new territory to remain colonial in style. Jefferson had other notions; he used not troops but hard cash, and made not only a great free society but a bargain. He bought the 820,000 acres of Louisiana for three cents an acre; it was "the biggest real estate deal in history," or in Talleyrand's words "a noble bargain." In 1804 it had about 50,000 inhabitants; by 1904 they numbered 20 million; and by 2004 they are likely to exceed 100 million. Once again the United States was the happy beneficiary of the diplomatic tensions of Europe.

This accession of territory, however vast and rich in resources, raised serious constitutional issues, for it was far from clear that the President had authority under the Constitution to acquire territory on this scale and in this way. Moreover, one who had opposed the "loose construction" views of Hamilton was now imposing arbitrary government in the new territory. The liberal could, it seemed, be both empire-builder and expansionist, and, of course, to the Republicans' advantage, for this clearly would be an empire for free men with votes. But the Senate approved the deal and the United States formally took possession of the new and as yet unmapped country in December 1803.

In his Third Annual Message to Congress in 1803, Jefferson laid out the background to the acquisition, and the measures Congress needed to take to secure it:

Congress witnessed, at their last session, the extraordinary agitation produced in the public mind by the suspension of our right of deposit at the port of New Orleans. ... Previous, however, to this period, we had not been unaware of the danger to which our peace would be perpetually exposed while so important a key to the commerce of the western country remained under foreign power. Difficulties, too, were presenting themselves as to the navigation of other streams, which arising within territories, pass through those adjacent. Propositions had, therefore, been authorized for obtaining, on fair conditions, the sovereignty of New Orleans, and of other possessions in that quarter interesting to our quiet. ...

The property and sovereignty of all Louisiana ... have on certain conditions been transferred to the United States ... While the property and sovereignty of the Mississippi and its waters secure an independent outlet for the produce of the Western States, and an uncontrolled navigation through their whole course, free from collision with other powers and the dangers to our peace from that source, the fertility of the country, its climate and extent, promise in due season important aids to our treasury, an ample provision for our posterity, and a wide-spread field for the blessings of freedom and equal laws. With the wisdom of Congress it will rest to take those ulterior measures which may be necessary for the immediate occupation and temporary government of the country; for its incorporation into our Union; for rendering the change of government a blessing to our newly-adopted brethren; for securing to them the rights of conscience and property; for confirming to the Indian inhabitants their occupancy and self-government, establishing friendly and commercial relations with them, and for ascertaining the geography of the country acquired.

However, no one was clear about what "Louisiana" actually meant, since the treaty of cession merely quoted the nebulous provisions of the earlier, secret treaties. Furthermore, there was little detailed and accurate geological or geographical knowledge of the area. There had been earlier explorations of the new territory — in 1771 Samuel Hearne of the Hudson's Bay Company found that the Coppermine River led not to the Pacific but to the Arctic; and in 1789 Alexander Mackenzie too ended up in the Arctic, and found a chain of mountains between him and the Pacific. Did these mountains run the length of the continent? Was there a river — and the Missouri seemed the most likely — from which a short portage would carry an explorer to the Western ocean? Jefferson calculated that the portage would be some 20 miles in length; it proved to be several hundred. Were there other Indian tribes than the Arikaras, their numbers known to be weakened by smallpox, or the Sioux, closely bound to British fur-traders? It was this last factor, the fear of the growth of a Canadian fur trust, that led Jefferson to send his own team, and to try to keep their journey as secret as possible. Meantime, Jefferson saw it all as Indian country, to be put under military administration. As governor he appointed General James Wilkinson, US commander in the Southwest, whom we now know

had been in Spanish pay for years. Wilkinson became an ally of
Aaron Burr, and then suspect as a traitor. In the end he betrayed
Burr, who was arrested in New Orleans, brought back a prisoner
and tried for treason in Richmond. The Wilkinson appointment
was not in any event one of Jefferson's wisest appointments, since
the post combined military and civil functions. But the future proved
golden: Louisiana with its present boundaries was admitted as a
state in 1812, bringing with it its own institutions and its own
code of French civil law.

Louisiana was the greatest, but not the sole, example of Jefferson's readiness to bend his ideas in office; the philosopher could
be a pragmatist when it was necessary. The President who was
by nature sensitive and shy founded West Point, the US Military
Academy. Congress was ruled firmly by one who had claimed (and
continued to claim) to be a believer in the separation of powers.
A successful war was begun against the Barbary corsairs (1802–5)
by the most pacific-minded of men ("Peace is our passion," he
had said.) In advocating and encouraging internal improvements
to help the agricultural areas to get their supplies to market, the
Republicans were hard to distinguish from Federalists. If politics
makes strange bedfellows, office seems to make for inconsistency
in its occupants. But on exploration and interest in geology Jefferson had always been consistent. Louisiana for him was thus
a treasure trove. Its boundaries were uncertain. And into the vast
and unknown West he sent an expedition led by fellow Virginians
Meriwether Lewis, his secretary, and William Clark. Jefferson had,
in fact, been preparing to send his own expedition West even before the Purchase. He had chosen Meriwether Lewis to be his
private secretary in Washington in 1801, partly because he and
his ancestors were trustworthy neighbours in Albemarle County,
and he had tastes akin to his own; partly because of his military experience with Anthony Wayne in his campaign against the
Indians in the Northwest Territory; but primarily to prepare him
for an expedition West: with consultations galore with scientists
and astronomers, and much use of Jefferson's library. He relied
heavily on Jefferson's copy of Antoine du Pratz's *History of Louisiana*; Pratz was a French engineer who had been there from 1718
to 1734, and who also believed in a short portage between the
east-flowing and the west-flowing waters. Lewis even had a French
passport – since the plans were made before the American acquisition of Louisiana. Captains Lewis and Clark were each instructed to keep a detailed daily record of all they saw, as were
the other ranks, if they could write – seven of them did. They were

to record "what the Indians wore, what they ate, how they made a living, and what they believed in." The copious notes and documents they brought back record flora and fauna encountered, geographical and geological details, meteorological and climatological data, and the ethnography of the Indians. Much of this information had to be based on observation of the material culture, for the barrier of language (the interpreters were inadequate) made probes into religious beliefs, for example, difficult if not impossible. But the captains worked on languages, drawing up lists of words when time and circumstances permitted and attempting to identify language groups. In an epic two-and-a-half year journey they crossed the Rockies and by way of the Snake and Columbia Rivers reached the Pacific (November 1805), established a claim to the Oregon Country, and explored and mapped an area America was "destined to fill with arts, with science, with freedom and happiness."

This is one of the great adventure stories in American history. They lived off the country. The main Indian tribes on their route were the Arikaras and the Sioux, and both were hostile to European penetration into the heart of the continent, since they desired the role of middlemen in the fur trade. The Arikaras had been a very powerful people in Spanish and French experience, but had been weakened by a smallpox epidemic and by the migration of the Sioux. The Sioux had more reason to oppose Lewis and Clark than simply being "warlike;" they were closely bound to British fur-trading interests (British goods were better and cheaper than American) and susceptible to British political influence.

They were helped much of the way, and greatly impressed, by a remarkable Shoshone girl, Sacajawea, "the Canoe Launcher". She and her baby became the "pets" of the expedition, for whom her husband, the French Canadian Toussaint Charbonneau, was guide and interpreter. She had been captured in childhood by the Sioux, and had been bought from them by Charbonneau.

The expedition brought back reports of a land rich in furs and grizzly bears, of the majesty, scale – and terror – of the Rockies, and – wrongly – that this was the quick route to Cathay. Their map appeared in 1814, five years after Lewis's tragic death. It was a remarkable journey, well planned and well executed. It was planned at Monticello, and drew much from William Bartram's observation as botanist, and the skill of the members of the American Philosophical Society. And Jefferson's friend Dr Benjamin Rush in Philadelphia planned the hygiene of the trip. His notes included the sage counsel: "Lie down when fatigued." It was apparently carefully honored; of the 50 men in the "Corps of Discovery" only one died (from appendicitis), although one deserted.[10]

For Meriwether Lewis, it was a tremendous, an overwhelming, experience. At the outset he thought he was to travel through a garden – or was he saying so because he was hearing the echoes of his master's voice? He did count herds of buffalo 3,000 strong. But, as he proceeded, Nature he found to be awesome, even frightening, no idyllic garden but a land of "towering and projecting rocks ... every object here wears a dark and gloomy aspect." When he first saw the Rockies, they proved to be no replica of his familiar Blue Ridge but "broken" and snow-crested. The cactus and prickly pear shredded the men's feet; the river banks in what is now known as the Breaks of the Missouri were precipitous and dangerous; the Great Falls of the Missouri took three weeks to bypass. The short portage was a myth: it took two months to reach the upper reaches of the Columbia River. The winter of 1805/6 was spent in the constant rains of the North Pacific coast. They did not reach St Louis again until 23 September 1806. The West was no garden of Eden, but full of hazards and horrors. He had so many horrors to recount, from being accidentally wounded by his own men, to a bloody encounter with a grizzly bear and to a skirmish with Indians, that there are gaps in his diary (as from August 1805 to January 1, 1806). Nature in Montana could be malevolent in a fashion alien to forest-cleared Albemarle County; even perhaps a threat to the balance of an imaginative traveller's mind. Three years later, in 1809, when returning to Washington from St Louis, the territorial capital, along the Natchez Trace from his governorship of the Louisiana Territory, Lewis died – either of suicide, as Jefferson believed, or of murder by bandits. He was returning to Washington to explain discrepancies in the Territory's accounts. He was only 35.

In 1806 Zebulon Pike similarly explored the Southwest. Although he failed to find the source of the Mississippi, he led a party up

---

[10] For Lewis and Clark, see Donald Jackson's superb edition of *Letters of the Lewis and Clark Expedition* (Urbana, University of Illinois Press, 1978), and Bernard De Voto's readable *The Course of Empire* (Boston, Little, Brown, 1952), and his own edition of the *Journals of Lewis and Clark* (Boston, Houghton Mifflin, 1953); also James P. Ronda, essay review, "'The writingest explorers,' the Lewis and Clark Expedition in American historical literature," *Pennsylvania Magazine of History and Biography*, 112.4 (Oct. 1988); idem, "Dreams and discoveries, exploring the American West, 1760–1815," *William & Mary Quarterly*, 46.1 (Jan. 1989), pp. 145–62; and William Goetzmann's essay review, "Chronicling the Second Great Age of Discovery," *Pennsylvania Magazine of History and Biography*, 114.1 (Jan. 1990).

the Arkansas River and sighted the peak in Colorado that now
bears his name. Jefferson's interest in Western land and his certainty of American destiny were as striking as Washington's. He
wanted not only to avoid entangling alliances with Europe but to
keep Europe – if possible – out of America, North and South and
West. This was not easy, and in fact was only made possible because of the generation-long Revolutionary and Napoleonic struggle
in Europe, which kept it totally preoccupied. Jefferson believed that
America was not only distant from Europe, but distinct. It was
indeed a garden. To him the most striking feature of America was
its abundance of land, conferred on the former not by the state
but by a beneficent Nature, and by man's own enterprise and skill
in mixing his own labor with it. This made of it the "property"
that Jefferson valued as much as any contemporary. Jeffersonian
democracy was rooted not in equality and socialism, but in land
and its availability. Jefferson saw the New World as different from
the Old, in its natural resources, geology and wild life, its animals
and its people. He even suggested a design for an American order
of architecture: a column fashioned like a bundle of cornstalks, and
a capital in the shape of the leaves and flowers of tobacco. These
were its distinctive crops, growing in native soil.

Consistency is no monopoly of academics-turned-politicians, if
that is an adequate description of Thomas Jefferson. Indeed, for
them consistency is a rarity. So it was with him. Recent studies
of him have made it plain. He gave jobs to many of his people,
if he was too restrained to suit all who proclaimed their allegiance.
He worried over but ignored constitutional niceties in order to
double American territory. Nothing in the Constitution authorized
the acquisition of foreign territory, much less its incorporation with
the Union. He drafted a constitutional amendment – "an act of
indemnity" – to sanction his action retroactively. Congress did not
deem it necessary.

Some recent students of the Revolutionary period recognize that
there is much that is myth (or, more accurately, rhetoric for pamphlet and propaganda) about the citizen-soldier as the bulwark of
the Republic: Cincinnatus is in fact more efficient at his plow than
with his musket. Despite his natural pacifism, and despite the indictment Jefferson drew up in 1776, in order to win in 1756–63
and again in 1776–83, the new nation had had to train a professional army, the Continental Line. After a long war, and successive
frontier crises, once in authority Jefferson had to abandon reliance
on militia armies. Hence the foundation of West Point in 1802,
and the dramatic increase in the size of the army. Antony Wayne's

anti-Indian force was a legion, and with a distinct style. Moreover, Jefferson had to cleanse the army of its Federalist taint, and to turn it into an instrument of service for the new democratic republic. He kept Wilkinson in command in the Southwest only because he had no senior qualified Republican to replace him. In 1808 he needed trustworthy and trained Republicans for command should the crisis come. He came to believe in a professional cadre, which in a crisis would be expanded by enlisted men. So it had been, so it would be again. Inconsistent with his creed perhaps: but, once again, intelligent, cool and immensely rational.[11]

A searching analysis of Jefferson's ideology is that by Joyce Appleby. Jefferson's language remained that of 1776, that of a nostalgic agrarian radical with a taste for apothegms and epigrams. But behind the phrases he realized that America offered an opportunity for ordinary people to prosper in an Atlantic market. From 1783 the Jeffersonian Republicans were urging policies of making new lands available to farmers and of developing internal improvements. Such policies were "neither regional, nor strictly speaking agrarian;" they did not pit rich against poor, or the commercially inclined against the self-sufficient, but sought a freely developing economy that would benefit all, would eradicate privilege and stimulate the natural harmony of interest among the propertied that Locke had assumed. This was forward-looking, not nostalgic; liberal and capitalist, American not Civil War England nor France of 1789. They saw the future and realized that it worked.[12]

[11] Theodore J. Crackel, *Mr Jefferson's Army: Political and social reform of the military establishment 1801–1809* (New York, New York University Press, 1987); Lawrence D. Cress, *Citizens in Arms: The army and the militia in American society to the War of 1812* (Chapel Hill, NC, University of North Carolina Press, 1982); John E. Ferling, *A Wilderness of Miseries: War and warriors in early America* (Westport, Conn., Greenwood Press, 1980); Richard H. Kohn, *Eagle and Sword: The Federalists and the creation of the military establishment in America, 1783–1802* (New York, Free Press, 1973).
[12] Joyce Appleby, *Capitalism and a New Social Order: The Republican vision of the 1790s* (New York, New York University Press, 1984); "Commercial farming and the agrarian myth in the early Republic," *Journal of American History*, 67 (1982), pp. 833–49; and idem, "Republicanism in old and new contexts," *William & Mary Quarterly*, 43.1 (Jan. 1986)), pp. 20–34. cf. Isaac Kramnick, "Republican revisionism revisited," *American Historical Review*, 87 (1982), pp. 629–44, and Lance Banning, "Jeffersonian ideology revisited: liberal and classical ideas in the new American republic," *William & Mary Quarterly*, 43.1 (Jan. 1986), pp. 3–19.

4 JEFFERSON'S SECOND TERM

Helped by Aaron Burr's intrigues and by his murder of Hamilton, which threw the Federalists into chaos, and with an impressive first term record, in the election of 1804 Jefferson won every state except Delaware and Connecticut. In 1800 he had had 73 votes in the electoral college; in 1804 he had 162 out of 176. As Vice-President, Burr was dropped in favor of George Clinton of New York – and thereafter Burr became the thorn in the side of the Administration, an ambitious intriguer in the New West. In the 1806 congressional elections the Republicans elected four-fifths of the senators and five-sixths of the congressmen.

In his second term, as in his first, Jefferson was bedeviled by the problems of Europe, and this time the experience was less happy and much less successful. By 1806 Napoleon's attempt to defeat Britain by invasion or by sea battle had failed, and the emperor was forced to reduce the power of the island by economic blockade. Blockade bred counter-blockade by Britain, first of France and then of all French-controlled Europe. This was a war between land and sea, between the Elephant and the Whale. Moreover, this was war – as in 1776–83 – at the expense of the trading neutrals, especially of the fledgling United States. In such a struggle the little neutrals went to the wall. British mercantile interests were in any event alarmed at the rapid growth of American commerce and shipping after the ending of the Truce of Amiens. A series of British decisions made neutral trade increasingly difficult. In the Essex case (1805), British courts held that a neutral ship laden with enemy goods, destined ultimately for an enemy port, could not change the character of the voyage by landing at a neutral port and making a pretense of trans-shipping the goods. American ships, loading in French or Spanish West Indies with goods destined for France or Spain, could not make the shipment a neutral one by breaking the voyage at an American port. Taking full advantage of its superior sea-power, Great Britain issued several orders which crippled the neutral traders quite as much as the enemy. The Fox Blockade of April 1806 closed the ports of northern Europe from the south of the Elbe to Brest; an order in Council of January 1807 forbade coastwise trade between ports in the power of France or its allies; and an order of November 1807 blockaded all European ports from which the British flag was excluded, and forced neutrals to trade with the continent through Great Britain.

The right of stopping and searching American ships and removing suspected seamen became a matter of tension, and of national pride. The most flagrant example was the case of the *Chesapeake* in 1807. This American frigate was approached ten miles from the mouth of Chesapeake Bay by a British warship, the *Leopard*, with a request to allow a search to be made for a British deserter believed to be aboard. The presence of deserters was denied and the demand was rejected; after the boarding party had returned, the *Leopard* suddenly loosed three broadsides at the *Chesapeake*, which, with 20 serious casualties, was forced to strike her flag. A second British boarding party found deserters, including a malcontent ringleader, who were on board unknown to the American commander. Such insults as these, or the searching of ships at the very mouth of New York harbor, provoked American resentment. The situation was complicated by the superior conditions in the United States fleet and the lax United States naturalization laws.

The British policy was the occasion for retaliatory decrees issued by Napoleon, which equally seriously hindered neutral carrying trade. The Berlin Decree of November 1806 forbade all commerce with the British Isles and ordered the seizure of ships coming from Britain or her colonies to ports under French control. The Milan Decree of December 1807 declared that all ships which paid a tax to the British government were "good prize." By subsequent decrees – Bayonne (1808), Rambouillet (1810), and Trianon (1810) – Napoleon sequestered American vessels in French ports and confiscated their cargoes.

The warfare of orders and decrees seriously injured, though it did not ruin, the American carrying trade. Jefferson was convinced that some form of economic boycott would bring the belligerents to the point of honoring American neutrality; they had been, after all, the devices used in "his" war, 30 years before. The Non-Importation Act (1806) excluded important British manufactures from American ports. The Embargo Act of December 1807 forbade all American vessels from sailing to Europe, and Federal agents were given the right to search out and seize ships and goods suspected of violating the law. However, this policy, labeled "peaceable coercion," was at once noble, intelligent – and disastrous. Not only the merchants but many who depended on them turned bitterly against the Administration. "Embargo" written backward was seen to spell "O grab me," which provided a text for many hostile cartoons. In New England, Federalists roused themselves to denounce the scheme as a Southern plot to ruin the political as well as the economic influence of the North. Jefferson had over-estimated the economic importance of the

United States in British trade. British traders, the "shopkeepers" of whom Napoleon was so unwisely contemptuous, smuggled goods into America over the Canadian border, and opened alternative markets in South America, which, after the overthrow of the Spanish monarchy in 1808, enjoyed under various *juntas* complete freedom of trade. The enforcement of the Embargo constituted at home a direct invasion of private liberties. Jefferson was driven to enforcing his policy by federal intervention; another volte-face for the drafter of the Kentucky Resolutions and the President who had promised in his first inaugural "the support of the state governments in all their rights, as the most competent administrations for our domestic concerns and the surest bulwarks against anti-Republican tendencies." "You infernal villain," wrote one New Englander to the philosopher-President. "How much longer are you going to keep this damned embargo on to starve us poor people?" It hurt the trade of New England and drove it into High Federalism, and into bitter secessionist talk and plotting voiced by Timothy Pickering, formerly Adams's secretary of state, by the "Essex Junto" in Massachusetts, and by the "River Gods" of Connecticut, whose capital and chief port, New Haven, was wrecked by the controls. Bankruptcies were common. New York ceased to be Republican political territory. The word "secession" was heard — and would be heard more loudly later.

The embargo brought the wartime prosperity of the United States to a sudden end. Exports for the year 1808 dropped suddenly to $22,000,000 from $108,000,000 in 1807; customs revenue fell from 16 to 7 million dollars. It has been estimated that more than 150,000 men (mostly sailors, merchants, and laborers) lost their jobs as a result of the embargo. Some merchants reverted to the colonial practice of smuggling to avoid a law they thought unjust. Hard times spread over the once prosperous land. The army was strengthened, and some curious and unseaworthy gunboats were built for the fleet, designed for defense, not offense. The Federalists improved their political position in the 1808 election; and a few days before Jefferson left office, Congress decided to replace the Embargo by a Non-Intercourse Act: trade was reopened with other countries, but not with Britain or France; but the new President, James Madison, was authorized to resume trade with whichever of the two belligerents agreed to respect American rights. When obligingly, in August 1810, Napoleon announced that he would rescind his decrees affecting American trade, the US invoked Non-Intercourse only against Britain.

As would happen again in World War I, the effort to preserve both American neutrality and American rights abroad was high-minded but heavy-handed, and was hard to reconcile with liberalism at home. Equally hard to reconcile with Jefferson's earlier anti-British record had been his readiness in 1803 to "marry ourselves to the English fleet and nation;" it was equally hard to reconcile this with his First Inaugural Address and his arguments against "entangling alliances." Indeed, Jefferson found himself indirectly and unintentionally encouraging the very industry he feared, because American capital, cut off from investment in overseas commerce, was switched to manufacturing. On all sides, the agrarian order seemed to be threatened. "We must now place the manufacturer by the side of the agriculturist," said Jefferson. He can indeed be called, however reluctant he might be, almost a Hamiltonian, almost a father of the factory system.

This policy, which after 1808 his successors Madison and Monroe continued, was, in its nationalism, its preparedness, its protective tariffs, its second Bank and its centralized character, hard to distinguish from Federalism itself: the old High Federalists of Essex County in Massachusetts, tempted by secession, found themselves by 1814 in an unnatural alliance of protest with Southern liberals, in opposition to this new and strange Democratic-Republicanism. This pattern too was to recur, as in 1940, when F. D. Roosevelt's Democratic party showed itself in office more sympathetic to centralized power than it had ever been in opposition. On both occasions, the shift of ground was a reflection less of political inconsistency than of the permanence of sectional economic interests. Jefferson's second term had left his reputation tarnished. Henry Adams summarized its contradictions thus:

He had undertaken to create a government which should interfere in no way with private action, and he created one which interfered directly in the concerns of every private citizen in the land. He had come to power as the champion of states' rights, and had driven states to the verge of armed resistance. He had begun by claiming credit for stern economy, and ended by exceeding the expenditure of his predecessors. He had invented a policy of peace, and his invention resulted in the necessity of fighting at once the two greatest powers in the world. [13]

Jefferson's genius shone brightest in opposition.

From his most acute problems in his second term, he was in part rescued by his critics' own personalities. John Randolph of Roanoke, his party leader in the House of Representatives in his

---

[13] Adams, *History of the USA*, vol. II, p. 281.

first term, erratic and unstable in all his eloquent invective, criticized his attempt to acquire Spanish West Florida because it
amounted, he contended, to bribing France to bully Spain; but
Randolph damaged his own reputation beyond repair in 1805 by
his mismanagement of the impeachment of Samuel Chase, a Federalist member of the Supreme Court whom Jefferson sought to
remove because of his political bias. Randolph lost his case, and
Chase was acquitted. Jefferson's first Vice-President, Aaron Burr,
killed Hamilton in 1804, and went into exile in 1805 in the unmapped West, seeking to detach it from the American republic
or to attack the Spanish West. Could a President arrest a former
Vice-President if he suspected him of treason? If he could, should
he? When Burr's co-conspirator, General James Wilkinson, the
territorial governor of Louisiana, who had himself been in Spanish
pay ("agent 13") revealed the supposed plot, Burr was tried for
treason in 1806 — and acquitted for lack of evidence. The judge
who presided was no less than the chief justice, John Marshall,
another Virginian (and indeed a cousin of Jefferson), whom Jefferson nevertheless now saw as his most entrenched enemy. It was
not true. John Marshall, one of John Adams's last appointments,
was Adams's best legacy to the US. Nevertheless, Burr was — as
throughout his long and stormy life — his own worst enemy. T. P.
Abernethy thought him not guilty on the evidence, but guilty on
intent. He was with all his gifts of inherited ability, his charm and
his devotion to his daughter, extravagant, reckless with money (his
own and everyone else's) and with words, plausible, imprudent —
and hungry, even greedy, for the affection of men and women. After
the duel with Hamilton he was a financial and political bankrupt.
He told so many tales and dreamt so many dreams that he came
to believe many of them himself. The West, still unmapped and
unexplored, was for him and his generation an opportunity for
adventure, riches and fame. He had plans for the separation of
the West, for the liberation of Mexico (in which his only error
perhaps was to be, as he thought himself, a generation ahead of
his time), for aid to Bolívar and his compatriots, for aid for the
French Creoles and the "Mexican Association," for new republics
or even empires (when in his European exile he was talking to
agents of Napoleon) to suit his legion of listeners in America and
Europe. Heavily involved as Burr was in the Floridas and Texas
before and after his trial for treason, and ambitious as he was for
the West's growth, and his own, he was not guilty of plotting treason against the United States. In less fevered times the charge would
not have been brought; before the War of 1812 was fought, and

even after it, the allegiances of the men of the Western waters was not to the United States, nor to Spain, nor to Britain, but to themselves; whether frontiersmen, soldiers, or scouts, they were intriguers all the time. Patriotism hardly yet existed. Theories of states' rights, arguments of self-interest, markets for furs and cotton, for corn and whiskey, distrust of eastern finance, indeterminate geographic boundaries and ambitious leadership, all produced a series of plots in the West from the Blount affair in Florida, to the Burr "conspiracy,' that came close to destroying the new state. The charge of treason may even have been in large part the product of President Jefferson's ready imagination.[14]

Jefferson was all too aware of the problems his second term was presenting. Burr was only one of them; slavery was another, and a constant anxiety. When the Constitution was drawn up, the complicated compromise over slavery had left the African slave trade open for a further 20 years. At the end of that time, Congress had the power to close it – and was expected to do so. By 1808, however, a significant proportion of the burgeoning produce of American agriculture, including its rapidly increasing exports of cotton, was the result of slave labor. Southern representatives now spoke for a section which saw the future in terms of an expanding, slave-based economy. The three-fifths compromise of 1787 no longer appealed to them. However, Southern opposition was not powerful enough to prevent Congress from closing the foreign slave trade in 1808.

Jefferson, unhappy in his second term and glad to be out of office after 1809, reverted thereafter to a more natural and more consistent liberalism. He was more at ease with Horace under his own trees at Monticello, than with Hamilton, Burr – or his cousin Judge John Marshall. He cited as precedent for only holding the presidency for two terms the magic name of Washington. It was probably an excuse, but it established a myth that endured until 1940. If he was happy to go in 1809, as he had been as executive in Virginia in 1781, he left the country prosperous. Merchants and shippers found the trade of the West Indies extremely profitable now that the British fleet kept French and Spanish vessels from trading with their own colonies. Americans also made money by exporting flour, tobacco, and cotton direct to Great Britain or the Continent,

[14] T. P. Abernethy, *The Burr Conspiracy* (New York, Oxford University Press, 1954), Milton Lomask, *Aaron Burr: The conspiracy and years of exile 1805–1836* (New York, Farrar, Straus and Giroux, 1979) Mary-Jo Kline and Joanne Wood Ryan (eds), *Political Correspondence and Public Papers of Aaron Burr*, 2 vols (Princeton, Princeton University Press, 1983).

because the war raised prices. The exports of the United States nearly doubled in the four-year period from 1803 to 1807.

From 1809 Monticello was the center of Jefferson's life. After his presidency, Jefferson lived in retirement there, busy with his estate, his many intellectual pursuits, the writing of letters (1,000 hand-written letters a year), and as elder statesman advising his successors in the presidency. His "harbor", he called it, from which he looked out on "his friends still buffeting the storm, with anxiety indeed but not with envy." He was for many years president of the American Philosophical Society, the most important organization of the time in the promotion of science. He was the founder of the University of Virginia, and carried on an extensive correspondence with learned men in Europe on a host of themes. Whatever information he could obtain regarding inventions of value to farmers in the raising of crops or in caring for livestock, he passed on in laboriously written letters to agricultural societies or to those who he knew would make use of the knowledge.

He turned back to his old interest in education and in local government. It was perhaps a more appropriate role for him than executive leadership. Yet the philosopher "on the tempestuous sea of liberty" had been remarkably successful: an administration more open than its predecessors, with the president more a policy-maker and a working executive than his predecessors, spending more time at his desk and less prone to delegation. New York Senator DeWitt Clinton affirmed: "Never did I before see realized a perfect view of the first Magistrate of a republican nation." Jefferson came to oppose immigration and foreign travel, to set the compass west by south and keep it so. For man's mind, reason was the oracle, he told his young friend Peter Carr, and the uprightness of a decision mattered more than its rightness. But about the future of America there was more assurance. He wanted "free commerce with all nations, political connections with none, and little or no diplomatic establishment." He saw the future of his country as agrarian, a continent-wide settlement of self-supporting farms with few cities and none of them large, a society of little government, run economically by self-reliant and self-contained farmers. "Those that labor in the earth" he said, "are the chosen people of God – if ever he had a chosen people."[15] He believed in democracy, though only in a long-term sense. In practice, government would be by the aristos of merit, not of birth. He was as a prophet utterly inaccurate,

[15] *Notes on the State of Virginia in 1785*, Query XIX, in Saul Padover (ed.), *The Complete Jefferson* (New York, Duell, Sloane and Pearce, 1943), p. 678.

and failed to foresee not only the scale of commercial enterprise, but its liberating – and indeed equalizing effect. In his day only 5 percent of the American people lived in cities of more than 8,000. Today 80 percent live in 150 vast metropoli. But he was a man of hope. Much of his creed indeed reflected his own wonderful health, his easy optimism: "We shall go on, puzzled and prospering beyond example in the history of man."[16]

In his retirement in Monticello, from which he did not stir far in his last 17 years, under the encouragement of Benjamin Rush, he began that long correspondence with also-retired-President John Adams, opponent gradually becoming reminiscent friend. The correspondence continued until they died – as they did within hours of each other, Jefferson aged 83, Adams 91, and as if by a special sign of grace, on 4 July 1826. John Adams's last words were: "Tom Jeffers still lives." It was not actually true, since Jefferson in fact went first, and pietists say that his last words were: "all eyes are opened, or are opening, to the rights of men;" but it is true of him as architect, educationalist, and democratic philosopher. Jefferson left his own summary of his achievement carved on his gravestone at Monticello: the author of the Declaration of Independence, of the Statute of Virginia for Religious Freedom, and founder of the University of Virginia.

5 JAMES MADISON AND THE WAR OF 1812

Jefferson was succeeded as President by his fellow-Virginian, his close friend of many years and his secretary of state, James Madison: the shy, small-boned bookish westerner from Orange County in the foothills of the Blue Ridge (Washington Irving called him "but a withered little apple-john"), who was the principal author of the Constitution. If Jefferson was a philosopher-king, his successor was the political scientist as president. He was eight years younger than Jefferson, and would – despite his poor physique and constant complains of ill-health and "biliousness" – live ten years longer. The Virginians were good survivors. By 1808 Madison was married to an ambitious and social-minded widow, Dolley Payne, physically

---

[16] For a fresh view of the Jeffersonians, see Appleby, *Capitalism and a New Social Order*; and for Thomas Jefferson as executive, see Noble E. Cunningham Jr., *The Process of Government under Jefferson* (Princeton, NJ, Princeton University Press, 1978). For a recent assessment, see Bailyn, "Jefferson and the ambiguities of freedom," American Philosophical Society, *Proceedings*, paper read April 1993.

taller and a much more dominant personality than her frail-looking uncharismatic husband. But the scholarship, the ultra-realism implicit in the Constitution-making, the subtlety and parliamentary skill, the width of experience availed him little in his two terms as President, which were marked by open war with Britain, in the "War of 1812," which is sometimes called "The Second War of Independence."

Napoleon's invasion of Spain in 1808 precipitated a wave of revolts in Latin America and further undermined Spain's declining colonial power. In 1810, a group of American settlers in the area east of New Orleans declared themselves independent, and asked for annexation by the United States. Madison, quite willing to take by force what neither he nor Jefferson had been able to acquire by diplomacy, joined this portion of West Florida to the Territory of Orleans, which became the state of Louisiana in 1812. The balance of West Florida was occupied when the war with Great Britain began.

Troubles with Britain were a legacy of Jefferson's second term. The program of commercial non-intercourse with Britain and France, which succeeded the Embargo, was ineffective; and the Erskine Agreement, the work of the British Ambassador in Washington, which provided for the restoration of trade with Great Britain in return for repeal of her offensive orders in Council, was rejected in London. A replacement of the ineffective Non-Intercourse Act was the final American effort to use commercial coercion. Enacted in May, 1810, it restored commerce with the world, but offered to invoke non-intercourse with either France or Britain if the other would withdraw its regulations injurious to American commerce. Napoleon shrewdly indicated his willingness to suspend the Milan and Berlin Decrees; Madison had already re-established non-intercourse with Britain before he discovered that the French Emperor's offer had been so qualified as to be meaningless. Madison was simply too credulous. Years of warfare, blockade, and trade interruptions had taken their toll in Britain. The government was therefore prevailed upon by British mercantile interests to revoke the orders in council on June 16. Before the news reached America, however, Madison had asked Congress to declare war (June 18, 1812). In other words, the War had lost its "cause" before it began; and its main and most costly battle would be fought after the peace terms had been agreed.

Not maritime grievances, but Western expansionism precipitated the war with Britain; the sections most vociferous for "freedom of the seas" and the most enthusiastic about the conflict, were the most inland and land-locked; those with most to lose in trade, mainly the seaports, were against. An Indian uprising in the Northwest, led by Tecumseh of the Shawnees and his brother, "The Prophet," collapsed after William Henry Harrison's quasi-victory at Tippecanoe in Indiana in 1811; but on finding British-made weapons on the battlefield the settlers in the region were convinced that the British were responsible for the native outbreak; the only way to guarantee peace, they held, was to add Canada to the United States. "Agrarian cupidity, not maritime rights, urges the war," was the view of John Randolph of Roanoke in Virginia. In the Southwest, similar suspicions were entertained about the Spanish, and Florida was an object of frontier aspirations. The Congress which convened in November, 1811, included a number of young politicians who represented this exuberant mood of frontier expansionism. Though a minority, they succeeded in electing the charismatic Henry Clay, of Kentucky, Speaker of the House. John C. Calhoun, of South Carolina, was their most eloquent and intellectual voice; with Felix Grundy of Tennessee and Peter B. Porter among them, they were labeled the "War Hawks." Taking up the cry of "freedom of the seas," because it offered an excuse for belligerency, the "War Hawks" denounced commercial coercion as a cowardly course, and demanded war. This was especially true of Clay, whose Kentucky Bluegrass constituency had been drawn into flourishing hemp production for the international market by way of New Orleans, and Calhoun, whose South Carolina upcountry was undergoing a heady transformation into a land of cotton plantations. Such areas of recent economic boom, based on the production of agricultural staples for national and international markets, shared the cosmopolitanism, progressivism, and nationalism of the older commercial-minded areas and might be characterized as agrarian commercial in spirit. From such areas was beginning to emanate a new-style Republican nationalism whose spokesmen *par excellence* were Clay and Calhoun.

The vote for war was by no means unanimous: 19–13 in the Senate and 79–49 in the House. Almost all Republicans voted for war; not a single Federalist did so. The South and the West backed it; New England, New York, and New Jersey did not. Congress then adjourned, without voting war credits or providing for increases in the army and navy; for the "War Hawks" were confident that a short campaign would be sufficient to win Canada and Florida, after which peace could be restored.

The War of 1812 was not a popular war. The Federalists were bitterly opposed to the conflict, and they realized that the Republican party had actually been dragged into it by its radical frontier wing. They had suffered under the trade embargo, when the word "secession" was first heard. Now, when the war blocked out all commerce, ships lay idle in New England's harbors, and men stood idle in the street — or drifted West. Wharves were abandoned, and warehouses steadily emptied. Only the solid support of the West and the South, with its slave population over-represented through the three-fifths constitutional ratio, re-elected Madison in the fall of 1812, the commercial states voting strongly for DeWitt Clinton, the Federalist mayor of New York, and peace. Madison secured 128 electoral votes to Clinton's 89: had the latter won Pennsylvania, the "peace" ticket would have won. Many Americans felt that it was wrong to attack Britain at the very time when Napoleon's fortunes seemed at their peak; certainly until 1814, the British were entirely too busy in Europe to divert troops and supplies to the New World struggle. When news of the declaration of war reached Boston, flags flew at half-mast.

There were three theaters of war: the North, the South, and the Atlantic; and three issues: what the President called "maritime rights and national honor;" agrarian imperialism pointed particularly at Canada; and the removal of an Indian threat from the Western frontiers. Though in population and military manpower the United States far surpassed Canada (with a population of 7½ million as against 500,000), the American army of 7,000 was poorly equipped and badly led, and the 400,000 militiamen who were called to the colors during the war proved either unresponsive or ineffectual. General James Wilkinson, the senior officer, was corrupt and unpopular. Secretary of War John Armstrong was incompetent and disobedient; and until the emergence of Andrew Jackson, no American commander distinguished himself. The effort to invade Canada in 1812 was a fiasco. Scheduled to advance from Michigan Territory, William Hull permitted his force to be surrounded by a Canadian and Indian army at Detroit, and General Isaac Brook, the British commander, persuaded and threatened him into surrendering without a battle. Shortly afterward, Captain John E. Wool led a small American force across the Niagara River, killing Brook in the skirmish which followed. The New York militia refused to cross to Wool's aid, however, and he was soon defeated. Several changes of command brought no improvement in the situation.

The diminutive American navy made a more impressive showing. Numbering 16 men-of-war and some smaller vessels and gunboats, the fleet was no match in massed combat for the scores of heavy warships and hundreds of lesser craft of Britain. In small engagements, however, American ships gave an excellent account of themselves, the three 44-gun frigates, *Constitution*, *Constellation*, and

President, being faster and more powerful than any of the enemy ships. Such spectacular victories as that of the *Constitution* over the *Guerrière*, in August, 1812, angered the British but did wonders for the sagging morale of the United States. In the end, however, numerical strength prevailed. By 1813, the British were blockading the American coast, and one vessel after another was captured, destroyed, or forced to remain in port. The *Essex* was destroyed in the South Pacific after a successful raid upon British whaling ships. At the war's end, only the *Constitution* and a handful of other vessels carried the American flag upon the high seas. On the Great Lakes and Lake Champlain, however, the Americans established and maintained control, and when Oliver Hazard Perry described his victory on Lake Erie in September 1813 as "We have met the enemy and they are ours," he added another to the roster of famous and belligerent national quotations. The War of 1812 is richer in such quotes than in achievements.

In 1813, an American force invaded Canada and burned several buildings in the city of Toronto, then quickly retired. This wanton destruction was strongly denounced in Canada and Britain.

The surrender of Napoleon in 1814 permitted Britain to send more than 10,000 seasoned veterans to America. The effort to invade northern New York was thwarted by an American victory in a desperate naval battle on Lake Champlain, but the British campaign against Washington was more successful. The militia of the surrounding area failed to respond to the call, and the small force which made a stand before the capital was badly directed and easily routed. After burning some public buildings, however – the Capitol building, the Treasury office, the War office – in retaliation for events at New York, the British retired, and their effort to capture Baltimore and Fort McHenry succeeded only in inspiring Francis Scott Key to write "The Star-Spangled Banner," which became the national anthem. By the end of 1814, British conquest of the United States had been demonstrated yet again to be impractical.

A third British expedition was dispatched to New Orleans late in 1814. By stern disciplinary measures, Andrew Jackson organized the militia defenders into an effective fighting force, and his choice of a defensive and entrenched position was a wise one. He was abetted – or so legend has it – by the pirate Jean Lafitte, expert as smuggler in navigating the bayous. The major victory of the war made Jackson a national hero. Happily, Wellington had not sailed with his regulars, but sent his brother-in-law Sir Francis Pakenham instead (for he and most of his senior officers were killed in the battle, along with 700 of his men.) Otherwise, who would have won

Plate 6   General Jackson's Victory at New Orleans, 1815.
(The Mansell Collection, London.)

at Waterloo? On January 8, 1815, the over-confident British were repulsed and routed, losing 2,000 to the Americans 13. It was a great victory indeed. Unfortunately – or otherwise – the war had in fact ended two weeks before: but the news of the treaty of peace signed in Ghent at Christmas 1814 had not yet reached New Orleans.

Whatever its causes – the land hunger of the West, the aggressiveness of War Hawks like Henry Clay or John Calhoun, the problems of British impressment or of neutral rights at sea – the War of 1812 was a war that should never have begun, and in which the last battle should, of course, never have been fought, since the peace treaty had already been signed. It was, as wars are, a story of coups and blunders, cowardice and courage, and chance governed its course also. When, in mid-August 1814, a forest of masts and sails appeared off the Virginia capes, the American cause had looked hopeless. The economy was in ruins; with Napoleon now a prisoner, the British regular army was available for new campaigns; and the war – as in 1776 – should have been an easy matter for the redcoats. Admiral Sir Alexander Cochrane, blockading Baltimore and the coves and yards from which came privateers, himself an expert in patronage and intrigue, assumed that he would have available some

15,000 regulars from Wellington's army, and thought that there
was no limit to what he could do. "I am confident," he wrote to
the Admiralty, "that all the country South West of the Chesapeake
might be restored to the dominion of Great Britain if under the
command of enterprising generals."[17] His plans now seem wild; they
ranged from kidnapping political leaders to stirring up the slaves
to join the British cause. "The blacks," he wrote, "are all good
horsemen;" they would be "as good Cossacks as any in the European
army." In view of the fact that only 120 blacks appear to have
been recruited, his strategy was a piece of fantasy. Not that the
American cause was any better led – it was a strange mixture of
folly and confusion. It was out of this mêlée, however, that a sense
of national identity emerged, and it was this identity and the heroic
defence of Baltimore against the British that produced "The Star-
Spangled Banner," and "The dawn's early light." The symbolism
is apt: the confusion and excitement of Fort McHenry and of the
struggle in the Chesapeake, even more than the Battle of New
Orleans, was the real turning point of the war. Moreover, because
it was unsought by one side, and only half-sought by the other,
it was a war devoid of any grand strategy, and became dozens of
local clashes, often contested only at battalion strength. As a result,
more generals were closer to front lines in the war than is usual
among the professionals. At sea, however, where the only issue of
principle arose (the rights of neutrals in war), it was a different
story: over 1,000 British ships were captured or sunk, and American
privateers operated – to enrich the East Coast ports and Baltimore
in particular – as close as the English Channel. It was only in 1814,
after the first capitulation of Napoleon, that the Royal Navy could
spare the resources to deal with the Americans.[18]

---

[17] H. L. Coles, *The War of 1812* (Chicago, University of Chicago Press, 1965),
p. 42.

[18] Fred W. Hopkins, *Tom Boyle: Master privateer* (Cambridge, MA, Tidewater
Publications, 1976); Jerome R. Garitee, *The Republic's Private Navy: American
privateering business as practiced by Baltimore during the War of 1812* (Seaport,
Mystic, 1977).

Bradford Perkins, in *Prologue to War* (Berkeley, University of California Press,
1961), is critical of the Republican leaders and challenges the argument that the
expansionists fueled the drive for war – the argument most forcefully voiced by
Julius W. Pratt, *Expansionists of 1812* (New York, Macmillan, 1925). Also critical
of Pratt are J. C. A. Stagg, *Mr Madison's War: Politics, diplomacy and warfare
in the early American republic* (Princeton, NJ, Princeton University Press, 1983) and
Reginald C. Stuart, *United States Expansionism and British North America* (Chapel
Hill, NC, University of North Carolina Press, 1988).

The treaty of peace which was finally signed at Ghent said very little about any of the Anglo-American issues; all that it secured was a termination of the war. There was no mention of neutral rights, of indemnities for seizures, or of the impressment of American seamen. The American delegates, despite the able leadership of Albert Gallatin, and their own talents, had disagreed among themselves more than with Britain. Subsequent negotiations were required to settle the outstanding controversies: the question of naval forces on the Great Lakes and the issues involved in the Oregon boundary dispute. The war, in other words, resolved nothing; but the Senate unanimously ratified the treaty in February 1815, and thus ended the War that should never have been begun. Its aftermath, however, was a euphoric wave of national unity, and of triumph over Britain, now for a second time. The President and Henry Clay advocated an "American System" under which domestic manufacturing would be stimulated by protective tariffs, and by improvements in transport. In the longer economic run, the War of 1812 benefited New England, for it compelled a diversification of economic activity and led to many new manufacturing ventures.

Most New Englanders, however, were conscious rather of the immediate loss of commerce, and of the accompanying depression in the port cities. They blamed the war on the West and South, and found little comfort in the prospect of having their influence in the federal government diminished as more and more states were created on the western frontier. Ever since the split and defeat of the Federalists in 1800–1, New England's mercantile interest, and to a lesser extent New York's, New Jersey's, and Pennsylvania's, which between them dominated the coastal and the international trade of the United States, had felt themselves victimized by the Republican party, with its base in agriculture among the farmers of the West and the South, and various under-privileged groups in the Northeast, notably the poorer sections of New York city, organized by Tammany Hall. What the Founding Fathers had worked so hard to avoid, the tyranny of the mob, might certainly seem to have come about, when such laudable measures as the excise or, in 1811, the first United States Bank, were swept aside to gratify West Pennsylvania moonshiners or Western speculative financiers; when foreign policy was clearly opposed to the interests of the Federalist minority, as in the Embargo Act or the spending of taxpayers' money on the Louisiana Purchase, or in the declaration of war itself, many became convinced of partisan victimization. Following the example set by the South and the West when the Federalists were in control they began to talk about states' rights – and its derivative, secession.

The British blockade of Massachusetts, begun in 1812, was not effective – perhaps on purpose to encourage secession? – until the spring of 1814, and so those goods which were imported or exported were channeled through her ports, to her merchants' advantage. Far more important than this in the long run, however, was the stimulus of decreased English exports to industry in New England, with its numerous well-watered rivers available to supply power, and its large population whose income from farming was more and more threatened by the opening up of the more fertile lands in the West. The industrial expansion, mainly in textiles, can be seen in the increase in the number of spindles from 8,000 in 1807 to around half a million in 1814, in which year the first power loom was installed at Waltham, Massachusetts, by Francis Lowell. In any event, men of enterprise, and experienced in smuggling, could always defy blockades. New England supplied most of the food for the British army in Canada. But smuggling, and, in war, collusion with the enemy, had always been good business practice along the New England coast.

These industrial developments, however, were less obvious to the men of the time. Apart from anti-war meetings in New York, and puritanical umbrage in Massachusetts, more effective non-cooperation arose when Connecticut refused to send its militia to fight for the Union, when the financiers refused to contribute towards the war loan, and when the remaining New England militia refused to fight. The climax of New England's unrest came at the end of 1814 with the Hartford Convention.[19]

In October, 1814, the legislature of Massachusetts voted to call a convention to meet at Hartford, Connecticut, in December to consider measures to strengthen Federalism in a time of Republican-caused unrest. Only the Rhode Island and Connecticut legislatures responded, but popularly-elected delegates from New Hampshire and Vermont also attended. The preliminary talks were of a revision of the Constitution, or even of secession, but no serious propositions of this sort were made; the call went out for a ban on all embargoes lasting more than 60 days. The moderates, however, led by Harrison Gray Otis, a Boston lawyer with a Harvard background, and George Cabot, a wealthy Boston merchant who controlled the Convention, were content to issue a protest against the activities of

---

[19] David H. Fischer, *The Revolution of American Conservatism: The Federalist party in the era of Jeffersonian democracy* (New York, Harper, 1961); and Fischer, "The myth of the Essex Junto," *William & Mary Quarterly*, 21.2 (Apr. 1964), pp. 191–235.

the Administration. News of Jackson's victory at New Orleans at the beginning of 1815, with New Orleans and the Mississippi Valley now firmly American, and the wave of national pride that it provoked, killed the proposals of nullification put by the Hartford commissioners in Washington, since they now appeared as examples of contemptible disloyalty. The Treaty of Ghent was signed nine days after the Convention met. Federalism as a political and vote-winning force was permanently weakened by this Convention, even if it could be argued that Otis and Cabot sought only to allow Federalist extremists to let off steam. Nor did Democratic-Republicanism emerge with much credit. If the war could be seen as, in a fashion, a second round with Britain (with New Orleans matching Yorktown in significance), it was devoid of the heroism of the War of Independence, and of the tragedy of 1861.

The War of 1812 was not for white men only. During it Tecumseh of the Shawnees tried to build an Indian confederation of midwestern and southern tribes to drive out the invaders, and to end the steady encroachment on Indian lands. To strengthen this Indian confederacy, Tecumseh planned to form an alliance with the British in Canada and the Spanish in Florida. He traveled from the Great Lakes to the Gulf in quest of allies. He was backed by the revivalist preachings of his brother, a medicine man, Tenskwatawa, "The Prophet." But while Tecumseh was absent in the South recruiting the Creeks to his cause, US forces, under William Henry Harrison, the Governor of Indiana Territory, defeated The Prophet and destroyed his settlement and its food supplies (the Battle of Tippecanoe, at the junction of the Tippecanoe and the Wabash Rivers, November 1811). Frontiersmen naturally saw the British as instigators of Indian attacks. When the War of 1812 began, Tecumseh assisted the British to capture Detroit. He was killed by American forces again under William Henry Harrison at the Battle of the Thames in October 1813, and the Great Lakes tribes were driven west. Of Tecumseh's bravery, his oratory and his attempts at federalism, an American legend was born. One of his legacies was pacific – but it too was ultimately unsuccessful.

After the War of 1812 the "five civilized tribes" in the Southeast – the Cherokee, Creek, Choctaw, Chickasaw, and Seminole peoples – gave up fighting and concentrated on agriculture. Many were converted to Christianity, and tried to reconcile the Indian and European cultures. One of their number, Sequoya, without speaking or writing English, devised a Cherokee alphabet or syllabary of 86 characters. By memorizing these, reading and writing became available; the Cherokee became a rarity, a literate Indian people. Here indeed was civilization as the Europeans understood it; these Indians were neither savages nor heathens, but a literate tribe, with newspapers, books, and the Bible in Cherokee.

In 1814 the Creek Indians were badly beaten by Andrew Jackson at Horseshoe Bend on the Tallapoosa in what is now eastern Alabama. They were compelled to admit their war-guilt — whatever that meant — and to cede by "treaty" two-thirds of their territory. Over the next 40 years the federal Government sold off the land, and made over $11 million by doing so. After the War of 1812, Jackson invaded Spanish Florida to continue his campaigns against the Seminoles. Such wars brought profit — and fame.

It mattered not at all. As the whites increased in Georgia and adjacent states, they came to covet the lands of the civilized tribes and to demand possession — whatever their literacy. The Indians protested. They pointed to their treaties with the white men. They called attention to their progress and their interest in Christianity. They appealed to the courts, and won some court cases (e.g. *Worcester* vs. *Georgia*, a Supreme Court decision written by chief justice John Marshall in 1832). They lost out, however, to American nationalism, to race prejudice, to greed for land, in a now consistent and relentless sequence. And when Andrew Jackson reached the White House, they would be driven from their lands, as legacy of his wars with the Seminoles (1834–42) and the Black Hawk War with the Great Lakes Indians (1832), and pushed westward along the "trail of tears" to what is now Oklahoma. It had not been Jefferson's way nor his intention, but it was dreadfully effective in wiping out people.[20]

6 THE ECONOMIC CONSEQUENCES

In domestic policy, the Administration had shown itself unwilling to adapt to the needs imposed by its own nationalism. Before the outbreak of war, but when it was already obvious that the government was going to need all the strength it could command, Republican attitudes were responsible for a serious weakening of the banking system. The Bank of the United States came to the end of

[20] Glenn Tucker, *Tecumseh, Vision of Glory* (Indianapolis, Bobbs Merrill, 1956); R. David Edmunds, *Tecumseh and the Quest for Indian Leadership* (Boston, Little Brown, 1984); Alvin M. Josephy, "Tecumseh, the Greatest Indian," in *The Patriot Chiefs* (London, Eyre and Spottiswoote, 1962), pp. 131–73.

its 20-year term in 1811. Pure Republican doctrine had consistently denounced it as a source of illicit wealth and a new "paper aristocracy." The Swiss-born treasurer, Albert Gallatin, who understood the need for a central financial agency, and had profited in land speculation, never shared these views, and when the renewal of the charter was debated, enough members agreed with his attitude to produce a tied vote in the Senate. In this situation, George Clinton, the Vice-President, adhering to narrow Republican and anti-Hamilton precepts, cast his vote against rechartering of the bank and brought its life to an end. He died himself in 1812.

The results were sudden and spectacular. The country was in a ferment of economic expansion and hungry for savings. In bank credit, people had discovered "a new source of energy." In the absence of a strong central institution to exercise control, a crop of new banks sprang up to meet local demands. In 1811, there were 88 state banks in existence; by 1815, there were 208, and a year later 246 — many of them inadequately funded, poorly run, if not corrupt. Bankruptcies were frequent. The Republicans, whose dogmas were at least partly responsible for the instability, found that their theory was out of date. In the War itself, the absence of a Bank deprived the Administration of ready cash, of a depository for its funds and of any machinery for raising loans. As a result, in Madison's second administration, a new national bank was planned. Indeed, the signing of the Act to bring the Second Bank of the United States into existence in 1816 was one of his last acts. The first Bank, incorporated in 1791, was supported by the North; the second, of 1816, was supported by the South and opposed by the North.

Although the peace concluded with Britain by the Treaty of Ghent in December 1814 had been ratified in February 1815, the closing years of Madison's presidency were beset with economic emergencies. The war had no sooner ended than cheap British manufactures poured into the American market, overwhelming the weak, newborn industries and draining valuable currency from the country. In face of the flood, first of cheap goods, and then of goods that were dumped rather than merely sold in hard competition, American workshops failed. The effects were unevenly distributed, and agriculture felt fewer adverse effects, particularly as American agricultural produce gained renewed access to European markets. But the distress of the cities began to bring home, even to the Republicans, the fact that the federal government could be held responsible for economic policy — a view that would not disappear. The result was the Tariff Act of 1816, the first distinctively protective American tariff. Republican majorities and Republican administrations had thus introduced a new national bank and a national protective tariff. Clearly the Republicans had learned a great deal about government since the early days of Jefferson's presidency. Madison's last message to Congress in 1816 revealed the scale of the change. "However wise the theory may be which leaves to the sagacity and interest of individuals the application of their industry and resources, there are ... exceptions to the general rule." Hence, items likely to be unavailable from abroad during a national emergency, industries needing support in their infancy, and manufactures using materials "extensively drawn from our agriculture," might be protected by tariffs. Madison believed generally in free trade, but conceded that circumstances might at times require a modification. On internal improvements, Madison noted that there was no country "which presents a field where nature invites more the art of man to complete her own work for his accommodation and benefit." Not only was federal support necessary to do what the states alone could not, but canals and roads were economically beneficial, of universally acknowledged utility, and honored a "wise and enlarged patriotism which duly appreciates them." Finally, better transportation would "bring and bind more closely together the various parts of our extended confederacy." The President stressed, however, that a constitutional amendment might be needed for the projects "which can best be executed under the national authority." He still tried to be loyal to the charter he had drafted 29 years before when he had been the first of the Federalists. But to "Old Republicans" in Congress, the President's message, and the nationalistic fervor of Calhoun and others in upholding it ("Let us conquer space"), was a complete surrender to Federalism. John Randolph of Roanoke, back in Congress after a two-year absence, declared that the President "out-Hamilton's Alexander Hamilton," and that the question was "whether or not we are willing to become one great, consolidated nation, or whether we have still respect enough for those old, respectable institutions to regard their integrity and preservation as part of our policy." Madison, Randolph insisted, was now merely a Federalist in disguise.[21]

When Madison's retirement approached, the old caucus system still served to select for President his fellow Virginian, and former rival, James Monroe. The Federalists could no longer offer serious opposition, and the election virtually went by default, with Monroe

---

[21] Adams, *History of the USA*, vols V and VI; Coles, *The War of 1812*; Pratt, *Expansionists of 1812*.

gaining 183 votes to Rufus King's 34. The first party system had collapsed. The situation seemed almost to have returned to the kind of harmony to which Jefferson had once aspired. Apart from the tariff and the Bank, government was as light as Jefferson could have wished, and the growth of the country gathered pace with little show of central direction, restraint, or even supervision. The Federalists felt, to employ the phrase used of Disraeli, that the Republicans had caught the Federalists bathing and run away with their clothes. [22]

Madison's period in the White House had not been easy. In the course of it, he had moved away from the extreme nationalist stance of his Constitution-making in the 1780s. A believer in "balanced" government, he then had seen the threat to it in the passions of men, in sectional clashes, in localism, in legislative licentiousness or "democratic despotism," in the power of a selfish majority or in demagoguery. The test of war, for him as for Jefferson, however, had made deference to Congress and the protection of civil liberties, the Whig principles, hard to honor. After the implementation of Hamilton's system, and after his own experiences close to or on the throne were behind him, he saw the threat again as that of ministerial despotism, "executive encroachments," and excessive centralism. "The censorial power," he said, "is in the people over the Government, and not in the Government over the people." He steadily reverted to the Jeffersonian position of the paramountcy of the rights of the states: an important shift as the slavery problem developed, but a view that he had not held when himself in office. As an executive, he saw his role as that of "the Guardian of the people," and he played it as well as he could, in all its varieties and all the inconsistencies between the "Ins" and the "Outs." Yet the end of the two presidencies, of Jefferson and of Madison, revealed the more disturbing truth that:

certain Republican axioms were ill-suited to the Napoleonic era. A belief in executive forbearance, fiscal predilections that abhorred debt, a faith that standing armies and navies necessarily corroded freedom, a reliance on militia, an adherence to commercial coercion, and a long-range view that America was impregnable were, however correct and virtuous by themselves, dangerous when insisted upon categorically in a world at war. Thus

---

[22] The best study of the financial issue is Bray Hammond, *Bank and Politics in America: From the Revolution to the Civil War* (Princeton. NJ, Princeton University Press, 1957.) Cf. T. P. Abernethy, *The South in the New Nation 1789–1819* (Baton Rouge, University of Louisiana Press, 1961).

the Jeffersonians merely asked Congress for defense appropriations, and they tried every alternative to a regular army and to a fleet. They placed debt reduction above national defense, and they persisted in the Embargo long after both their countrymen and foreign powers had recognized its failure. The result was to leave the United States virtually helpless in a world it could not compel to accept republican precepts. By learning too slowly the exigencies of power, the Republicans endangered national survival. The great miscalculation of the Jeffersonian administration, for which Madison shared general, if not direct, administrative responsibility, left a chasm between the principles it proclaimed and the power and means necessary to give them effect. The Jeffersonians' fault was not cynicism or lust for power or infidelity to constitutional principles or partiality toward France or agrarianism or sectional bias; rather, it was a republicanism that left them disarmed in a hostile world. [23]

Madison retired to his home at Montpelier, with books piled on every table and on every chair. Before leaving Washington, he and Dolley gave a party: "Members of Congress and officers of the army and navy, greasy boots and silk stockings, Virginia buckskins and Yankee cowhides, all mingled in ill-assorted and fantastic groups." The First Lady, "very tall and corpulent ... manners ... easy rather than graceful, and pleasant rather than refined ... distributed her attentions and smiles with an equal and impartial hand." He and Dolley entertained almost as lavishly at home; indeed too lavishly, for some of their guests stayed for months, and, as the years passed, their debts compelled retrenchment. He died in 1836, Dolley in 1849.

"Era of Good Feelings" or not, being elected President was Madison's tragedy, not his triumph. His mind was richly informed and agile, but not decisive. Senator Plumer thought in 1806 that he was "too cautious, too fearful and timid to direct the affairs of this nation." Later he assessed him:

No man was more tenacious of his opinions than he was — he would die sooner than give them up; but then no man was more ready to waive for the present, their application to existing circumstances ... if permitted to have the whole arguments for himself, he seemed less anxious about the immediate adoption of the measure which he then deemed necessary. It was the same with all other measures — if you agreed with him in the abstract he would not contend much with you about particulars. Nothing would have induced him to surrender the neutral rights for which he so

[23] Ralph Ketcham, *James Madison: A biography* (New York, Macmillan, 1971), p. 471.

ably contended in his pamphlet and in his correspondence with England — but he was willing to pass them over — to say nothing of them — to put 'em in abeyance — to waive them for the present — with a caveat as to our rights; to maintain the argument and assert our principles, but to forbear their application. Something of this disposition is no doubt seen in most men, but it was remarkably characteristic in Mr Madison, and forms the true explanation of his conduct in more than one important transaction.

Madison's triumph had been 49 years before his death, in drafting the Constitution, and in his contributions to *The Federalist Papers* justifying and explaining it. Essay No. 39 is the clearest definition of a federal republic ever written, and No. 10 is a charter of American optimism, explaining why the US has not been torn apart by pressure groups, as Washington feared, and as Lord Macaulay predicted. The Declaration of Independence and the Gettysburg Address are more eloquent, Hamilton's *Report on Manufactures* is more ingenious, Calhoun's *Disquisition on Government* is more rigidly logical, but none of these political documents sums up the basic American theory as clearly as these two. They are fundamental to any understanding of the American system of government. [24]

7 JAMES MONROE

James Monroe, the fifth President and the third and last of the "Virginia Dynasty," is best known for the Doctrine named after him — but he wrote very little of it. As secretary of state and then as President, he earned the reputation of being a foreign policy specialist — yet all of his own diplomatic missions were failures. His presidency acquired the name of "The Era of Good Feelings," for it was the age before slavery and industry posed their special problems to the American people; yet within 30 years of his death, the country would be torn apart by Civil War. Monroe was in fact the last president to have direct experience of a pre-industrial age, of the years before independence was won. [25]

Few political careers equal Monroe's in length and variety. In his first days as politician, he was a controversial figure; in the end he

[24] For an excellent assessment of Madison after his presidency, as an exemplar of the Jeffersonian Enlightenment see Drew R. McCoy, *The Last of the Fathers: James Madison and the Republican legacy* (London, Cambridge University Press, 1989). For Senator Plumer's views, see Ketcham, *James Madison*.
[25] *Columbian Centinel*, July 12, 1817.

was universally respected. Monroe was born of Scottish stock on April 28, 1758, in Westmoreland County, Virginia, of the farmer rather than the planter class. He left William and Mary College to join Washington's army, and was wounded at Trenton, one of the four casualties; he reached the rank of lieutenant-colonel. He became a student of law under, and a close associate of, Thomas Jefferson, in whose long shadow his life was spent; he practiced law in Fredericksburg and he made his home at Ash Lawn, then known as "Highland," on its 500-acre estate in the mountains, within three miles of Jefferson's home at Monticello. It does not have the grace of Monticello: Monroe called it his "cabin-castle."

He served from 1783 to 1786 in Congress, and as a Senator from Virginia from 1790 to 1794. As a Jeffersonian, he stood for states' rights; he opposed a strongly centralized government, even in 1788 the Constitution itself, and was critical of the Bank of the US that Hamilton proposed. He was less the student and more the man of affairs than Madison, and more the Democrat and states-rightist.

In 1794 Monroe was sent by Washington as minister to the government of Republican France in the hope that his pro-French sympathies would secure for him a favorable hearing. It proved a testing assignment. Robespierre was dead, the future uncertain. Monroe got off to a good start, with a stirring reception before the whole Convention; he laced his speech with appropriate cries of "Vive la République," even though he was the emissary of a neutral government. But the French knew of the similar Jay mission to Britain, and were justifiably suspicious that Monroe was there merely to placate them. The terms of the Jay treaty when published seemed to confirm their fears that the ally of 1778 had sold out to the Old Enemy, Britain. To try to offset these fears, Monroe went too far the other way, and had to be rebuked for his enthusiasm. He was recalled in 1796.

He served from 1799 to 1802 as governor of his state, but in 1803 was again despatched on a mission to France. While not responsible for the Louisiana Purchase, since Napoleon had already offered the ex-Spanish West to American minister Robert Livingston before Monroe arrived, he showed himself prompt in accepting the obvious bargain, and precise in working out the details. Later in 1803 he replaced Rufus King as US minister in London, an assignment he did not enjoy. He tried to end the British practice of impressing American seamen into the British Navy, and to obtain commercial concessions, but he had as little success as John Jay 11 years earlier. His treaty got no concessions from Britain on impressment, and no indemnities for losses; indeed, President Jefferson and Madison, his secretary of state, deemed it prudent not to submit the document to the Senate for ratification. Monroe had by this time, in one role or another, spent nearly six years abroad on diplomatic missions; his actions in Paris had been repudiated by Washington, his treaty in London was repudiated by Jefferson. It had been a strikingly unprofitable series of sojourns.

In January 1811 he became once again governor of the state, but only for two months. In March, Madison invited him to become secretary of state, a post he held until his own election to the White House in 1816.

His term as secretary was as unfortunate as had been his foreign missions. Although he sought to avert the war of 1812, he knew enough of British opinion to judge its unwillingness, as he believed, to abandon the practice of impressment. The declaration of war on June 18, 1812, largely owed its form to a draft of Monroe's. Yet the War need never have been fought; Britain had repealed the orders in council two days before the War was declared; it was bitterly unpopular in New England, which saw it as "Mr Madison's War;" and this was not meant as tribute; in its Convention at Hartford in 1814, New England had threatened to secede from the Union. Monroe's real task was to try to end the War as soon as possible.

The War was a grim experience for Americans. In 1813 the British navy advanced on Washington unopposed, and Monroe, along with the President and Cabinet, left the city in a hurry – the event satirised in "The Blaydonsburg Races." The American government was in hiding and bankrupt, Washington was burned by the British, New England talked ominously of rebellion. American trade was practically at a standstill. But the news of British reverses at Plattsburg and Baltimore led Britain to be willing to negotiate; after 20 years of war in Europe; and a heavy burden of debt and taxes, she was tired too. With Napoleon safely, it seemed, on Elba, the case for ignoring the rights of neutrals and this sideshow struggle lapsed. The American War had been, as Castlereagh called it, "a millstone."

The terms of the treaty made at Ghent by the negotiating team Monroe chose were very simple. British demands were dropped. Not a word was said on maritime rights, impressment and the rights of search or seizure. Nor were there any references to territory. Neither side gained or lost. It was peace without victory.

The ending of the War of 1812 was only in part Monroe's achievement, but it was his greatest good fortune. It initiated the era of good feelings, of which he was the principal beneficiary. Though a sectional war in its origins, it had a nationalizing effect.

It taught the US the need for an army and navy, for a national Bank, for protection against British competition, for the encouragement of domestic industry, and for a system of internal communications. On these issues all the sectional leaders were – for a few years – in harmony. Both Clay and Calhoun supported the tariff of 1816; both South and West agreed in 1816 on the need to charter the Second Bank of the US. Madison himself realized that the days (and the dreams) of strict construction and government economy were over. A wave of national unity and nationalism swept the country, fostered by pride in the military and naval victories in the War, especially those at sea and at New Orleans – it is significant how much the songs and phrases of American nationalism are product not of Washington's War but of Mr Madison's. It was the result also of the invention of the cotton gin and the prospect of a rapidly expanding cotton culture in the South, and of the turnpike and canal craze that offered the prospect of a quick linking of East and West. The Cumberland Road, linking the Potomac and the Ohio, was pushed on to the Mississippi – at federal expense, and to Yankee complaints at the squandering of taxpayers' money. There seemed likely to be assured markets for Western produce, and even under some Republicans, assured money for internal communications. In the next decade six new states would come into the Union. The mood was optimistic, expansionist, and brash.

The presidential election of 1816 was thus held in a mood of pride and relief. Monroe was the Republican choice, though there were now signs of opposition to the Virginia dynasty in the Republican party caucus that in effect named the candidate. In securing the nomination, he defeated William Crawford of Georgia, who was also a Virginian by birth and had been a minister to France, by 65 to 54. The vice-presidential candidate was the former governor of New York, Daniel D. Tompkins. The Federalists were discredited by their conduct during the War, by the succession of political defeats, and by the evidence of what seemed the near-treason of some of their leaders. In December, Monroe was elected in a landslide, with 183 votes in the electoral college to 34 cast for the Federalist candidate, the brilliant Senator Rufus King of New York; the latter won only three states, Massachusetts, Connecticut, and Delaware. The country had never been so united. Nor was it ever to be so again.

As a result, it was possible for Monroe to select a cabinet largely freed from party pressures, and a strong and happy one it proved to be. John Quincy Adams of Massachusetts, the son of a Federalist president, became secretary of state, the first non-Virginian to hold the post since 1801; William H. Crawford of Georgia became secretary of the Treasury; John C. Calhoun of South Carolina, secretary of War; the charming and loyal lawyer, William Wirt of Virginia, who had acted as the prosecutor in the trial of Aaron Burr in 1805, attorney general. It could well be argued that this was a team each one of whom was abler than the President, but there was no attempt by any of them to challenge his authority. Indeed, the strongest influences in the Cabinet were those of two men who were not there at all – Jefferson and Madison. From them came floods of advice on every item, from the different kinds of wine to be got from France to opinions on the latest escapades of the irresponsible General Jackson. Monroe received a letter from Jefferson, long, eloquent, avuncular, and detailed, every fourth day throughout his Administration.

Monroe's popularity was helped by two goodwill tours, and in 1820 Monroe's second election was unchallenged. The Federalist party offered no candidate and Monroe got all the electoral votes but one, which was cast for John Quincy Adams. It is sometimes said somewhat lyrically that the dissenting vote in 1820 cast by elector William Plumer of New Hampshire was deliberately cast, so that only Washington should have the honor of unanimous election. This was what Plumer said in public. Actually Plumer would not have voted for Monroe under any circumstances – his letters and those of his son reveal a bitter dislike. But in 1820 at least it seemed that Washington's warning against political parties had been heeded, and that real unanimity could exist.

Politically, Monroe's was then an important administration. Old John Adams once called it an "administration without a fault." Economically, its most important feature was the American system. Henry Clay was the chief spokesman for those Americans who recognized the emergence of new sectional tensions, and sought to devise a program which would unite all parts of the nation by bonds of self-interest. The protective tariff, to appeal to the North, and internal improvements, to appeal particularly to the West, were cardinal tenets of what Clay called "the American system." Clay wanted to see "a chain of turnpikes, roads and canals from Passamaquoddy to New Orleans," roads criss-crossing the nation and "intersecting the mountains, to facilitate intercourse between all parts of the country, and to bind and connect us together." Such a program should be federally funded. Behind it, legacy of the War of 1812, should be a standing army of 10,000 men and an increase in the navy. This was Hamilton's policy brought up to date: the use of central government and its resources, aided by a national bank, to build up the nation's infrastructure and its economy. But the appeal to the West was new. The Tariff Act of 1816 was happily timed to gain maximum approval, for American industry faced the threat of being swamped by the goods which British merchants "dumped" in the United States at the end of the War of 1812. Massachusetts' commercial interests opposed the measure, but even in the agrarian South it received much support.

Westward expansion increased the problems of communications and transportation, and when the steamboat on the Mississippi began to divert overland trade between East and West, the demand for roads and canals increased rapidly. New York began constructing the Erie Canal, which after 1825 carried much merchandise between the Great Lakes region and the Atlantic; other states undertook internal improvements, with somewhat less spectacular success. Clay's program, however, was to construct turnpikes and waterways with federal funds, mainly the profits from the Banks, since only in this way could the thinly populated Western states receive those projects which they needed. The Cumberland Road was constructed from Fort Cumberland to Wheeling by 1818, but Madison's veto of a bill for internal improvements in 1816 forestalled further Federal undertakings during this period.[26]

Even in the midst of the era of good feelings, problems arose. Two of these were important, the Panic of 1819 and the Missouri Compromise. The Panic of 1819 was due to two factors; first, the opening up of new lands in the West, with new farms needing capital for the purchase and first years of operation – all on the easy credit provided by the wildcat banks of 1811; and, second, the consequences of tariff protection of 1816. Even the Bank of the United States at first followed an easy credit line. The policy of over-expansion resulted in inevitable collapse in 1819, when the second Bank of the United States, in a sudden panic for its own safety, demanded that the state banks redeem their obligations to it in specie. Immediately arose the protests so often heard before and since, of the Western debtor against the Eastern creditor. "All the flourishing cities of the West," cried the fire-eater Senator Benton of Missouri, "are mortgaged to this money power. They may be devoured at any minute. They are in the jaws of the Monster." As

[26] Daniel Walker Howe, *The Political Culture of the American Whigs* (Chicago, Chicago University Press, 1979); and his edition *The American Whigs: An anthology* (New York, Wiley, 1973); Thomas Brown, *Politics and Statesmanship: Essays on the American Whig party* (New York, Columbia University Press, 1985).

mortgages and debts could not be met, the US Bank found itself a huge absentee landowner, owning, for example, the greater part of the city of Cincinnati on the Ohio. Economic nationalism, as seen in the conflict between the Western farmer and the Eastern banker, re-emerged. The panic resulted in an investigation and reorganization of the bank. It brought the Land Act of 1820, which abolished the system of purchasing public lands on credit, liberalized the land policy by reducing the amount of land that must be purchased from 160 to 80 acres, and lowered the price from $2 an acre to $1.25. The acquisition of farms became easier, but the agrarian depression continued until 1824, and won converts for Jacksonian Democracy.

Another conflict was destined to be more serious; the problem of slavery as against free labor. Since 1789, a sectional balance had been maintained in the senate by admitting an equal number of slave and free states; but the Northern and Western states were growing more rapidly and thus were in control of the House of Representatives. Missouri had applied for admission to the union in 1818, and, when the debate opened in the following year, Congressman James Tallmadge of New York proposed an amendment that, as a condition of its admission, the further introduction of slavery in Missouri be prohibited, and that slave children be freed there when they reached the age of 25. The House, with 105 Northern Congressmen against 81 Southerners, passed his amendment, but the Senate, with two Senators from each state and thus strongly representing the South, rejected it. There were many reasons why the south opposed his proposal so bitterly. Since the invention of Eli Whitney's cotton gin in 1793, cotton production had become very profitable and was becoming the economic mainstay of the South. There were 11 free and 11 slave states in the Union, so that the Tallmadge amendment would have given the North control of Congress. Although only some 6,000 of its 66,000 people were slaves, Missouri's white population were Southerners, and mainly cotton-growing. Missouri was the first state wholly west of the Mississippi, and would set a precedent for the rest of Louisiana territory; it was largely north of the Mason-Dixon and Ohio River Line, which previously had divided the free states from the slave. Aware now that there existed a determined anti-slavery faction in the North, the South grimly resolved to defend its "peculiar" and cherished institution. The South contended that Congress had no power to ban slavery from the Louisiana Purchase Territory, because it had existed under Spanish and French rule, and the treaty of purchase guaranteed that the inhabitants would be protected in their "liberty, property and religion." They held, moreover, that Congress

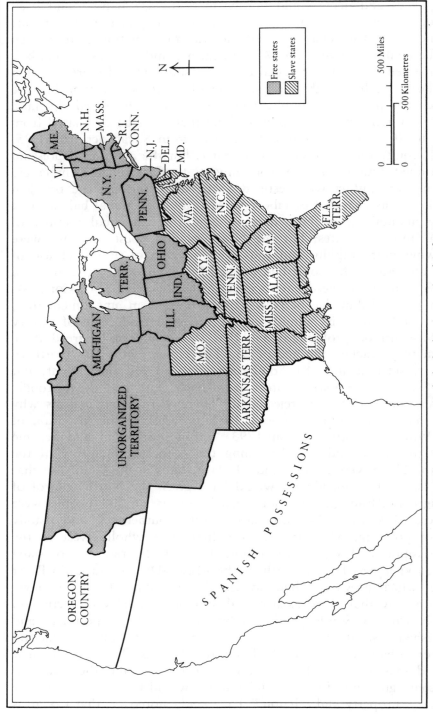

Map 3 The Missouri Compromise, 1820. The Compromise forbade slavery north of 36° 30′, except in Missouri; but it was repealed in 1854.

could impose no restrictions on a state, and that Missouri had the same powers as the other states. The deadlock was broken by admitting Maine (since 1677 part of Massachusetts) as a free state and Missouri as a slave state, but slavery was excluded from all the Louisiana Territory north of 36° 30', except Missouri itself. This arrangement, known as the Missouri Compromise, settled the question until 1854, when the Compromise was repealed. The South was content: it saw and welcomed the prospective admission of Arkansas and Florida. The anti-slave forces for their part had won recognition of Congress's right to control slavery in the territories. The basic question – whether or not Congress had the right to impose qualifications, other than those set forth in the Constitution upon applications for statehood – was sidestepped. Slavery as a national issue, however, had now become important. In Jefferson's phrase, the country had heard the sound of the firebell in the night. It would be heard more loudly, and with shattering effect, in the next generation.

If one problem was raising its head, another – the Northern and Southern boundary – was being settled. By the Rush-Bagot agreement of 1817, Britain and the United States pledged themselves to keep the Canadian-American border unfortified and to keep no armed war vessels on the Great Lakes, except those involved in customs control. The next year the United States rectified the northern boundary of Louisiana Territory. The boundary was to extend along the 49th parallel from the Lake of the Woods to the Rocky Mountains; Oregon was to be held by joint occupation for ten years. American fishing rights off Newfoundland and Labrador were recognized.

These diplomatic settlements between the United States and Great Britain in the years following the war of 1812 were the more remarkable because of the inconclusive character of the Treaty of Ghent and the continuing bellicosity of many citizens of both countries. Lord Castlereagh, the British foreign secretary, was the first British statesman to see the advantages of preserving harmonious relations with America, and Madison and Monroe met his overtures half-way. Adams, the secretary of state, was less enthusiastic, but his Yankee skepticism and ardent nationalism did not prevent his recognizing worthwhile opportunities. Since the occupation of West Florida in 1810 (as far east as the Pearl River), the United States had been trying to obtain the rest of Florida. During the war of 1812, another slice of land was annexed, extending beyond Mobile Bay east to the Perdido River (now the coastal reaches of the states of Mississippi and Alabama). American desires were whetted by the fact that the British used East Florida as a base for operations in the War of 1812, and that after the war British officers had incited Indians and runaway slaves to make attacks on American border settlements. At any rate, when Seminole Indians raided across American borders, General Jackson invaded Florida and seized every Spanish fort except St Augustine, drove the Indians into the Everglades, and executed two British subjects, Arbuthnot and Ambrister, for inciting Indians. Spain protested, demanding the punishment of Jackson and the restitution of the forts. Monroe agreed on the latter, but John Quincy Adams insisted that Jackson be upheld. Adams gave Spain an ultimatum, demanding that it police Florida or cede it. Since the king of Spain found himself unable to exert any real authority over Florida and recognized the implicit threat, he deemed it best to sell. By the Treaty of 1819, the Adams-Onis Treaty, the United States obtained all of Florida — for $5 million, this being the amount its citizens claimed from Spain. The western boundary of Louisiana was also agreed upon (from the mouth of the Sabine River, on the Louisiana-Texas border, northwest along the Red and the Arkansas Rivers to the 42nd parallel, and then west to the Pacific.) In effect, Spain abandoned its claims to the Pacific Northwest. For its part, the United States abandoned its claim to Texas. After probing the unsavory activities of the two British subjects, Castlereagh made no protest.

During the Napoleonic Wars the colonies of Central and South America had rebelled against Spain, and for several years the mother country had been helpless to recover control. Following the final overthrow of Napoleon, the victorious powers — Austria, Russia, and Prussia — decided to form a league, the Holy Alliance, to prevent the spread of the principles of the French Revolution. The Holy Alliance succeeded in suppressing popular revolts in Italy in 1820 and in Spain in 1822. It was evident that the next step would be intervention in the New World and the suppression of the new Latin American republics. In 1822 Monroe recommended to Congress that the new states be recognized as independent.

The one great power in Europe which had little sympathy with the Holy Alliance and a great deal with the Latin American republics was Great Britain. Great Britain did not relish the principle of intervention against revolution, and welcomed the rich commercial opportunities opened up by the overthrow of Spanish authority in South America. Great Britain hoped to secure the support of the United States against possible French designs to discourage newly independent republics from being drawn towards the US, and also to discourage the United States from seizing Cuba. American critics of the new British foreign secretary, George Canning, Castlereagh's successor after his suicide in 1822, feared a new British Caribbean empire of trade, if not dominion, replacing Spain's.

The first member of the Monroe cabinet to show alarm over the possibility of European encroachment in the New World, and especially over the Tsar's invitation to the United States to join the Holy Alliance, was John Quincy Adams. Adams had come to think of North America as the special preserve of the United States, from which the rest of the world ought to be excluded. In July 1823 he informed the Russian minister that the Americas were no longer subject to any new colonial establishments by European powers.

The first step in the actual formulation of the Monroe Doctrine was taken in August 1823, when Canning, speaking to the American minister in London, Richard Rush, suggested a joint announcement by Britain and the United States agreeing to recognize the new republics, and to warn France to stay out of Latin America. Jefferson and Madison, when consulted, favored a joint Anglo-American pronouncement. Adams, on the contrary, thought that the United States ought to act independently of Great Britain, and persuaded Monroe to follow his views. In the first place, he argued, Canning wanted America to share the British pledge against territorial expansion, an undertaking which might seriously embarrass the United States in the future. Furthermore, a joint declaration would place America in the role of a diplomatic satellite of Britain. Again, it was just as desirable to check England in the New World as to curb the other powers of Europe. Having convinced the President of the desirability of a unilateral declaration of policy, Adams then had to limit it to the objectives which he thought important. It was important to warn Russia, for in 1821 the Tsar had pushed the Alaska boundary south to the 51st parallel, and his diplomacy was becoming increasingly reactionary and anti-republican. Monroe, however, wanted to go further, reproving France for interfering in Spanish affairs, and endorsing the Greek war for independence. Adams opposed any effort to involve America in European affairs.

The Monroe Doctrine consists of three broad principles. The first, the non-colonial doctrine written by Adams and directed to Russia, states that "the American continents ... are henceforth not to be considered as subjects for future colonization by any European powers." The second, written by Monroe, the isolationist doctrine, was a warning to the Holy Alliance:

The political system of the allied powers is essentially different ... from that of America ... we should consider any attempt on their part to extend their system to any portion of this hemisphere as dangerous to our peace and safety. With the existing colonies or dependencies of any European power, we have not interfered, and shall not interfere. But with the governments who have declared their independence, and maintained it, and whose independence we have ... acknowledged, we could not view any interposition for the purpose of oppressing them, or controlling, in any other manner, their destiny, by any European power, in any other light than as the manifestation of an unfriendly disposition towards the United States.

The third principle, the non-intervention doctrine, was the proposition that the United States did not intend to interfere in European affairs, and they did not want the European powers to extend their political systems to the New World.[27]

The Doctrine, to which history has given Monroe's name, was but three paragraphs in a 51-paragraph message to Congress on December 2, 1823. If it took 30 years to be known as his doctrine, the President won popular support at home from it, and the respect of liberals abroad. European governments, notably Metternich's in Austria, deplored its non-colonization and its pro-republican theses and its "arrogant" tone. Canning deplored the unilateral declaration, but considered the non-interventionism a useful barrier against the proposed European congresses on Latin American affairs: "The effect of the ultra-Liberalism of our Yankee co-operators on the ultra-despotism of our Aix-la-Chapelle allies, gives me just the balance that I wanted." In his statesmanship there was also some pique — that the President had got his blow in first — and some fear of the US as a commercial rival in Latin American markets. In Latin America itself, Simon Bolívar, the Liberator, completely ignored the President's declarations in his correspondence; Latin American leaders continued to see Britain and its navy — and its trading companies (there were 39 set up in Buenos Aires by the end of 1824) — as the chief bulwark against any revival of European intervention. What the Doctrine revealed, in all its Americanism, was the twin paths of Anglo-American diplomacy, despite 1776 and 1817, at a time when all the rumors were that France would cross the Atlantic to suppress the rebellions in Spanish colonies. The two British foreign secretaries, Castlereagh and Canning, were of one mind with Adams and Monroe. The Americans turned down an offer of

[27] Monroe's Seventh Annual Message to Congress, Dec. 2, 1823, in H. J. Commager (ed.), *Documents of American History*, 5th edn (New York, Appleton-Century-Crofts, 1949), p. 235.

cooperation, because they did not wish to play the role of satellite, "to come in," in Adams's words, "as a cock-boat in the wake of a British man-of-war,[28] and they struck out on their own." Monroe's message of December 2, 1823, in Dexter Perkins's words, "completed the work of the Declaration of Independence."[29]

We now know that the Holy Alliance had no intention of intervening in Latin America, and, furthermore, that they had no particular reason to respect the American army or navy. Russia had never been serious about the *ukase* of 1821 and in 1824 a treaty was concluded whereby the Tsar accepted 54° 40' as the southern boundary of Alaska. On the last day of 1824, the British government recognized the independent regimes in Mexico, Colombia, and the United Provinces (Buenos Aires). The US had done so already.

Monroe was not the most gifted nor the most subtle of the Virginians, nor was his experience abroad very successful. He came to the presidency almost by inheritance. But he brought to all he did a transparent integrity – and no small quantity of *amour-propre*. Jefferson noted the attention he paid "to his honor and grade" – the mark, no doubt, of a Virginian who was never as much at ease socially as were his peers. In attitude and intent he seemed a man of a distant and historic age. Jefferson, his leader and friend, said of him that if his soul were turned inside out, not a spot would be found on it. His dress and style, his knee-length pantaloons and white topped boots, were all the features of an earlier day. But his own tastes as President were simpler than those of his predecessors: the touch of democracy was creeping in. If he was not striking or flamboyant in manner and did not arouse the devotion that his predecessors did, he could rise above sectional conflicts and could choose excellent lieutenants – which could not be said of all who preceded him, notably Madison; and he could show administrative ability of a higher order. On his work as statesman the Doctrine put the seal. It was not all his own doing, nor was it novel. It owed its origins to John Quincy Adams, his secretary of state. But Monroe gave expression, in a form he chose himself, to a nationwide popular sentiment. He was able to tap a national mood, and to sense the will of the people. His doctrine became the cornerstone of American foreign policy and of the view that

[28] John Quincy Adams. *The Memoirs of John Quincy Adams*, edited by his son Charles Francis Adams (1874–7), vol. VI, pp. 177–9.
[29] See Dexter Perkins, *The Monroe Doctrine 1823–26* (Cambridge, MA, Harvard University Press, 1927).

prevailed through most of the nineteenth century, that the interests of the US and of Europe were quite distinct.

Monroe found public service demanding and unrewarding. Like some of his predecessors, notably Jefferson, he left the White House in debt. Congress voted him $30,000 in 1826, but it was not enough to meet the claims. He was forced, on his wife's death in 1830, to sell his home (now owned by William and Mary College), and to leave Virginia to live with his daughter in New York. There he died, on July 4, 1831. He died on a hallowed day. On that date, five years before, both Jefferson and John Adams had died. And 55 years earlier the Declaration of Independence had been signed. Monroe's death was indeed the end of America's Revolutionary era.[30]

8 JOHN QUINCY ADAMS

Ever since the formation of political parties during the administration of Washington, it had been customary for the presidential candidates to be nominated by a caucus of their party members in Congress; the national convention method had not yet been devised. By 1824, however, in an age when local and sectional democratic sentiment was strong, and newspapers became more numerous and more vigilant, the caucus had fallen into disrepute. That disrepute was equally true of the caucus in state politics, whereby a group in the legislature ran the state, and gave "jobs to the boys." Since the Senators sitting in Washington for six-year terms were themselves elected by their state legislatures – and this remained so until 1913 – American politics at the national and state levels was in the hands of a handful of power barons. The caucus – King Caucus" as it was called – was exclusive, and, as the franchise widened, was seen as remote from popular control. Senator Nathaniel Macon of North Carolina refused to attend because, he said, "it produces so much electioneering among the members of Congress that it seems to border on intrigue and bargain, and is not known to the Constitution." Rufus King in the Senate attacked this "new, extraordinary self-created central power, stronger than that of the Constitution." As the role of the caucus declined, presidential recommendations by state legislatures or by public meetings grew in importance and popularity.

[30] The best recent study of Monroe is Harry Ammon, *James Monroe: The quest for national identity* (Charlottesville, University of Virginia Press, 1989).

In 1824 William H. Crawford of Georgia, the secretary of the Treasury, was named as a candidate by the Democratic-Republican caucus, but only 68 of the 261 members of Congress had bothered to attend; Crawford himself had, six months before, suffered a paralytic stroke, and was for a time blind. He was a Virginian by birth, now a Georgian, a skillful financier and the leader of the slave-holding cause, the close-run rival to Monroe for the presidency in 1816, the choice – in essence – of the Republican machine. In 1820 he had secured the passing of a 4-year-tenure Act, and had filled the Treasury with his own personal following: he was the father of the "spoils system." John C. Calhoun, aged 42, the other Southern candidate, likewise held a Cabinet position, serving Monroe as secretary of the War Department. Calhoun was Scotch-Irish in background, his grandfather an immigrant from County Donegal to Pennsylvania; his branch of the family had remained in the Carolina uplands and had grown up with the section, and with family legends of Indian frontier clashes, instead of crossing the Appalachians into Kentucky as so many others did. A friend of Henry Clay and a leading War Hawk in 1812, he was an eager nationalist; he helped to establish the Second Bank of the United States, and his bonus bill would have led to the building of a network of roads and canals had not President Madison vetoed it. He had grown to manhood with relatively few outside contacts, with the mind of a Calvinist, cold, stern, and metaphysical. By background a Jeffersonian Democrat, there was in him none of the liberalism and little of the cultivation of the Master. Harriet Martineau, the English social reformer and abolitionist, traveling in the South in 1834, describes him as "the cast-iron man, who looks as if he had never been born and never could be extinguished. I never saw anyone who gave me so completely the idea of possession." Clamoring for internal improvements and voicing the sentiments of the nationalistic West, Calhoun was at the same time the chief, and the most eloquent, leader of the South. As the years passed, he became more and more a Southern advocate.[31]

Out of the West, as favorite sons, came Henry Clay and Andrew Jackson. Clay, the Kentuckian, was the epitome of all that state, at least in anecdote, represented: sporting blood, whiskey, honor, and poker; and to Adams he was "in politics, as in private life, essentially a gamester." He was certainly no Puritan. But though Kentuckian by adoption, and of poor origin (or so he always

---

[31] Mrs Martineau cited in Walter Allen (ed.), *Transatlantic Crossing* (New York, William Morrow, 1971).

claimed, not quite accurately) he too was a Virginian by birth, trained as George Wythe's amanuensis at Williamsburg. He had the Virginian virtues; charming, frank, suave, and courteous: he could sway his followers with his magnetic personality and his qualities of leadership. His easy mastery in debate, and the fact that his best work was done with the inspiration of an audience, had caused him to make of the Speakership of the House one of the most important of American offices, one from which the occupant might aspire to the presidency. Although he lacked Adams's diplomacy and skill, and Calhoun's learning, he had a considerable reputation as a *bon viveur*, and as a conciliator. Almost continuously Speaker since 1811 he attributed his skill in the chair and the ability to make firm and rapid decisions, to the habit of stating them without ever giving reasons. He had learnt the politician's tricks: to state a position wins support, to debate the causes produces the opposite. Ever since his War Hawk days in Congress, when he had been so influential in promoting war with Britain, Clay had been a bold champion of constructive legislation. In his vehement, at times petty, opposition to Monroe, he had forged a new set of American political issues: the gospel of Western expansion and internal improvements at federal expense, the United States Bank, the tariff, and the recognition of and good relations with the South American republics. He gave the National Republicans a program and pushed it hard. A slave-holder himself, he disapproved of the system and advocated gradual emancipation – but with the resettlement of the freed people in Africa. More than any other candidate, he was precisely the man around whom would crystallize the elements of a new political party. As statesman, he had no love for Jackson; it was Jackson who blocked his way to the presidency. Clay, probably the most deserving man who never got the presidency, though he ran for it on three occasions, was the most popular and the most influential figure of his age. But, as it is in politics, he could be hated too.

While Clay represented and appealed to the progressive business and property interests, Andrew Jackson was the embodiment of the rough and rampant West, the coonskin-capped frontiersman. Jackson disliked Clay because he never "risked himself" for his country. Jackson's phraseology, said Harriet Martineau, indicated that "his time had not been passed among books." He was the poorest educated of all the presidents. Born in the Carolina backwoods to an immigrant farming family from Ireland, he fought as a youngster against the British; almost all of his family died in the War of Independence. A poor and lonely teenager, he was intensely ambitious, and saw the law as his ladder of opportunity. He served as a delegate to the Tennessee constitutional convention, as its first elected congressman and as a US Senator. Comparatively unknown outside his native Tennessee, this gaunt, lantern-jawed, choleric soldier had sprung into fame as a result of his campaign against the Creek Indians and then with his heroic and opportune defeat of the British at New Orleans in 1815. It happened again in 1818, when the over-reckless zeal of the military hero brought Monroe's administration to the brink of war with Spain over the capture of the Florida posts. Jackson had a short spell as the first military governor of the Florida Territory. His subsequent conduct in Florida, involving the imprisonment of the governor, accorded with the secret inclination of the country. He was free from promises, unworried by the test of consistency that afflicts politicians, and he could be all things to all men. A slave-holder, cotton planter, and shrewd business man, yet he could inveigh against the Bank and the "money-power." A self-made simple citizen soldier, yet he lived as an aristo. He was a gambler, and a duelist, a man of impulse and a winner of battles. Without training and experience in statecraft, he sat silent and uninfluential in the Senate, but swept all before him in Washington. Everybody expected, he said, "to see me with a tomahawk in one hand and a scalping knife in the other." In fact, to a commanding presence he added courtesy, and a firm Christian faith. He had a public personality, material for legend, and for political salesmanship.

In January 1822, the newspapers, at the behest of William B. Lewis, began urging Jackson's candidacy. Lewis, the clever and unscrupulous master of the art of winning the support of the illiterate and the impressionable, was determined to become the Tennesseean's campaign manager, and to manufacture a poor man's latter-day Washington. With growing literacy, many newspapers and their editors became Jackson's vehicles: Isaac Hill (*The New Hampshire Patriot*), Mordecai Noah (New York *Enquirer*), James Watson Webb (New York *Courier*), Amos Kendall (*Argus of Western America* in Kentucky), Thomas Ritchie (the Richmond *Enquirer*), and Duff Green's new, Washington-based *United States Telegraph*. Jackson became the political idol of a popular movement, national in its sweep. The "image" was tailor-made: poor boy, Indian fighter, victor over the "auld enemy." His record showed what he was against. As a personality, and in the end a president, he was made for and by the media of the day.

Two years before the election of 1824 there were before the public five candidates for the presidency, representing four sections of the Union and nominated by members of state legislatures, by mass meetings, and by the congressional caucus. In 1824, 18 of the 24 states still chose their presidential electors by popular vote. By 1828, all but South Carolina would do so; there they were still chosen by the legislature. The beginnings of Jacksonian Democracy can thus be found not in the General's election in 1828 but in the 1824 election campaign. Crawford's defeat marked the end of the congressional caucus as a method of election; apart from its remoteness from "the people," it had made the nomination of the executive dependent on the legislature, as the Founding Fathers in 1787 had expected to happen as realists, but which they had not specified in the document. For a time, state conventions seemed likely to replace the caucus; but they might not, and did not, agree on the same men for the same offices. It was not until 1832 that the national convention was summoned.

Calhoun withdrew from the race in 1824 to run for Vice-President, unopposed. If the issues were far from clear, if there was only one party, and that breaking up, at least there was no shortage of colorful candidates; and each had a following of *devots*.

When the electoral college ballots were counted in 1824, Jackson had 99, Adams 84, Crawford 41, Clay 37. Since no candidate had an overall majority, the election went to the House, voting by states, as the Constitution prescribed, and choosing only from the three highest. Clay, now ineligible, cast himself, as Speaker of the House, in the role of president-maker, and threw his support to Adams, who was elected by the House. Adams promptly announced that Clay was to be secretary of state. John Randolph described this as a union of "the Puritan and the blackleg, Clay was so brilliant and so corrupt that like rotten mackerel in the moonlight, he shines and stinks," and an inconclusive duel followed.[32]

The opponents of Adams had suspected some sort of "deal," and a Philadelphia newspaper printed a letter accusing Clay of a "corrupt bargain." Clay challenged the writer, who turned out to be a Congressman named Kremer, a tool of the Jackson supporters. The Jackson party had at first counted upon Clay's favor, but when they learned of his partiality for Adams, they decided to discredit him or compel him to support Jackson. Kremer failed to appear before a congressional investigating committee, and Adams went through with his plan to appoint Clay. The upshot of the matter was the division of the Republican party into the Adams-Clay wing and Jackson-Calhoun wings. The former became known as National

---

[32] Robert V. Remini, *Henry Clay, Statesman for the Union* (New York, Norton, 1991), p. 293.

Republicans, the latter as Democratic Republicans – or, gradually, simply as Democrats.[33]

The split imperiled the Adams presidency, and left a legacy of bitterness on which the Jackson campaign for 1828 fed. The hero of the West had, it seemed, been denied his rightful place by a corrupt bargain, by an "unholy coalition." "The sovereign will of the people, the almighty voice of this great nation ... has been set at defiance." Jackson was a popular hero in the Western states, where most of the qualifications for voting and for office-holding had been removed, and where – in a still largely illiterate Western population – many local officials were elected by oral approval, and where political issues were voiced in alcoholic turbulence. But the newspapers were also very much on his side. John Quincy Adams by contrast was a president's son, Harvard-educated, a linguist with long diplomatic experience in Europe, as well as secretary of state. He was austere and assiduous, and had the indifference to popular acclaim of the Adams clan. To Clay, Jackson was a mere "military chieftain," or worse; Jackson replied in kind, but with a soldier's venom: Clay was now, he said, "the Judas of the West." Jackson was re-nominated for President by the Tennessee legislature in 1825; he accepted the call, and a renewed and savage three-year campaign began. It was seen now as a nation-wide and popular vindication, an effort to rouse not caucuses but people to ensure that the "wrongs" of 1824 were righted. There was no need for a program or a policy: now personality was all. But in constructing an alliance, a program was implicit: strict construction, opposition to federal internal improvements as advocated by Adams and Clay as an expansion of federal power and favoring the wealthy and the privileged, Western expansion, majority rule, rotation in office, all on the assumption that plain folk could do the people's business. But the 1824 result carried another message also. Unlike his opponents, Henry Clay at least had a program to sell: the American System: the Bank of the United States, internal improvements, and the protective tariff. Clay won the electoral votes of Kentucky, Ohio, and Missouri, three states which were then committed to internal improvements and the protective tariff, if not convinced by the case for the Bank. By

[33] M. J. Heale, *The Presidential Quest: Candidates and images in American political culture 1787–1852* (London, Longman, 1982); William G. Morgan, "The 'corrupt bargain' charge against Clay and Adams: an historiographical analysis," *Filson Club Historical Quarterly*, 42 (Apr. 1968), pp. 132–49, and "Henry Clay's biographers and the 'corrupt bargain' charge," *Register of the Kentucky Historical Society*, 66 (1968), pp. 242–58.

contrast, where these issues were unwelcome he made little impact: New England, New York, and the Southwest. It was the American System as well as its advocate who went down.

As statesman, John Quincy Adams was distinguished, experienced, and intelligent. To his compatriots, however, he appeared a stiff Yankee and too much his father's son; certainly he was more successful before he became President than during his single term: witness his drafting of the Monroe Doctrine and the acquisition of Florida from Spain, his achievements as secretary of state. His plans were splendid: wide-ranging, imaginative, and constructive. His first message to Congress as President envisaged a national program that was in large measure an extension of Alexander Hamilton's ideas: a federally funded system of internal improvements, of turnpikes and canals, a national university and government assistance to the arts, to science and to observatories, a national banking system with a uniform currency, and not least – and basic to it all – a protective tariff to provide the funds. This splendid vision of a Whig before his time was, however, easier to draft than to translate into effect in an intensely regional America, where intensely state-based and state-bound political barons reigned.

From the start, the Adams presidency was torn by these personal, factional, and regional clashes. Jackson's lieutenant, Martin Van Buren of New York, opposed every measure, regardless of its merits; and Calhoun was coming to be loyal only to his section. Like his father before him, the President was too honest and straight-laced to use patronage to build up a party machine; he even insisted on retaining Jackson supporters in public office. The manner of his election, his refusal to compromise, and his own austere style made him unpopular with friend as well as foe. He refused to reward his own folk – there were only two removed from office in four years. It was an age of Good Feelings. His plans sounded academic, even unrealistic. From the start many Southerners and advocates of states' rights frowned on his Federalist notions, and Adams gradually had to abandon them. Indeed, on every important issue the Administration found itself hamstrung by the opposition, and by the growing sectionalism. Monroe's successor lived in an Era of Hard Feelings.

Three distinct incidents revealed the split. First, in 1825 the United States was invited to send envoys to a Pan American Congress at Panama. The slave-holding interests in Congress denounced the Panama Mission as a step that could lead to Negro insurrection in the United States, since they were, according to their agenda, to consider the liberation of Cuba and Puerto Rico from Spain, and the ending of slavery in them, although this was plainly a misrepresentation of the purposes of the Panama Congress. In fact, the protests that the Mission would involve the US in entangling and potentially revolutionary alliances was obviously insinuous and spiteful. The envoys were finally confirmed by the Senate, but one died of fever on the way to the Congress, and the other, also fearing fever, contrived to arrive too late. This was a miserable outcome for a President whose own expertise – and success – had been in diplomacy. But his support for Caribbean America brought him some popularity. The isolationist towards Europe appeared as an expansionist in the Americas.

A second embarrassment for Adams was the Georgia-Indian episode. In 1802 Georgia had ceded land to the federal government, and the latter agreed to extinguish the Indian claims. In 1825 the United States paid the Creeks for their land, and Governor Troup began to survey the region. The treaty had not been honest and the Creeks repudiated. Adams ordered Troup to wait for new arrangements, but Troup defiantly refused, declaring that Georgia was sovereign on her own soil. Receiving no support from Congress, Adams was helpless and Troup continued the survey.

As the pro-Jackson campaign mounted, it found an ally in Martin Van Buren, "the little magician": a small, balding, affable man, with his base in New York's Tammany Hall, among the immigrant Irish. By profession a trial lawyer, agile and pragmatic, Van Buren's special skill was in detecting rising stars, and attaching his own chariot to them. He had been an ally of Aaron Burr in his campaign against the great families of New York, then an aide of Governor DeWitt Clinton. He then became a rival-turned-enemy of the last, and from 1821 a Senator from New York. When he became active in Washington, his friends were active on his behalf in Albany (the so-called Albany Regency): Edwin Croswell, editor of the *Albany Argus*, William L. Marcy, Benjamin Butler, Silas Wright, and John Dix, all with long careers ahead as smoothers and fixers. When Crawford's health collapsed, Van Buren became a liege man to the Tennessee demagogue. He saw a rising tide – he would not have been there otherwise. At the mid-term elections in 1826, the Jacksonian Democrats won control of both Houses of Congress and a majority of the state governments – the result in part of manhood suffrage replacing property qualifications for the suffrage in many states; between 1824 and 1828 the electorate doubled. This was the writing on the wall for John Quincy Adams. Indeed, the ex-Crawford-now-Jackson machine – Northern and Western liberals and farmers plus Southern planters – were to win all but two national elections between 1828 and 1860.

Thirdly, no event more clearly revealed the rising sectional feelings than the tariff episode of 1828. From the beginnings of the
independent state, its main source of revenue had been the tariff.
Clearly, in wartime and with interruptions in trade, funds fell, and
new devices had to be found: excise taxes, loans, and the ever-
expanding proceeds of land sales (revenues from which rose from
$1.5 million in 1829 to $25 million in 1836). To the Jeffersonians
the great financial objective was the simple one: to retire the national
debt and, for revenue, to rely entirely on land sales and the tariff,
increasing the latter as necessary. Except in the war years, when
receipts fell off, and in the immediate postwar deluge of British
imports and the consequent depression, the economy was blooming.
Given the wealth of land, it was only peace that was required; in
each of the 21 years from 1815 to 1836 there was a Treasury surplus. The tariff was used increasingly, however, not only for revenue
but for the protection of American industry, which gave still further
stimulus to sectional rivalry.

Until 1816 not only Northern manufacturers, but Western farmers
and Southern planters too, had all alike supported the tariff. Vermont, Kentucky, and Ohio – sheep country – also wanted protection against imports of British woolens and of Scottish hemp. Only
maritime and trading New England opposed the tariff. After 1816,
with the rapid growth of industry in the North, especially in New
England, their manufacturing interests now sought tariff protection.
In particular the speed of the textile boom was electrifying: Lowell
started production in 1822, Nashua was founded in 1823, Waltham
was flourishing. The water-power of the Fall River brought prosperity to the Providence-Pawtucket area. There was a near-matching
growth along the Hudson, Mohawk, and Delaware valleys. The age
of household manufacturing was coming to an end. And protection
helped. Importers became manufacturers. Daniel Webster, who, as
New Hampshire-born, was a states' rights man, and an opponent
of the War of 1812, by 1827 as a Senator for Massachusetts became an advocate of federal action to stimulate the economy by the
"national" program: protective tariffs, internal improvements, and
a national Bank: as State Street Boston went, so did he. A deal
was made with the Western states, which wanted higher duties on
imports of raw wool, iron ore, and hemp, and the tariff was raised.
Even this was not fully satisfactory: the manufacturers claimed that
the duties were inadequate; the sheep-raisers of the West, looking
for a home market, and fearing the competition of British wool,
supported them; and in contrast the woolen manufacturers wanted
imported woolens savaged. A bill raising the rates on woolens was

defeated only by Vice-President Calhoun's casting vote in 1827. By that year Calhoun himself had gone the other way: he was a free-trade Southerner, and wool was needed in the South – if only for Negro clothing.

By this time many Southerners, like Calhoun had come to realize that their section would never (well, hardly ever) become industrialized, and that a protective tariff was detrimental to their interests. Higher duties would raise the cost of the planter's bill for clothing and implements, and also offend Britain, their major trading partner. They denounced the protective tariff as unconstitutional, as a tax on the South to help the North. The tariff bill introduced in 1828, which provided protection not only for wool but for glass, iron, flax, and other commodities, was to them and all free traders, "The Tariff of Abominations." In other words, the economic rivalry lay between a pro-tariff alliance of the ironmasters and ironworkers of Pennsylvania, the wool-growers of Ohio and the Middle States, and manufacturing interests everywhere (home-market school plus infant-industry-protection school) against the free-traders: the South's cotton growers and the North's shipping traders. The caustic Virginian John Randolph saw the tariff as the work of Jacksonian politicos. It referred, he said, "to manufactures of no sort or kind, but to the manufacture of a President of the United States." The Southerners tried to kill it by making it distasteful to New England. They raised the rates on wool, iron, and hemp to exorbitant levels, and added duties on cordage and molasses. Ultimately from this clash of sections came a civil war.

Adams was a nobler figure than his one-term presidency suggests; he was an honest man with an independent mind. "I am a man," he said of himself, "of reserved, cold and forbidding manners." His father's son, and schooled in his image, he was widely experienced from his youth in Europe (he went to school in Amsterdam) and had seen service in Paris, the Hague, Berlin, and St Petersburg – where he had been Madison's envoy from 1809 to 1814; as the arbitrator at the Treaty of Ghent (1814); and as ambassador in London from 1815 to 1817. His *niche* was diplomacy, not partisan in-fighting; intelligent, intellectual, courageous, moral – with "a tortured, not to say tortuous, morality" – but a puritan too, suspicious, irascible, ambitious and mean.[34] He practiced law in Boston,

[34] George Dangerfield, *The Awakening of American Nationalism* (New York, Harper Torchbooks, 1965), p. 28.

and served as Washington's minister to the Netherlands in 1794 and as his father's minister to Prussia in 1797. On Jefferson's election to the presidency in 1801, he resigned, and two years later was elected a Federalist Senator from Massachusetts. But he never was comfortable in a party harness. A Federalist until 1808, when he broke with the Essex County right-wingers in supporting the Embargo as an alternative to war, one reason for his choice as a presidential candidate was to prove that others than Virginians could be called to the highest office. During his term, he was in fact steadily working back to his original faith: a supporter of John Marshall on the sacredness of contracts in *Fletcher* vs. *Peck*, he was clearly a nationalist, despite his affection for Britain, and a partisan of the Bank and of the cause of sound money.

Again like his father, he was a believer in the notion of public service as an honorable activity for the good citizen. Public office should be accepted, but not striven for. You "stood," you did not "run." "The principle of my life has been never to ask the suffrage of my country, and never to shrink from its call." On returning to Quincy, to his farm and his books, he expected to live quietly among Federalist Whigs who would, he feared, ostracize him as one who could turn his coat; in fact he was elected; as a Whig, to the House of Representatives, where he served for 17 years; and by any measurement he was its wisest and its most experienced member. He opposed the annexation of Texas and war with Mexico – just as he had in 1803 seen the Louisiana Purchase as "a flagrant violation of the Constitution." He saw it as a sacrifice of Northern freedom to slavery and the South, and as the purchase of Western support by the plunder of public lands: "Slavery and democracy, especially a democracy founded, as ours is, on the rights of man, would seem to be incompatible with each other; and yet ... this democracy of the country is supported chiefly, if not entirely, by slavery." He went further in 1842: should this issue lead to war with the South, in a state of war the military authority – president or commander-in-chief – could, he believed, order the universal emancipation of slaves. Certainly there should be no extension of slavery. He campaigned single-handedly against a Southern-dominated House for the right of anti-slavery groups to bring petitions. In his efforts to defend a constitutional right, he was thwarted by a gag rule and by threats of expulsion. But in the end, in 1844 the House repealed its gag rule and the right of petition was restored. To the end, this was a man standing single. In the same year, in his address to his constituents, he left his political testament, a remarkable survey of the years since he had left the White House. He became, to his generation, "the old man eloquent" – although he was in fact no orator. After his death in 1848, he was buried where he had been born 80 years before, in Quincy, Massachusetts. Perhaps the most appropriate verdict on his long and unusual career is that of Theodore Parker, not normally a chivalrous assessor of others, who saw Adams as "the one great man since Washington whom America had no cause to fear."[35]

9 JEFFERSONIAN AMERICA

Until 1828 the new nation was headed, as it had been discovered and explored, by gentlemen. Four of them were Virginians; two, father and son, were from Massachusetts – and Harvard. All were Tidewater men, and all but the first college-educated; three of them, the second, third, and fourth, were scholars too. They all had or had acquired a Roman *gravitas*, but all linked an aristocratic unpretentious of manner to a republican simplicity. Whatever their differences or ideology, all shared a non-partisan view of the presidency. None of them saw their role as active initiators of legislation, though they made their proposals on policy as part of the piety of their annual messages to Congress. They saw themselves as presiding officers, with a primary interest in foreign affairs, so it was usual that each should be succeeded by his secretary of state. The role of government they saw as limited. Jefferson and his Virginian successors saw their function as the strong right arm of the Congress. As the third President put it in his first annual message, "Nothing shall be wanting on my part to inform, as far as in my power, the legislative judgment, nor to carry that judgment into faithful execution." Although their intentions, like those of the Constitution-makers, gave priority to the Congress, the fact that the presidency was not an hereditary but an elective office and held for a relatively short term made it competitive; and Washington's and John Adams's sense of the dignity of the office thrust it – however unwillingly they said this was – into the political arena. Each quadrennial

[35] See Adams's son Charles Francis Adams's edition of *The Memoirs of John Quincy Adams* (1874–7), and Samuel Flagg Bemis's biography, *John Quincy Adams and the Foundations of American Foreign Policy* (New York, Knopf, 1949). For brief biographies of the Federalists in the age of Jefferson, see David Hackett Fischer, *The Revolution of American Conservatism* (New York, Harper Torchbooks, 1965), and cf. George Dangerfield, *The Era of Good Feelings* (New York, Harcourt Brace, 1952).

contest was the most conspicuous feature of the similar contests for the House, for one-third of the Senate seats, and for the state governorships, and it was the campaign for the presidency that caught the national imagination. The President – or the strongest members of his cabinet team – provided the initiative, and was, in Alexander Hamilton's phrase, "the engine" that drove the state. They had their henchmen in the Congress; they rewarded the faithful, they relegated to oblivion the disloyal or the independent men. [36]

Their country – whose many locales would be "run" by men like themselves – they all believed, had not only unique institutions but a God-given mission.

The station which we occupy among the nations of the earth is honorable, but awful. Trusted with the destinies of this solitary republic of the world, the only monument of human rights, and the sole depository of the sacred fire of freedom and self-government, from hence it is to be lighted up in other regions of the earth, if other regions of the earth shall ever become susceptible of its benign influence. All mankind ought then, with us, to rejoice in its prosperous, and sympathize in its adverse fortunes, as involving everything dear to man. [37]

These legacies of the Jeffersonians were binding on their successors: no more than two terms for any president (only broken once, in 1940); a council of state, now called Senate, that had a distinct identity, and did not merely sit in attendance on the man on the throne; and, despite the first secretary of state's early pro-French sympathies, Washington's rule held: no entangling alliances, no foreign adventures; and it would be binding until 1898, with foreign affairs constitutionally delegated to executive leadership. It was the achievement of John Adams to hold to this view of the peculiar distinctness of the United States and to avert intervention in Europe; within a decade he found his policy being reinforced by the embargoes of Jefferson; in this as in so much else, and especially so of foreign policy, the third President was right to say, in his first Inaugural: "We are all Republicans, we are all Federalists."

[36] For an excellent discussion of the nature and challenges of the early presidency, neither "popular" nor "partisan," see chapter 11, "Executive power and the non-partisan ideal," in Ralph Ketcham, *Presidents above Party: The first American presidency, 1789–1829* (Chapel Hill, NC, University of North Carolina Press, 1984), pp. 215–35.

[37] Jefferson, March 4, 1809, on leaving the presidency; quoted in Leonard Levy, *Jefferson and Civil Liberties: The darker side* (Cambridge, MA, Belknap Press of Harvard University Press, 1963), pp. 21–2.

If in 1812 both isolation and neutrality were abandoned, to many the War of 1812 was fought with the wrong enemy. At Springfield, Massachusetts, in 1812, a meeting could declare: "We hold in utter abhorrence an alliance with France, the destroyer of old republics." The principles of 1776 had not been those of 1789. After reading and translating the long article on the two revolutions by the young Friedrich von Gentz that appeared in 1800 in the Berlin *Historisches Journal*, the still younger John Quincy Adams wrote to Gentz in June of that year congratulating him on having vindicated the American Revolution from "the imputation of having originated or been conducted upon the same principles as that of France." That of 1776, it seemed, was defensive and not for export; that of 1789 was offensive. By 1800 the United States had opted out of revolution. Miranda and Bolívar fought the fight unaided. That its cause was no longer the cause of all mankind America demonstrated by its later rejection of Tom Paine. He who had first used the words "the United States of America" was in 1806 denied the right of being an American citizen.

By the end of the War of 1812, Great Britain was ready to accept the permanence of the United States and to look for advantage in flourishing trade between the two countries. Seeing great commercial opportunities throughout the Americas, British ministries observed with satisfaction the crumbling of the Spanish Empire, the last great colonial empire in the New World, and resisted any efforts by other European powers to extend their influence across the Atlantic.

This amicable turn in British-American relations was signaled when the outstanding questions between the two countries were settled by the Rush-Bagot Agreement of 1817. And when Florida was ceded to the United States by a treaty signed in 1819, though not ratified until 1821, the country could now turn West, in the knowledge that Britain and the US were, in diplomacy at least, of one mind. Vermont won statehood in 1791, Kentucky in 1792, and Tennessee in 1796. From the Northwest Territory, Ohio was carved out as a state in 1802. Illinois, west again of Indiana, was admitted to statehood in 1818. In the South, Louisiana qualified for statehood in 1812 – the first to be shaped from the Louisiana Purchase. Mississippi came in in 1817, Alabama two years later. The sequence was orderly and swift – and practically all had manhood suffrage. Every ten-year census confirmed the optimism: more acres, more products, more people. The movement West was reflected in the steady drift west of the state capitals too: Albany replaced New York City as the capital of "the Empire State;" Harrisburg became the capital of Pennsylvania instead of Philadelphia; Columbia eventually supplanted Charleston in South Carolina; in Virginia the seat of government shifted from Williamsburg to Richmond during the Revolution, and after the War of 1812 the western counties did their best to have it shifted again, to Winchester. In Georgia the constitution of 1795 arranged to transfer the state government inland from Savannah to Louisville. Within ten years this change was superseded by an agreement to make a capital out of a brand-new town to be called Milledgeville. The refusal to move Massachusetts' capital further west from Boston angered many citizens. The argument about location was a recognition that citizens expected their state government now to be active in promoting the economic development of all the state.

At the first census in 1790, the population of the 13 states was 3.9 millions, and by 1800 5.3 million – an increase of a third in a decade, and most of it by natural increase, since revolutionary wars at home and abroad had curbed immigration to some 4,000 a year, and Britain had tight restraints on the loss of skilled men. (Never the less, by 1837 it became 100,000 per year, and in the peak year of 1854 it was 427,600.) By 1820 there were 9.6 million; in 1830, 12.9 million. Although the importing of Negro slaves was prohibited by law in 1807, 20 years after 1787, as the Constitution had prescribed, the 700,000 slaves of 1790 had become about 2 million by 1830. The total population was thus doubling every 23 years and likely to go on doing so – for in 1830 nearly one in three of the total white population was under the age of ten. By 1850 the population would reach 23 million. By 1860, it reached 31.5 million (of whom 4.5 million were Negroes), and thus exceeded Britain's, and almost equaled that of France or Germany. And by 1850 half of the population lived west of the Appalachians. Better food, improved city sanitation – of which Philadelphia served as model – medical advances and increased resistance to disease, especially vaccination against smallpox, were the main causes of longer and healthier lives. As the population doubled, and doubled again, so the electorate had tripled in the 20 years before 1850, as the qualifications for the suffrage were widened – and lowered. There was now also a large class of industrial wage-earners.

For the Negro, however, the growth in sectionalism and the Western advance halted the promises implicit in 1776. By 1792 there had been anti-slavery societies in every state of the Union. Schemes for gradual emancipation were introduced in Pennsylvania (1780), Connecticut and Rhode Island (1784), New York (1785), and New Jersey (1786). In 1783 the Massachusetts courts, following the logic of the state constitution of 1780 ruled that the phrase "all men are born free and equal" must automatically abolish slavery there. The Northwest Ordinance stipulated that the territory north of the Ohio was never to permit slavery. Even in the South, where no abolition laws were passed, at least the continuance of slavery was deplored. A number of prominent citizens, George Washington among them, owning 150 slaves in his own name, and another 150 on his wife's plantations, arranged in their wills to free their slaves. But to free the labor force was to threaten the economy; for cotton and tobacco needed manual workers. The fund of goodwill was being sapped by invention also. The cotton engine (or "gin"), separating the fiber from the clinging seeds, transformed the South. When the Yankee, Eli Whitney, sojourning by chance on the plantation of Catherine Greene at Mulberry Grove, produced his simple machine the flood gates were opened. When Whitney patented his "gin" (short for "engine") the Patent Office was only four years old. The constitutional government of the United States was so new that the people of the more remote states scarcely knew what federal law meant. But they knew what upland cotton meant, and what the gin meant, as soon as the news of it leaked out. Inevitably the invention was stolen. Gins more or less on Whitney's design were being built in the carpenter shops of every plantation in Georgia, before Whitney's manufactory was set up in New Haven.

The cotton gin did not merely promise a vast cotton boom. There was the growing conviction among whites that whites and blacks could not coexist in the same country unless the whites were the masters. Humanitarianism therefore turned increasingly to the idea of freeing slaves in order to send them back to Africa. The Virginia legislature, for instance, passed four colonization resolutions between 1800 and 1816. But prejudices in the South were deeply rooted. In his *Notes on the State of Virginia*, written in 1781–2, Jefferson advanced it "as a suspicion only" that blacks "whether originally a distinct race, or made distinct by time and circumstances, are inferior to the whites in the endowments both of body and mind." Winthrop D. Jordan concludes that Jefferson's writing on the Negro "constituted, for all its qualifications, the most intense, extensive, and extreme formulation of anti-Negro 'thought' offered by any American in the thirty years after the Revolution."[38] This view is

---

[38] Winthrop D. Jordan, *White Over Black: American attitudes toward the Negro 1550–1812* (Chapel Hill, NC, University of North Carolina Press for IEAHC, 1968), pp. 439, 481.

buttressed by William Cohen. After studying Jefferson's slave holdings, his treatment of slaves, and his actual transactions, Cohen
concludes:

In his daily life there were few differences between Jefferson's behavior
as an owner of men and that of Virginia plantation masters who opposed
his antislavery speculations. His bondsmen were well fed and clothed,
and their work load was comparable to that of white freemen ... Nevertheless, when he dealt with runaways, sales of slaves, breeding, flogging,
and manumissions, his behavior did not differ appreciably from that of
other enlightened slaveholders who deplored needless cruelty, but would
use whatever means they felt necessary to protect their peculiar form of
property.[39]

Nowhere in the new nation did black-white equality become genuine. Below the Mason-Dixon line slavery continued and increased.
This was again mainly by natural increase, for large families were
the fashion. And as cotton boomed, and slave numbers grew, so
there grew the Southern awareness of their peculiar institution, and
of the investment of the plantation owner in his slave property. If
emancipation were to come, what of their loss of capital as well
as of labor? And could there, would there, ever be adequate compensation for the loss?

Behind the factional political in-fighting that one-party rule always
breeds, the Era of Good Feelings saw the virtual disappearance of
the Federalists – except in pockets of New England – and the
adoption by the Republicans of many of the features of Hamiltonian
nationalism. The protective tariff of 1816 and the second United
States Bank (1816) were symptoms of the conversions of the Jeffersonians. The Embargo and the War of 1812 stimulated industry,
especially iron manufactures, and agriculture, especially cotton.

The peace brought new immigrants, some of whom – British,
Germans, French, and Swiss in particular – were more accustomed
to work in industry than on the farm. Among the immigrants were
those with skills, like Samuel Slater at Pawtucket, Rhode Island. But
the early stages of the American Industrial Revolution depended
much more on the employment of women and children: the first
textile factories in New England, at Waltham and what is now
Lowell, employed women and children – even children under 12.
And, given the temporary slump in overseas trade, even sea-captains

[39] William Cohen, "Thomas Jefferson and the Problem of Slavery," *Journal of American History*, 61 (1969), pp. 514–15.

and shipowners turned to manufacturing: Salem and Providence, Rhode Island, became manufacturing towns. Industry developed fast where there were ample supplies of water and/or mineral resources: the Mohawk and Hudson valleys, the Jersey shore (Newark, Paterson), Philadelphia, Rochester, Pittsburg, and the Ohio valley. By 1820 Philadelphia's population reached 110,000, but it was now surpassed by New York City with 120,000.

The emergence of strong industrial interests in New England and the trend toward political democracy, particularly in the west, were major features of the years between Jefferson and Jackson. By 1830, however, they had contributed also to the formation of a new sectional division in American politics, which persisted until the Civil War. North opposed South, and both struggled to control the West, or at least to win its support. Under these conditions, efforts to form national parties, appealing to all classes and interests, became increasingly difficult, and politics became in large measure a series of sectional bargains. The great extent of the country was as much stimulus to sectionalism as to nationalism; as Tocqueville said later, these were "like two distinct currents flowing in contrary directions in the same channel." The size of the Republic brought, on the one hand, pride and prosperity; it brought, on the other, diverse climates, economies, and social patterns under a single political framework. What at one stage were embryo territories became, within a generation, sections with policies of their own, so that compromises had continually to be remade, with heart searchings and alarms. The sectionalism of Northeast and of Southeast is most strikingly displayed in the careers of Daniel Webster of Massachusetts and John C. Calhoun of South Carolina.

Calhoun, a South Carolinian of Scotch-Irish background, secretary of war in Monroe's Cabinet; and elected Vice-President in 1824, resigned in 1832 to serve as Senator from South Carolina. Early a nationalist, as in his support of the views of the War Hawks of 1812, Calhoun later came to symbolize Southern resistance to the tariff and abolitionism, as seen first in his anonymous *South Carolina Exposition and Protest* of 1828, affirming the Southern position on the so-called Tariff of Abominations of 1828, and asserting the right of a state to nullify or make void any act of the federal government that it saw as a violation of its constitutional sovereignty. His essentially sectional, pro-slavery, anti-majority, agrarian views determined the rest of his later public life and his writings. There should be some restraint, he held, on the unbridled majority control of government; otherwise nullification was legitimate, after a decision on it was taken by a special convention of an aggrieved state.

Calhoun was supremely the logician, an austere and easily angered man. He became the abiding and eloquent apologist for the slave interests, and he idealized the Southern system by likening it to that of classical Athenian democracy, which was also based on slavery.

By contrast, Daniel Webster voiced the attitudes of what was becoming the "North." An able, active lawyer, Webster was considered one of the greatest orators of his time. Notably in his speeches in 1830, in reply to Senator Robert Hayne of South Carolina, he defended the supremacy of the national Constitution against those who would permit its nullification by individual states. The Constitution was founded by the people of the United States, he held, not by the several states. Webster assailed the theory of nullification as unconstitutional. "The right of a State to annul a law of Congress cannot be maintained, but on the ground of the inalienable right of man to resist oppression; that is to say, upon the ground of revolution."

Of the two men, Webster was the greater orator, indeed probably the best in American history. "No man," it was said, "could be as great as Daniel Webster looked." With a face that seemed to have been hewn from his native granite, his eyes, said Thomas Carlyle, were "dull anthracite furnaces waiting to be blown." Though he was not born in a log cabin, an elder brother and sister were, and he never tired of boasting of the fact. During the period of the Embargo Act, he came into prominence as a champion of the New England shipping interests. The Federalists, who saw something of his potential, backed him in a successful candidacy for Congress; at the same time, he was building up a successful law practice in Boston. It was his good fortune to appear on the scene as a spokesman for New England at a time when both oratory and legal maneuvering were at the summit of their popularity. Holiday orations had succeeded Puritan sermons as the key efforts in invocation, and as occasions for festival, eloquence, and bunkum flourished side by side. The landmarks in Webster's life were his important speeches: for example, his Plymouth oration of 1820 and his Bunker Hill oration of 1825. In 1827 he was sent to the Senate (which he preferred to the House because of its better acoustics.) It was there, in 1830, that he delivered his famous "Reply to Hayne," which ended with a notable peroration on the grandeur of the union and the necessity for its preservation. Webster was, however – or he became – addicted to adulation, pompous and hungry for applause.

There was one other orator, who, unlike these two, saw himself as the great compromiser, as in 1824 he had been, in making a President. Henry Clay was in many ways the most representative

American of his time. He was born in Virginia and taken to Kentucky as a child. He early served in Congress, where he was a leader of the War Hawks of 1812. He then directed his energies chiefly toward the development of, and the argument for, the "American System." Clay began his political career as a spokesman for the agrarian West, but in time he became the champion of the Western moneyed interest which eventually settled into alignment with those of the East. He was the "Great Compromiser," and the most affable, the most genial and the most popular – with women as well as men – of the trio. He was defeated for the presidency in 1824, 1832, and 1844, and failed to secure party nomination for the contest in 1839 and 1848. [40]

There was one other lawyer – and American politics was already overwhelmingly a game (or is it more than that?) played by lawyers and won in law-courts – of major importance. He began as a Virginian, in fact a cousin of Thomas Jefferson, but became more a nationalist than all the others; and his legacy was to add a third branch to the federal government, far beyond the notions of any of the Founding Fathers. Moreover, he was a rarity, in that he remained consistent in his interpretation of the Constitution through all his years, and notably during his long and decisive chief justice-ship, from 1801 to 1835. Like his cousin, John Marshall was tall, loose-limbed, with "lax, lounging manners," casual in dress and style. But the cousins were poles apart in every other respect. A veteran of the War and of Valley Forge, like his frontiersman father – and convinced by that experience of the need for a strong government – he retained the tastes of a sociable soldier, addicted to whist, backgammon, and the race-track. He became, however, businessman, urbanite, and land speculator, unlike the scholarly and idealistic agrarian of Monticello. He was neither an eager student, nor a visionary; but shrewd, forceful and at ease in the real world. Secretary of state in John Adams's team, he was one of the "midnight judges," appointed just before Adams gave up his office.

Marshall's 34 years on the bench were as decisive for domestic America as was Hamilton for financial policy, and Monroe for American diplomacy. When the Capitol was being designed, no place was provided in it for the Court, which had to use an unassigned room in its basement. By the time Marshall died, his Court would be as important as either the House or the Senate. Throughout, he sought to strengthen the federal government, to hold the quickly

[40] Remini, *Henry Clay, Statesman for the Union.*

growing country together against the sectional tides. Republican presidents filled vacancies with states' rights Republicans, but all of them, even the able Justice Story, soon fell under the spell of Marshall's ideas. In those 34 years, Marshall dissented from the majority on his court only eight times, and he himself wrote 519 of 1,106 opinions handed down. This place he attained not because of legal learning — he had had only three months' training in law — but because of very definite opinions regarding the function of state and national governments, an ability to state these beliefs clearly and logically, and the strength to carry his associates with him. Basically, he was a frontiersman and a soldier, like Andrew Jackson, and thus had no innate distrust of strong government. He wrote his opinions as one might compose an essay on constitutional government, and then handed them to more learned men to justify. "Brother Story," he is reputed to have said on one occasion, "will add the citations." If the Federalist party never won another national election after 1796, the Supreme Court under Madison's lead expounded Federalist constitutional principles for a period that spanned the administrations of six presidents. By ingenuity and force of personality more than knowledge of legal texts, he made the Court a coordinate branch of government, and extended federal power at the expense of the states.

Marshall held to two central themes. First, that the Constitution, which created the government of the independent state, was "superior paramount law," unalterable by federal or state legislative act, or by executive order; and that it was the function of the Supreme Court to uphold it. This gave the Court, on appeal, a claim to judicial review of legislation. But, he argued, the federal government could follow any policy that was not specifically prohibited by the Constitution (the doctrine of "implied power"), and was not just the creature of the states to do as they prescribed. ("Let the end be legitimate, let it be within the scope of the Constitution, and all means which are appropriate ... are constitutional.") Thus, in *McCulloch* vs. *Maryland (1819)* he held that the federal government was entitled to establish the Second Bank of the United States, despite the objections of Maryland, which had taxed the banknotes of its Baltimore branch; the Bank, he held, was not subject to such state regulation. The center for him, unlike for John Calhoun, was greater than the parts.

By the same token, Marshall held to the supremacy of the judiciary not only over the states, but over the federal legislative power, as in the case of *Marbury* vs. *Madison (1803)*, in which he held that, while Madison, Jefferson's secretary of state, had no right to withhold the appointment to office of William Marbury, one of John Adams's last-moment appointments, that clause of the Judiciary Act of 1789 under which Marbury had sued was itself invalid as being contrary to the Constitution. The Supreme Court, that is, could declare Acts of Congress unconstitutional – a decision that, though not at the time of much effect, was ultimately extremely significant. Not until 1857 (in *Dred Scott* vs. *Sandford*) would the Court again strike down a law of Congress. Before the Civil War, judicial review was exercised almost exclusively against state laws, a power resting on reasonably solid textual ground – the prohibitions on the states recited in Article I, section 10, together with the clause of Article 6 declaring "the Constitution, laws, and treaties of the United States to be the Supreme Law of the Land."

In two cases, *Martin* vs. *Hunter's Lessee* (1816) and *Cohens* vs. *Virginia* (1821) Marshall also established the authority of the Supreme Court over its state courts. Implicit in all his cases was the wish to enhance the authority of the federal government. In the case of *Gibbons* vs. *Ogden* (1824), the so-called "Steamboat Case," he defined the nature of interstate commerce and its relation to the states. The New York legislature had granted Livingston and Fulton a monopoly of the steamboat business on the Hudson. Ogden secured a license from them. Gibbons, his competitor, operated steamboats under a federal license, and Ogden sought to restrain him. Marshall declared that commerce is intercourse and navigation; that commerce is interstate when it concerns more states than one; that Congress has complete power over such commerce and may exercise it within a state. Accordingly, the New York statute granting the monopoly was void. By implication, this gave the federal government ultimate authority over railways (which began to be built in 1825), water transport, and posts, and later over telegraph, radio, and television and air travel. Commerce became, that is, something more than buying and selling.

Secondly, Marshall believed in the sanctity and inviolability of private contracts, no matter what their ethical calibre – as evidenced in the case of the Yazoo frauds in Georgia, and in the Dartmouth College case. In the first of these, *Fletcher* vs. *Peck* (1810), despite the charges that speculators as well as Georgia legislators had acted fraudulently, and that the legislature had then properly annulled the land grants so made along the Yazoo River, the Court held that the sale to innocent investors was legally a contract which the Georgia legislature could not constitutionally invalidate. Again, in *Dartmouth College* vs. *Woodward* (1819), a charter of incorporation was held to be a binding contract within the meaning of the

Constitution, and could not be amended by a state legislature to bring that institution under state control. In each case, state laws were held to be unconstitutional – a view important for the future when private franchises and business corporations rather than colleges were the objects of state regulatory interference.

Moreover, Marshall left legacies that were not only in judicial judgments. He left protégés, in Joseph Story and James Kent. Joseph Story was a Salem lawyer, a professor of law at Harvard, and eventually an associate justice of the Supreme Court. He came from a family active in the Revolution, a family of radical traditions and ardent republicanism (his father had taken part in the Boston Tea Party). In his youth, Joseph Story was himself a liberal, but as he grew in years and honors, his attitude crystallized into reaction. His philosophy of government remained static, while changing conditions changed yesterday's liberalism into today's conservatism. His *Commentaries on the Constitution of the United States* set forth an ultra-conservative interpretation of the document. Story too revered George Washington, in the latter's Federalist aspect, and believed in an almighty national government. The principle of governmental checks and balances, capitalism, and the English common law were to Story the foundations of a sound society. Naturally enough, Story detested the Jacksonian regime, which he called "the reign of King Mob." James (Chancellor) Kent was of the same stamp as Marshall and Story. A New Yorker, he attended Yale College, and then practiced law in Poughkeepsie and New York City. He taught in the Columbia law school, was a member of the New York state court, and became chancellor of the New York Court of Chancery. This had been a judicial position of minor status, but Kent made it one of considerable importance. The creator of equity jurisdiction in the United States, Kent was always an ardent apostle of the common law, and a devotee of Blackstone; his *Commentaries on American Law* are heavily tinctured with Blackstonean conservatism. Kent was strongly devoted to the conservative tenets of John Locke, especially the doctrine sacred to him, as to Marshall, that a cardinal function of government is the preservation and protection of private property. This would, when slavery became a national issue, become a doctrine for the preservation of slavery, since slaves were property and owned by a master. Kent made nonsense of the view that the United States was a unique and peculiar society; democracy, he believed, had brought trouble to the Old World, and a wide suffrage jeopardized both property rights and liberty. In 1821 Kent aided in the revision of the New York state constitution and sought, not very successfully, to have it rewritten on Hamiltonian principles. Only the propertied classes, he held, should participate in government; and he too, of course, abhorred Jacksonian democracy.

The problem facing the judges – like the politicians – after 1787 was that of reconciling the need for stability with the inevitability of change. In the early years of the republic, there was also much heated discussion: should American law continue to pay allegiance to the English code? Should it be based on natural equity alone? Should an original American law, based solely on the law of nature, be created? Should French legal principles, which were derived from Roman law, be adopted? It was the triumph of John Marshall, Joseph Story, and James Kent that they succeeded in anchoring American law to English common law, equating the common law with the law of nature, which they defined as an ideal universal body of rational principles. And it would be the judges rather than the politicians who would define what those principles were. One Virginian drafted the Declaration of Independence, another led its armies to win separation from Britain, and another drafted the United States's Constitution. The fourth, not the least among them, put his own stamp on that document by insisting that all subsequent acts of the federal or of the state governments, or of their political leaders, would be assessed and if necessary thwarted by the judges as guardians of the covenant.

In 1901, on the centennial anniversary of the day Marshall took his seat as chief justice of the United States, a tribute was paid by another great judge, Oliver Wendell Holmes, then Chief Justice of the Massachusetts Supreme Judicial Court:

There fell to Marshall perhaps the greatest place that ever was held by a judge ... If American law were to be represented by a single figure, skeptic and worshipper alike would agree without dispute that the figure would be one alone, and that one John Marshall.[41]

At the human level, there was in this period a Franklinesque emphasis on hard work, on utility, ingenuousness, and human shrewdness. There was more concern with plain living than with high

[41] The still-standard life of Marshall is by A. J. Beveridge, in 4 vols (Boston, Houghton Mifflin, 1916). A briefer and more readable treatment is David Loth's *Chief Justice John Marshall and the Growth of the Republic* (New York, Norton, 1954). Nor should one omit to note the valuable chapters on Marshall in Alfred Kelly and Winifred Harbison, *The American Constitution, its Origins and Development* (New York, Norton, 1948), and the varied assessment in Thomas C. Shevory (ed.) *John Marshall's Achievement: Law, politics and constitutional interpretation* (New York, Greenwood Press, 1989).

thinking. Indeed, there was a certain Rousseauist distaste for the intellectual and an emphasis on the solving of practical problems that has always marched a trifle self-consciously, but assertively, in North America alongside the concern with education. If two of the Presidents and many more Congressmen were lawyers, all were farmers, accustomed to horses, ploughs, crops, and the importance of planning the planting. A virgin nature reinforced this by demanding the pioneer virtues. The emphasis was on a republican simplicity; Jefferson spoke of "the unquestionable republicanism of the American mind;" and when Sarah Franklin Bache, daughter of a distinguished father, found her children being treated as "young ladies of rank," she replied with hereditary verve: "There is no rank in this country but rank mutton."

The frontier conditions and habits of provincialism, of rough manners and rougher sports — from bear-baiting to gouging — and of personal isolation, contrasted with (and often caused) gregariousness at festivals and fairs, at barn-raising and harvests. The availability of land produced extensive land-grabbing and land speculation at all social levels, and at the same time reinforced a Whig belief that property, so easily acquired, was basic to political stability; extensive property ownership made American democracy possible in the eighteenth century and profitable in the nineteenth, and was to be its major source of conservatism in the twentieth. Being abundant, land was abused; just as no society in history has been so rich in resources as the United States, so none was for a century so prodigal with its wealth. Conservation came late in American development, and the American economy has long been geared not only to abundance but also to waste. This is one European impression of America that has stayed constant through the years.

If a legal-minded, it was not yet a particularly law-abiding society; neither was it a very cultured or a very tolerant one. Toleration triumphed in the end, as always, not from conviction but from necessity; it emerged from the clash of mutual intolerances of race or creed. The cultural leadership came, as always, from the aristocracy of talents, who had in this environment an easier road to the top, but who, being an elite, were never quite so fully respected as in Europe. But the second, third, and fourth Presidents were remarkably learned men; scholars as well as politicians. It was a society of free individuals, standing on their own feet, on native ground. Those who were not free had at least the opportunity to become so. It did believe in liberty; and liberty in 1800 it enjoyed as it had not 40 years before. It was discovering that with independence there came problems not so different from those faced by the Old World: of capitalist versus agrarian, of debtor versus creditor, of town versus rural frontier, and of party controversy.

There was by 1828 at the popular level a now-pervasive nationalism. It was rooted in distance and isolation from the Old World, in the long interval of European revolution which kept the Old World preoccupied, and in the heady stimulus of victory in the War of 1812. It was symbolized in the opening of the Erie Canal in 1825, using the Mohawk valley to link Buffalo with Albany on the Hudson River 360 miles away, which owed everything to the initiative of Governor DeWitt Clinton, and gave New York City access to the West. Although the issue of federal aid to build "internal improvements" became partisan and divisive, the Erie became a model, and a symbol, as did the steamboat on the Mississippi and, in 1828, the Baltimore & Ohio Railway. In 1787, 2 percent of the population lived in five cities (places, that is, of more than 8,000 inhabitants). In 1800 the percentage was 16, and there were 141 cities of more than 8,000 people; New York now had 1,175,000, Philadelphia 560,000, and Baltimore 200,000.

Wars provided slogans: "I have not yet begun to fight," said John Paul Jones off Flamborough Head in 1779; the XYZ affair of 1798 produced "Millions for defense, but not one cent for tribute;" the North African war was fought for "our country right or wrong;" and the British attack on Washington produced "The Star-Spangled Banner." The American eagle – modeled on the Roman – appeared on furniture and in newspapers, just as "Uncle Sam" replaced the earlier "Yankee Doodle" and "Brother Jonathan." From 1815 onwards, Washington's birthday (February 22) and the Fourth of July became national holidays, and occasions for fireworks. From 1818 it was established that the national flag would have a new star for each new state. The coincidence of the deaths of Thomas Jefferson and John Adams within hours of each other on the fiftieth jubilee of the Declaration of Independence stirred imaginations and stimulated a wave of republican pride and national self-consciousness. The first volume of George Bancroft's 10-volume *History* appeared in 1834, a story of uniqueness and wonder.

If there was no response to repeated presidential calls for a national university, the lexicographer Noah Webster argued that the American language was distinct from the English, and did his best to make it so:

As an independent people our reputation abroad demands that in all things we shall be federal; be national; for if we do not respect ourselves, we may be assured that other nations will not respect us ... America must be as independent in literature as she is in politics, as famous for arts as for arms.

   As a Yale graduate, who tended not to move far from Hartford, Webster took the Connecticut accent to be standard, and campaigned to make it so; he disapproved of the New Englander's *keow* and of the Marylander's *oncet* and *twicet*. His taste for Connecticut was reinforced by the fact that it was the first state, and for a time the only state, to have a copyright law. In spelling he used "s" for "c" in "defence," "offence," and "expence," and dropped the superfluous "u" in "labour" and "ardour;" and he reversed "re" in "theatre", "centre," and "lustre," to accord with their pronunciation. He spread the new words not only in his *Dictionary* (pron. Dictionerry) but in spellers and readers, and his *Spelling Book* in 1837 is estimated to have sold no less than 15 million copies. He did more: "he taught millions to read and not one to sin:" some good Anglo-Saxon words disappeared – "stink," "spew," and "womb"; and a new delicacy was born – girls were "betrayed" not "seduced", "legs" were "limbs", and "breasts" were "bosoms." He dotted his *Speller* with adages and proverbs, on Franklin's lines: "He that lies down with dogs must rise up with fleas."
   Perhaps Noah Webster was not only the most influential orthographer but the most thorough Federalist of them all. He scorned regionalism. He adopted Indian words as good American: *squash*, *moccasin*, *raccoon*. He took over familiar Dutch: *scow*, *sleigh*, *stoop*. But he made little money by his many activities as teacher, editor, salesman. When he decided to marry, he looked for a ready and steady income. He opened a law office.

6

Jacksonian Democracy

It has become essential to the office of the presidency of the United States that around its occupant myths and legends should gather. It is not, of course, so written in the Constitution. But the capacity to arouse popular emotion and to generate political excitements has come to be one of the tests of greatness in the man. He is indeed a successful President to whom most easily legendry adheres, however remote from truth it be. He must be more than life-size, and touched, if not by divinity, at least by the exotic. Thus Washington never told a lie, Lincoln was always quick with the apt anecdote and the tall tale, the story of John F. Kennedy will be permanently linked to "the curse on the Kennedys" and the un-fulfilled promise of a Camelot that never was. And even if there is, as in our own day, total information, if the fullest publicity is available, if all the processes are open and democratic, still the legends grow. The greater the President, the more he will be in danger of being lost in his own mythology. Of Washington, of Lincoln, of Theodore and Franklin Roosevelt, of J. F. Kennedy, this is true. And it is particularly so of Andrew Jackson.

1 THE MAN FROM THE WEST

Jackson was the first of the really strong presidents, opinionated, explosive, forceful. He was the first President to be chosen by processes recognizably democratic. He was perhaps the first President to voice, and to be ready to defend by force, the idea of American national unity. And, though a wealthy cotton planter with a real scorn for the mob, he could claim with justice to be the first truly popular President. As the only federal official now nominated, and certainly now elected, by the people as a whole, he was convinced that he was the tribune of the people, since he was elected by everybody. In his two terms – and he could have had a third had he wished – the power of the presidency was greatly enhanced. All his predecessors combined had vetoed only nine Congressional measures, usually on the grounds that they were unconstitutional. Jackson vetoed 12, and not merely on constitutional grounds. And the threat of a presidential veto itself became a powerful sanction to keep recalcitrant legislators in line. Both for what he did, and for what he is often portrayed as having done, Jackson's career is at once important and fascinating.

The seventh President of the US was born in 1767 at Waxhaws in the South Carolina backwoods. He came of poor Scotch-Irish stock, his father having left Carrickfergus just two years before; but the father died two months before the son was born. Two of his brothers were killed in the frontier war with Britain, and he himself, though a mere boy, took part in the battle of Hanging Rock. He trained as a lawyer, but his schooling was inadequate, and his spelling always idiosyncratic. He was a tall, hatchet-faced, high-tempered young man, and age never dulled the spirit: he was prompter with his fists than with words, and he had to his discredit at least one fatality in a duel. He was as proud of his dueling wounds as of the scar on his head earned from the British at Hanging Rock.

He moved west with the frontier, and settled at Nashville, then a village of log cabins. He lodged in the home of the widow Donelson, whose husband had been a Virginia land speculator and who was one of Nashville's founders. The daughter of the house, Rachel, had made an unhappy marriage with Lewis Robards; the friendship of Jackson with Rachel led to her divorce, but their own marriage took place before the divorce decree was granted. To his wife Jackson was devoted, and about the marriage and its scandal he was always sensitive; there was, thereafter, always in him a Wellingtonian promptness to defend women about whom gossip played. His marriage was happy; and socially it brought him up in the world a notch or two.

The lawyer turned cotton planter and farmer; he bought and sold land; and he built his own home on the Hermitage tract. In 1796 he was a member of the Tennessee convention which formed its first constitution, and he served for a spell in the House and the Senate in Philadelphia. But neither legislating nor debating were to his taste. In 1802, however, he was elected major-general of the

Tennessee state militia — by the casting vote of the new governor, his friend Archibald Roane, who had come West with him. This was a decisive turning point. The job was no sinecure, for in the West the militia were often on call. Jackson made his reputation as a frontier soldier, like Washington before him; but behind the images, he too was a wealthy landowner, an owner of slaves — and foxhounds; he could be decisive, dignified and determined. When one of his slaves was asked if he thought that Andrew Jackson would go to Heaven, his verdict was that "The Gen'll go to Heaven if he wants to."

In the War of 1812, when the Creeks rose in support of Britain, the Tennessee militia were called out. Jackson defeated the Indians at the battle of Horseshoe Bend on the Tallapoosa River in March 1814: not in itself a great victory, but an achievement of logistics, of hard slogging along difficult untamed trails, and of the holding together of reluctant volunteers by the effort of a superior willpower. He lost 50 dead, and 150 were wounded. Nine hundred Creeks were killed and the Creeks surrendered. Jackson now became a major-general in the Army of the United States. And by the Treaty of Fort Jackson, the Creeks were required to surrender 23 million acres of land, or roughly three-fifths of the present state of Alabama and one-fifth of Georgia. When many Creeks took refuge in Spanish-held Florida and stirred the Seminoles into raids across the American frontier, they gave any American government justification for counter-raids in defense.

Jackson was called on again in 1814 to defend New Orleans against the veterans of the Peninsular War — called on in fact, as we saw earlier, to fight an unnecessary battle in an unnecessary war. He chose his ground well, and the British forces, hemmed between marsh and river, were forced to attack on a narrow untenable front. Over 2,000 British lives were lost: American casualties were 8 dead and 13 wounded. Again, Jackson's skill lay in holding together a motley crowd of volunteers, prominent among them Jean Lafitte and his Bay pirates. The victory of January 1815 had no bearing on the treaty with Britain, which had already been signed, but it made Jackson's name now a legend back East as well as on his native ground. Aged 48, he was now a figure of national importance. And, as with a not dissimilar Western-oriented figure — and almost as ill-educated — of 40 years earlier, Jackson had qualities to match. About both Jackson and Washington there was the same directness, the same high temper, the distaste for words, the absolute loyalty to friends, the same expectation of an equal loyalty in return — and a private life beyond reproach. The road to the White House now became a clearer trail than the Natchez and New Orleans Traces.

Nor was it checked by the clash with the Seminoles. In 1818 Jackson chased the Seminoles back across the line into Spanish Florida, and in an excess of zeal hanged two British traders, Ambrister and Arbuthnot, that he allegedly mistook for spies. They had been tried and found guilty in a military court of giving aid to the Seminoles. When Florida was in turn acquired in 1821, Jackson was to be for a short time governor of the new territory.

There gathered around this powerful image — soldier, Indian fighter, Western expansionist with a Western program of a protective tariff and internal improvements — a group of friends who saw in Jackson the first serious candidate for the White House from the West. They included his former fellow-lodgers at the Donelson house, John Overton, William Lewis and the latter's brother-in-law John Eaton: the nucleus of his later "kitchen Cabinet." They began the hard work of politics, feeding the press with stories, persuading, cajoling, making contacts in other states. Jackson became the presidential choice of the Tennessee legislature in 1822, and in 1823 once again a Senator for Tennessee.

In 1824, the United States had in fact a one-party system. Under the successive Virginian Presidents — Jefferson, Madison, Monroe — and aided by the long years of isolation from Europe and by the War of 1812, partisan politics had all but disappeared. Against Monroe's selection in 1820 only one electoral college vote had been cast. Jefferson's party, the Republicans, was all but the party of all the people, and was called by some Democratic Republicans.

Ever since the formation of political parties during the Administration of Washington, it had been customary for the presidential candidates to be nominated by the Congressional caucus. By 1824, in an age when democratic sentiment was strong, the caucus had fallen into disrepute. In 1824 William H. Crawford of Georgia, the secretary of the Treasury, was named as a candidate by the Democratic Republican caucus, but only 68 of the 261 members of Congress bothered to attend; and Crawford himself had suffered a paralytic stroke. Other Republicans — John Calhoun, Henry Clay and John-Quincy Adams — as well as Jackson aspired to the White House. Clay, champion of the "American System" and of the South American republics, was the "favorite son of Kentucky." Adams was secretary of state, and was the only candidate known to oppose slavery. Calhoun withdrew from the race to run for Vice-President, unopposed. If the issues were far from clear, there was no shortage of candidates, and personality was all-important. But by 1828 the situation had changed. Clay withdrew from the race, though not with benevolence. He hoped Jackson would kill someone during the campaign. "How hard it is to keep the cowhide from these villains," stormed Jackson, and was with difficulty dissuaded from challenging Clay to a duel. Called everything from murderer to adulterer, Jackson always contended that the bitterness of the campaign caused his wife's death. She died in December 1828, just over a month after the returns were in.

By 1828 Crawford too, a sick man, was not a serious candidate. So the struggle became a straight clash between Jackson and Adams, between "the man who can fight and the man who can write." Crawford's major ally of 1824, Martin Van Buren of New York, turned to Jackson, and carried with him the Crawford groups of Virginia and Georgia. This was powerful support, though it stored up rivalry for the succession between Vice-President Calhoun, running again for the vice-presidency, and Van Buren. But in 1828 the result was impressive: Jackson's popular vote was quadrupled over that of 1824. He carried every state west of the Alleghanies and south of the Potomac, plus one-half of New York and all Pennsylvania. In the electoral college, it was 178 to 83.

2 KING MOB

Jackson's victory over Adams in the election of 1828 is usually regarded as a great popular triumph. It was marked as such by the crowds that cheered him on his journey in mid-January 1829 from Nashville, first by steamboat down the Cumberland River and up the Ohio to Pittsburgh, then overland to Washington; and still more by the mob violence of his Inaugural, when some 20,000 "supporters," stimulated by the tubs of punch placed over-abundantly on the White House lawn, invaded the house, destroying rugs, curtains, and furniture in their enthusiasm. The retiring President deemed it prudent to be absent – as his father had boycotted Jefferson's Inaugural. To Supreme Court Justice Story, no supporter of the President, "The reign of King Mob seemed triumphant."

The fact is that Jackson's success was made possible by the over-representation of the South in the electoral college. And by 1828 the Jackson machine (Lewis, Van Buren of New York, and James Buchanan of Pennsylvania) had won over the Crawford and Calhoun groups in the South. The South had no love of the common man or of the hero of the West, but it hated the tariff and feared Adams's nationalism. In 1828 it seemed as if Jackson's political strength

Plate 7 The election of General Jackson, 1828.
(The Mansell Collection, London.)

rested on an alliance of South and West – on, that is, lower tariffs for the South, and liberal land policies and internal improvements for the West. The Northwest deserted Clay because of his advocacy of the Bank, and swung to Jackson because he wanted to eliminate the Indian menace. For four years he had preached that the "people" had been defrauded in 1824 by a corrupt bargain. He preached it at rallies and barbecues and in the columns of the newspapers. He appeared to be but the symbol of a tidal wave of democratic and nation-wide discontent.

Two other major developments contributed to Jackson's victory, and to the success of his party through the next decade. The first of these was the rapid growth of the West and the influence of the Western states in promoting democracy. The political codes of the Western communities called for manhood suffrage, frequent elections, rotation in office, and popular control of the judiciary. The seaboard states were in turn compelled to abolish political and economic privilege, and by 1840 only Rhode Island retained colonial franchise restrictions.

The other major development which strengthened democracy was the introduction of the factory system in the Northwest. The new laboring masses, suffering from political and social discriminations, began to organize in the 1820s, forming labor unions and labor parties. The new labor organizations were formed not in the new textile factories where mainly women and children were employed, but in the handicraft trades, now selling to a larger and steadily expanding market. The new labor organizations typically consisted of printers and hatters – that is, of craft societies. The first trade union in the world was formed in Philadelphia in 1827 – though there had been some organizations among Philadelphia shoemakers since 1792. Their interest was in shorter working hours rather than higher wages, since the availability of cheap land in the West kept Eastern wages high. Union membership reached 300,000 by 1836. As early as 1828, the extension of the franchise made it possible for the wage-earners of the East to throw their support to the Democratic party of Jackson, to make of it essentially a farmer-labor party. The labor movement reached flood-tide in 1828–9 and the election of Jackson was only one of its consequences.

Many factors explain, then, the Jackson victory. But if Jackson was the product of this new democratic spirit, he also knew how to capitalize on it, and to use the new masses of voters to political advantage. He was uneducated and ill-informed about banking and finance, but he regarded himself as the tribune of the people, owing no deference to the other branches of the government. When the

Cherokees carried their case against Georgia to the Supreme Court and obtained a verdict, Jackson, who sympathized with the state and the white settlers, declared: "John Marshall has made his decision, now let him enforce it."

In his first two messages to Congress Jackson kept returning to the theme; "To the people belongs the right of electing their chief magistrate." His alliance with the bosses and machines, his use of the spoils system, his campaign against the Bank, all illustrate the popular nature of his administration. He was "King Andrew," as his critics called him, by the will of the people – and his own; he was an autocrat disguised as a democrat.

3 THE SPOILS SYSTEM

One of Jackson's first acts as president was to dismiss many office-holders and replace them with his loyal followers. The "spoils system" had already appeared in several of the states, especially New York and Pennsylvania. What Jackson did was to extend it to the federal administration. He had a precedent to follow, thanks to that wily but now ailing politico, William Crawford. The latter had introduced a four-year tenure law in 1820, making a number of officers and naval agents, registrars in land offices. Each presidential election was thus followed by the re-appointment of the entire civilian personnel of the federal government. Behind each Presidential candidate's banner there thus marched armies of job-holders or aspirants. This, of course, was thoroughly in accord with the democratic principle, so cherished in the West, of rotation in office. It rested not only on the code of rewards for loyalists after years in the wilderness, and of the adhesive quality of public plunder, but on the view that the duties of all public functionaries were so simple that any intelligent man could perform them. In fact Jackson did not abuse the "spoils system" during his administrations. Though the figures are disputed, it seems that he removed between 10 and 20 percent of the approximately 10,000 holders of federal offices, and something over a third of the 600 officials whose appointment was the direct concern of the President. By later standards the total was modest and the application was in general honest. Only with William Barry's appointment as postmaster-general in 1829 did the spoils system become rampant. If until 1861 the role of government was small, its payroll grew steadily.

Security and comfort, however, brought neglect; the system was inefficient, not least in the diplomatic services; federal employees were seen as armies of votes, commanded by party bosses (notably the post-master general, who from 1829 was in the Cabinet). Yet those who saw themselves as superior (like John Quincy Adams) were defeated; and one President, James A. Garfield, was shot in 1881 by a disappointed office-seeker. In practice, as used by "strong" men, it meant that postmasters and customs collectors now used patronage as a weapon for creating a well-organized Jackson machine which ensured Jackson's re-election in 1832.

The man who expected to succeed Jackson, the heir apparent to any alliance of South and West, was John Calhoun. Running again for the vice-presidency in 1828, Calhoun had given his support to Jackson, and expected (like Hamilton in Washington's, and Seward in Lincoln's administration) to have the deciding voice in the administration. Jackson's friendship for Calhoun dated back to the time of his invasion of Florida, for he always believed that Calhoun, then secretary of war, had upheld him. In 1830, however, a break occurred between the two men. In the first place Jackson learned that in fact in 1819 Calhoun had proposed to discipline him, and when Calhoun tried to explain away his attitude, Jackson became embittered. A social quarrel in the Cabinet widened the rift. John Eaton, secretary of war (whose appointment Calhoun had opposed) had a second wife, Peggy Eaton, who, because of a somewhat tarnished reputation as the daughter of a Washington saloon-keeper and a "merry widow," was ostracized by Mrs Calhoun and the wives of other Cabinet members, and by his own favourite niece, Emily Donelson, his hostess in the White House. Jackson was fond of Mrs Eaton and remembered his own wife had been similarly maligned; he was pleased when Van Buren, a fashionable and easy-mannered widower, (known as "Matty Van" or "Petticoat Pet"), treated her with gallant courtesy. Finally, Jackson, a staunch defender of the Union, suspected Calhoun of championing the doctrine of states' rights.

It was Van Buren who reaped the advantages from the feud between Jackson and Calhoun. In 1831 the Cabinet was reorganized, and the friends of Calhoun were replaced by men in sympathy with Jackson and his policies. Calhoun resigned the vice-presidency to become a Senator from South Carolina, now an open leader of nullification. Van Buren was nominated to be ambassador to England, and when the Senate rejected him (by Calhoun's exercise of his casting vote) Jackson determined to avenge the affront by making him his running mate in 1832. Van Buren, a smooth politician from New York, where he had been a county court judge, had built up a powerful political machine, "the Albany Regency," and had cleverly identified his own cause with that of Jackson, the leader of the Democratic Party. His nicknames indicate the man: as well as "Petticoat Pet" he was dubbed "the American Talleyrand" – or later, after the Depression of 1837, "Martin Van Ruin." John Calhoun said that "he was not of the race of the lion or the tiger; he belongs to the lower order, the fox;" for John Randolph, "he rowed to his object with muffled oars." Mrs Eaton at least accompanied her husband as minister to Spain, became a favorite of the queen, and married one daughter to a Randolph of Virginia and another to the Duc de Sampajo; a grand-daughter became Baroness Rothschild of Austria.

The quarrel between Jackson and Calhoun was far more than a personal feud. Jackson's "policies" were the product of an instinctive egalitarianism and a Jeffersonian agrarianism. Chastened by the bankruptcy of 1819 that ended his own land speculations, a believer in the agrarian values of hard work and paying off all debts, including the national debt, he had enemies: the Bank, and easy credit. The President found a new ally in Van Buren, and a new alignment: of Southern planters with the plain Republicans of the northern towns, who could agree on opposition to "internal improvements" – for New York wanted no federally backed competition for its own state-financed Erie Canal – and to the Bank, to New Yorkers an unwelcome Philadelphia-based rival to Wall Street. Calhoun's disgrace thus signified that the South had lost political influence, and that the Western farmers and Eastern laboring masses were becoming the dominant elements in the Democratic Party. On no issue did this fact become more obvious than on the nullification question.

4   NULLIFICATION

After the War of 1812 Calhoun and Southern spokesmen such as William Lowndes and Langdon Cheves of South Carolina had advocated the nationalist program: the tariff, internal improvements, and the Bank of the US. But industry was developing slowly in the South; it lacked skilled labor, fuel, and water power; its white population increased much more slowly than that of the rest of the country, and there was a steady exodus to the new, richer and cheaper lands in the South and West, and it was increasingly hurt by protective tariffs imposed, it seemed, for Northern benefit. Higher duties raised the planter's costs for clothing and tools. Moreover, the depression of the 1820s ended the uninterrupted half-century of boom conditions in South Carolina, where rice, indigo, and sea island cotton had created a wealthy low-country aristocracy, and where a matching cotton culture spread to the uplands. As cotton spread to the cheap and fertile lands of the Gulf states, however, an era ended for Charleston. "States' rights," once synonymous with democratic-mindedness, now became a lament, and in the end a call to arms, in 1828 as in 1861. Calhoun, and his South with him, became savage critics of the tariff, and in 1828 he drew up his Exposition and Protest, a statement of the states rights case. Until then Jackson himself had shared this point of view: he vetoed a bill authorizing the government to buy stock in a company to extend the road from Maysville on the Ohio to Lexington, Kentucky, without which Lexington would be bypassed by Western travel; he was all for this road being extended, but he doubted if it was constitutional for a purely internal improvement within one state to be built at federal expense. But when states' rights items were pushed to the extravagant lengths of Calhoun's claim that a state could nullify the will of the federal government, Jackson drew a firm line. On April 13, 1830, at the annual Jefferson birthday banquet, angered by no less than 24 toasts to nullification, Jackson's proposition was: "Our Federal Union, it must and shall be preserved." It is easy enough to label the issues by the dinner toasts — and to cite Daniel Webster's "Liberty and Union, now and forever, one and inseparable." Jackson held that the theory of state sovereignty would threaten the union, and be a recipe for chaos — as it was. In historical fact, the union had begun as one of several states, as Webster himself argued in 1814. But as its principal architect, James Madison, had seen in 1787, its growth was its own best security. It was visibly stronger in 1832 than in 1814, or in 1787. Yet with expansion the seams in the fabric were now showing.

In 1832, when Congress passed a high tariff measure, a special session of the South Carolina legislature declared it null and void, and said that if the US used force against it the state would secede. Force was precisely what Jackson intended to use. The President was voted full control over army, navy and militia to bring South Carolina into line; an act, said Calhoun, "to enforce robbery by murder." In the South a medal was struck: "John C. Calhoun, first President of the Southern Confederacy." Clay introduced a compromise tariff law in 1833 securing step-by-step tariff reductions over the next ten years, and South Carolina thereupon rescinded its ordinance of nullification But if the President had won, the issue was but delayed for 30 years. Calhoun and the Nullifiers dominated the South. The Democrats in the West developed a political-economic program of their own: cheap land, an end to the Indian menace, internal improvements at federal expense – and protection. Northern Democrats agreed with Western on the need for tariff protection; but on nothing else. To them cheap land in the West led to depopulation and high wages.

5 THE BANK OF THE US

Jackson, a strong Federalist where secession was concerned, was a states' rights man where the Bank was concerned. He believed that the Bank had been used to block his victory in 1824 and to oppose him in 1828; he had the Westerner's fear of a big monopoly which kept interest rates high and milked the poor and the debtors' classes; the banks bred speculation, he believed, and transferred money from the many to the few. On this issue he was ignorant and prejudiced, but so were most Westerners. The Bank Charter did not expire until 1836, but his opponents, especially Clay, his presidential rival again in 1832, demanded its re-charter before the election, so that the Jackson veto would become an issue in the campaign. Indeed it did: and the more open political processes indicated that Jackson had a popular following on this issue. The candidates were now being nominated in national conventions, and the first Democratic convention in May 1832 in Baltimore had identifiably modern features. A so-called "spontaneous" call to a national convention of Democratic-Republicans was put out for May 1832 in Baltimore, organized by Van Buren, Amos Kendall, and Major Lewis. This, the first Democratic National Convention, set a pattern; representation in it was apportioned on the basis of 1 vote for each electoral vote of the state; 344 delegates in all attended from every state in the Union except Missouri. The Jackson nominating convention, however, was not the first. In 1826 an ex-Mason, a certain William Morgan, had disappeared and it was assumed that he had been murdered, allegedly for revealing the secrets of Freemasonry; a bitter anti-Masonic movement resulted, culminating in the formation of an Anti-Mason political party. In the various enquiries between 1827 and 1831 it emerged that practically all the office-holders in New York were Masons, and Andrew Jackson was one too – a revelation that his opponents were quick to exploit. In September 1830 the Anti-Masons, largely Roman Catholics and urban immigrants, held a national convention at Baltimore and nominated William Wirt, a Virginian lawyer, for the presidency. They thus became the first "third party" in the history of the US.

Following this precedent, the supporters of Adams and Clay and the various nationalist and anti-Jackson forces met in the same city in December 1831; but only 156 delegates attended, and none at all came from South Carolina. Adopting the name National Republicans, this convention endorsed the Bank and nominated Clay. The National Republican platform, later drawn up by Clay, called for protective tariffs, the Bank, internal improvements, a civil service, and the final arbitrage of the Supreme Court. It denounced the sins of Jackson, which were numerous but popular. In the 1832 campaign Clay decided to force the Bank issue. Nicholas Biddle, the Philadelphia financier who was president of the Bank, was induced by Clay to apply for a new charter, though the existing one would run until 1836, and a bill to that effect was introduced into Congress. Clay felt that Jackson was now faced with a dilemma: if he signed the bill, he was guilty of inconsistency; and if he vetoed the bill, Clay felt confident he would defeat him at the polls. But when the Bill to re-charter the Bank was passed by Congress in the early summer of 1832, Jackson, a better judge of public opinion than Clay, did veto the Bank bill: he would "cripple the monster." "Mr Biddle's Bank" became the major issue in the election. Jackson's indignation was strengthened by the fact that the Bank was spending lavish sums of money to defeat him, that Clay got easy loans from it, and that Webster was on its payroll as counsel. Louis McLane, secretary of the Treasury, was friendly to the Bank, and was therefore promoted out of the way to the State Department. His successor, William Duane, was dismissed when he would not remove the government's deposits from the Bank. The third incumbent, Roger Taney, was in sympathy with Jackson, and ordered that public funds be deposited in 23 specified state banks, known as "pet banks." This, of course, compelled the Bank to contract its loans and a period of financial stringency ensued. Petitions and deputations came to Jackson to plead for the Bank, and continued to do so through his second term – but in vain.[1]

When Congress convened in December 1833, Clay led the attack on the administration by requiring the Senate to demand Jackson's statement to his Cabinet advising the removal of deposits. Jackson

[1] Robert V. Remini, *Andrew Jackson and the Bank War* (New York, Norton, 1968); John M. McFaul, *The Politics of Jacksonian Finance* (Ithaca, NY, Cornell University Press, 1972); Paul Goodman, *Towards a Christian Republic: Antimasonry and the Great Transition in New England 1826–1836* (New York, Oxford University Press, 1988); William P. Vaughn, *The Antimasonic Party in the US 1826–1843* (Lexington, University of Kentucky Press, 1983).

was well within his rights in rejecting this demand. Thereupon the Senate passed Clay's resolutions, one declaring that Taney's reasons for removal of deposits were unsatisfactory, and one censuring Jackson, by a vote of 26 to 20, for having assumed authority and powers not granted by the constitution or the laws.

Is there a senator who can hesitate to affirm ... that the President has assumed a dangerous power ... not granted to him by the Constitution and the laws?

The eyes and the hopes of the American people are anxiously turned to Congress. They feel that they have been deceived and insulted; their confidence abused; their interests betrayed; and their liberties in danger. They see a rapid and alarming concentration of all power in one man's hands. They see that, by the exercise of the positive authority of the Executive, and his negative power exerted over Congress, the will of one man alone prevails and governs the Republic. The question is no longer what laws will Congress pass, but what will the Executive not veto. The President, and not Congress, is addressed for legislative action.

And then, in the grand manner, the peroration: "The land is filled with spies and informers, and detraction and enunciation are the order of the day. People, especially official incumbents in this place, no longer dare to speak in the fearless tones of manly freedom but in the cautious whispers of trembling slaves. The premonitory symptoms of despotism are upon us; and if Congress does not apply an instantaneous and effective remedy, the fatal collapse will soon come on, and we shall die – ignobly die! base, mean, and abject slaves – the scorn and contempt of mankind – unpitied, unwept, unmourned!"[2]

Jackson responded:

The resolution of the Senate ... presupposes a right in that body to interfere with [the] exercise of Executive power ... If by a mere denunciation – the threat of censure – the President should ever be induced to act in a matter of official duty contrary to the honest convictions of his own mind in compliance with the wishes of the Senate, the constitutional independence of the Executive Department would be as effectively destroyed and its power as effectually transferred to the Senate as if that end had been accomplished by an amendment of the Constitution.[3]

---

[2] *Register of Debates*, 23rd Congress, 1st session, p. 718.
[3] Robert V. Remini, *Henry Clay, Statesman for the Union* (New York, Norton, 1991), p. 451.

President Jackson lost; he became the only President of the United States ever to be censured. Three years later, on January 16, 1837, the resolution of censure was expunged.

In 1832 the President, with Van Buren now as his running mate, was re-elected by a larger popular vote than in 1828 (687,000 as against 530,000 for Clay and Wirt together); in the electoral college he won 219 as against 49 for Clay (Massachusetts, Connecticut, Rhode Island, and Kentucky) and 7 from Vermont for Wirt, and made incursions into the hitherto alien territory of New England. The Bank duly went out of existence – but its disappearance, and the distribution of its funds among the states, which promptly dissipated them, was a disaster – though hidden for a while by the boom of the Jackson years.

Jackson's war on the Bank, nevertheless, was an economic disaster for the United States. As the end of the national Bank drew near, hundreds of local banks sprang up like mushrooms and issued vast quantities of unsecured and worthless paper notes. Jackson, who knew next to nothing about banking, hoped to substitute gold coins for enormous issues of paper notes then in circulation. Bullion, of course, could meet only a fraction of the needs of a country enjoying an extraordinary business boom. The period 1830–7 was one of unusual prosperity. This was due in part to the expansion of domestic trade, in part to heavy investment in road, canal and railroad projects, and finally to the re-opening of American trade with the West Indies in 1830.[4] Indeed, so great was the prosperity that the national debt was extinguished in 1835, and in 1836 the Treasury had a surplus of $32 million. Congress voted to distribute this surplus among the states according to their population, and the states promptly applied the money to reckless schemes of internal improvements. Such prosperity encouraged demand for tariff reduction and the Western demand for reduction in the price of land.

The business boom of the early 1830s included three unhealthy elements: over-issue of banknotes, over-investment in internal improvements, and over-speculation in Western land. Between 1830 and 1836 receipts from the sale of land rose from $1,880,000 to $24,877,000 – most of it purchased by speculators with the worthless notes of the hundreds of "wildcat" banks recklessly chartered by state legislatures. Western states were plunging themselves into

[4] Since 1783 Britain had refused to allow the US to trade with the British West Indies. After Jackson threatened retaliation, Britain opened the trade to the US in 1830.

debt in order to carry out grandiose schemes for canals, turnpikes, and railroads, which were constructed far in excess of reasonable needs.

The needle that pricked this bubble of fictitious prosperity was Jackson's "Specie Circular," ordering land offices to accept only gold or silver in payment for public land. The President issued this order because the government was getting nothing out of the land sales except an accumulating amount of credit in a number of unstable banks. The effect of the Specie Circular was the immediate depreciation of the state bank notes which the land offices had been accepting for public land and depositing in the "pet banks." As these bank notes became worthless, land sales ceased, land values collapsed, and the wildcat banks called desperately for specie to meet their notes and at the same time contracted their loans. Inevitably these local banks had to close their doors, and by 1837 every bank in the United States had suspended specie payment. The distribution of the Treasury surplus only aggravated the credit problem, for it involved the withdrawal of millions of dollars from the deposit banks at the very moment that more currency was needed to sustain credit. The new entrepreneurs relied on easy credit from local banks, and were hurt by tight money policies.

What is less familiar is that, of his kitchen Cabinet — though most of them had started off as poor farm boys and Van Buren began work helping his father run his tavern — most were businessmen, except for Major William Lewis, the Tennessee planter who came to live with the widowed Jackson in the White House, and James K. Polk, also of Tennessee, himself later President of the United States. Martin Van Buren became a lawyer-turned-investment banker; and David Henshaw, Jacksonian boss of Massachusetts, though himself a banker, was quick to rail at those he called "aristocrats" or "capitalists" — to him synonymous — by whom he meant the old families, the Appletons and Lawrences of the earliest Industrial Revolution in Massachusetts. Samuel Ingham, Jackson's first secretary of the Treasury, was a Pennsylvania paper manufacturer-turned-banker. All sought to kill the bank of the US, since it stopped the state banks from lending as freely as they might otherwise do. For all of them, however poor their origins, saw credit as the life-blood of industrial investment in a new country with limitless resources to exploit. And all lived by trade, including foreign trade — and customs dues were still then the principal source of federal income. Since most of this trade came from and in New York, it was natural for Amos Kendall, ablest and longest-serving of all Jackson's liege-men, complex and chronically ailing, to say that

paying the Bank of the United States located in Philadelphia was
"a wrong done to New York in depriving her of her natural advantages." It was mere chance that the attack on the Bank of the
US could be personalized in an attack on its president, Nicholas
Biddle, himself a Philadelphian, and a pampered product of wealth:
elegant, literary, intellectual – and aware of his qualities. In the
end his Bank of the US was broke, and he was tried on criminal
charges, to be released on a technicality, but to die a broken man.
Amos Kendall, later Jackson's postmaster-general, was a Jacksonian
in another sense, as a Jeffersonian also: "The world is governed too
much." All were aware that from New York or elsewhere money
passed from local banks, for fines, excise, postage and import duties,
to federal agencies, and from them went as government expenditure,
often to distant places: army posts on frontiers and Indian agents
in the territories, or to owners of public debt, largely foreigners.
So, the Jacksonian attack was no mere frontier and agrarian protest:
in his case the attack came from a Westerner hostile to an Eastern
monopoly that played politics and conferred privileges on chosen
individuals in response to persuasiveness from the businessmen and
would-be entrepreneurs closest of all to King Andrew's throne.

It was fortunate for Jackson that the ill effects of the Specie
Circular did not become manifest until after he had left the White
House. Indeed, the campaign of 1836 was too far advanced to
be affected. Jackson had no difficulty in securing the democratic
nomination for his right-hand man, Van Buren. The opposition
consisted of many heterogeneous elements who had little in common
save hatred of "King Andrew." The old National Republicans, the
party of property led by Webster, Clay, and Adams, resented the
sustained attack on the Bank and the Maysville veto. States' rights
Democrats like John Tyler were offended by the treatment of South
Carolina. Nativists joined because they disliked the Irish immigrants,
Roman Catholics and Masons, who were being welcomed by the
Democratic politicians and city machines. As these diverse groups
were linked only by hatred of Jackson, they adopted in 1834 the
name "Whig" to signify their opposition to the "tyrant" in the White
House. Unable to agree on a candidate or platform, the Whigs
merely tried to prevent the election of Van Buren, and in this they
failed. The consequences hit only his successors, with local bank
failures, an end of land sales, and all but universal bankruptcy in the
panic of 1837. For the "Bank War" was reflected in similar bank
wars in every state.

Jackson was a strong, vigorous and contradictory being, quick-
tempered, rich in prejudice and passion. On nullification, he was a

Unionist and an authoritarian, and on the strength of it he got an honorary degree from Harvard – to John Quincy Adams's horror. When the Harvard students shouted "Give us a speech in Latin, Doctor," he replied: "E Pluribus Unum." On the Bank he was a Westerner. On internal improvements he was a states rights man. On the Indians he was all of these. He made 94 treaties with the Indians, and opened up for white settlement millions of acres. When the Indians were slow to move, he was not: he harried the Seminoles in 1819, and when they repudiated a treaty he wiped out those who stayed behind in Florida. Hostilities with the Seminoles in Florida continued until 1842, at a cost of 1,500 lives lost, and of $20 billion. Creek, Choctaw, and Cherokee were pushed across the Mississippi; when the Sauk and Fox Indians in Illinois under Black Hawk were slow to move in 1831 they were ruthlessly massacred.

Jackson was by nature an authoritarian who treated his Cabinet as executive clerks, aware – as with many Westerners – that the people have a taste less for democracy than for leadership, and a straightforward affection for character. He knew from instinct the truth of that aphorism of William Penn's: "Let the people think they govern and they will be governed" (*Some Fruits of Solitude*, 1693). The West may have been the seed ground of equality, but it produced very unequal beings. Jackson was a natural leader who can best be described, in T. P. Abernethy's words, as an "opportunist" or as "a demagogic aristocrat." He owned slaves, and slavery seemed not to worry him at all. He came up the hard way, and never paused to reflect on theory or justification. He was the first Westerner to become President, the first genuinely popular incumbent of the White House, and the most colorful and masterful politician between Jefferson and Lincoln. Unlike the Jeffersonians, he represented a democracy not afraid of a strong central government, and which insisted that at least some of the people should rule as well as vote.

He retired in 1837 to "The Hermitage," a Victorian Monticello outside Nashville, where he died in 1845. He was buried in his own garden alongside his wife Rachel. He had, he said on his deathbed, only two regrets: that he had not hanged John Calhoun and that he had not shot Henry Clay.

6 THE POLITICS OF DEFEAT IN JACKSON'S WORLD

Among nineteenth-century Americans, few commanded the reverence and respect accorded to Henry Clay of Kentucky. One of the

greatest orators of the century, he equaled or surpassed his contemporaries Daniel Webster and John C. Calhoun. Clay, the Speaker
of the House for longer than any man in the century, was a major
character in the drama of the new nation. He wielded almost
unimaginable power through his wit, biting satire, and golden voice.
He was a beloved figure whose compelling presence in Congress,
more than any other, helped preserve the Union in the antebellum
period. Indeed, it was his proposal to avert division that resulted
in the compromise of 1850.

A pamphlet of 1844 entitled Henry Clay's *Moral Fitness for the
Presidency* declared that "The history of Mr Clay's debaucheries
and midnight revelries in Washington is too shocking, too disgusting
to appear in public print." A handbill from the same election portrayed Clay as "that notorious Sabbath-breaker, Profane Swearer,
Gambler, Common Drunkard!" Clearly character was at stake in the
political world described by Robert Remini, a world of oratorical
feats and battles in Congress as well as the rough and tumble of
electioneering, a world in which consistency was an issue, conspiracy
and duels common.[5]

Clay (1777–1853) was one of the most brilliant figures in this
world, a Virginian who sought opportunity by hiking west, and
made his way as a lawyer in Kentucky. The new world in the West
was open to talent. Elected to the Senate at 29, Clay became a
long-serving speaker of the House of Representatives, and also held
office as secretary of state. Yet he was defeated for the presidency
in 1824, 1832, and 1844, and failed to secure party nomination for
the contests in 1839 and 1848.

As Speaker of the House, Clay championed a vision of a prosperous United States whose people were fully represented in governmental decisions. But he suffered enormously their repeated
rejections of his bid for the presidency. If he failed in any area, it
was not his purported womanizing, his gambling or drinking but
his towering ambition for what he perceived to be his destiny. His
defeat by Andrew Jackson in 1832 was due to a lack of the populist
instinct, an inability to reach the general public, while in 1840
Harrison's "nonsense and shout" were preferable to lofty statements
about the objects and purposes of government. Four years later
James K. Polk, a politician of conspicuously fewer talents, was
seen as more acceptable than Clay. Clay emerged as a great Congressional orator who failed to appreciate the democratization of

---

[5] Remini, *Henry Clay*.

society and politics that democracy brought. In 1840 his inability to appreciate the strong popular desire to gain Texas was fatal to his campaign.

It was not only politics that brought disappointment and despair. Clay, a brilliant and witty companion, an eloquent and virile man, suffered many ailments, and numerous personal tragedies. All six of his daughters and one of his sons predeceased him; one son was a severe alcoholic, two were committed to asylums. The death of his favorite son led him to turn to religion. Earlier in his career he had serious financial problems and had to borrow from John Jacob Astor. An able man held back by the widespread preference for mediocrity and brought low by hubris: the theme is an attractive and familiar one. But there was more to his story.

Clay was on many occasions an able populist, keen to speak and seek support throughout America, and the very fact that he won nomination on three occasions revealed his appeal as a candidate. In 1844 Polk's percentage of the popular vote was a mere 1.4 percent over Clay's. Clay's failure was not an inevitable product of his personality or of the voting system. Different factors were at work in each of his defeats. No one could have beaten Jackson in 1832. Clay's career is an account of the play of contingency, rather than the working out of fate. It is also fascinating because of the issues he addressed. A champion of Latin American independence, Clay saw the potential of America as a great nation, sought to provide a framework for economic growth, and strove to avoid seeing the Union wrecked on the issues of slavery and states' rights. These helped to cost him the presidency.

The bitter sectional divisions within America made it increasingly difficult for a national politician not to arouse hostility. Clay fought in Congress for the compromise of 1850, which helped to postpone secession and civil war, but neither compromises nor talk of common interests could hold the Union together. Instead, there was to be a brutal war that revealed the bankruptcy of federalism. Lincoln could present Clay as an inspiration, but one of his sons fought for the Confederacy.

7   THE POLITICS OF THE JACKSONIANS

The characteristics of the 12 stormy years between 1829 and 1841 are clear: first, an extension of democratic privileges to the common man on a scale without parallel in American history (360,000 voted in the presidential election in 1824; 1.5 million in 1832; 2,400,000 in 1840; 2,870,000 in 1848; over 4 million in 1860), and expressions of sympathy for votes for women (as in Emerson, Horace Greeley, and Lincoln): second, attacks on monopoly that arrayed the masses against the classes and roused the shades of Jefferson and Hamilton; and, third, a bold federal challenge to any talk of nullification or secession from the Union. Behind the images were the image-makers: the phenomenal growth of newspapers and rallies, of the lyceum lectures and P. T. Barnum's circuses, and of barbecues and of party machines — ideal tools as they would become to control the immigrant urban votes as they grew in number. The Democratic Party from the 1840s onwards was a curious alliance of low-tariff South and high-tariff Pennsylvania, of (ex-Puritan) New England and Boston's Catholic Irish, and anti-Catholic and anti-Indian rednecks from Georgia, of frontier Tennessee and sophisticated New York. All that could hold such an alliance together was spoils, the "pork barrel," "the cohesive power of public plunder." Elections were about serious issues, and an ever-increasing number of them; they were entertaining and boisterous — and frequent; for local, state, and federal decision-making required mass meetings and barbecues, banquets, parades, and speeches galore. Since the national parties were carefully constructed and steadily oiled alliances of local groups, the national reflected the local, and vice-versa. All were occasions for fun and frolic, for feud and riot.

Before the Revolution, when the mob had played a key role in politics, it was usually hired by a patrician leader or by a radical group to do a master's bidding. By Jackson's day, in an open-market economy, mobs now became the often spontaneous action of individuals expressing the conflicting loyalties of social, ethnic, racial, and religious groups. This was especially so in cities — particularly New York. Rioting became a means of expressing and redressing group grievances at the expense not only of public order but also by inflicting pain on rival groups. Most rioters were now drawn from "the very bottom of society" and were motivated by hostility towards immigrants, Catholics, Jews and blacks — though the tension between the last and the newly arrived Irish Catholics was acute. The emergence of a labor movement accelerated this trend, with labor problems most acute each spring regardless of the general state of the economy.[6]

Jacksonian politics is closer to the twentieth-century pattern than to Jefferson's world. Indeed, Jefferson was forthright: "I feel much

[6] Paul A. Gilje, *The Road to Mobocracy: Popular disorder in New York City 1763–1834* (Chapel Hill, NC, University of North Carolina Press, 1987).

alarmed," he wrote in 1824, "at the prospect of seeing General Jackson President. He is one of the most unfit men I know for such a place." The President did not "emerge" from the smoke-filled meetings of a Congressional caucus, but openly and dramatically as the chosen one of a succession of noisy and open state conventions, attended by party activists, many of whom had party jobs, or expected them. Marshalled by the postmaster-general, who became the officer in charge of jobs, rewards, and punishments, party organization took on the nature of a well-drilled and disciplined army; and party "machines" formulated political opinions for the increasingly literate masses, and reaped votes for the chosen leaders. The party managers became the American Tadpoles and Tapers, to use Disraeli's characters, the "pullers" who were aware that the game would ultimately be won by popular clamor.[7]

Jackson, who had come up a new way, as well as a hard one, did not regard his Cabinet as an advisory body, but merely as a group of executive clerks, and soon discontinued its meetings. He sought and secured necessary advice from his kitchen Cabinet, a small group of cronies consisting of editors, minor office-holders, and personal acquaintances; this group, always available to the President, acted as his chief lieutenants, supplying secret information and advice. During his second term, his critics called themselves "Whigs" in opposition to "King" Andrew. The Whigs were made up of the National Republican followers of Clay and Webster, plus the Anti-Masons and all those dissatisfied with the outcome of the nullification and Bank controversies and the high-handed executive policies of Jackson. They had the support of sound-money men, of business and – for a time – of those larger southern planters whose staple crops involved them in the commercial network. In short, the Whigs represented a curious combination of political wanderers bound together by a common anti-Jackson feeling; they were a cross-class and cross-section alliance, seeking continuous national growth by government encouragement. This strange party was in the main the descendant of the old Federalist Party, and bridged the gap between Federalism and the rise of present-day Republicanism in the 1850s. Because of their diverse elements and interests, the Whigs were seldom able to agree upon a set of principles, and only once, in 1844, did they select a candidate committed to a platform. But, as is now a cliché in American politics, a platform is not something you stand on, it is something you get in on.

---

[7] Benjemin Disraeli, *Coningsby* (Oxford, Oxford University Press, 1982), p. 409.

The Jackson party now assumed the name of Democrats, and thus for the next 20 years the old parties of Jefferson and Hamilton battled as Democrats and Whigs. In 1836 Jackson could have been re-elected for a third term, but he declined the honor. With a final flourish of leadership, he selected his successor; and the Democrats, the majority of them party officials, customs officer, and postal managers – the "payroll" vote – dutifully nominated Martin Van Buren, the smooth New York politician and Jackson's Vice-President. The Whigs hoped to defeat Van Buren by throwing the election into the House. Their plan was to nominate three leaders, each of whom would carry his own section, and thus prevent any candidate from getting a majority of electoral votes. Accordingly, the sectional candidates on the Whig ticket were Daniel Webster in New England, the Virginia-born General William H. Harrison in the Northwest, and Senator White in the Southwest. Jackson's hold on the people was demonstrated when Van Buren received more popular and electoral votes than his opponents combined. The Democrats also carried both houses of Congress. To the surprise of the Whigs, "King" Andrew and the "people" still ruled.

Van Buren took office with the announced purpose of following in the footsteps of his "illustrious predecessor," but it was soon evident that he could not maintain the pace. Of no more than average ability, he was soon swept off his feet by a storm not of his own making. The wild speculation and inflation which had marked the close of Jackson's presidency burst like a bubble soon after Van Buren entered office, and the country suffered the worst panic experienced until then. In May 1837 every bank in the US suspended specie payments; by early 1838 nine out of every ten factories were closed, and almost all the state governments – especially those which had borrowed heavily to finance roads, canals, and "internal improvements" – were bankrupt. The public followed its invariable practice and held the administration responsible; in democratic and media-influenced politics, the public knows what it is against (or thinks it ought to be against) more often than what it is for. Aside from the Independent Treasury system, Van Buren seemed to have little to offer. As the election of 1840 approached, the blight of panic was still on the country. The Democrats, blaming all on the "money power," renominated Van Buren and knew what they were against: the banks, the tariffs, and "internal improvements." The Whigs passed over Henry Clay, their leader, as a man previously defeated for the presidency (1824 and 1832), and nominated the Westerner, General Harrison – the best Whig vote-getter in 1836 and the "hero" of Tippecanoe. Harrison seemed cast in the Jackson image; and he had other claims to fame. He was a medical school dropout from the University of Pennsylvania, and a former minister to Colombia (1828–9), where he had hoped to earn enough money to pay off the debts of his 2,000-acre estate at North Bend, Ohio, where, with cash or without it, he lived like a lord. For the vice-presidency the Whigs nominated John Tyler, a Virginian Democrat, a Southern Nullifier and an anti-Jackson man. The campaign that followed was one of wild hysteria.

Neither the Whig candidate nor the party had a platform, but they agreed on the slogans "Down with Van Buren," "Tippecanoe and Tyler too." They whipped up enthusiasm with monster rallies, torchlight parades and log-cabin symbols galore:

> Let Van from his coolers of silver drink wine
> And lounge on his cushioned settee
> Our man on his buckeye bench can recline
>   Content with hard cider is he —
> The iron-armed soldier, the true-hearted soldier
> The gallant old soldier of Tippecanoe.

The Whigs promised the return of prosperity on banners reading "Matty's policy, fifty cents a day and French soup; our policy; two dollars a day and roast beef." They accused Van Buren of being an aristocrat, of eating with gold spoons and of perfuming his whiskers. Unwittingly, a Democratic editor in Baltimore furthered the confusion by stating that Harrison would be happy the rest of his life if he had a pension of $2,000 a year, a barrel of cider, and a log cabin. The Whigs seized upon this remark and made a virtue of Harrison's simple tastes. Log cabins and barrels of cider on tap marked future Whig meetings and parades, as the enthusiasts burst into their favorite song of "Tippecanoe and Tyler too," ending with "Oh! Van ia a used-up man!" When the votes were in, the un-popular Van Buren was swept out of office to the tune of 234 electoral votes to 60, even losing his own state of New York, Jackson's Tennessee, and traditionally Democratic Pennsylvania. Harrison's victory was complete, for the Whigs captured both houses of Congress. Slogans and symbols — and entertainment — matter more than principles.

However contrived, the election of 1840 became a portent. Only 27 percent of the eligible voters had voted for the president in 1824; the Jackson-Adams contest of 1828 had raised the figure to 56 per cent, but the contest of 1840 brought out 78 percent of the eligible electorate, a proportion that may never have been equaled since. This dramatic rise in political interest was a result of the full development of the two-party system, however constructed, and a massive skill in ensuring turnout. By 1840 the two parties were almost equally strong, not only at the national level, but also in every section, in most of the states, and in a majority of counties. This meant closely contested elections for all offices from sheriff to president. Each party maintained an elaborate network of stridently partisan newspapers in Washington, the state capitals and countless villages and towns. Rival orators stumped every neighborhood for months before every election. Competing systems of party committees at county, state, and national levels issued a constant stream of broadsides and pamphlets, organized parades and rallies, and made sure that no voters stayed away from the polls on election day. This incessant political activity not only brought voters to the polls in droves, but also made politics a leading form of American recreation, which, now abetted by radio and television, it still remains.

But the parties were as much affected by the new voters as they affected them. The new-style democratic politicians of both parties developed an acute sensitivity to shifts in public opinion, and became expert in building coalitions that would yield a majority or near-majority. The Whigs continued to appeal more strongly to businessmen and the well-to-do, to manufacturing interests and large planters, while the Democrats attracted smaller farmers, workingmen, and frontier areas. The Whigs – like Republicans after them – tended to nominate military heroes, the Democrats "dark horses." But both parties needed additional support to achieve a majority, and both quickly learned the techniques for constantly adjusting their positions to changing public moods. As a result the parties tended not to differ sharply in normal times and to maintain a nearly even balance of strength.

Yet 1840 proved to be an empty victory. Within a month of his inauguration, President Harrison was dead (the first President to die in office). He had made not a single decision. But his legacy was striking: twice married, he produced more grandchildren (48) and more great-grand-children (106) than any other President, and one of his grandchildren (Benjamin) would become the 23rd President. John Tyler became the first Vice-President to succeed an incumbent President. Like almost all his successors as Vice-Presidents, he was chosen too quickly, with little expectation that he might in fact succeed, and with bitter recriminations afterwards. He was personally impressive: a tall, loose-limbed Virginian, a violinist – like Jefferson – and like him, and like his own father, a governor of Virginia in his day (1825–7). He was put on the ticket as a Southern

states' righter to balance Harrison's more nationalistic views. Disowned by the Democrats and unsympathetic to the Hamiltonian
program of the Whigs, however, Tyler was soon a man without a
party. Vetoing the pet measures of the Whigs, including their Bank
bill, Tyler ("Old Veto"), in the past the good Jeffersonian Democrat
and at heart a Nullifier, was at constant loggerheads with Congress.
"He looked somewhat worn and anxious," thought Charles Dickens,
"as well he might, being at war with everybody." He was the first
President against whom impeachment was planned. For two years he
tried to rally the Whigs to his states' rights cause; like his father
before him, he was an obstinate and proud man, and no compromiser. In 1861 he would became a member of the Confederate
Congress.

Harrison was not the only loser. He, the oldest individual ever
elected president, died from over-indulgence not in hard cider but
in ice-cold milk, spiced with rum, consumed after a long Inaugural
– his 8,000-word speech took nearly two hours to deliver, and the
wind was chill; he was unused to such harshness – his "log-cabin"
had been panelled in walnut, and was book-lined, looking out on
his broad acres. The other loser was Henry Clay, who for a whole
month had acted as Harrison's king-maker from his Senate seat, and
appointed his friends to major Cabinet posts (especially Daniel Webster as secretary of state). In fact the one-term Tyler presidency was
reduced to an open war between Tyler and Clay.[8] Yet it was Clay's
resolutions, offered in the Senate in June 1841, that became the
platform of the Whig party. They called for the repeal of the Independent Treasury Act, which had been in operation only for a
year, the re-charter of the Bank, the distribution of the proceeds of
public land sales, and the upward revision of the tariff.[9]

The Independent Treasury Act was soon repealed, but the revenue distribution bill encountered opposition. Tyler feared that the
loss of revenue would be an excuse for increasing tariff rates. Clay
had to yield on the protection issue and agree to the proviso that
the tariff should not rise above the 20 percent level set in 1833.

[8] Robert J. Morgan, *A Whig Embattled: The presidency under John Tyler* (Lincoln,
Nebr., University of Nebraska Press, 1954). For the individual presidencies of
Harrison, Tyler, Polk, and Taylor, see the American Presidencies series published
by the University of Kansas Press: studies by Norma Lois Peterson, *Harrison and
Tyler* (1989), Paul Bergeron, *Polk*, (1987), Elbert B. Smith, *Taylor and Fillmore*
(1989).
[9] For Clay's American System, see Daniel Walker Howe, *The Political Culture
of the American Whigs* (Chicago, Chicago University Press, 1979); Remini, *Henry
Clay*.

Another concession gave the squatter the right to buy his land at a minimum price of $1.25, and that by a series of deferred payments – a measure of vital importance in the settlement of the West. The distribution bill became law in 1841. The Whigs then tried to raise the tariff, and twice Tyler vetoed the bills. In 1842 the Whigs abandoned the distribution principle and enacted a tariff law restoring the protectionist rates of 1832.

Clay's efforts to revive the Bank precipitated an open break with the President. When the President vetoed a "Fiscal Bank" bill and then a "Fiscal Corporation" bill, every Cabinet member resigned except Daniel Webster, who wished to complete negotiations with Britain over the Maine boundary. The Maine boundary line, in dispute since the treaty of Paris of 1783, was finally compromised on, as was also the line between Lake Superior and the Lake of the Woods. Of the territory in dispute in Maine, the United States obtained 7,000 of the 12,000 square miles, including the fertile Aroostook valley, now the most important potato region of the East. The circumstances surrounding the eventual agreement were not without irony. An American historian had discovered in the official French archives a map, believed to have been prepared by Franklin for the French foreign office, which supported the extreme English claims. Concealing this from the English, Webster showed it to the Senators from Maine, and the treaty was ratified. At the same time a map formerly belonging to Henry III was discovered in the British Museum; on it the line, as described by the British peace commissioners of 1783, supported the extreme American claims, and this map was produced in Parliament when the treaty was attacked there. In this "battle of the maps" each side held the information most needed by the other, and by distorting it, secured a compromise; the United States was fortunate in securing the most valuable area. The real legacy of the Tyler presidency, the settlement with Britain, was the work of the man who owed his appointment to Clay, not Tyler: Daniel Webster. It was his good fortune that the fall of the Melbourne government in Britain brought Sir Robert Peel to office as prime minister, with Lord Ashburton replacing the xenophobic Lord Palmerston; and Ashburton was a member of the banking house of Baring, long involved in American (and Webster's own) finances, and with an American wife. The goodwill was useful, since Britain, which had abolished the slave trade in 1833, claimed a right of search to free slaves when the traffic in them was a feature of the South Atlantic and the American eastern shore. When the negotiations with Britain were concluded, Webster resigned as secretary of state, and all his other Cabinet colleagues had already abandoned Tyler; two years later Webster returned to the Senate, to be its "God-like Daniel," the arch-nationalist, to his death in 1852; his call for unity at all costs became the rallying-cry of the Union troops in 1861: "Liberty and Union, now and forever, one and inseparable."

Economic influences were also at work. Most important of all was the growing reliance of industrial Great Britain, plagued by a succession of bad harvests, upon American wheat and cotton. That gave a false economic optimism alike to the Midwest farmers and to the South's plantation owners, both groups sure that their crops were the guarantee of foreign support, should tensions increase between the sections. Not that the South was otherwise optimistic. In August 1831 the Nat Turner Rebellion in Southampton County, Virginia, was responsible for the deaths of 55 whites before it was suppressed, and a Virginia convention of that year narrowly voted against the emancipation of slaves. Thereafter the South tightened its control over Negroes.

There was one other feature of the 1840 election result: 7,000 anti-slavery votes were cast for James G. Birney. With these votes, opposition to slavery became the cause of a national political party which under different names would steadily gain followers until its objective was attained – though by war, not by the ballot box.

The Jacksonian period, usually seen as an age of *laissez-faire*, in fact saw much government intervention: tariffs, patent laws, the sale of public land, Indian removals, and the Bank. Individual states granted charters lavishly, notably Massachusetts and Pennsylvania, Missouri and Georgia, and subscribed heavily to, or owned outright, banks and enterprises.

Nor is there evidence that in the Jackson years any large number of the poorer classes were very much better off. In Philadelphia, Brooklyn, and Boston, only 2 percent of the Jackson era's urban elite had been born poor. There were examples in abundance of rags to riches – Jackson, John Jacob Astor, William E. Dodge – but the men who led the parties that monopolized politics and office before the Civil War "were out of the same inordinately prestigious and economically privileged cloth" as their predecessors of Jackson's and Jefferson's, and colonial, days; "and they did nothing to jeopardize great wealth-holdings;" the political leaders, not surprisingly, were invariably wealthy men. Despite De Tocqueville's much-repeated views ("In America, men are nearer equality than in any other country in the world"), those who owned the land were usually those who had been born to it; the distribution of wealth remained dramatically unequal. When Tocqueville visited the US – he stayed only nine months and described "the tyranny of the masses" – New York City had about 100 persons each worth $100,000 or more, Boston 75 worth at least that; a decade later New York City's tax data disclosed that John Jacob Astor and Peter G. Stuyvesant were millionaires, while 300 others were each worth $100,000 or more. Jacksonian democracy – much of which was demagogic rhetoric – did not mean any more than a minute advance towards egalitarianism. [10]

If there is a consensus here, it would seem to be that, at least as measured by urban growth, by the construction of roads, railways, and steamships, by the availability of land, by continual invention of labor-saving devices, by ready credit, and by much government encouragement, the New World was indeed booming. The suffrage was extended widely, in the new states and in the old – "the people", overstated Alexis de Tocqueville, "reign in the American political world as the Deity does in the universe." There was less direct participation in government by the very wealthy, and a sharp decline in the notion of *noblesse oblige*, precisely because they did not see a threat to their interests; and indeed in banks and railways, steamboats and factories, they saw all-but-unlimited opportunities for profit. If there was wider participation in American life, there was a decline in the efficiency of its administration; it was pro-slavery and ruthlessly anti-Indian (as Tocqueville, in all his sympathy, was most eloquent in describing the tragedy of the forced migration of the Choctaws), it was less competent and less honest than in Jefferson's day; hypocrisy, demagogues and humbugs abounded. [11]

8 THE CREATION OF THE MARKET ECONOMY

"Jacksonian democracy" means many things, to many people. Bray Hammond, banker and historian of banks, finds it in the attempt to liberate business, to make available to the many the entrepre-

[10] Edward Pessen, *Jacksonian America: Society, personality and politics*, rev. edn (Homewood, Il, Dorsey Press, 1979), and his "Wealth in America before 1865," in W. D. Rubinstein (ed.), *Wealth and the Wealthy in the Modern World* (London, Croom Helm, 1980), pp. 167–88; de Tocqueville, *Democracy in America*, 2 vols (1835–40).

[11] Leonard D. White, *The Jacksonians: A study in administrative history* (New York, Macmillan, 1954); George W. Pierson, "The M-Factor in American history", *American Quarterly*, 14 (summer 1962).

neurial opportunities that hitherto were confined to the few. Professor Arthur M. Schlesinger Jr finds it in the attempt on the part of the other sections of society, including the working classes born of the new industrialism, to restrain the power of the business community. Professor Marvin Meyers finds it in the attempt to restore the virtues of an earlier Jeffersonian republican society. Lee Benson of the University of Pennsylvania has even argued that the concept itself is specious, and should be discarded altogether. In his examination of New York politics, he found that its citizens voted for or against Jackson for purely local and selfish reasons, not for great issues of democracy, egalitarianism, or national purposes. David Hackett Fischer argues for a profound shift in the half-century following the Revolution in attitudes toward the aged as well as in their treatment. Colonial society, he argues, was gerontophilic; age was revered. By the 1820s, however, America had become gerontophobic; the elderly lost many of the privileges they enjoyed in politics and society. No longer correlated with wisdom, age was attacked as another unjustified form of social inequality. Among Fischer's indicators are the introduction of mandatory retirement laws, age-related fashions in dress, pejorative meanings of words related to age, age preference in censuses, and child-naming patterns. Charles Sellers sees it in a market revolution, the transformation of an economy based on production for home use into one geared to buying and selling in a capitalistic market place; from it came the cotton kingdom of the South, reviving the once-decaying institution of slavery and, in the West, stimulating an agrarian empire based on shipping wheat and corn to distant markets. What is not debatable is that – behind, and in part cause of the party turmoil and maneuvring – American economic life in these years was being transformed by six interrelated phenomena.

One was the expansion of the United States, the movement outward from settled society, a centrifugal movement great in numbers and vast in space across the face of the continent. It is hard to remember that when Jefferson was inaugurated in 1801, the population of the United States was confined east of the Allegheny ridge. Since the settlement of Jamestown in 1600 and Boston in 1630, it had taken almost 200 years to get that far. Then, in one generation, Americans burst out of their colonial space; by 1850, they were already in California, and the frontier line of settlement was across the Mississippi River. As part of the process, Jackson signed some 90 treaties with the Indians, compelling them to surrender millions of acres and move across the Mississippi. The legal justification for the violence was the Indian Removal Act of 1830, which was approved by the House of Representatives by 5 votes (102 to 97). It was arrogant, racist, and doomed the chances of survival of the First Americans of all.

During the very same years, a second social movement was changing the internal structure of American society, a centripetal movement toward the factory and the city, the first and crucial stage in the development of an industrial and capitalistic society. By 1840, the United States had made the great transformation from a relatively backward economy of self-subsistence agriculture, organized around small farms, artisan workshops, commercial towns, and household industries, to the first stages of self-sustaining industrial growth. The great bulk of the population was still on the land, and, quantitatively, the major sources of power were still human and animal labor. The New England cotton mills, employing mainly young women, who were housed in paternalistically-managed company boarding houses, and many of whom were lost on marriage, were not fertile ground for labor organization. But in the skilled crafts — shoemaking, building, printing — unions established themselves, and as industries and cities grew in size, so did their power grow. Workingmen's parties strove for local or state-wide social legislation in New York and Pennsylvania, in Massachusetts and Rhode Island. They were preoccupied not with the formation of a national political party, since the federal government had a small role to play in their, or any domestic concerns, and not with wages and hours; but with the issues of free public education, anti-convict labor laws, the abolition of imprisonment for debt, and recognition of the right of collective bargaining.

The Panic of 1837, however, and the Depression that followed, brought widespread unemployment, reductions in wages, and the near-collapse of the trade union movement. Only a few desperate strikes occurred during the succeeding years, and workers in considerable numbers turned from unionism to various social and economic panaceas. Producer and consumer cooperatives as well as communistic-type settlements appeared. Robert Dale Owen, fresh from his failures at New Harmony, Indiana, and Frances Wright, "the harlot of infidelity," joined the New York Working Men's Party in 1829, and urged its endorsement of "national, rational education." Their reputation as much as their language discredited the party in the eyes of the press and public, and, with the secession of the printers' union, the party collapsed. Thereafter, units of the movement began to collaborate with the Democrats on such issues as the United States Bank, and were able to secure the abolition of debt imprisonment in New York. They put increasing emphasis on

Plate 8 Bound Down the River.
(The Mansell Collection, London.)

such direct methods of improving working conditions as strikes, closed shop agreements and city-wide confederations of trade unions. By 1836 they had secured the 10-hour day in many municipal governments, and in the Navy Yard. The achievements were Factory Acts limiting the hours of child labor, and, in Massachusetts in 1842, the legalization of unions and of strikes. Horace Greeley's advice to young men – "Go West" – was not a practical alternative, because the minimum tract purchasable from the government, a quarter-section, cost $200. Efforts were made to make land available at a more reasonable price, but the first free homestead bill was defeated in Congress in 1846, and a Wisconsin proposal to limit land inheritance was so vehemently opposed by speculators that it failed in the state legislature in 1851.

The third, fourth, fifth, and sixth features were in a measure by-products of the first two: steam power, improved transportation, credit facilities, and the exploitation of natural resources that each made possible. America was developing from a subsistence to a market economy; much is made by economic historians of the entrepreneur and his role, but in essence the development was done on credit, in part on word-spinning and blarney – and was thus prone to the recurrent panics and depressions that were the obverse of the optimism (as in 1819, 1837, 1854, and 1857, when many banks failed, railroads went bankrupt, and land values fell.) And at the roots of the boom-and-slump times, paradoxically, lay a yearning for the old-time values, of simplicity, equality, and *laissez-faire*. With the nostalgia for what was past (and had rarely existed) was born national identity, national pride, xenophobia, and a sense of manifest destiny.

Jackson was right to see the America of growth and opportunity as the America of the Mississippi and the Ohio. Canals such as the Erie, joining New York City to the Great Lakes via the Hudson River and 364 miles of canal, or that linking Philadelphia to Pittsburgh, lifting barges 2,000 feet by a series of locks and cable cars, linked East and West. So did the steamboats (of which Robert Fulton was the pioneer on the Hudson in 1807) that plied the river-systems of the Mississippi and the Ohio, carrying cotton and, reaching up the Missouri, facilitating the fur trade – slow-moving, however, on rivers that could freeze in winter and run dry in Western summers. In appearance, the river steamboats were rococo palaces of highly florid construction, boasting whistles and calliopes to herald their passage. They were the haven of gamblers and confidence men, and were, in some instances, floating brothels. Mark Twain's *Life on the Mississippi* catches the flavor of the pilot house, but glosses over the more unseemly aspects of riverboat life. There was a fierce sense of competition between rival packet companies, and races between boats were not uncommon. They were sometimes carried on in a recklessly wanton manner, and the river traffic was spotted by some terrible disasters; the average life of a Mississippi riverboat was only three to four years, and the mortality rate among pilots was inordinately high.

The depression years of 1837–43 delayed the railroad building that had begun in the 1830s. Nevertheless, the Baltimore & Ohio Railroad, which in 1831 had 3 miles of track, by 1840 had 3,000 miles. The Erie Canal, backed by New York State (and nicknamed "Clinton's Ditch" after its governor), was financed by tolls – how else? The railroads were private companies; but by the 1850s the federal government was making lavish grants of land to the western states for railroad construction. As late as 1848 the country had only 6,000 miles of track. Mileage doubled in the next four years and reached 30,000 by 1860. Between 1850 and 1860 the federal government granted 18 million acres of public lands to aid the construction of 45 railroads in ten states. By 1857 the country had invested $1 billion in railroads, two-thirds of it during the preceding seven years. Railroads expanded rapidly just before the Civil War. In 1853 several New York lines coalesced to form the New York Central. In 1854, the Rock Island & Chicago was built as a link between the Great Lakes and the Mississippi. The Erie Railroad connected New York City with the Great Lakes; the Baltimore & Ohio reached the Ohio River at Wheeling, Virginia (now West Virginia.) Particularly important was the completion in the early 1850s of five great trunk lines connecting the Atlantic ports of Boston, New York, Philadelphia, Baltimore, and Charleston with the Ohio and Mississippi valleys by way of Albany and Buffalo, Pittsburgh, Wheeling, and Atlanta and Chattanooga. From these terminals the Eastern trunk lines rapidly developed connections by new Western railroads to the emerging transportation and commercial centers of Chicago, St Louis, and Memphis. By 1855 a passenger could travel in two days from one of the Atlantic cities to Chicago or St Louis for a fare of $20. Chicago became the major inland terminal of the railroads, and by 1860 the city was served by 100 trains a day. Between 1850 and 1860 the population of the city trebled.

The building of American railroads was marked – and marred – by that form of politics known as politicking. Eastern magnates sought legislative favors from the states of the West, and in 1850 the federal grant of public lands to the Illinois Central and the Mobile & Ohio Railroads – to facilitate the building of a line to link the

Great Lakes with the Gulf of Mexico – resulted in the transference of railroad lobbying to the Congress at Washington. Congressmen and other federal officials were granted free passes – a practice the ethics of which was questioned, although James Buchanan was the only president who did not take advantage of it. Meanwhile, the railroads were greatly enhancing the economic development of the United States. On the eve of the Civil War, the first sleeping arrangements on trains were introduced; and the Negro porter was already an institution.

At first, the South had lagged far behind the North in railroad building, but in the 1850s a spurt of construction increased Southern mileage from 2,000 to 10,000 miles – still less than that of the North, however. The most extensive railroad building took place north of the Ohio River, between the Alleghenies and the Mississippi. This development in transportation shifted the axis of the nation's trade; in the steamboat age, traffic had flowed from north to south, but the railroads diverted the flow into an east-west channel. The economic alliance that resulted between New England and the North-west led to a new cultural alignment of the country, reflected in sides taken by the sections in the Civil war.

If the US looked west, its links with Europe improved also. Nathaniel Bowditch, as a scientist a second Benjamin Franklin, the son of a poor cooper in Salem, taught himself Latin in order to read Newton's *Principia*, and to become America's leading mathematician and astronomer. He published the *New American Practical Navigator* in 1802. As simply "Bowditch" it became the navigator's bible, and American ships became the swiftest that had ever sailed. In 1818 the Black Bull Line ran regular scheduled sailings from New York to Liverpool. By the 1850s a larger sailing ship, the Yankee Clipper, of over 1,000 tons, dominated the North Atlantic – and the China trade; and more than three-quarters of the vessels registered in New York were New England built. But a sailing ship still required at least four weeks for the crossing, and by the 1840s regular Cunard steamers were able to cross the Atlantic in ten days.

The laying of the Transatlantic cable owes much to the work of Matthew Fontaine Maury, a Southerner, the father of the scientific study of oceanography. In 1847, Maury published his *Wind and Current Chart of the North Atlantic*, which saved much time for the sailing ships. He later published similar charts for the South Atlantic, Pacific, and Indian oceans. The use of Maury's chart could shorten the 180-day passage from New York around the Horn to San Francisco by as much as 50 days. Maury worked out a profile of the Atlantic floor for the purpose of laying a transoceanic cable –

an enterprise finally completed in 1858 by Cyrus W. Field after many disappointments. Shortly thereafter this cable broke, but it was soon re-established permanently. The consequence was an upsurge of immigration from abroad, especially from Ireland and Germany after the potato famine created widespread destitution in 1846. Immigrants to the United States had not numbered more than 10,000 a year before 1823, but reached an annual level of around 400,000 in the early 1850s. Between 1844 and 1854 nearly 3 million new Americans arrived from abroad.

In Jackson's day, however, the Mississippi was still the effective limit of settlement; beyond were Indians, trappers, and US army posts. West of the Appalachians the population was sparse, lands dotted with log cabins, the people wearing linsey-woolsey homespun, the diet mainly hog and hominy grits. But Cincinnati and Detroit, Chicago and Milwaukee, grew rapidly as the railroads began to thread their way west; Germans in particular established themselves there and in the farmlands of Wisconsin and Iowa. The inventions were abundant: the threshing machine began to supplant the flail and the roller; and the grain drill and the mechanical reaper of Cyrus McCormick's devising, the corn planter and the corn sheller, and equally importantly the sewing machine, were invented.

If Southern cotton crops increased by 60 percent in the 1840s and by 100 percent in the 1850s, if Louisiana's sugar production rose fourfold between the 1830s and 1859, with a matching fourfold increase in the price of a field hand, the increases in the Northern farm belt were even more striking. The advance of the agricultural frontier north into Wisconsin and west across Iowa into eastern Kansas and Nebraska, coupled with the widespread use of McCormick's reaper, pushed Northwestern wheat production from some 30 million bushels in 1850 to almost 100 million bushels in 1860. Meat packing and the production of corn and hogs expanded almost as spectacularly.

By 1847, Richard Hoe's rotary printing press was in use and lowered newspaper costs. Samuel Colt's new munitions factory in Connecticut was to play a large part in supplying the Union armies during the Civil War; Charles Goodyear's process for vulcanizing rubber was extending the use of that product. New mineral discoveries – notably of coal and oil in Pennsylvania – were made, under the leadership of the distinguished Yale geologist, Benjamin Silliman, and to J. D. Rockefeller's benefit. Nicholas Longworth introduced grape-growing into the Ohio valley, where the development of new species of grapes furthered American viticulture. If cotton textile manufacturing was the pioneer of American industry, and Francis Cabot Lowell's Boston Manufacturing company at Waltham, Massachusetts, the first large-scale manufactory enterprise, with imitators wherever water power was available, by the 1840s, steam power was replacing water. By 1850 the value of manufactured products for the first time exceeded the value of agricultural products, and between 1850 and 1860 it nearly doubled: from just over $1 billion to just under $2 billion.

It was not only Chicago, St Louis and Memphis that suddenly boomed. Industry located in cities, indeed bred them: for example, Newark, Lowell, and Lynn. By 1860, 5 of the 15 largest cities had more than 10 percent of their populations engaged in manufacturing. By 1860, 1 in 5 of the American people lived in centers with more than 2,000 people; New York City had 1 million people; only then did Boston, with the coming of the Irish, cease to be the colonial and British city it had remained for 70 years. And with the cities came riots – notably in New York City – and department stores. Alexander B. Stewart opened a splendid one on Broadway. In 1862, in fulfillment of the urgent need for better agricultural education, grants of land were made to aid in the financing of state agricultural and industrial colleges (marking the beginning of the "land-grant" colleges). In 1862 the passage of the Homestead Act, which granted title to 160 acres of land after five years' residence thereon, sent many squatters West. Between 1812 and 1852 the population rose from just over 7 million to over 23 million, and they were now inhabiting a continent almost the size of Europe, its territory having increased from 1,700,000 to almost 3 million square miles. Yet the fantastic growth was not the product of the federal government; the United States became the only major industrial country without a publicly-owned railroad or a national fiscal and banking system. *Laissez-faire* as well as cotton was king.

The land was fertile and seemed almost limitless; and in all of it, thanks to roads and canals, railways and telegraph, the US had a new economic weapon: unity. In 1837, when goods crossing Italy paid tolls every 20 miles, and Germany was not yet organizing the Zollverein, all 26 North American states formed a single economic unit. Southern cotton went north, or abroad, to textile mills. The West became a granary, shipping wheat and corn to the Northeast and the South. And to both, the Northeast supplied its manufactured goods, its timber, and its ships. Even a century and a half ago, the US was a single market, which superimposed on the map of Europe would have covered more than 20 separate and warring states, and would have stretched from Bordeaux to Bucharest, from Hamburg to Naples. This was a powerful, if still a sleeping, giant And in 1861 it was linked coast to coast by 50,000 miles of telegraph lines.

Behind "Manifest Destiny" lay perhaps the only period of isolation the US has ever enjoyed: from 1820 to 1850. Steamship transportation across the Atlantic was very slow and irregular; there was as yet no overseas cable. Relatively fewer Americans were living or traveling in Europe during this period than at any other time. The flow of European immigration was also at its lowest ebb. Between 1650 and 1850 the American population doubled every 25 years, partly through the birth rate and partly through immigration. Before 1820, these two forces had acted in very nearly equal measure; between 1820 and 1850, however, the birthrate moved far ahead of immigration as a source of the growth in population. Behind this, and reinforcing the Monroe Doctrine of 1823, was a Western-oriented nationalism, and a new sense of geographic and intellectual divorce from the Old World.

To this, from the mid-1830s onwards, came one distinguished exception: a wave of European, mainly Irish and German, immigrants who, among other features, fed American nativism and xenophobia. For until they came, the United States had been overwhelmingly an Anglo-Scottish country. From 1830 to 1850, about 2,500,000 immigrants entered the United States; over half this number arrived between 1845 and 1850, when revolutions and famine in Europe gave special impetus to emigration. This influx of unsifted newcomers dealt a mortal blow to the earlier New England hope for a selected immigrant population. The demand for labor was simply too great to permit the application of any such principle of selectivity. Moreover, in the prevailing view, the United States was regarded as a sanctuary for the oppressed. No efforts were made to limit immigration, naturalization was easy, and immigrants received land rights in the public domain equal to those enjoyed by the native born.

Most of this immigration was still largely from the traditional British sources of American population – England, Scotland, and Wales – until in the late 1840s many thousands of Irish and Germans emigrated to the United States. The majority of the Irish were wretchedly indigent peasant farmers who arrived in the United States with no resources, ready to take any kind of work they could find. Therefore the flood of Irish immigration tended to congest in Eastern cities, particularly Boston (until then still decisively "English" in character), instead of spreading out over the countryside. They were forced to become day laborers, factory workers, and domestic servants, employed at very low wages. On the whole, they were resented; their whiskey (the Irish) and their beer (if they were German) made the cities to which they swarmed more riotous, more congested and more disease-prone than ever: the notion of the "wicked City" became a recurring American literary theme. The poverty of the Irish immigrants embarrassed and irritated the more fortunate citizens, while their Roman Catholic faith was identified in the Protestant mind with the hated monarchical principles of the Old World. In Boston in particular, in one decade (1845–55), they doubled the number of employees in industry, mainly clothing manufacture; and with numbers in congested slums came smallpox (which had disappeared, but returned in 1845), cholera (1849), tuberculosis, drunkenness, crime, and prostitution. But the Irish proved highly adaptable, and their aptitude for politics was remarkable. They had captured Tammany Hall in the 1820s, and in the 1840s they became influential in municipal governments throughout the Northeast. They were egalitarians, and generally strong supporters of Jackson. When their hope of securing federal aid for parochial schools was abandoned, the Irish campaigned to make the public schools strictly nonsectarian, opening a controversy that has lasted ever since. Their newspapers, Church-controlled, pro-Democratic, pro-slavery, and rabidly anti-English, kept them loyal to the Old Cause and the Old Sod.

By contrast, the German immigrants were mainly farmers, mechanics, musicians, and intellectuals, many – especially Catholics and Bavarians – escaping from the failure of the 1848 Revolution in Europe. They were better educated than the Irish; many had modest resources; all were liberals and many radicals, avowedly waiting until the opportunity was ripe for a return to a more democratic Europe. They avoided the nativist North and the equally nativist South, and settled mainly in the farm belt of the Middle West. Most of them stayed there, and in the end, as the "Forty-Eighter Germans," radicals and republicans, they would fight for a new liberal cause in the land of their adoption; some of them, like Carl Schurz, to fight at Second Bull Run and at Gettysburg, and to be enrolled in Lincoln's service.

Not only was there a change in an awareness of ethnic differences among whites, and in urban congestion, but a new *homo Americanus*, with changes in the family, in law, and in social values. As Charles Sellers has shown, the expansion of production for the market rather than family subsistence fostered an ethos of competitive individualism that rejected old hierarchies and fostered a democratic egalitarianism. At the same time, however, the market economy generated unprecedented wealth for some entrepreneurs, but economic disaster for those submerged in its wake — subsistence farmers on poorer lands and urban craftsmen eclipsed by factory production. The market generated enthusiasm among some Americans and fear among others. These contradictory attitudes were reflected in the era's politics, with some political leaders, such as Henry Clay, avidly promoting market development, while others, like Andrew Jackson, sought to mobilize the population to oppose the inequalities the market produced. Sellers pursues his theme well beyond the confines of politics. "Lawyers," he writes, "were the shock troops of capitalism;" and in an interesting section he shows how changes in legal doctrines enshrined market assumptions (such as the primacy of property rights over traditional values) in the law. Moreover, the competitive marketplace was said to be the "sphere" of men, while the household, allegedly immune to the market's pressures, was to be presided over by women. In the end, Sellers argues, the market revolution produced not simply a new middle class, but a new middle-class culture, in which self-discipline, temperance, and other forms of psychological repression honed the qualities thought to guarantee success in the competitive turmoil of a market economy: "The 'business man' — originally a man conspicuously busy — became the archetype of a culture of busyness." [12]

9   EXPANSION

The years from Andrew Jackson's entry into the White House in 1828 to the outbreak of the Civil War in 1861 have three all-embracing themes: the appearance of Democracy — political, egalitarian, economic, and humanitarian; the noise of "the firebell in the night," as Jefferson described the issues presented by the steady growth of slave numbers; and the westward movement. [13]

For Jackson's political victory was more than the triumph of an impulsive, bluff soldier-man and of a new political tactic. He was the first President to be the product of a non-Eastern background, and to whom the East was remote, alien and snob. Born in abject poverty, he was raised in Tennessee; he fought in the Revolutionary War in which his two brothers died, and he fought Indians in

[12] Charles Sellers, *The Market Revolution: Jacksonian America 1815–1846* (New York, Oxford University Press, 1990).
[13] Jefferson to John Holmes, Apr. 22, 1820, in P. L. Ford (ed.) *The Writings of Thomas Jefferson*, 10 vols (New York, G. P. Putnam's Sons, 1891–9), vol. X, p. 157.

Florida; he was frontier lawyer, planter and merchant, a man of parts, and — in the end — of wealth, and a perfervid nationalist. He saw the America of growth and opportunity as the America of the Mississippi and the Ohio. "Hi-o, away we go, floating down the river on the O-hi-o" was the theme of the migrations West; canals like the Erie, railroads like the Baltimore & Ohio, became the spokes of the continent; and the spokes now ran firmly east and west. Pittsburgh and Cincinnati, St Louis, Kansas City, and Council Bluffs became the staging posts of a great folk-wandering. Within a half-dozen years, six states were created: Indiana in 1816, Mississippi in 1817, Illinois in 1818, Alabama in 1819, Maine in 1820, and Missouri in 1821. The first frontier had been tied closely to Europe, and the second to the coastal settlements, but the Mississippi valley was independent and its people looked West rather than East. The Jacksonian movement was part of the Manifest Destiny that the United States should inherit, if not the earth, at least a continent deemed virginal.

Let me live where I will [wrote Thoreau], on this side is the city, on that the wilderness, and ever I am leaving the city more and more and withdrawing into the wilderness. I should not lay so much stress on this fact if I did not believe that something like this is the prevailing tendency of my countrymen. I must walk toward Oregon and not toward Europe.[14]

The sentiments were voiced more vehemently by others: in 1845 by John L. O'Sullivan, editor of the *Democratic Review* of New York, the first to use the phrase "Manifest Destiny"; and by Mayor Davezac at the New Jersey State Democratic Convention in 1844:

Land enough — land enough: Make way, I say, for the young American Buffalo — he has not yet got land enough; he wants more land as his cool shelter in summer — he wants more land for his beautiful pasture grounds. I tell you, we will give him Oregon for his summer shade, and the region of Texas as his winter pasture. (Applause). Like all of his race, he wants salt too. Well, he shall have the use of two oceans — the mighty Pacific and turbulent Atlantic shall be his ... He shall not stop his career until he slakes his thirst in the frozen ocean. (Cheers).

William Henry Seward, in a speech at St Paul, Minnesota, in 1860, believed that the future capital of the US would be somewhere "not far" from that point. And even more "spread-eagle" orators

---

[14] Henry David Thoreau, *A Week on the Concord and the Merrimack Rivers* (1849).

could see the country's boundaries as "in the North, the Aurora Borealis, in the South, the succession of the Equinoxes, in the East, the primeval Chaos, in the West, the Day of Judgment."[15]

The facts are that American settlers moved into Texas at the invitation of the Mexican government when it became independent of Spain in 1821, and by 1830 the "Old 300" had become a colony of 20,000. By 1836 when they revolted against Mexico they numbered some 30,000. Texas became the 27th state in the Union in 1845; victory in the Mexican War in 1848 brought in New Mexico and California also; half the Oregon country was acquired up to the 49th Parallel in 1846. Between 1840 and 1865, the US became a geographical area five times the size of France.

On the concept "Manifest Destiny" itself, there is now a daunting literature. Given the speed and ease of the expansion of territory and the growth of population, it is easy to see it as a cover phrase for imperialism, or for sectional greed; Manifest Destiny has been the plea of every robber chief since Nimrod, said Senator Tom Corwin of Ohio.

> They just want this California
>   So's to bring new slave-states in
> To abuse ye, an' to scorn ye
>   An' to plunder ye like sin.

This was the view of James Russell Lowell in *The Biglow Papers*.[16] It is possible to trace its roots: to Jefferson's and de Crevecoeur's sense of America's geological and botanical difference from and superiority to Europe; to Tom Paine's republicanism and his faith in the superiority of American institutions; to the War of 1812 as a "second War of Independence," and the Monroe Doctrine as a second Declaration of Independence from the Atlantic and from Europe –

> (Have the elder races halted,
>   Do they droop and end their lesson
> Over there, beyond the seas,
>   We take up the task eternal,
> The burden and the lesson,
>   Pioneers, oh Pioneers)

---

[15] Both quoted in A. K. Weinberg, *Manifest Destiny* (Baltimore, Johns Hopkins University Press, 1935).
[16] "Mr Hosea Biglow Speaks." The North saw the Mexican War as a pretext for extending slave territory.

– to the obligation resting on a superior culture to extend its benefit to the lesser breeds without the law, all the way to the Pacific along the 49th Parallel (and ideally at some later date, north of it?); and to the appeal of the West to the land-hungry, to the plantation owner, to individualists and eccentrics – to the Mormons in their quest for security –

> No more shall Jacob bow his neck
>   Henceforth he shall be great and free
> In Upper California,
>   O that's the land for me;

and to Parson Wilbur's more realistic view of the western movement; "Half of its ignorance, and the other half's rum." And later critics (like A. K. Weinberg) have been able to view it, rightly or wrongly, in terms of the disrepute that in the 1930s, as later, have become attached to the word "Imperialism." Weinberg detected that it had 15 themes: natural right, geographical predestination, the destined use of the soil, extension of the area of freedom, the true title, the mission of regeneration, natural growth, political gravitation, inevitable destiny, the white men's burden, paramount interest, political affinity, self-defense, international police power, and world leadership. Are some of these not merely synonymous terms? Or do they not themselves omit some of its features, not least its trebling of American territory in less than a century? Here population in 1790 was 4 million; in 1870 it was 40 million.[17] In fact the phrase "Manifest Destiny" belonged to the 1840s; only 15 years before, in 1825, the idea of the acquisition of Oregon and of much of Mexico would have been seen as ludicrous.

10 THE TEXAS STORY

The Texas story is not now seen as especially controversial, though it was controversial in the nineteenth century. The Mexican War, and the whole expansion into the Southwest, was thought of by many Northerners, by abolitionists, and by their historians as a wicked conspiracy plotted by Jackson and his Tennessee protégé Sam Houston, to bring Texas and Mexico into the US in order to provide a covey of slave states that would perpetuate slavery in the Union.

[17] Weinberg, *Manifest Destiny.*

A later "school" of historians – Justin Smith, Eugene Barker, W. C. Binkley – has shown that the US government had nothing to do with the settling of Texas or with the Texas "Revolution." Whatever shadowy claim to Texas the United States might have acquired with the Louisiana Purchase was formally surrendered to Spain in the treaty of 1819, but the ink was scarcely dry on that document before agitation to gain – or regain – Texas began. President Adams went so far as to send Joel R. Poinsett to Mexico in 1825, with an offer to purchase the territory for $1 million, making the Rio Grande the boundary. Later, Jackson, who became convinced that Texas had to become American as a defense against Mexicans and Indians, increased the offer to $5 million, with the Rio Nueces as boundary. Mexico said "No" to both proposals, claiming that Louisiana had been surrendered by Spain under pressure from Napoleon, and it had had no right to do so. Senator Thomas Hart Benton, Jackson's ally in his campaign against the Bank ("Old Bullion" Benton), and Missouri's most distinguished Senator for 30 years (1820–50), advocated government support for all frontier explorations, and stressed that Texas was at least four times the size of New England, and much more fertile; from it some four or five states could be carved, thus offsetting the Northern gains in the Missouri Compromise of 1820 and ensuring a Southern dominance in the Senate. Immigration into this vast and empty region was pioneered by Aaron Burr's fellow-conspirator in plotting Western secession, General James Wilkinson, who in 1806 signed the Neutral Ground Treaty with Spain (by which he promised that the US would stay west of the Sabine River); by horse traders and horse thieves and merchants intriguing with the Indians, like Philip Nolan; by Bernardo Gutierrez and Augustus Magee in 1819, claiming that Texas was in law American; and, making similar claims, by James Long, who had married a niece of General Wilkinson and had an ally in Jean Lafitte, the pirate-turned-American-hero at the Battle of New Orleans. All such ambitions and such raids were, at least in law, ended by the Florida Treaty of 1819, whereby the US not only surrendered its claims to Texas but agreed that the Sabine and the Red Rivers were the boundary between American and Spanish territory. By the time that the treaty became effective, however, Mexico itself had become independent of Spain (by the Treaty of Cordoba of 1821) – with the aid of a number of American adventurers, be it said – and itself claimed the territory.

Between 1823 and 1836 there was an uncontrolled movement of Western pioneers attracted by the climate and fertility, and by the lure of former Spanish and now Mexican land grants and tax exemptions. By a law of 1825, a man could buy a *sitio* of 4,428 acres for $200 less than the cost of 160 acres of public land in the United States. Vast grants were made to agents (*empresarios*) if they would bring in and settle within six years a number of families. Stephen F. Austin, a Connecticut Yankee, led a group to Texas under a grant issued to his father, Moses Austin, in 1821; within a decade several thousand Americans had crossed the Sabine River or the Red River into the Mexican domain. Because the land was ideal for cotton and the labor supply was short, slavery was introduced. While Mexico by this time had itself abolished slavery, Austin was able to gain an exception to the law and separate judicial and executive authority for the settlements in Texas. The insecurity of slave property, however, was one factor which inspired dissatisfaction with Mexican rule among American settlers. Though Austin as an honorable man tried to keep his colony loyal to Mexico, there were many causes for friction – racial and linguistic, economic and political. Furthermore, the first organized groups of settlers were soon outnumbered by freelance adventurers like Sam Houston, the Bowie brothers, and Davy Crockett, who felt no obligation to Mexico. What in 1820 had been an American (in fact mainly *mestizo*) population of some 4,000 had in ten years become an unmanageable population of some 30,000 white American settlers with 5,000 slaves, all of them alien to the Mexicans in language, religion, and habits of government. Naturalization, acceptance of Spanish as the language of law and trade, and nominal acceptance of Roman Catholicism as the state religion did not change the frontiersmen, many of them Southerners. Uneasily alongside them were some 5,000 Mexicans and 12,000 Indians. Friction developed further over restrictions on further immigration, and the cutting down of tax exemptions. Perpetual turmoil in Mexican political affairs complicated the situation, and when General Antonio Lopez de Santa Anna came to power in 1835, bent on centralizing authority and canceling all such special local privileges, Texan discontent flamed into revolt. Originally, they even had some Mexican support against a seemingly gaunt and frail man, whose appearance belied the ruthlessness of a Machiavelli.

The "Texas Rangers" chose Sam Houston as their commander-in-chief and claimed to be seeking their rights within a "federal" Mexico. If it was a short conflict, it was a bloody one. Santa Anna massacred 400 Texans after they surrendered to him. When on March 6, 1836, his trumpets called the *deguello* (no quarter), his troops stormed the Alamo, the mission church across the river from San Antonio, and killed all 180 of the defenders, and in doing so lost

Plate 9 The Alamo, where Davy Crockett died.
(The Mansell Collection, London.)

400 of his own men. As thousands of women and children fled east, the Mexicans were defeated by Houston near the San Jacinto River in a surprise attack on April 21, 1836. In a battle that lasted only 18 minutes, Houston's force, outnumbered two to one, lost only 8 men, against over 600 Mexicans killed, 300 wounded, and 700 captured, including President Santa Anna. The battle-cry "Remember the Alamo!" went into history. The Independence of Texas had been proclaimed on March 2, 1836, four days before the Alamo fell, though for more than a decade Mexico stubbornly refused to recognize it. The Rio Grande from its source to its mouth became the boundary.

Many American volunteer (and violent) soldiers went to the aid of the Texas revolutionaries, but the United States government remained officially neutral: the Republic of Texas was not diplomatically recognized until a few days before Jackson left office. But for a heated controversy in Congress on the slavery question, the Texas overtures for annexation by the US might have been accepted at once. Benjamin Lundy's tract, *The War in Texas*, had painted a lurid picture of pro-slavery designs on the area, and Northern Congressmen argued that the admission of Texas would disturb the carefully contrived balance of power between slave and free states. At the time there were 13 free states and 13 slave states in the Union. The South, however, was determined to obtain Texas, for a number of new states would soon have to be admitted in the Northwest, and, with the exception of Florida, the Southwest offered the only region from which new slave states could be created. But Congressman and ex-President John Quincy Adams filibustered an annexation resolution to kill it in 1838, and Texas had to wait seven years longer.

European interest in Texas was a powerful argument for annexation. As soon as France and Great Britain recognized the Texan Republic, Sam Houston – twice elected president of the Texan Republic – began to bargain between these powers and the United States. He probably wanted annexation most, but he would have accepted a joint Franco-British guarantee of Texan independence, which would have tied the infant republic to Europe politically and economically. The British government, keen to secure markets, and cotton supplies, and resenting the US tariff on their manufactured goods, also offered to guarantee the Mexican boundary against American aggression, in return for Mexican recognition of Texan independence – and even the offer of California to Britain; but to acknowledge the loss of Texas would have been political suicide for any Mexican government, so the offer was rejected. Any understanding between Texas and Britain was hampered by the British desire that slavery be abolished. The possibility that Texas might do so, thereby establishing a refuge for runaway Negroes on the flank of the South, was another factor behind Southern zeal for annexation. Tyler openly declared that the mere hint that Texas contemplated emancipation would be justification for American annexation, but this argument lost more support than it won in the United States, and nothing was done. Texas and Mexico were – like everything else – involved in the slavery question. Had there been no slavery issue, and had successive short-lived Mexican governments been able to concede the surrender of Texas and Upper California to the US, and had Britain helped persuade Mexico to make this deal (as Tyler and Webster urged her to do in 1842), the US would have been prepared to surrender territory to Britain and make the Columbia River the boundary between the US and Canada – as in geography and geology it appears to be.

In the election of 1844, the Democrats made national self-interest and Manifest Destiny the bases of their expansionist program. The "re-annexation" of Texas and the "re-occupation" of Oregon, and " 'Fifty-four forty or fight' ", were campaign slogans rather than an argument, but they won enough free – and slave – state annexationist votes away from the Whig candidate, Clay, who sat on the fence (though very eloquently) on the expansionist and slavery questions, to win the election for James K. Polk. Van Buren had expected to win the Democratic nomination, but was defeated on the ninth ballot of the convention by a "dark horse," Polk. "Who is James K. Polk?" sneered the Whigs, and with justice. His name had not even been on the first seven ballots. His "magic" was that "Young Hickory" (he came from Jackson's state of Tennessee) had been an able Speaker of the House of Representatives as a successor to Henry Clay (1835–9), and had strongly urged the annexation of Texas. He won (by 170 electoral votes to 105) 6 free and 8 slave states against Clay's 7 free and 5 slave, but his popular majority was less than 40,000. Clay's pussyfooting on Texas, despite vast oratorical effort on the principles of Whiggery, lost him the support of anti-slavery Whigs, enough of whom in New York and Michigan swung to the abolitionist candidate, James Birney, to throw those states to Polk: a slaveholding expansionist was in fact elected (by the bare 5,000 votes of New York) by New York abolitionists. The first "dark-horse" candidate to be elected President, Polk effectively tapped the expansionist sentiments engendered by the Westward Movement. Many Americans saw in the West the chance to recoup their losses in the Panic of 1837, and they voted for the man who promised to clear the way. Congress responded quickly. Polk saw his election as a mandate for the annexation of Texas and Oregon.

Since it would have been impossible to secure two-thirds support for a treaty in the Senate, both Houses of Congress passed resolutions for the admission of Texas (a device that would be repeated in the procedure to annex Hawaii in 1959). Thus Tyler harvested part of the fruit of Polk's victory by signing the resolution which admitted the Lone Star State on 1 March, 1845, three days before he left office. Texas came in as the 27th state in the Union: from it five states might be carved, and in it slavery was permitted by the application of the terms of the Missouri Compromise.

The 1844 election was typical of what had been heralded in 1828, and repeated in 1840: songs, buttons, snuffboxes (Clay was a notorious snuff-inhaler), banners and parades, barbecues and "Clay Clubs".

> Get out of the way, you're all unlucky
> Clear the tracks for Old Kentucky.

But this was a campaign with a difference. There were portents of a more disturbing kind. Not least in New York and Philadelphia, many Whigs appealed to nativists, conscious of the waves of Catholic Irish and German incomers. Clay as a slaveholder and hemp-producer had been evasive on slavery, and lost abolitionist support. More than this: if one-third of Birney's votes in New York had gone to Clay, and the Kentuckian had reached the White House, there would have been no annexation of Texas, no Mexican War, no territory to fight over for or against slavery, and no Civil War.[18] When a Whig from Vermont saw a Democratic victory banner waving over the slave market in Washington, he prophesied: "That flag means *Texas*, and *Texas* means *civil war*, before we have done with it."

Polk, behind the slogans, had also resolved the Oregon question. The US and Britain negotiated the boundaries of the Oregon territory, which, as jointly administered by them since 1818, extended from the 42nd parallel to the 54° 40' line, although the British had long been willing to concede the territory south of the Columbia River. Democrats in Congress demanded "the re-occupation of Oregon," and President Polk asked for authority to end the joint occupation. By 1846 the British were ready to compromise, partly because of the decline in the beaver trade, and partly because, after

---

[18] Roger Fischer, *Tippecanoe and Trinkets Too: The material culture of America's presidential campaigns 1828–1984* (Urbana, IL, University of Chicago Press, 1988), pp. 49–59.

the repeal of the Corn Laws, they wanted to import American grain. Polk had warned that in one year the US would end the joint occupation of Oregon and thus extend America's northernmost boundary to the 54° 40' line. The British countered by offering to divide the territory at the 49th parallel. Despite his pledge – "Fifty-four Forty or Fight"[19] – the Oregon Treaty (the "49th parallel treaty") was agreed with Britain, and the Senate ratified this treaty in 1846.

Polk was a lawyer with a trained mind, and had experience as Speaker of the House and governor of Tennessee, and he selected a well-qualified Cabinet, with the annexationist James Buchanan of Pennsylvania as secretary of state, and George Bancroft, the historian, as secretary of the Navy. Tenacious, methodical, and serious-minded, he drove himself hard; he pursued in foreign affairs a program somewhat reminiscent of that of John Quincy Adams, but with greater success. He was, however, cold, humorless, and unimaginative. In domestic affairs, Polk was committed to reduction of the tariff, establishment of an independent treasury, and acquisition of Oregon and the Southwest. All these he achieved, while keeping slavery comparatively in the background. The price he paid was his own death, from overwork, a few months after leaving office.

11 THE MEXICAN WAR

To the lands between Texas and the Pacific, the United States had no claim. Many Americans, however, viewed Manifest Destiny as a force transcending mere law, and the fact that Great Britain was suspected, albeit without justification, of having designs on California – and on Cuba – only magnified Polk's interest in the region. Polk's Mexican policy was a combination of war plans and efforts to negotiate, complicated by the fact that Mexico had severed diplomatic relations in protest at the annexation of Texas. Had the President been content with the acquisition of Texas, there probably would not have been a war. Mexico was not unaware that his interests went much further.

While General Zachary Taylor was being stationed at the Nueces River, Commodore John D. Sloat, commanding the Navy's Pacific Squadron, was receiving orders to occupy San Francisco in the event

---

[19] See Edwin A. Miles, "Fifty-four Forty or Fight – an American political legend," *Mississippi Valley Historical Review*, 44 (1957), pp. 291–309.

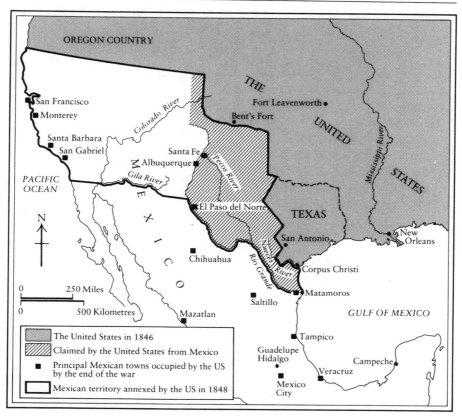

Map 4 Expansion: Texas and Mexico. On March 28, 1845, the US agreed to annex Texas, and to consider the Rio Grande as the Texas-Mexico frontier, not the Nueces as Mexico claimed. In the ensuing war around 17,000 Americans and 4,000 Mexicans died before Mexico abandoned all claims to Texas and surrendered California and New Mexico in return for $15 million by the Treaty of Guadalupe Hidalgo.

of war, and Captain John C. Fremont, Senator Benton's son-in-law, was making, with or without authority, barely camouflaged military reconnaissances in California (and writing them up in his *Exploring Expeditions*). Polk tried diplomacy. A considerable number of American financial claims against the Mexican government constituted his bargaining weapon, and John Slidell, of Louisiana, was his agent.

Prior to 1846 the United States had paid little attention to its citizens' private claims against Mexico, though the European powers had applied considerable pressure to collect debts due to their nationals. (In the French bombardment of Vera Cruz, in 1838 – the so-called "Pastry War" – a cannon ball had deprived Santa Anna of a leg and made him a national hero.) In 1843, Mexico had acknowledged its American obligations, but frequent changes of government led to suspension of remittances. The best indication of the chaos that reigned in Mexico City is that Antonio Lopez de Santa Anna was president on 11 separate occasions between 1833 and 1855, and on four of them had dictatorial powers. Polk was aware of the Mexican political situation, but resolved nevertheless to press for a settlement. Late in 1845, Slidell arrived in Mexico City, authorized to offer American assumption of the claims obligations in return for Mexican acceptance of the annexation of Texas, and also to offer $5 million for New Mexico, and $25 million for California. Mexican public opinion, however, remained a bar to negotiations, and Slidell was not even received. Mexicans believed that the US army was undermanned and inexperienced; Europe was expected to support them, with commerce raiders sailing under Mexican commissions; and, as evidence, they cited the London *Times*, which forecast American disasters in the deserts and the mountains.

Learning, in January 1846, of the rejection of his minister, Polk ordered General Zachary Taylor ("Old Rough and Ready") with an "Army of Observation," to advance from the Nueces to the Rio Grande, ignoring the Nueces as the proper southwest boundary of Texas. This gesture convinced the Mexicans of the desirability of discussing the Texas question, but Polk now wanted the land to the Pacific too, so he dismissed the offer to negotiate, on the grounds that it was insincere. The President's Cabinet was lukewarm to his proposal of a declaration of war on the grounds that the Mexican government had refused to receive his minister and settle the outstanding claims. A war message, however, was finally approved on 9 May, 1846, to be submitted to Congress three days later. At this critical juncture, the Mexicans came to Polk's aid by conducting a foray across the Rio Grande and killing or capturing several of Taylor's men. Upon hearing the news, the President advanced the delivery date of his war message to May 11, and two days later Congress declared that as a consequence of Mexico's action in invading American territory, a state of war existed between that nation and the United States, and it was "by the act of Mexico itself." This view earned for Polk the epithet "Polk the mendacious," and Whig Congressman from Illinois Abraham Lincoln introduced into Congress the "Spot Resolution," requiring the President to name the spot on American soil where American blood had been shed.

The West was enthusiastic, and many volunteers were forth-coming. The North, already suspicious of the rising influence of the West and of a slaveholders' conspiracy, remained indifferent or critical. Many Southerners were skeptical of a venture which pro-mised once again to upset the territorial balance between slave and free states, for the bulk of any acquisitions from Mexico would prob-ably lie north of a westward extension of the Missouri Compromise line, 36° 30'. The Whigs opposed the War on both sectional and political grounds, and did their best to embarrass the administration abolitionists, who, fearing the addition of all Mexico to the slave domain, were bitterly critical. A strange alliance – Webster and Clay, each of whom lost a son in Mexico, Calhoun and Van Buren, abolitionists and high tariff men – joined in denouncing and trying to block "Jimmy Polk's War." Polk expected that an easy victory could be won by the 7,500 men of the regular army and 20,000 volunteers. The Texas War suggested to him that wars are won by enthusiastic civilian amateurs, dressed in a variety of uniforms. Lest the Mexican hope of aid from Britain be realized, he hastened to complete a settlement of the Oregon boundary question along the compromise line proposed by the amicably disposed government of Lord Aberdeen in London.

In the Mexican War, California was remote from the main thea-ters of operations, and only a little fighting occurred there. Fremont hastened down from the north to join his efforts with the short-lived "Bear Flag" revolutionaries, whose Californian Republic survived only three days, Commodore Sloat's naval forces occupied Monterey and held it against some resistance from Spanish-Californians. Stephen Kearney, leading the "Army of the West" (300 regulars, 2,400 vol-unteers), took Santa Fe. San Diego, Los Angeles, and San Francisco were taken, and by the end of 1846 the United States was in control of New Mexico and California. Taylor crossed the Rio Grande and in October 1846 won a victory in a three-day battle at Monterey, which made him, as a successful general, potential Whig presidential timber. Lest further victories give the colorful general too much political stature, and since Democratic losses in the Congressional elections were worrying, Polk placed a less spectacular Whig, Win-field Scott, in command of the major American offensive – an over-land march from Vera Cruz to Mexico City, in 1847. "Great Scott," "Old Fuss and Feathers," may have been pompous and petulant, but he was an experienced soldier (as in the War of 1812), able, sensible, and generous. Persuaded that Santa Anna, who was at the moment in enforced retirement in Havana, could arrange a nego-tiated peace, Polk granted him safe passage through the American lines in August 1846. The wily Mexican soldier-politician ignored his pledges and threw himself into the defense of his country, only to be narrowly beaten by Taylor at Buena Vista, in February 1847. American troops took Sante Fe in New Mexico, El Paso, and Chihuahua. The campaign which began at Vera Cruz in March 1847 was well planned and executed, and provided training and experience for many young officers (notably the engineer-officer Robert E. Lee) who were to lead Confederate and Union forces a few years later. By August 1847, following the route of Cortez three centuries before, Scott's troops were before Mexico City, and after vicious fighting on the hill of Chapultepee, a battalion of US Marines took over the halls of Montezuma.

Within a decade, the military lessons of the War were to be seen as important as the acquisitions of territory. The US won because it had a 3 to 1 superiority in numbers of troops, and outmatched the Mexicans in discipline, training, and equipment. But the Americans were at the end of a long and perilous line of communications, and they lost many to yellow-fever, typhus and dysentery, in an age when preventive medicine was all but unknown. Of the 90,000 troops who served in Mexico, 11,300 died of disease and accident, and another 12,000 had to be discharged as unfit; 6,700 deserted, and 1,550 were killed in action. And if some reputations were made or enhanced, many more were lost: the generals quarreled with the politicians, and Fremont emerged as a glory-hunter, at odds with his so-called colleagues, to be court-martialed and dismissed the Service, involving his father-in-law, Senator Benton, in consequent disputes with President Polk. General Scott refused the call to become dictator of Mexico, Santa Anna having gone – again – into exile; and four years later became lieutenant-general of the US Army, the first since Washington.

The shadow of slavery hovered over the Mexican War. When Polk requested the House to supply the resources needed in the negotiation of the treaty, David Wilmot, a Pennsylvania Democrat, added an amendment known as the Wilmot Proviso. Under its terms, "neither slavery nor involuntary servitude shall ever exist in any part" of the territory to be acquired as a result of the war. The House approved the Proviso, but Southern votes in the Senate defeated it each time it was presented. In these votes party lines were shattered as the South and North acted as units.

In the treaty signed in the village of Guadalupe Hidalgo (February 1848) (the shrine of the Virgin of Guadalupe, the patroness of Mexico), the United States secured not only the disputed territory between the Nueces and the Rio Grande rivers, but also the vast Mexican Cession – present-day California, New Mexico, Arizona, Nevada, Utah, and parts of Colorado and Wyoming – in return for which Mexico was paid $15,000,000, and some $3,000,000 of her debts were assumed by the United States. Here was a new territory in which to stage the struggle between free and slave interests.

The movement of expansion was not simply westward, but outward, pressuring northern and southern as well as western borders. It had begun soon after the Revolution with the drive to control the lower Mississippi. Neither manifest nor controlled by destiny, expansion continued "by purchase and violence," tripling US territory by mid-century. Traders, farmers, boosters, squatters, speculators, gold rushers, politicians: all erased one "natural" barrier after another. After the completion of the Louisiana Purchase, the Continental Divide had seemed a natural boundary, the Great American Desert so clearly impassable and uninhabitable. As the west proved accessible, the Pacific seemed formidable – but in time that barrier, too, yielded to improved technology and escalating ambitions, as the pressures to annex the Hawaiian Islands demonstrated. Like the term "virtual reality," natural boundary soon meant exactly the opposite of what it pretended to mean; it was rendered visible – or invisible – always through the lens of nationalism and expansionism.

But not only was the creation of a continental United States not natural, inevitable, and foreordained; it was highly problematic, to say the least. Hailed as essential to "the development of the great experiment of Liberty and federated self-government entrusted to us," territorial acquisitions exacerbated precisely those conflicts that resulted in the Civil War. To those who claimed that western expansion would ease sectional tensions by weakening slavery, Daniel Raymond replied sharply, "Diffusion is about as effectual a remedy for slavery as it would be for smallpox."

Even more obvious, every step of this experiment in liberty, from Jamestown to Santa Fe, from Louisiana to Oregon and beyond, entailed the dispossession, reduction, removal, deformation or extermination of captive peoples, primarily, although not exclusively, Native Americans. The particular character of American imperialism forms one of D. W. Meinig's major themes, as do the consequences of Americans' refusal to recognize themselves as imperialists. As Josiah Royce observed in the 1880s, "The American as conqueror is unwilling to appear in public as a pure aggressor. ... The American wants to persuade not only the world but himself that he is doing God's service in a peaceable spirit, even when he violently takes what he has determined to get."

With the extension of the country's borders to this tropical sea, a whole circuit of coasts — Florida, Cuba, Yucatan, Mexico, Texas — suddenly took on new meaning for Americans, and before long such places were being declared to be of compelling national interest. For the Gulf of Mexico was an inner compartment, "a Mediterranean with two outlets," as the geographer Alexander von Humboldt put it, guarded by Havana, an American Gibraltar "strongly defended by nature and still more strongly fortified by art." Unlike its European counterpart, one could not sail outward past this bastion directly into the Atlantic but had to skirt a broad and a dangerous archipelago to the north and east or pass the whole length of Cuba and other large islands extending 1,000 miles to the south and east before reaching the open sea. So it was necessary also to bring the Bahamas, Jamaica, Hispaniola, and Puerto Rico into this new American view.

This was not a tranquil prospect. Through Louisiana the United States stepped directly into an arena that had been the scene of intense European imperial activities and immense geographical changes for 300 years. The young republic immediately asserted claim to a major role in that theater and found itself participating in a tumultuous drama involving three European powers and a dozen American peoples.[20]

[20] D. W. Meinig, *The Shaping of America*, vol. II, *Continental America 1800–1867* (New Haven, Conn., Yale University Press, 1993), p. 24.

7

Those Who Did Not Belong

1 MAKERS AND SEEKERS

Of the egalitarian and politically progressive in the Jacksonian
world-view, of its romantic faith in the judgment of unlettered
people, and its suspicions of the past, of tradition, and of the
wealthy, there were many critics. They opposed the brutal treatment
of Indians and slaves, and in the 1840s the war with Mexico; they
disliked North America's incipient industrialism. "Things are in the
saddle and ride mankind," lamented Ralph Waldo Emerson. And
in the America he visited, Alexis de Tocqueville recognized that in
the United States public opinion was a tyrannical God, and that the
central intellectual problem posed by the country's experience was
that of the place of the individual in what was becoming a mass
society. The common theme of writers and intellectuals, in all their
own diversity, was rejection of, and alienation from, Jacksonian
America: a movement known as Transcendentalism. If it had a center, it was just outside Boston, in Concord. Living in Concord, or
spending much time there, were persons all of whose names are now
familiar: Ralph Waldo Emerson, Henry Thoreau, Bronson Alcott,
George Ripley, Margaret Fuller, Theodore Parker, William Ellery
Channing, and others. There were some themes common to all of
them, individualists though they were. The mature American of
1830 had seen stripped of their power all the establishments which a
generation or so earlier had seemed to represent order: the Church,
the Bar, the Federalist party, and the eastern merchant aristocracy.
"In all my lectures," Emerson declared, "I have taught one doctrine,

namely the infinitude of the private man." It was an age, too, which throbbed with the impulse to reform.[1]

A familiar view of the age is that expressed by Henry James, writing later of Nathaniel Hawthorne's world, and of what it lacked:

The negative side of the spectacle on which Hawthorne looked out, in his contemplative saunterings and reveries, might, indeed, with a little ingenuity, be made almost ludicrous; one might enumerate the items of high civilization, as it exists in other countries, which are absent from the texture of American life, until it should become a wonder to know what was left. No State, in the European sense of the word, and indeed barely a specific national name. No sovereign, no court, no personal loyalty, no aristocracy, no church, no clergy, no army, no diplomatic service, no country gentleman, no palaces, no castles, nor manors, nor old country houses, nor parsonages, nor thatched cottages, nor ivied ruins; no cathedrals, nor abbeys, nor little Norman churches; no great universities nor public schools — no Oxford, nor Eton, nor Harrow; no literature, no novels, no museums, no pictures, no political society, no sporting class — no Epsom nor Ascot! ... The natural remark, in the almost lurid light of such an indictment, would be that if these things are left out, everything is left out.[2]

Edgar Allen Poe is the obvious example of this — in his scorn for the moralistic and didactic poetry then fashionable, in his view of science as the destroyer of the mythic, in his creed that the purpose of art is the creation of beauty — and sometimes of terror. But Poe's fame came posthumously and not as a Transcendentalist; he was sufficient to himself. He was born in Boston but raised in Baltimore, and lived — off and on — in Richmond, to become a self-proclaimed Southerner; he was a drug addict, prone to alcoholism, to bouts of melancholia and even madness, and, aware that "less than a little was with him too much," he lived a life shaped by the darker side of man's nature.[3]

It was not Poe's Baltimore, nor Charlottesville, where for a single term he studied, but Calvinist-turned-Unitarian Boston, with Concord and Walden within a 20-mile range of Harvard, that became a Mecca and a "Literary Emporium:" writers, philosophers, and activists with the pen lived within reach of each other. Living

---

[1] *Journals of Ralph Waldo Emerson*, ed. Edward Waldo Emerson and Waldo Emerson Forbes (Boston, Houghton Mifflin, 1900–14), vol. V, p. 380.
[2] Henry James, *Hawthorne* (New York, Harper, 1879), pp. 42–3.
[3] Kenneth Silverman, *Edgar A. Poe, Mournful and Never-ending Remembrance* (London, Weidenfeld and Nicolson, 1992).

in a city bypassed in population growth by Philadelphia and New York City, whose Erie Canal left Boston isolated, a city with little industry and no agriculture, these writers were concerned with quality, not wealth, which many of them inherited, and with quality more than equality. They founded the Boston Public Library and the Athenaeum, the *North American Review* (1817), the *Dial* (1840–4), the *Liberator* (from 1831), and the *Atlantic Monthly* (from 1857). Although Emerson feared that the fortunes being made in the mills of Lawrence and Lowell and Lynn would foster plutocratic rule in the United States at the price of the poverty of the mill-girls, and Herman Melville turned out savage literary caricatures of the new rich, and crusaded against the industrial slavery of Northern sweat-shops, benefactors were in fact numerous. The gifts of the Astor Library (the nucleus of the New York Public Library,) the Lowell Institute in Boston, Girard College, the Lawrence School in Mas-sachusetts, the Perkins Institute for the Blind in Boston (the first school for the blind in America,) George Peabody's grants to Balti-more, Harvard, and Yale, and his Education Fund for the South, were notable examples of capitalist philanthropy. Indeed, so com-mon and lavish were such gifts that in 1860 the New York legislature found it necessary to pass an Act stating that anyone survived by near relatives could bequeath no more than one-half of his property to charitable organizations. It was in Boston that de Tocqueville found the best features of the new society. And even Dickens thawed, in his *American Notes* (1842):

The golden calf they worship at Boston is a pigmy compared with the giant effigies set up in other parts of that vast countinghouse which lies beyond the Atlantic, and the almighty dollar sinks into something com-paratively insignificant, amidst a whole pantheon of better gods.

What to Sam Adams had been a Christian Sparta was now replac-ing Philadelphia as the Athens of America, with Faneuil Hall as its Acropolis. Boston's illuminati were many, and varied in their views. For four years they had the quarterly journal the *Dial*; Brook Farm (1841–7) and Fruitlands (1843) were their experiments in com-munal living. They included what might be called the professional-professorial poets of Cambridge, Henry Wadsworth Longfellow (a professor of modern languages at Bowdoin at 18) and James Russell Lowell, providing a literature of uplift and protest; the Everett brothers and the Prescotts, father and son, George Ticknor, William Ellery Channing, and Andrews Norton (whom Carlyle would describe as "The Pope of Unitarianism"); the historians George Bancroft,

Jared Sparks (Harvard's first professor of History) and Francis Parkman — the United States's first truly nationalist and patriotic chroniclers; Emerson, for whom Truth could be captured not by reason but by intuition, and by communing with nature; and Henry David Thoreau, who took the doctrine (the Oversoul, the Transcendental) so far as to live for two years in his private utopia in isolation at Walden Pond (1845–7), and whose essay justifying civil disobedience (after spending a night in jail for refusing to pay his taxes as a gesture of opposition to slavery and to the Mexican War) has ever since become a sacred text for all critics of parties, groups, or organizations. The doctrine of the individual's self-sufficiency became with him indistinguishable from anarchy — anarchy, but in his case with morality attached. Thoreau never locked his door at Walden, and lost only one item: his copy of Homer. He deplored the wanderers who in the spring came to intrude, particularly those he called the shanty-Irish, the latest waves of the sea. When, during the Civil War, Thoreau lay dying of tuberculosis, a neighbor asked him, "Henry, have you made your peace with God?", he replied, "We have never quarreled." In fact he was no back-to-Nature primitive, but a Harvard-educated man of letters, who was surveyor and natural historian as well as romantic, and who studied Charles Lyell's *Principles of Geology*, Ovid's *Metamorphoses*, and — in 1860, when it was acquired by Concord Town Library — Darwin's *The Origin of Species*. He was the most Transcendentalist of them all: the best government is not merely the least (Jefferson's view), but one that governs not at all. Loyalty is to be given to the individual, not the state. And for him that utopia was best that was no more than an easy walk from the comforts — and the libraries — of town.

There are other exotics: Orestes Brownson was born a Presbyterian, but became America's most famous convert to Catholicism, in his quest for authority and hierarchy as the only guarantors of eternal religious truth. *En route* he was a supporter of the Brook Farm community, then a Unitarian minister, all to no avail; he also founded and edited the *Democratic Review* and, later, his *Quarterly Review* (after 1844). He saw class war between capital and labor as inevitable, and sought the abolition of the wage system, and of the hereditary transmission of landed property; but he also saw states' rights as the guardian of political liberty. Theodore Parker was a Unitarian turned lyceum-preacher, with a Boston congregation of 7,000; an opponent of slavery and of the Mexican War, but advocating peaceful and rational change, not violence. Not least of these was Oliver Wendell Holmes: the epitome of the nineteenth-century "Boston Brahmin." He was the son of a clergyman, and the father of a celebrated jurist. He achieved fame as a wit, a man of letters, and a physician. Trained first as lawyer, then in medicine at Harvard and Paris, Holmes published a prize-winning monograph on fevers. From 1847, he taught at the Harvard Medical School. He was the exponent of a rational, easygoing, fun-finding attitude toward life. But, for all his nonchalance, through his investigations into childbed fever, which had previously not been known to be contagious, he revolutionized obstetric care in the United States. His novel, *Elsie Venner* (1861), shows a remarkable understanding of abnormal psychology. Holmes lived by faith in the New Science, with its emphasis on speculation, individualism, and progressivism. He combined iconoclasm, urbanity and levity — witness his *Autocrat of the Breakfast-Table*, which appeared in the *Atlantic Monthly* in 1857–8. But in him the Brahmin Boston clubman displaced the Transcendalist.

As an intellectual revolution, Transcendentalism developed between 1815, when William Ellery Channing was maturing the liberal gospel of Unitarianism, and 1836, when Ralph Waldo Emerson's first important book, *Nature*, was published. The "movement" — if such a name can be given to a rich collective of sharply distinct individuals — sprang from Unitarian soil; the Unitarians had abandoned the Puritan theology of hell and damnation, and had turned to a more creative, human view, believing that man was a rational being capable of improvement, and that God was all-beneficent. But, intellectually, Unitarianism was "a sterile rationalism;" and the Transcendentalist movement was a revolt against the "icy system," to use Lyman Beecher's words.

As befitted a movement with a New England heritage, Transcendentalism had a moral foundation, and took an ethical view of the world and of man's place within it. It was in fact religion masquerading as philosophy. To the Transcendentalist, the material world was only a veil for the divine, a doctrine recalling the Quaker belief in the "inner light," as does the other tenet of stressing the intuitive rather than the reasoned knowledge. God is indwelling in the universe, in the natural world around us, and in man ("I am part or parcel of God.") Therefore, Emerson reasoned, man himself is the true source of moral law. Nature, he said, is "the dress God wears, the shadow he casts upon our senses." The "movement" owed much to Coleridge, Carlyle, Victor Cousin, and German philosophers such as Fichte and Hegel. In the early nineteenth century, many New England youths were trained at German universities, where they studied German mataphysics; Everett, Longfellow, and Ticknor all studied in Germany on being appointed professors, and all had many European friends and correspondents. Channing was greatly influenced by Wordsworth and Coleridge, and very much at home in the English Lake District. Ticknor was a personal friend of Macaulay and Sydney Smith, Talleyrand and Metternich. But Ticknor always called himself a Federalist, and Edward Everett became a Whig politician, and succeeded Webster as secretary of state in 1852; Bancroft, Fenimore Cooper, and Hawthorne, however, were dedicated Jackson men. Transcendentalism stressed the individuality of man, self-asserting and self-transcending. If this "movement" had leaders, they were Channing, the Unitarian, and – largely by self-appointment – Emerson, scion of seven Puritan ministers, schoolteacher turned Unitarian minister who found the lecture platform more congenial than the pulpit, and whose essay on *Nature* became a Bible to many Transcendentalists – and to Yankee idiosyncrasy. Like all of them, behind his apparently simple credo, Emerson was a man of paradox. He certainly was often contradictory; he worshipped power, but maintained a respect for the moral values; he believed in a theoretical democracy but was temperamentally an aristocrat; an idealist, he could nevertheless give very practical advice; although he professed to ignore and despise material things, he was a very shrewd businessman. He was consistent only in his conviction that consistency was "the hobgoblin of little minds."

The pessimism of the Transcendalists was shared but pushed further by two literary giants, Herman Melville of New York and Nathaniel Hawthorne of Salem, each with a vivid Puritan awareness of the Satanic forces at work among men. Hawthorne's ancestors had persecuted Quakers and hanged witches, and his *The Scarlet Letter* (1850) and – the story he liked best – *The House of the Seven Gables* (1851) are rich in an awareness of a guilt, a remorse – and a tragedy – that had occurred on native soil. They lived in the real world too: Hawthorne was an admirer of Jackson, and a lifelong Democrat. For four years he served as US consul at Liverpool, England (1853–7). He recognized the need for political compromise with the South, and in *The Celestial Railroad* (1843) and *The Blithedale Romance* (1852) he satirized Brooke Farm and easy Utopianism. There was for him, in a world of good and evil, no easy way to grace; man's own spiritual pride was the main source of sin. Melville experienced boyhood poverty, the brutality of life on a whaler – a whaleboat, he said, was his Harvard and his Yale – and he lived among the cannibals of Typee in the Marquesas (*Typee*, 1846, *Mardi*, 1849). *Moby-Dick* (1851), drawing on the reports of Mocha Dick, the great white killer-whale whose deeds were seamen's talk for 20 years or more, drew also on his own 18-month voyage on the whaler *Acushnet*; it is dedicated in admiration to his friend Hawthorne. Though he lived for 40 years after writing *Moby-Dick*, Melville died in obscurity. Only the posthumous discovery of his short novel *Billy Budd* led to the later appreciation of his style, and of his tragic vision.

This small group of New Englanders, many of them friends, were prolific, penetrating, wide-ranging, and disturbing writers. Their themes were universal, but their knowledge of their own country and of their own countrymen brought a power – and an originality – hitherto missing from American literature.[4] By contrast, the earlier tales of Washington Irving, though set in the Hudson valley, were German in concept (and derivation); and if James Fenimore Cooper, in the Leather-Stocking tales and in the character of Natty Bumppo or "Hawkeye," dramatized that central theme in the US, the confrontation between civilization and savagery, his Indians are over-simplified and stylized, and critics, beginning with Mark Twain, have been savage over his largely European-conceived and somewhat condescending portrayal of the hunters and trackers of the forest. Cooper's Indians were fictional – unlike his first hero, the peddler turned spy. They are noble, eloquent, and chivalrous; and their heroes, Chingachgook and Uncas, were of course the white men's friends and allies.

Cooper was raised at Cooperstown in the Fingerlakes country of Central New York (founded by his self-made father, an able land speculator), and saw himself, like his father before him, as a lord of the manor – part pioneer, part gentleman, silkhose but leather-stocking too. Cooperstown, now a baseball shrine in a still rural setting, became the Templeton of the Leather-Stocking tales. He had indeed no affection for New England; in his latest books, it provided him with his villains; for him, Plymouth Rock was "Blarney Rock." Cooper became a writer when he moved to farm at Scarsdale in New York State, and thus became a neighbor of the now 75-year-old and anecdotal John Jay. From Jay he got the story of the true adventures of a patriot spy, who emerges as the hero Harvey Birch (in reality the then 77-year-old Enoch Crosby) in *The Spy, a tale of the Neutral Ground* (1821). Thereafter he spent too much time

[4] For Hawthorne, see Edwin Haviland Miller, *Salem is My Dwelling Place: A life of Nathaniel Hawthorne* (London, Duckworth, 1992). For the epic narratives and burlesques of Washington Irving, James Fenimore Cooper, and William Prescott, *see* John P. McWilliams Jr, *The American Epic: Transforming a genre 1770–1860* (New York, Cambridge University Press, 1989).

abroad, was depressed by the America he found on his return from a triumphal tour, and became as prolific in quarrels as in novels. Where, however, he had a real-life model to draw on – as he used the stories, now near legends, of Daniel Boone to draw Natty Bumppo – he created a wilderness hero, perhaps the first in American literature. By contrast, Melville's and Hawthorne's worlds are their own, real and grim, but haunting and disturbing, aware of "the great power of blackness" in a wolfish world.

Walt Whitman was no Bostonian, and no Transcendentalist, but the most Jacksonian or rather Jeffersonian of them all ("In this wide and naturally rich country, the best Government indeed is that which governs least;" to him Jefferson was "the greatest of the great;" one of his brothers was named Thomas Jefferson, another Andrew Jackson). In origin half Long Island democrat, and half New York Dutch, his training was, like Franklin's, at the printing press; he became a romantic troubadour of the notion of equality but also a devotee of "grand individuals" and "higher men," and of the great orators, and the "democratic despots" Rossuth and Garibaldi; he was a lover of all mankind, its women and its men. His interest was "the bulk of the average," the nobility of the people in all of the states of the Union. Which did not mean that he had any illusions; nor was it a matter of "rights." Democracy was simply, he held, the only effective way to train people to rule themselves. In his eyes the Jacksonian form was simply the use of populist rhetoric by the educated and professional, not the common, man. When the War came, the Northern workers would discover their democracy in the process of defending it, and would free themselves as well as the slaves. It meant that, as well as author and editor, he himself also worked for Tammany Hall and the Free-Soil Democrats.

2 WITH PEN, PRINT AND SPADE

Among the Bostonians there were, then, not just creative writers and critics, but reformers. It was, in Boston at least, a heady world for visionaries of all causes. The most colorful of them attempted to carry out the theories of the European utopian socialists, Robert Owen and Charles Fourier. If they had a single American progenitor, it was Albert Brisbane (1809–90), who had studied in Europe with Hegel, Goethe, and Fourier, and on returning to America in 1840 became the advocate of Fourier's ideas as an answer to the Depression of 1837 and the problems of an industrial society. His *The Social Destiny of Man* caught the attention of Horace Greeley, editor of the *New York Tribune*, who printed many of Brisbane's articles. A number of communistic settlements or "Fourierist phalanxes" were established, though – Amana, Harmony, and Oneida apart – without permanent success. In the 50 years from 1805 to 1855, no less than 99 different social experiments were begun in the United States, 45 of them in the Old Northwest (Ohio, Indiana, Wisconsin, Illinois, Michigan), and another 28 in western New York. All these experiments were Middle Western rather than strictly frontier phenomena. Indeed, the availability of land weakened rather than strengthened them ("The lust for land," said John Humphrey Noyes, "leads off into the wilderness ... Almost any kind of a factory would be better than a farm for a Community nursery.") Again, almost all the leading creeds among them, like their leaders, came from Western Europe.

The best publicized among these settlements was Robert Owen's community at New Harmony, on the Wabash River in Indiana, which attracted a thousand people, from philosophers to idlers, had seven forms of government in the two years of its existence, and ended when Owen's interest – and his money – ran out. Owen's description of it was: a "Heterogeneous collection of radicals, enthusiast devotees to principle, honest latitudinarians and lazy theorists, with a sprinkling of unprincipled sharpers thrown in." Some deserted him because he was agnostic, others because he was teetotal; the latter founded a settlement of their own, Feiba Peveli, so named since they held that names of towns should indicate their geographic location by degrees of longitude and latitude – thus they renamed New York Otke Notive and London Lafa Vovutu. Owen himself soldiered on in his socialist crusading; he died aged 87, in the course of giving a lecture on "The Human Race Governed without Punishment."

Owen's predecessor, George Rapp, a German Lutheran, was cleverer; a believer in the imminent second coming of Christ, he led his 900-strong community from Württemberg, Germany, first to Butler, Pennsylvania, then to Indiana. Since Christ had to be well-endowed for his mission on his return, members on joining the community had to relinquish all their property to Father Rapp, acting as his John the Baptist, and pledge themselves to celibacy, so there would be no rival heirs. He sold the 20,000 acres of land with its orchards and mills, craft shops and hospital, to Owen for $150,000, which enabled him to move his now rich group to Economy (now Ambridge, Pennsylvania, northwest of Pittsburgh), where it was even more prosperous than in Indiana; it survived for 100 years. But with material success, and/or from the preaching of celibacy, came trouble: Rapp's experiment had a turbulent history; after his death in 1847, when the movement found it harder to resist the appeals of marriage, of a livelier secular life and other worldly temptations, its credulous flock fell victim to the fraud who called himself Count Leon.

There were 30 or more Fourierist phalanxes, of 300 to 1,800 people, most notably that at Brook Farm, founded by George Ripley, an ex-Unitarian minister. With a common workshop, granary, and dining hall, and a large farm efficiently and communally run, it would prove superior to scores of private enterprises. It was co-operative, not communist, preferring the married to the single state, and was little touched by sexual scandal – which made it unique among utopias. Its objective was no less than "to combine the thinker and the worker, so far as possible in the same individual ..." Its school was unique in its high standards. But the experiment lasted only six years. Of the avowedly Fourierist experiments, only one, the North American Phalanx at Red Bank, New Jersey, lasted more than a decade; all were capitalist-and profit-motivated, and commitment to celibacy, while encouraged, was not required. The successive failures were due less to Utopianism than to inactivity – Fruitlands, Bronson Alcott's community farm, where little Louisa Alcott spent some of the most unhappy days of her far-from-happy childhood, was held together by the doctrine that "a pure soul, by the laws of its own nature, adopts a pure diet and cleanly customs, nor needs detailed instructions for daily conduct." It survived but a single summer. Icaria in Iowa (1848–59) was largely the handiwork of Etienne Cabet, who had been Louis-Philippe's attorney general in Corsica, and another failed French revolutionary; it featured compulsory marriage. Cabet died not long after reaching his New World, and his experiment died with him: not surprisingly, since his *Voyage en Icarie* envisaged a society sharply un-American: his utopia was to be classless and totally egalitarian, with military order and discipline, and a uniform was to be worn appropriate to "every condition;" no one could eat anything which the Republic did not "approve;" and women as well as men would work at trades – but, happily, retain their true function: they would cook all the meals.

J. H. Noyes's Oneida was established in the Fingerlakes Country of Central New York in 1848. Noyes sought to build a communist society, with no private property, modeled on what he believed was the first-century Church, with himself as interpreter of "Bible Communism." As he saw it, the monogamous family bred selfishness, hence his "complex marriage." This was not the "free love" of some utopias or the male paramountcy of the Mormons, but a community in which every male was married to every female, and vice-versa. "Complex marriage" not only allowed freedom of choice of husbands by wives, but required that propagation be the result of preliminary discussion by the community. Birth control and eugenic experiments were part of the community code; partners were chosen to form "scientific combinations." Their newspaper, the *Circular*, carried religious exhortation into the small ads:

To Jewellers: A Single Pearl, of great price. This inestimable jewel may be obtained by application to Jesus Christ, at the extremely low price of all that a man hath.

As a communist experiment it ended in 1879, but as a commercial enterprise Oneida became the most successful of all, producing splendid and still profitable cutlery and silverware.

In the end practically all the experiments failed: though not for the usual reasons. The ardours – and hardships – did not deter. Communal life in itself did not stifle industry or initiative. The members of the communities were more industrious, more abstemious, and more honest than their neighbors; they were quite as resourceful in manufacturing and agriculture, and for a while even more dedicated. ("Hands to work, Hearts to God," was the Shaker faith.) Their lives were frugal. Their schools were usually superior to the average, their morality almost invariably better. The underlying causes of failure were, socially, the inability long to maintain patches of communism in a strongly individualistic society, to which it was always too easy to escape; and human nature itself. *Labor* did not *vincit omnia*. As Hawthorne put it, after six months' experience of Brook Farm: "labor is the curse of this world, and nobody can meddle with it without becoming proportionately brutified." After pitching hay all day, and digging for potatoes, he was too tired to write. The intellectual and the manual functions were hard to marry. The most successful – Oneida apart, a triumph of capitalism – were Amana in Iowa, rooted in Christian marriage; the oldest-established German and Mennonite groups in Pennsylvania, notably at Ephrata Cloister in Pennsylvania, which called itself a monastery, and was celibate, hard-working, and with strong local ties; the Shaker communities, despite their celibacy, and despite a strange creed of belief in the bisexual nature of God, and in a Day of Judgment that had already come; and, not least, the Mormons, who, repeatedly attacked, moved first to Ohio, then to Missouri, then to Illinois, and then out into the wilderness, where at least – they hoped – there were no other Americans, only Mexicans. The last was the most communal and the most successful of the American utopias.[5]

3 WITH HANDCARTS

The founder of the Mormon Church was Joseph Smith, who was born in 1805 in Sharon, Vermont, into a family of frontier drifters and faith-healers. The family eventually settled near Palmyra, New York, where Joseph grew up in an atmosphere of fervent religion. Beginning in 1820, he had a series of visions; in 1823 he stated that an Angel, "Moroni," had told him that he was to be God's agent in restoring His Church on earth. Smith claimed to have unearthed, at Moroni's direction, a book of gold plates buried (conveniently) in a hillside two miles from his home, and written in "Reformed Egyptian" hieroglyphics. He dug up also — with equal convenience — some magic spectacles (called "Urim" and "Thummin"), with which he was able to read them. From these plates he dictated, from behind a curtain, the "Book of Mormon," published in 1830 — a religious fantasy-history. As translated though Urim and Thummim, the Book of Mormon is a history of the colonization of America by the Jaredites, who were led from the Tower of Babel at the time of the confusion of tongues. First they flourished and then they degenerated, until 600 BC, when their decline was arrested by the arrival of a great part of the tribes of Israel, who had fled from Jerusalem just before the Babylonian captivity. These people were the Nephites, who were destined to build Zion in America. But, like their fathers before them, they were a stiff-necked people with the sin of pride in them; and as the result of a grave disobedience a branch of the tribe, the Lamanites, were cursed and, like the children of Ham, given dark skins. These were the ancestors of the American Indians. But it was the Redskins who multiplied, and in the year 385 AD, they rose against the remnant of the pale-faced Nephites and extirpated them. The last prophet of the Nephites was Mormon, who, when he saw the fate that was coming, wrote the history of his people on gold. And Moroni, his son, who was the only survivor of the massacre, hid the plates, for Joseph Smith to find in 1823.

This melange could be described as a catchall of frontier religious doctrine, and yet another product of the revivalist area around

---

[5] In 1992 there were 11 surviving Shakers, in two communities, one at Sabbathday Lake, in Maine, the other in Canterbury, New Hampshire.

Rochester, New York, so swept by religious enthusiasms that it earned the name of "The Burned-Over District" (a name given it by the English traveller, William Hepworth Dixon in 1870). The Book of Mormon was at once an anachronistic history of early America, and in style a naive parody of what in Britain is called the Authorised Version, but in the US is the King James Version, of the Bible. It reflects also the contemporary interest in the origin of the American Indians (whom many saw as descendants of the lost tribes of Israel), and in the Indian mounds near Lake Ontario. Shortly after publication of this book, Smith founded at Fayette, NY, the Church of Jesus Christ of the Latter Day Saints, popularly known as Mormons. Smith and an assistant, Sidney Rigdon, moved in 1831 with a group of followers to Kirkland, Ohio, where they attempted an experiment in communal living, and built a tabernacle. The group were attacked for setting up an unauthorized bank, and they left hastily for Independence, Missouri, in 1838. When a guerrilla war broke out there in 1840, between the Mormons and the other settlers, Smith and his followers moved on to Commerce, Illinois. Renaming the town Nauvoo, the Mormons applied themselves to the land, and for some time they were left in peace – for Illinois politicians saw that the Mormon votes might be important. Some 4,000 converts came from England and Wales, led by, among others, Brigham Young. In 1844 Smith had another visitation from Moroni, who persuaded him of the blessedness of polygamy, to the steady multiplication of his group; this novelty attracted some, but alienated many. Smith was making himself more and more objectionable to outsiders, and to some Mormons as well. He further alienated Democrats and Whigs by offering himself as a candidate in the presidential election of 1844. When, although he had 27 wives, he decided to marry a 28th, already the mate of a fellow Mormon, a riot followed, and a mob stormed Nauvoo, whereupon Joseph and his brother Hyrum gave themselves up to the authorities in return for the promise of a fair trial. Too many of his flock were on tour, campaigning for his presidency, to be available to support him. He and his brother were taken to the jail in nearby Carthage, Illinois. Given insufficient protection, the brothers were removed from the jail by a hostile throng and lynched on June 27, 1844.

"The blood of the martyrs" served to encourage the Mormons to continue their fight. The leadership was assumed by Brigham Young (1801–77), who led the exodus via Iowa (1846–7) to the region of the Great Salt Lake, not then under US jurisdiction (but later acquired in the Mexican War). Columns of poor factory-folk,

Plate 10 Salt Lake City looking westwards (1858).
(The Mansell Collection, London.)

many of them English and Welsh, struggled across plains and mountains, with white-roofed wagons and ox-teams, handcarts and wheelbarrows, to their distant Canaan. By 1848 there were 5,600 there. President Millard Fillmore (who had succeeded to the presidency on the death of Zachary Taylor in 1850) appointed Brigham Young governor of Utah Territory in 1850, but he was removed from office in 1852, when he in turn proclaimed polygamy. His wives (who may have numbered 27 or more, though some may have been only doctrinally allied, that is, wives in name only,) bore him 56 children. He was a remarkably able and remarkably autocratic leader, who planned the lives of his people in minutest detail. He was all but uneducated and all but illiterate, yet in social and economic terms he was an organiser of genius. Bloodthirsty, unscrupulous and lustful, preaching sermons more often of hate than love, yet he could be benevolent, and was, in his fashion, devout. His religion was born in a forested wilderness, and grew up in a desert, the two seed-beds of many strange faiths.

For a long time, the Mormon commonwealth existed as a separate entity, distant from federal interference. Salt Lake City was and remains a splendidly planned city with an excellent educational system. Through thrift and industry, and tithes to the Church, the community grew prosperous, making part of its profits by selling supplies to California-bound migrants. It owed most of all to the Civil War, which diverted Federal forces to face other foes; and it owed something also to the railroad, which Mormon builders completed in the late 1860s. In 30 years the population of the settlements grew from 6,000 to 200,000. The practice of polygamy was continued until 1893, for it was well-adapted to a patriarchal, agricultural community; after 1893, only some small and isolated Mormon villages stayed fundamentalist. The Utah Territory prospered as a polygamous theocracy in the midst of an equally prosperous monogamous democracy. It is a gripping story, and hard to credit that it all happened only a century ago, and that what is today an impressive state and a magnificently planned city with an abstemious and responsible citizenry should have had so exotic and erotic a founder.[6]

4   CRUSADERS

The Mormon faith was exotic. It was sharply distinct from the characteristics of the North of the 1840s and 1850s; industrializing, urbanizing, and more and more commercial. As slavery was becoming the distinctive feature of the South, so reform of institutions – and of people – became the common theme of the North; legacy of the Jeffersonian Enlightenment and of its Jacksonian reflections, the new middle class of American prosperity set an optimistic tone in the now flourishing newspaper and periodical press; professional men, shopkeepers, merchants, independent farmers and artisans believed in progress and the perfectibility of men – and of women. By this time, both Democrats and Whigs advocated universal manhood suffrage, which ceased to be a real issue in American politics. Both parties advocated *laissez-faire* economic policies, espoused the ideal of equal opportunity for all, opposed special privilege and praised the self-made man. The Whig candidate in 1840 was lauded as an example: General William H. Harrison, the hero of Tippecanoe, the log-cabin candidate for the presidency. The religious revivalism in upstate New York, stirred by the preaching of Charles Finney, the Unitarianism of Boston, the Depression of 1837, all roused the

---

[6] Stanley P. Hirshson, *The Lion of the Lord: A biography of the Mormon leader Brigham Young* (London, Dent, 1971); Fawn Brodie, *No Man Knows My History* (London, Eyre and Spottiswoode, 1975); Mark Holloway, *Heavens on Earth: Utopian communities in America 1680–1880* (New York, Library Publishers, 1951).

social conscience — of employers as of employees. Economically, the early nineteenth-century American liberals were advocates of *laissez-faire* and of the doctrines of Adam Smith. They believed that labor creates wealth, and that labor has a right to the fruits of its toil; but, the communist Utopians apart, the reformers were for the most part conservative, not socialist. There was no significant sentiment in the early nineteenth-century American reform movement against the institution of private property. They did not support labor organizations, strikes or boycotts. They did not even attack child labor.

Among the many reform movements, spiritualism and mesmerism flourished also, witness Owen's *Footfalls on the Boundary of Another World*. Attention was given to the care of the inmates of penal and health institutions. Dorothea Dix, the shy, ill Bostonian, visited hundreds of jails, poor houses, and insane asylums, and induced many states to provide more modern facilities. There was a campaign against public executions, which became private matters in Pennsylvania in 1834 (unlike in Britain, where they continued to be public festivals until 1868). Still another group of reformers organized an anti-war movement, and in 1828 many local pacifist organisations merged into the American Peace Society. Elihu Burritt, prominent in the American movement, attended several European peace congresses until the outbreak of the Crimean War smashed the hopes of the peace advocates. Americans were equally sympathetic to the plight of foreign peoples under autocratic rule. Louis Kossuth — symbol of the nationalist and democratic aims not only of Hungary but of central Europe — received great popular acclaim in America, and there was much compassion for the Cubans, seen as languishing under Spanish tyranny. Ideas of economic revolution, however, were not as striking in the United States as were those of constitutional political change. The principles of Marxist socialism, brought in by European immigrants, served only to add political fuel to the fires of religious prejudice, fanning the flames of nativism as expounded by such groups as those popularly known as the "Know-Nothing" party. The Order of the Star-Spangled Banner, a secret society which sought to abridge the political rights of the newcomers, answered all public inquiries into the nature of their activities with the phrase, "I know nothing." As politicians began to make capital out of this nativist movement, the title "American party" was adopted, but the nickname stuck. Between 1852 and 1856, the Know-Nothings won considerable support in both the North and the South, drawing most of their votes from members of the old Whig party, to which almost none of the German and Irish immigrants belonged. In 1854, the American party elected a governor and gained control of the legislature in Massachusetts, and almost carried New York. Two years later its nominee, Millard Fillmore, the former President, ran a poor third in the presidential election; the party declined rapidly thereafter, as the slavery question pushed alien-baiting off the political stage.

When Jackson was elected, women enjoyed no civil or political rights. Agitation for women's rights was begun by a Scottish feminist, Frances Wright, who was aided by such Americans as Lucretia Mott, Mrs Elizabeth Cady Stanton, and the Grimke sisters of South Carolina. These brave agitators widened their activities to include labor reform, temperance, and anti-slavery. Marriage reforms — including more liberal divorce laws and provisions for allowing married women to retain control of their own property — were advocated. In 1848 a women's rights convention met at Seneca Falls and issued a "Declaration of Independence" for women. In the 1840s a few states accorded women the right to control property. In 1857 Mount Holyoke College opened its doors, and thereafter a few colleges dared to admit women students.

The second quarter of the nineteenth century thus teemed with various humanitarian crusades. In order to discourage the universal use of hard liquor, abstinence societies were formed, and when these proved effective, the reformers demanded state legislation. As a result of the efforts of Neal Dow, Maine passed a prohibition law in 1841. By 1860, 13 states had become prohibitionist: all New England, and those from Ohio to Iowa — where beer and whiskey were associated with the waves of German and Irish immigrants. New York and Pennsylvania held out, as did the South, firmly resistant to all such "isms," and varied as their local preferences were, from mint juleps in the elegant Tidewater to Monongahela red-eye on the banks of the Ohio or the Mississippi.

"Parson" Weems had joined the Temperance Movement in 1812, when he published the *Drunkard's Looking Glass*. There his Golden Receipts Against Drunkenness included:

1. Drink no longer water but use a little wine for thy stomach's sake. Also, cyder, ale, beer etc.
2. Never fight *duels*. Nine times in ten memory of the murdered drives the murderer to the bottle.
3. Never marry but for love. Hatred is repellent; and the husband saunters to the tavern.
4. Provide against *Old Bachelorism*, Age wants comfort, and a good wife is the second best in the universe.
5. Hot coffee in the morning is a good cure for *dram-craving*.

Forty years later Timothy Shay Arthur put the message over more vehemently. His *Ten Nights in a Barroom* (1854), a lurid melodrama on the evils of drink, enjoyed a tremendous success, both as a novelette and as a play. Arthur brought an insider's knowledge: he was a friend of Edgar Allen Poe, in Baltimore.

The central reform of all, and the most far-reaching, was in education. In Jefferson's day, the notion prevailed that education was needed only by a few, and that it should be provided by the Church or by private enterprise. Free schools were regarded as charitable institutions, and the quality of instruction was poor. With the coming of manhood suffrage, politicians like Abraham Lincoln, Thaddeus Stevens, and DeWitt Clinton pointed out the need to educate the electorate, almost contemporaneously with similar Liberal movements in Britain. Labor gave its support, as did educational leaders like Horace Mann and Henry Barnard. The contest between friends and foes of free, public education was sustained and bitter, and for a time compromises were tried: subsidies for pauper schools, land grants for endowments. Eventually state after state provided for tax-supported education, and by 1850 – except in the South – the battle was won. At the same time the curriculum was enlarged, many private colleges and state universities founded, and women admitted to a number of institutions of higher education.

5   THE LYCEUM

The influence of the public school system and the newly founded colleges was to be in the future; for the moment other forms of education were more important. One of the great educational forces of the second quarter of the century was undoubtedly the lyceum. It originated with Josiah Holbrook of Darby, Connecticut, who in 1826 contributed to the *American Journal of Education* an article on the subject of "associations of adults for the Purpose of Mutual Education." To illustrate his ideas he organized in the same year, in Millbury, Massachusetts, "Millbury Lyceum, No. 1 Branch of the American Lyceum." By 1834 at least 3,000 lyceums had been established with state boards, and in 1839 there was even a national convention. In New England there was hardly a village of any size but boasted its lyceum. The lyceums were especially valuable as a means for the wider dissemination of new scientific knowledge – platforms where Benjamin Silliman of Yale lectured on chemistry, and Edward Hitchcock of Amherst and Louis Agassiz on geology. Henry Thoreau, Nathaniel Hawthorne, Ralph Waldo Emerson,

Daniel Webster, Oliver Wendell Holmes, Henry Ward Beecher, were professional performers on these platforms; many of them, Emerson in particular, modified and popularized their style, and their subsequent publications, for a popular audience. Although political controversy and the Civil War destroyed fully 90 percent of the lyceums, they left a legacy in the form of literary societies, lecture bureaus, Chautauquas, and such permanent foundations as Cooper Union in New York, the Peabody Institutes in Baltimore and Boston, and the Lowell Institute, also in Boston. In Emerson's words, the lyceum offered "a pulpit which makes all other pulpits ineffectual." And yet the lyceum movement flourished only in New England, New York and the upper Mississippi valley, particularly Ohio. Conservatives in Pennsylvania were skeptical of the value of its legacy, the campaign for free public education; and in the South the scattered towns and the lower levels of public education hindered the development of that intellectually curious middle class that was the basis of the lyceum movement.[7]

Even more important than the lyceums were the newspapers, which began to take on the characteristics of the modern "daily" and to reduce their price to an amount within the range of the masses. By 1850 there were some 1,500 newspapers, daily, weekly or twice or thrice-weeklies. The New York *Herald*, founded in 1835 by James Gordon Bennett, was the first to print financial news, to report social affairs, and to discuss the theater. Bennett, a Scot by birth and education, schooled in Latin and Greek, "had the perspective of an educated professional not that of a self-educated craftsman," as Benjamin Franklin and the Bradfords had been. To him news was "a commodity." William Cullen Bryant, the poet, became editor of the New York *Evening Post* in 1828; Horace Greeley in 1841 founded the New York *Tribune*, and in 1851 the New York *Times* was established under Henry J. Raymond. In Boston there were 40 bookshops and more than a dozen publishers; one of them, the bearded and Falstaffian James T. Fields, an intellectual impresario, made of the old Corner Bookstore on Washington Street not only a salon but a think-tank.

Central to the explanation of the flowering and the follies of New England was that this was a world far away in spirit from the politics of Jackson's home in the Hermitage in Nashville, or Van Buren's in Kinderhook, New York. The interlocked directorate of Boston's intellectuals produced some splendid history, and much

[7] Carl Bode, *The American Lyceum: Town meeting of the mind* (New York, Oxford University Press, 1957).

penetrating and psychologically-rooted creative writing; and it was the driving force behind a wave of social reforms, including not least the campaign against slavery. They wrote books, built and administered schools and colleges, but they were of little use in clearing the rock and scrub required in building utopias. Moreover, it is easier to preach socialism than to get along with the neighbors next door. Or as Louisa May Alcott put it, in "Transcendental Wild Oats," her satire on Fruitlands, the life of a woman in a commune was scarcely different from her life anywhere else. She had to do "the many tasks left undone by the brethren, who were so busy defining the great duties that they forgot to perform the small ones."

6 THE ECCENTRIC AND THE EDUCATOR:
FANNY WRIGHT AND HORACE MANN

Two of this very varied company can perhaps be seen as its true polarity: Fanny Wright of Dundee, Scotland, and Horace Mann.

Frances Wright was born to wealthy but free-thinking radical parents, who died before she was three. The dominant influence on her youth was her grandmother's brother, the radical professor of moral philosophy at Glasgow University, James Mylne. She toured the US first in 1819 producing her play *Altorf*, dealing with the Swiss fight for independence, and then in 1824 accompanying Lafayette, whom she greatly admired, and who seems to have admired her in return. She was introduced to Jefferson and Madison. They encouraged her to establish the Nashoba Community near Memphis in Western Tennessee (1825–8), designed to train slaves in the skills they would need for emancipation, and then to colonize them. On its collapse after four years – though some free blacks did reach Haiti – she took to the lecture circuit, advocating women's rights, free marital union, easy divorce, birth control, the corrupting influence of the Church in politics – but the divine inspiration of the Bible. Owen's *New Harmony Gazette* was transferred to New York City, to be edited by her as the *Free Enquirer*. She bought the Ebenezer Church in the Bowery, and it became her headquarters, renamed as the Hall of Science. Her estate on the East River became the free-thinking headquarters for New York.

Even on straightforward topics she bred controversy: after an address in Philadelphia, on "A Geographical and Historical Sketch of the North American United States", the mayor banned her speaking there again. An address in New York in support of Jackson led to her platform being destroyed beneath her. She was nearly mobbed on a number of occasions. The New York Workingmen's party, however, did not survive long after she and Robert Dale Owen joined it. Her marriage (1831–5) to William D'Arusmont did not last. She campaigned for Andrew Jackson and advocated the abolition of all banks; capital of all kinds should be held by the state, by which all citizens should be employed. A fiery redhead ("the red harlot of infidelity," "the female Tom Paine,") she carried controversy with her as her banner, and wrecked all she touched. But she had imagination, initiative, and extraordinary courage, moral as well as physical.[8] Her critics outnumbered her admirers: James Fenimore Cooper's wife thought that her face "looks now like that of an old bottle-bruiser – and I do not know which is the most disgusting, her appearance or her doctrines." Even Robert Dale Owen, her collaborator in New Harmony and New York, saw in her "much to admire," but "nothing to love." Contemporary versifiers were even more blunt:

> For she had gold within her purse
> And brass upon her face.
> And talent indescribable
> To give old thoughts new grace.
> And if you want to raise the wind
> Or breed a moral storm
> You must have one brave lady-man
> To prate about reform.

Fanny Wright was an eccentric. But there were other women, not authors or foreign journalists, who went West, and not merely as consorts to restless land-hungry husbands. Trained and enrolled by the National Board of Popular Education, nearly 600 single women teachers went to the new schools in the West between 1846 and 1856, and two-thirds of them stayed on to settle. Whether single or married, the West was for them a grim experience.

Writing from Kansas in 1859, Sarah Everett thanked a sister-in law in Western New York State for sending dress trimmings. She then added: "It was two or three weeks before I could make up my mind to wear anything so gay as that lining and those strings. I am a very old woman," Sarah explained "My face is thin, sunken and wrinkled, my hands bony withered and hard – I shall look strangely I fear with your nice under-sleeves and the coquettish cherry bows."

[8] A. G. J. Perkins and Teresa Wolfson, *Frances Wright, Free Enquirer: The study of a temperament* (New York, Harper, 1939).

The woman who wrote those lines was 29 years old. "Whether we take her protests as exaggerations or, more probably, as accurate assessments of the physical toil of pioneering, one crucial fact emerges. "Sarah Everett's fear of growing old before her time, of losing the capacity for feminine coquetry, was a fear that most women (and men) associated with westward emigration." Pioneer men ranged over the countryside around the newly built cabins, enjoying the richness of wildlife and scenery; women toiled indoors, deprived not only of neighbors but even of the simple joy of looking at the sunlight, of enjoying the seasons.[9]

At the other pole was Horace Mann, the founder of the American public school system. He was able, generous, dedicated, gifted with a taste for ornate rhetoric, and – unusual for a zealot with a sense of duty – he had also a sense of humor. A poor boy, his father died when he was 13; and for a time he worked on the family farm. He was a convert to Unitarianism, a star graduate of Brown University, a Baptist institution; he became a lawyer and in 1827 was elected a member of the Massachusetts Legislature. When he persuaded it to establish a State Board of Education, he then resigned his political role to serve from 1837 to 1849 as secretary of the Board. Until his day, there had been no efficient and regular distribution of funds to schools; authority was decentralized. In some of the poorer parts of the state, the school term was only two months long; school buildings were dilapidated, and were more crude one-roomed cabins than the "little red schoolhouses" of legend; many teachers were inefficient, and all of them were poorly paid. One sixth of Massachusetts school children attended private schools, while one third of them had no educational opportunities whatsoever. Although tax-supported and non-sectarian schools existed in some areas, there was no agreement on discipline, curriculum, attendance, or teacher preparation in Massachusetts or any other state. Yet as immigrant numbers and social tensions rose, the role of the school became important. It would replace family, church and village in shaping the character of the child. "The Common School," Mann said, "is the greatest discovery ever made by man ... in a Republic, ignorance is a crime." Yet there was no automatic support for free public education. The wealthier contended that it would prove costly and would destroy the self-respect and self-reliance of the working man. Others held that it would make the workers more stable, and hence, they hoped, more conservative. The mass of Americans themselves wanted more and more of it. Mann took the

---

[9] Annette Kodolny, *Fantasy: Experience of the American Frontiers 1630–1860* (Chapel Hill, NC, University of Carolina Press, 1984).

Prussian and Swiss schools as his models; education was a state responsibility and pedagogy a new science. His authority as secretary of the State Board of Education was only that of a publicist; nevertheless he aroused public opinion in Massachusetts sufficiently to achieve many reforms. The first Normal School in the United States was founded; a law was passed providing for a minimal school term of six months; around $2,000,000 was raised for equipment; other school appropriations were more than doubled, and teachers' salaries were greatly increased. More children began to enter public school, while the enrollment of private schools fell off.

In 1848 Mann succeeded John Quincy Adams in the US Congress as an anti-slave Whig, and in 1852 ran (unsuccessfully) for the governorship of Massachusetts on the Free Soil (anti-slavery) ticket. By his second marriage (to Mary Peabody, herself an advocate of good causes, and not least of kindergartens) he became a brother-in-law of Nathaniel Hawthorne, and brother-in-law too of Elizabeth Peabody, who from the Peabody Bookshop, the cultural center of the Brook Farm group, ran her two brothers-in-law and much else of Boston's over-zealous philanthropies. In all his warmth of spirit, Horace Mann brought a deep rooted Calvinist-become-Unitarian drive to his work; a Puritan without a theology, he disapproved of smoking, drinking, and frivolities – which for him included the ballet. He could not help preaching and moralizing. But he never preached narrow dogmas and pious generalities. He could state imperishable truths with eloquence;

If we do not prepare children to become good citizens; – if we do not develop their capacities, if we do not enrich their minds with knowledge, imbue their hearts with love of truth and duty, and a reverence for all things sacred and holy, then our republic must go down to destruction, as others have gone before it; and mankind must sweep through another vast cycle of sin and suffering, before the dawn of a better era can arise upon the world. It is for our Government, and for that public opinion, which, in a republic, governs the government, to choose between these alternatives of weal and woe.[10]

By the time of his death in 1859, the basic shape of American education had been determined: free public primary and secondary education provided as a community responsibility and no longer as "charity;" compulsory school attendance; special training for teachers; superintendents of education established in some states, and even

[10] Quoted by Louise Hall Tharp, *Until Victory: Horace Mann and Mary Peabody* (Boston, Little, Brown, 1960).

in some cities – Buffalo being the first. There were 80,000 elementary schools with over 3 million pupils, and 6,000 high schools and/or academies with 250,000 students. And – portent of things to come – Bronson Alcott, when he became superintendent of schools in Concord (1859), introduced singing, dancing, reading aloud, and physiology.

Moreover, though not free, higher education was spreading steadily if erratically. To the colonial college foundations of Harvard, William and Mary, Yale, and New Jersey, were added Brown, Dartmouth, Bowdoin, Williams, and Amherst; and the first state universities (Pennsylvania 1791, and Virginia 1819, followed by Indiana 1821, Michigan 1837 and Wisconsin 1848), with their land-grant backing, and all scientific and secular in their emphases. There were some unusual and pioneering institutions in scientific engineering and technical training; West Point Military Academy (1802), the Sheffield School at Yale and the Lawrence at Harvard; Rensselaer Polytechnic (1824); Oberlin College in Ohio (1833), a liberal, private Congregational institution open to students of either sex and "irrespective of color;" and progressive Antioch (1854), of which Horace Mann was for a time president. Alongside the Smithsonian Institution in Washington DC were institutes offering practical instruction in science and commerce to young working men (the Franklin in Philadelphia, the Lowell in Boston, the Peabody in Baltimore, the Cooper Union in New York.) The main drive, however, behind the wave of college-building in the decades before the Civil War was still strongly religious: in 1860 the Presbyterians could boast 49 colleges, the Methodists 34, the Baptists 25, the Congregationalists 21, and the Episcopalians 11; while by that time the Catholics had founded 14 colleges and theological seminaries, notable among them St Louis University in Missouri and Fordham in New York City. But then, as de Tocqueville had noted in 1831, "The religious aspect of the country was the first thing that struck my attention." Moreover, though Mann had a fellow-enthusiast, Barnard, in Connecticut, the energy was in individual states, not in the federal government. Indeed, in the South, colleges were being outnumbered by military academies, some of them distinguished, like the Virginia Military Institute at Lexington (1839) and the Citadel in Charleston, SC (1843). South of the Mason-Dixon line (the boundary between Pennsylvania and Maryland), where the tobacco and cotton plantations were the sources of wealth and of status, all reform, however well-intentioned, was suspect, and abolitionism was seen as especially disruptive and revolutionary, as it was. The South marched to a different drum.

8

Was Destiny Manifest?
How the West Was Won

Even before the Lewis and Clark expedition had returned in 1806, Lieutenant Zebulon Pike, with a small group of men, was sent by his superior officer, General James Wilkinson, at the request of President Jefferson, to find and survey the headwaters of the Mississippi. A year later he was assigned an even more difficult task; to ascend the Arkansas River to the region of the present city of Denver. When he reached the upper Rio Grande his force was captured, and he was imprisoned as a spy and then deported by Spanish authorities; when he returned to the East he could at least report on Spanish Santa Fe and its economic opportunities, and on the Indian tribes in its vicinity: Navahos, Utes, and Apaches. His third expedition into the Colorado Rockies (1806–7) was less successful, and he pronounced the Peak that now bears his name to be "unscalable;" a road now goes to the top – 14,000 feet above sea-level. In 1819–20 Major Stephen Long, an assistant professor of mathematics at West Point, who had transferred to the Topographical Corps, explored the Great Plains between the Platte and the Canadian rivers. The "haunt of bison and jackal," whose "sole monarch" was the prickly pear, was unsuited, he reported, to agriculture; this was "the Great American Desert." Between Pike's true picture of some 40 peaks rising to 14,000 feet, and Long's fanciful picture of a great desert, lay the truth.[1]

[1] See W. Eugene Hollon, *The Lost Pathfinder* (Norman, University of Oklahoma Press, 1949); Maxine Benson (ed.), *From Pittsburgh to the Rocky Mountains: Major Stephen Long's expedition* (Golden, Fulcrum, 1988).

Plate 11 *Western Landscape*, by John Mix Stanley.
(Gift of Dexter M. Ferry, Jr. © The Detroit Institute of Arts 1990.)

1 BUFFALO COUNTRY

From eastern Ohio running almost to Oklahoma is the tall-grass prairie, where the grasses once grew as high as, or higher than, a tall man. Kansas is wheat country; wheat and oats, rye and barley, and not least corn, are, after all, grasses, the first plants cultivated by man. One thousand miles west rise the Rockies, "those stupendous mountains," as Lewis and Clark described them, and in approaching them the grass becomes short and all but treeless. Between Kansas and the "great Stony Mountains" are the Great or the High Plains; as the land rises so does the rainfall decrease; the sunflower – the state flower of Kansas, growing man high there – becomes a tiny wildflower in the West. This was buffalo country: perhaps some 60 million buffalo fed on the plains when the first white settlers reached them – so many, said the Spaniards, that they could only be compared to the fish in the sea. To the Indians they were the only source of their economy: food, bedding, clothing, tools and household utensils, for theirs was a buffalo not a maize culture; buffalo and worship of the sun were the bases too of their religion, and of their view of Nature. Lewis and Clark's column of 40 men, plus Sacajawea, needed a buffalo a day to survive. Buffalo Bill Cody's first job was to feed the workers on the Kansas Pacific Railway; he killed 4,280 buffalo in a year and a half. The first railroad tracks were laid along the buffalo trails. But this could be a windswept country too, swept by dust storms, tornadoes, blizzards; and in winter the northwind blows cold indeed. It is a land of great distances, where the sky seems vast: "A nameless blue-green solitude, flat, endless, still, with nothing to hide behind."[2]

The whole of the westernmost world, from the Great Plains to the Pacific, is dominated by mountain ranges and a few rich valleys, like the Sacramento and the Willamette. Relief controls climate, vegetation and soil, drainage, water power and mineral wealth. This is far more true than of the Appalachians, across which the main east–west lines of climate, river, and vegetation freely move, albeit with a salient for the Smokies. In the West, climate and vegetation have the north–south orientation of the mountains, and the main contrasts are between windward and leeward slopes, between northern and southern aspects, and between lower and higher altitudes. The West was alien in history and geology, in its rugged mountains

[2] O. E. Rolvaag, *Giants in the Earth: A saga of the prairie* (New York, Harper Collins, 1991).

and inadequate rainfall. Neither in navigable rivers nor in splendid harbors could the Pacific coast rival the Atlantic; had the country been discovered from the Pacific, it might not have been explored, nor settled, for centuries: witness the trials of that pioneering geologist John Henry Powell on the Colorado river. Its one great inlet, however, the Golden Gate, is one of the most beautiful harbors in the world, and it was its gold, its timber, and its furs that were magnets; in its gold rush in 1849, as again a half-century later in the still less accessible Klondike farther north, the dream of Coronado and of the Seven Cities of Cibola stayed alive. The Columbia, however, more than 1,200 miles long, is more impressive than any river of the Atlantic Tidewater; it runs north between the Rockies and the Selkirks, then after its great loop around the northern end of the Selkirks, south across what is now the state of Washington, and west through the Cascade Mountains to the Pacific. It was a source of salmon for Indians, and the first explorers went along it in canoes: Lewis and Clark in 1805, and then in 1811 David Thompson, voyaged down its entire length. And far to the south of it, where it is hot and dry and cold in winter, is true desert country. Here water was and is the most precious resource. But here too it is the limitless horizons that are striking. Texas has been described as a country where you can travel farther in a straight line, and see less, than anywhere else in the Union – or on earth?

2   THE MISSIONS

The West was explored, opened up and mapped by the mountain men and by the army's Topographical Corps. But they had, of course, been preceded as discoverers of California by the Spanish, moving across by lateral routes of their own, from Florida and Texas and New Mexico, and by sea. The first Spanish missions north of Mexico were established in New Mexico with the Juan de Onate expedition of 1598, hunting for the fabled silver mines, whose wealth would be the basis of his colony; he was accompanied by a team of 10 Franciscans outnumbered by some 400 soldiers. Some thousands of Pueblo Indians were "converted," but stayed truculent; Santa Fe was built by Pueblo Indian labor and established as capital in 1609 by Onate's successor, Pedro de Peralta. It was well placed: on the central route north via the Pass of the North, and on the south bank of the Rio Grande; but the Pueblo Revolt of 1681 expelled settlers and missionaries. It was not recovered for a decade. It was even harder going among the Pima and Apache of

Arizona, though by 1700 there were missions at Trumacacori and San Xavier del Bac, the work of Father Eusebio Kino, the "padre on horseback." By 1767, when the Jesuit missionaries were expelled from all Spanish possessions by order of Charles III of Spain, the area had only eight missions, all in Sonora. And Franciscan efforts on the route to Upper California led to the Yuma Revolt in 1781. The first Texas mission, San Francisco de los Tejas, was set up in 1690 by Spanish friars, but abandoned in the face of Indian hostility. It was reopened in 1716 to counter the French settlements along the Gulf Coast; and two years later a mission and *presidio* (garrison) were built at San Antonio, which gradually became the principal Spanish settlement in Texas. But warlike and nomadic Indians made the deserts unwelcoming and stony ground. By 1800 there were only six functioning missions with nine missionaries in Texas; and in 1793 the San Antonio mission was secularized, and its lands distributed.

Spain's outposts of empire, its missions and *presidios* in the Southwest, were never strongly held, and Santa Fe was the only town of consequence prior to the nineteenth century. Alongside the missionary and the mining motives, the political purpose was to forestall the threat of the French moving down the St Lawrence and of the Russians in northern California; the number of Spanish settlers was never large. The missionary centers did usually become trading towns; each year traders from Chihuahua drove their pack train via Santa Fe and Taos to the French settlements on the Mississippi, as later they did to Texas, Kansas, and Utah. As the French moved down the Mississippi, to Natchitoches on the Red River and to New Orleans, the Spaniards founded not only San Antonio (1718) but Los Adaes, 20 miles west of Natchitoches and within present Louisiana, which became the Spanish capital of the new province of Texas (named after the Tejas Indians). Indians and *mestizos* were Hispaniolized and brought up as Christians and/or as scouts (*genizeros*, after the Turkish janissaries); or bought and sold as articles of commerce. From 1700 the Spanish inland frontier was the province of Coahuila, and its edge lay on the Rio Grande: the permanent enemy proved to be not the French but the Apaches and Comanches, a sharp contrast with the Pueblo Indians or the Hopis, erratically unwelcoming as they had been.

Meantime, along the Sierra Madre Occidental, Jesuit missionaries worked their way into Sonora and Arizona. In 1768, under the lead of the Spanish viceroy José de Galvez and the Franciscan Fray Junipero Serra, missionaries from what is now Mexican Lower California moved north, partly by sea, partly by land, on what was

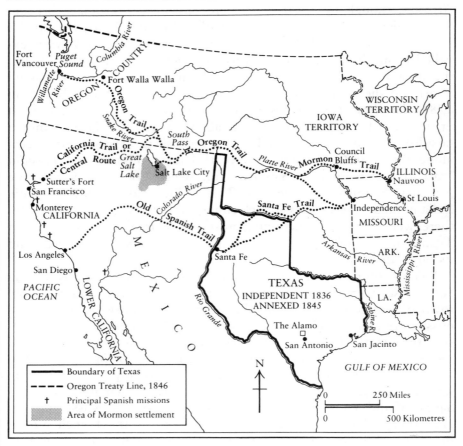

Map 5 The opening of the West.

known as the Sacred Expedition. In moving inland from Monterey
Bay, Don Gaspar de Portola by chance found San Francisco Bay.
The best known of the missionary leaders, Father Junipero Serra
was born on Majorca (where his home was in 1923 given to the
City of San Francisco). A scholar with a tiny physical frame, he had
been sent as a missionary to Mexico; he walked from Vera Cruz
to Mexico City when he was 36, after which he was permanently
lame and had an ulcerous leg; yet he constantly scourged himself.
He became Father and President of the Lower California Missions
in 1760, then promptly went as religious leader on the Sacred
Expedition to the North. Not having enough soldiers to protect
his missions, he went back to Mexico City to plead for more. The
first coastal missions were established by Father Serra at San Diego
and Monterey, and at San Francisco in 1776, the year when a

Declaration of Independence was signed 3000 miles away, in a very alien world. In 1781 El Pueblo de Nuestra Señora Ia Reina de Los Angeles de Porciuncula was established by a team of two Spaniards, 10 Indians and *mestizos*, 10 Negroes and mulattoes, and a Chinese; Santa Barbara came a year later. Before his death in 1784 Father Serra had founded 9 missions, and his successors built 12 more. In the end there were 21 missions along the Pacific coast, to the 21st and last at Solano, north of San Francisco. Each had the same pattern: priests and soldiers in uneasy partnership, with semi-Christianized Indians as farm laborers, cultivating vineyards, orchards, and olive groves, with sheep, goats, horses, and herds of long-horned cattle. By the time of secularization, some 60 friars mostly Spaniards, and 30,000 Indians provided most of the food for Upper California. And those settlers privileged to have royal grants built up vast *haciendas* and ranchos. As the missions were broken up and auctioned after Mexican independence – in Spanish-American California as in Tudor England – a few families did well in the free-for-all. Yet the padres' carefully-kept records showed more deaths than births among Indians.

Some quarter of California's 300,000 Indians were converted. But there were serious Indian revolts – at Yuma and at San Diego in 1775, at Santa Barbara in 1825, and in Taos in 1847. The brutal treatment of Indians by whites was recorded by Helen Hunt Jackson in her *A Century of Dishonor* in 1881, and in her even better-known romantic novel *Ramona* (1884). For a short period, however, the missions provided security, and some measure of training, for the non-warlike Indians in oases that were surrounded by a constant conflict between "Anglos," "Chicanos," and "Indios," and amid revolutionary "constitutional" changes (usually by wars or coups.)

Mexican independence from Spain (1821) was attended by no tightening of political control in the Southwest. The missions, however, were secularized. And the 1820s and 1830s, it was American traders and then settlers, far more than Spanish-Americans or Mexicans, who began to penetrate the area in numbers – from Texas to the Pacific Coast; and within a single generation it became a part of the United States. The North American continent was taken by men, mainly British, moving from the eastern seaboard; it took three centuries to master, and the final stages of that mastery was later to be made easy by European inventions, by barbed wire and the Colt revolver, later by the laying of railroad tracks and the use of dynamite, and later still by Irish and Chinese labor.

3   THE INDIANS

The Plains and mountain Indians, in all their distinct tribes and languages, were as varied as those in the East, but by the nineteenth century largely nomadic. The indigenous tribes of Plains Indians seem to have been few in number – Shawnee, Osage, Wyandot, and Delaware – and agriculturalists, without buffalo. Only with the acquisition of the horse from the Spaniards did the non-plains Indians move in: tepee-dwelling nomads who made the buffalo their commissariat, and did little farming. Some had migrated West voluntarily, driven from the East by the wars and weapons of the invaders. Much of present-day Kansas and Nebraska began as "Indian Territory," the reservations for the Five Civilized Tribes, or for the Cherokees and Choctaws, Creeks and Seminoles, driven from Georgia and the Southwest by Andrew Jackson's men.

In 1832 came a new flare-up of hostility. Black Hawk, a Sauk, led a band of his people who refused to move, saying that they had not been party to the treaty which the rest had approved. But it was too late. The Potawatomi, the Kickapoo, and the Winnebago refused to support him. Black Hawk was taken prisoner, and put in chains on a Missouri river boat. The defeat of his Sauk and Fox in Iowa and Wisconsin saw the end – except in isolated pockets – of organized armed resistance east of the Mississippi, though some have seen Black Hawk as an Indian George Washington. All the tribes, or the remnants of them, moved across the great river. By 1832 there were at least 300 tribes and they probably numbered half a million people or more. Those already driven west from Georgia or the Florida Country were driven on again, to the Indian Territory (which became Oklahoma); many of the longer-settled – the Wyandot, Delawares, Shawnee, and Osage – were bought out by incoming whites. The Arapaho and Cheyenne arrived very late on the scene. They occupied land which wiser Indians, like the Pawnee, and more indigenous ones like the Ute, had inspected for several centuries and found unproductive. They were cultural nomads whose way of life was transformed by the horse – and the gun. With these they created an entirely Indian culture based on the hunting of buffalo. From their earliest days these societies, forced to protect their land and food supply against increasing competition from other Indians dispossessed by white settlement, existed almost permanently on a war footing, trained as horsemen, developing a powerful warrior ethos and considerable military skill. They now looked on apprehensively as the growing network of trails, protected by chains of forts, bisected their hunting territories, disturbing their game and seriously threatening their survival.

Yet what is striking is not the similarities, but the immense diversity of culture, product of the great distances and the range of climate, of topography, and of flora and fauna. The 300,000 western Indians lived in more than 500 village states, many of them mobile, all independent of each other; 30 distinct Indian languages were spoken west of the Rockies – more than on the east coast; some of them were, in the linguists' terms, "isolate," spoken by only from 500 to 5,000 people, related to the eight main groups of Indian languages or language "families." These were Algonquian (from the Atlantic coast south to the Carolinas); Eskimo-Aleut (spoken across the Arctic regions of the North as far as Alaska); Siouan, overwhelmingly in the Missouri River valley and the Great Plains, which included the Winnebagos in Wisconsin, the Osages, the Omahas, the Crows, and the Mandans; Iroquoian (in the lower Great Lakes and upstate New York area, and from which the Cherokee, Tuscarora, and the five languages of the Iroquois "civilized tribes" had broken away); Muskhogean in the Gulf of Mexico region, which included the Seminoles, the Choctaws, the Creeks, the Tuskegees, and the Natchez, who had a royal family and an hereditary nobility; Uto-Aztecan (in Mexico and Southern California, which included the Shoshonean as well as the Aztecs); Athapaskan, which included Apaches in Canada; Navahos and Salish in the Pacific northwest, which included the Flathead of western Montana. Inside these family groups, the tribes did not, however, always know their relationship, and they might be separated by long distances, and even by enmity. Of them all the Pueblo Indians of New Mexico and Arizona, who had four language groups and additional dialects, were the most highly civilized, living in villages of apartment-like structures, often housing thousands of dwellers. Shortly before the Spaniards arrived, the semi-nomadic Apaches moved into the Southwest, to become the permanent foe of Hopis and then also of Spaniards. Many Plains Indians communicated by hand signs and arm signalling, not by speech, almost to the point that the gesture language of the Indians formed a distinct form of communication in itself.

If the Northern Californian Indians – because isolated? – were village-dwelling and salmon-fishing, matrilineal and status-bound (with captive Indians treated as chattel slaves) and some of them with a clear class system based on ancestry, the Colorado River and Mojave Desert Indians, driven together by the desert as much as by white men, could be warlike; the Mandans lived in permanent villages and practiced agriculture; the Southwest Pueblos had been

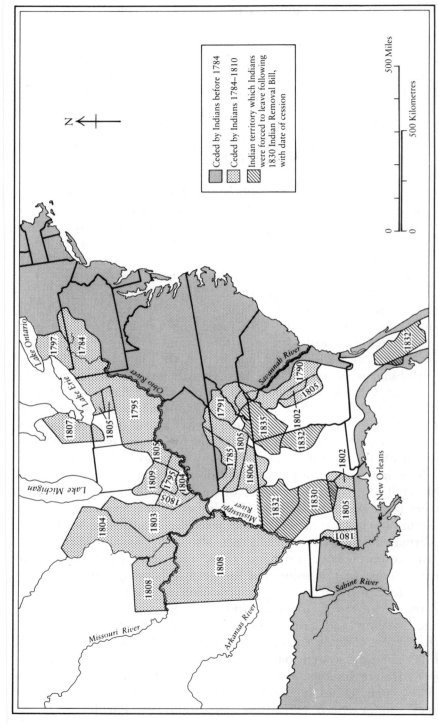

Map 6 The expulsion of the Indians, 1784–1840. By war or negotiated treaties, the Americans gradually pushed the Indians further and further West.

settled for centuries, living in multi-storied houses of stone or adobe, irrigating, weaving, excelling in poetry – and in their worship, saluting Rain more than Sun; and the Navahos – widely scattered – were shepherds and weavers of the wool. The mission Indians were protected – but not from the white men's diseases. Indeed, the whites had but to appear as peaceful traders to leave death behind; the invaders soon realized that their most powerful weapon was the deadly and invisible one. Smallpox swept the Missouri country in the 1830s as it had New England 200 years earlier (from trading contacts before the Puritans' coming in the 1620s); in each case it was seen as divine intervention, to the whites a mark of God's blessing, to the red man a form of magic. The Missouri visitation reduced the most militant tribe, the Blackfeet, by three-quarters; the Mandans were reduced from 1,600 to 31 in a single winter. Behind smallpox came tuberculosis, venereal disease, and the anomie and despair that led to many suicides. And behind the intended benevolence of the missions came the peonage of the Mexican-American ranches, and the open war of the plains and of the gold camps. Like the smallpox, the miners, the railroads and visitors of the next decades, who massacred the buffalo, decimated the tribes; sometimes – such was their invisible magic – without weapons.

The US federal government, like the British before it, saw Indian "policy" as a federal, not a state or colony, matter. President Jackson and his successors refused to treat the tribes as independent nations; the Removal Bill of 1830, after bitter debate in the press and in Congress, authorized the President to negotiate the removal of the tribes West, and then West again. The Treaty of Fort Laramie (1851) was an attempt to bring peace to the Plains: it had no effect in Oregon and the Northwest. The gold rush led to clashes in the Willamette and Lower Columbia valleys: the Cayuses' destruction of the Whitman mission, the Rogue River War, the Yashima war. And the independent white trader, profiting from both sides, and as often illicit gun-runner as merchant, was the hardest of all to discipline. In 1849 the responsibility for Indian affairs was transferred from the War Department to the newly created Department of the Interior, where it still remains.

With horses, the buffalo hunters could range more widely; and with better food, their own numbers grew. The Comanches moved out of their Colorado foothills to cover much of the southwestern plains, the Blackfeet to dominate Montana, the Sioux west from the Minnesota lakes. From permanent villages with their own corn as substance, they launched two or three buffalo hunts each year. Some smaller tribes – Osage and Pawnee – became totally nomadic. In the decade of the 1850s, with the US and not Mexico now "sovereign," a small settled area around Sante Fe and the Pueblos was surrounded by raiding tribes; Navahos, Utes, Apaches, Chiricahuas, Aravaipas, and others. The coming of the miners and of the *rancheros* added new fuel; and US Governor David Meriwether had a stormy time. California's first years of statehood, too, were marked by savage anti-Indian policies. In the East, so it was to be again in the West.

The final Indian chapter, legacy of the "peace" that followed 1865, would be the bloodiest of all. With the Indians confined to isolated reservations, presumably it is the last chapter? Although as Mexicans move back across the Rio Grande licitly and illicitly, into what they call Azteclan, one recalls that *Navaho Times* cartoon, of a large family of young children in a crowded yard, and the comment: "You take the pill. We re-take the country."

4   THE MOUNTAIN MEN

The first Americans to follow the trail of Lewis and Clark were not primarily soldiers or explorers or adventurers, although they were soon to fulfil the functions of all three, but traders looking for a profit. The mountain men, traders, trappers, and – later – scouts, were almost entirely responsible for opening up the whole of the country northwards from the Arkansas River to the Canadian border. Until the late 1830s furs remained the most valuable and market-able produce of the American West, but the men who sought them, either by trading with Indians or by hunting themselves for pelts or buffalo robes, brought back, when returning East, knowledge of other natural resources. Concern for the souls of heathen Indians brought missionaries across the continent, and they were quickly followed, just as the fur trade was simultaneously confronted with dwindling supplies and an even more swiftly contracting demand, by agriculturists who reckoned 'Oregon' afforded fresher woods and newer pastures than the prairies and plains immediately to the west of the Mississippi. It all began with Lewis and Clark, in August 1806, when Private John Colter, one of the ablest hunters of the group, obtained the captains' permission to travel back upriver to the mouth of the Yellowstone, where he spent the winter trapping, and trading with the Indians. Next year, he was back in St Louis in time to guide the first large scale fur-trading expedition under the Spanish-born Manuel Lisa to the Yellowstone. There he helped to build the first trading post in the area, at the mouth of the Bighorn River (Fort Manuel), and, the following winter, he made a solo trip across the Rockies, becoming the first white man to see the present Yellowstone Park region. It was much later that geologists would find scientific proof for his description of the boiling springs and geysers of the Yellowstone as a "bubbling Hell."

It was with the establishment of the Rocky Mountain Fur Company by William Henry Ashley and Manuel Lisa in the midst of Blackfoot Indian enemies that the trade became thoroughly organized, with teams of trappers going out each spring from St Louis, operating at a chain of fur-posts. In 1823 another group, which included Jim Bridger, Tom Fitzpatrick, and Jedediah Smith, working for Lieutenant Governor William Ashley of the new state of Missouri, crossed the Continental Divide through South Pass, and found a new wealth of beaver pelts in the friendly Shoshone country. The route would become the emigrant highway to Oregon. Thereafter, larger and larger columns of traders would make spring hunts and gather their spoils at fixed rendezvous, meeting supply trains of trade goods and stores of tobacco and liquor sent out from the headquarters of the trade in St Louis. After Ashley had made a fortune from his company, and with it begun a political career, Jedediah Smith and two colleagues bought him out (and sold out themselves in 1830). Two rival companies came into being: Astor's revived American Fur Company – the "Company" or the "Trust" to the mountain men – and the revived Rocky Mountain Fur Company (Ashley's original), which was taken over by its rival in 1834. Six years later, the beaver were so scarce and the prices in St Louis so low that, in essence, the fur trade was over. The 1840 rendezvous was the last, and the "Company" turned with zeal to that other market, buffalo hides – which ensured sustained Indian enmity, and in the end spelt doom for the tribes, who were totally dependent on the buffalo for meat, clothing, tents, and *tipis*. The trappers and mountain men found new careers. In 1840 Tom Fitzpatrick led the first emigrant train to Oregon, and in 1842 Kit Carson guided Lieutenant John C. Fremont's team of US Engineers on their mapping expeditions. As, in the 1840s, with routes clearly marked, the emigrants came, so the mountain men became guides and agents. And when the army followed, they became scouts and interpreters and mapmakers. Then came the genuine emigrants: farmers and artisans from Missouri and Kentucky, Ohio and Illinois, starting out on the 2,000 mile-or-more slog that would take them to a new life in the land of promise on the Pacific Coast.

The mountain men are now part of the legendry of the west. They were drawn from every station in life and every nationality on the Continent. They needed physical toughness, nerves of steel, and more than average intelligence if they were to survive. Sometimes they were on safari for two or three years. To manage the Indians, both friendly and hostile, the mountain men had to be masters of primitive psychology. Even the neglect of the smallest precaution in treating with friendly tribes — Crows, say, or Pawnees or Shoshones — could mean the disappearance of the horse herd and the loss of the season's catch. And hospitality itself was dangerous, if the supplies of firewater were too lavish.

Inevitably, to survive required an Indian life-style: wearing fringed buckskin and moccasins, and, as like as not, sleeping in a tepee wrapped up in a buffalo robe. The mountain man took an Indian squaw for his wife, partly for the comforts of married life, partly for occupational security, partly with the expectation of monopolizing the beaver catch of the tribe. He made war like an Indian, scalping his victims with as much dexterity as any Blackfoot or Comanche. And, as was said of Old Bill Williams, killed by a war party of the Utes, who were his own blood-brothers, he was "seldom sober and never wrong."

The stories told of them are of rare courage and all but incredible endurance; the story of Jim Clyman, for instance, cut off from his companions by hostile Indians in unfamiliar country. He had no food and only 11 bullets for his rifle; the only geographical data available to him was that civilization lay to the east. So he started walking in that direction. Eighty days and 700 miles later, he tottered into Fort Atkinson, more dead than alive but still on course, doggedly marching east. Or of Tom Smith, soon to become known throughout the West as Pegleg, cutting off his own leg after it had been shattered by an Indian bullet; or Jedediah Smith, his scalp nearly torn off by a wounded grizzly, gulping down a bolt of Taos Lightning while the boys sewed him up again; or Kit Carson and five companions forting up behind their dead mules and holding off a 200-strong Comanche war party for 12 hours.

If two of the mountain men were to be selected as specially striking, they would be Jedediah Smith and Jim Bridger. Smith was not only the discoverer of South Pass (no narrow defile but a wide and low gap in the mountain chain) as a route to California, but the first man to reach California overland from the American frontier (through the Mojave Desert), the first to cross the Sierra Nevada from west to east, the first to travel the length and width of the Great Basin (the desert area east of the Sierra), and the first to reach Oregon by a journey up the California coast (1827).

Smith did all these things within a period of eight years after he signed on with William Ashley's expedition up the Missouri in 1822 as a young greenhorn from Ohio. And he did them because the fur trade demanded a relentless search for fresh beaver grounds. His drive and skill paid off. In a year he was head of a trapping party, in three years he was Ashley's junior partner, and in four he could join with David E. Jackson and William L. Sublette to buy out Ashley. Moreover, he hunted and trapped as far west as the Coastal Range of California and as far north as Vancouver. The trail to the mountains was his way to wealth. He achieved his goal by fidelity to the maxims that guided the Virtuous Apprentice – sobriety, industry, perseverance. Having liquidated his interest in the partnership of Smith, Jackson & Sublette – amounting to $30,000 or $35,000 – he bought a farm in the Ohio community where he had spent his boyhood, a house and a lot in St Louis, and two Negro slaves for house servants. He placed one of his brothers in college near St Louis, and arranged for two others to be put in school back in Ohio. Then he embarked on the Santa Fe trade, a much less risky occupation than trapping beaver. But this heroic voyager was not destined to the life of a merchant, even a Santa Fe trader. He was killed by Comanches only a short distance out on his first trip to New Mexico when riding ahead of his party, on May 27, 1831. Despite his abilities and experiences, though, he was incapable of communicating his experiences or his emotions in moving language. He can use only clichés: "Providence has made me Steward of a small pittance," or again (from "Wind River, East side of the Rocky Mountains"), "Oh when Shall I be under the care of a Christian Church? I have need of your prayers." Smith was unusual among the mountain men: alongside rifle and pack he treasured a collection of books, a Bible, a hymnal, a collection of sermons entitled "Evidences of Christianity" and – his most treasured possession – an account of the travels of Lewis and Clark. And throughout his life he abstained from tobacco, profanity, and the company of squaws.

Jim Bridger's story is a microcosm of the economic history of the US. A distant cousin of President Tyler, his father was a tavern-keeper in an inn near Richmond, Virginia. But in 1804 business was poor and Virginia's tobacco land exhausted. When Jim was eight, his parents and two boys went West (1812): by Conestoga wagon along the new National Road to the Ohio, then by flatboat to St Louis, at the confluence of the Missouri and the Mississippi rivers. Here he worked as a blacksmith, to be excited by the tales of the mountain men and the fur-trappers from the Northwest, with their descriptions of the western mountains. He joined the fur-trading expeditions of William Ashley's Missouri Company, then of the Rocky Mountain Fur Company; he mastered Indian languages, though illiterate; he discovered the Great Salt Lake in 1824; he survived an Indian arrowhead that was embedded in his back for three years, before it was extracted at the 1835 rendezvous by Dr Marcus Whitman, the Oregon missionary pioneer; and he had three Indian wives – a Flathead, a Ute, and a Shoshone – and several half-breed children. In 1843 he built a fort and supply base (Fort Bridger) on the Black Fork of the Green River, to the west of South Pass, on the best route to the Great Salt Lake, Oregon, and California, over 1,000 miles from St Louis. There he made a fortune, quarreled bitterly with Brigham Young – who relied on Mormon relief columns for his supplies – and found his fort burnt to the ground by Mormon "destroying angels." Thereupon, Bridger became a guide and Indian interpreter in the US Army, helped map and build roads, notably the Bozeman Trail and the route through Bridger's Pass, west of the North Platte in southern Wyoming. He left his name on maps. When his second wife died in childbirth, he had the girl sent East to be convent-educated, only to die in 1847 when the Cayuse Indians destroyed the Whitman mission in Oregon; his third wife he married after the white man's law. In 1875 he went totally blind; but when he died in 1881, aged 77, he was still a lean, rawboned figure over six feet tall. He was perhaps the model "Old Man of the Mountains," illiterate but shrewd, superstitious but sensitive, a spinner of yarns – to Indians and to whites. And "Ned Buntline" (E. Z. C. Judson), later the partner of and advertising man for the Buffalo Bill Wild West Shows, without adding much to his tales, wrote him up in fiction.

But bandy-legged and matter-of-fact Kit Carson, being literate (though only just, and that very late in life), was a better salesman of himself by way of dictation of his alleged heroic deeds and by way of dime novels; Joshua Pilcher became better-known as a superintendent of Indian affairs; Sacajawea's son (European-educated) was a better linguist; and James Water, originally a mountain man, built the first opera house in southern California. The secret weapon of this rich collection of lovable and unlovable folk, was, of course, that they coincided with the printing press, and so they were able to appear only slightly disguised in a host of fugitive writings. Almost every Colonel Cody had a Ned Buntline around to chronicle and embroider. And, one notes, the hardy wives of the early waggon train missionaries riding sidesaddle from New York to Fort Vancouver up to 45 miles a day, some pregnant, found time to write their diaries as they went, Apache or no Apache.

Democrats? Aristos? They were anti-Mexican, and thus anti-feudal, anti-monopolist, anti-Indian (and free from all illusions about "noble savages"), and anti-Eastern, from which came supplies of money and goods. They were tough, adventurous and expectant capitalists, fascinated by the West. In political terms, the acquisition of the trans-Missouri West owed most to the drive of Senator Thomas Hart Benton of Missouri, and four others: Senator John Tyler of Virginia; Senator Franklin Pierce of New Hampshire; Representative James K. Polk of Tennessee; and Representative James Buchanan of Pennsylvania. Each became President, and each, when he assumed office, took steps to incorporate the West. But it had been explored and mastered by the only-just-literate mountain men. They made their own distinctive contribution to the legend: hard-working, self-reliant, restless, ambitious, suspicious of banks and moneyed men, and of all in the East who grew comfortably off by handling other people's money. They confirm another of de Tocqueville observations of the Americans he met: "They love change but they abhor revolution."

The abiding legacy of the Mountain Men was the opening of three main routes to the Pacific Coast: the Oregon or California Trails, or Northern Route (later US 30), which closely followed the old Lewis and Clark Trail, via South Pass in Wyoming, via the Snake River across southern Idaho, then across the Blue Mountains to the Columbia River and by raft to the Willamette, or southwest to the headwaters of the Rumboldt River in the northeast of present Nevada, and over one or other of a number of passes over the Sierra to California and Oregon – a 2,000-mile trek from Independence in Missouri that took the first settlers (in 1843) six months to travel – between spring and autumn, before the snow fell; the Southern Route, the Santa Fe Trail from Independence, Missouri, via the Arkansas River and the dry high plains, where the Comanches and Pawnees lived, across the Cimmaron Desert of southwestern Oklahoma to Santa Fe, then from the Rio Grande (there known as the Rio del Norte) through the Gila River region to either San Diego or Los Angeles, the route with the largest number of variations, one of them across the Mohave Desert; and the Central Route, opened by Jedediah Smith, which ran in a southwesterly direction from the Salt Lake region to the San Gabriel-Los Angeles area. This last was the more popular of the direct routes to California, especially after the outbreak of the Civil War, since it ran through Union country. In 1858 a regular semi-weekly stagecoach service began, pioneered by John Butterfield and his American Express Company (a 25-day schedule through the Southern Route via Arkansas and El Paso to Tucson, San Diego, and San Francisco.)

The great appeal of California, the Ultima Thule of the West, was largely the result of prolific advertising. The overland men, the trappers, and the ship captains vied with one another in praising the climate, fertility, wealth, and accessibility of California, as well as its abundance of wild game, natural resources, and scenic beauty. Richard Henry Dana's *Two years Before the Mast* (1840) was copious in its praise of California, and that work is still the most widely circulated account of the early history of the state. The earliest American settlers in California were not the overlanders, however, but American whalers, merchants and hide-and-tallow men, who reached the coast of California early in the nineteenth century, the majority finding it to their advantage to become Mexicans. With few exceptions, they took Spanish-Mexican wives, learned and used the Spanish language, adopted the California mode of dress, and applied for naturalization as Mexican citizens. Because of their astute business sense and exceptional energy, many of these men became wealthy landowners and influential figures in local affairs, not least a number of Irish — such as the Irish priest Eugene McNamara, Surveyor-General Jasper O'Farrell, or John Reed, who married a Spanish widow and became a *ranchero* in Marin County. By contrast, the overland emigrants wanted ranch life, rather than commercial activities in the coastal towns. They did not intermarry with the Spanish-Californians, rarely associated with them, and were slow — and reluctant — to assimilate.

The interest of the nation back East was at first centered primarily upon Oregon (which had recently been claimed by the US government), with emigrants to Oregon outnumbering those going to California 10 to 1. Even so, California benefited from the Oregon publicity. The pioneer settlers of 1841 and thereafter are distinguished from the earlier visitors and emigrants for their more frequent utilization of the overland trails; by their coming almost unanimously from the Midwest; by their preference for the unsettled, inner, agricultural areas of California; and by the presence of women and children in their parties. Senator Benton's son-in-law John Charles Fremont arrived in Oregon in 1842 on the first of his three pathfinding probes as an officer in the army's Topographical Corps. In 1843, on his second exploratory expedition, Fremont came to California via Fort Hall, the Columbia River valley, Carson Pass, and the Sacramento valley. After recuperating his men at Sutter's Fort, he explored the San Joaquin valley, then crossed Tehachapi

Pass and proceeded to Utah. His reports of this expedition fanned still more the "Oregon fever" that swept the East. His third expedition in 1845 led him into a still-Mexican California, and involvement in the Bear Flag Revolt and its brief republican experiment.

Since 1818 the region north of California and west of the Rockies had been jointly occupied by the United States and Great Britain, though British fur traders were the only inhabitants whose numbers were significant. Although in 1811 John Jacob Astor had established a fur-trading post at Astoria on the Columbia River — the river named after US Captains Kendrick and Gray's ship, which in 1792 had sailed into the wide mouth of a great river — but he sold out to the British North West Company, which in turn was absorbed by the Hudson's Bay Company. For a quarter-of-a-century Dr John McLoughlin, the Hudson Bay Company's agent, from his head quarters in Fort Vancouver, ruled a trade empire extending from San Francisco Bay to Alaska, with a host of log forts, exporting furs (as far as Canton) and lumber (as far as the Hawaiian Islands.) Only a few trappers, among whom Kit Carson was a notable figure, were familiar with the routes through the Rockies prior to 1840. The Oregon Trail was blazed by Nathaniel Wyeth, from Massachusetts, in 1833–4.

The rush to Oregon in the 1840s was precipitated by a group of Protestant missionaries from New England, who were not very successful in converting the Indians, but who inadvertently did a splendid job of advertising the fertile soil and mild climate of the Northwest. Their efforts were abetted by Washington Irving's popular *Astoria* (1836) and *Adventures of Captain Bonneville* (1837) and by the writings of Hall Kelley of Boston. Thousands of Americans followed the Oregon Trail, and by 1844 it was apparent that some governmental organization would soon have to be provided in the region of the Willamette and Columbia Rivers. Terms had first to be made with Britain, for the popular slogan of the settlers, "Fifty-four forty or fight," claiming possession of all Oregon to the Alaskas, was a diplomatic weapon with no legal justification. Indeed, of the two nations, Britain had the better claim to the whole of Oregon, despite Captain Gray's discovery, Lewis and Clark's explorations, and Astor's trading. By 1846, however, the Hudson's Bay Company had abandoned its posts south of Vancouver, and in that year the boundary between British and American territory was agreed as being the 49th parallel (i.e. what is now Oregon, Washington, Idaho, and Montana), with a small deviation in Puget Sound allowing Britain Vancouver, while Britain received title to the area between the 49th parallel and Alaska. "Fifty-four forty or fight" was forgotten, and the natural advantages of the Columbia as a boundary were ignored. Oregon became a territory in 1848, and a state in the Union in 1859.

American interest in the Far West grew out of trade and furs, exploration, and, increasingly, settlement. But it was not all a smooth story. Nine overland expeditions had reached California successfully, but the tenth, led by the Donner brothers of Illinois (1846), ended in tragedy. This party of 87 men, women, and children tried to find a short-cut south of the Great Salt Lake. Crossing dry desert, it took them 21 days to cover 36 miles, and they became lost. Their loss of oxen necessitated the abandonment of essential equipment and supplies. Destitute, disorganized, and far behind schedule, they turned to quarreling as the snows fell and blocked the passes. James Read set out toward Sutter's Fort to find help, but the snow blocked the return with supplies; starvation and death by freezing came at Donner Lake; the survivors were reduced to eating the flesh of the dead. Four rescue attempts were necessary in order to bring out the 45 survivors (of the 79 who reached Donner Lake) to safety in April 1847. Thirty-five had died in the Sierra, five earlier, and one died after arrival in the Sacramento valley. But one survivor, Patrick Breen, did manage to keep a diary to tell the grim tale — for a trim and true tale made the best legend of all.[3]

6 THE COMPROMISE OF 1850

State Department clerk, Nicholas P. Trist, a Virginian who had married Jefferson's granddaughter, had been sent along with General Scott to help handle the peace negotiations with Mexico. His efforts to induce the Mexicans to surrender New Mexico, California, and Texas (to the Rio Grande), and to grant to the United States the right to construct a canal across the Isthmus of Tehuantepec, were at first unsuccessful, but after Scott's forces fought their way into Mexico City in September 1847, the Mexican president, General Santa Anna, resigned, and the new government agreed to negotiate. By this time Trist had been recalled; but, in violation of his orders, he remained to complete the Treaty of Guadalupe Hidalgo, signed on February 2, 1848; for Scott's fear was of a rebellion in Mexico. The Rio Grande boundary was recognized, and New Mexico and Upper California, including all the territory that lay between them,

[3] George R. Stewart edited Breen's diary and used it as the basis for his *Ordeal by Hunger* (Boston, Little, Brown, 1936; repr. 1960).

were ceded to the United States, in return for assumption by the United States of the outstanding claims of American citizens against Mexico, and the payment of $15,000,000. Many American, among them two members of Polk's Cabinet, Robert Walker of Mississippi and Secretary of State James Buchanan, now demanded that the United States annex all of Mexico, but Polk refused to be swayed by their arguments, and the Senate ratified the treaty without change (38 to 14). The Treaty was thus the work of an unauthorized agent, and was submitted to a dissatisfied Senate by an accidental President: but by it the boundaries of the United States were brought approximately to their present limits, only the Gadsden purchase of 1853 remaining to be added (an area equivalent in extent to the State of Pennsylvania, bought for 10 million dollars to permit a railroad to be built to the Gulf of California.) Polk renounced a second term, and refused to permit his Cabinet officers to campaign either for him or for themselves. As he foretold, the Whigs won the 1848 election with the war-hero Zachary Taylor as their Presidential candidate, and Polk retired to his Nashville home, where he died a few months later.

The prospect of gaining land from Mexico raised the question of the status of slavery in the new territory. Northern Congressmen were bitter because, having agreed to support the Southern demand for Texas to the Rio Grande even at the cost of war, they had received little Southern support for a "Fifty-four forty or fight" settlement of the Oregon question; consequently, they were determined to resist the extension of slavery to all of the Southwest. When President Polk, in 1848, asked Congress for funds to implement the negotiations with Mexico, Congressman David Wilmot of Pennsylvania moved to attach to the appropriation bill a proviso that slavery be forbidden in all the territory so acquired. All but one state legislature in the North formally endorsed the Wilmot Proviso, but just as solidly did the South rally against it. After an effort to extend the Missouri Compromise line to the Pacific had failed, Wilmot's resolution was narrowly defeated in the Senate. An attempt to settle the question of slavery in the territories was made in the Clayton Compromise of 1848. Oregon was to have complete territorial government, with its legislature having the authority to determine the slavery issue; California and New Mexico were to be administered by a governor, secretary, and Supreme Court judges, and there the courts would determine on slave or free. The measure, however, was rejected by the House. So divided was Congress that, although the Oregon Territory was organized as a free territory in 1848, until 1850 no territorial government at all could be established

for New Mexico, Utah, or California — which in that year became
a state.

It had long been believed that Congress could legislate slavery
into or out of the territories, and several laws based on that conviction had been enacted. By 1850, however, new legal theories were
being formed, embodying sectional views. Northern abolitionists
held that Congress had the moral duty to prohibit slavery in its
jurisdiction. Southerners contended that Congress not only could not
prohibit slavery, but was under obligation to protect it, as property,
in the territories. Southerners led by Calhoun contended not only
that slavery was legal and constitutional, but that federal action
should curb the mounting abolitionist agitation, that fugitive slaves
should be returned to their masters, and that all the new territories
should be freely opened to the emigration of the slaveholders. The
Missouri compromise was denounced as illegal, it being held that
American citizens had the right to the protection of their property
— including slaves — anywhere within the jurisdiction of the federal
.government. In 1857 the Dred Scott decision would read this interpretation into the Constitution.

A new anti-slavery movement, the Free-Soil party, made its appearance in the presidential election of 1848. Composed of numerous
abolitionist groups in the North, and the radical wing of the New
York Democratic party, or the "Barnburners," the Free-Soil party
("free soil, free speech, free labor, free men") carried no states, but
its candidate, Martin Van Buren, won enough votes from the strong
expansionist and Jacksonian Democratic nominee, Senator Lewis
Cass, the former governor of Michigan, to permit Zachary Taylor to
carry New York and the election. Cass was a man of ambition and
energy — he had in 1820 explored the headwaters of the Mississippi
— and a nationalist: he would resign the secretaryship of state under
President Buchanan (1857–60) when the President refused to reinforce Fort Sumter. He had, however, no strong views on slavery
other than that each state legislature should pronounce on it (the
"popular sovereignty" thesis), and thus earned the soubriquet of
"doughface" — "a Northern man with Southern principles." His fence-
straddling — he was what later journalists would call a "mugwump,"
a chap with his mug on one side of the fence and his wump on the
other — reflected the deep division in his party and in the country.
One group — including Polk — thought the only solution was to
extend the Missouri Compromise line of 1820 all the way to the
Pacific. Another, including Wilmot, wanted the exclusion of slavery
from the territories. Another, the Calhoun-Davis type, denied the
power of Congress to prohibit slavery in the territories. Yet another

(Cass, Zachary Taylor and, later, Stephen Douglas) believed in popular or "squatter" sovereignty: the right of settlers to choose. Even in the Democratic party, one group (Calhoun's) was pro-slave, another (Thomas Hart Benton and Van Buren) anti-slave. The compromisers (Cass and, later, Douglas) were slow to learn that the surest way of having a collision is to drive down the middle of the road.

Zachary Taylor, "Old Rough and Ready," was a war hero, with 40 years' army service; he had defeated Santa Anna at Buena Vista in 1847 – in the battle where Henry Clay's eldest son was killed. One of his fellow-officers there was his son-in law Jefferson Davis; as it happened, also a Southerner (reared in Kentucky) and a slave-holder. His party for the fifth time passed over the claims of Henry Clay to run for President. And again, as it happened, Taylor died 16 months after winning the election, like General Harrison eight years before. Politically, his death was no loss: he was honest, but had no political experience, and had indeed never voted in an election. To him, slavery was an academic question, since the peculiar institution was, to him as to many Southerners, a fact of economic life. He died of gastro-enteritis, and was succeeded by his Vice-President, Millard Fillmore. But the poet Stephen Vincent Benet put it differently,

> Zachary Taylor was President T.
>   One very warm day in July,
> When he called for a bowl of ripe cherries and milk,
>   With a greedy old gleam in his eye.
> Now cherries and milk when the weather is hot
>   Make even the strongest turn paler
> And they proved more effective than Mexican shot
>   For they finished poor Zachary Taylor.

His death, like Harrison's, left behind a Vice-President unable to control his party, just when the most difficult issues were coming forward.

With the discovery of gold in California, a new and ugly dimension was introduced. It was found at the mill of a German-speaking Swiss, John August Sutter, who had become a Mexican citizen, and lived in the hitherto idyllic meadows of the Sacramento valley. His vast *rancho* was – like those of Austin's Texans – a distinct community, larger than the whole Swiss canton where he was born, to which he gave the name Nueva Helvetia. It consisted of a fort with cannon, orchards and vineyards, cotton and indigo, worked by Indian labour; he had a semi-independent state acted as

"General" and "Captain of the Royal Swiss Guards," and dressed the garrison of the fort in a uniform of blue and green with red trims, armed with the ancient flintlocks left behind in Russia by Napoleon's retreating troops. He enforced his own laws. It was all a sharp contrast to his original flight to New York ten years before to escape the debts and the enemies he had left behind in Europe, and to his years as a trader on the Santa Fe trail. His group sought absorption by the US, but were Spanish-speaking rather than Anglo. Sutter supported the Americans in their conquest of California; and when, by the Treaty of Guadeloupe-Hidalgo, Lower California was restored to Mexico, the north became American, so Sutter's community's future seemed assured. Then came gold – and with it an inferno. Sutter's workmen and his garrison deserted him for the mines, and squatters took over. Some 80,000 greedy immigrants swept in, and justice swept out; riots became normalcy and gangs appeared, many of veterans of the Mexican War, anti-Spanish and looking for loot, or ex-Australian convicts, escaping from prison ships – the "Hounds," the "Sydney Ducks." The only justice was provided by local groups of vigilantes, "the Law and Order party." Since civil government had become a matter of urgency, the American settlers called a convention at Monterey, and framed a state constitution – excluding slavery. They sought from Congress admission to the Union as a free state, without serving an apprenticeship as a territory. They claimed not only to need governing, but – unusual for a new state – that they could afford it. Their state motto was, appropriately, "Eureka."

The good fortune did not hold, however, for John August Sutter, nor for his employee and partner, John Wilson Marshall, in whose pan the precious tiny nuggets had been seen. Sutter's property was ruined by mobs, and he spent the rest of his life in a Moravian colony in Pennsylvania suing Congress – unsuccessfully – for redress for his losses. His fort, rebuilt, is now a historical monument in downtown Sacramento. He died broke in 1880. Marshall too died a pauper. And the pathfinder John Fremont, who had abandoned both the army and his dreams of political glory, went broke operating a gold mine. There is a moral here. As Melville expressed it in *Mardi*: "Gold is the only poverty; of all glittering ills the direst ... But men still will mine for it; and, mining, dig his doom."

The South was incensed by the proposed state constitution, and at the prospect that one-half of the Mexican cession would thus be lost to slavery. South Carolina prepared to secede, but delayed in the expectation that other Southern states would soon join it. Actually, the South had little cause for complaint. It held half the Senate and a majority of the Cabinet and Supreme Court posts, and President Taylor was by birth a Virginian. Furthermore, the low tariff was in the Southern interest, and to the increasing fury of abolitionists, the slave trade was permitted in the District of Columbia. Abolitionist agitation in the North was magnified into a threat to Southern existence, and secessionists had visions of a great Cotton Empire, solidly founded upon slavery and extending into the Caribbean, free from Northern economic, political, and social interference.

The intensity of sectional feeling in the Congress which convened in December 1849 was demonstrated in the fact that sixty-three ballots were required to elect a Speaker of the House. The territorial question was the first order of business. Though Taylor had recommended that California be admitted as a free state and the rest of the Mexican cession be left unorganized until ready for statehood, and had indicated his intention to prevent secession, by force if necessary, Clay believed that sectional differences could be reconciled by compromise. The "omnibus bill" which he introduced in January 1850 provided for:

(a) Admission of California as a free state.
(b) Organization of Utah and New Mexico as territories, without reference to slavery — though there was no expectation that slavery would flourish there.
(c) Enactment of an effective Fugitive Slave Law, to be administered by the federal government.
(d) Abolition of the slave trade, but not slavery, in the District of Columbia.
(e) Adjustment of the boundary between Texas and New Mexico.
(f) And Congress should formally declare that it had no power to interfere with the interstate slave trade.

The month-long debate in the Senate had a powerful effect upon public opinion during subsequent years. Clay defended his program with a stirring appeal for unity, which pointed out that the North would gain most of the objectives of the Wilmot Proviso, while the Fugitive Slave Law would be a great assistance to the South, and slavery could still expand to the West if the people desired it; secession, he declared, could not be permitted. Calhoun persisted in his extremist position, insisting that the South could remain in the Union only if fairly treated, and demanding not only the admission of slavery into New Mexico and California, but also the termination of abolitionist agitation in the North. The Constitution, he argued, had become an engine of repression and tyranny — thanks to Northern power and reiterated reformist propaganda. His view had substance – but in fact until 1860 the federal government was Southern in character, as were ten of the first Presidents. Webster again struck the note of national unity, which he had so effectively sounded against Hayne 20 years before. The laws of physical geography in any case made a cotton-slave economy unlikely in the Southwest. The Compromise, however, was not due to Webster's oratory, but to President Taylor's death. Millard Fillmore, a quiet and largely self-taught lawyer from Buffalo, New York, was a friend of Clay's, and no believer in William Henry Seward's (and thus Taylor's) view that there was "a higher law" than the Constitution. Clay's bill was modified, but accepted by Congress.

Both sides reaped certain advantages from the Compromise. The new fugitive slave law benefited the South. No jury trial was allowed to the Negro claimed as a fugitive. Master or agent had simply to present an affidavit before a federal judge or commissioner, whose fee was doubled if he decided in favor of the claimant. The whole community was bound by federal law to come to the aid of the commissioner to prevent the rescue or escape of the condemned fugitive, and the US Marshal was liable to a fine of $1,000 and a civil suit for the value of the slave if the latter got away or was rescued. The law was *ex post facto*, and thus to lawyers unconstitutional, in that it applied to slaves who had fled from their master at any time – even years before. The Northern abolitionists simply refused to obey the Act, and they redoubled the activity of the slave escape route known as the "underground railroad." Emerson, Whittier, and Longfellow gave their arguments a lyrical and rhetorical appeal.

On the other hand, the North secured the abolition of the slave trade in the District of Columbia, and the admission of California as a free state. By the latter provision the balance between the free and the slave states, which had been maintained in the Senate since the days of the Missouri Compromise, was broken, and both branches of Congress were now controlled by the free-soil states. Henceforth there were no more slave states admitted to the Union.

The Compromise of 1850 postponed secession for a decade, a decade of fantastic Northern growth. On the advice of Calhoun, a convention of Southern delegates had been called to meet at Nashville, Tennessee. He died before it met. Only nine states were represented and a majority of the delegates voted to wait until after the session of Congress. A "rump" convention of 59 radicals reassembled after passage of the compromise and passed resolutions urging the South to boycott the North. The South, however, accepted the Compromise heartily. The extremists in each section, Northern nullifiers and Southern secessionists, were repressed by the moderates.

In the election of 1852 both parties were pledged to maintain the Compromise. The Whig party, weakened by the steady growth of anti-slavery sentiment in its northern branch, turned for a third time to a military hero, General Winfield Scott. The latter was the favored candidate of William Seward, the Whig governor of New York, and was suspected of being a Free-Soiler. Leading Southern Whigs, like Robert Toombs and Alexander Stephens, bolted the ticket. The result was the overwhelming election of Franklin Pierce, the Democratic candidate. The Whig vote in the South dropped from 138,369 to 81,775; its disintegration had begun. In 1856 it, the party of compromise, was not able to put a candidate forward.

The industrial and transportation revolutions seemed to strengthen political compromise. Railroads and canals were linking the nation together, while a flood of immigrants was arriving to farm the new lands and to man the new factories. Westward expansion and industrial growth combined to raise wages, and craft unionism was appearing on a national basis, its program being economic rather than political. Although the first Marxian socialists were coming from Europe, the radical movement was not conspicuous in the economic picture of the early 1850s.

Though secessionist sentiment declined for a few years, the South's sense of solidarity continued to grow. Among the poor, emancipation was opposed because of racial prejudice and fear of competition from free Negro labor, while the booming cotton trade increased the plantation owners' conviction of the benefits of slavery. Moreover, in contrast with the clarity of presidential direction during the first seven presidencies, the 20 years from 1840 to 1860 are confusing. Party control changed every four years, and the elected leader on two occasions died too quickly, so that lesser men were thrust into leadership. Between 1840 and 1856 seven different individuals were in the White House. Given the spoils system, this meant a clean sweep every four years, frequent shifts in policy, and government by inexperienced men. There was a succession less of presidencies than of directories, since around each leader was an influential adviser or mentor: witness Zachary Taylor's dependence on Seward and Thurlow Weed, Pierce's on Jefferson Davis and Caleb Cushing, James Buchanan's (President 1856–60) first on Southerners, then on Northerners. The nominating conventions now put forward the names of non-committed men. Calhoun said of Webster that he was "too great a man ever to be made President," and the Whigs in 1852 ordered him to choose – despite the precedents of 1840 and 1848 – yet another soldier, Winfield Scott. The Democrats chose "unknowns" – Pierce in 1852 was selected on the 49th ballot – or trimmers like Buchanan. Although government touched the lives of ordinary people much less than today, the deliberate choice of advocates of evasion was culpable when two issues were paramount, and one of them moral: the government of the new states, and the question of slavery. Moreover, at every turn the tradition of *laissez-faire* and the distrust of federal power blocked any constructive solution of national questions. A railroad to the Pacific could not be built because sectional jealousies entrenched themselves behind the old shibboleths. Land settlement could not be judicially promoted. Urgently needed laws to exclude unfit immigrants could not be passed. Agriculture could not be given efficient guidance. The history of the period is incomprehensible unless its pervasive belief in the evils of strong government, its regard for local and state autonomy, and its faith in unfettered individualism as the mainspring of progress are clearly grasped: "We are going to do nothing this session, and a great deal of it," said Horace Greeley in 1849.

The Compromise of 1850 thus gave a false sense of security. There was optimism and prosperity: cotton prices were high, and cotton was the whole country's major export. The South was not yet distinct, and if railroads and manufacturers were to develop there, using its own resources of iron and granite, Unionist sentiments there would grow.

Yet, though they were the authors of the Compromise, the Whigs were growing weaker, not stronger. The steady increase in attacks on Southern institutions by Northern Whigs made it difficult to remain a Whig in the South. The tariff protection and internal improvements that so obviously favored the North made little appeal South of the Mason-Dixon line. And in 1852 the two Whig leaders who alone commanded national prestige – Clay and Webster – both died. By 1856 the Whigs were no longer a party; and the Democrats were no longer democrat, but a coalition of national conservatives, directed by Southern planters, but maintained in office by Northern votes.[4]

---

[4] There are three excellent studies: Joel Silbey, *The Partisan Imperative: The dynamics of American politics before the Civil War* (New York, Oxford University Press, 1985); Richard L. McCormick, *The Party Period from the Age of Jackson to the Progressive Era* (Chapel Hill, NC, University of North Carolina Press, 1986); and Holman Hamilton, *Prologue to Conflict: The crisis and compromise of 1850* (Lexington, University of Kentucky Press, 1964).

7 THE FRONTIER IN AMERICAN HISTORY

In 1893, a young professor from Wisconsin, Frederick Jackson
Turner, delivered to the American Historical Association what has
been called "the most influential single piece of historical writing
ever done in the United States." This was his paper *The Significance
of the Frontier in American History.*

Turner wrote in reaction to the teachings of his mentors at The
Johns Hopkins University in Baltimore, leading proponents of the
then generally accepted "germ theory," which saw the source of
"The American way" in institutions transplanted from Europe. And
he gave his paper in Chicago in the year that the US was holding
in that city the world's Columbian Exposition to mark the 400th
anniversary of the voyage of Columbus. He was offering a comment
on a long history.

Though later generations have sought to qualify his conclusions,
Turner's theses are now taken almost as gospel:

The existence of an area of free land, its continuous recession and the
advance of American settlement westward, explain American development
... The true point of view in the history of the nation is not the Atlantic
coast, it is the Great West.

Moreover, he argued that "The advance of the frontier has meant
a steady movement away from the influence of Europe, a steady
growth of independence on American lines." It was the source of
America's rugged individualism, its egalitarianism, and of its sense of
national rather than local or sectional loyalties. In the revolutionary
era, the frontier was a melting-pot for many different nationalities;
the broadening of the franchise in the early period of the Union
was the work of western radicalism; the tariff, land, and internal
improvement policies were dictated by the needs of the West; the
slavery question was a less important cause of the Civil War than
the future of western lands. The growth of the power of the federal
government over the prerogatives of the individual states was the
result of western influence.

Again, each frontier had similar, recurrent features:

The Atlantic frontier was compounded of fisherman, fur-trader, miner,
cattle-raiser, and farmer. Excepting the fisherman, each type of industry
was on the march toward the West, impelled by an irresistable attraction.
Each passed in successive waves across the continent. Stand at Cumberland
Gap and watch the procession of civilization, marching single file — the

buffalo following the trail to the salt springs, the Indian, the fur trader
and hunter, the cattle-raiser, the pioneer farmer — and the frontier has
passed by. Stand at South Pass in the Rockies a century later and see the
same procession with wider intervals between. The unequal rate of advance
compels us to distinguish the frontier into the trader's frontier, the rancher's
frontier, or the miner's frontier, and the farmer's frontier. When the mines
and the cowpens were still near the fall line the trader's pack trains were
tinkling across the Alleghenies, and the French on the Great Lakes were
fortifying their posts, alarmed by the British trader's birch canoe. When
the trappers scaled the Rockies the farmers were still near the south of the
Missouri. [5]

The consequences were clear: such a land attracted all types;
the gifted, the ruthless, the enterprising, the ne'er-do-well, the perennial misfits, and the vagabonds. Western America became even
more a melting-pot, even more polyglot than the increasingly urban-
ized East. In the 1840s, 100,000 immigrants a year were reaching
the New World — in 1854 it was almost 500,000 — and although
the British, and the Irish particularly, stayed firmly in the Northeast,
the majority of German immigrants settled west of the Appalachians.
In 1790 only 5 per cent of the population (250,000) lived west of
the mountains; in 1850 it was 45 per cent (14 million).

Moreover, men moved West not only or indeed mainly from
Europe, but from the upland South also, and from this stock sprang
future President Abraham Lincoln, born in a Kentucky log cabin.
Scotch-Irish, Pennsylvania Germans, New Englanders, and men of
other origins played their part. By 1830, more than half the people
living in America had been brought up in an environment in which
the Old World traditions and conventions were absent or very weak.
Men in the West were valued not for their family background or
for inherited money but for their physical stamina, ingenuity, and
inventiveness, which mattered more than accent or book-learning.
Skill with axe and rifle mattered more than literacy: survival depended on being able to master the hostile environment. Individual
and local self-reliance mattered more than distant government or
banks or even law. Both east and west of the Pecos, in Regulator
North Carolina as in Mexican Texas, even justice was home-made.
This was rich material for fiction and for myth, and for poetic re-
telling. In the end Gary Cooper walked alone in *High Noon*, and
John Wayne as "Ringo" in *Stagecoach* although in each case helped
by a "good woman;" at the OK Corral, or other remote locations,

[5] *The Turner Thesis concerning the Role of the Frontier in American History*,
ed. George R. Taylor (Boston, D.C. Heath, 1949), pp. 5–6.

a man was himself alone, *contra mundum* and *contra* evil. Families helped, if they were good with muskets; usually they were far away back East.

Again, land was cheap, when it had to be bought. Farms could be had for a price well within the reach of any thrifty person; government land after 1820 could be obtained for $1.25 an acre, after 1850 for a dollar an acre, and, after 1862, for merely settling on it. And tools for working the land were easily available too. It was a time when, as the journalist Horace Greeley said, young men could "go west and grow up with the country." Certainly they could go there to escape ... so that the frontier was a safety-valve for urban strains, economic depressions, and class conflicts; and the US was freer from class awareness than was the Old World. The equality of economic opportunity reinforced the sense of social and political equality, and gave home-bred natural leaders a chance to come quickly to the fore, like Daniel Boone and John Sevier earlier, like Jefferson on the piedmont frontier, Andrew Jackson on the Tennessee frontier, Abraham Lincoln from the Old Northwest. The tariff, internal improvements, and land policies owed most to the needs of the West. And the West itself was in constant change. There were indeed many frontiers – the cattlemen, the rancher's, the cowboy's, the miner's ... and distance and mobility produced easy adaptation to many environments.

The challenges to Turner's interpretation have been many. Individualism? Thus Daniel Boorstin: "Of all American myths, none is stronger than that of the loner moving west across the land ... The pioneering spirit, we are often told, is a synonym for 'individualism' ... but, in fact, early settlers, those who took one-way passage and became the backbone of new western communities, generally went together."[6] On the frontier, cabins were built by a group, not by a lone settler. The wagon trains moved in convoy. The problems of the new settlements were solved communally, as were those of Philadelphia in Franklin's days. In his day, fire companies, fire insurance, libraries, colleges, hospitals, a defense militia were all the product of advertising, donors – and collective action. So in the West: the log-rolling, the harvesting and cabin-raising, the repulse of Indians and the capture of brigands, the education of the young, the care of the sick and the erection of a common place of worship were done in and by groups.

[6] Daniel Boorstin, *The Americans: The national experience* (New York, Viking Press, 1965), p. 75.

Plate 12 Broadway in Yankton, capital of Dacotah Territory, sketched by M. K. Armstrong. (The Mansell Collection, London.)

Egalitarianism? "The great illusion of historians of the frontier," writes Schlesinger,

has been that social equality produces economic equalitarianism. In fact, the demand for economic equality is generally born out of conditions of social inequality, and becomes the more passionate, deeply felt and specific as the inequality becomes more rigid ... The fur capitalists of St Louis and the land speculators of Mississippi were as characteristic of the west as Andrew Jackson.[7]

Three major qualifications on Turner's thesis are certainly required. It was not as easy as Turner assumed for an immigrant to move to and settle in the West. In 1822 a wagon able to cross the Appalachians cost at least 40 dollars, a good horse cost more. He needed money to buy land and support a family until the harvest came in; and he was reliant on himself, his family and his neighbors to build a cabin. The settler, that is, needed at least 100 dollars to move West. If he had not ready money, and raised credit back East, that was easier in good times than bad. But did he want to move at all in good times? A leading student of the frontier, Ray Billington, estimates that few 80-acre farms were available that did not cost their owners some 1,500 dollars.[8] This was far beyond the reach of the average Eastern working man. Two conclusions follow: either fewer went West than the usual figures indicate, or – more likely – they lived in very poor conditions for at least a decade or more; and their wives, not least in pregnancies, suffered acutely.

If this view is true, it in turn throws in doubt the customary view of the waves of western migration coinciding with economic slumps: did the post-Revolution slump lead to the foundation of Kentucky (1792) and Tennessee (1796)? Was it the post-Napoleonic depression that caused the statehood of Louisiana (1812), Mississippi (1817), Alabama (1819), Missouri (1821), Indiana (1816), and Illinois (1817)? Was it the depression of 1837–45 that led to the statehood of Michigan (1837), Iowa (1846), Wisconsin (1848), Arkansas (1837), Texas (1845), and Minnesota (1858)? Or were other factors responsible?

The pioneers were freedom-seeking; they were also land-seeking and conservative. First settlers were prompt to organize claims clubs, to secure title to land that they settled that had not yet been organized by national law. So too in the mining regions once the first

[7] F. L. Olmsted, *The Cotton Kingdom* (New York, Knopf, 1953).
[8] Ray Allen Billington, *America's Frontier Heritage* (New York, Holt, 1966).

wild scramble was over. By 1866 there were over 1,100 such self-governing districts in the eight western states and territories. Indeed, many of those who came to the West were conservative members of Eastern communities who wanted to re-establish the sort of order they believed was being undermined by liberal domination of their homelands. They founded churches and schools in the first days of community-building. Henry Ward Beecher noted in the 1850s that the frontier settlers "drive schools along with them as settlers drive flocks. They have herds of churches, academies, lyceums and their religious and educational institutions go lowing along the western plains as Jacob's herds lowed along the Syrian hills."[9]

Moreover, the democratizing of state constitutions was quite as much an Eastern as a Western process. The roles of protestantism, the traditions of English parliamentary parish government and Puritan congregations constitute rival sources of democracy. And as Thomas Perkins Abernethy stressed, mindful of the frontier leaders from John Sevier and Judge Richard Henderson to Jackson, Houston and Lincoln, the West bred natural leaders, even *aristos*, of its own. And, if they did not found the landed and entailed dynasties of Boston and Virginia, they were usually men with broad acres of their own. As David Potter and J. K. Galbraith have demonstrated, American democracy was as much the product of the abundance of land and resources as of men's enterprise in harnessing and exploiting them.[10]

More than this the land was not free for the white man's taking, as all historians of the American Indian have emphasized. The

[9] Henry Ward Beecher, as quoted in Billington, *The Frontier and American Culture*, pp. 7–12. See also Louis B. Wright, *Culture on the Moving Frontier* (Bloomington, University of Indiana Press, 1955), *passim*; Richard C. Wade, *The Urban Frontier* (Cambridge, MA, Harvard University Press, 1959), p. 315; Boorstin, *The Americans*, p. 75; and Philip Paludin, "The American Civil War considered as a crisis in law and order," *American Historical Review*, 77.4 (Oct. 1972), pp. 1013–34.

[10] David M. Potter, *People of Plenty* (Chicago, University of Chicago Press, 1954); John K. Galbraith, *The Affluent Society* (various edns; first published 1963, New York, NAL-Dutton); Henry Nash Smith, *Virgin Land* (Cambridge, MA, Harvard University Press, 1950), Ray A. Billington, *The Genesis of the Frontier Thesis: A study in historical creativity* (San Marino, Huntington Library, 1971); Thomas P. Abernethy, "Democracy and the southern frontier," *Journal of Southern History*, 4 (1938), pp. 3–13 ("Jackson never really championed the cause of the people; he only invited them to champion his"); Fred A. Shannon, "A post-mortem on the labor-safety-valve theory," *Agricultural History*, 19 (Jan. 1945), pp. 31–7; and George Wilson Pierson, "The frontier and American institutions," *New England Quarterly*, 15 June 1942, pp. 224–55.

Indians were immensely mobile, most of the tribes themselves incomers. But there, as in the East, the pale faces, "the owl-eyes,"
rested their case on their role as cultivators, whereas the Indians
ranged over but rarely tilled the soil — though almost every Indian
village had its tiny farm, worked by the squaws. The land that was
"waste" or *vacuum domicilium* in English eyes was, to the Indians,
covered with property and jurisdictional rights. The white men never
recognized Indian sovereignty *de jure*, even though for convenience
they dealt with *sachems de facto*. There was in the peninsula of
India the same clash of views over the role of the *Zemindar* and
the similar failure of the East India Company to understand communal property rights. What in eastern North America were a succession of entrepreneurial jurisdictional disputes ending in conflict,
became in the open plains of the West simple and often instant conflicts. The conflict of laws and guns was buttressed by the mythology
of "civilization" plus Christianity versus "savagery." Moreover, in
the West, when the buffalo were destroyed the Indian lost not only
his property and his right to range but his food supplies, his clothing
stores, and his role. Given the number of Indian languages and the
mobility of the Indian life-style, it is perhaps not surprising that
serious study of the Indians came only in the late twentieth century.
To their contemporaries the only good Injun was a dead Injun.[11]

Is there any consensus? Writing of the Missouri frontier in the
1830s, Alexander Majors, the founder of one of the most powerful
overland freight companies in the West, wrote:

The first settlers in the Mississippi valley were as a rule poor people, who
were industrious, economizing, and self-sustaining. From ninety-five to
ninety-seven per cent of the entire population manufactured at home almost
everything necessary for good living. A great many of them when they
were crossing the Ohio and Mississippi to their new homes would barely
have money enough to pay their ferriage across the rivers, and one of the
points in selling out whatever they had to spare when they made up their
minds to emigrate was to be sure to have cash enough with them to pay
their ferriage. They generally carried with them a pair of chickens, ducks,
geese, and if possible a pair of pigs, their cattle and horses. The wife took
her spinning wheel, a bunch of cotton or flax, and was ready to go to
spinning as soon as she landed on the premises, often having her cards and
wheel at work before her husband could build a log cabin. Going into a

---

[11] See Francis Jennings, *The Invasion of America: Indians, colonialism and the
cant of conquest* (Chapel Hill, NC, University of North Carolina Press for IEAHC,
1975), and his "Virgin land and savage people," *American Quarterly*, 23 (1971),
pp. 519–41.

land, as it was then, that flowed with milk and honey, they were enabled by the use of their own hands and brains to make an independent and good living.

While the people as a rule were not educated, many of them very illiterate as far as education was concerned, they were thoroughly self-sustaining when it came to the knowledge required to do things that brought about a plentiful supply of the necessities of life. In those times all were on an equality, for each man and his family had to produce what was required to live upon ... There was but little stealing or cheating among them. There was no money to steal, and if a man stole a piece of jeans (cotton fabric) or cloth of any kind he would be apprehended at once. Society at that time was homogeneous and simple, and opportunities for vice were very rare. There were very few old bachelors and old maids, for about the only thing a young man could do when he became twenty-one, and his mother quit making his clothes and doing his washing, was to marry one of his neighbor's daughters. The two would then work together, as was the universal custom, and soon produce with their own hands abundance of supplies to live upon.

... There is one remark that I will venture here, and it is this, that while the white people were in the power of the Indians and understood it, we got along with the Indian a great deal better than when the change to the white people took place. In the early days white men respected the Indian's rights thoroughly, and would not be the aggressors, and often they were at the mercy of the Indians, but as soon as they began to feel that they could do as they pleased, became more aggressive and had less regard for what the Indian considered his rights.[12]

But, whether in the eighteenth century or in the nineteenth, indeed whether in the US, Canada, Asia, or Australia, all visitors noticed the recurring traits among the white frontiersmen: the faith in democracy, the preaching of egalitarianism, the social mobility, the familiarity, the optimism, the enthusiasm, the urgency, the self-importance, the inventiveness, and the anti-intellectualism, the materialism, and the wastefulness. Indeed, the last is the thesis of *People of Plenty* where David Potter advances the theory that the dominating factor in American development has been abundance – both the presence of enormous natural wealth, and the widespread opportunity to exploit it. He sees the frontier as one vital source of this abundance: the presence of free, virgin land, relatively easily available for settlement and exploitation. But, he argues, the frontier was not the only source: "as early as mid-century, if not earlier," he writes,

[12] Alexander Majors, *Seventy Years on the Frontier* (1893).

America's industrial growth, relying upon the use of other forms of abundance than soil fertility, began to compete with the frontier in the opportunities which it offered, and the migration of Americans began to point to the cities rather than to the West ... The frontier ceased to operate as a major force in American history ... when the primary means of access to abundance passed from the frontier to other focuses of American life.[13]

One feature was central to the concept of the frontier: behind the sense of security on the Atlantic – thanks more to the British fleet, and thus coming free of charge, than to the Monroe Doctrine – this was a society that was recurrently expansionist. Behind the relatively easy settlement of successive boundary disputes with Britain (Florida 1819, the Maine boundary 1842, the Oregon Settlement, the Codfish War of 1852, the Reciprocal Treaty of 1854), behind the American role in Canada in 1837, lay a popular nationalism that ignored all frontiers. The New York *Tribune* advocated the outright annexation of Canada, which in its view cost Britain one and a half million pounds a year and provided asylum only for a few politicians and noblemen. Lewis Cass, long-time governor of the Michigan Territory and Michigan Senator, and Jackson's secretary for war, in planning his Democratic presidential bid in 1848 contemplated as slogans "the annexation of Canada, and of the Yucatan peninsula of Mexico." In 1850 Stephen Douglas introduced a bill for opening the St Lawrence and its canals to American commerce, with a view to the slow and peaceful annexation of Canada. Again, when James Gadsden negotiated his 1853 settlement with General Santa Anna, only the anxiety of Congress over the $15 million proposed, and its reduction of the price to $10 million, led to the abandonment of the original dream of the cession of the whole of the Colorado River; this would have simplified the problem of later irrigation projects in the Southwest, and secured for the US control of the Gulf of California, a more "natural" and more easily defensible frontier.

Cuba too was an object of diplomatic design, because of its possibilities as a slave state. Polk's efforts to purchase the island in 1848 were defeated by the Whigs, but upon their return to power in 1852, the Democrats sought an excuse for gaining Cuba, either by bargain or by war. The seizure of the American vessel *Black*

---

[13] Potter, *People of Plenty*. For parallels with other frontiers, see Owen Lattimore, *Studies in Frontier History* (New York, Oxford University Press, 1962); for Australia, H. C. Allen, *Bush and Backwoods* (Westport, Conn., Greenwood Press, 1959).

Warrior by Cuban customs officials in 1854 might have served as such an excuse, but the Spanish government apologized and made reparations before an annexationist program could be launched. A few months later, the American ministers to France, England, and Spain collaborated on the "Ostend Manifesto," which proposed that Spain sell Cuba to the United States and claimed that America had a natural right to Cuba and should take it by force if Spain refused to sell; but the maneuver decreased American prestige abroad and Democratic prestige at home, without accomplishing any positive results.

The acquisition of California and Oregon had increased American interest in a canal across Tehuantepec, Nicaragua, or Panama, but England's Caribbean influence was too strong to permit unilateral action. By the Clayton-Bulwer Treaty of 1850, Great Britain and the United States agreed that they shared an equal interest in any such canal.

Manifest Destiny was thus the major impulse in American foreign policy from 1812 to 1860. But it also had other characteristics. There was support for the American merchant marine: Spanish and British colonies were opened to American traders, Dutch and French later. A federal grant was given to the Collins shipping line to compete with Cunard. Whaling was extended from the Atlantic to the Pacific, and, with it, backed by missionaries, an interest in Hawaii began. American clippers competed with British in the China trade. Caleb Cushing negotiated the first treaty between the US and China in 1844. Japan was opened up by Commodore Matthew Perry, leading to the treaty of 1854. And – though the US had declared the African slave traffic unlawful in 1808 and made it piracy in 1820 – the slave trade continued, usually via Brazil and Cuba rather than directly to the American states, and in American (i.e. mainly Yankee) ships.

Behind the traders and the exporters were the ideologues and the demagogues. Democracy in the 1840s, unlike the 1790s, was now for export. If American democracy was superior to any European alternative, would the US be safe so long as the European monarchies remained? Even in the Monroe Doctrine, there was explicit support for Greece in its nationalist struggle in the 1820s against the Ottoman Empire. Ypsilanti, Michigan, is named after a Greek who fought in the War of American Independence, and whose sons were engaged in what was seen as Greece's own War of Independence. The 1848 Revolutions in Europe evoked a chorus of approval, and by 1852 the German and Irish votes were eagerly sought in the presidential election. Whigs vied with Democrats particularly in support for Hungary, and the visit of Kossuth in 1851–2 evoked a response mindful of Lafayette's visit in 1824. America's emotional and democratic national imperialism was born in these years, stimulated rather than offset by the language barriers, or by the poverty and Catholicism of many of the immigrants. It was further stimulated by the adverse comments on American manners of European visitors such as Charles Dickens or Harriet Martineau, and by dependence on European, mainly British, capital for the building of internal improvements such as the Erie Canal. And the optimism, the pride, and the successes of the Mexican War fed the xenophobia, the chauvinism, and the violence of Americans – of the South as well as of the North and West. The absence of social external restraint that Crèvecoeur had extolled meant that freedom was frequently synonymous with anarchy. Abraham Lincoln, in his lecture to the Springfield Lyceum in 1838, deplored "the increasing disregard for law;" it could lead to the appearance of "an Alexander, a Caesar or a Napoleon." He was a frontiersman himself; his grandfather had been killed by Indians.

The violence needs no stress. Indians, abolitionists, immigrants, Negroes, Mormons, Masons, all received their share of it. Abolitionists were attacked by "gentlemen of property and standing" for threatening the existing economic and racial *status quo*. Indians were seen as savage threats to the expansion of a prosperous and comparatively well-organized society. Mormons outraged the morals of their neighbors, and Negroes who forgot their assigned place knew that their punishment would not be restrained by charity. Vigilantism is "as American as cherry pie;" it is, as Richard M. Brown argues, socially conservative – an attempt to secure and maintain a society that respects property, stability, and order. Michel Chevalier saw this in 1833 and thought that it was admirable. Local saloon-keepers, he observed, were often the "police commissioner," and the tavern regulars "would in any case of necessity be ready to act the part of constables."[14] This was not a tolerant society – popular and near-illiterate democracy rarely is. As a result Fanny Wright's meetings were wrecked; the Mormon leader Joseph Smith and his brother were lynched by the mob, as was the abolitionist advocate Elizah

---

[14] Leonard L. Richards, *Gentlemen of Property and Standing* (New York, Oxford University Press, 1970); Richard Maxwell Brown, "The American vigilante tradition," in Hugh Davis Graham and Ted Robert Gurr (eds), *Violence in America: Historical and comparative perspectives* (3rd edn, 1989, Newbury Park, CA, Sage), pp. 121–70; Michel Chevalier, *Society, Manners and Politics in the United States* (New York, Kelly, 1966), pp. 321–2.

Lovejoy at Alton, Illinois. And, in turn, abolitionist crusaders could be themselves violent men, as was John Brown at Pottawatomie, Kansas, and again in 1859 at Harper's Ferry. Not a house, unless it was a Quaker's, was "without its sword, pistol, musket or rifle." In the slave country, they were kept handy – and would stay so, as a necessary part of the lobby furniture, for many decades.

The lawlessness was not just the result of fear of slave risings. The last Indian war – with the Seminoles – lasted six years; so to the South and West violence, not peace, was the "norm." The challenge to a duel was a feature of the career of almost every public figure: thus Aaron Burr killed Alexander Hamilton in 1804; in 1806 Andrew Jackson killed one man in a pistol duel outside Nashville, and in 1813 met two other challenges; in 1826 John Randolph of Roanoke exchanged shots with Secretary of State Henry Clay; in 1845 William L. Yancey of Alabama was interrupted in a duel with a fellow Congressman from Kentucky; when Benjamin F. Wade of Ohio entered the Senate in 1851 he thought it prudent to put a brace of pistols on his desk, as a warning to hecklers. Lawlessness was as conspicuous in urban areas: product of group clashes, nativism, of the over-exuberant rivalries of fire companies; in New York, the result of the private wars of police gangs, each more concerned to smash the other than to curb crime; plus – in Boston, Philadelphia, and New York – the Irish *versus* the Know-Nothings, in San Francisco the gold-rush gangs *versus* the vigilance committees that arose to protect the men of property (there were over 100 murders in San Francisco in the first six months of 1856); vigilance committees were themselves violent, but at least they provided their own primitive law and order, where there were no courts or judges available.

There was one obvious cause of the propensity to brawn and brawl, whether in town or out of it: the demon drink. Foreign visitors saw in America a nation of drunkards. It was not that public drunkenness was especially common, but that, as the shrewd Scot Peter Neilson noted, the citizenry "was in a certain degree, seasoned." Anne Royale wrote; "When I was in Virginia, it was too much whiskey – in Ohio, too much whiskey – in Tennessee, it is too, too much whiskey!" The high point was 1820, when the annual *per Capita* consumption of distilled liquors exceeded five gallons, a rate triple that of today. However, two-thirds was consumed by the adult males – although Fanny Kemble noted that New York ladies visiting the public baths were "pretty often" supplied with mint Juleps. The stagecoaches stopped regularly, "to water the horses and to brandy the gentlemen." And, as a Kentucky politico put it, the way to men's hearts is "down their throats." Alcohol was so much an accepted part of American life that in 1829 the secretary of war estimated that three-quarters of the nation's labor force drank at least four ounces of distilled spirits daily. Water, by contrast, was not only usually unfit for human consumption, it lacked what was called "food value." One view of it was that it was very good for navigation but was too "common" to drink. Or, as Benjamin Franklin put it, if God had intended man to drink water, He would not have made him with an elbow capable of raising a wine glass. [15]

The frontier added the special boastfulness of the mountain man, "half-horse, half-alligator," usually without culture, without status, without currency, but unbounded in his egotism and in his appetites, standing between civilization and savagery. If Daniel Boone and Davy Crockett are almost as much figures of fiction as Paul Bunyan, all are remembered for their claims – and for the voraciousness of their appetites. Davy Crockett boasted that he could "yell like an Indian, fight like a devil, spout like an earthquake, make love like a mad bull and swallow an Indian whole without choking ...". So with the distances they covered, the animals and the "Injuns" they killed, in a world where these long hunters were themselves hunted. But Davy Crockett was a special case: he took hailstones for "Life Pills," picked his teeth with a pitchfork, and could drink the Mississippi dry. And, as he explained in his *Autobiography*, when he held office as a squire in the canebrakes, he gave his decisions on the principles of common justice and honesty between man and men, and relied on natural-born sense, and not on "law learning to guide me: for I had never read a law book in all my life." There were many frontier lawyers like him. And when they relaxed, over a chew of tobacco or of "stewed Yankee and pork steak," even their games and sports were as violent as pulp fiction said their lives were; in the Rockies as on the Mississippi, rough wrestling and fisticuffs, ear-chewing and eye-gouging, were a legitimate part of any game. At the core of the braggartry and of the humor was the violation of Nature itself and of the land, and the accumulation of its goods, of bears and furs. All was more than life-size. And the motive in the West as in the East was: profit. With their profits, the mountain men who survived all adopted civilized careers. From them, Ned Buntline could write down their tales, editing and bowdlerizing as much as embroidering. And some needed no ghost-writers, and told their own yarns, like Roy Bean, Justice of the

[15] W. J. Rorabaugh, *The Alcoholic Republic: An American tradition* (New York, Oxford University Press, 1979).

Peace, keeper of the saloon in West Texas that he called "Langtry" after the Jersey Lily. He dispensed hard liquor and hard justice, and the line between the two was often thin. He was "the law west of the Pecos."[16]

The frontier's is a colorful as well as a boisterous history. The single decade before the Civil War witnessed at least a dozen "characters" cross California's stage. Not only John August Sutter or the Pathfinder Fremont, not only the Irish adventurers who got lavish land grants from the obliging thirteenth and last Mexican governor of Alta California, Manuel Micheltorena; he became commanding general in (more or less) peaceful Yucatan, only to find that the Indians there were equally violent men. Not the least colorful was that Irish girl, "merciless in her man-eating propensities," as one of her admirers described her, who arrived with a miner-husband from New York, but had before that been mistress of Liszt, and what was politely described as a protegée of a king of Bavaria; Lola Montez. She stayed only a year, playing herself in the mining camps, and was asked to move on to yet another world to conquer: empty Australia. In 1858 she returned – to New York. There she lectured on history, and its heroines, got religion and died in Brooklyn, "a Magdalen just turned forty."[17]

The West produced others than adventurers and exotics, brigands and Byronic heroes, actors, actresses and writers. Benjamin Louis Eulalie de Bonneville was Paris-born, and first moved to America as a boy in care of Tom Paine. He became a US Army officer, who in 1832–4 was given a two-year leave of absence to lead a party of 100 trappers and traders into the Rockies; in 1832 he took the first wagons over South Pass in the Rockies. A detachment of his men, led by Joseph Walker, were the first white men to make a westward crossing of the central Sierra Nevada (1833), and probably the first to see Yosemite and the Sequoias. Bonneville's maps were expertly drawn and provided the first accurate knowledge of the mountains. His function, like those of Pike and Long, is likely to have been that of an intelligence gatherer as well as that of map-maker. One of his company, a Pennsylvania-born trapper and mountain man, wrote up his story in *The Narrative of Zenas Leonard* (1839). Albert Abraham Michelson, born in Prussia but raised in Virginia City,

---

[16] See Richard Slotkin, *Regeneration Through Violence* (Middletown, CT, Wesleyan University Press, 1973); Marcus Cunliffe, *Soldiers and Civilians: The martial spirit in America 1775–1865* (London, Eyre and Spottiswoode, 1969), pp. 82–98.

[17] Van Wyck Brooks, *The Times of Melville and Whitman* (New York, Dutton, 1947), pp. 204–5.

Nevada, and San Francisco, was, via the US Naval Academy and the University of Chicago, to be the first American scientist to receive a Nobel Prize in 1907. And a German pastor's son, who spoke 18 languages, went to the Californian mines to make his fortune; not by digging, but by setting up a bank to purchase gold-dust. That way he made his fortune. His wealth allowed him to leave, and in doing so, he was able to say that "among those who leave this Country there is hardly one in a hundred thousand who has done as well as myself." Like Benjamin Franklin before him, his fortune allowed him the freedom to be himself. He became an archaeologist, and 20 years later discovered Troy and the treasures of Priam. His name was Heinrich Schliemann.

9

The Old South: Slavery
And Secesh

THE PRO-SLAVERY ARGUMENT

I hold that in the present state of civilization, where two races
of different origin, and distinguished by color and other physical
differences, as well as intellectual, are brought together, the
relation now existing in the slaveholding states between the two
is, instead of an evil, a good — a positive good.
                                        John C. Calhoun

THE ABOLITIONIST VIEW

The slaves in the United States are treated with barbarous in-
humanity ... they are overworked, underfed, wretchedly clad and
lodged, and have insufficient sleep ... they are often made to
wear round their necks iron collars armed with prongs, to drag
heavy chains and weights at their feet while working in the field
... they are often kept confined in the stocks day and night for
weeks together, made to wear gags in their mouths for hours or
days, have some of their front teeth torn out or broken off, that
they may be easily detected when they run away ... they are
frequently flogged with terrible severity, have red pepper rubbed
into their lacerated flesh, and hot brine, spirits of turpentine,
&c., poured over the gashes to increase the torture ... they
are often stripped naked, their backs and limbs cut with knives,
bruised and mangled by scores and hundreds of blows with the
paddle, and terribly torn by the claws of cats, drawn over them
by their tormentors.
             Theodore Dwight Weld, Slavery As It Is, *1839*

1 SLAVERY

The states now known as United have lived through three revolutions: first, the struggle for Independence (in two wars, from 1775
to 1783, and from 1812 to 1815); second, the War Between the
States of 1861–5, which determined that not two federal states but
a single united nation should emerge on the North American mainland south of the 49th parallel and north of the Rio Grande; and

third, the all-but-peaceful revolution since 1954 during which, not only in law but in fact, Black has come to be treated as equal to White. Of course, it can be argued that the third revolution has not yet been completed, that many whites do not regard African-Americans as equal, and that some African-Americans insist that they should be treated as separate – or, indeed, be treated with special favor in order to offset the centuries of discrimination. Whatever the qualifications, however, at the price of a few ugly riots in the 1960s in a few (Northern as well as Southern) towns, a civil war, the third revolution, was fought and won. It is one of the US's great and too-little chronicled achievements. Moreover, if now legally settled, the quest for genuine parity for the African-American remains the major domestic issue in the United States, and – not merely because of the scale of the Civil War – the major continuous moral problem in American history. For African-Americans, there remain the ambiguities of what W. E. B. Du Bois called his "double consciousness," as black and as American.[1]

If the problem of Black and White has been central in the American story since 1783, it was not seen as a major issue at the outset. When the first blacks were landed in Virginia in 1619 – before the Pilgrim Fathers sailed – their status was similar to that of white indentured servants who, like them, were bound to a master for a term of years. These first blacks were freed after seven years, and one of them became a landowner. In 1668 there were at least ten free Negro households in Northampton County, Virginia, the only county for which there are full records. By 1671 there were only 2,000 blacks in Virginia.

Tobacco in the seventeenth century, however, like King Cotton 150 years later, required a biddable workforce, accustomed to all-year-round routine work in the heat, unable to complain, and, if they ran away, easily detectable because of their color. So in 1661 black slavery was sanctioned by law in Virginia, and in 1663 in Maryland: a life sentence, and hereditary. From its foundation in 1672, slaves were increasingly supplied direct by the Royal African Company from West Africa, or as re-exports via the Caribbean. They were packed like cattle on ships that brought fortunes to shipowners in Glasgow and Liverpool, Bristol and Newport, Rhode

---

[1] See David B. Davis, *The Problem of Slavery in the Age of Revolution 1770–1823* (Cornell University Press, 1975), and his essay "Slavery and the post-World War II historians," identifying five "turning points" in the historiography, in Sidney W. Mintz (ed.), *Slavery, Colonisation and Racism* (New York, Norton, 1974), pp. 1–16.

Island, and to those of New York, Nantes, and La Rochelle also. The institution of slavery, and a system of racial segregation, became the basis of the Southern economy from about 1680 until 1861 though it was not until 1691 that Virginia banned intermarriage of black and white, and miscegenation. Slavery did not take root in the North, whose hard winters and rocky soil, far more perhaps than any liberalism of spirit, forbade the plantation crops of the South; there family farms, and then mills and factories, required skilled artisans rather than field hands. But the Puritans had not hesitated to enslave Indian captives, or to buy and sell slaves. At the time of the Declaration of Independence, there were fewer than 20,000 blacks among some 700,000 people in the region east of the Hudson River; at that time no colony/state prohibited slavery.

Many blacks were loyal to George III in 1776, and in Virginia Lord Dunmore raised his Ethiopian Regiment, to the horror of most Virginians. Reports of it led Washington to change his mind: whereas in 1775 he directed recruiting officers not to enrol "any stroller, Negro or vagabond," by 1776 he relaxed and agreed to enlist free Negroes; later, after Valley Forge, slaves were welcome too, if used essentially only as labor battalions, since with weapons they were suspect. Five thousand blacks fought on the Patriot side; and two blacks, Oliver Cromwell and Prince Whipple, were at the oars when Washington crossed the Delaware on Christmas Day 1776, as Emanuel Leutze's painting records. Rhode Island, short of men, did raise two black regiments, and Salem Poor of Massachusetts was one of a handful of black junior officers. Some blacks were given their freedom, others escaped to Canada and Florida, others still went back with the British, and a few hid out and raided their ex-masters. In the difficult months before Yorktown, the young John Laurens, son of a planter and former slave-trader, proposed the formation of a black battalion, but South Carolina vetoed the project. But there were many like Captain Mark Starlin, the only Negro naval captain in Virginia's history, who made daring night raids on British vessels at Hampton Roads, only to be rewarded by being re-enslaved, to die in slavery.

Yet South Carolina and Georgia refused to permit the recruitment of blacks, and they were carefully excluded from militia service. When the good liberal Thomas Jefferson declared that "all men are created equal," he meant white men only – and men only. No appeal was made to the island colonies to join the Americans, just because their populations were largely black. Jefferson's God seemed to discriminate. Moreover, the original words in the Declaration of Independence were "among these rights are life, liberty and property."

(It was only after some discussion, and Franklin's persuasions, that "property" was replaced by the ambiguous phrase "pursuit of happiness.") Interference with slavery violated the sanctity of private property. This inconsistency seriously worried Abraham Lincoln, who considered compensating slave-owners for the loss of their slaves, as did Tsar Alexander II in Russia, who was emancipating his serfs at the same time (and without a civil war). Jefferson was acutely embarrassed by the issue, and sought to blame it all on the slave traffic, on the British "who brought them here," and logically therefore – however inaccurate with respect to the facts – on George III. "He has waged cruel war against human nature itself" was a clause in the Declaration of Independence struck out at the request of South Carolina and Georgia. One of the first to die for Independence, it is stressed nowadays, was Crispus Attucks, a black seaman and fugitive slave, one of the five shot by British troops in the so-called Boston Massacre of March 5, 1770. But one distinguished historian has seen the "apotheosis of Crispus Attucks" as reprehensible, since the victims of the massacre were simply "hooligans." Jefferson remained uneasy. In 1781 in his *Notes on the State of Virginia*, he advanced it "as a suspicion only" "that the blacks, whether originally a distinct race, or made distinct by time and circumstance, are inferior to the whites in the endowment both of body and mind."[2]

Despite the contradictions between the pieties of the Declaration and the reality (and prejudices) of life around them, slavery was in 1776 only an embarrassment. It was largely localized; 60 percent of the slaves were in Virginia and Maryland. On many small farms, white owners and black slaves worked alongside each other. Slavery earned the disapproval only of individuals. Indeed, in large measure, Americans were able to finance their independence with the labor of slaves; American-French relations during the War of Independence can be called "King Tobacco Diplomacy." To the Revolutionaries of 1776, North and South, to talk of giving slaves (or industrial workmen) their freedom was ideological nonsense: without property, they had learnt from John Locke and continued to believe, no one was or is free; any form of dependence, regardless of color, was seen as slavery.[3]

[2] *Notes on the State of Virginia*, ed. W. Peden (Chapel Hill, University of North Carolina Press, 1955), p. 143.
[3] Edmund Morgan, *Journal of American History*, 59 (June 1972), pp. 5–29, and his *American Slavery – American Freedom* (New York, Norton, 1975); Winthrop D. Jordan, *White over Black: American attitudes to the Negro 1550–1812* (Chapel Hill, NC, University of North Carolina Press for IEAHC, 1968), pp. 429–81.

There was, however, a potentially powerful issue here. At the Constitutional Convention in 1787, the important division between the states was not one of size (Virginia had 750,000 people, Massachusetts 400,000, Rhode Island and Delaware approximately 60,000 each) but of views on slavery. The Constitution says nothing on race and avoids the use of the words "slave" and "slavery;" until 1857 (the Dred Scott case) there was no consistent policy on whether the Negro was a citizen. The states were left to do as they pleased. To Southern planters the slave was property, and as property-owners, they wanted their ownership protected by law; more, they should have extra votes because of their extra property, since – in the US as in Britain – the suffrage depended on property, on a "stake in society," not on a mere counting of heads. In Northern eyes, no such extra power should be given to the South, and, if it were, they should be taxed because of it. From this clash came the "three-fifths compromises:" three-fifths of the slaves were to be counted in determining the population, and thus for apportioning of representation in Congress – although of course only free white property-holding males would actually vote for the representatives allotted.

The three-fifths clause – the "federal ratio" – was more than a compromise formula. It reflected the awareness that the wealth, the freedom and now the independence of at least the Chesapeake colonies rested on the coerced labor of others; not, since the Greeks invented what is called "democracy," that there was anything unusual in that. As Edmund Morgan has demonstrated, the central paradox of American colonial and Revolutionary history is that the rise of liberty and equality coincided with the rise of slavery. Black slaves replaced landless and lawless white indentured servants. And not only the tobacco colonies benefited: New England's prosperity rested on its carrying trade with the slave isles of the Caribbean; Massachusetts had only some 5,000 slaves, but its West Indian trade employed some 10,000 seamen; and its 60 distilleries produced the rum that was the currency of the seaboard. Land and crops, ships and trade – all had slavery as base.

In the 1770s to 1780s, mainly among Quakers, Baptists and Methodists, an abolition movement began, opposing slavery on moral and religious grounds. Its leaders, if often Scottish-educated, were mainly Philadelphia-rooted. Quakers underlined three wrongs in slavery: the sinful motivation of the master, the sinfulness forced on the slave by his condition, and its violation of the spiritual brotherhood of man. John Woolman played a large part in persuading the Society of Friends to free their slaves:

Placing on men the ignominious title, SLAVE, dressing them in uncomely Garments, keeping them to servile labor, in which they are often dirty, tends gradually to fix a Notion in the Mind, that they are a Sort of People below us in Nature, and leads us to consider them as such in all our Conclusions about them.

In 1773, the Edinburgh-trained physician, Benjamin Rush, elaborated on the new spirit of Environmentalism:

I shall allow, that many of them are inferior in virtue, knowledge and the love of Liberty to the inhabitants of other parts of the World: but this may be explained from Physical causes. Human Nature is the same in all Ages and Countries: and all the difference we perceive in its characters in respect to Virtue and Vice, Knowledge and Ignorance, may be accounted for from Climate, Country, Degrees of Civilization, form of Government, or other accidental causes.[4]

John Allen, writing in 1774, was outraged by the hypocrisy of Americans:

Blush Ye pretended votaries for freedom! ye trifling patriots! who are making a vain parade of being the advocates for the liberties of mankind, who are thus making a mockery of your profession, by trampling on the sacred natural rights and priviledges of the Africans; for while you are fasting, praying, non-importing, non-exporting, remonstrating, resolving, and pleading for a restoration of your charter rights, you at the same time are continuing this lawless, cruel, inhuman, and abominable practise of enslaving your fellow-creatures.

Or, as Dr Johnson put it, according to Boswell; "How is it that we hear the loudest yelps for liberty among the drivers of Negroes?"

The abolitionist cause was Atlantic-wide, European even more than American, and product of the Enlightenment. It was voiced by middle-class reformers, who saw it as yet another campaign for yet another freedom. As with Wilberforce and Granville Sharp in Britain, and Brissot de Warville, the founder of the *Société des Noirs* in France, abolitionism came from the egalitarianism of the *philosophes* as well as from the Quakers and the Methodists; it owed its shaping to Montesquieu (to whom slavery was contrary to

[4] Philips P. Moulton (ed.), *The Journal and Major Essays of John Woolman* (New York, Oxford University Press, 1971), p. 322; L. H. Butterfield (ed.), *Letters of Benjamin Rush*, 2 vols (Princeton, NJ, American Philosophical Society/Princeton University Press, 1951), vol. II, p. 130.

natural law) and to the Scottish Enlightenment as much as to the pity and the simplicities of the Quakers and of Benjamin Rush. It was possible for the Philadelphia Quaker Anthony Benezet, and, later, the men – and women – of Boston, Cincinnati, and New York to attack slavery as part of their attack on what appeared as a surviving relic of a quasi-feudal and agrarian past, out of place in their emerging new industrial order, and which, in their sophisticated world-order, branded the US as uniquely reactionary.[5] In some states laws were passed requiring slave children to be set free at 21. This manumission movement meant little in the Northern states, where slavery was already being abolished, as in Vermont (1777) and Pennsylvania (1780), or where gradual abolition was a constitutional pledge – Rhode Island, Connecticut, and Massachusetts (all in the 1780s), New York with its 20,000 slaves (1799), and New Jersey with some 10,000 (1804). The Ordinance of 1787, which organized the Northwest Territory, barred slavery from what became Ohio, Indiana, Illinois, Michigan, and Wisconsin. Urban free blacks and fugitive slaves in Boston; New York, and Philadelphia gradually began to establish two-parent nuclear households, to organize black institutions, to engage in domestic and maritime employment, and to choose new surnames in an effort to break with their slave past. The Revolution effectively put slavery in the Northern states, as well as the Western territories of that day, on the road to ultimate extinction. If the "peculiar institution" became more deeply entrenched in the Chesapeake region, especially in Virginia, and in South Carolina and Georgia, even in this latter region, because of the disruptions of the war, slaves also managed to gain a degree of autonomy, and to accumulate personal property to an extent unparalleled elsewhere on the North American mainland. Nor do geographical boundaries overrule individual judgments. Both Alexander Hamilton and John Jay favored abolition. And John Jay did more than agonize, for he was an honourable man: "I purchase slaves, and manumit them at proper ages, and when their faithful services shall have afforded a reasonable retribution." It was the fashion among many Southerners to free many house slaves when the owner died, as did both Washington and (to a lesser degree) Jefferson. Many Southerners admitted to horror of the institution, but could see no solution, given their need for slaves as their major labor force, and given also what seemed the helplessness,

---

[5] See David B. Davis, *The Problem of Slavery in Western Culture* (Ithaca, NY, Cornell University Press, 1966) and Duncan Rice, *The Rise and Fall of Black Slavery* (London, Macmillan, 1975), ch. 5.

even inferiority, of the slaves. What Jefferson deplored about the idea of freedom for the slave, which as an idea he welcomed, was their lack of "the habits of industry;" "they chose to steal from their neighbors rather than work." The eccentric John Randolph of Roanoke, who treated his slaves as members of his family and refused to sell them – "men cannot have property in men" – told his fellow-Southerners that slavery was "the cancer in your face." "We have the wolf by the ears," wrote Jefferson in 1820, "and can neither hold him nor let him go." There was a general awareness that the Ethiopians, in Colonel William Byrd's words, "blow up the pride and ruin the industry of our White people who ... detest work for fear it should make them like slaves."[6]

In 1782 there were several thousand free blacks, and by 1860 half a million (but only in Massachusetts, Maine, and New Hampshire could they vote.) In Maryland free blacks outnumbered slaves; in Delaware they formed 92 percent of the black population. But, as new state constitutions, product of Jacksonian democracy, extended the suffrage, they did so to white property-holders; or, as in New York when the suffrage was attended to all whites, Negroes had to hold property before acquiring the right to vote. The free Negro, however, needed to protect himself by carrying with him his certificate of freedom, and to ensure its regular renewal, or he ran the risk of forcible re-enslavement, since color of skin implied condition. Solomon Northrup's *Twenty Years A Slave* (1853) is the account of the kidnapping of a free black in the North, who was sold South into slavery, and spent 20 years as such. Yet many free blacks prospered, especially in towns: in Charleston, in 1850 they included 122 carpenters and 77 tailors, and Jehu Jones, the wealthy hotelkeeper; in Natchez, William Johnson, son of a white father and a mulatto mother, became a wealthy Mississippian, operated three barbershops and was himself a slave-owner. Thomy Lafon of New Orleans and his fellow-Louisianian, Cyprien Ricard of Iberville, were deemed the wealthiest free Negroes, the latter owning a plantation with 92 slaves. Opportunities in New Orleans, however, were more abundant than anywhere else: there were many free men of color there – *les gens de couleur libres* – legacy of its French century, and of mixed marriages of French fathers and quadroon mothers.

---

[6] Arthur Zilversmith, *The First Emancipation: The abolition of slavery in the North* (Chicago, University of Chicago Press, 1967), p. 167n.; Leon F. Litvack, *North of Slavery: The Negro in the United States 1790–1860* (Chicago, University of Chicago Press, 1961).

The African slave trade was abolished in 1807, as prescribed in the Constitution. Had slaves continued to be available at the same price and on the same terms as in Cuba and Brazil, the whole history of the United States would have been different. Not only would there have been more blacks, but they would have been employed in different ways, and probably not only in the South. Following the outlawing of the trade, however, the traffic from Africa to the US officially ceased. There are no records of Africans being directly imported in the 1830s and 1840s, although some million slaves were carried to the New World during those years. Nevertheless, despite a law which prescribed the death penalty for citizens convicted of slaving, and despite the presence of a US squadron and of British anti-slave patrols off the coast of West Africa after Britain banned the trade in 1806–7, and after slavery was banned in the British Empire in 1833, some Americans did engage in this traffic. There were well-authenticated cases of slavers being outfitted in New York and other northern ports, Newport in particular. More significant was the frequent use of the US flag by slavers of indeterminate nationality, to evade capture by British cruisers. The US consistently refused to enter into a bilateral treaty with Great Britain allowing a mutual right of search until Lincoln finally agreed to one in 1862.[7]

It seemed equally clear that, in the optimism of the 1820s, some blacks would, anyway, be shipped back to Africa; the first meeting of the American Colonization Society was held in Washington in 1816, and Liberia, land of liberty, was set up in 1822 with its capital Monrovia named after President Monroe; it was to parallel Britain's establishment of Sierra Leone, and then of Freetown. Since only free blacks could go, the project was designed to remove an ambiguous element in the slave-holding community, and thus to serve as a safeguard for slavery itself; since it promised to make manumission more feasible, however, it was promoted in the North as part of an anti-slavery program. The basic problem remained untouched by it. In 1847 the society surrendered control to the independent republic of Liberia. By 1852 only 8,000 had been transported "home;" by 1860, 15,000 in all had gone; and a number of them had been liberated from captured slave ships without ever seeing the New World. Such numbers were minute. To the black slave masses, in any case, America, not Africa, was home. "This land," wrote Bishop Richards Allen (himself a Philadelphia slave

---

[7] H. Temperley, *British Anti-Slavery 1833–1870* (London, Longman, 1972); Rice, *Rise and Fall of Black Slavery*, ch. 7.

who had bought himself freedom and became founder of the African Methodist Episcopal Church), in one of the first issues of the first newspaper published by Negroes, "This land which we have watered with our tears and our blood, is now our mother country."

Before the invention of the cotton gin, and the expansion of the cotton kingdom, before the South became defensive of its peculiar institution, and before the issues of race, miscegenation, and morality bedeviled the whole Union, the labor problems of slavery may have been slight, but already they were worrying enough. Consider one estate as an example. The largest of George Washington's four estates at Mount Vernon, the River Plantation, had the following groups: 1 male overseer, his wife, 10 male laborers, 17 female laborers, 23 children. In addition, a grist mill on the estate demanded the attention of 1 miller and 3 coopers. Weavers, tanners, carpenters, and blacksmiths were all on the payroll. There was a ferry and a fishery. The manor house had a large retinue: 13 house servants, 16 skilled artisans of both sexes, 6 stablemen and wagoners, 7 laborers, 3 old people and 26 children. Martha Washington had to supervise the preparation of food — and preserving it, smoking as well as cooking the meat, soap-making, sewing, and weaving. There fell to her also the care of the sick, slave and free, at all hours. In Mary Boykin Chesnut's words, "there is no slave like a wife."[8] To direct this microcosm of the South's economy the planter's task called for a farmer, a horticulturist, a builder, a businessman, and an accountant — all in one; and for steady industry, experience, authority over men and women — and, always, tact.

Washington's main crop was tobacco, which he tried to diversify with wheat, since tobacco left him dependent on sales abroad — and on the "factors" who acted as intermediaries. When he added his wife's plantation to his own, he had, in 1775, 135 slaves. He treated them well, for on their health and industry his own prosperity depended. He followed the general practice in Virginia in his day of not selling a slave if the slave was unwilling to be sold, and believed no more should be imported — it was, he said, "a wicked, cruel and unnatural trade." But it would not go away of its own

---

[8] Mary Boykin Chesnut, *The Private Mary Chesnut: The unpublished Civil War diaries*, ed. C. Vann Woodward and Elisabeth Muhlenfeld (New York, Oxford University Press, 1984), Introduction and p. 20. For a critical view of women in the slave household, see Elizabeth Fox-Genovese, *Within the Plantation Household: Black and white women of the Old South* (Chapel Hill, NC, University of North Carolina Press, 1988).

accord, nor could slave-owners abandon it, since their slaves represented a large part of their property and investment, and without them there would be no crops for sale. "It introduces more evils than it can cure," he considered, but only "legislative authority" could end it, and that "only by slow ... and imperceptible degrees." Whatever the political theory might be, white and black alike had to live inside a complex situation, in which the black did not seem prepared for independence and adulthood, and the institution itself was not very profitable. By the time of the Revolution, it was no revolution in morals, but the exhaustion of the soil that was destroying the basis of slavery, as the tobacco yields dropped remorselessly in the Tidewater colonies. The Founding Fathers' account books were the source of their conviction that slavery would wither away. But the reality was grim enough. A Polish visitor to Mount Vernon in 1797 was in awe of the great man and appreciated his sincere dislike of slavery. But he found the slave huts "more miserable than the most miserable cottages of our peasants. The husband and wife sleep on a mean pallet, the children on the ground; a very bad fireplace, some utensils for cooking ... A very small garden, with vegetables ... they may not keep either ducks, geese or pigs." Their rations were a peck of corn per person per week, and 20 salt herring a month; field hands got some salt meat at harvest-time; and clothes were a homespun jacket and a pair of breeches yearly.[9]

What transformed the problem was the invention of the cotton gin by ingenious Yankee Eli Whitney in 1793, while relaxing, after the exhaustions of Yale, on the Savannah plantation of Washington's ablest soldier, Nathaniel Greene. By the mechanical separation of the seed from the short-staple fiber, and by permitting slaves to devote their time to planting and hoeing, cotton became a major

---

[9] The meticulous records kept by the Founding Fathers have allowed meticulous study of their plantations; and not least of the ambiguities of Thomas Jefferson. See David B. Davis, *Was Thomas Jefferson an Authentic Enemy of slavery?* (New York, Oxford University Press, 1970); Boyston Merrill Jr, *Jefferson's Nephews: A frontier tragedy* (Princeton, Princeton University Press, 1976); John Chester Miller, *The Wolf by the Ears: Thomas Jefferson and slavery* (New York, Free Press, 1970); Fawn M. Brodie, "Thomas Jefferson's unknown grandchildren: a study in historical silence," *American Heritage*, 27 (1976), pp. 28–33, 94–9; and Mary Beth Norton, Herbert G. Gutman, and Ira Berlin, "The Afro-American family in the age of Revolution" in I. Berlin and G. Hoffman, *Slavery and Freedom in the Age of the American Revolution* (Charlottesville, University of Virginia Press, 1983), pp. 175–91; Julian U. Niemcewicz, *Under their Vine a Figtree: Travels through America 1797–9* (New Jersey Historical Society *Collections* XIV, Grassman Publishing, 1965).

product, and it spread steadily through the South and into the black belt. The land was worked, and then abandoned as the plantations spread into virgin territory with longer growing seasons. They grew in size; so did their profits. Slavery brought prosperity; and, like sugar along the Mississippi above New Orleans, and rice in the Carolina Tidewater, the Cotton Kingdom needed more and more capital and more and more slaves. So their price rose. Negroes were bred like animals; families were parted; "fancy girls" were sold on the auction block ("This is truly a No. 1 woman" read the advertisements); Thomas Jefferson Randolph, grandson of Thomas Jefferson, calculated in 1832 that Virginia had been exporting 8,500 each year for the last 20 years. He was moved to call Virginia "this ancient dominion ... converted into one grand menagerie, where men are to be reared for market oxenlike for the shambles." By 1860 a good field hand would fetch $1,800. This was now a new problem.

Despite the official ending of the slave trade in 1807, large numbers were smuggled in; and a considerable internal slave trade developed. Between 1830 and 1860 over 700,000 slaves were moved from the border states to the more profitable lower South, by the movement of the planter himself, by the migration of a younger son, or − 70 percent of them − by the internal slave trade, by being sold "down the river."

Along with domestic breeding, the slave population rose remorselessly from 700,000 in 1790 to 4 million in 1860 (almost all of them in the South, and forming more than one-third of the South's population). Not that there was a total contrast with the North. The North was no Eden. There the Negro was free, and had opportunities for self-expression; and he could help the escape of slaves. But the "Liberty Line" ran mainly from the border states or the lands just south of the Ohio rather than from the Deep South. Indeed, the Underground Railroad was probably more important to those operating it, in maintaining their zeal, than actually in its work of liberation.[10] But in most states the free black could not vote; and where they could − in Massachusetts, Maine, New Hampshire, and Vermont − there were not many of them. The "Jim Crow" system of segregation and discrimination − on transport, in hotels and bars, theaters and churches − applied everywhere. In

[10] The US Census Bureau estimated in 1860 that only 1,000 of the more than 3,000,000 slaves were fugitives. Senator Quitman of Mississippi, a fire-eater, thought that the South had lost 100,000 in the 40 years from 1810 to 1850, an average of 2,500 per year.

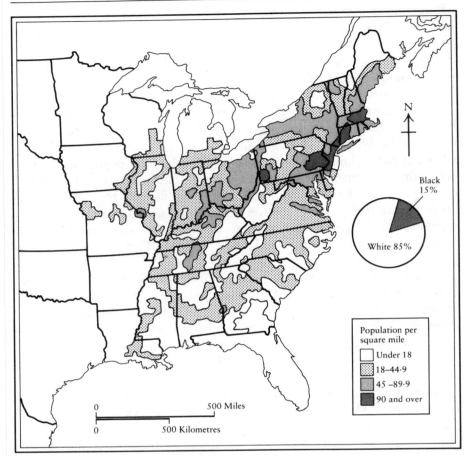

Map 7   Total population in 1850.

1851 Indiana, and in 1857 Oregon, banned the admission of Negroes, and they could enter Ohio and Illinois only on producing
evidence of good conduct, or a bond as its guarantee. Trade unions
refused admission to them. As de Tocqueville observed in 1831,
"The prejudice of race appears to be stronger in the states which
have abolished slavery than in those where it exists."

   There were many "Souths," and many varieties of slavery. Virginia had two and a half times as many blacks as in all 16 of the
"free" states — yet in its Western Appalachian counties there were
hardly any. In South Carolina, Louisiana, and Mississippi, blacks
outnumbered whites; and in Adams County, Mississippi, there were
50 blacks to every 1 white. In 1840 there were already as many
slaves in Alabama and Mississippi together (448,743) as in Virginia

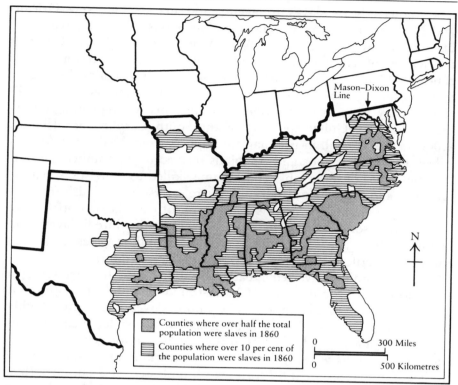

Map 8 The slave population in 1860.

(448,987). During the next 20 years, the number of slaves in the two Gulf states, Alabama and Mississippi, almost doubled (871,711) as against a tiny increase in Virginia (490,865). Moreover, the interstate commerce clause of the Constitution was invoked – as in 1850 – to permit the domestic slave trade, although half a century later it was used against lotteries, prostitution, child labor, and other social evils. Indeed, the notion of a "federal police power" that was derived from the commerce clause in the Supreme Court's decision in the Lottery Case in 1903 could have halted the domestic slave trade, and indeed that extension of slavery to the territories that became the overt cause of the War.

By 1860 the slaves of the Atlantic states were practically all natives of the states where they were owned; whereas in the newer cotton states, half of the slave population had been brought in from other states by immigrant owners, or through the domestic slave trade, or came directly from Africa. The major firm involved, Franklin and Armfield, of Alexandria, Virginia, shipped or sent by land thousands of slaves to agents and markets in New Orleans and Natchez. In so far as generalization is possible, the slaves were brought overwhelmingly from West Africa and the Guinea Coast as the legacy of African tribal raiding of their own interior, where capture of and trade in their own kind was the major feature of their economy; they more often came via the West Indies than directly. They were of many tribes, speaking many languages. Among the present-day Gullah-speakers of the South Carolina Sea Islands, 4,000 words are still in use that are imports from 21 distinct African tribes. In Virginia, Ibos and Angolans seemed to outnumber the rest. If some were house servants and became skilled as domestic servants, artisans, and craftsmen, and some were overseers and drivers with their long cow-hide whips as badges of office, the majority were field hands; some were urban slaves, some were hired slaves; and in the 1850s there were some quarter of a million black ex-slaves, enjoying a perilous and, for a few, an exotic freedom.

Clearly conditions varied greatly, from still-near-frontier Georgia and Florida to sophisticated Charleston and Tidewater Virginia, from plantation to plantation. The house slaves were often highly trained, sometimes skilled craftsmen, and responsible; their families might serve master and mistress in the Big House for generations. By contrast, as we have seen, the field hands working in hoe-gangs were clothed in homespun, fed on corn-bread, molasses, and salt pork (like the poor whites), with small vegetable patches; and they lived in cabins that were often windowless shanties. Many advertisements for runaway slaves mentioned their decayed or rotten teeth. A resident slave-owner, aware of the human investment slavery represented, might well treat his slaves kindly; an overseer, himself usually a poor white working for an absentee master, or a slave "driver" or foreman directing a gang in the fields and working to please his overseer, could be more tyrannical than any white. The psychology has been likened by Stanley Elkins (perhaps over-imaginatively?) to the concentration camp. Jefferson's indictment was the major one; slavery was "a perpetual exercise of the most boisterous passions; the most unremitting despotism on the one part, and degrading submissions on the other." "Indeed, I tremble for my country when I reflect that God is just; that his Justice cannot sleep for ever." For Henry Clay, slavery was "a curse to the Master, and a wrong to the slave."

Perhaps the most lyrical view of "the peculiar institution" came from Governor Hammond of South Carolina:

And our patriarchal scheme of domestic servitude is indeed well calculated to awaken the higher and finer feelings of our nature. It is not wanting in its enthusiasm and its poetry. The relations of the most beloved and honored chief ... are frigid and unfelt compared with those existing between the master and his slaves — who served his father, and rocked his cradle, or have been born into his household, and look forward to serve his children — who have been through life the props of his fortune, and the objects of his care — who have partaken of his griefs, and looked to him for comfort in their own — whose sickness he has so frequently watched over and relieved — whose holidays he has so often made joyous by his bounties and his presence, for whose welfare, when absent, his anxious solicitude never ceases, and whose hearty and affectionate greetings never fail to welcome him home. In this cold, calculating, ambitious world of ours, there are few ties more heartfelt, or of more benignant influence, than those which mutually bind the master and the slave, under our ancient system, handed down from the father of Israel.

But, he then added — less lyrically:

Allow our slaves to read your writings, stimulating them to cut our throats! Can you believe us to be such unspeakable fools?[11]

A more realistic view came from Frederick Law Olmsted, whose book, *The Cotton Kingdom*, was compiled from three earlier books describing his journeys through the South from 1857 to 1860. Responding to the comment of a friend who claimed that the South "must be rich" because "their last cotton crop alone was worth two hundred million," Olmsted noted that:

my own impression of the real condition of the People of our Slave States gave me, on the contrary, an impression that the cotton monopoly in some way did more harm than good; ... I went on my way into the so-called cotton states, within which I travelled over, first and last, at least three thousand miles of roads, from which not a cotton plant was seen, and the people living by the side of which certainly had not been made rich by cotton or anything else.[12]

[11] James Henry Hammond, *Letters on Slavery in the United States* (1845), and see also James K. Paulding, *Slavery in the United States* (1836) cited in Larry E. Tise, *Proslavery: A history of the defense of slavery in America 1701–1840* (Athens and London, University of Georgia Press, 1987), p. 328.
[12] Frederick L. Olmsted, *A Journey in the Seaboard Slave States* 1856); *A Journey through Texas* (1857); and *A Journey in the Back Country* (1860); and idem (ed. and introd. Arthur M. Schlesinger Jr) *The Cotton Kingdom* (orig. published 1861; this edn, New York, Knopf, 1953).

Slavery took many forms. Slaves formed the plantation workers, but in 1860 20 percent of the population of Southern cities were slaves; and in the country as a whole half a million slaves worked in factories and on railroad construction, as lumberjacks and stevedores, and on riverboats also. They were waiters and cooks, craftsmen, nurses, and prostitutes too. The majority, however, worked on plantations and as field hands. In South Carolina the slave codes limited the working hours to 16 in summer, 15 in winter: and from dawn to dusk, "from kin to kaint." On the sugar plantations of Louisiana, where the long process of production could be ruined by a delay in cutting, milling, boiling, or curing, and the work was done in large gangs, conditions were similar to those in Jamaica or Brazil; owners were usually absentees – and slaves outnumbered whites by 10 to 1, and would have little contact with white men. In contrast, in Virginia the numbers of free and unfree were approximately equal, and the typical tobacco plantation employed about 20 slaves. And in further contrast, cotton did not require elaborate preparation or processing, could be grown on small-scale farms, and an owner often worked in the field alongside his 10 or 12 slaves.

The slave codes were elaborate, and followed most of the prescriptions of the Virginia code of 1705. The most severe were those of South Carolina. Slaves could be punished by whipping, branding, ear-cropping, and imprisonment; no intoxicants could be sold them; they could not leave a plantation without written permission nor carry any weapon; by the Fugitive Slave Act of 1850, runaways had to be returned to their owner. Marriages between slaves did not legally exist, and families could be broken up and sold. Nevertheless, whether "legal" or not, the fact of marriage was a reality in the slave quarters, with large families from a settled partner being general. The break-up of such marriages often led to what Herbert Gutman calls "sequential polygamy," and thus to elaborate if often unrecorded kinship networks, often extending across the black as well as the white South. What has also to be noted is the further moral issue: since offspring should always follow the status of the mother, breeding became a minor industry, and some owners (like Jefferson's father-in-law) saw little wrong in fathering children by his slave women, so that many blacks became to a greater or lesser degree white. But few could "pass," and all mulattos were officially "Negro." The sexuality of slavery is a topic recent writers have juicily explored, and even Jefferson's own reputation has been challenged. Certainly, it was a society with a double standard. Mrs Chesnut, the wife of a South Carolina planter, could be savage:

Like the patriarchs of old, our men live all in one house with their wives and their concubines; and the mulattoes one sees in every family party resemble the white children. Any lady is ready to tell you who is the father of all the mulatto children in everybody's household but her own. Those, she seems to think, drop from the clouds. [13]

The 1860 census showed that there were 518,000 Negroes of "mixed blood" in the United States, or 1 in 17 of the country's black inhabitants.

In economic as well as human terms, the South was peculiar, and made so by the plantation economy: it was at once a debtor and an expansionist society. The price of cotton was determined by the world market, and most of the American crop was exported. Since the South had no merchant marine of any size, the profits of the carrying trade went to Northern merchants. Manufactured items were imported by Northerners who sold them in the South, reaping the profits of the middlemen. Because of the scarcity of capital and labor there was very little industry in the South; in 1860 the South produced scarcely one-tenth of the amount of cotton manufactures produced by New England. The South blamed its economic troubles on the North and became selfconscious of its minority status; selfconscious, defensive, proud, and afraid.

Controversy is especially acute over the profitability of slavery. By Jefferson's time, slavery in the older planting states, especially in Virginia, where the soil was over-worked, had become less profitable than in the past; but the settlement of the black belt, the Gulf states and the acquisition of the Louisiana Purchase opened up thousands of square miles, fertile and cheap, to cotton culture, and did make it profitable: at least for a time, and depending on the size of the plantation and the skill and luck of managers and overseers. Some scholars are firm that it was profitable, but others differ. To Lewis Gray, and the cliometricians, the former. [14] But Charles Sydnor argues that there was less return on investment in slaves in Mississippi in 1860 than could be obtained from other properties:

---

[13] Mary B. Chesnut, *Diary from Dixie*, ed. T. Williams (Boston, Houghton Mifflin, 1949). Cf. Woodward and Muhlenfeld (eds), *The Private Mary Chesnut*.
[14] Lewis C. Gray, *History of Agriculture in the Southern United States to 1860* (Washington, Carnegie Institution, 1933).

"From an economic standpoint, it is very questionable whether slaves were a good investment year in year out even in Mississippi."[15]

Abolitionist sentiment first blossomed from gradualism to "immediatism" in the North in the 1830s: in Boston, as voiced by Wendell Phillips, "abolition's golden trumpet," by the fanatical though pacific William Lloyd Garrison, editor of the *Liberator* ("harsh as truth, uncompromising as justice"), calling for immediate abolition in the language of an extremist, by ex-slave Frederick Douglass, with his own weekly, the *North Star*, and by David Walker, who was born free in North Carolina, and who preached violence; in New York, where it was led and financed by the wealthy respectable silk-mill owners, Arthur and Lewis Tappan; in Philadelphia, where Lucretia Mott and the wealthy black sailmaker James Forten were among its leaders; and at Oberlin College, Ohio, the first college to admit both blacks and women.[16] It had begun, however, among the Quakers and the men of the Enlightenment in the 1770s; in 1815 Charles Osborn, a Quaker preacher, founded the Tennessee Manumission Society; and in 1819 Elihu Embree began the *Manumission Intelligencer*, renamed the *Emancipator*, in Jonesboro, Tennessee. In 1827 there were over 100 emancipation societies with 5,000 members in the slave states, and only 24 (with 1,475 members) in the free states. The Abolitionists were especially active in organizing slave escape routes – the so-called Underground Railroad – and in trying to thwart the South's call for ever tighter fugitive slave laws. The Fugitive Slave Law of 1850 was a great irritant in the Northern towns. Although there were in fact only a dozen prosecutions under the Act in the 14 years of its existence (some of them including a number of dependents), mobs appeared to free the captured fugitive, and it sometimes required – as in Boston in 1850 – martial law and troops to escort him back to slavery. One Virginian slave-owner complained in 1859 that it cost him more than 600 dollars to recover a fugitive from Ohio. Another Virginian lost his life to a mob

---

[15] Charles S. Sydnor, *Slavery in Mississippi* (New York, D. Appleton, 1933), p. 200; cf. Ralph Flanders, *Plantation Slavery in Georgia* (Chapel Hill, NC, University of North Carolina Press, 1933), pp. 299–300; and Stanley Elkins, *Slavery: A problem in American institutional and intellectual life* (Chicago, University of Chicago Press, 1959), Appendix B.

[16] For a vivid description of the hiding of a runaway by a professor there, of his "rescue" by his Kentucky owners, and of his liberation by an angry mob, see Nat Brandt, *The Town that Started the Civil War* (New York, Syracuse University Press, 1990).

in Pennsylvania when he was attempting to return several slaves to his plantation.

The American Anti-Slavery Society was founded by Theodore Weld in 1833; within a decade it had a team of 70 lecturers spreading the gospel, with 200,000 members in 2,000 branches. His *American Slavery As It Is* (published in 1839) is a carefully documented collection of documents that stressed the brutality of slavery; it was compiled from statistics and from scores of Southern newspapers, mainly by the Grimke sisters of Charleston (one of whom, Angelina, Weld married), and was probably the most powerful anti-slavery tract ever published. From it Harriet Beecher Stowe drew some of her ideas. Over the years 1836–44 anti-slave petitions poured in on the House of Representatives. Indignant Southerners then secured the passage of the "gag rule," which specified that such petitions be laid on the table without debate or other consideration (1836). Ex-President John Quincy Adams, now an anti-slavery Congressman, protested that this violated the constitutional right of petition (the First Amendment to the Constitution.) In 1840 anti-slavery leaders founded the Liberty party, which put its chief emphasis on restriction of slavery in the territories. Its presidential candidate, James G. Birney, was a former Alabama slaveholder converted by Weld. Slavery was inconsistent, he became convinced, with "the Great Truth that all men are created equal ... as well as the great rule of benevolence delivered to us by The Savior Himself that in all things whatsoever ye would that men should do unto you do ye even so to them."[17] In 1840 he polled only 7,000 votes, but in 1844 his vote rose to 60,000. An anti-slavery party contested every election until 1860 when Lincoln was elected. By 1850 the movement was militant, its language that of fire and brimstone; it demanded immediate abolition of slavery without any compensation to slave-owners; and Northern businessmen were ready to support a cause that would destroy the competition of the slave-powered Southern economy. As Fanny Wright put it, as early as 1829, "Hatred of the planter seemed oftentimes to be a stronger feeling than interest in the slave." So much so that Weld, the ablest organizer of them all, in the end withdrew from the movement.

In 1853 Harriet Beecher Stowe, daughter of one fire-eating Evangelical reformer and married to another, wrote *Uncle Tom's Cabin*. It sold 300,000 copies in the first year, and was translated into 37 languages. Here were, for all to see, the archetypical figures: the

---

[17] Betty Fladeland, *James Gillespie Birney: Slaveholder to abolitionist* (Ithaca, NY, Cornell University Press, 1955), p. 83.

sadistic planter, Simon Legree (born a Yankee, as it happened), the superhumanly patient and forgiving Uncle Tom – whom Dickens called "an impossible piece of ebony perfection" – and little Eva, the quintessence of sentiment. The book made a fortune, on which its author bought a plantation in Florida (where she lived after the War); and its popularity – so Charles Sumner said – ensured Lincoln's election; Lincoln himself described it as "the book that made the war." The reform movement of the North used pamphlets, platforms, petitions – and pulpits; it introduced the words "right" and "wrong;" being distant, and bred on Calvinism, it could afford the indulgence of moralism. The South was made to feel guilty – and guilty of what, in a North now dominated by a popular press written for a more-and-more literate and more-and-more racially mixed and immigrant society, could appear as the race prejudice of whites. That came, of course, before abolitionism, with the first colonists; it was made to appear now as the second sin of Adam.[18]

In the South, in rebuttal, a bitter defensive psychology grew. John C. Calhoun, the "Puritan apostle of slavery," proclaimed that slavery was "a positive good," declaring that inequality of status was a spur to progress, and maintaining that under the slave system the interests of capital and labor were united in the master; he drew a caustic comparison between the amenities of Southern slavery and the harsh conditions of "factory niggers" under Northern industrialism. His arguments and justifications were more sophisticated – and, it could be claimed more intriguing, even more relevant? – than the simpler emotionalisms of the abolitionists. Indeed, Calhoun's indictment of class conflict, wage slavery, and the evils of industrialism have led some to see him as Karl Marx before Marx. He was the philosopher of states' rights, and perhaps the United States' only true philosopher of conservatism: he recognized, like Edmund Burke, that the strength of national identity lay in loyalty to "the little platoon you belong to." Aristides, perhaps? Or Cato? He was certainly also a Jeremiah turned Cassandra.

The War Hawk and anti-British nationalist of 1812 had, by the time of his death 38 years later, become the leading sectionalist. Indeed, just before he died, in March 1850, as the Compromise of that year was being planned, he predicted the dissolution of the Union: "I fix its probable occurrence within twelve years or three presidential terms. The mode by which it will be done is not so clear; it may be brought about in a manner that no one now foresees. But the probability is, it will explode in a presidential election."

---

[18] Jordan, *White over Black*.

Unlike John Taylor of Carolina, Calhoun was more than an agrarian radical seeking to put the clock back. He was a skillful and experienced politician. He held every important office except the presidency: Congressman (chairman of the Foreign Relations Committee), secretary of war (under Monroe), Vice-President (under both Adams and Jackson), Senator, and secretary of state (under Tyler). As a politician, he was vastly more effective in South Carolina than elsewhere. He was one of the sponsors of the re-chartering of the Bank of the United States, and unlike many of his Southern contemporaries he never came to doubt the Bank's constitutionality. Again, he favored federal power to promote internal improvements. What he objected to was the use of federal power to benefit exclusively one part of the nation. Had he not been so intense a Southerner, and so protective a sectionalist, he might have seen that there was an alternative strategy, of an alliance of the conservative and large-propertied interests on either side, of Southern cotton producers and Northern cotton manufacturers, of those whom Charles Sumner called "the lords of the lash and the lords of the loom." His first major piece of writing was published anonymously, *The South Carolina Exposition* (1828), a criticism of the inequities of the tariff. He believed, however, that sectional reciprocity was lacking. His hostility to the Northern policies of high tariffs, and his view of the need to protect the slave society of the South, produced his two famous tracts, *The Disquisition on Government* and the *Discourse on the Constitution and Government of the United States*, published after his death in 1850. Calhoun recognized that the (white) South was a minority, and his preoccupation was with the political devices to protect a minority in the nation from the powers (and potential tyranny) of the majority. It is no small irony that the same problem has been a major issue on the national agenda in this last half-century, once in the late 1950s with conservative Southerners still hostile to the claims of black Americans, but more frequently with the Supreme Court using its powers to protect a vastly different minority than that that Calhoun had in mind.

Calhoun had already in 1832 brought forward one ultimate argument, nullification. This was an extension of the ideas expressed in the Virginia and Kentucky Resolutions of 1798. Here Calhoun used the standard states' rights argument: in organizing the US in 1787, the independent states had delegated certain powers to the federal government, but had not surrendered their sovereignty. There could therefore be no such thing as an "implied power" in what the Founders had set up in 1787. The states, which had given the central government its authority, had the sole right to determine

the constitutionality of federal Acts; the Supreme Court, as a creature of the federal government, could have no such function. According to the theory of Nullification, if the federal government
should pass an Act which was regarded by a state as unconstitutional, the state would call a convention representing the sovereign
will of its people. Should the convention delegates decide that the
Act was unconstitutional, they would declare it null and void, and
of no effect within the limits of the state. If the federal government
should resort to coercion, the state would be warranted in seceding
from the Union. In the face of a nullifying ordinance by a state,
the federal government might do one of two things: repeal the
objectionable law, or submit a constitutional amendment to the
states, embodying the authority necessary to enact such a law. (Since
the South represented more than one fourth of the states, it could
block the ratification of any objectionable amendment.) To the
doubts over the "workability" of Nullification, Calhoun responded
as politician: the very process of Nullification, and its availability
as an ultimate remedy, would provide the atmosphere, and the
psychology, of compromise.

Calhoun's speeches in the Senate in December 1837 and January
1838, in clarification of his *Resolutions*, reveal the Madisonian
depth of his thinking; the central thesis remains, that "the States
retained, severally, the exclusive and sole right over their own domestic institutions and police, and are alone responsible for them."
To this, Calhoun now added another doctrine. He agreed that in a
democracy there is a danger that the majority will tyrannize the
minorities. To protect the planter minority, he proposed that federal
laws should be passed not by a simple majority of all the members
in Congress, but by a concurrent majority – a majority of the
Southern legislators and a majority of legislators from the non-
slave states. The "concurrent" or "constitutional" majority regards
"interests" as well as "numbers," and acts as a "cease-and-desist"
order by aggrieved minorities. To him vetoes, interpositions, nulli-
fications, balances of power, were all part of the constitutional process. By this device, only those bills which were beneficial to the
whole country would become law.[19]

[19] The states' rights view was at the center of the thinking of Alexander Stephens
of Georgia, vice-president of the Confederacy and the architect of its Constitution; see his retrospective *A Constitutional View of the Late War Between the
States*, written (2 vols) in 1867 and 1870. See also Edmund Wilson, *Patriotic Gore:
Studies in the literature of the American Civil War* (New York, Oxford University
Press, 1962), pp. 395–437. Calhoun's career has been thoroughly explored: crit-
ically by Richard Current, seeing him as "philosopher of reaction," favorably by

Calhoun as a politician was aware of the need to hold his own troops in line. In the 1820s there were more anti-slavery societies in the South than in the North. Indeed, the first systematic reasoned – and temperate – argument in defense of slavery came in 1832 from Professor Thomas R. Dew of William and Mary College, addressing a group of Virginian legislators who had proposed compensated emancipation and the deportation back to Africa of free Negroes. The debate on slavery in the Virginia legislature in the winter of 1831–2, triggered by Nat Turner's rebellion, was the fullest debate on the subject in the Old South: the moment when a great reaction began, and a series of doctrinal defenses for the system were generated. Emigration, Dew argued, would cost too much; and cotton demanded more slaves, not fewer. The line between North and South, however, was not always clearly drawn: as in 1776, this was a brother's, or at least, a cousin's war. And until the 1830s there were many abolitionist groups in the Upper South, and some 300 in the South as a whole. In his last years Calhoun was even driven to question the principle of majority government itself. He proposed a dual-executive system for the US: one president from the North, one from the South, with the assent of both to be required before any Act of Congress could become law. Professor Dew was not a greatly troubled apologist. But he wrote:

A merrier being does not exist on the face of the globe, than the negro slave of the U. States. Let the wily philanthropist but come and whisper into the ears of such a slave that his situation is degrading and his lot a miserable one ... and that moment, like the serpent that entered the garden of Eden, he destroys his happiness and his usefulness.

By the emancipationists in the Virginia legislature, as elsewhere, Dew was alarmed:

Charles Wiltse's 3-vol. study (Indianapolis, Bobbs-Merrill, 1944–51), and by Margaret Coit's single-volume study (Boston, Houghton Mifflin, 1950); and with unusual detachment by John Niven of the Claremont Graduate School in his *John C. Calhoun and the Price of Union* (Baton Rouge, Louisiana State University, 1988). For an inclusive and varied view, see John Taylor (ed.), *John C. Calhoun: A profile* (New York, Hill and Wang, 1968); and for an especially stimulating one, Richard Hofstadter, "John C. Calhoun: Marx of the master class," in his *The American Political Tradition and the Men Who Made It* (New York, Knopf, 1948).

They are admirably calculated to excite plots, their murders and insurrections; whether gradual or rapid in their operation, this is the inevitable
tendency.[20]

And in 1837 William Gilmore Simms insisted:

Perhaps there is nothing in the world that the people of the South less
apprehend, than ... the insurrection of their negroes. The attempts of this
people at this object have been singularly infrequent, and perhaps never
would be dreamed of, were their bad passions not appealed to by the
abolitionists or their emissaries. They are not a warlike people; are, indeed,
rather a timid race. ...[21]

Simms was out of date. Southern nationalism was evident in the
change of view of Calhoun, and in the narrow defeat in the Virginia legislature of the bill for the gradual extinction of slavery in
1832 – west of the Blue Ridge voting solidly Aye, the east equally
solidly No. If the new "Southernism" had identifiable parents, they
were Garrison's vehement language in his journal the *Liberator*, and
Nat Turner's insurrection in 1831, in which over 100 died – the
one seen as the "trigger" for the other.

As abolitionist criticism grew, the constitutional proposals and
persuasions of Calhoun were buttressed by older and more emotional
arguments. They drew on many roots. Historically, it was argued
that every superior civilization had been based on slavery, which
freed the upper classes for intellectual activity; Aristotle and Burke
were drawn on, to buttress the case for order in society. Various
"scientific" evidences were cited to show that the Negroes were
an inferior race, whose natural and logical status was slavery. By
virtue of their white skins, even the lowliest of the non-slaveholding
Southerners were thus superior to the Negroes, and slavery served
to keep an inferior caste in its place. George Fitzhugh's *Sociology
for the South* and his *Cannibals All!* were lawyer-journalist's apo-
logies for slavery, and for authority and hierarchy as more "natural"
than liberty, and important glosses on Jefferson's Declaration of
1776 – "Men are not born physically, morally, or intellectually equal
... their natural inequalities beget inequalities of rights." ... "It would

---

[20] "Professor Dew on Slavery," reprint of Dew's *Review of the Debate in the
Virginia Legislature of 1831 and 1832*, in Tise, *Proslavery*, pp. 70–1, 388.
[21] "The Morals of Slavery," in ibid., p. 344. Simms, novelist and *littérateur* of
Charleston, edited the *Southern Quarterly Review*. This essay originally appeared
in the *Southern Literary Messenger* in 1837 as a review of, and attack on, the
writings of Harriet Martineau and others.

be far nearer the truth to say that some were born with saddles on their backs, and others booted and spurred to ride them – and the riding does them good." Fitzhugh and Henry Hughes both use Auguste Comte's newly-coined word "sociology" – and the latter's style show how early the new word produced its own jargon. The Bible, too, was cited in justification of slavery, notably by Reverend Thornton Stringfellow of Culpeper, Virginia.

There were texts galore to draw on: were not the black races sons of Ham, cursed by Noah? A considerable number of pro-slave defenders were ministers of religion in the Border states and the North, who found their views no obstacle to advancement to college presidencies. More than this, it was contended that the institution had been the means of civilizing and Christianizing the natives of darkest Africa. They were obviously better off in North America than in Africa. There was the recurring and persuasive argument that living conditions among the Negroes were superior to those of the white factory workers, who were being exploited as "factory niggers" by the "wage slavery" of the North. The Yankee mill-owner degraded people of his own race and culture. "Why, you meet more beggars in one day in any single street of the city of New York," said Governor Hammond of South Carolina, "than you would meet in a lifetime in the whole South." It was not, indeed, difficult for Fitzhugh and Dew, for George Frederick Holmes and Henry Hughes, to make a case that outright lifetime bondage in a paternalist society was the humane and rational solution for the subordinated orders. Again, energetic yeomen farmers could rise to membership in the planter aristocracy; hence it was in the interest of the Southern farmers to defend rather than attack slavery. Calhoun could defend slavery in terms of egalitarian ideals: "With us the two great divisions of society are not the rich and poor, but white and black; and all the former, the poor as well as the rich, belong to the upper classes, and are respected and treated as equals." The abolition of slavery would, again, place the white farmers in competition with 4,000,000 freedmen. And world trade itself upheld slavery, for Cotton was King, not only in the South but in Lancashire, England, with mills in endless need of the major Southern crop. To cotton and to slavery the South attributed its prosperity, and its gracious living. By 1860 it produced three-quarters of the world's cotton, and employed 3 out of every 4 negroes in the US to grow it. On the masthead of his New Orleans journal, *De Bow's Review*, the editor James Dunwoody Brownson De Bow proudly and repeatedly proclaimed that Cotton was King. Mary Eastman in *Aunt Phillis's Cabin or Southern Life As It Is*, a reply to Harriet Beecher Stowe, wrote that slavery was "Authorized by God, permitted by Jesus Christ, sanctioned by the apostles ... and by good men of all ages." Basic to all the references was the conviction that the black was not only different from, but inferior to, the white. Jefferson said so himself, as a "surmise":

Blacks whether originally a distinct race, or made distinct by time and circumstances, are inferior to the whites, in the endowments both of body and mind.

And so even did Lincoln, who at one point came close to apartheid:

Your race suffers greatly, many of them by living among us, while ours suffers from your presence. In a word, we suffer on each side. If this is admitted, it affords a reason why we should be separated.

There grew up a dangerous romanticism in the South — what Mark Twain called "The Sir Walter Scott disease of chivalry," with high-flown lyricism about the "South" and the code of honor, with tournaments, dueling, and the exaltation of the military. Indeed, some of the Civil War characters step out of an almost fictional Dixie, with almost fictional names; the impulsive and argumentative Pierre Gustave Toutant Beauregard, the Creole-born superintendent of West Point who left it to join the South, and under whose orders the first gun was fired against Fort Sumter; the lawyer-turned CSA officer Lucius Quintus Cincinnatus Lamar who, in fact, always opposed secession; the tall, bearded Louisiana planter-turned-general Braxton Bragg, who made many more enemies than friends on both sides of the divide; and the fighting bishop-turned-general Leonidas Polk, the founder of the University of the South at Sewanee, and a friend and West Point classmate of Jefferson Davis; he was killed at Pine Mountain during the Atlanta campaign in June 1864, when he was 58.

Contemporary British visitors were both appalled and fascinated by the South. Mrs Trollope found it bewildering:

I had indeed, frequent opportunities of observing this habitual indifference to the presence of their slaves. They talk of them, of their condition, of their conduct, exactly as if they were incapable of hearing. I once saw a young lady, who, when seated at table between a male and a female, was induced by her modesty to intrude on the chair of her female neighbour to avoid the indelicacy of touching the elbow of *a man*. I once saw this very young lady lacing her stays with the most perfect composure before a negro footman. A Virginian gentleman told me that ever since he had married, he had been accustomed to have a negro girl sleep in the same chamber with himself and his wife. I asked for what purpose this nocturnal attendance was necessary: 'Good heavens!' was the reply, 'if I wanted a glass of water during the night, what would become of me?'"

Dickens wrote in scathing terms of slavery and much else ("Washington may be called the headquarters of tobacco-tinctured saliva"), and detected an "air of ruin and decay wherever slavery sits brooding;" he visited the US in 1842, and was fêted in (and therefore impressed by) Harvard and Yale; for the rest he was disenchanted. In *American Notes* he drew heavily on Weld's compilation, *American Slavery As It Is*, though without acknowledgment, supplemented by his own recollections of Washington, Richmond, St Louis, and Pittsburgh. William Makepeace Thackeray, who visited Virginia in 1853, drew quite a different impression, and noted:

Of course, we feel the cruelty of flogging and enslaving a Negro — of course they [the Virginians] feel here the cruelty of starving an English labourer, or driving an English child to a mine — Brother, Brother, we are kin.

In law, this system altered in 1863, when, by his Emancipation Proclamation, President Lincoln freed the slaves in those states that were at war, or which, in his view, were in a condition of civil rebellion against what he saw as the legitimate government of the United States. The Union Army, sometimes in despite of itself, liberated the slaves, and in the end 186,000 blacks, many of them just out of slavery, joined it. In July 1861, in the person of the egregious John C. Fremont, the pathfinder of the Rockies, the liberation of the slaves was premature, and became almost hilarious. Appointed a major-general, as commander of the newly created Western District, he brought his drama with him — as with his whole career — to the delicate politics of largely German-American St Louis, Missouri. Having been the Republican party candidate for President in 1856, he thought he had authority to award contracts — often to dishonest contractors; he surrounded himself with a motley collection of gaudily-attired staff officers, many of them German-Americans or Hungarian-Americans; he won no battle; and he declared all slaves in his District free. When Lincoln rescinded the order as — at least — premature, and dismissed him, he posted guards to prevent these instructions reaching him; and he sent his wife, the formidable Jessica Benton Fremont, to Washington to plead — and further harm — his cause. From June 1862 he spent the war "awaiting orders;" the war was won without him. T. Harry

Williams is generous, in his *Lincoln and his Generals*, in describing him as "sincere and attractive," "giddy and fumbling," but he adds that in Missouri, Lincoln "had sent a boy to do a man's work."[22]

In 1865, the 13th, 14th and 15th Amendments to the Constitution translated victory into law. In form, slavery no longer existed. But then, as now, the laws go but a little way. The slave remained desperately poor, and needed employment, if he was capable of it. The master lost his labor force, and got no compensation for his loss of his property. And the evidence of history was partisan, and mainly oral. Historians of slavery face vast difficulties: in 1865, and still. There is not a single slave diary as such; and letters written by slaves obviously were rare – more than 90 percent of them were illiterate. Frederick Douglass's *My Bondage and My Freedom* (1855) is an unusual, almost unique, piece of autobiography. Or, more accurately, one of three autobiographies. In itself it becomes the microcosm of the blacks' struggle for freedom: born on the eastern shore of Maryland, son of a white master and a slave mother, he took a different surname to show his distinctness (using the name of Walter Scott's hero in *The Lady of the Lake*); an escapee who learnt to read and write, he became one of the most eloquent and active propagandists in the abolitionist cause, from a base in upstate New York. There are two other useful narratives: David Wilson (ed.), *Narrative of Solomon Northrup* (1853), and Kate E. R. Pickard, *The Kidnapped and the Ransomed, being the Personal Recollections of Peter Still and his Wife, Vina, after Forty Years of Slavery* (1856). Almost all such narratives, as with the tales of Solomon Northrup (actually a New York freeman kidnapped and sold to the sugarcane horrors of Louisiana), of Henry "Box" Brown, and of *J. Henson, Formerly a Slave* (1849), were edited by abolitionists. "Box" Brown earned his name, since his journey to freedom from Richmond was made nailed up inside a packing case 3 feet long, 2 feet wide and 2 feet 6 inches deep, which – despite the instructions on the lid – was loaded upsidedown; he survived a journey lasting 3 days to Philadelphia; and Henson – or was this an editorial gloss? – was said to be the original "Uncle Tom." The bulk of the vast literature

---

[22] Frances Trollope, *Domestic Manners of the Americans* (1832; New York, Knopf Vintage, 1949), pp. 250, 271; Clement Eaton, *Freedom of Thought in the Old South* (Durham, Duke University Press, 1940); Joseph Dorfman, *The Economic Mind in American Civilization 1606–1865* (New York, Viking, 1946), vol. II, pp. 881–956; Charles Dickens, *American Notes* (1842; London, Macmillan, 1925), pp. 98, 116; Michael Slater (ed.), *Dickens on America and the Americans* (Brighton, Harvester Press, 1979); T. Harry Williams, *Lincoln and his Generals* (New York, McGraw Hill, 1967).

is thus on the other side — in defense of the institution. Variety of view, therefore, of the Negro "personality" is hardly surprising; some historians simply contradict each other. The Marxist Herbert Aptheker claims that rebelliousness was common among, "even characteristic" of, Negro slaves; Elkins disagrees: the majority of them were "not rebels but Sambos," i.e. docile, loyal but lazy, addicted to lying and stealing, and to acting as children. The laws treated them as property. Moreover, slavery was a "closed system," that gave them no chance of escape and offered limited contact with white society, and no prospect of ever becoming part of it. The peculiar institution was also a paradoxical institution:

Slaveholders who considered Afro-Americans to be little more than sub-human chattels converted them to a religion which stressed their humanity and even their divinity. Masters who desired and expected their slaves to act like dependent children also enjoined them to behave like mature, responsible adults ... Whites who considered their black servants to be little more than barbarians, bereft of any culture worth the name, paid a fascinated and flattering attention to their song, their dance, their tales, and their form of religious exercise. The life of every slave could be altered by the most arbitrary and amoral acts. They could be whipped, sexually assaulted, ripped out of societies in which they had deep roots, and bartered away for pecuniary profit by men and women who were also capable of treating them with kindness and consideration and who professed belief in a moral code which they held up for emulation not only by their children but often by their slaves as well.[23]

To this, yet another paradox has to be added. In Virginia, the state that became the chief battleground of the War, and suffered the greatest devastation, three-quarters of all its white inhabitants owned no slaves. Lee called it a "moral and political evil," and had long before 1861 emancipated the slaves that he inherited from his mother. "Stonewall" Jackson owned two, both of whom he purchased at their own request; to both of them he accorded the right to buy their freedom, one of whom accepted; the other chose to remain as his house servant. A. P. Hill and Joseph E. Johnston never owned a slave, and each was strongly opposed to slavery. J. E. B. Stuart inherited one and purchased one, but gave them both their freedom several years before the War. The leading Virginian soldiers were neither slaveholders, nor defenders of the institution.

[23] Lawrence W. Levine, *Black Culture and Black Consciousness: Afro-American folk thought from slavery to freedom* (New York, Oxford University Press, 1977), p. 114.

2   INTERPRETATIONS

The civil rights campaign that dominated American politics after 1954 has transformed the views of the 1850s. A century and a half ago slaves were seen primarily as but a form of property, and the laws and customs of the day enforced that view. Today's emphases are on the "rights" of the African Americans, and thus on the moral, human, and emotional problems of the lives of slaves – and free-men. In the wake of this profound social revolution, which some have labelled "Reconstruction II," the history of the years before the coming of the Civil War has been itself rewritten in an unprecedented outpouring of scholarship. The historians of these years have seen themselves as the keepers of the nation's conscience, aware that for many Americans, the promise of freedom made in 1776 had been unfulfilled. Sociologists have been similarly preoccupied with the issue of race prejudice. The slave was too easy to identify, since he was identified by his color; was the barrier against him his status as unfree, or – more disturbing – the color of his skin, and the awareness of racial difference? Each study of this theme, of which there have been many, has tried to be more anti-racist than its predecessors. Progressives and left-inclined scholars, seeing slavery as peripheral to the major forces of class war and collective-versus-individual themes, have eagerly explored the slave's eye view of history. In their contemporary anxieties over black–white tensions and in their "presentism," all have minimized, or even forgotten, that seen in the long view it is not slavery but free labor that is the peculiar institution: since time began the vast majority of mankind have worked under compulsion – as victims of war, status, or debt, or under many forms of fear.

When, after World War II, a new generation of historians examined the ante-bellum South and slavery, they had one book as a target for attack. The Southerner, Ulrich B. Phillips, the first to base his research on actual plantation records, thought the system inefficient and uneconomical, but he saw the black as childlike, and emphasized the general and paternal side of an economically unprofitable regime. The cost of newborn pickaninnies, as of super-annuates, had simply to be added to the master's bill. To Phillips, the Tuckahoes of the Tidewater outmatched the Cohees of the Valley; the aristos knew and worked and loved the land, but were not of the earth, earthy; they were strong on their awareness of cousinhood and kinship, but hospitable to all who passed. He recognized that as the cotton culture spread to the deep alluvial, because largely tideless, deltas of the Gulf, the "society" of New Orleans was shoddier than that of Richmond or Charleston; Caesar and Cicero were more likely to be the names of Negroes in the yard than of authors on the shelves; and if there were revolts (the 1739 Stono revolt, 1800 Gabriel's uprising, 1822 Denmark Vesey's, 1831 Nat Turner's), they were strikingly few. There may have been "injustice, oppression, brutality and heartburning," but there was also "gentleness, kind-hearted friendship and mutual loyalty – to a degree hard for him to believe, who regards the system with a theorist's eye and a partisan squint. ... On the whole the plantations were the best schools yet invented for the mass training of that sort of inert and backward people which the bulk of the American negroes represented."[24]

In the era of the Progressives, in the first quarter of the twentieth century, and despite all their social liberalism, the black was seen as inferior, the Civil War as a mistaken product of Southern fire-eaters and Northern abolitionists. Historians were aware of "Jim Crow," even though such segregation was product of the 1890s, not of the 1850s. Much of this comes through in the classic silent film-making of D. W. Griffith, notably in *Birth of a Nation*. But in Kenneth Stampp's *The Peculiar Institution*, published in 1952, a book that re-worked the material used by Phillips, a new view appeared. Slavery was neither a charitable enterprise nor a viable educational system, but a harsh and highly profitable labor system, that survived because it made money. And its profits were due to its major features: the price of slaves, their longevity and long working hours, their natural increase, the price of the product, and the returns on alternative investments. Stampp argued that the slaves were ordinary human beings, "white men with black skins," and it was the nature of slavery that forced humane people, the slave-masters and overseers, to be cruel; if a slave-owner's profits demanded it, he would enforce discipline and instill subordination. Some owners lived happily alongside their slaves, others indulged their sadism. Slavery was resented by blacks, and they struck back. Although murder of slaves was murder, and state laws forbade excessive punishments, nevertheless no slave or freed slave could testify against his master, and

[24] Ulrich B. Phillips, *Life and Labor in the Old South* (Boston, Little, Brown, 1929), and his *American Negro Slavery* (1918, repr. New York, Peter Smith, 1959). For assessment of Phillips's slave writings, see Eugene Genovese, *In Red and Black: Marxian Explorations in Southern and Afro-American History* (2nd edn, Nashville, University of Tennessee Press, 1984), pp. 345–58; and A. Winkler, "Ulrich Bonnel Phillips: a re-appraisal," *South Atlantic Quarterly*, 81 (1972), pp. 234–45.

deaths from "moderate" punishment did not count as "murder." The Southerners became the victims of their own "peculiar institution;" and they did not need it – since the plantation preceded slavery, and continued after its abolition. Nevertheless, it was a many-sided system: white men did perform much of the South's heavy agricultural labour – and many Southern women worked in the fields. Stanley Elkins took a different view; whereas Stampp stressed the anger and rage of the slave, Elkins saw his dependence, his passivity, and his acquiescence; he became a "Sambo," child-like and irresponsible; his protests were not revolts but "go-slows," his attitudes luddite. Elkins goes so far as to compare the place of blacks in the plantations of the South with that of Jews in Nazi death camps – and holds that the impact on their personalities was likely to be similar. In the writing of Stampp and of Elkins, there is thus a new realism in the view of slavery.[25]

What have been the main emphases of this re-writing? First, there has been an attempt to give a slave's-eye view, to portray the reality of the lives lived by the slaves, a nation within a nation, with a distinct Afro-American, rather than African, subculture. The slave accommodated himself to living in two worlds, at once both an accommodator and a rebel; if he was seen as "Sambo," then Sambo he would be – he would be happy to be "puttin' on ole massa;" house servants in particular had loyalties both to the Big House and the slave quarters. If he played the part of Sambo, he played other parts at other times. Those in between master and serf – the foremen of the slave gang, the mammy with a large family who might be nurse, even wet nurse, to the master's children – played crucial roles, and wielded much authority. Slavery was always a spectrum, ranging from the ruthless to the benign. It compelled the slave-owner also to living in two worlds: if his attitude was complaisant to the work done in the fields he courted financial failure, and thus to selling his slaves to meet his debts. The skillful master was he who knew when to crack the whip – or, more accurately, when to get his driver to do it for him. And as Frederick Douglass noted, "he who was whipped oftener was whipped easiest."[26] Planter paternalism not only adjusted to the slaves as human beings, when it came to such matters as work rhythms, the cultivation of their own

[25] Kenneth Stampp, *The Peculiar Institution: Slavery in the ante-bellum South* (New York, Knopf, 1956), pp. 383–418; Elkins, *Slavery*; Harold D. Woodman, "The profitability of slavery – a historical perennial," *Journal of Southern History*, 39 (Aug. 1963), pp. 308–25.

[26] Frederick Douglass, *Life and Times* (1881), p. 62.

gardens, and their familial relationships, but usually permitted the slaves enough autonomy — such as allowing them to meet together alone even when laws forbade this — to enable them to develop their own culture and community. Around the Big House they could be skilled craftsmen. There was a sense of solidarity among the slaves — even between field hands and house servants — and the black bondsmen developed a "world view" that was no imitation of the white man's. And as their spirituals testified, the outgoing emotional and often explosive Christianity of the slaves on the one hand strengthened their ties to their "white folks," and voiced humility, but also strengthened their love for each other, their sense of community, and their pride in being black people. It expressed joy in the coming of the promised land; not for it the sophistications of guilt or shame. In their rich oral culture, their faith drew sustenance from magic, from songs and spirituals, and not least from the trickster tales in which the weak outwit the strong. If they had a recurring folk-hero, it was Brer Rabbit, or Anansi the spider. In their sacred world-view there was a fusion: the concepts of Moses, who led a people to freedom, and of Jesus, who suffered on behalf of all mankind, became intertwined, with the result that "the slaves transformed the promise of personalized redemption ... into the promise of deliverance as a people in this world as well as the next."[27] From their pulpits would come their political leaders in the twentieth century.

Secondly, and somewhat in contradiction, the cliometricians have moved in, led by Robert W. Fogel and Stanley L. Engerman, whose work one historian, William N. Parker, called "the *Das Kapital* of the literature on American Negro Slavery." For them, history is, first and last, a quantitative science, and its major tool economic statistics; their concern is less with the slave than with the institution of slavery and its profitability. They contend that plantation slavery was the most efficient form of agriculture and the most profitable investment in the US, that slave farms were more efficient than Northern, and that blacks as well as whites benefited materially from it.

---

[27] Eugene Genovese, *Roll Jordan Roll* (New York, Pantheon, 1974), p. 660. Other writers who explore this slave subculture are John W. Blassingame, *The Slave Community: Plantation life in the ante-bellum South* (New York, Oxford University Press, 1972), and (ed.), *Slave Testimony* (Baton Rouge, Louisiana State University Press, 1977); Herbert Gutman, *The Black Family in Slavery and Freedom* (Oxford, Blackwell, 1977); and Leonard Levine, *Black Culture and Black Consciousness* (New York, Oxford University Press, 1977).

Black slaves were the first group of workers to be trained in the work
rhythms which later became characteristic of industrial society ... Black
plantation agriculturalists labored under a regimen that was more like a
modern assembly line than ... many of the factories of the antibellum
era.

The large slave plantation was, in essence, a factory in a field.
Southern agriculture as a whole was about 35 percent more efficient
than Northern agriculture in 1860. The large slave plantations of the
Old South, producing cotton, tobacco, and sugar, exceeded the efficiency of free Northern farms by 19 percent, while the slave plantations of the newer Southern states exceeded the average efficiency of
free Northern farms by 53 percent. The South was richer than any
of the countries of Europe except England. Only Sweden and Japan
have been able to sustain long-term growth rates substantially in
excess of that achieved by the ante-bellum South between 1840 and
1860.[28]

On this basis, the authors dispute the notion that slavery left
blacks crippled intellectually and culturally. On the contrary, they
say, slavery succeeded economically because the slaves developed a
high level of skill; they worked at least as hard as free farmers and
ate well; they maintained stable family lives and even prudish sexual
mores; and they were whipped only enough to maintain production,
not excessively or out of sheer cruelty; they had distinct "career
prospects" of rising to become craftsmen, or drivers. The implication
is that the destabilization of the black family, and the absence of
a father-figure, so often cited as the cause of black troubles today,
occurred in the post-Civil War period, especially during the Depression of the 1930s; and that therefore the blame for today's race
tensions cannot be consigned to the small Southern aristocracy of
a century and a half ago. However, after Emancipation, whites
had no interest in the profitable employment of Negroes, who were
accordingly squeezed out into the most menial and unskilled jobs.
It follows that the caste system of twentieth-century America, especially the deterioration of the African-American family, is the legacy,
not of slavery, but of Emancipation, or of the Progressive period
of the 1890s which, equally paradoxically, bred "Jim Crow" and

[28] Robert W. Fogel and Stanley L. Engerman, *Time on the Cross* (Boston, Little,
Brown, 1974), vol. I, *The Economics of American Negro Slavery*, vol. II, *Evidence
and Methods: A supplement.* For a rebuttal of *Time on the Cross*, see Herbert
Gutman and Richard Sutch, *Reckoning with Slavery* (New York, Oxford University
Press, 1976), esp. pp. 55–93.

segregation.[29] That the book has been savaged by critics, does not weaken its impact. Even the critics agree that the life expectancy of a slave at birth was 12 years longer than that of a child born in Northern cities in 1830 – or in Manchester, England, in 1850; that slave population was doubling every 20 years; and that some 12 percent were skilled craftsmen and 7 percent occupied foremen or managerial jobs. Slave degradation and suffering were probably more psychological than physical. The brutal economic facts were, however, that, certainly on the large plantations, they worked longer hours for less pay than in a free society – the result of rationalized rhythms of field work and of a wide spectrum of inducements, only rarely calling for the whip.[30]

And, as a third theme, there has been much analysis of the pro-slavery arguments used in self-defense by the South. It is clear now that there was a traditional body of relatively standardized pro-slavery arguments based on concepts of black racial inferiority, on interpretations of the Bible, and on the economic benefits of slavery for whites and slaves. These doctrines were not original to Americans. Almost every pro-slavery argument, including the supposedly uniquely Southern "positive good" theory, was elaborated by British and West Indian authors in the eighteenth and early nineteenth centuries. Indeed, the defense of slavery had its origins in the admiration of classical republics that was one by-product of the American struggle for Independence. Although many of these writers viewed slavery as an evil, their doctrine of an ordered society and the superiority of classical republics logically led to an acceptance of slavery, since the classical republics were based on it. When the abolitionist crusade appeared a danger after 1835, Southern proponents of slavery were intellectually ill-equipped, and they had to be aroused by a Burkean federalist advocacy of slave-holding, a conservative, hierarchical social system. The defense of slavery in fact owed more to Northern than Southern influences. Two hundred and seventy-five clergy wrote pro-slavery tracts; and roughly half of them were educated in Congregational or Presbyterian colleges and seminaries with impeccable Yankee origins or influences. The defense of slavery was based on a nationally held body of ideas which Larry Tise labels "conservative republicanism." Philosophically, the South was part of the Union.[31]

---

[29] C. Vann Woodward, *The Strange Career of Jim Crow* (New York, Oxford University Press, 1955), pp. 13–95.
[30] Herbert Gutman, *Slavery and the Numbers Game* (Urbana, University of Illinois Press, 1975); for the "profitability "argument, see also Elkins, *Slavery*, Appendix B.
[31] Tise, *Proslavery*; William J. Cooper, *The South and the politics of Slavery*

A fourth emphasis in recent scholarship can be detected, an awareness that all situations involving human relations are psychological rather than objective and factual, matters not only of enforcement of slave-codes but of human judgment. In all the legal disfranchisement, slave revolts were few, and were usually led by outsiders — freedmen, wandering preachers, and artisans — not by those who were "inside" the system. In fact, in the US there were few rebellious "Nats," and very many docile "Sambos." If the Protestantism of the US emphasized that in law the slave was property (Aristotle had described him as "property with a soul,") the majority of the planters, and the majority of their slaves, accepted, adjusted, and survived. And the abolitionists were themselves equally exotic: rarely members of Congress, but opinion-shapers, academics — but more often from small and isolated liberal arts colleges; the reformers held to Emerson's doctrine, "the infinitude of the private man." There was only one Garrison, only one Weld, only one John Brown. Even so, to practically all Southerners and to many Northerners, they were anathema.

Moreover, slavery in the US meant Negro slavery. In contrast to Catholic Latin America, slavery in the ante-bellum South meant caste, and was made visible by the color of the skin. Color and subordination emerged together, and were seen as all but synonymous. Runaways on their own were visible, bewildered — and distinct.

To which, add physical condition. However prosperous the ante-bellum South, every known disease existed, and was passed on easily; typhoid fever and dysentery, not to mention the epidemic visitations of smallpox, cholera, and yellow fever. To the last, blacks were more resistant than whites. To tuberculosis they were very susceptible. Crowded conditions, dirt floors, poor food (little more than "hog and hoecake") made things worse. Yet material conditions among North American blacks were superior to those in the Caribbean, Latin America — or the African homeland. Witness the remarkable natural increase of the slave population: elsewhere in the New World it failed to reproduce itself, and needed the constant injection of new slaves from Africa. In the US there was a near balance of the sexes, whereas in slave populations elsewhere there was a heavy preponderance of males. And, after 1808, as it came to depend on its own resources for future supplies, it was in the interests of the South to provide at least satisfactory living conditions.

1828–1856 (Baton Rouge, Louisiana State University Press, 1978). For recent reprints of these arguments, see the Bibliography to this chapter.

There was yet another theme: the growing turmoil, and a propensity to violence in American society, North and South. It had many causes: the waves of non-English immigrants, many living in poverty and not familiar with civic life; the growth of cities themselves, with saloons and licentiousness and prostitution, offset by the appeals of evangelical preaching and of camp-meeting crusades against the demon drink and the empire of Sin in all its forms; lynch-law and the struggle to survive on the frontier, in the all-too-frequent absence of any other law enforcers; the unreliability of juries and courtroom justice; nativist and anti-Catholic riots in Boston, New York and Philadelphia, plus, in the South, the honor code, the ready availability of weapons, and the settlement of disputes among gentlemen – including editors – by resort to a duel. Young Horace Mann drew the conclusion that the South was a place "where they have an idle habit of making small holes thro' a man at the distance of ten paces." In fact duels, or at least challenges, were as frequent in New York; but if the event took place in the South, or on Navy Island in the Niagara River near the Canadian line, legal intervention was less likely. And legal duels had their own roll of honor, with names like Andrew Jackson, Aaron Burr, Alexander Hamilton, John Randolph, and Henry Clay among them. New Orleans had a special reputation: July and August inflamed tempers, and the summer was the high season there for duels – unless they coincided with epidemics which were also frequent; public hangings there were popular occasions: in 1838 four steamboats of spectators came south for the fun; and in Baltimore 20,000 watched the execution of Henry McCurry in 1845. The violence was turned on the abolitionists: Garrison was almost lynched in Boston in 1835, the Tappan brothers' property in New York was attacked, the hall used by them in Philadelphia was burnt, the anti-abolitionist editor Elijah Lovejoy was murdered when pro-slavery rioters in Alton, Illinois, tried to destroy his press. The Kansas-Nebraska riots and Harper's Ferry had their grim precursors.

And, be it noted, this propensity to violence – towards other whites, and towards Indians (from both of whom vice-versa) – swept blacks less frequently than whites. In contrast to many revolts in the Caribbean and Brazil, and notably the French Revolution-inspired revolution in Santo Domingo led by Toussaint L'Ouverture, there were only three abortive slave uprisings in the American South: the Gabriel Prosser Revolt of 1800 in Virginia; Denmark Vesey's rising in Charleston in 1822, when a mulatto carpenter bought his freedom after winning a lottery, and inspired a group of slaves with the idea of seizing the City (37 slaves were hanged before the revolt began); and the only one major revolt, that of Nat Turner in Virginia in 1831, in which 100 whites were killed. Its combination of Messianic fervor and total ruthlessness was unique – but after it no white man or woman was ever free from the fear of another Nat Turner arising.[32] All were urban, not plantation, phenomena; and their leaders were exceptional, and skilled men: Gabriel a blacksmith, Vesey a devoted Christian and a carpenter, Turner a preacher, with the gift of words. Slave revolts were organized by "outsiders," and, more striking, there was no slave uprising in the South through the four years of war.

Moreover, the settlement of argument by war, as in Texas, Mexico, and California, was an outgrowth not only of the exhaustion of all compromise, but of the speed with which news could now be circulated. As yet there was no "national" newspaper; the country was too big, and growing too fast; but there was an active local and state press, and in the decade of the 1850s the numbers of newspapers doubled, from 1,500 to over 3,000. Most of them were reformist in tone, notably the *Tribune*, the New York *Evening Post*, the San Francisco *Bulletin*. And, even more impressive, there was a steady growth of book publishers: Harper's 1817, Appleton's 1831, Putnam's 1840, Scribner's 1850, and in Boston, Little, Brown in 1837. Appleton's New American *Cyclopaedia* appeared in 1857, the US's first rival to the *Britannica*.

Perhaps, as coda, a final point should be made. Until the compromise of 1850, the role of the federal government had been limited, even negative; no major foreign crises had erupted since 1815; the war with Mexico was an escapade in a distant land; the armed services were small; indeed, the largest army hitherto commanded by an American general had been Winfield's Scott's force of 14,000 men in its march on Mexico City in 1847; law and order were mainly local matters. Major single issues, even the creation of new states, could be settled by negotiation. Bargain and compromise had thus far averted collision. The compromise of 1850, however, though a rag-bag, was a collection of major issues; the decisions made or not made by the federal government were now becoming dauntingly important: it could stimulate, subsidize, and direct development of roads and railroads, it could foster or discourage by its tariffs and by banking and currency legislation; and many of the problems it met now – like slavery – transcended state boundaries. Moreover,

---

[32] Eugene Genovese, *From Rebellion to Revolution: Afro-American slave revolts in the making of the modern world* (Baton Rouge, Louisiana State University Press, 1979).

the old political parties, themselves for long coalitions of local groups, were themselves breaking up; and the new loyalties being born were to sections and/or to single issues. Even each church — Episcopalian, Baptist, Presbyterian, Methodist — broke apart into separate wings, as did the missionary societies. This was a loosely organized and fragmented society — if a single society it was. Senators and Congressmen saw themselves as emissaries from their little sovereignties, meeting only occasionally, and not yet aware of being part of an "Establishment;" had they been so, and taken pride in it, their constituents would probably not have voted for them again. Henry James's lament, written as a naturalized Englishman when he commuted between Rye, Kent, and Cheyne Row, Chelsea, recorded the absence in the United States in 1890 — and still more therefore in 1861 — of national institutions on English (British?) lines, in which old school or old college ties, professional associations, common acts of worship, or sporting meetings would provide settings for personal contact, for talk — and for political adjustments and decisions. Seward's attempt in 1861 to talk to some Southern leaders was contrived, done by intermediary — and could easily be disowned. Lincoln was right. The House was divided; only war would settle the division. And in 1776, so in 1861, the War made two nations.

3   THE WORLD OF THE SLAVEHOLDERS

By 1850 the South was becoming a distinct region, almost a nation on its own, living by its own legends and its own codes. It was, Southerners like to think, founded by English *aristos* in exile, fleeing from the civil and religious wars of seventeenth-century England; they lived elegant lives in stately white-columned homes, maintained by a squad of loyal and admiring house servants, and looked out on broad acres of cotton, planted and picked by equally devoted field hands. There were a number of military academies, and many Southerners carried arms. Dueling was a feature on matters seen as points of honor. The South was separate, self-centered, prickly, and defensive.[33]

The South in fact was settled by the same kind of people who came to the North. Bluebloods were extremely rare; a large proportion of the colonial migration, to the South, as to the North,

---

[33] For the creation of the legends, see William R. Taylor, *Cavalier and Yankee* (New York, Doubleday, Anchor paperback, 1963).

was lower middle class, while the lowest social classes were well
represented among the indentured servants. A tight little aristocracy,
of humble origins, did develop in the Virginia Tidewater, and in
the environs of Charleston, South Carolina. A few had been Crown
favorites rewarded with lands in the West. But the majority of
Southern planters lacked the "culture" of these groups. The new
cotton areas of the Deep South were not far removed from the frontier, socially as well as geographically. Illiteracy was by no means
unknown among the planters. In many respects Andrew Jackson was
a typical representative of the Southern "aristocracy." The nullification crisis of 1832 nevertheless lost Jackson many Southern
supporters, who never forgave him his strong tactics against South
Carolina, or his acceptance of the Tariff of 1832. Led by Calhoun,
the anti-Jackson conservatives joined the Whig party, and although
Calhoun returned to the Democratic fold after the retirement of
Jackson, he was unable to bring all the Southern Whigs back with
him (the so-called "cotton Whigs.")

The census returns disprove the legend of the great landed estates
worked by slave legions. Of the 8 million white inhabitants in
the 15 slave states in 1860, only 383,000 were slaveholders. Of
these, half owned fewer than five, but 10,000 owned at least 50
slaves, and 1730 owned 100 or more. This elite of large plantation
owners wielded enormous political and social influence; they were
the magistrates and mayors, sheriffs and judges, but they formed
only a small group in the total population. In other words, taking
into account the members of their families, only 20–25 percent
of the people of the South were directly connected with slavery.
Furthermore, one-half of the slaveholders owned no more than four
slaves, and five-sevenths owned no more than nine. Only the 15
percent who owned 30 or more Negro slaves – 10,000 or 15,000
planters – could qualify for the Southern aristocracy of fiction and
films. The typical slaveholder was a successful farmer who worked
along with his slaves. The 1860 census returns show that fewer
than 3,000 Southerners owned more than 100 slaves, that only 14
owned more than 500 slaves, and that only 1 owned more than
1,000. Of Virginia's white population of just over 1 million, only
114 owned as many as 100 slaves; its largest slaveowner, Samuel
Hairston, had 1,600 on his numerous plantations; his largest in
Henry County was "likened to Paradise." Moreover, whereas in 1850
one in three Southern whites were directly or indirectly concerned
with slaveholding, this proportion had by 1860 declined to one in
four. The overwhelming bulk of Southern cotton was produced by a
small number of very large plantations. Moreover, the rarity of very

large plantations and the presence of masters on their estates are features in sharp contrast to those of the West Indies and Brazil, which in turn explains why major revolts – though they did occur – were few in the American South.

Most cultivators were not wealthy; but they were engaged in agriculture, and 80 percent of them owned their own land. Their lands were usually not well-suited to the large-scale production of the great commercial crops – cotton, tobacco, rice, and sugar; or if in the mountain-sheltered valleys south of the Shenandoah they might be remote from markets; but they were suitable for producing the family's own food, for diversified self-subsistence agriculture, and perhaps for a small cash crop of cotton or tobacco. These Southern yeoman farmers were very much like those of New England, Pennsylvania, and the Old Northwest: self-sufficient and independent on their 80–160 acres, on the basis of their own and their family's labor. These were the most "typical" Southerners. They were much in awe of the people in the Big Houses. [34]

The true "poor whites" were relatively isolated families, cut off from markets, living on submarginal lands – exhausted, barren, or swampy – or in erosion-gutted clay hills or the piney woods of the coastal plains. They had no opportunity to develop diversified agriculture. Very often what farming they did was carried on by the womenfolk, tending patches of corn, sweet potatoes, and collards, while the men spent their days hunting and fishing. Those who lived in the Alleghenies, especially in the valleys of the Blue Ridge and the Smokies, often opposed both secession and the War as lowland movements – as the history of West Virginia and eastern Tennessee testifies. Many of the "mountain people" were sallow, debilitated, and unambitious; and many were disease-ridden. Much of their lack of energy and ambition was due to malaria, to pellagra, to dietary deficiencies, and especially to hookworm, a disease that was not even recognized until late in the nineteenth century. The poor whites were at the bottom of the Southern social ladder: "po' white trash" in Virginia, "squatters" in Alabama and Mississippi, "people of the barrens" in Tennessee, "sandhillers" in South Carolina, "crackers" in Georgia; everyone – even Negro slaves – looked down on them. William Byrd in 1730 had found them in what he called "Lubberland;" they would recur in twentieth-century

---

[34] Genovese, *From Rebellion to Revolution*; US Census Office, Eighth Census, *Population of the US in 1860* (US Government Printing Office, 1864), p. 247; Gavin Wright, *The Political Economy of the Cotton South* (New York, Norton, 1978), pp. 79–81.

fiction as stock characters, in Jeeter Lester of Erskine Caldwell's *Tobacco Road* and in William Faulkner's Snopeses. Although the real ante-bellum South was thus a far cry from the South of legend, it was a unique section of the US. The South was overwhelmingly rural and agricultural. New Orleans, "the city of legitimate sin" was its only large, cosmopolitan, commercial city. Richmond, Mobile, Savannah, and Charleston were no more than towns. The border cities — St Louis, Baltimore, and Louisville — were as much Northern or Western as Southern in character.

In 1860, only 10 percent of US manufactures were produced in the South. Southern agriculture was devoted to the production of cash crops for export to the North and to Europe. Cotton was by all odds the most important; but tobacco, rice, indigo and sugar cane were also produced in quantity. Of the 2,500,000 slaves directly employed in agriculture, 1,815,000 were producing cotton, 350,000 tobacco, 150,000 sugar, 125,000 rice, and 60,000 hemp. In 1860, more than half the exports of the US were from the South, with cotton forming 60 percent of US exports — even if it was carried in Northern ships. The dependence of British (and North American) mills on Southern cotton was the most striking economic fact of the mid-nineteenth century. The 119 British cotton mills of 1787, at American independence, had become 1,800 by 1840, employing a quarter of a million people; and by that time more than 80 percent of the cotton spun in Britain came from the American South. As with Lowell and the mills along the Merrimack in Massachusetts, so with Burnley and Manchester in England. As Samuel Watt wrote, on March 27, 1843, three years before the British repeal of the Corn Laws:

Who are the slaveholders of America? The planters — No. The overseers? The feculent dregs of society? No. The slaveholders of America are the City of London! ... If Great Britain would buy no slave-raised produce, slavery would not last one year! ... Repeal your Corn Laws! Repeal all duties upon the products of our free states — Discriminate between Liberty and Slavery! Impose a duty upon cotton!

It was thus the plantation system, rare though it was outside the Deep South, that was the unique form of economic organization. Its labor force was unfree and unskilled; being so, it relied on repetition, producing a single crop; because land was plentiful, little care was taken to restore the fertility of the soil. Edmund Ruffin, a self-taught scientist, on his plantation on the James River, established that the exhaustion of the soil was due to acidity; experimented with marl and limestone from the shell deposits of eastern Virginia to neutralize the acidity; his Virginia farms Marlbourne and Beechwood became laboratories to prove the value of calcareous manures; his essay-turned-into-book, "An Essay on Calcareous Manures" (1832), and his decade of editorship in the 1830s of the periodical *The Farmer's Register*, like his encouragement of agricultural associations and fairs, came too late, however, to save the worn soils of Virginia and South Carolina. Moreover, cultivation was crude and was more like mining than careful husbandry; single crops, easily sold in world markets, were grown, and sandhills and uplands were too many.[35] Nor was land expansion any guarantee of security. More land and the prospect of cotton made slaves more valuable, but an increase in the supply of cotton drove its price down, and tended to depress the value of slaves. The equation ceased to balance almost with each new acre, or with each new crop. But observers from outside saw the cotton kingdom as ever-expanding, and could become obsessive about it. And insiders, whose soils were so quickly overworked, were constantly tempted by the mobility of their labor force to go South and West, and risk it. Prosperity seemed tied to the possession of slaves. Visitors were as often shocked by what they saw, as was Frederick Law Olmsted on his *Journey in the Seaboard Slave States* in 1856:

I went on my way into the so-called cotton states ... And for every mile of roadside upon which I saw any evidence of cotton production, I am sure that I saw a hundred of forest or waste land, with only now and then an acre or two of poor corn half smothered in weeds; for every rich man's house, I am sure I passed a dozen shabby and half furnished cottages and at least a hundred cabins — mere hovels, such as none but a poor farmer would house his cattle in at the North.[36]

Yet, when the two short depressions of 1854 and 1857 came and many banks failed, railroads went into bankruptcy, and land values fell, when there was widespread unemployment in the cities, and criminal activity mounted, when it became fashionable for the wealthy to give "poverty parties," the South, with its agricultural

[35] Avery C. Craven, *Edmund Ruffin, Southerner* (Baton Rouge, Louisiana State University Press, 1966).
[36] Olmsted, *A Journey in the Seaboard Slave States; A Journey through Texas; A journey in the Back Country; The Cotton Kingdom.*

economy and world market for cotton, was much less affected by these crises than was the North. Its survival gave it further false optimism. Moreover, the Upper South was part of it. The South in 1860, with 39 percent of the population, produced 52 per cent of the nation's corn, 29 per cent of its wheat, and no less than 90 per cent of its sweet potatoes. The Upper South was farming more than cotton country.

The South was dependent upon the outside for tools, clothing, furniture, and luxuries. Many of the planting areas were not self-sufficient even in foodstuffs, importing meat and grain from the Northwest. For capital also, the South was dependent upon other areas, particularly the Northeast. The coal and iron of what became Birmingham, Alabama, was not exploited until after 1865. Since capital was tied up in land and slaves, most of the planters were dependent upon Northern funds to finance the production and marketing of their crops; it was a debtor section. Northerners also provided most of the shipping facilities, the insurance, and the other services incidental to the staple-crop economy, for few Southerners engaged in commercial enterprises. The South by 1860 had only one-fifth of the shipping tonnage of the North. In many respects, the relation between North and South in the Jacksonian period resembled that which had existed between Great Britain and the American colonies a century earlier; the South had become an economic colony of the North.[37]

Dependent – and defensive; and complex. So complex that little attention was paid by abolitionists or slaveholders to the question of the cost of emancipation. Clearly the property-losers would require compensation. Slaves might be (would be?) willing to purchase their freedom, but would need to work "like slaves" for the rest of their lives to pay off their debt. The government could issue bonds, given to the slaveholders as token of their loss, but the cost of amortization would be high. To free the slave seemed likely to cost $3 billion, in an economy in which the GNP was only some $4 billion per year. Moreover, the bill would be borne by the non-

---

[37] The most vehement contemporary description of this dependence is in Hinton B. Helper's description of Cotton as King, but its products were manufactured in New England or Old England: "It is carried in their ships, spun in their factories, woven in their looms, insured in their offices, returned again in their own vessels, and with double freight and cost of manufacturing added, purchased by the South at a high premium. Of all the parties engaged or interested in its transportation and manufacture, the South is the only one that does not make a profit. Nor does she, as a general thing, make a profit by producing it." Hinton B. Helper, *The Impending Crisis of the South: How to meet it* (1860).

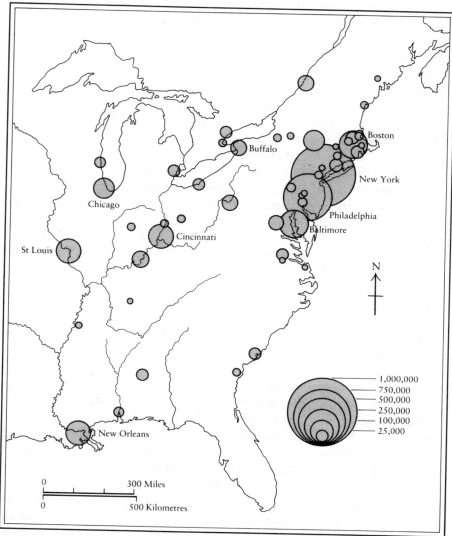

Map 9   Major cities in 1860.

slave and the non-slaveholders, by an electorate which would, it seemed, gain nothing from it. As a result emancipation was not conspicuous on any party's agenda – except for a handful of dedicated abolitionists. Indeed, the abolition societies defeated their own purposes: to them it mattered not that the Southern economy would be wrecked and the planters left destitute without compensation: for them it was sin, not economics, that mattered.

Again, apart from the Negro, the South was more purely native and English than was the North. The nineteenth-century immigrations of German, Irish and Scandinavians avoided the South, objecting to the competition of slave labor and the lack of industrial employment. Not only did the population of the North grow more rapidly than that of the South; it also benefited from the cultural contributions of the new national groups. The main shipping lines ran to Northern ports. The Southern legend to the contrary notwithstanding, the South was dominated by a small conservative aristocracy, whose members for the most part stubbornly resisted new ideas. Family knew family, and individuals mattered. The intellectual innovations of Europe and the reform movement of the North were viewed with suspicion, and resisted vigorously if they seemed to threaten the *status quo*. The South remained fundamentalist in religion long after the repercussions of the scientific revolution had been felt in the churches of the North. Fewer books, papers, and magazines were published below the Mason-Dixon Line than above it. The American literary renaissance of the first half of the nineteenth century occurred in New England, not in the South, and William Gilmore Simms' romances were published by a Northern company, Harper's, in Boston. Only *De Bow's Review*, the New Orleans business journal, and the Southern *Review*, a Charleston literary publication, had quality. The obligation on the state to develop free elementary education that marked Massachusetts in the 1840s came late in the South. Only in South Carolina was the establishment of schools mandatory, and nowhere was attendance compulsory. The small number of towns in the South hindered professional education. A good medical school needs close links with a large hospital: New York and Philadelphia medical colleges attracted Southern students, and the same held true almost to the same extent for the law. Subsequently subscribing to Northern journals, Southern professional men became as colonially dependent as were Southern bankers, Southern brokers, and Southern cotton planters. As private institutions, however, there were in 1860 over 200 colleges and academies, some 1,500 teachers and some 25,000 students; and in 1865 the roll-call of the alumni of the University of Virginia, founded by Jefferson, is hard to distinguish from a roll-call of Confederate officers and veterans.

The most distinctive educational features of the South were indeed the military academies. The two most conspicuous, the Virginia Military Institute at Lexington, founded in 1839, and the South Carolina Military Institute (the Citadel) founded in 1841 were both, in a measure, the reaction to Nat Turner's revolt; their conspicuous

stress on drill and ceremonial were designed in part to overawe
the slave population. But by 1860 every Southern state except the
newest, Florida, had its own miniature West Point, or supported
a college by financing military instruction there; Kentucky (1845),
from which in 1860 its students left to go North as well as South;
Arkansas at Tulip (1850); Jefferson College, near Natchez, in Mississippi (founded in 1802, and attended by Jefferson Davis), which
had a military division after 1829; Georgia Military Institute at
Marietta (1851); Tennessee at Tyree in 1835. Alabama had two
military academies; North Carolina's was founded at Charlotte
in 1859; and the first superintendent of the new Louisiana State
Seminary of Learning and Military Academy (now Louisiana State
University) was no other than that future scourge of the South,
William Tecumseh Sherman. By 1860, the Virginia Military Institute
could proudly claim to have produced 400 officers – many of whom
would reveal their skills on Southern battlefields. The South also
sent disproportionate numbers to West Point itself – conspicuously
Jefferson Davis (class of 1828), Robert E. Lee (class of 1829), and
Stonewall Jackson (class of 1848). The federal government itself
had at times sent military instructors from "the Point" to teach
tactics at the Virginia Military Institute, and at the University of
Tennessee's military school. There were, of course, similar institutions in the North. Indeed, the military school could actually be
said to be a Northern invention, since it was Alden Partridge's
academy at Norwich, Vermont, beginning in 1819, that became a
model; and it had its Northern parallels at Mount Pleasant, New
York, the Highland Military Academy in Worcester, Massachusetts,
and in Hamden, Connecticut. Crowning them all, of course, was
West Point on the Hudson, a disproportionate number of whose
students came from the South; but 64 percent of its graduates in
the decades before the War were Northerners. If a large number
of its graduates before 1861 became civilians, that was in part
a tribute to its quality as an engineering academy: the skills acquired there were in demand in the age of railroad-building. It
was seen as an academy rather than as a military apprenticeship.
Probably the most distinguished American military theorist was
Henry Wager Halleck of New York (West Point, class of 1839),
later General Grant's chief-of-staff; and General George McClellan
(second in his class in 1846), had had an impressive baptism in
the Mexican War, an observer-role in the Crimea, and a spell as
engineer-in-chief on the Illinois Central Railroad before Lincoln
called him to command in 1861. Military training was no Southern
monopoly in the years of the Mexican War, when every frontier

called for the qualities bred in the military school and even on the parade ground.[38]

There are, nevertheless, obvious reasons for the emphasis on the military academy in the South. The continuing frontier folk culture in the Old South, accompanied by a spirit of preparedness and defense against hostile Spaniards and Indians, was an important unifying thread in the history of the South during most of the antebellum period. Less than one generation transpired between the removal from the South of the Cherokee, the Choctaw, the Chickasaw, and the Seminole, and the bombardment of Fort Sumter. Legends of Indian fighting, the social role of the militia muster, and the popularity of volunteer clubs, of medieval-style jousting tournaments, and of military titles, all captured the imagination of young Southerners soon destined for the battlefields of San Jacinto, Buena Vista, and Chickamauga. Moreover, as a Southern editor put it, "every plantation is a small military establishment." As the organizer and manager of a large agricultural establishment employing slave labor, the planter of the Old South was forced by his location to play the role of a military executive. Writing on the management of slaves, a planter in 1860 stated that "as a general thing, the Army Regulations as to the disciplines in Forts is the best mode of managing negroes that I know of."[39] Many Southerners

[38] A challenging view of the Southern military tradition is in Marcus Cunliffe, *Soldiers and Civilians: The martial spirit in America 1775–1865* (Boston, Little, Brown, 1969), ch. 10. Compare with it, however, James C. Bonner, "The historical basis of Southern military tradition," *Georgia Review* (spring 1955), pp. 74–85, and John Hope Franklin's writings mentioned above, emphasizing the belligerence ("militance" is a politer word) of the South. Neither Cunliffe nor Franklin add the point that Jefferson Davis, as secretary for war in 1853–7, rejected the Georgia submission that there should be a federal military academy in the South, on the grounds that it would tend "to create and increase sectional jealousies." No more than Lincoln did Jefferson Davis want war.

[39] John Hope Franklin, "Slavery and the martial South," *Journal of Negro History*, 132, 36 (Jan. 1952); and idem, *The Militant South 1800–1860* (Cambridge, MA, Harvard University Press, 1956). George Featherstonhaugh, the British traveler, noted one feature of the South that was the legacy of military schools: the frequency of titles. When using a ferry *en route* to Winchester, Virginia, he overheard a conversation: "Major, I wish you would lead your horse a little forward," which he did, observing to the man, 'I am not a major, and you need not call me one.' To this the ferryman replied, 'Well, kurnel, I ax your pardon, and I'll not call you so no more.' Being arrived at the landing place he led his horse out of the boat and said, 'My good friend, I am a very plain man, and I am neither a colonel nor a major. I have no title at all, and I don't like them. How much do I have to pay you? The ferryman looked at him and said: 'You are the first white man I ever crossed this ferry that warnt jist nobody at all, and I swear I'll not charge

lived under real apprehension of a slave insurrection, and there were only 11 years between 1800 and 1860 in which there were not, somewhere in the South, grave rumors of a slave revolt; in every plantation home a collection of muskets was always available in the hall. Governor Robert Y. Hayne of South Carolina told his legislature in 1833 that "A state of military preparation must always be with us. ... A period of profound peace and consequent apathy may expose us to the danger of domestic insurrection." After Denmark Vesey's conspiracy in Charleston in 1822, the work of an intensely religious – and prosperous – free black, and after the Nat Turner rebellion in Southampton County, Virginia, in 1831, there was a new terror walking abroad in the South. Throughout the South in periods of alarm, patrol squads rode the highways at night to keep Negroes in their cabins and to take precautions against uprisings, while in the larger towns and in the cities special guards were employed to patrol Negro sections at night.

This tradition was one of preparedness, of defense of home, family and kin, rather than of drill-ground precision. The Confederate army, mainly of young men of rural background, was not distinguished by the quality of its staff work. What did recur was the skilled use of cavalry and the role of the free fighter, as exemplified in the exploits of such men as Mississippi cotton planter turned cavalry raider, Nathan Bedford Forrest, or University of Virginia lawyer turned ranger, John Singleton Mosby; or West Pointer (class of 1837) but Virginian Confederate commander, Jubal Early, or another (and strikingly handsome) West Pointer (1857) cavalry raider, J. E. B. Stuart, who was killed, aged 30, in the Wilderness Campaign of 1864. Again, the common soldier of the Confederacy, as revealed in his letters and diaries, was often thrown upon his own resources, and his ingenuity, for survival. In culture, Southerners were consumers rather than producers – and consumers more of newspapers, and still more of their editorials, than of books. Opinion was largely made by newspaper editors or owners, such as Thomas Ritchie, editor of the Richmond *Enquirer*, or by R. Barnwell Rhett of the Charleston *Mercury*. The balanced Ritchie – to quote the acerbic John Randolph of Roanoke – was a man of seven principles, and they were five loaves and two fishes; by contrast Robert Barnwell Rhett owned two plantations and 190

you nothing." See also Don Fehrenbacher, "The new political history of the coming of the Civil War," *Pacific History Review*, 54 (1985), and Don Higginbotham, "The martial spirit in the antebellum South," *Journal of Southern History*, 58 (1992).

slaves, crusaded unyieldingly for secession for almost 30 years, and wanted the slave trade restored.

Cotton was King, certainly; it was Emperor too. It expanded steadily to the Gulf states and the lower Mississippi valley, where the price of good field hands went up by 100 percent. There was a steady internal migration from the Tidewater to the West and the Deep South. The Lincoln and the Davis families were but typical; no fewer than 227 men born in Virginia before 1810 served in Congress from other states. Southern capital, however, went almost exclusively into land and slaves; almost all proposals for the building of mills and factories were doomed by the slave–plantation system. On the eve of the Civil War the South was manufacturing only 4 percent of its cotton crops. The exceptions were the Tredegar Iron Works in Richmond, established in 1837, managed by ex-West Point engineer Joseph Reid Addison, and employing mainly slave labor; the model village founded by Daniel Pratt at Prattville, Alabama, using both black and white workers; and William Gregg's similar (and similarly successful) experiment in the Graniteville Manufacturing Company of South Carolina. All of them exploited the South's coal and iron, lead and copper; in 1860, against its population of 30 percent of the United country, the South had 22 percent of its manufacturing, 17 percent of its labor force, and 16 percent of its output. Prior to the invention of the cotton gin in 1793, the general expectation had been that slavery would soon disappear; the Northern states all abolished the institution in the generation following the Revolutionary War, and leaders like Jefferson, Madison, and Washington hoped and expected that it would soon be gone in the South. But the cotton gin made profitable the cultivation of short-staple cotton, and the westward expansion of the South brought vast new areas into the slavery economy in the first decades of the nineteenth century.

The people of the South, and certainly their politicians, were conscious of their economic imbalance, and of their minority status in the Union – in population, in wealth, and in representation in Congress. Until 1850 they had kept even with the free states in representation in the Senate, but with the admission of California they lost this last check upon the federal government. Nevertheless until then, the South had done well from the Union. For 49 of the 72 years since 1789 the President had been a Southerner, and a slaveholder. After the civil War a century was to pass before another true Southerner was elected President. In Congress, 24 of the 36 Speakers of the House up to 1861, and 25 of the 36 Presidents *pro tempore* in the Senate, were Southerners. For the first half-century after the outbreak of the War, no Speaker nor President *pro tempore* was from the South. From 1789 to 1861, 20 percent of the 35 Supreme Court justices were from the South; in the next half-century only 5 of the 26 appointed to the Court were Southerners. As Seward pointed out in 1856, King Cotton "practically chooses thirty of the sixty-two members of the senate, ninety of the two hundred and thirty-three members of the house of representatives, and one hundred and five of the two hundred and ninety-five electors of president and vice-president of the United States." In addition, the South had five of the nine justices of the Supreme Court. If a minority section with a lopsided economy, the South had skillfully exploited its role – until 1850.[40]

From 1850, the South went on the defensive, espousing the ideas of men like Calhoun, in an effort to protect itself from oppression by the majority. It needed to do so, for its distinctiveness was being enhanced by the industrial and transport changes of the decades after 1850. For the era of railroad building revolutionized American economic and political geography. The old lines of trade ran North and South by the coastline routes and canals of the Atlantic seaboard, and by the Mississippi River system. The products of the Northwest went down the Mississippi to Memphis, Natchez, and New Orleans. In 1840 New Orleans was the fifth city in size in the country, and second only to New York in the export trade. The coming of the railroad shifted the routes of trade; wheat could be brought more cheaply from the Northwest by lake and rail across the Alleghenies to the Atlantic ports. By 1860 the export of grain from New Orleans had dropped to 2,189 bushels. The once enormous export trade of the Queen City of the South was now confined to cotton, rice, sugar, and tobacco. Political allegiance followed material interests. In 1850 the Northwest was affiliated by economic ties with the South; by 1860 the Northwest was affiliated with the Northeast.

It was, then, the plantation economy, and its peculiar institution slavery, that made the South unique and isolated in the world, and increasingly distinct from the Northern and Western United States. In 1860 there were approximately 4 million Negroes in the South, the overwhelming majority of whom were slaves. They were the South's major investment, and were probably worth 2 billion dollars in 1860. Southern leaders lived in constant fear of a black insurrection, which they tried to obviate by repressive measures. Floggings,

[40] J. McPherson, "Revolution and counter-revolution in the American Civil War," Commonwealth Fund Lecture, University College London, Jan. 1982.

lynchings, and other forms of violence increased in the decade preceding the war. After the Nat Turner revolt of 1831 all the Southern states strengthened their laws for the control of slaves. The slave codes were tightened to keep the Negroes under discipline: they were forbidden to carry weapons, to leave their owners' property without permission, even to learn to read, so that Northern inflammatory propaganda would not reach them. And the abolitionists got the blame.

In Virginia, a state which in the early nineteenth century had been prone to apologize for slavery as a necessary, but transient, evil, the general attitude changed steadily after 1830, as the cotton economy became firmly rooted in the South. Thenceforth, slavery was regarded, in Virginia and the rest of the South, as permanent, as a lasting good, as a system vindicated by history and religion. Racial myths and a code of cultural isolation prevailed throughout the South. The claims of Cavalier descent and pure Anglo-Saxon blood came to be voiced in Southern circles, and Sir Walter Scott's romances became regular reading. The burning of anti-slavery books began. The fear of white apostasy from the orthodox Southern creed was ever-present. During the 1850s, Southern youths began to forsake Northern colleges for those in the South, which taught the "pure" Southern doctrine (the enrollment of such Southern colleges doubled during the decade 1850–60). Even Southern textbooks took on a sectional coloring. The myth of the Southern Cavalier, living in a land of magnolias and mint juleps, was product not only of the reading of Sir Walter Scott, but of the writing of John Pendleton Kennedy's *Swallow Barn* (1832), and of the historical novels, especially *The Yemassee* (1835), of William Gilmore Simms of Charleston. Pride in the South as distinctive flourished. It was identified with, and especially visible, in Virginia. For those condemned to live in the new cotton belt of the Mississippi and in "costermonger times," but who were raised in Virginia, "coelum non animum mutant qui trans mare currunt"; "patriotism was for a Virginian a noun personal – it is the Virginian himself and something over." And even if he was not fortunate enough to come from Richmond, Albemarle, or the Valley, but from its Western extension, even Heaven itself was described as a "Kaintuck" of a place. And as well as proud, the Virginian was magnamimous: he never threw up at a Yankee the fact of his birthplace. Similar gentlemanly style was evident in Charleston. In fine, Southern loyalties were gradually transferred from the federal government to the section or to the individual state. Southerners began to demand that the slave trade be reopened, or that new slave territory be set up in the West. The devising of some generally acceptable scheme to safeguard minority political rights, as Calhoun argued, or the opening of new slave states – even in the Caribbean – were seen as the only remedies short of war. The American situation as it stood was quite untenable: the oldest of economies, a staple-crop agriculture using forced labor, was joined with the newest, an industrialized capitalism based upon wages, in one political union.

That the conflict was "irrepressible" was W. H. Seward's view in 1858; as a prominent Whig and ex-governor of New York, he was Lincoln's Republican rival for the presidential nomination, and became his secretary of state after his election in 1860. The conflict certainly seemed so in economic terms. The plantation–slave system had saddled a one-sided economic life upon the South, which proved profitable only so long as there was fresh land available into which to expand; even more, it required cheaper slaves, which could be obtained only by the reopening of the African slave trade. The South wanted direct trade with Europe. It wanted cheap money and lower costs for moving and financing cotton. It wanted free trade. But by 1860 the limits of slavery expansion were fixed, despite the Dred Scott decision of 1857, which denied citizenship to blacks, and slavery was ceasing to be profitable. That this fact was known to some Southerners is clear from the appearance in 1857 of H. R. Helper's *The Impending Crisis of the South*. Written by a middle-class white, one of the large group of non-slaveholding Southerners in a state, North Carolina, where large plantations were unusual, it argued that the planter class engrossed the best land, few men of middle rank survived in the system, and the Old South had only three "classes:" the planters, the slaves, and the "po' white trash." Unless the South abolished slavery its economic future was doomed; dependence upon the North must be ended, by diversifying crops and introducing manufacturing into the South. The South, however, continued to worship at the throne of King Cotton. As late as 1858 Senator Hammond of South Carolina held cotton to be indispensable. Should the South produce no cotton for three years, he told Senators, "England would topple headlong and carry the whole civilized world with her, save the South. No, you dare not make war on cotton. No power on earth dares to make war upon it. Cotton is King."

4   THE FAILURE OF COMPROMISE

The war that occurred in 1861 was due to political failure: the inability to compromise. For until then all clashes between North

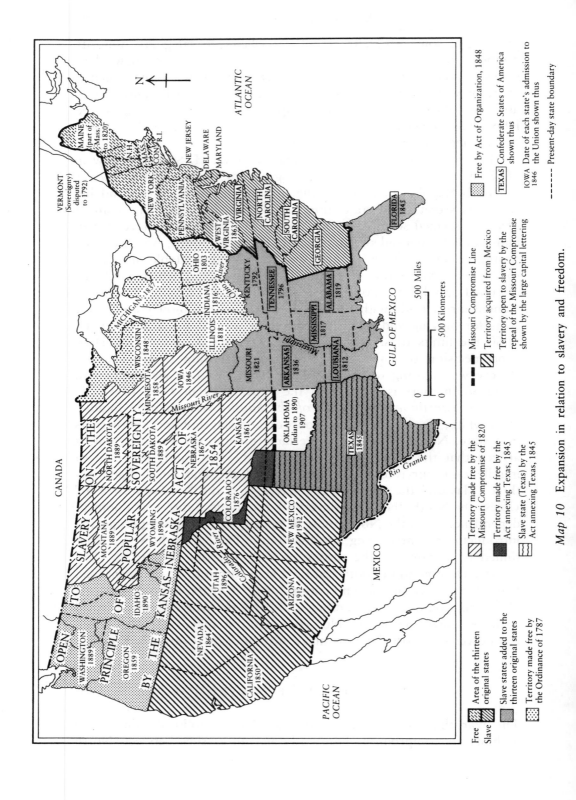

Map 10 Expansion in relation to slavery and freedom.

and South had been adjusted: and it was the role of politicians, and of political parties, to do the adjusting: in 1787, in 1820, in 1833 involving Nullification, and in 1850. In each case, the South was concerned that Southern institutions might be damaged or destroyed by an ever more powerful North. The Constitution itself was built on compromise: the three-fifths ratio to recognize the South's slave numbers, the prohibition of export taxes, which would hurt Southern staples, the requirement that treaties needed a two-thirds vote in the Senate, seen as the defender of each state's economic interests.

Up to and including 1850 the political balance in the Senate between North and South had been maintained by the admission of equal numbers of free and slave states, as in 1820. While allowing slavery in Missouri, the 1820 Compromise had barred slavery from all future states carved out of territory North of 36° 30' (Missouri's Southern boundary). In time, the free states would outnumber the slave states and the North would dominate the Senate as well as the House. Each new census registered population growth, and a reapportionment of seats in the House of Representatives; and in each reapportionment, the free states gained. By the 1850s the free states had 144 members, the slave states only 90. In the Nullification controversy of the 1830s, under the direction of John C. Calhoun, the state of South Carolina defied the national government, declaring the tariff law of 1832 unconstitutional, hence null and void and unenforceable in South Carolina. Calhoun maintained that sovereignty was indivisible and belonged to the states. In the Compromise of 1833, to please Calhoun, the tariff rates of 1832 were reduced. But, given the Force Act, Nullification could not be used again. The slave states would have to obey national laws while they remained in the Union. Through the 1830s and 1840s, the South managed to maintain the balance in the Senate. With the admission of Missouri and Maine in 1820, the Union contained two dozen states, half free, half slave. Six more states came in during the next two decades, three with slavery (Arkansas, Florida, Texas), and three without (Michigan, Iowa, Wisconsin). During the Mexican War a Pennsylvania Democratic Congressman, David Wilmot, proposed that any territory obtained from Mexico should be forever free. After a bitter struggle, the Northern-dominated House of Representatives twice voted for the Wilmot Proviso. It did not get through the Senate; but on it the party unity cracked: Southern Whigs against, Northern Whigs for; and many Northern Democrats, including ex-President Martin Van Buren, broke party ranks on it.

Compromise was managed with difficulty in 1850, after the acquisition of territory from Mexico, in a war seen by many Northerners as a slaveholder's conspiracy, by an army thick with Southerners. Some in the Deep South – the Knights of the Golden Circle – had a dream of a Caribbean Slave Empire, with new slave states and plans for an inter-oceanic canal. Sentiment in the North ran ever higher, with mounting abolitionist agitation, and with slave pens within walking distance of Capitol Hill. Northern extremists, like William Henry Seward, the Whig Senator from New York, opposed making any concessions whatever to slave-owners. Many Northern Congressmen stood on the Wilmot Proviso principle of barring slavery from the territories. Others demanded the abolition of the slave trade and slavery itself in the District of Columbia. But Calhoun died after attacking the bill, and compromisers won the day, including the Whig leader Henry Clay, who had helped arrange the earlier Compromises in 1820 and 1833, the old Whig Daniel Webster, and the rising young Illinois Democrat, Stephen A. Douglas.

As finally worked out, the Compromise of 1850 offered something to each side. To please the North, (1) California was admitted to the Union as a free state; (2) the slave trade was barred in the District of Columbia; and (3) the slave state of Texas was prevailed upon to give up its claims to New Mexico. To satisfy the South, (1) the Wilmot Proviso was definitely shelved, and the principle of popular or squatter sovereignty was applied to the new territories of Utah and New Mexico (that is, Congress neither forbade nor encouraged slavery, but allowed the residents of each territory to vote for or against the institution when they sought admission to the Union); (2) slavery was retained in the District of Columbia; (3) the United States assumed some Texas debts; and (4) Congress adopted a new fugitive slave law, which required state officers and other citizens to help the return of runaways to their masters; and those so charged were denied jury trial.

Despite this last provision the Compromise of 1850 favored the free states. They had won control of the Senate once and for all (with the admission of California, there were 16 free and 15 slave states, and two more free states were admitted in the next decade, Minnesota in 1858 and Oregon in 1859). "Popular sovereignty" gave the planters a chance in Utah and New Mexico, but those areas were not by nature suited to plantation agriculture. The North was further aided by the fact that the Compromise of 1850 postponed disunion for ten years. During those ten years the free states would enormously increase their economic power and thus be able to crush the South in 1861–5. It might have been different had the slave states seceded a decade earlier. The last great compromise did not satisfy the South, though it was happy to have won its struggle against the protective tariff and internal improvements; while business interests were pleased at the return to "normalcy," the federal requirement that fugitive slaves be returned to their masters stirred up a storm of Northern opposition. Prominent Northern leaders like William Seward advocated civil disobedience, stating that if the Constitution were found to conflict with the moral law, the latter was to be honored in defiance of the former. The Wisconsin Supreme Court declared the Fugitive Slave Law null and void. William Lloyd Garrison, the editor of the *Liberator*, despaired of saving the Union by any political action, and – like Calhoun in reverse, as it were – advocated the secession of the free states from a Union that they no longer controlled. Until 1850 – even when the Methodist and Baptist churches were breaking up into separate Northern and Southern wings – the two major political parties (Whigs and Democrats) had been organized on a national basis, even if each was – as always – a faithfully oiled and loaves-and-fishes-fed coalition. There were conscience Whigs, people with hearts; many of them became Free-Soilers, as did Charles Sumner and Charles Francis Adams. There were also cotton Whigs: New York merchants, New England textile manufacturers, transoceanic shippers, all needing and using Southern cotton, all for trade, and opposed to abolitionists and those who would rock the boat. Some of them, attributing Pierce's victory in 1852 to his recruitment of foreign-born voters, joined the nativist Know-Nothing lodges, believing that "Americans should rule America." As each new problem arose, both parties continued to seek compromises rather than solutions. But the unity was disappearing now. By 1860 the Whigs had disappeared, the Democrats were split – and the war came. Popular relief over the compromise achieved in 1850, however, was enough to allow the election of two easy-going Democratic Presidents, Franklin Pierce in 1852 and James Buchanan in 1856. Each accepted the compromise of 1850. And the decade promised prosperity with the discovery of gold in California, with a golden age for river steamboats on the Mississippi, and a steady extension of communication. In 1857 John Butterfield began his semi-weekly mail service from the Mississippi to the Pacific, and a year later a stagecoach and mail service covered the ground in 25 days. In 1860 the freight company of Russell, Majors, & Waddell inaugurated the pony express (St Joseph to Sacramento in ten days), and in October 1861 Western Union established a transcontinental link.

The 1852 election was the last presidential election until 1880 in which slavery and its aftermath would not be the central issue. Opposition to slavery was steadily rising in pitch and volume. In

1852, Harriet Beecher Stowe's *Uncle Tom's Cabin*, the most influential novel of all time, was published; though implausible, sentimental, and theatrical, it was tremendously effective in arousing antislavery sentiment, and in its intensely human portraits of blacks as well as whites. The South attempted to refute Mrs Stowe, and some 14 pro-slavery novels were published in response to *Uncle Tom's Cabin*, among them one by William Gilmore Simms, the editor of the Charleston *Southern Quarterly Review*, and the best Southern writer of the period. *Uncle Tom's Cabin* was, thundered Professor George Frederick Holmes in the *Southern Literary Messenger*, "fiction in its form with falsehood as its end." A black minister in Maryland was given a 10-year prison sentence for owning a copy. For a long time the South had glorified the orator, the statesman, the planter, and the soldier, scorning the artist and poet; and now it paid the price of its neglect, for after Calhoun's death in 1849, it had no political philosopher or propagandist able to respond to the abolitionist deluge from the North. And the major publishing houses themselves, as we have seen, were in the North.

Two factors in the 1850s widened the gap between the sections still further: abolitionism, and railroad rivalry. Abolitionism had its precursors: Jefferson had ensured through the Northwest Ordinance of 1787 that slavery would not be introduced into the Northwest Territories (later to become the states of Ohio, Indiana, Illinois, Michigan, and Wisconsin). A federal law in 1807 prohibited trading in African slaves after January 1, 1808 (although some smuggling occurred). The American Colonization Society was founded in 1817 for the purpose of transporting freed blacks "with their consent" to Liberia, an African colony that it established for them, and 15,000 were so transported, back "home," or as unsuited to "civilization." Most slaves regarded themselves as Americans, however, and did not want to go to Africa; blacks who did go repeatedly conflicted with the indigenous tribesmen; and finally, the white South, which had once been enthusiastic, withdrew its support. The emotions aroused by abolition now defied all compromise.

Until the late 1840s the arguments, if blunt, had been realistic, as in Calhoun's contentions that the slave was backward, an "African barbarian;" that the wage slavery of the North was worse, in that it involved the ill-treatment of people of the same race; that Southern planter and Northern manufacturer needed each other — and had certainly done so in an earlier generation when each had been a Federalist. In allowing abolitionists to separate them, the capitalists, North and South, were being attacked, it was argued, by socialists and by social revolutionaries. More than this, mechanical inventions and the increasing value of land were likely to make slavery unprofitable — just as it was already declining in importance in Maryland and Kentucky, and even in Virginia. The lands north and west of Missouri were unsuited to rice, cotton, and sugar, and thus unsuited to slavery. At the realistic level, the level of practical politics, extension of slavery North and West was unlikely. In the census of 1860, taken just before the War began, and despite the lifting of restrictions that followed from the Kansas-Nebraska Act and the Dred Scott decision, there were less than 100 slaves in the then seven territories (Colorado, Dakota, Nebraska, Nevada, New Mexico, Utah and Washington); and there were many more (7,369) held as slaves by the Indians in the Indian Territory. There was disturbing truth in the contemporary ironical remark, that the whole controversy "related to an imaginary Negro in an impossible place."[41] Politicians — always compromisers — would kill slavery slowly; provided moralists, using the language of "sin" and "wickedness," were kept out.

The abolition movement that from 1831 was the most conspicuous aspect of New England reformism, had three centers: Boston, New York, and Oberlin College, Ohio. In Boston it was headed by William Lloyd Garrison. He did not come from the intellectual, Unitarian upper class, which long remained aloof from the slavery issue, but he did win some support from the Boston elite, particularly from Wendell Phillips. He became a fervent evangelical Protestant, motivated by a strong, almost Calvinist, sense of sin. The North, he argued, should do the seceding from a wicked alliance with evil. Before a Fourth of July assembly in 1854, he burned a copy of the Constitution, saying "so perish all compromisers with tyranny." In New York, where the abolition movement was better organized, though less radical, than in Boston, it was headed by a pair of wealthy silk merchants, Arthur and Lewis Tappan. They too were extremely pious and moralistic, and regarded the slavery issue as part of a campaign to save the country from sin and sinners. They fought with equal vehemence against drinking and sexual incontinence. Oberlin College in Ohio, financed by Arthur Tappan, was a center of the abolition struggle; its doors were open to Negroes and it was a station on the Underground Railroad. When Lane Theological Seminary, in Cincinnati, where the spell-binder Lyman Beecher was principal, attempted to quash student agitation in the community for immediate abolition, the students, supported by the

---

[41] Quoted by James G. Blaine in his *Twenty Years of Congress*, 2 vols (1884 and 1886), vol. I, p. 272.

Tappans and the evangelist Charles G. Finney, moved to Oberlin. Verse for every crisis came from John Greenleaf Whittier, the Quaker hymn-writer. And, though Charleston, SC, was not an abolitionist center, from it came the Grimke sisters, Angelina and Sarah, militant crusaders against slavery, who repudiated their planter background and recalled their Huguenot origins; Angelina married Theodore Weld of New York, in many ways the intelligence chief of the abolition crusade; he had converted the Tappans, and his anonymous tracts, *American Slavery As It Is* were the inspiration and the source-book for *Uncle Tom's Cabin.*

The novel was both cause and symptom of Northern vehemence against slavery; in turn it convinced Southerners that they and their institution would never be seen impartially in the North; and in turn again, Northerners began to deny, not the legality of the Fugitive Slave Law, which was on the statute book as part of the compromise of 1850, but its constitutionality – it denied jury trial to the accused – and its morality, since it was ran counter to a "higher law." In New England and New York, mobs rescued fugitives from the authorities – witness the Anthony Burns incident in 1854. Burns was a fugitive slave arrested by federal marshals in Boston. A mob led by a Unitarian minister tried to rescue Burns from a courthouse where he was detained. His master then identified him and he was escorted to a ship by a battalion of artillery, 1,000 militia and four platoons of marines, through streets filled with hissing and frustrated spectators. The enforcement of the law cost the federal government $40,000. He was the last Negro returned from Massachusetts. Many people shared the abolitionists' frustration; Northern legislatures passed personal liberty Acts to counter the Fugitive Slave Law, and to their cause a coalition of strangely named local groups gave allegiance: the Barnburners of upper New York, the ultra-Jacksonian Loco Focos of New York City, and the Conscience Whigs, all agreeing that a "Higher Law" denied the spread of slavery. There were others of that ilk. In an open letter to the abolitionists, George Fitzhugh asked:

Why have you Bloomer's and Women's Rights men, and strong-minded women, and Mormons, and anti-renters, and "vote myself a farm" men, Millerites, and Spiritual Rappers, and Shakers, and Widow Wakemanites, and Agrarians, and Grahamites, and a thousand other superstitious and infidel isms at the North? ... Why is all this, except that free society is a failure?

On another occasion Fitzhugh stated: "I do not believe there is a Liberty man in the North who is not a socialist." A Northern paper, the Catholic Boston *Pilot*, charged that wherever you found an abolitionist you found "an anti-hanging man, woman's rights man, an infidel frequently, bigoted Protestant always, a socialist, a red republican, a fanatical tee-totaler, a believer in Mesmerism, and Rochester Rappins." The Richmond *Enquirer* felt that abolitionism fostered "lectures against marriage, licentious phalansteries, Oneida haunts of communism, agrarian doctrines and anti-rent practices, free love saloons, Mormon states and Quaker villages," which would soon displace the "moral, religious, and law-abiding" ideals of Southern society.[42]

By 1840 there were 2,000 abolitionist societies, with some 200,000 members. Abolitionism in the North and Northwest, like slavery in the South, was splitting existing parties. In 1852, it took 53 ballots to nominate a Whig presidential candidate, General Winfield Scott, and when he expressed mild anti-slavery views, many deserted him in his campaign.

In opposition to all-out and, at times, violent, abolitionism, there were only three distinct policies open to practical politicians – even if they all were likely to destroy the Whig and to threaten the Democratic party. First, allegiance to the Liberty party, which was founded at Albany, NY in 1840, and which in 1848 merged with the Free-Soil party; it wanted no further expansion of slavery. Its main spokesmen were James G. Birney of Kentucky, who freed his slaves, moved to Ohio, and left the Whigs in order to be the Liberty party presidential candidate in 1840 and 1844 – he too was a convert of Weld's; Salmon Chase of Ohio, an anti-slave zealot, who was also aloof and humorless, abstemious and prayerful; he left the Whigs on this issue, sat in the Senate as a Free-Soiler from 1848 to 1854, and in 1855 became Republican Governor of Ohio; and ex-President Martin Van Buren, who in 1848 bolted the Democratic ticket, and won 10 percent of the presidential vote as a Free-Soil candidate – he had already earned his title of "the little fox." William H. Seward, the ambitious, erratic but able governor, then Senator (1849–61) of New York, was sympathetic to this view on his journey from Whiggism to Republicanism: Free-Soil became a Republican party plank in 1856 and 1860, though Seward, who had opposed the Compromise of 1850, held also that there was a "higher law than the Constitution" that forbade slavery.

---

[42] Harvey Wish, *George Fitzhugh, Conservative of the Old South* (Baton Rouge, Louisiana State University Press, 1938), pp. 15, 141; and Russell Nye, *Fettered Freedom: Civil liberties and the slavery question 1830–1860* (East Lansing, Mich., University of Michigan, 1949), pp. 13, 20.

Second, the Liberty party's Southern counterpart was states' rights: notably as voiced by Calhoun, who opposed both the Compromises of 1820 and 1850 on these grounds. On his death in 1849, its political spokesmen were the arch-secessionists Robert Barnwell Rhett of South Carolina, Representative, then Senator, and owner of the Charleston *Mercury*; William Yancey of Alabama, who would leave the Democratic party in 1860 on the issue; and John Quitman of Mississippi, who as an ex-governor of Mexico City wanted slave expansion. In the years after Calhoun's death, leadership fell not to these "fire-eaters," but to merchants and editors, small planters and yeomen, who saw the South developing more rapidly as independent than as a section confined by a Northern alliance; if independent, it would be able to reopen the African slave trade and expand into the Caribbean. The cry now was "white supremacy;" abolitionists were simply "nigger-lovers." They saw Charleston, Mobile, and New Orleans as rivals of New York, Philadelphia, and Boston: in the 60 years from 1790 to 1850 Charleston had doubled its population (from 16,000 to 30,000), but New York's had gone up 15-fold, and by 1850 it had half a million people.

And, third, in distinction from each of these, and still giving a hope of another compromise, were the advocates of popular sovereignty: "squatter sovereignty" seemed likely to defuse the issue; to many, both North and South, it seemed to be the way out. Especially did this appeal to Senator Stephen Douglas who made it the cornerstone of his policy, with dire consequences, in Kansas and Nebraska, in 1854. He was the Democratic Senator from Illinois and chairman of the influential Committee on Territories. As such he controlled all bills coming forward in the Senate on the undeveloped regions of the country. Democracy and the railroads in alliance might just solve the problem.

The prospect of a transcontinental railroad stimulated sectional rivalry still more. Already four lines were in operation from the east coast to the Mid West. The route for a line to and across the Rockies would require federal government financial aid, foreign investment – and political stability without which neither of the others was likely. The War Department survey of 1853 undertaken while Jefferson Davis was secretary of war, strongly supported a Southern route, which had the advantage of being based on New Orleans and of going through territory which was at least politically organized. It was the shortest route and with the best contours. When it was found that the best southern route lay south of the Gila River border of the Mexican cession, James Gadsden was sent to Mexico to purchase the needed strip (1854). It cost $10 million and is now the Tucson region of Arizona. The northern area – by the upper Mississippi and the upper Missouri and through what are now the states of Montana, Wyoming, and the Dakotas – was seen as too arid or too mountainous to be of value for settlement in 1850. It was the area west of Missouri that lay astride the most likely rail routes (the Central, from St Louis via the Kansas and Arkansas Rivers, crossing the Rockies to the Great Salt Lake, and on to San Francisco, and the 35th parallel route from Memphis via Santa Fe and the Apache country to Los Angeles), and which was tempting bait for free and for slave settlers alike. The spokesmen for the Southwest, among whom Senator David Atchison of Missouri (and president *pro tempore* of the Senate) was the most prominent, and for the Mid-West, of whom Senator Douglas was the most prominent, began campaigning for a central railroad to the Pacific, which would exploit the grain wealth of the Mid-West, enhance land values, and make Chicago (Douglas hoped) or St Louis (Senator Atchison hoped) its national capital. By 1850 agricultural machinery was making possible the development of the vast grain belt west of the Mississippi; by 1860, 100,000 McCormick reapers were in operation, built in his great factory in Chicago, and he had competitors; in Hiram Pitt, in John Deere in Moline, Illinois, and Obed Hussey in Cincinnati; the traditional subsistence farm of the frontier was already becoming a memory. Rising wheat prices in Europe as in America were a particular stimulus to settlement of the Great Plains during the ante-bellum decade. Moreover, Mid-Western grain, which had hitherto gone down river to New Orleans, now went East; the South would be more isolated than ever. In 1817 a journey from Cincinnati, Ohio, to New York City – by boat, wagon, and horse – had taken 50 days. By 1850, and allowing for a number of changes on some routes, it only took 6 – by rail. By 1860 New York to St Louis or Chicago was down to 2. The railroads were at once the cause and the effect of prosperity, and of the ever-tighter bonds between the Atlantic coast and the trans-Mississippi West.

Stephen Douglas, "the little giant," short and stocky, confident, persuasive and shrewd, was ambitious for himself, his state, and the development of the West; he was also – who was not? – a land speculator. Though a New Englander by birth and a resident in Chicago, his political strength lay in Southern Illinois ("Egypt,") whose settlers were mainly Southerners. They – and Douglas – did not want any extension of slavery to the territories beyond them, but were not for any interference with it where it existed – in the South from which they had come. "I have no sympathy with abolitionism," he said; but, he cynically told his people, "If slavery be a blessing, it is your blessing." To make his railroad possible, it was necessary to provide a government in, to encourage white settlement in, and to eliminate Indian claims in the upper Louisiana Territory. Under the Missouri Compromise, the land north of 36°30' (which thus included Kansas and Nebraska) was free territory; in order, however, to win Southern support for his railroad project and to have Atchison's support, Douglas proposed a bill early in 1854 re-opening the slave issue. In the previous session a bill organizing what was then called the Nebraska Territory had failed only because it did not secure enough Southern support in the Senate. In its final form, Douglas's bill provided that Louisiana between 37° and 49° latitude be divided, at the line of 40°, into the territories of Kansas and Nebraska, and that the new states carved therefrom "shall be received into the Union with or without slavery, as their constitution may prescribe at the time of their admission." This was identical language to that of the Compromise of 1850, which was drafted by Douglas, and had been applied then to Utah and New Mexico. Let the people through their territorial legislature choose whether or not slavery shall be extended, said Douglas; surely local democracy, or "popular sovereignty," would be acceptable to all? The restriction of slavery by a geographical line" as in 1820, he held, was out of date anyway; the Act declared the Missouri Compromise Line of 36° 30' "inoperative and void." More than 30 years before, Jefferson had warned of the danger of fixing a line that coincided with a "moral and political principle." Douglas expected that Kansas, just west of Missouri, and suitable for hemp and tobacco, would come in as a slave state almost immediately, and that Nebraska and other states to the north would be "fed" from Iowa and would come in as free states some time, probably decades, later. And Kansas, a slave state, would restore the political balance of power at 16 states to 16.

The bill aroused prompt and angry opposition from Northern Whigs and Free-Soilers, who saw the proposal as a device to end the Missouri Compromise, and to permit slavery north as well as south of 36° 30'; and now there was no moderator like Henry Clay to reconcile the conflicting points of view. Add to the mixture a touch of mischief. It was the explicit recommendation of the repeal of the Missouri Compromise — an addition that was largely Seward's doing — that caused anger; by it, in his devious and Machiavellian style, Seward had hoped to make the measure so objectionable (as a piece of crafty Democratic politics) that the campaign against it would help repair Whig fortunes. Hopeful of winning new lands for slavery, Jefferson Davis, then serving in Pierce's Cabinet (and its ablest member), and other Southern leaders joined Douglas in urging President Pierce to support the measure. The Nebraska issue — in its final form the Kansas-Nebraska issue — thus became a Pandora's box of political storms. Abolitionists and Free-Soilers saw the new lands not only being opened up to masters and slaves, but thereby being made unattractive to free settlers and to immigrants from the Old World — by that time forming the majority in New York City and the near-majority in a number of Eastern cities. In the same session of Congress, Southern votes in turn blocked the bill to give free homesteads to farmers, and President Pierce responded to Southern pressures by vetoing a river and harbor improvements bill; Southern votes compelled the lowering of the tariff; the Gadsden Purchase, and William Walker's filibustering expeditions against Lower California in 1853 and in Nicaragua in 1855, were evidence of Southern plans to expand south as well as west. Walker, to the joy of the Deep South, declared that slavery would be legalized in his domain. Perhaps Pandora's box is not the most appropriate metaphor: Kansas-Nebraska was, rather, a volcano. After the eruptions, the old party contours had disappeared — and so had the little giant. The original Pacific railroad proposal was forgotten in the heat of the debate over Kansas, the South arguing that slavery could be extended anywhere within the federal jurisdiction, the slavery-sensitive North vehemently denying it. Douglas could hardly have anticipated the furor which his "popular sovereignty" doctrine created, but he defended the Kansas-Nebraska bill with great ability: with the help of presidential pressure, he was able to bring into line enough Democrats to secure passage of the measure in May 1854. Two territories were to be created, Kansas and Nebraska, each much larger than the present states of those names, hopefully to balance each other, as had been done in 1820: Kansas, adjoining Missouri, seemed likely to become a slave state; Nebraska, and other states that might emerge to the North, were seen as unsuited to slavery and would, though later, come in as free. The Senate passed the measure comfortably, 37 to 14, the House more narrowly by 113 to 100. President Pierce signed it into law.

Popular sovereignty sounds good grass-roots democratic doctrine. But it rests on the premise that the minority will accept the will, and the vote, of the majority. This proved not to be true when the issue was freedom *vs.* slavery inside a state, or in the states adjoining. Douglas had expected that his bill would "raise a hell of a storm" but had not foreseen, or had minimized, intra-state and inter-state ethnic division. So would wiser men after him. Douglas

Plate 13   The Last Moments of John Brown, by Thomas Hevenden.
(The Mansell Collection, London.)

had sensed the strength of Northern sentiment against repeal of
the Missouri Compromise, but he had supposed that once the first
storm had blown itself out, the extension of slavery would be left
to popular sovereignty, and agitation would cease. But the storm
did not blow itself out. A more accurate prophet was William H.
Seward of New York, who had warned that the bill would "end

a cycle in the history of our country." Never before, one Washington newspaper reported, had "a public man been so hounded and hunted." As Douglas said himself, he could have traveled from Boston to Chicago by the light of his burning effigy. Into a territory largely uninhabited except by Indians, there poured Free-Soil and abolitionist groups, backed by emigrant aid societies in New England; from Missouri and Arkansas came planters ("The Border Ruffians") with their slaves, all seeking to obtain control of the territorial government: it became Bleeding Kansas, where free-soilers *vs.* pro-slavery men engaged in a five-year Civil war that became a herald of things to come. A pro-slave raid on Lawrence in May 1856 and the sacking and burning of the town roused John Brown, acting as surveyor and militia captain at Osawatomie, to lead his four sons and two others like-minded into the murder of five pro-slave men on the banks of the Pottawatomie; they were, as it happened, very poor and innocent, and sleeping in their beds when murdered.

Brown's activities in the guerrilla war led to plans for an invasion of the South to free the slaves: all was a model of what would happen at Harper's Ferry in 1859 — ballots if possible, but otherwise bullets; and all because, he said, God willed it so. It mattered little that Brown was a bigot, with a strain of insanity in his family, which he passed on to one of his 20 children. Compromise now no longer worked; ethnic differences or advocates of different ethnic blocs defied the democratic code. There were two rival governments at war in Kansas and two rival capitals: Lawrence (free) and Lecompton (slave). "Popular sovereignty" — superficially a democratic solution — had become mob violence. Federal troops went in in 1856 to keep the peace — but clashes recurred in 1858. By repealing the Missouri Compromise, which many Northerners saw as a sacred text, and by restoring Southern hopes of restoring the balance of power with slave expansion, Douglas had stirred the abolitionist North to fever heat. And none of the presidentially-appointed governors had any capacity to cope with the rough and tumble. What misled Douglas was his own materialism. Having no moral repugnance to slavery himself, he could not understand the depths of Northern resentment. He was in fact too realistic and judged by that index only:

Whenever a territory has a climate, soil and productions making it the interest of the inhabitants to encourage slave property, they will pass a slave code, and give it encouragement. Whenever the climate, soil and productions preclude the possibility of slavery being profitable they will not permit it. You come right back to the principle of dollars and cents.

Everything should turn on the views of white people in a locality. Between the white man and the Negro, he said, he favored the white man every time; and as between the Negro and the crocodile, he favored the Negro.

The echoes of the struggle were heard in Congress. In the spring of 1856 the learned and usually urbane Senator Sumner of Massachusetts, in his "Crime Against Kansas" speech, mercilessly insulted the South and its leaders, especially the elderly Senator Andrew Butler of South Carolina. "He has chosen a mistress ... who though ugly to others, is always lovely to him ... the harlot slavery." Two days later, Representative Preston Brooks, a nephew of Butler, caned Sumner into bloody insensibility as he sat at his Senate desk after adjournment: "You have libeled my State and insulted a relative." Sumner barely escaped with his life, and it took him nearly four years to recover. His seat stayed empty: his state's eloquent rebuke to the South. Brooks resigned his Congressional seat, but was immediately returned by his constituents by a practically unanimous vote; and he received numerous canes to replace the one he had broken in "punishing" Sumner. The "slave power" was seen as barbarous and violent. Although the newly elected President Buchanan instructed all Democratic Congressmen to ensure the acceptance of the Lecompton (pro-slave) constitution, it was repeatedly rejected by the free-state voters in Kansas itself, and Congress found it impossible to make an impartial decision on the Kansas question. Douglas now denounced the pro-slave constitution as a violation of his doctrine of popular sovereignty, and broke with his party, looking for support now to Northern Democrats. Finally, after the South had withdrawn from the Union, Kansas came in as a free state (1861), the 34th, with its capital at Topeka. By that time other free states had joined the Union — Minnesota in 1858 and Oregon in 1859 — and the "Little Giant" was dead. His motives had been varied: presidential ambitions to bring the railroad to Chicago, where he lived and where he had invested heavily in real estate; indifference to the moral issues involved in slavery; and a genuine belief that a local vote should settle the matter. He was cocksure and brash, and something of a hustler. He was also personally opposed to slavery, and was one of the intelligent few who believed that it could not be adapted profitably to the climate and soil of the plains country, manifestly inhospitable to cotton or tobacco culture. By temperament an adjuster rather than an agitator, he expected the logic of geography to preclude a theoretical debate on the dominant moral and political question of the day. He was too sensible, too much the realist; the men who stood on either side of him were not willing to let nature make policy. [43]

With the Whig party hopelessly divided over slavery, party affairs were in confusion. Northern anti-slavery radicals – Free-Soilers, Liberty party men, "conscience Whigs," and anti-Nebraska Democrats disenchanted with Douglas – were casting about for a common program and for leadership. Since the presence of slavery, and conditions on plantations, had never attracted the – mainly Irish and German – immigrants of the 1840s and 1850s, Northern politicians like Chase and Seward were aware that the notion of a free society included items – planks in a party platform? – that went beyond the issue of slave or anti-slave. It attracted temperance advocates – and nativists also. While Congress was debating the Kansas-Nebraska bill, representatives of these varied groups gathered at Ripon, Wisconsin, in February 1854, and called for a new party line-up. After the bill was passed, the "antis" met in a large mass meeting in an oak grove near Jackson, Michigan, on July 6, 1854, organized a state-wide party, and adopted the name "Republican," thus appropriating the name but not the principles of Jefferson's party. Their platform, calling slavery a "moral, social and political evil," denounced the repeal of the Missouri Compromise, and demanded repeal of the Kansas-Nebraska Act and the Fugitive Slave Law.

The Republican movement of 1854, pledged to an undying opposition to the further extension of slavery, and the political legacy of Douglas's misjudgment, quickly spread to other Northern states. With the slave issue its chief plank, the new Republican party was also Hamilton's policy revived: it sought governmental aid to commerce through river and harbor improvements, a tariff to protect industrial labor, improved marketing for the corn and wheat farmer, and aid to business by governmental encouragement of a continental railroad. The early Republican party had much of the flavour of Jacksonian populism, and prominent in its counsels was the old Jacksonian warhorse, Francis Preston Blair, and his two sons, Francis Preston Jr of Missouri, and Montgomery of Missouri and Maryland, at once Free-Soilers in sentiment but slaveholders in fact. They were a powerful clan, and indeed if Republican followers were numerous in Pittsburgh and Philadelphia, the tactical headquarters of the party was the Blair estate at Silver Spring, outside Washington – where

[43] James A. Rawley, *Race and Politics: "Bleeding" Kansas and the coming of civil war* (Philadelphia, J. B. Lippincott, 1969); David M. Potter, *Impending Crisis 1848–1861* (New York, Harper Torchbooks, 1976).

Lincoln would spend much time in the war years. Faced by the combined opposition of the Republicans and the "Know-Nothing party" (of anti-Catholic and anti-immigrant groups who, when asked about their politics, found it wise to say "I know nothing," but swept through Northern cities in ugly – mainly anti-Irish – riots.) In 1854 the votes for the House were Republicans 108, Democrats 83, Know-Nothings 43. Indeed, that new House, after two months of debate, would elect a Republican Speaker, a former Democrat alienated by the Kansas-Nebraska Act. Though some Democrats, after election day, took solace in the disintegration of the Whig party, the Republicans had emerged as serious rivals, while the Democrats themselves, as never before, were separating into Northern and Southern camps. The irony of Douglas's miscalculation had become apparent. In introducing his bill, and in bending to Southern amendments to it, he had inadvertently damaged the party – and the nation – he meant to strengthen, had weakened the candidacy he wanted to serve, and had revived the issue he proposed to bury.[44]

The strength of the new Republican party was further tested in the presidential election of 1856. The Democrats, rejecting Pierce and Douglas as too closely associated with the Kansas-Nebraska Act, nominated James Buchanan of Pennsylvania, who, as minister to Britain in 1854–6, had avoided making enemies over Kansas, and as a pro-Southern Northerner, earned the name of "a doughface." A party regular schooled in diplomacy seemed the man for a difficult job. His most recent biographer sees him as "Mr Pliable." Buchanan had always shown a talent for shifting positions under political stress, and the balancing of issues had been a major part of his success. The Democratic platform upheld popular sovereignty as the "only sound and safe solution of the slavery question." The Republicans passed over their obvious leaders, Chase and Seward, and nominated a former Democrat, John C. Fremont of California, the colorful if erratic Western explorer. The Republican platform had no intention of interfering with slavery where it existed in the states, but held that Kansas must come in as a free state. To the cries "Free soil, free labor, free speech, free men, Fremont," this new party demanded that Congress should prohibit in the territories

[44] Eric Foner, *Free Soil, Free Men and Free Labor: The ideology of the Republican Party before the Civil War* (New York, Oxford University Press, 1970), pp. 11–12; idem, "Politics, ideology and the origins of the American Civil War," in George M. Fredrickson (ed.), *A Nation Divided* (Minneapolis Burgess, 1975); and William E. Gienapp, *The Origins of the Republican Party 1852–1856* (New York, Oxford University Press, 1987), p. 70.

"those twin relics of barbarism — polygamy and slavery." The Democratic response was that if "a Black Republican" were elected, the South would secede from the Union. The threat led Northern conservatives yet again to avoid a "final solution," and to vote for Buchanan (174 electoral votes to Fremont's 114); but Fremont carried every free state in the North except New Jersey, Pennsylvania, Illinois, Indiana, and California. The combined votes of Fremont and the Know-Nothing candidate, ex-President Millard Fillmore, totaled 55 percent of the popular vote, and the Republicans captured 92 House seats and 20 Senate seats.[45]

Two days after Buchanan's inauguration, the Supreme Court handed down its decision on the case of Dred Scott, a Missouri slave owned by an army surgeon, who had sued for freedom on the grounds that periods of residence in the free state of Illinois and the free territory of Wisconsin (now Minnesota), where his master had been posted, had ended his bondage. A majority of the Court, including Chief Justice Taney, denied his petition on four grounds: Scott, as a Negro, was not a citizen, and hence had no right to sue in the Federal courts; as a resident of Missouri, Scott had not been affected by the laws of Illinois; temporary residence in free territory did not make him free; and, most important of all, his residence in a territory made free by Act of Congress had not liberated him, for the Missouri Compromise from the beginning had been an unconstitutional effort by Congress to deprive citizens of their right to property without due process of law; as such, it was contrary to the Fifth Amendment. Congress, in other words, had never had the constitutional power to exclude slavery from the territories. This verdict was hailed in the South as a guarantee of the right to hold slaves in all the territories. Northerners denounced the decision as part of a conspiracy by the "slave power." Douglas's "squatter sovereignty" doctrine was rendered obsolete, for, according to the Court's reasoning, Congress had no power to regulate slavery in the territories anyway; and even the people of a territory could not pass a law barring slavery. Dred Scott was a symbol — though, in fact, as a person, he was illiterate and ignorant; he much enjoyed his unmerited fame. It was the timing rather than the content of the judgment that was important — for there were many legal precedents for its findings. Even the shock of the Court's pronouncement on the unconstitutionality of the Missouri Compromise needs to be offset by the simple fact that Congress was engaged in over-

[45] Elbert B. Smith, *The Presidency of James Buchanan* (Lawrence, University Press of Kansas, 1975), p. 31.

turning that Compromise anyway in its Kansas-Nebraska Act. But it was – to Chase and to Seward – yet more evidence of the grip of the "slave power;" Chief Justice Taney, himself a planter's son and an old-style Jacksonian, was after all a Marylander, and five of the nine justices came from slaveholding states (though none of them held slaves.) Taney had almost as long a "reign" as his predecessor as Chief Justice, John Marshall, but differed totally in his interpretations. To Abraham Lincoln of Illinois, Taney was the arch-enemy. He did not know that, four years later, Taney would invite him to take his oath of office as President.

Before the Kansas controversy, Abraham Lincoln was merely a frontier politician, who had served for one term as a Conscience Whig member of Congress (1847–9) during the Mexican War. About 1854, he began speaking in opposition to the expansion of slavery, though without the fanaticism of the abolitionists. Within a short time, he became a well-known figure in the Northwest, thanks to his contest with Douglas for the Senate seat in Illinois in 1858, and the seven public debates throughout the state between the two men. Douglas's interest was not only in the Senate, but in the presidency in 1860. Douglas and Lincoln were totally different in appearance and in style, but good and old friends on the circuit. Douglas was probably the most popular and most brilliant politician of his day, four years younger than Lincoln but a sitting Senator, eloquent and witty, as clever a business operator as he was a manipulator of men, advocate of popular sovereignty as a solution of the slavery question. He lived in Chicago, and wanted it to flourish; he had shaped and backed the Compromise of 1850; he wanted expansion of territory and trade, and had no sympathy with abolitionism. Lincoln, in contrast, was six feet four inches tall, hollow-chested and raw-boned, gangling and awkward, and a slow, clumsy, and drawling speaker. The man of sorrows, with his sad gray eyes, was, however, a ready speaker and a tavern jokesmith. His views were – almost – orthodox, for his neck of the woods: leave slavery alone where it existed, but it should not be extended to the territories, where it would exclude free farmers. But, he added, and it was the quality that would later give him greatness – and martyrdom, it was a national as well as a local issue, a moral question that flouted all principles of justice, and which jeopardized the liberties of those who were already free. On some issues there could be no flexibility.

I have stated upon former occasions … what I understand to be the real issue in this controversy between Judge Douglas and myself. On the point of my wanting to make war between the Free and the Slave States, there has been no issue between us. So, too, when he assumes that I am in favor of introducing a perfect social and political equality between the white and black races. These are false issues. ... The real issue in this controversy — the one pressing upon every mind — is the sentiment on the part of one class that looks upon the institution of slavery as a wrong, and of another class that does not look upon it as a wrong. The sentiment that contemplates the institution of slavery in this country as a wrong is the sentiment of the Republican party. ... They look upon it as being a moral, social, and political wrong; and while they contemplate it as such, they nevertheless have due regard for ... the difficulties of getting rid of it in any satisfactory way and to all the constitutional obligations thrown about it. Yet ... they insist that it should, as far as may be, be treated as a wrong; and one of the methods of treating it as a wrong is to make provision that it shall grow no larger.[46]

In opening his campaign for Douglas's senatorial seat in 1858, Lincoln made his famous "House divided" address, which held that the Union could not survive "permanently half slave and half free — but I do expect it will cease to be divided. It will become all one thing, or all the other." The series of debates which followed, one in each Congressional district, precipitated Lincoln into the national limelight, though they did not secure his election to the Senate.

Lincoln's primary goal was to tie Douglas to the issue of "popular sovereignty" — the doctrine he had advocated in fathering the Kansas-Nebraska Act. A notable feature of the debates came to be known as the "Freeport Doctrine," expressed by the "little giant" in reply to Lincoln's question in their Freeport debate, on August 27, 1858, as to whether or not the people of a territory could, if they desired, forbid slavery? For Douglas to say "Yes" would flout the Dred Scott decision, alienate the South, and lose all chance of a Democratic presidential nomination in two years time. For him to say "No" would deny his own "squatter sovereignty" thesis of 1854, alienate many Illinois voters, and lose the Senate race. Douglas replied with a politician's dexterity that the Supreme Court was right: slavery could not be barred from any territory. Slavery, however, could not exist anywhere without "friendly local legislation:" by refusing to enact a slave code, a territorial legislature could in effect exclude slavery, since no owner would take his slaves into a territory where local police regulation did not protect his property. Slavery, that is, could not be forced on an unwilling people. This

[46] Abraham Lincoln, speech at Alton, Ill., October 15, 1858.

sound doctrine, which helped to ensure the election of a legislature favorable to him, nevertheless constituted a rejection of the Dred Scott decision, which clearly stated that the Constitution guaranteed the right to own slaves. Douglas held to his doctrine firmly, implying approval of local opposition to slavery and (in the light of Kansas's experience) to the bloodshed that might follow; it would deprive him of most of his Southern following, should he – as was expected – be a presidential candidate in 1860. For his part, Douglas sought to portray Lincoln as the "friend of the Negro." Lincoln made his views clear – too clear to many –

I am not, nor ever have been, in favor of bringing about in any way the social and political equality of the black and white races ... there is a physical difference between the black and white races which I believe will forever forbid the two races living together on terms of social and political equality.[47]

Lincoln succeeded in increasing anti-slavery sentiment by arguing that the institution was morally undesirable, but emphasized that there would be no interference with it where it existed; Douglas remained noncommittal on this point, lest he alienate the South completely. In other words, Douglas was still trying to be a compromiser. His obvious absence of moral scruples – he did not care, he said, whether slavery was "voted down, or voted up" – may well have convinced many that he was not fit for the presidential nomination in 1860. There was more than personal rivalry and Senator-making, or even President-making, in these debates. It is unlikely, indeed, that in 1858 Lincoln ever dreamed of being a candidate in 1860. Two able debaters, with command of words and of courtesy, faced each other, and their theme was – almost to the exclusion of all else – slavery. They faced up to a question, however, that every President had evaded, or on which he had compromised. Their state was important, separated only by the Ohio from the slave South; and neither candidate emerged as an outright champion of the rights of blacks. "Illinois as the home of free white men" was almost an anthem for both. And what the reaction of their large audiences revealed was anxiety, concern – and bewilderment. Americans were now seeking the eradication of the perplexing

[47] Allan Nevins, *The Ordeal of the Union*, 8 vols (New York, Scribner's, 1947–61), vol. III, p. 386; Don E. Fehrenbacher, "Lincoln, Douglas, and the 'Freeport Question,'" *American Historical Review*, 66.3 (Apr. 1961), pp. 599–617.

and distasteful peculiar institution; but, with matching intensity, they did not concede social and economic equality to the blacks. Probably few Americans realized that the dilemma of 1858 would not be resolved even by War itself. But the publicity, and the crowds that attended the debates, attested to the stature of the men and the scale of the issue. Election to the Senate lay not with the audience but with the Illinois legislators: what was at issue were 87 legislative seats, and whoever won a majority of them would control the votes necessary to choose a US Senator. Douglas would be narrowly elected to the US Senate by the Illinois legislature, but Lincoln made his reputation. And now the South campaigned actively for federal protection of slavery in the territories.

Though Congress witnessed a bitter battle in 1858 over the admission of Kansas as a slave or a free state, it was clear that the majority of the settlers there were anti-slavery, and the South was forced to look elsewhere for room for expansion. For the most serious political/economic/moral aspect of the 1850s was not race, since there were few abolitionists who strongly argued the case for racial equality, as a fact or as a goal, but the South's hunger for more land and for more slaves, outside if not now inside the United States. If they seceded, that would still be true. A number of prominent Southerners – including John Slidell and Pierre Soule of Louisiana (former US minister to Spain) and John A. Quitman of Mississippi – were abetted by expansionist Northern merchants, and by John Louis O'Sullivan, the New York editor, in their dreams of a Caribbean slave empire. The Knights of the Golden Circle, a secret society strong among Southerners in the Middle West, were held to share those dreams of a Caribbean slave empire. President Buchanan, like Pierce before him, showed interest in William Walker's filibustering activities in Nicaragua, which were Southern-backed, and made another effort to purchase Cuba, just as he had done at Ostend in 1854, when he was minister to Britain; but such territorial expansion was opposed by the North, except by those manufacturers there who expected to gain from the plan of constructing an Interoceanic canal across Nicaragua that attracted interest in Britain, Europe, and the USA – here at least might be an area where the South and the industrial North might ally? Similarly, proposals to revive the slave trade in order to reduce the cost of Negro laborers were opposed in Congress, and Southern feelings of frustration mounted. Sentiment in the North ran high over the compulsory return of fugitive slaves, and over the sight of slave pens within walking distance of Capitol Hill. In 1857 the Supreme Court's decision in the Dred Scott case implied that Congress had no power to prohibit slavery in the territories. The prospects of slave extension seemed limitless.[48]

Rising sectionalism had been further manifested in Wisconsin in 1854 when the rescuer of a runaway slave was acquitted, and the state Supreme Court upheld the decision on the ground that the Fugitive Slave Act of 1850 was unconstitutional. When the United States Supreme Court in 1859 overruled the decision in a strongly nationalist ruling, noting that this was the first time a state court had asserted supremacy over the courts of the United States – and implying that it would be the last – Wisconsin then talked of secession, and the legislature passed resolutions recalling the Kentucky and Virginia Resolutions of 60 years earlier. The cleavage between North and South had now gone beyond constitutional arguments, and the will to compromise was being eroded on all sides.

By the time Congress met in December 1859, sectional lines were drawn so tight that it took two months to elect a Speaker of the House. Prospects of a Republican victory in the coming presidential election were improving, and talk of Southern secession was in the air.

By 1860 the Republican party was a movement based upon sectional sentiments rather than a purely anti-slavery movement. Its convention was held in a vast hall known as the Wig-Wam in Chicago. Its platform offered a homestead law, a Pacific railroad, and internal improvements to attract support in the West, and a protective tariff to win the industrial states; upon the slavery question it stood in opposition to extension into the territories, in opposition to Dred Scott but not for abolition. The fanatical John Brown was roundly condemned. It needed to collect other than abolitionist votes if it was to win.

To run on this platform, which combined Hamiltonian federalism with Jeffersonian humanitarianism and idealism, Lincoln was nominated on the third ballot; he seemed less extremist than the radical Whig, Senator William Henry Seward of New York, who had expected the nomination; and he benefited as a local boy, with a shrewd manager, David Davis, who, instructed to make no deals, made them all the same, with patronage pledges to the delegations

---

[48] When Walker moved on to attempt the conquest of Honduras, he was captured by the British Navy and turned over to a Honduran firing squad. Ollinger Crenshaw, "The Knights of the Golden Circle: the career of George Bickley," *American Historical Review*, 47 (Oct. 1941), pp. 23–50. In the Civil War, they became a group of "peace Democrats and "Copperheads," hostile to the Union.

from Indiana, New Jersey, and Pennsylvania. "I authorize no bargains and will be bound by none," Lincoln instructed. Davis's comment was simple: "Lincoln ain't here, and don't know what we have to meet." The hall was packed with stentor-voiced Lincoln men, hired for their skill as noise-makers. As Murat Halstead of the *Cincinnati Commercial* reported: "Imagine all the hogs ever slaughtered in Cincinnati giving their death squeals together, a score of big steam whistles going (steam at a hundred and sixty pounds per inch) and you conceive something of the same nature."

Lincoln won not because of his merits, which were still largely unknown, but because in 1860 he was the most "available" man whom the Republicans could find. To his supporters he was "Honest Abe." To the South he was a Black Republican. To himself he was not quite either. It was the extension of slavery into the territories that was, in Lincoln's eyes, the fundamental test. He was willing to compromise on all else. He did not, he said, know how to solve the slavery problem. "If all earthly power were given me," he said, "I should not know what to do as to the existing institution." He was a compromiser almost all the way, but always a Unionist. "If I could save the Union by emancipating all the slaves I would do so; if I could save it by emancipating none, I would do it; if I could save it by emancipating some and not others, I would do that too."[49] He did know that slavery must not be allowed to extend outside the South, even though he promised no interference with it inside the South itself. There would be – he said – no abolition by force; his preference was for gradual compensated emancipation, and for voluntary colonization outside the US. Moreover, he was sufficiently moderate to attract dissident Northern Democrats and to win Pennsylvania, Indiana, and his own Illinois – which had been lost in 1856.

Douglas was still the leading Democrat, but he had lost the extreme South by his Freeport speech, and by his opposition to the admission of Kansas under a fraudulent pro-slavery constitution. The Democratic Convention at Charleston in April split. Although Douglas, a party nominee for President, led on all 57 ballots, he could not muster the necessary two-thirds majority, and the convention adjourned. When it reassembled in Baltimore, Douglas was chosen – but only after many Southern delegates had withdrawn; the radical Southerners wanted, and failed to get, an endorsement

---

[49] Lincoln to Horace Greeley, Aug. 22, 1862, in *Collected Works of Abraham Lincoln*, ed. Roy P. Basler (New Brunswick, NJ, Rutgers University Press, 1953), vol. V, p. 388.

Plate 14 Abraham Lincoln. "Soon afterwards there entered, with a shambling, loose, irregular, almost unsteady gait, a tall, lank, lean man, considerably over six feet in height, with stooping shoulders, long pendulous arms, terminating in

of their demand for a congressional slave code, protecting slavery in the territories. The Douglas men were aware that their survival in Northern constituencies depended on the preservation of popular sovereignty. They agreed only to accept Supreme Court jurisdiction in any disputes – aware that this left many doors open. Eventually Douglas headed one (the Northern) ticket, while Buchanan's Vice-President, John C. Breckenridge of Kentucky, headed another (the Southern), renewing the demand for a federal slave code in the territories. Only Douglas could possibly have won the election for the Democrats; a divided campaign guaranteed a Republican victory.

The Democratic chances were further undermined by the formation of a Constitutional Union Party, composed of conservative Whigs and others of the American Party ("the Know-Nothings"), strong in the Upper South and eager to keep the Union intact, which nominated Senator John Bell of Tennessee and Edward Everett of Massachusetts; it had, however, no permanent organization.

While the Republican platform made a wide appeal by repeating its demands for aid to commerce and industry, and adding other pledges in the form of free land for those who would work it and the protective tariff, the issue of the hour was slavery. Demanding a free Kansas, the Republicans took a firm stand against the further extension of slavery into the territories. However, they hastened to add that they would make no move against slavery in the states. The Douglas Democrats stood for popular sovereignty, while the Southern Democrats stood squarely by the Dred Scott decision. The Constitutional Unionists did not mention the burning issue of slavery, but called for the "Constitution of the country, the union of the States, and the enforcement of the laws." Thus the Southern vote was split three ways.

Plate 14 (*continued*)

hands of extraordinary dimensions, which, however, were far exceeded in proportion by his feet. He was dressed in an ill-fitting, wrinkled suit of black, which put one in mind of an undertaker's uniform at a funeral; round his neck a rope of black silk was knotted in a large bulb, with flying ends projecting beyond the collar of his coat, and above that, nestling in a great black mass of hair, bristling and compact like a ruff of mourning pins, rose the strange quaint face and head, covered with its thatch of wild republican hair, of President Lincoln. The impression produced by the size of his extremities, and by his flapping and wide-projecting ears may be removed by the appearance of kindliness, sagacity, and the awkward bonhomie of his face; the mouth is absolutely prodigious ... the nose ... a prominent organ ... the eyes, dark, full, and deeply set, are penetrating, but full of an expression which almost amounts to tenderness." From William Howard Russell, *My Diary, North and South* (1863).
(The Mansell Collection, London.)

The four-cornered campaign was fought spiritedly, though the Republicans could not conceal a natural confidence in the outcome. Vermont and Maine — voting early as usual — went Republican in September. A sense of pending doom seemed to be in the air, and everywhere there was fear for the Union. Only Douglas campaigned across the whole country. When the ballots were counted, Lincoln had 180 electoral votes, as against 123 for his opponents (Douglas 12, Breckinridge 72, and Bell 39). But the popular votes told a vastly different story. He had one million fewer votes than the combined votes of his opponents. Of 4,500,000 votes cast, Lincoln received only 39 per cent. Although Douglas received only 12 electoral votes, he received 30 per cent of the total popular vote: Lincoln 1,866,452; Douglas 1,376,957; Breckenridge 849,781; Bell 588,879. Four things were clear: one, Lincoln, the "Black Republican," was a minority President as the result of a sectional vote, in which he won every free state except New Jersey, but not a single vote in ten Southern states, and only a handful of popular votes in the border states. In the whole of American history, no other candidate has carried the electoral college with so small a percentage of the popular vote. Two, Breckenridge, who won the Deep South, in fact won only 7 of the 15 slave states. In the 14 slave states that voted by individual ballot (South Carolina still determined its electors through the legislature) Breckenridge received some 570,000 votes to his opponents' 705,000. Three, the Republicans failed to win a majority in either House. The minority President had Congress against him: no novelty in American history, but putting a heavy burden on an unknown President's unknown skills as persuader-in-chief. And four, every candidate pledged loyalty to the Union; the country, in all its complexity, was not offered a choice — at the polls — for any break-up. But it was also clear that as the free states went, so went the nation. Or so it seemed.

Lincoln was elected in an election honestly won, marred neither by fraud or by violence. He would not take office until March 4, 1861. Could he, could President Buchanan, in his last four months, avert war?[50]

[50] Nevins, *Ordeal of the Union*, vol. III, p. 412, and *The Emergence of Lincoln*, 2 vols, (New York, Scribner's, 1950); Roger J. Ransom, *Conflict and Compromise: The political economy of slavery, emancipation and the American Civil War* (Cambridge, Cambridge University Press, 1989), pp. 160–6; William E. Binkley, *American Political Parties* (New York, Knopf Borzoi, 1954), pp. 202–34.

5   AN IRREPRESSIBLE CONFLICT

Was the War Between the States inevitable?

In 1858 Lincoln spoke of a House divided. In December 1858, Seward went farther:

Shall I tell you what this collision means? Those who think that it is accidental, unnecessary, the work of interested or fanatical agitators, and therefore ephemeral, mistake the case altogether. It is an irrepressible conflict between opposing and enduring forces, and it means that the United States must and will sooner or later, become entirely a slaveholding nation or entirely a free-labor nation.

No conflict is ever inevitable: it is caused not by "destiny" or by economic forces moving as though by their own volition, but by the decisions of men. Thus far, a compromise had been found to reconcile the distinct economic interests of North and South. The first such compromise was the Constitution of 1787 itself, in devising the three-fifths clause as a measure of the value of a slave for voting purposes, and resolving that the traffic in slaves should end after a further 20 years. The new state sought to live with the reality that, although the Declaration of Independence declared that "All men are created equal," slavery was permitted to continue in the South — for, without it, the Southern states would not have joined the new nation. Even as the peculiar institution became a feature of the South, and slave numbers grew remorselessly, the compromises had been repeated in each generation: in 1820, and again in 1850, by the device of balancing off slave states against free. In the crises of the 1830s and 1840s, Oregon had been linked with Texas, to preserve the balance. But after 1850, the balance had gone when California, Minnesota and Oregon came in as free states. After the great compromisers — Clay and Webster — had died, the last great compromise of Senator Stephen Douglas, popular sovereignty ("I care more for the great principle of self-government, the right of the people to rule, than I do for all the Negroes in Christendom"), had been wrecked less by the Kansas-Nebraska Act, which repealed the anti-slavery prohibitions of the Missouri Compromise, than by the violence inside Kansas, when the introduction of Northern abolitionists and Free-Soilers and of some 5,000 Southern slaveholders (mainly Missourians) denied the validity of local choice.

In the civil war in Kansas, and again in John Brown's raid on Harper's Ferry, Virginia, in 1859, abolitionism had revealed its violent streak. Alongside the moral reformers, the church-based anti-slavery evangelicals and the Liberty party abolitionists, there clearly was a small minority who considered armed resistance to slavery to be just, necessary, and honorable. Stimulated by the scale of the repressive measures against anti-slavery activists in both North and South, and by Federal enactments to return fugitive slaves, some among the abolitionists campaigned not only for local personal freedom laws, but for war against the South, to block its insistence on the extension, as well as the preservation, of a peculiar institution that made human beings a form of property – and no more. Slavery as a moral as well as political issue was now dividing the forces that still made for national unity – not least the churches. The Southern brethren split from the Northern: the Presbyterians in 1838, the Methodists in 1844, the Baptists in 1845. The South, indeed, sought to ban the import of all "isms" – except, significantly, temperance; Dixie, not Massachusetts, was now the citadel of puritanism; and many of its yeomen farmers and its mountain people were pentecostal in their worship. And the geological differences between the Blue Ridge and the Tidewater in Virginia, and between east and west Tennessee, were revealing of the extent of the gap between the distinct economies inside a single state.

Nevertheless, slavery as such did not make war inevitable. In his first Inaugural, Lincoln undertook to protect and respect the rights of slavery in the slave states. In the North, abolitionism was never much more than the cause of *dévots*; and again the Republican party in 1860 sought to divert attention from abolition by including other planks in its platform. Moreover, in the course of the war itself, abolition as such was never a strong political aim; the Emancipation Proclamation did not come until two years after the call to arms, and even then it did not apply to slavery in the Unionist Territory. Only those slaves got their freedom whose states were at war with the North; it was a war measure, designed to weaken the enemy. In the South only one family in four owned any slaves, and Lee, the Southern hero in the war, regarded the institution as a "moral and political evil." Why, anyway, should the South secede when its peculiar institution was protected both by the Dred Scott judgment and the Fugitive Slave Law? Why should the Southern Democrats reject Stephen Douglas, who had said that he cared not whether slavery was voted up or down?

The revisionist historians contend indeed that the war was avoidable, being the work of tiny groups of extremists in North and South; they cite the apathy on the part of the North once quick victory was denied; they blame Lincoln for his uncompromising silence during the interregnum from November 1860 to his Inaugural; they claim that the war settled none of the fundamental problems. Far from being, in the words of Seward, "an irrepressible conflict," they claim that the war was both repressible and unnecessary. To Marxists and near-Marxists, the irrepressible conflict was not between slavery and freedom, but between the industrial and commercial civilization of the North and the agrarian civilization of the South. The industrial North demanded a high tariff so as to monopolize the domestic markets; it demanded a national subsidy for its shipping system, trading in mainly Southern crops; it demanded internal improvements at national expense to furnish roads, railroads, and canals, for the transport of its goods to Southern and Western markets which were already hedged around for the benefit of the North by the tariff wall. "And all the favors thus asked by the North were of doubtful constitutional right, for nowhere in the Constitution were these matters specifically mentioned ..."[51]

The issue was resolved, and the war came, because the newly elected President refused to compromise on one point: there would be no extension of slavery beyond its existing boundaries; there would be no interference with slavery as such; but thus far, and no farther. When Douglas was making it plain that he was not pro-slavery but was ready to permit slavery in the territories, Lincoln was making it equally plain that he was not an abolitionist, but that he was opposed to slavery in the territories. Douglas's stand could only win support in the South, and on the Southern border — and tepid support at that. Lincoln's could win approval everywhere outside the South. And in his opposition to the extension of slavery to the territories, Lincoln was always firm and consistent. A thread of certainty was now appearing; and a strong thread it was, for it was Lincoln's refusal to sunder it that caused the Civil War. If he were nominated as a Republican candidate for President, and if that new party won the 1860 election, the heavens could fall.

This gives, however, an over-simple view of the man from Springfield, Illinois; and Lincoln, despite his lack of a formal education, was nevertheless the reverse of simple. In his own way, and with a command of language of outstanding clarity and elegance, Lincoln's early career, and his speeches, reflect the agonies of his country. He came to the emancipation of the slaves very late, and with marked reluctance. Born in a log cabin in Kentucky — within 100 miles (and 8 months) of Jefferson Davis — the family moved from

[51] Frank L. Owsley, "The Irrepressible Conflict," in *I'll Take My Stand*, by "Twelve Southerners" (New York, Harper, 1930), pp. 74, 75.

Kentucky to Indiana and finally to Illinois; Lincoln had been a jack-of-all-trades — farm laborer, rail splitter, flat-boatman on the Mississippi, storekeeper, postmaster, assistant surveyor of roads. He held no job for long, but he came to know people and to be known by them. So odd was his appearance that he was described as "the offspring of a happy marriage between a derrick and a windmill ... He can hardly be called handsome though he is certainly much better-looking since he had the smallpox." To Edwin Stanton, later his secretary of war, he was "the original gorilla ... the original ape" — though he did not hold these views long, or repeat them. Lincoln was phenomenally strong and striking, however ungainly. Not until his election for Sangamon County to the Illinois State Legislature (at the second attempt) in 1834, did he begin the serious study of law. And as his later law partner William Herndon records, he rarely spent long reading law books; despite the poor schooling, the droll manners, and the lack of grace, he had political ambitions.

Not only ambitions but skill, and some success. His prominence in state politics — he served four terms in the state legislature — derived largely from the fact that he helped to have the state capital moved to the county seat, Springfield. This was politics — then as now — that his county could appreciate; it mattered more than policies or principles. Where principles were concerned, what was striking about Lincoln in Illinois politics in the 1830s — the heyday of Jacksonian Democracy — was that he was, after all, not a Democrat but a Whig. Raised on the frontier, he was yet no agrarian. He cast his first vote in 1832 for Henry Clay; he preferred "the American system" — the program of internal improvements, stable currency, and high tariffs — to the program of equality and reform; he held the Jacksonians to be traitors to Jefferson's ideals. The poor boy was in the rich man's party; he was ultimately to marry into it; and his wife, a Todd from the Lexington Bluegrass, was never to allow him to forget the social gulf between them. In all the emphases of Lincoln as a product of American democracy, his most noticeable feature was his determination to rise by his own boot-straps, and to become not only successful, but dignified. He was embarrassed in 1860 by the propaganda about his origins, and by the rail-splitter image. Prone to tell a folksy tale, he did not really welcome replies in kind. As Seward was to learn, he could keep his own counsel. "He was not a social man," says William Herndon, his law partner and close friend; "too reflective, too abstracted," a "reticent, secretive, shut-mouth man." Behind the rough exterior he was never a Jacksonian. Despite the Turner thesis, the frontier has in fact produced as many natural aristocrats as it has produced conformists.

Always compassionate, Lincoln detested the institution of slavery; equally he deplored the campaigns of the abolitionists who fought slavery by extra-constitutional means, just as he deplored the riots of those who sought to deprive the abolitionists of the right to speak their minds. It was at Alton, Illinois, that Elijah Lovejoy had been murdered. The abolitionists, especially their leader in the West, Theodore Dwight Weld, were far more a problem in the 1840s and 1850s than the pro-slavery advocates; Weld, indeed, a more important figure, it now seems, than Garrison. And Lincoln faithfully reflected in these years the viewpoint of his section. The tale that when, on his second visit to New Orleans, when he was just 21, he saw a mulatto girl being sold on the block, that "the iron entered his soul," and that he vowed to "hit slavery hard," is now suspect among Lincoln scholars. In fact, during his formative years, he appears not to have been particularly concerned about slavery. He lived in an area where slaves were rare; his family hailed from Virginia, and if this did not make him pro-Southern, at least he seems to have shared the contemporary Southern belief that slavery would gradually disappear. When serving in the state legislature he did nothing to interfere with the severe laws that were in force against free Negroes or runaway slaves; he did not denounce – as so many did – the Fugitive Slave Law, despite the obvious hardships to free Negroes: "I confess I hate to see the poor creatures hunted down ... but I bite my lips and keep quiet." When the Illinois legislature denounced abolitionists, and came down on the pro-slavery side, Lincoln refused, it is true, to support the majority; but he afterwards justified his position by the unexceptionable statement that "the institution of slavery is founded on injustice and bad policy but ... the promulgation of abolition doctrines tends to increase rather than abate its evils." As a good lawyer, Lincoln respected the Constitution; slavery where it existed must be left alone, and allowed to die a natural death – if it would. It is not surprising, but often forgotten, that such moderation, at a time when tempers ran high, brought him no distinction – and some obloquy. To Wendell Phillips he was "that slavehound from Illinois." However inaccurate this was, Lincoln was certainly no crusader.

Lincoln was slow to condemn slavery as such. He did so now and then, but never formally until 1854, and always accompanying his condemnations by a frank avowal that he did not know what to do about it. There was, then, distaste for the institution, a firm front against its further extension, and a frank avowal of uncertainty of how to curb it without offending the South – or the law of the land. But there was something more than this, greatly appealing to

Illinois: and that was the theme that the Western states, like the territories, were for white men – free men but white men. Alongside every sentence in every speech condemning the wickedness of slavery and stressing the superior merits of a free to a slave society, there is the equal emphasis that the Negro must not be given political or social equality. The Negro might be the equal of the white: but he must not be given citizenship. The Republican party in the Northwest inherited both Free-Soil sentiment and, in some degree, nativism; if not as cold-blooded about slavery as Douglas's, it did not want Negroes, free or slave, on its borders. Its theme-song in Missouri, as advocated by Frank Blair on the masthead of his *Daily Missouri Democrat*, was "White Men for Missouri and Missouri for White Men."

Lincoln at Peoria in 1854 spoke of the future of the territories:

We want them for homes of free white people. This they cannot be, to any considerable extent, if slavery shall be planted within them. Slave States are places for poor white people to remove from, not to remove to. New free States are the places for poor people to go to, and better their condition. For this use the nation needs these Territories.

The argument, which he used repeatedly in the next six years was an argument not for equality – of black and white – but for freedom – for whites. It was the fear of poorer whites, almost all of them immigrants into the West and many of them of foreign origin, that they might now have to compete in hitherto-free states with the labor of slaves, that brought them into the Republican party in the Northwest. It was not difficult for the Republican party to build around this theme those other planks – free homesteads, a railroad to the Pacific, a protective tariff – that were in the end to make of it the party of progress, expansion, and the full dinner pail. The pioneer of the 1850s was, after all, often the father of the entrepreneur of the 1890s. If Lincoln's father was an illiterate nomad, Lincoln's son was ambassador to the Court of St James and president of the Pullman Car Company. The generation that lived in the sod-house – like that which fought the Indian – was very short; but if short in actual span of years it too has been long in legends. Lincoln was, said Douglas, "jet black" in the North, "a decent mulatto" in the center, and "almost white" in the South. And the charge was true: in Chicago it was "all men are created equal;" in the South "the superior position must go to the white race." Lincoln was still a moderate – opposed to abolition, opposed to the repeal of the Fugitive Slave Laws, opposed to Negro citizenship and to social and political equality of white and black. The free Negro, H. Ford Douglass, thought his program no better than that of Stephen Douglas. But in all his dexterity, Lincoln never abandoned the central argument: that slavery must not be permitted to expand. If the Dred Scott decision of the Supreme Court in 1857 were permitted to stand – that slavery could not be excluded from the territories – where could slavery be halted? "Popular sovereignty" could not be reconciled with the Dred Scott decision. The Democratic party had become a "conspiracy ... for the sole purpose of nationalizing slavery."

For Lincoln the Dred Scott decision of the Supreme Court in 1857 was decisive. It held that "blacks had no rights which the white man was bound to respect." Lincoln offered a sharp and superbly phrased dissent in his speech at Springfield, Illinois:

I think the authors of the Declaration intended to include all men, but they did not intend to declare all men equal in all respects. They did not mean to say all were equal in color, size, intellect, moral developments, or social capacity. They defined with tolerable distinctness, in what respects they did consider all men created equal – equal in "certain inalienable rights, among which are life, liberty and the pursuit of happiness." This they said, and this they meant. They did not mean to assert the obvious untruth, that all men were enjoying that equality, nor yet, that they were about to confer it immediately upon them. In fact, they had no power to confer such a boon. They meant simply to declare the right, so that the enforcement of it might follow as fast as circumstances should permit. They meant to set up a standard maxim for a free society, which should be familiar to all, and revered by all; constantly looked to, constantly labored for, and even though never perfectly attained, constantly approximated, and therefore constantly spreading and deepening its influence, and augmenting the happiness and value of life to all people of all colors everywhere.

Invoking the Book of Proverbs, Lincoln said that the principle of equality in the Declaration of Independence was like the apple of gold inside a frame of silver – the frame being the Constitution. But the skill of the analysis also reveals a politician dancing on a tightrope between moral conviction and political expediency. And even as president he urged a group of blacks to find a black colony in central America – "it is better for us both to be separated."

The 1858 debates gave Lincoln a national platform. Throughout 1859 he campaigned as the leading Western Republican, in Ohio and Indiana, Iowa and Wisconsin. When he delivered the Cooper Institute speech in New York in February 1860 – the speech and the photograph that in retrospect he thought gave him the Republican nomination – he held to the same note: denial of abolitionism; distaste for John Brown's radicalism; sympathy for the South – but no support for any proposed extension of slavery to the territories of the United States. This was for Lincoln the central precept, ordained by the Founding Fathers.[52]

6 AND THE WAR CAME

South Carolina made the election of Abraham Lincoln the occasion for an ordinance of secession, which was passed by a special convention in Charleston on December 20, 1860. South Carolina was as unique as was the Republican party, but dramatically different. It still lived under the constitution of 1790, with no elections for an area larger than the Congressional district, with the legislature choosing governor, state officials, and presidential electors. It was ruled by an aristocracy based on rice and cotton, with Charleston a gracious city state where, as the residents on the Battery proudly boast, the Ashley and the Cooper Rivers unite to form the Atlantic Ocean; here states' rights was the cover-word for state sovereignty. When its leading citizen John C. Calhoun had gone to Washington as Vice-President or as secretary of state, Charleston had seen him as a diplomat on a mission to a neighboring but friendly power. Calhoun's successor as Senator, and the state's major advocate, was Robert Barnwell Rhett, owner of the Charleston *Mercury*, master of two plantations and of 190 slaves, the most fiery of the "fire-eaters;" it was his call for secession in 1860 on the news of Lincoln's election that was decisive for what some called "Rhettsylvania." Enthusiastic mass meetings elected the overwhelmingly secessionist convention which met in Charleston on December 20, 1860, to agree without any dissenting vote that "the union now subsisting between South Carolina and other states, under the name of 'The United States of America' is hereby dissolved." Most Southerners had long been sure that the United States was a league of sovereign independent states, and any member had a right to secede if and when it chose.

By February 1, 1861, by the vote of similar specially summoned conventions, the other six states of the lower South – Mississippi, Florida, Alabama, Georgia, Louisiana, and Texas – had also left the Union. Two nations were emerging, and two economies. Propaganda

[52] Don E. Fehrenbacher, *Prelude to Greatness: Lincoln in the 1850s* (Stanford, Stanford University Press/Oxford University Press, 1962).

reinforced the separation. "A surrender to Secession is the suicide of Government," said Cincinnati. "Crush treason," said Roxbury, Massachusetts. "We have a civil war on our hands," declared the New York *Tribune*. The secessionist conventions which met during the winter of 1860–1 rehearsed their own long series of grievances against the North; the prohibition of the slave trade after 1808, assistance to fugitive slaves, resistance to the extension of slavery to the territories, and now the election of a man who was an avowed opponent of slavery. Slavery was the *only* issue which received significant mention at these gatherings. Subsequently efforts were made to include the tariff among the causes of the War between the States; in fact, the tariff was low in 1860, and the higher Morrill Tariff of 1861 was enacted only after the Southern Congressmen had already withdrawn. By 1861 there was evidence of a "now or never" sentiment. The North and West were growing more rapidly than the South, and the ties between them were drawing tighter. If secession were to succeed, prompt action was necessary. There was considerable doubt even in 1860 that the Southern states would be permitted to depart from the Union peacefully.

Though the leaders of secession acted upon premeditation, rather than impulse, there were still many Southerners who argued for giving Lincoln a chance. Alexander H. Stephens, for example, argued that to secede now was folly, since the South was strong enough in Congress to block radical Republican enterprises at least until 1863. By seceding, the South lost all the territories, and all protection under the Fugitive Slave Act. Remaining in the Union posed no real threat to slavery where it then existed, for a Constitutional amendment could easily have been defeated by the Southern states; and the free states would not have resorted to war to secure abolition. Secession, on the other hand, invited war, with the likelihood that abolition would be the result of a Northern victory. Southern extremists professed to believe that the North would not fight to preserve the Union, and that, if war came, the South would be victorious. Was not cotton king of the nation's economy? Did not the South possess the most experienced military and political leaders?

On February 4, delegates from six of the seven states of the Deep South, later joined by Texas, met at Montgomery, Alabama, to consider united action. They were moderate men – a "fire-eater" like William L. Yancey did not secure a place in the Alabama delegation. Within a week a temporary constitution was ready for the "Confederate States of America," and within five weeks a permanent document was not only drafted but accepted, and submitted to the state conventions for their approval. Unlike 1787, the preamble of the new constitution explained that it derived its existence from "the people of the Confederate States, each state acting in its sovereign and independent character." This constitution had two fundamental bases: first, it recognized the sovereignty of the states as expressed in the Articles of Confederation of 1778, and, second, slavery was specifically made a lawful institution. Indeed, the word "slave" was openly used, instead of the anguished circumlocutions of 1787. The protection of slavery in any territories of the Confederacy was guaranteed. The three-fifths ratio as the basis of representation in the lower house of Congress was retained, but the foreign slave trade was banned. If, in its general form, it parallelled the federal Constitution, its differences were important and specific: bounties and protective tariffs were prohibited, internal improvements for sectional benefits were ruled out and there was no power in Congress "to provide for the general welfare;" the President was elected for six years (a final fulfillment of a Jeffersonian dream), but was ineligible for re-election; unlike the federal president, he was empowered to veto separate items of appropriation bills. Jefferson Davis, the Confederate president, vetoed 38 measures during the war, only to have 37 of them passed over his veto. As in the British Parliament, Cabinet members could sit in Congress, but – unlike Westminster – they could only speak on their department's affairs. Unlike the document of 1787, product of a skeptical age, the Confederacy invoked "the guidance of Almighty God."

The Founding Father of the Montgomery Constitution of 1861 was less Alexander Stephens than "St Calhoun:" the delegates were revising the document of 1787 in the light of their bitter experience. The powers they conferred on their Congress were not "granted" – as in 1787 – but "delegated." The Southern argument was that the Union was a confederation, in which the states were sovereign; this had the history of 1787 on its side, but left it difficult to explain the status of the Western states since they were created by the federal government. Under the Articles of Confederation, the states clearly had been sovereign. Were they still so in 1787? Was the creature born in that year one – or a confederal – animal? In any event, by 1860 it was vastly larger, not 13 now but 33, urban as much as rural, resting on two oceans and two inland seas, a complex mosaic of plural, overlapping, and competitive sovereignties; and, like any adolescent, it was the product as much of its own experience, history, and environment, as of its inheritance. What was the nature of the Union that Lincoln was prepared to fight to maintain? By 1860, serious insistence upon the primacy of states' rights in the South was being made only in Virginia, Georgia, and

South Carolina; states' rights had become the sectional issue of "Southern rights," but it would be invoked in the war to bedevil the Confederacy. In the North, and particularly in the West, national loyalty ranked first, except for occasional utterances by radical minorities.

In all the Southern states, as voiced in their conventions, the issue was not whether to secede but how to do so; there was a clear majority for secession in each of the State conventions; and in Texas, where (alone) secession was put before the voters, it won a clear majority there. It seems likely that it would have been the same in every state of the Deep South. The Montgomery convention became a Congress, and Jefferson Davis of Mississippi was elected President, and Alexander H. Stephens of Georgia, Vice-President. Davis was a cotton planter, and a West Point graduate, but of Kentucky yeoman stock, and owed his rise to the wealth and the backing of a successful elder brother; as colonel of the Misssippi Rifles he received a wound, and fame, at Buena Vista, and a bride also, since he married the daughter of his commanding officer Zachary Taylor. In so far as he wanted a job he sought the post of commander-in-chief, not the presidency; and he did not curb a taste for intervention in exclusively military matters. He wanted a strong South more than he wanted secession, with expansion into the Caribbean; he had campaigned for a New Orleans–Pacific Railroad and had inspired the Gadsden Purchase to make it possible. To his distinction in the Mexican War, he could add his role as a leader in both houses of Congress, and as Pierce's secretary of war. But, slight in build, egotistic° and neuralgic, industrious and testy, he was not made for political leadership. He was totally devoid of that imperative for all politicians: a sense of humor. Stephens, long a Unionist, had served his state loyally for six years in the legislature and 15 years in Congress; his parchment-like face and tiny, skeletal frame, indicated his own poverty of origins and his ferocious industry. He was no ally of Davis, but he was the principal architect of the constitution. Himself more philosopher than politician, he was outspoken in his view that its foundations rested "upon the truth that the Negro is not equal to the white man, that slavery – subordination to the superior race – is his natural and normal condition." Unfortunately, he was in effect an absentee Vice-President; in the two years from October 1862, he visited Richmond only twice. His home in Georgia became the states' rights think-tank of the opposition to Davis. It was the election of Lincoln that swung the Georgia Unionists, and advocates of the Compromise of 1850, into secession: Alexander Stephens, Howell Cobb, and Robert Toombs – and only the last was a wealthy planter. So it proved to be also with Davis's Cabinet: its ablest member, Judah Benjamin, a New Orleans lawyer, was British West Indian born, the son of a small merchant; his Treasury secretary, Christopher Memminger, was a German immigrant brought up in an orphanage; and his Navy secretary, Stephen Mallory, a Connecticut Yankee by birth, had helped his widowed mother run a boarding house in Key West. The planters were inconspicuous here.

At Montgomery the Confederate government was devising not only a constitution but a strategy, for Davis believed – correctly – that "there would be war, long and bloody." The Congress adopted a flag of "stars and bars" to replace the stars and stripes. An army of 100,000 men was voted, a $15 million loan authorized, and a small export tax on cotton levied to cover the loan. Davis was instructed to secure Fort Sumter, the Federal fort in Charleston Harbor, and at the same time a committee was appointed to go to Washington to negotiate a treaty of friendship with the federal government.

The themes of the state conventions were familiar. If union continued, the Southern "nation," with its values based on its agrarian economy, would be sacrificed to the economic demands of the North. Its federal taxes would be spent on internal improvements which would make the North progressively richer; its cost of living would be further increased by higher import tariffs to protect Northern industries; immigration would be encouraged to supply the Lords of the Loom with wage slaves, and the swelling of the population in the North would increase its political representation in Washington. Secession, it was argued, spelt economic independence: free trade with Britain would bring cheap imports with the abolition of discriminating taxes and tariffs, higher profits for cotton, lower prices for slaves. Why should the South continue to profit Yankee middlemen? Republican triumph in 1860 in any case would end the effective control of the federal government by Southerners, and herald another protective tariff, a homestead Act and a railroad linking the Pacific Coast with the Old Northwest, measures which the South had consistently opposed. Moreover, Lincoln's election had been preceded by the violence of John Brown's raid on Harper's Ferry, which to many Southerners indicated what might be in store from Republicans. And they argued that if the Union had a Republican President, slavery would be doomed, and the South would be Africanized by the following Republican strategy: first, Lincoln would "abolitionize" the border slave states, and then prevent the further expansion of slavery into the territories; eventually, three-quarters of the states would be free, and the abolitionists would then abolish slavery by constitutional amendment.

The immediate secessionists argued that if the states passed secession ordinances legally, they would be able to leave the Union peacefully. War was not in anyone's interest. An attack on the South would merely unite the Southern states, and the practical Northerners would quickly recognize the folly of war. The immediate secessionists were fond of comparing the South's size and resources to those of the smaller countries of Europe. If Switzerland, Belgium, and the Netherlands could survive among their larger neighbors, surely, they said, the South could survive in North America. The South would even grow stronger economically, since it would no longer be dependent upon Northern manufactures. Finally, they said, secession need not be a permanent solution; the South could return to the Union after it had won suitable concessions. They still heard the voice of St Calhoun. It would be a quick – and a defensive – war.

The more hesitant Southerners were reassured by the secessionists, who argued that the speed with which the South had recovered from the panic of 1857 proved the economic power of cotton and the soundness of the plantation economy. The North, threatened with the loss of cotton and the Southern market, would not dare forcibly to oppose secession. If war came, the South believed that it could count upon the intervention of Great Britain, anxious to save its textile industries, and the support of the Ohio valley, closely connected to the Cotton Kingdom by commercial ties.

President Buchanan, a lawyer, indeed a man who through his long life had prided himself upon his mastery of constitutional law, put his knowledge to work on defining the problem. Not knowing whom else he could trust, he turned to his fellow-Pennsylvanian, Jeremiah Black, another lawyer – who had been appointed to his Cabinet as attorney general but was now serving as secretary of state, or in effect as second-in-command. Buchanan, afraid of secession but surrounded by Southerners, reasoned that since the Constitution made no provision for its own liquidation, no state could unilaterally withdraw from the Union. The Founding Fathers, when composing the Constitution, had made no specific provision for meeting that which was impossible. There was no lawful right to secede, and the federal government had no right to coerce. Therefore, and quite plausibly, he resolved that the only grounds upon which the federal government could meet the crisis would be if the seceded states were to interfere with the duly constituted rights and powers of the federal authority. The outgoing President had established a point of critical significance for his successor. If war was to come, it could only occur as a result of Southern aggression, a deliberate

Southern infraction of duly constituted federal powers. His was the impeccable reasoning of an able lawyer, and the hesitancy of one not endowed with executive *brio*. Surrounded by a Cabinet in which Southern influence was predominant and some members of which were avowed secessionists, he refused to send reinforcements to Fort Sumter, whose supplies were running short, or to take steps to collect customs and enforce the laws in the seceded states. All he could suggest was yet another compromise, and the soothing of the South by a constitutional convention to frame amendments guaranteeing slavery in the states and territories, and assuring the recovery of runaway slaves.

Numerous similar schemes for reconciliation were proposed during the winter of 1860–1. They were especially sought by the border states. The House set up a Committee of 33, the Senate a Committee of 13 – in each case the old, not the newly elected chambers, serving their last "lame-duck" session. The most important proposals were the Crittenden Compromise and those of the Virginia Peace Convention. The essence of the plan advocated by Senator J. J. Crittenden of Kentucky, was contained in five "permanent" amendments to the Constitution: (1) protecting slavery in the states where it was legal; (2) sanctioning the domestic slave trade; (3) guaranteeing payment by the United States for escaped slaves; (4) forbidding Congress to abolish slavery in the District of Columbia without the consent of Virginia and Maryland; and (5) reviving the Missouri Compromise line and extending it to the Pacific. Crittenden, a Kentucky Senator for 18 years, opposed secession – like the majority in his state, he wanted to stay in the Union. In that he was successful; but one of his sons, George, became a Confederate general; another, Thomas, who fought at Shiloh and Chickamauga, and a nephew, were Union generals. At Lincoln's insistence, however, the Republicans refused to endorse any compromise which permitted the extension of slavery into any federal territory; the Crittenden proposals did not get beyond congressional debate. The Peace Convention of February 1861 was attended by representatives from 21 states, who similarly worked for a month to formulate a program of conciliation. Their final proposal, the addition of a constitutional amendment, virtually identical with the Crittenden proposals, passed both Houses but was never ratified by the states. The reasons for the failure are clear enough: the Union was now breaking up. By the end of January the Congressmen of the Deep South resigned their seats and went home, as did Buchanan's Southern Cabinet ministers. Every Republican voted against the Crittenden Compromise: the North had conceded enough; now it must stand up for its principles.

Lincoln was convinced that nothing but a complete surrender of Republican principles would placate the South; hence he took relatively little interest in compromise proposals. To compromise would be to concede that the election of a Republican President, or even more the dominance of the Republican party, was a menace to the Union; the South, it seemed, was demanding the suicide of the Republican party. More than this, from November 1860 to February 1861, Lincoln said nothing in public, but he wrote letters to key Republican congressmen whose tenor was uniformly against compromise. He argued that the crisis would have to be met sometime, and that he did not want to experience the humiliation of begging or buying a peaceful inauguration. His letters were decisive in maintaining the Republican opposition to compromise. Moreover, Northerners, aside from their objection to secession as illegal, had practical reasons for opposing it. Northern farmers did not want to lose access to the mouth of the Mississippi, for then the Old Northwest would be landlocked. Northern businessmen did not wish to give up their investments and markets in the South. Finally, many feared that the secession of the Deep South portended the Balkanization of America. People talked seriously of a Pacific Confederation and of a Northwest Confederacy, and in New York businessmen thought that New York City itself should become an independent nation, and trade with both sides. To others, it seemed that war with the South was inevitable anyway, so one might as well fight for a restored Union.

Lincoln left Springfield for Washington on February 11, 1861. Because of reports of likely attempts at assassination he entered the city secretly, at night. His speeches *en route* had done nothing to placate the South. General Winfield Scott had been ordered to be ready to "hold or retake" the forts in the South as circumstances might require. But the Inaugural Address was conciliatory. Lincoln once again disclaimed any intention of interfering with slavery in the states. All federal laws must be observed — including the laws compelling the return of fugitive slaves; the Union, however, must and would be preserved. But there was no way in which the oath to maintain the Constitution and preserve the Union could be squared with secession. "In your hands, my dissatisfied fellow-countrymen, and not in mine, is the momentous issue of civil war. You have no oath registered in heaven to destroy the Government; while I shall have the most solemn one to 'preserve, protect and defend' it."

Lincoln won his election not by moral greatness, or by compassion for white or black, but by political skills of a high order. He was to reveal greatness in the years ahead, moral as well as political.

Earnest he was, with remarkable insight into the essence of the controversy; and firm he was to show himself. But little of this was evident in 1860, least of all to his Cabinet. The ill-dressed and awkard figure, with a high nasal inflexion in his voice, was – to Seward as to the country – an unknown quantity, even perhaps a "Simple Susan." But he had shown uncanny skill in compromising on many questions. He had also shown that there were for him some issues on which there could be no compromise, and no surrender.

Edmund Ruffin, the Virginian editor of the *Farmers Register*, who had devoted much of his life to campaigning for the restoration of fertility to worn-out tobacco lands by the application of marl, was so ardent a secessionist that he left his native Virginia to live in South Carolina. In 1859, at the age of 63, he attended John Brown's hanging clad in the uniform of a Virginia Military Academy cadet. In 1860, he had written *Anticipations of the Future*, forseeing a long war, the continuing loyalty of the slaves, the development of Southern industries and Southern victory in 1867; New York City would be destroyed by a mob of "undigested foreigners" and Washington would become the capital of a new Southern republic. As a volunteer in the Palmetto Guards, he was invited to pull the lanyard to fire the first shot on Fort Sumter, on April 12, 1861.

10

The War Between The States

---

1 LINCOLN AT THE FOX RIVER

When in February 1861 President-elect Abraham Lincoln made the long journey from Springfield, Illinois, to Washington, DC, he was met by many people; some came to cheer, one or two perhaps planning to kill. The endless questioning was on the theme: would there be war? To all such, he used his skill as *raconteur* — that is, as evader. In New York he told of his days as a young lawyer when he used to ride the judicial circuit in southern Illinois. Once during a rainy spell he and some companions found most of the streams along their way swollen far beyond their normal size. As they crossed these streams with mounting difficulty, the party became concerned about the Fox River, which lay ahead and promised to be even more turbulent than the creeks behind them. Night came on, and the men stopped at a tavern. There by chance was the local Methodist presiding elder, who traveled about the region extensively. Lincoln and his colleagues were eager to learn from this man about their prospects of fording the Fox. To their questions the elder replied: "O yes, I know all about the Fox River. I have crossed it often and understand it well; but I have one fixed rule with regard to the Fox River; I never cross it till I reach it."

Lincoln took his oath of office as President on March 4: until then he made no move. He was an unknown and untried quantity, a neophyte from the backwoods, the surprise choice of a sectional party, elected by a minority of the popular vote. His Inaugural was carefully moderate in tone:

I therefore consider that in view of the Constitution and the laws the Union is unbroken, and to the extent of my ability I shall take care, as the Constitution itself expressly enjoins upon me, that the laws of the Union be faithfully executed in all the States ... In doing this there needs to be no bloodshed or violence, and there shall be none unless it be forced upon the national authority. The power confided to me will be used to hold, occupy, and possess the property and places belonging to the Government, and to collect the duties and imposts; but beyond what may be necessary for these objects, there will be no invasions, no using force against or among the people anywhere.

Since "the Union of these States is perpetual," he saw his duty as the maintenance of the Union. There would be no interference with the institution of slavery in the Southern states, and the Fugitive Slave Act would be faithfully observed; but there would be no expansion of slavery into the territories of the US. In not compromising on this — unlike his predecessors in 1820 and 1850 — Lincoln was responsible for what followed. But he would not be the first to move. "You can have no conflict," he told the South, "without being yourselves the aggressors" —

In your hands, my dissatisfied fellow-countrymen, and not in mine, is the momentous issue of civil war. The Government will not assail you ... You have no oath registered in heaven to destroy the Government, while I shall have the most solemn one to "preserve, protect and defend it."

The border states had not yet seceded — nor had Virginia, North Carolina, Tennessee, and Arkansas. Lincoln's own Cabinet covered the usual wide cross-section of opinion and geography, a collection of all the leaders of all the factions, if not of all the talents; the product of diversities of interest, and of deals done. His Vice-President, Hannibal Hamlin of Maine, was a one-time Democrat. Only one member, Salmon P. Chase of Ohio, secretary of the Treasury, was an abolitionist; he had been an anti-Nebraska Democrat. Its leading figure — at least in his own eyes — was William H. Seward of New York, the "wily old scarecrow" as Henry Adams called him, a former anti-slavery or "conscience" Whig and Free-Soiler, now serving as secretary of state; he saw Lincoln as a "Simple Susan," and still felt that he should have been in Lincoln's place in the White House. Once the prophet of irrepressible conflict, Seward was now the champion of compromise, planning to preserve the peace by providing a cooling-off period, during which the South would return to its senses — and to the Union. "Mr Lincoln," says his secretary, John George Nicolay, "shared Seward's pacific inclinations, but not his optimism."

Lincoln was temperamentally a moderate, but on the integrity of the Union, to which he was now pledged by oath of office, as on the further territorial expansion of slavery, he would not compromise. Seward first followed his own private line to the Southern commissioners, then suggested that an aggressive foreign policy would reunite the country: better a foreign foe than a civil war. Once he realized that he was not to be the power behind the throne, he handled foreign affairs with a competence which needed only occasional checking by the President. In the end he became a sincere admirer and supporter of Lincoln. Salmon P. Chase was sympthetic to the Radicals, and injudiciously critical of Lincoln both as to his person and his policies; touchy and ambitious, he was also able and honest. The Navy Department was under an opinionated and crusty former Democratic editor, Gideon Welles of Connecticut, who wisely left technical affairs to be administered by the competent career man Gustavus Vasa Fox, who happened to be the brother-in-law of the new postmaster-general, Montgomery Blair of Maryland. Welles's *Diary* was to chronicle the inside story of Washington during the next grim four years.[1] Seward and Welles, along with Attorney General Edward Bates of Missouri and Montgomery Blair, from key border states, proved to be Lincoln loyalists. Caleb Smith and John P. Usher were undistinguished secretaries of the interior, owing their place to deals done in Chicago. There was one further member, Simon Cameron of Pennsylvania, in the War Department. Cameron was the boss of the Pennsylvania Republican machine, who sold army contracts — and much else — to the highest bidder; his definition of an honest politician was that he was one who, once bought, "stays bought." He resigned in January 1862, to be replaced by Edwin M. Stanton of Ohio, a Democrat. Stanton was the greatest, and probably the most industrious, war minister in American history, and without his administrative vigor the war might well have been lost. He was, however, ill-mannered and devious, and seemed to love mischief for its own sake. His decisiveness as administrator belied an erratic past: he had served in the last months of Buchanan's Cabinet, and in 1860 voted for Breckenridge. He was an ally of the Radicals; he greatly influenced public opinion by his military censorship; and he ruined the reputation of many a general.

[1] *The Diary of Gideon Welles*, ed. John T. Morse Jr, 3 vols (Boston, Houghton Mifflin, 1911).

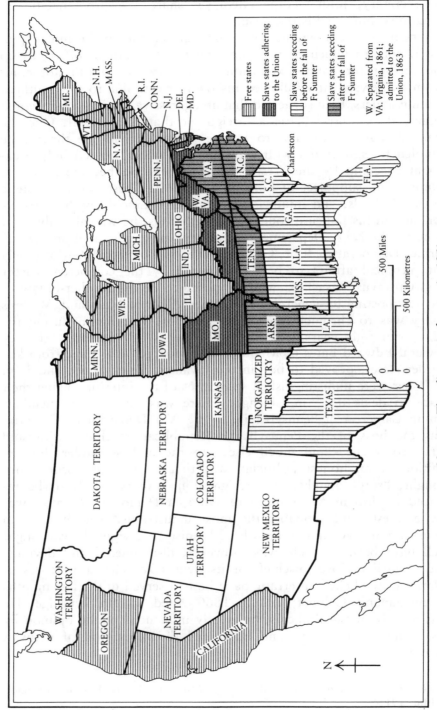

Legend:
- Free states
- Slave states adhering to the Union
- Slave states seceding before the fall of Ft Sumter
- Slave states seceding after the fall of Ft Sumter
- W. Separated from VA. Virginia, 1861; admitted to the Union, 1863

WASHINGTON TERRITORY
OREGON
NEVADA TERRITORY
CALIFORNIA
UTAH TERRITORY
DAKOTA TERRITORY
NEBRASKA TERRITORY
COLORADO TERRITORY
NEW MEXICO TERRITORY
KANSAS
UNORGANIZED TERRITORY
TEXAS
MINN.
IOWA
MO.
ARK.
LA.
WIS.
ILL.
IND.
OHIO
MICH.
KY.
TENN.
MISS.
ALA.
GA.
S.C.
N.C.
VA.
W. VA.
FLA.
PENN.
N.Y.
VT.
ME.
N.H.
MASS.
R.I.
CONN.
N.J.
DEL.
MD.
Charleston

500 Miles
500 Kilometres
0

Map 11 The alignment of states in 1861.

There was no unity in such a group: only three were on friendly terms with the rest. But that mattered little, for they met irregularly, and did little serious business. When they were summoned, as for their views on the Emancipation Proclamation, they heard the President read a document already drafted; its style was his; what he wanted was their views on its timing. That suited the President: his system was devoid of system, and what mattered was what suited him. For in the Constitution, executive power is vested in the President alone. As Edward S. Bates put it, it was "not an administration, but the separate and disjoined action of seven independent officers, each one ignorant of what his colleagues are doing." At the 37th Congress, the President was similarly aloof: it met for three sessions only in its two years. His party was strongest, since the Southerners were absent.

On March 5, 1861, Lincoln received a message from Major Robert Anderson, commanding at Fort Sumter in Charleston Harbor (previously artillery instructor at West Point to P. G. T. Beauregard, the Southern commander at Charleston), that his garrison of 128 men could hold out without reinforcement only for 40 days. It would need a force, he reckoned, of 20,000, with the navy to support, to relieve him. The commander of the US Army, the 74-year-old corpulent veteran of both the War of 1812 and the Mexican War, General Winfield Scott, "Old Fuss and Feathers," counseled that it would take eight months to prepare a relief expedition: the total US Army was only 16,000 strong, and mainly scattered along the distant Mexican frontier. General Scott recommended the reinforcement of Fort Pickens, at Pensacola, the other fort in much the same situation as Sumter; all the other forts in the South had been quietly evacuated, except remote Key West and the Dry Tortugas. Reinforcement at Pickens was thought to be more feasible, more expedient, and less dangerous than aid to Sumter; a relief force was already standing off Pensacola. Lincoln was assured that a token display of Union strength there would do the job: Sumter could then be quietly abandoned — and with this evidence of goodwill, Virginia (and other hesitant states?) might then be persuaded to remain in the Union. A state for a fort seemed to Lincoln a good bargain. There were, after all, large minorities in Louisiana, Georgia, Texas, and Alabama who had opposed secession — those in northern Alabama wishing to recreate the state of "Nickajack," the old Indian name for the region. So it was ordered.

It was not until April 6 that Lincoln learnt that the reinforcement order of March 12 had not been carried out; this delay is often held to have profoundly affected his decision on Fort Sumter.

Meantime Seward was in contact (though not face to face) with three Confederate Commissioners, who were visiting Washington to discuss the peaceful separation of North and South; and he probably assured them, or at least allowed them to conclude, that there would be a discreet abandonment of Sumter; to the President he unhelpfully suggested a declaration of war or the threat of a declaration of war on France, or perhaps on Spain, as a method of reuniting the house divided – and thereby giving him as secretary of state the primary role in government. The President gave his own – equally private – orders for a Sumter relief expedition to be outfitted in New York. Lincoln's single thesis – no extension of slavery beyond its present limits in the slave states – was advanced as a solution to a moral and political dilemma. In the Crittenden-Seward discussions during this interregnum (1860–1), the only proposals which both Houses endorsed, and which Lincoln would have supported, was for an amendment to the Constitution, guaranteeing no federal interference with slavery in the states where it existed; but it was soon abandoned as Southerners withdrew from Washington. Yet this was the answer, as geography itself ensured. The Census of 1860 showed that there were precisely two slaves in Kansas, and only a handful more in the remaining territories. When, in 1861, the new territories of Colorado, Nevada, and Dakota were being organized, the Republicans did not even feel it necessary to impose a ban on slavery; climate alone made it unnecessary: this was not tobacco or cotton country. By 1860 slavery had reached its economic boundaries. In the old cliché, the Civil War was fought about an imaginary Negro in an impossible place.[2]

On April 6, Lincoln sent a message to the governor of South Carolina, Francis Pickens, by a special courier who reached Charleston two days later. Lincoln warned the governor that an attempt would be made to supply the Sumter garrison with provisions only. No effort to throw in men or arms would be made, unless the relief force, or Fort Sumter itself, were attacked. Lincoln had thus resolved his own dilemma over evacuation or relief, by forcing the Southern leaders to face a similar problem – to shoot first or to be humiliated. The Sumter expedition finally sailed on April 8–9, and was due to assemble off Charleston on April 11–12. After consulting his Cabinet, Jefferson Davis, the Confederate President ordered Beauregard to demand the surrender of Sumter before relief could reach it. On April 10, Anderson rejected this demand;

[2] Charles W. Ramsdell, "The natural limits of slavery expansion," *Mississippi Valley Historical Review*, 16 (Sept. 1929), pp. 151–71.

but he admitted that his tiny force would be starved out in a few days.

2 FORT SUMTER

At 4.30 a.m. on April 12, the first shot was fired. The bombardment lasted for over 30 hours until Anderson was compelled to surrender. Fort Sumter was badly battered, but, astonishingly, there was not one fatal casualty on either side; the only death among Anderson's small force occurred after the surrender, when a soldier was killed while firing a ceremonial salute to the flag. The North saw April 12, the date of attack on Sumter, as a date which will live in "infamy," to quote President Franklin Roosevelt's description of 7 December 1941, when the Japanese attacked Pearl Harbor. (Edward Everett of the Constitutional Union Party called it a "day forever to be held in inauspicious remembrance.")

The South had thus fired the first shot. Lincoln now called for 75,000 militia to deal with "combinations too powerful to be suppressed by the ordinary course of judicial proceedings." They were asked to serve for 90 days. Many more than that responded, including Germans and Irish. Stephen Douglas, Lincoln's former rival, rallied round the flag — but he died of typhoid in June. And star orator Edward Everett, Vice-Presidential candidate of the Constitutional Union Party in 1860, delivered one of his famous addresses, "The Causes and Conduct of the Civil War," on 60 occasions within eight months, in 14 states of the Union, from Portland, Maine, to Dubuque, Iowa. Walt Whitman was impressed by the period of mobilization:

> To the drum-taps prompt,
> The young men falling in and arming,
> The mechanics arming, (the trowel, the Jack-plane, the
>   blacksmith's hammer, tost aside with precipitation),
> The lawyer leaving his office and arming, the judge
>   leaving his court,
> The driver deserting his wagon in the street, jumping
>   down throwing the reins abruptly down on the horses' backs,
> The salesman leaving the store, the boss, book-keeper,
>   porter, all leaving;
> Squads gather everywhere by common consent and arm.[3]

[3] "Drum-Taps" (1865).

Herman Melville saw it in cooler fashion:

> Youth must its ignorant impulse lend —
> Age finds place in the rear,
> All wars are boyish, and are fought by boys,
> The champions and enthusiasts of the state.[4]

General Winfield Scott, with the freedom from illusion of the professional soldier, predicted that it would take 300,000 men three years to defeat the South. All that the US had were 15,259 men and 1,105 commissioned officers, and they were widely scattered along the frontier and at a few coastal forts. On April 10, the Sixth Massachusetts, the first regiment to respond to Lincoln's call for troops, was attacked as it marched through Baltimore from one railroad station to the other. In the riot that developed, several soldiers and a larger number of civilians were killed. Temporarily, Lincoln ordered additional contingents to bypass Baltimore. But on April 27, 1861, he sent federal troops to occupy the city, authorized suspension of the writ of *Habeas Corpus*, and ordered the arrest of suspects. Union generals then arrested 19 members of the Maryland legislature, along with the mayor of Baltimore. Further orders called for the arrest also of Southern sympathizers who came to the polls in the autumn elections. Union candidates triumphed easily, and Maryland became and remained a loyal state. Thousands of Marylanders, "the blood-tubs," nevertheless volunteered for the Confederacy. But as Maryland went, so went Delaware. And access to Washington from the loyal states was assured.

Virginia, North Carolina, Tennessee, and Arkansas seceded, however, and joined the Confederacy. They could not conceive making war on the adjacent slave states. Fed by the Richmond newspapers, the *Enquirer* and the *Examiner*, influenced by Jefferson's grandson George Wythe Randolph, Virginians saw their state as the leading manufactory of the Confederacy, free now from anti-slavery agitation, and protected by a tariff from the competition of Northern industry. In Virginia's Convention, delegates who, on April 4, voted 88 to 45 against secession, on April 15 voted 88 to 55 in favor of it. However, the 48 western counties of Virginia then seceded from the seceders. Few large plantations and few slaveholders lay beyond the Blue Ridge. For years many of the people who lived there had resented the domination of the state government by the plantation

<hr>

[4] "The March into Virginia," in Hennig Cohen (ed.), *The Battle-Pieces of Herman Melville* (London, Macmillan, 1963), p. 43.

interests of the Tidewater region, and now they displayed a strong anti-Confederate sentiment. Capitalizing on this feeling, Lincoln in June ordered an army of 20,000 volunteers across the Ohio River and into western Virginia (or Kanawha). The original aim was to secure the line of the Baltimore & Ohio Railroad, but after the outnumbered Confederates were crushed the Administration encouraged the separatist tendency of the area. In November 1861, the western counties split away and, in an action of questionable legality but unquestionable effectiveness, formed a separate state. When in 1863 these became the new state of West Virginia, Virginia lost 35 percent of its territory and 25 percent of its population – but the new state excluded all Negroes, whether slave or free. The Union was the richer from the coal and lumber of the mountains, and from control of the Baltimore & Ohio Railroad route to Cincinnati and St Louis. With Virginia went Robert E. Lee, who would otherwise have been commander-in-chief of the Northern armies. He could not conceive not supporting his state, kin, and kindred in their hour of trial; with him the South acquired its most distinguished general.

Sentiment in Tennessee divided similarly, reflecting mountain *vs.* good bottom cotton land, east *vs.* west, white yeomen farmer *vs.* slave. The Knoxville *Whig* newspaper was suppressed, and its editor, "Parson" Brownlow, thrown into jail, when Nashville and the Tennessee legislature voted for secession. Andrew Johnson of Tennessee (later Lincoln's Vice-President in 1864, and his successor) was the only Senator from the South who refused to resign when his state seceded. Civil war broke out in Missouri and Kentucky, the motherland of both Presidents. In Missouri, Governor Claiborne Jackson was an ardent secessionist, but the strongly German population preferred to stay loyal. Lincoln authorized Congressman Francis P. Blair of Missouri to organize a pro-Union "home guard," which was drawn heavily from among German residents of the city. These troops, armed and sworn into federal service and led by Captain Nathaniel Lyon of the regular army, on May 10 forced the surrender of the militiamen whom the governor had intended to use to seize an arsenal for the Confederacy. Some 109,000 Missourians ultimately fought for the North, around 30,000 for the South. In Kentucky, Lincoln's astute program of conciliation finally overcame the influence of the secessionist Governor Magoffin, who had at first declared his state "neutral." Troops for both sides were recruited in Kentucky. In September 1861 a newly elected state legislature authorized a military force to drive out the Confederates. Three of Henry Clay's grandsons fought for the North, four for the

South. And though it did not secede, Kentucky provided the Confederacy with some able warriors – Simon Bolivar Buckner, John Bell Hood, and Albert Sidney Johnston, all West Pointers. The war had begun, even in the West. In the battle of Pea Ridge, Arkansas, over 300 Indians – all from the Old South nations of Creeks, Cherokees, Choctaws, Chickasaws, and Seminoles – fought for the Confederacy, and for some months the Stars and Bars flag flew over Albuquerque and Santa Fe. That flag had 13 stars; Southerners always saw Missouri and Kentucky as part of the Confederacy. "Hold fast," Lincoln had said, up to April. There would, he was implying, be no expansion of slavery. Now the stakes had broadened; and he had an oath to keep. "Both parties deprecated war," he said. "But one of them would *make* war rather than let the nation survive; and the other would *accept* war rather than let it perish." And the War came.

These 40 days of deliberation, tergiversation, intrigue, guesswork, or simply the hope that something would turn up, can be seen as the revelation of a statesman or a politician at work, or something else: Machiavelli – or Mr Micawber? It revealed much more, and the future would confirm it. Lincoln justified his actions in his message to Congress on July 4, 1861: as throughout, he would always try to explain. To the crucial delay of four months that then obtained between the President's election (November 1860) and his taking office (March 1861), he added another: he delayed the convocation of Congress from April 12, 1861, when Sumter was fired on, until July 4; and Congress, it should be remembered, was not Republican. Moreover, it was clear that it was the President, not the secretary of state, who made the decisions: as, before 1861 as after, it always would be. The phrase "the President as commander-in-chief," now familiar, was made so by Lincoln. In his months of executive grace, Lincoln ignored one law and constitutional provision after another. He assembled the militia, enlarged the Army and the Navy beyond their authorized strength, called for 40 regiments of volunteers for three years' service (and got more), spent public money without Congressional appropriation, suspended *habeas corpus*, arrested people "represented" as involved in "disloyal" practices, and instituted a naval blockade of the Confederacy – measures which, he later told Congress, "whether strictly legal or not, were ventured upon under what appeared to be a popular demand and a public necessity; trusting then as now that Congress would readily ratify them." By his caution, however, the President gained control of the Congressional factions, and so persistently and effectively did he press before the public the theme of "preservation of the Union" that in a comparatively short time he had the nation behind him too. Like Stephen Douglas, Buchanan and other Union Democrats rallied to Lincoln's support.

The initiative lay with the North, since in Lincoln's eyes there was a civil rebellion to suppress. When the war came, there were three theatres of war: first, Virginia, an area of 100 miles square, and later the whole Eastern seaboard south of the Virginia Capes; second, the Mississippi valley, a 800-mile line from the Ohio River at "Little Egypt" to the Gulf, which became two campaigns, first, the River, and the battle for Vicksburg, and second, the Tennessee campaign, affecting the seven Tennessee River states, and the battle for Chattanooga; and third, and throughout the war – the Atlantic, and the 3,500-mile-long Union blockade from the Chesapeake round to Galveston Bay in Texas. The impact of the blockade was obvious, steady, and remorseless. But the War was well under way before the importance of the West was realized – although two of the generals discovered there – Grant and Sherman – won the War.

From the regular army some 300 experienced officers resigned to take commissions in the Confederate forces; and at the outset the South was well ahead in military preparations. Only by trial and error was a Union army built, a basic mistake being the effort to keep the regular army intact, rather than to use it as the cadre of a larger, volunteer force. Regular *versus* volunteer was to be a discordant theme. Among the senior officers, the West Pointers favored their own kind, except that they had lost many of them to the South – and not always instantly: Frank Crawford Armstrong, one of McDowell's cavalry officers at Bull Run, joined the Confederacy a month later; a cousin of General McClellan's served as chief of staff to the Confederate generals J. E. B. Stuart and Wade Hampton; and George Meade, the victor of Gettysburg, was the brother-in-law of Confederate general Henry A. Wise, a former governor of Virginia. Some of the Union generals became political candidates. All of them had to keep contact with, even to cultivate or be cultivated by, the wartime Congressional (and radically oriented) Committee on the Conduct of the War, which was set up in December 1861. Its hearings and its demands kept pressure on Lincoln, who needed the Radicals' votes, and agitated the still divisive question of slavery among the people of the North, whose sentiments Lincoln wanted to direct uniformly to the issue of union. Grant and Sherman were remarkable among Union commanders in their distaste for political intrigue. Ironically, they it was who later became the political candidates. The vainglorious and ambitious (Fremont in 1856, McClellan in 1864) did not reach the White House: but the US has usually preferred the "Ikes" to the "Macs."[5]

The North at first expected a 90-day war, as Lincoln's first call for militia indicated. Had he named a longer term, the patriotic fervor of April 1861 probably would have given him just as large a number of volunteers; as it developed, the army had to be recruited again, after military reverses and the horrors of combat had somewhat diminished the zeal for a soldier's life. The various state militia, poorly organised, trained, and equipped, were at first incorporated bodily into the Union army; within a year, it was obvious that a more integrated organization was necessary. In contrast, led by men of ability and experience and made up of soldiers already at home with fire arms and life in the open, the Southern armies possessed certain natural advantages, not least in the use of cavalry. Union recruits soon learned military routine, however, and generally proved a man-for-man match for the Confederate soldiers. Such victories as the South won were attributable to superior leadership; but in time, Northern superiority in manpower and material proved decisive. Fighting was rarely on flat terrain, and the ratio of casualties to men engaged was higher in the Civil War than in World War I. As with Washington 80 years before, the short engagements of the militia compelled Lincoln into action. Only a quick end to the rebellion would ensure that there would be no foreign recognition of it, and no foreign aid for its armies. Moreover, when Virginia seceded, the Confederacy proclaimed that their capital would be transferred from Montgomery, Alabama, to Richmond, Virginia, less than 100 miles from Washington; there the rebel Congress would be summoned. The Northern newspapers pressed for decisive action: "on to Richmond" became their battle-cry. A quick blow must be struck at the Confederate army under General Beauregard at Manassas Junction, only 35 miles from Washington, by Winfield Scott's superior (and steadily growing) army — even if it was still untrained. The Union capital became — and remained for four years — a battle headquarters, and the President found himself all too literally a commander-in-chief, and — unusual for such — not far from the front line.

---

[5] T. Harry William, "The Macs and the Ikes: America's two military traditions," *American Mercury*, 75 (1952), pp. 32–9.

3 NORTH AND SOUTH: AN OVERVIEW

The War Between the States is the central, and the most emotion-stirring event, in American history. It was tragic, heroic, and romantic, with each side betrayed by its virtues even more than by its vices. And the debate continues; was it necessary anyway?

Perhaps the best summary of the situation in April 1861 is that of Allan Nevins to whom it was a "needless war:"

> The War, when it came, was not primarily a conflict over State rights, although that issue had become involved in it. It was not primarily a war born of economic grievances, although many Southerners had been led to think that they were suffering, or would soon suffer, economic wrongs. It was not a war created by politicians and publicists who fomented hysteric excitement; for while hysteria was important, we have always to ask what basic reasons made possible the propaganda which aroused it. It was not primarily a war about slavery alone, although that great institution seemed to many the grand cause. It was a war over slavery and the future position of the Negro race in North America. Was the Negro to be allowed, as a result of the shift of power signalized by Lincoln's election, to take the first step toward an ultimate position of general economic, political, and social equality with the white man? Or was he to be held immobile in a degraded, servile position, unchanging for the next hundred years as it had remained essentially unchanged for the hundred years past? These questions were implicit in Lincoln's demand that slavery be placed in a position where the public could rest assured of its ultimate extinction. [6]

Or perhaps Mary Chesnut's *Dixie Diary*, dated July 24, 1861, recording a conversation in Mrs Jefferson Davis' drawing room, after the first battle of Bull Run, is more vivid:

> Somebody said he did remember ladies' presence, for the habit of our men was to call them 'Damn Yankees.'
> ... And then somebody told a story — little girl came running to tell on her brother: "Oh Mama, Charlie is using bad language — curse words."
> "What is it?"
> He says "Damn Yankees are here, prisoners."
> "Well, Mama, is not that their name? I never hear them called anything else." [7]

[6] *The Emergence of Lincoln* (New York, Scribner's), vol. II, pp. 470–1.
[7] C. V. Woodward (ed.), *Mary Chesnut's Civil War* (New Haven, Yale University Press, 1981).

The America that went to war in 1861 was, in its nature, fragmented and invertebrate, to use Allan Nevins's word — he also calls it "sprawling," "inchoate," "unformed" "a veritable jellyfish." Government played a small part in it. Nevins's description cannot be bettered.

Like China in 1940 ... it was an agricultural history with a long historic belief in individualism, far more attached to the principle of self-reliance than to that of association. The shrewd French observer, Auguste Laugel, who wrote a book on the United States during the war, correctly stated, "There is a horror of all trammels, system, and uniformity." The population still lived close to the soil. Of the 8,200,000 whose occupations were noted by the census of 1860, 3,300,000 were farmers, planters, farm laborers, or stockmen, while as many more were indirectly connected with agriculture.

A few facts are significant of the lack of organization: The country as yet had no standard time — Boston, New York, Philadelphia, and Washington each had its own time. It had no accepted gauge for railroads, the eight or more gauges ranged from three to six feet. The postal system was so wretched that in New York in 1856 ten million letters were delivered privately in contrast to one million carried by the government. In 1860 the American population slightly exceeded that of Great Britain, but that year Americans posted 184 million letters, while Great Britain posted 564 million. It had no national labor union worthy of the name; the typographers, iron molders, and hat-makers possessed unions, but they were shadowy bodies which did little more than meet and pass resolutions. The panic of 1857, indeed, had paralyzed the infant movement toward labor organization. It had few other organizations. Not one state bar association had been formed. Only two American cities in 1865 had paid fire departments. In all of New England in 1860 there were only three hospitals; in the entire South, four or five. The American Medical Association was twelve years old, but when the hour struck to establish medical and surgical services for the war, it was so feeble that nobody thought of using it. Three trunk-line railways had been established, for the Pennsylvania, the New York Central, and the Baltimore & Ohio could be termed interstate railroads. But ninety-five percent of such manufacturing as existed was on a local basis and managed in small units. In fact, state laws of the time generally forbade corporations to hold property outside their own states except by special charter. Most business firms were managed as family affairs. Another significant detail is that in a country where whole libraries now groan with books on business organization and management, down to 1860 not one book — not one pamphlet — had been published on these subjects.

Modern organization, apart from politics, education, and religion, is built mainly on the machine, which is effective only with and through it. A mechanized country is of necessity an organized country; a land without machines is unorganized. Great Britain in 1860, with approximately the same population as the United States, was much better equipped with machine industry, and in consequence far better organized. With us, the industrial revolution was hardly beyond its beginnings. The partially mechanized area extending from Boston to Philadelphia was learning what organization meant, but learning slowly.

In just one broad field can the nation be said to have developed a considerable degree of organization before 1860: the field of westward expansion. Since the main fact in American life was the movement of population toward the setting sun, the major energies of the nation were channeled into its promotion. The building of highways, canals, steamboats, and railroads to carry people west; the manufacture of plows, axes, drills and harvesters to maintain them there; the production of arms to help them deal with Indians and wild beasts; the extension of churches, schools and post offices to keep them linked with the older communities – all this was fairly well organized. Yet westward expansion was itself to some extent a disorganizing process, spreading civilization thin and straining the bonds of society. [8]

A comparison of the strength of the two antagonists, on the eve of hostilities, seemed to promise a brief struggle. The North's resources were immeasurably greater. The North's white population was around 19,000,000; the Confederacy's total population was around 9,000,000, of whom 3,500,000 were slaves. The South had more acreage in farms, but the North's improved acreage was larger – 88,730,600 improved acres for the North and 74,380,000 improved acres for the South. In a war, foodstuffs are crucial. In 1860, the North had produced $167,295,000 worth of flour and meal as compared with the South's $55,849,000. Similarly, woolen goods for uniforms and blankets are part of the immediate necessities of an army in the field. In 1860, the North produced $64,270,000 worth of woolen stuffs; the South $4,596,000.

Communications – even more important in war than in peace – favored the North too: in 1860 it had 19,700 miles of rail track, the South had 10,500 – railroad mileage had increased from 5,000 to 20,000 between 1848 and 1857. The 11 independent local lines across New York state, which were consolidated in 1853 into the New York Central, found immediate competition in the Erie railroad, completed to Dunkirk on Lake Erie in 1851; in the Pennsylvania railroad, completed to Pittsburgh in 1852; in the Baltimore & Ohio railroad, which reached Wheeling in 1853; and in the

---

[8] Allan Nevins, "A major result of the Civil War," *Civil War History*, 5.3 (Sept. 1959), pp. 237–50.

Grand Trunk railroad, which joined Portland and Montreal in the same year. By 1850, 15 railroads reached Chicago. The chief feature of this new era of railroad-building was the development of "trunk-lines" connecting the Ohio and Mississippi valleys and the Great Lakes with the Atlantic seaboard. The Pennsylvania railroad, chartered in 1846, ran its first through train from Philadelphia to Pittsburgh in 1852. The Republican party was born in the year that the first lines reached the Mississippi. In 1860 Chicago, in which Lincoln was nominated, was a thriving city of 100,000 people; it had not existed 30 years before. As New York, Philadelphia, and Baltimore sent out agents to secure Western markets, so did Chicago, Cleveland, and Cincinnati send agents East; and every mile of track extended the weekly range of the *New York Tribune*. But, again, of the 30,000 total miles of American rail track in 1860, only 9,000 were in the South. Although there were two main lines running the length of the Mississippi, there were many separate companies, inadequate connections in the cities, and too many different gauges. The same held true of the North: if in 1861 the journey time by rail from New York to Chicago was only 36 hours, it was not an uninterrupted nor always a reliable ride; and if at least it was likely to be free from attacks from Southern armies, the 200-mile journey from New York to Washington was shared by three different companies and interrupted by ferries across the Hudson and the Susquehanna, and cross-town transfers in both Baltimore and Philadelphia.

Again, no better index of the prosperity of the country, helped by the discovery of gold and the sale of public land, could be found than the figures of the expansion of American commerce by sea and land. Northern commerce and industry, manned by free labor and encouraged by federal bounties and protective tariffs, developed manufacturing still more, and encouraged immigration to provide factory workers: in 1825, 11 percent of the American population was foreign-born; in 1855 it was over 55 percent. The North had over 100,000 manufacturing establishments against the South's 18,000, and its products were six times greater in value. The South was at a major disadvantage in the raw materials of war: in 1860 the South produced 36,000 tons of pig iron, the North 1 million tons; and 76,000 tons of iron ore out of a total of 2,500,000. The loss of the border states deprived the South of iron furnaces and forges, foundries and rolling mills. The capital investment in Northern manufactures was 1,131,600 compared to the South's 189,500. No less vital to each section's efforts were the draft animals needed to pull the wagons and other military vehicles, and to provide cavalry mounts – and fodder too. Again, the North had the advantage, owning almost 65 percent of the approximately 7 million horses, mules, and asses listed in the 1860 census return. No less formidable were the Northern maritime and naval advantages. Long a commercial region, it owned the bulk of shipping, and provided most of the naval manpower. The Yankee clipper ships challenged the British for the lucrative tea and spice trade with the Orient. Tonnage of American shipping in foreign and domestic trade aggregated over five million tons in 1860. The South's one apparent advantage – the great volume of its cotton exports (if they could be maintained, or the threat of a cotton embargo – proved not to be so: cotton exports to Britain dwindled until they had become negligible in 1862; in that year Britain was getting only 2.6 percent of its cotton imports from the United States, as compared with 80.2 percent in 1860.

The South foresaw, of course, a defensive war fought with interior lines of communication. Its superior training in and experience of cavalry, the response of its thousands of volunteers, and the number of experienced soldiers it could call on as leaders and N.C.O.s, would be hard to match. One-third of the regular army officers joined the Confederacy – many of them with Mexican War experience. Moreover, the South had a hidden advantage in its black landsmen. They provided the Confederacy with a huge reservoir of labor, allowing, as a result, a heavier proportional draft of white manpower. The slave system, in other words, increased the available ultimate reservoir of military reserves. During the opening phases of the war, the federal policy of not tampering with slavery ensured this Southern advantage. But as the drain upon Northern manpower grew, the originally reluctant Lincoln government turned to the slave manpower pool; eventually more than 180,000 black soldiers saw federal service.

The growth of the Republican party was an index of the extent of the political and economic alliance of North-East and West, and of its potential – almost half of the population of 31 million in 1860 lived west of the Allegheny-Appalachian mountain chain. And it brought a new twist to political convictions: the new party of and for free white men and free homesteads for them, for free soil and free land, wanted government support – for internal improvements and homestead bills; much of the railroad construction was government-aided. Congress granted millions of acres of land to the states, to be turned over to the railroads. States, counties, and cities supplemented the federal grants, while bankers and promoters borrowed heavily from the financiers of London and Paris.

The new party – like the old – was rooted in a faith in expansion, and in contradictions.

The contrast between North and South was, in part, that of free labor *vs.* slave, in part urban (or pre-urban) *vs.* rural, in part industrial *vs.* agrarian, and in part free, self-governing, and self-motivated individuals *vs.* an ordered hierarchical society. But as the future would show, there was more to it than this. The Republicans were nationalists, homogenizers, modernizers, and cosmopolitans. They were reformers, and sought to impose their reforms – including temperance even for Irish immigrants, and the end of slavery in the plantation South. By contrast the Democrats, like the Liberals in contemporary Britain, formed the party of regional and ethnical diversity. In his Lyceum speech of 1838 Lincoln condemned "the increasing disregard for law which pervades the country," the vigilantism and mob violence. In 1861, "the central idea of secession," he said, "is the essence of anarchy." There was substance in Stephen Douglas's plea for "diversity and dissimilarity," and in his objection to what he saw as Lincoln's belief that "there must be uniformity in the local laws and domestic institutions of each and all States of the Union." The North's ideology, however, was based on individualism, egalitarianism, and self-government; beliefs that transcended class lines, and which existed both among supporters and opponents of the War. Lincoln identified himself quite spontaneously with these core values; but to Jefferson Davis they were quite alien.[9]

4 BULL RUN

The first major battle of the War at Bull Run (its familiar name, though it was Manassas to Southerners – the creek is a tributary of the Potomac) on July 21, 1861, ended in the rout of a numerically superior Union force, under Irvin McDowell, by two Confederate armies led by Pierre G. T. Beauregard and Joseph E. Johnston. Johnston's arrival from the Shenandoah valley in the late afternoon, traveling part of the way by railroad (though, even so, not very quickly) transformed what might have been a Southern defeat into

[9] Eric Foner, *Politics and Ideology in the Age of the Civil War* (New York, Oxford University Press, 1980), pp. 22–5; Raimondo Luraghi, "The Civil War and the modernization of American Society," *Civil War History*, 18 (Sept. 1972), p. 242; Randall C. Jimerson, *The Private Civil War: Popular thoughts during the sectional conflict* (Baton Rouge, Louisiana State University Press, 1988).

a victory. It was the stand of General Thomas Jackson's brigade here which earned him and it the nickname of "Stonewall." On each side, there were over 400 dead and 1,000 wounded. The Congressmen – and their wives – who had come out to see what they expected to be a mere spectacle became part of an ugly and confused retreat back to the Potomac; two Congressmen were reported missing. As remnants of the shattered army dribbled back into the city, mostly "in disorderly mobs, some in squads, stragglers, companies," Walt Whitman wrote:

The dream of humanity, the vaunted Union we thought so strong, so impregnable – lo! it seems already smash'd like a china plate. One bitter, bitter hour – perhaps proud America will never again know such an hour. She must pack and fly – no time to spare. Those white palaces – the dome-crown'd capitol there on the hill, so stately over the trees – shall they be left – or destroy'd first? For it is certain that the talk among certain of the magnates and officers and clerks and officials everywhere, for twenty-four hours in and around Washington after Bull Run, was loud and undisguised for yielding out and out, and substituting the southern rule, and Lincoln promptly abdicating and departing.[10]

No longer did the North talk glibly of a 90-day war. George B. McClellan, a 34-year-old West Pointer, with service in the Mexican War and in Europe, who had reported successful campaigning in Loyalist West Virginia, was brought East and charged with the task of expanding and reorganizing the Union army. Despite his flamboyance, and a lack of tact which went as far as a frequent snubbing of the President, he did an excellent job of mobilizing and training an army of 100,000 men by the end of the summer, a task for which there were no West Point handbooks, and no strategic plans ready. In November he replaced Winfield Scott as general-in-chief. Meanwhile, though the victorious Southern armies were almost as badly confused at Bull Run as were the Union troops, many in the Confederacy became dangerously overconfident. But it was clear to each HQ that neither side was adequately prepared for sustained combat.

When Lincoln called for 75,000 militia on April 15, 1861, he also called Congress into session, but the session was not to start until 4 July. By that time the President had gone further. He wanted an increase in the regular army, and also 40,000 volunteers in 40 regiments, for a three-year term of service; thereafter came a series

[10] Whitman, *Prose Works* (ed. P. Stovall, 1892), vol. I, p. 27.

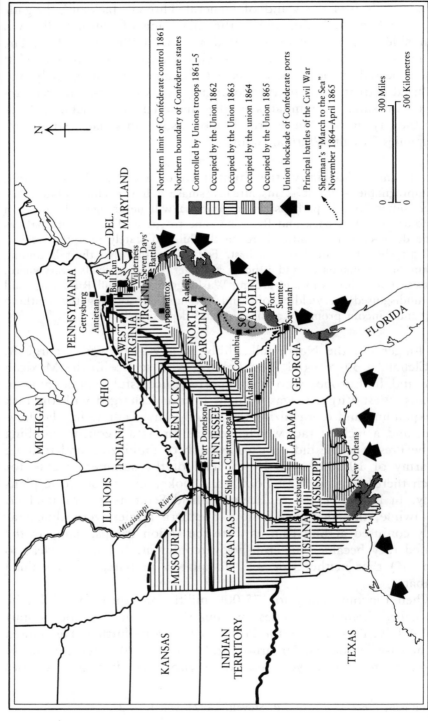

Map 12 The Civil War 1861–1865: the Union advance and major battles.

MICHIGAN

PENNSYLVANIA

OHIO

INDIANA

ILLINOIS

MISSOURI

KANSAS

INDIAN
TERRITORY

TEXAS

ARKANSAS

LOUISIANA

MISSISSIPPI

ALABAMA

TENNESSEE

KENTUCKY

WEST
VIRGINIA

VIRGINIA

NORTH
CAROLINA

SOUTH
CAROLINA

GEORGIA

FLORIDA

MARYLAND

DEL.

Mississippi River

New Orleans

Vicksburg

Shiloh Chattanooga

Fort Donelson

Columbia

Atlanta

Savannah

Fort Sumter

Raleigh

Appomattox

Gettysburg

Antietam

Bull Run

Wilderness

Seven Days'
Battles

N

Northern limit of Confederate control 1861

Northern boundary of Confederate states

Controlled by Unions troops 1861–5

Occupied by the Union 1862

Occupied by the Union 1863

Occupied by the union 1864

Occupied by the Union 1865

Union blockade of Confederate ports

Principal battles of the Civil War

Sherman's "March to the Sea"
November 1864–April 1865

0   300 Miles

0   500 Kilometres

of calls for more, and for varying periods. States and localities were assigned quotas, and local leaders took it upon themselves to act as recruiters, to be rewarded with captaincies and lieutenancies. When enough volunteers had been pledged, the governor of the state would enroll the company in the state militia. The President at first opposed the use of Negroes as troops, but in July 1862 Congress authorized Negro recruiting; in all 186,000 blacks fought in the Union army, of whom 100,000 were recruited in Confederate territory. The Confederacy, by an Act of March 1861, created an army of seven regiments; later, it raised troops through the states, some of which provided for conscription; in April 1862 the Confederacy itself adopted conscription for all men between 18 and 35, later broadened to 17 and 50.

However surprising in retrospect, though, the South's optimism after the first battle of Bull Run, and its gaiety, were natural enough. They were fighting on and for their own territory. The average Southerner was more familiar with guns and horses than many a Northerner. The peacetime militia was a familiar institution, quasi-social, quasi-political, and its officers were elected – as were those in the Confederate forces, to the detriment of military discipline, and accompanied by an orgy of electioneering. Only the high-ranking field officers were appointed by Richmond – and they came exclusively from the best and oldest families. These all, and some privates also, brought their slaves with them, to serve as batmen. The Confederate army, like the Old South, was devoted at once to democratic principles and to maintaining an aristocratic society. When Robert E. Lee took command of the Army of Northern Virginia in 1862, his troops were described as an "armed mob, ... magnificent material, of undisciplined individualists." The musket was now being replaced by the rifle, giving much greater accuracy and range. Confederate commanders were usually professional and experienced, often with Mexican War records; and cotton, it believed, would rapidly bring Britain in on the Southern side. That it was heavily outnumbered, and – the Tredegar Iron Works in Richmond and the foundries in Selma, Alabama, Macon and Fayetteville, apart – short of factories, and of food and railroads, did not at first seem significant, and was offset by the mood of ebullience. Southerners did not realize that the cotton boom of 1860 had already filled the cotton warehouses of Britain and of the North to overflowing, and that stocks there would survive any blockade or embargo; there was no cotton famine until the winter of 1862–3. Nor did they realize that Britain needed Northern grain more than Southern cotton, that Corn was a rival king. It was a war for the homeland, for Dixie, and there was a strong sense of Southern nationhood. Some English observers – including, be it said, W. E. Gladstone – were attracted by it. So were many British visitors, such as the London *Times* war correspondent William Howard Russell, who thought the South militarily impressive:

Secession is the fashion here. Young ladies sing for it; old ladies pray for it; young men are dying to fight for it; old men are ready to demonstrate it. The founder of the school was St Calhoun. Here his pupils carry out their teaching in thunder and fire. States' Rights are displayed after its legitimate teaching, and the Palmetto flag and the red bars of the Confederacy are its exposition. The utter contempt and loathing for the venerated Stars and Stripes, the abhorrence of the very words United States, the immense hatred of the Yankees on the part of these people cannot be conceived by anyone who has not seen them. I am more satisfied than ever that the Union can never be restored as it was, and that it has gone to pieces, never to be put together again, in the old shape, at all events, by any power on earth.[11]

Lincoln, he said, was shrewd, but temporizing and timid; Federal troops were "starved" and "washed-out-creatures," among whom were "flat-footed, stumpy Germans." His account of Bull Run was so scathing that, when it reached the US, *The Times* thought it discreet to recall its reporter. In all his matching savagery, Horace Greeley, for once, had pulled his punches.

But another British visitor, Edward Dicey, writing a few months later, was more perceptive of the potential of the North:

The general impression left upon me by my observations of the army of the Potomac was a very favourable one. All day, and every day while I resided at Washington, the scene before my eyes was one of war. An endless military panorama seemed to be unrolling itself ceaselessly. Sometimes it was a line of artillery struggling and floundering onwards through the mud – sometimes it was a company of wild Texan cavalry rattling past, with the jingle of their belts and spurs. Sometimes it was a long train of sutlers' wagons, ambulance vans, or forage-carts, drawn by the scraggy Pennsylvania mules. Orderlies innumerable galloped up and down, patrols without end passed along the pavements, and at every window and door-step and street corner you saw soldiers standing. You had to go far away from Washington to leave the war behind you. If you went up to any high point in the city whence you could look over the surrounding country, every hillside seemed covered with camps. The white tents caught your eye on all sides; and across the river, where the dense brushwood obscured

[11] W. H. Russell, *My Diary North and South* (London, 1863), vol. I, p. 153.

the prospect, the great army of the Potomac stretched miles away, right up to the advanced posts of the Confederates, south of the far-famed Manassas. The numbers were so vast that it was hard to realize them. During one week fifty thousand men were embarked from Washington, and yet the town and neighbourhood still swarmed with troops and camps, as it seemed, undiminished in number. And here, remember, I saw only one portion of the gigantic army. Along a line of two thousand miles or so, from the Potomac down to New Mexico, there were at that time Federal armies fighting their way southward. At Fortress Monroe too, Ship Island, Mobile, and at every accessible point along the Atlantic seaboard, expeditions numbered by tens of thousands were stationed, waiting for the signal to advance. At this time the muster-roll of the Federal army numbered 672,000 men, or, at least, that number were drawing pay daily from the Treasury, though a large allowance must be made for absentees and none-effectives. [12]

There was sound strategy in McClellan's determination to delay operations until his force, the Army of the Potomac, was strong enough to overwhelm Confederate resistance; superiority in equipment and numbers, in capital and rail facilities, augmented by the naval blockade, made attrition an advantageous Union policy, whereas a quick victory was the goal of Southern planning. Nevertheless, so slowly did McClellan's plans take shape that public opinion in the North became increasingly critical. He wanted an army of a quarter of a million men; in the course of training them, he became over-cautious, and too concerned with his men's creature comforts, as training officers often are; in the end he was unwilling to risk his men in battle, and became critical of the President for urging him to do so. He was misled in part by the reports of his friend Allan Pinkerton, the detective, employed as head of his intelligence service, who fed him inaccurate and inflated reports of Confederate numbers. The President, for his part, was worried about the vulnerability of his capital to a surprise attack by the Confederate forces poised across the river some 30 miles away, and refused McClellan's requests for more and more troops; what he wanted was a frontal attack via Manassas (Bull Run) on the enemy, and with the safety of his HQ thus ensured.

A radical wing of the Republican party, headed by Senators Benjamin F. Wade, Charles Sumner, and Zachary Chandler, and Representative Thaddeus Stevens of Pennsylvania, opposed the cautious policy of Lincoln and McClellan. They argued for arming the

---

[12] Edward Dicey, *Six Months in the Federal States* (London, 1863), quoted by Allan Nevins in *America through British Eyes* (New York, Oxford University Press, 1948), p. 276.

slaves, overlooking the fact that such an undertaking would have driven border states like Kentucky and Missouri into the Confederate camp. They sponsored a joint Committee on the Conduct of the War, which interfered in a wide variety of affairs. They pushed through Congress legislation abolishing slavery in the territories (without compensation) and in the District of Columbia (with compensation); the Confiscation Act of 1862 declared forfeit the property of everyone supporting the rebellion, and declared "forever Free" all slaves who escaped or were captured; and it succeeded in finding sufficient corruption in the War Department to warrant its reorganization. The new secretary of war, the Democrat Edwin M. Stanton, was an old-line Jacksonian, an uncouth, ill-tempered, and unpopular Quaker, but a strict disciplinarian and a good organizer. Symptomatic of the division in the Northern ranks was the fate of Lincoln's celebrated War Order Number 1. At length responsive to the public demand for action, the President ordered a general forward movement of the Union forces on Washington's birthday, 22 February 1862. McClellan ignored the order, and the advance on Richmond did not begin until April. He advanced, however, not directly but via the Virginia peninsula, confidently announcing his expectation of being in Richmond in ten days. However, decentralization of command and lack of War Department support deprived him of adequate reinforcements, and his plan failed. In the seven-day battle (June 25 to July 1, 1862) within five miles of Richmond, he inflicted 20,000 casualties upon the Confederacy, but a diversionary lunge by Stonewall Jackson in the direction of Washington prevented his driving home his advantage. McClellan withdrew his precious army to the Chesapeake, and they tented overnight and many nights on old camp grounds. McClellan's caution was such that he never lost a battle – but he never won one either. "To fight was not his forte," said Gideon Welles. [13]

John Pope, who replaced McClellan, tried a new vigor. He was indifferent to strategy and bases of supply; his headquarters, he replied to a reporter, would be "in the saddle" – which won the reply that his headquarters were where his hindquarters should be. He meant well. He was handsome, dashing, and a good cavalryman. But he angered Lee by prescribing harsh treatment for all sympathizers with the South that he encountered; and his attempt at psychological warfare and morale-building in issuing his address to troops on July 14, 1862, produced only bombastic and inflated prose:

[13] H. J. Eckenrode and Bryan Conrad, *George B. McClellan: The man who saved the Union* (Chapel Hill, NC, University of North Carolina Press, 1941).

Headquarters, Army of Virginia, Washington, DC, July 14, 1862.
To the Officers and Soldiers of the Army of Virginia:

By special assignment of the President of the United States, I have assumed the command of this army. I have spent two weeks in learning your whereabouts, your condition, and your wants, in preparing you for active operations, and in placing you in positions from which you can act promptly and to the purpose. These labors are nearly completed, and I am about to join you in the field.

Let us understand each other. I have come to you from the West, where we have always seen the backs of our enemies; from an army whose business it has been to seek the adversary, and to beat him when he was found; whose policy has been attack and not defense. In but one instance has the enemy been able to place our Western armies in defensive attitude. I presume that I have been called here to pursue the same system and to lead you against the enemy. It is my purpose to do so, and that speedily. I am sure you long for an opportunity to win the distinction you are capable of achieving. That opportunity I shall endeavor to give you. Meantime I desire you to dismiss from your minds certain phrases, which I am sorry to find so much in vogue amonst you. I hear constantly of "taking strong positions and holding them," of "lines of retreat," and of "bases of supplies." Let us discard such ideas. The strongest position a soldier should desire to occupy is one from which he can most easily advance against the enemy. Let us study the probable lines of retreat of our opponents, and leave our own to take care of themselves. Let us look before us and not behind. Success and glory are in the advance, disaster and shame lurk in the rear. Let us act on this understanding, and it is safe to predict that your banners shall be inscribed with many a glorious deed and that your names will be dear to your countrymen forever.

> John Pope
> Major General, Commanding

He was defeated by the Army of Northern Virginia under Lee and Stonewall at the second battle of Bull Run on August 30, 1862, and dismissed. Lee then advanced into Maryland. On September 17, 1862, Lee was halted by McClellan at Antietam Creek (or to Southerners, Sharpsburg). Sixty thousand troops were engaged and at the day's end one in every three had fallen in combat. It blighted McClellan's military career – but the heavy casualties forced Lee to abandon his invasion of the North. When Lincoln visited the battlefield and asked a friend "What is this?" he got the reply, "It is the Army of the Potomac." Not so," said the President, "It is only McClellan's bodyguard."

In November 1862, the handsome but hesitant Ambrose E. Burnside replaced McClellan in command of Virginia operations; he was in turn, however, decisively beaten at Fredericksburg, on December 13; and two years were to elapse before a strategy very similar to McClellan's original plan brought Union victory.

The first Union victory, in fact, had come in an unexpected quarter. Ulysses S. Grant, who had had a good record as a captain in the Mexican War and had then resigned to escape a court-martial for drunkenness, was in 1862 a brigadier-general in command of Illinois volunteers in the West. (He had, ironically, offered his services – unsuccessfully – to McClellan in Ohio in 1861).

Grant was stocky, careless in dress, painfully shy, stubborn, lonely, even forlorn, so grateful for any kindness shown him that he would return it with a doglike devotion. He was moody, subject to fits of gloom, whiskey-addicted but non-swearing; his drunken benders – at least during the War – were as often occasioned by the appalling scale of the casualties as by indulgence; he was a commander in an ugly war, who won in the end by sheer determination, and by the merciless sacrifice of men. Even his name went wrongly into the records. Born Hiram Ulysses Grant, the Congressman who put him forward for West Point could not recall the first name but could recall the second and third. He did remember Grant's mother's maiden name – so down he went as Ulysses Simpson Grant. Grant was of undistinguished family – his father was a tanner in Ohio, and he was born in a two-roomed cabin – and he had no scholarly bent. He never pretended to enjoy the military life; he was always more adept at managing horses than managing men. Neither the Mexican War nor six years' service in isolated Western posts altered his distaste for the peace time army. After a warning by his commanding officer that if he did not resign, he would be dismissed from the service, he then failed as a farmer and a businessman. When the War began, he was 39, and a clerk in his father's store. He was no politician – and, like many in his section, he had voted for Buchanan in 1856. But he had married the daughter of a St Louis slaveholder, and thus acquired two slaves. In 1861 the political influence of another old friend had secured him the rank of colonel in an Illinois regiment.

Having bottled up a Confederate force in Kentucky, Grant responded to the request for terms by replying "Unconditional surrender" – which provided his nickname and his slogan for the duration of the war. This victory on February 16, 1862, and – with the help of Flag-Officer Foote's river gunboats – the seizure of Forts Henry and Donelson on the Tennessee and Cumberland Rivers, gave Grant access to rivers reaching far into the South, and made the Confederate hold on Nashville untenable: he continued his advance. The Memphis-Atlanta-Charleston Railroad – as much the lifeline of the Confederacy as the Baltimore & Ohio was of the Union – was cut permanently at Corinth, Mississippi, in the spring of 1862.

But at Shiloh, in April 1862, Grant lost 13,000 of his force of 63,000, while barely holding the field against a Confederate force of 40,000, which lost 11,000 men. One of the Confederacy's ablest generals, Albert Sidney Johnston, a West Pointer who had served in Mexico and had been Jefferson Davis's friend and hero since his teenage years, was killed there; and such was the Confederate resistance that Grant said that it was at Shiloh that he became convinced that only "total War" and "complete destruction of the South" would save the Union. It was the bloodiest battle of the War so far; and Grant had his critics. Lincoln refused to replace him, however, despite those critics' complaints of his drunkenness. "I can't spare this man. He fights," said the President. "Tell me what he drinks, and I'll send a barrel to the other generals."[14]

New Orleans was taken on April 26, 1862, in an amphibious operation, and the Union naval force of David G. Farragut was then free to move up the Mississippi to support the land operations in the West. By the summer of 1862, the Confederates retained only the 125-mile "bridge" between Fort Hudson and Vicksburg on the Mississippi, the bridge through which they could obtain supplies from Texas.

New Orleans, appropriately, provided a hero – and a villain. David Glasgow Farragut was a colourful Spanish-North Carolinian by ancestry, a Tennessean by birth, and New Orleans bred; he was a swordsman and gymnast who did somersaults at the age of 60, for whom his naval service since the War of 1812, the Union flag, and the deck of a cruiser countered the appeal of his home in Norfolk, Virginia, and of his Virginian-born wife. He was reduced to changing his shore-address to New York City. The city's military governor was almost as exotic: the bald, fat, and one-eyed Benjamin Franklin Butler, Massachusetts criminal lawyer and politician, as raffish and unscrupulous as he looked, who had occupied Baltimore without opposition in May 1861, and captured Fort Hatteras in August; he contrived to anger and embarrass North as well as South during his six-month command in New Orleans. Butler built drains,

[14] Stephen Sears, *The Landscape Turned Red* (Boston, Ticknor and Fields, 1983).

suppressed banditry and gang war, and collected and spent tax money with abandon. He hanged William Mumford for pulling down the Union flag, and announced that anyone heard singing "The Bonnie Blue Flag" would be fined 25 dollars. He was accused of stealing the spoons when he was asked out to dine. When the Creole beauties of the South turned their backs on him, he is said to have commented: "These ladies evidently know which end of them looks best." He issued a notorious Order, no. 28, the "Women Order," that any female showing contempt for any officer or soldier of the US would be "liable to be treated as a woman of the town plying her avocation." When Lord Palmerston in the House of Commons offered the opinion that the order was unfit to be written in the English language, the commander replied that it had been taken almost word for word from an ordinance of the City of London. He was replaced in December 1862, and thought suitable for command in the Department of Virginia, where again he proved unwelcome. All of which may have been a suitable apprenticeship for the 13 years he was to serve as a Republican Congressman, for the governorship of the state of Massachusetts in 1883, and for his (happily, unsuccessful) candidacy for the presidency in 1884.[15]

6 THE ECONOMIES

By 1863 North and South were indeed becoming distinct societies. In each, war increased the role of government; so did the number of civil servants, endlessly enquiring; and, in each, criticism, even treason, grew. The North prospered away from the battlefield, notably in the flour-milling, ready-made clothing, meat-packing, and canning industries, and despite bread riots in some cities by the spring of 1863. Despite being deprived of much Southern cotton, Northern industry did not collapse; dividends in textiles went as high as 40 percent. The North had 80 percent of the whole country's factories, and most of the coal and iron. The Morrill Tariff Act of 1861 set higher protective duties, and in the following years they would go ever higher, with no Southerners now present in Congress to oppose them. Along with the tariff were excise taxes, the novelty of a personal income tax, loans carrying at least five different rates of interest, and not least paper money, or "greenbacks." David Wells, the special commissioner of revenue, likened it all to the Irishman at Donnybrook Fair: "Whenever you see a head, hit it; whenever

---

[15] Robert S. Holzanen, *Stormy Ben Butler* (New York, Macmillan, 1954).

you see a commodity, tax it." To attempt to bring order to a system that was no system, the National Bank Act of 1863 provided that new institutions could receive federal incorporation as banks, and could issue bank notes on the security of federal bonds, to which they would subscribe. Unlike the first and second Banks, which were centrally-controlled institutions with many branches, the system of 1863 provided for separate privately-owned national banks in different localities. After 1865 when the old state banknotes were taxed out of existence, the new banks had a national monopoly of note-issuing power. The War itself brought prosperity – and inflation. During the War some 1,500 banks chartered by 29 states issued some 7,000 different banknotes, of immensely varied value.

Immigrant labor filled the gaps left by soldiers, and the Contract Labor Law of 1864 allowed manufacturers to import cheap foreign labor under contractual agreements. (In 1862 only 72,000 immigrants entered the US, the smallest number for any year from 1843 to 1932). New machines, new packaging, and mass production resulted in a substantial enlargement of America's industrial capacity. At least ten national labor unions came into being between 1863 and 1866, including the first of the great railroad brotherhoods, the Brotherhood of Locomotive Engineers. Petroleum, discovered in Venango County, Pennsylvania, in 1859, had by 1865 virtually replaced whale oil as a lubricant – fortunately for the North, since, in 1863, most of the Northern whaling fleet had been destroyed by Southern raiders. The Morrill Land Grant Act of 1862 donated public lands to the states for support of agricultural and mechanical colleges, with provision for military training; from this source came 69 "land grant" colleges. No less than 15 colleges were founded in the War years, including Cornell, Swarthmore, and the Massachusetts Institute of Technology; many land-grant colleges later became state universities. The Western Union Telegraph Company, organized in 1856 by Hiram Sibley, became transcontinental in 1862, aided by a federal subsidy; it became a virtual monopoly by 1866. The news of victory or defeat came promptly, and nationwide.

The Homestead Act of 1862, granting 160 acres to any family settling on the public domain (Greeley's *Tribune* had long campaigned for "land for the landless") and public land for sale at $1.25 per acre, and the Conscription Act of 1863, each stimulated the westward migration of 300,000 Americans during the war years. The industrialization of the North involved a complete social revolution, "the replacement of improvisation by plan and organization," the growth of vast corporations, and "a sturdy new business system centred in New York." The War, as Allan Nevins put it, became a revolution that took the "shape of anvil, loom and piston." The mechanization of agriculture, the growth of trusts, the coming of cattle and wheat kings, the management of currency and credit, coincided with and were fostered by war; but it can equally be argued that the revolution in American economic life might have occurred even had John Brown not raided the Federal Arsenal at Harper's Ferry from his fastness in the Maryland hills, had not Beauregard fired on Sumter, nor Pickett's men made their charge across the field at Gettysburg.[16]

The response of men to join the armies, in both North and South, was remarkable. Up to the passing of the Draft Act in 1863, 800,000 volunteered in the North. Since a volunteer was given a cash bounty on enlisting, and a uniform, ("handsome, well made and will not drop off after two weeks' wear ..." declared the recruiting poster on Staten Island, "the finest camp ground in the State"), many men joined up for the money, and some of them deserted to enlist again for another bounty in another state, sometimes a wealthier one, paying more. (One man jumped bounty on 32 occasions.) There were bounty-brokers to organize the bounty-jumpers, sometimes bribing the recruiting officers to accept the physically unfit. In the North, as the supply of volunteers dried up, there was no alternative to conscription in March 1863. But for $300 a man could purchase exemption, or he could hire a substitute; until this provision was abolished, few rich men served in the Union Army. Draft riots chanting "Down with the rich!" occurred in New York, particularly among the Irish-Americans, which became anti-Negro and anti-abolitionist mid-July 1863; and large forces of soldiers had to be maintained in Northern cities to preserve order. Some 2,000 were killed in the draft riots. When workers went on strike because of the high prices, blacks were used as strike-breakers; the war fever cooled – except against blacks. Desertions were as high as 200,000 (1 in 7 enlistments).

The South had resorted to conscription in 1862, but overseers and owners of 20 slaves or more, professors and ministers, mailmen and blacksmiths, printers and newspaper editors, saltmakers and employees in cotton, wool, and paper mills, were, however, exempt: on both sides, the War began to appear as "a rich men's war but a poor man's fight;" however, the rate of desertion was slightly lower than that above the Mason-Dixon line – only 100,000 (1 in 9 enlistments). Both North and South found the enactment of

[16] Allan Nevins, *The War for the Union* (New York, Scribner's, 1959), vol. 310, 511, 528.

conscription a great inducement to volunteering. Indeed, in the South it was a matter of honor to volunteer before being drafted. The War developed a group of newly rich; Northern millionaires increased from less than a handful in 1860 to hundreds during the War, some by the sale of "shoddy" or inferior goods to the government at high prices. As the *New York Herald* put it on October 6, 1863:

The world has seen its iron age, its silver age, its golden age and its brazen age. This is the age of shoddy ... They are shoddy brokers in Wall Street, or shoddy manufacturers of shoddy goods, or shoddy contractors for shoddy articles for a shoddy government. Six days a week they are shoddy businessmen. On the seventh day they are Shoddy Christians.

While Southern railroads sank into uselessness, with tracks from branch lines torn up to be used elsewhere, the North was increasing its mileage. In 1862 Congress at last authorized the long-discussed transcontinental railroad, granting 30 million acres and millions in federal bonds to the Union Pacific and Central Pacific Railroad Companies: the lines would run west from Omaha across the plains and the Rockies, and east from the Sacramento River, now that the Southerners were not there to counter the proposal. New York and St Louis were linked by a one-gauge railroad. In short, the War greatly strengthened the industrial life of the North, while in the South the plantation-slave system was under immense strain. In one respect only did the North suffer materially. Southern privateers and high insurance rates had largely driven the United States merchant marine from the sea.

7 THE CONFEDERACY

Less divided in sentiment during most of the War than was the North, the Confederacy nevertheless experienced the fragmenting influence of "states' rights" policies, and the breakdown of its inadequate railroad system. The Northern blockade steadily tightened. Shoes, blankets, soap, and medicine were lacking: Lee at Antietam was held up by his stragglers — too many of his men were shoeless. Rations had to be reduced. The transportation system broke down, because supplies for the maintenance of the railroads, for locomotives and freight cars, were not available. The South's rail "network" was not only vulnerable but primitive: 113 small companies, all single-track, and with 11 different gauges. There was, however, a

continuous five-foot gauge on the line running from New Orleans,
Mobile, and Memphis to Chattanooga and then to Petersburg: a
Southern bread-line. The route from Chattanooga over the mountains to Richmond was interrupted at Lynchburg by a difference
of gauge; and each company was a jealous hoarder of its own cars.
Augusta, Lynchburg, and Charlotte did not connect. The shortages
became universal: of small arms – many fought the war equipped
with smooth-bore muzzle-loaders – and especially of artillery, of
medical supplies, and of food. The usual ration was moldy meat and
hardtack – usually with the initials BC (Boston Cracker) which for
the troops was seen as an accurate record of the biscuit's age. The
South was short of industry and transportation. The Confederate
government itself undertook to set up and operate mills, mines, and
factories. The central and state governments subsidized key private
industries, and took a share in blockade-running. Not least came a
shift of acreage from cotton to food crops. Unlike the North, it
was not until February 1865, two months before the end, that the
Confederate Congress authorized the secretary of war to take control
of any railroad needed for military purposes.

The blockade was by no means the only factor responsible for
the misery of the Confederacy. The Conscription Act of 1862 was
bitterly resisted. With the blessing of his Congress, Davis suspended
the writ of *habeas corpus*, and invoked martial law in some areas
of the Confederacy. Military commanders could and did impress
private property for the use of the army. The Confederacy also
levied an income tax, and a tax-in-kind (10 percent of the gross) on
agricultural commodities. Its War Department took an active part
in the economy by controlling draft exemptions for laborers, transportation priorities, and raw materials allocations. But whereas
Lincoln exceeded his power in the Vallandigham case and others,
Davis allowed his critics a free hand in voicing their opposition. He
had neither the will nor the wile of a dictator – though he was so
described. There was no censorship, even of soldiers' mail. He suffered accordingly: the price of democracy. And when Varina Howell
Davis played the role of "first lady" and gave festive luncheons
instead of visiting hospitals, she reaped bitter criticism for doing the
very things Southern "belles" were supposed to do in ante-bellum
times; it would take a long war to reconcile Richmond ladies to
being queened over by anyone from Mississippi. Prominent newspapers attacked Davis as incompetent and despotic. The seaboard
states, where the doctrine of states' rights was strong, denounced the
"unconstitutional acts" of the Richmond Cabinet. North Carolina
demanded the return of its volunteers for the defense of the state,

and hoarded its own supplies of food, uniforms, and blankets, even though Lee's men needed them desperately; its 40 cotton mills were one-third of the South's total number. South Carolina proposed to forbid the Confederate Government to raise troops in the state except by voluntary enlistment. Fractious governors like Joseph E. Brown of Georgia and Zebulon B. Vance of North Carolina, abetted by Vice-President Stephen in Georgia, defied President Davis. They tried to prevent the Davis government from controlling troops and supplies; they resisted martial law, interfered with conscription, and talked of tyranny. To make matters worse, hopes of British and French intervention failed, as the preliminary announcement of the Emancipation Proclamation in September 1862 gave pause to European sympathizers with the Confederacy.[17]

There was one exception to this catalog: the achievement of General Josiah Gorgas, Confederate chief of ordnance – a Pennsylvanian Southerner, by way of marriage to a girl from Alabama (and the parents of the victor over yellow fever in Panama 40 years later). Gorgas got rifles and muskets to the troops, 90 percent of them from Europe and through the blockade; and he established armories and gunpowder factories not merely in the ironworks at Richmond, Fayetteville, and Selma, but also in Charleston, Columbus, Macon, and Atlanta. During the war, the Tredegar Iron Works employed 2,500 men, the majority of whom were slaves.

8 EMANCIPATION

In the North the radical Republicans, or the "Vindictives" – men like Stevens, Wade, and Sumner – felt from the outset that the War must be made a war to end slavery. On the other hand, the conservative Republicans, led by Lincoln, supported in the Senate by Orville Browning of Illinois and John Sherman of Ohio, maintained for a considerable time that the War was only a war to preserve the Union. In the summer of 1861, Congress passed a first Confiscation Act, providing that slaves used by Confederates to aid the Rebel war effort – for example, in building fortifications – would be free upon their capture by Union forces. Subsequently, a second Confiscation Act provided that the slaves owned by persons who voluntarily aided the Confederate war effort should be free. Lincoln's personal wish by 1862 was for a federally compensated

[17] F. L. Owsley, *States Rights in the Confederacy* (Chicago, University of Chicago, 1925), pp. 113–22, 124–9, and 149.

and gradual emancipation, not for the unconditional abolition which the more extreme abolitionists had been demanding since 1830. By gradual he meant 1865 – or, in one version, as late as 1900. He even tried to persuade black leaders to consider colonization of Chiriqui, a province of Panama, if it could be acquired by the State Department, or of Cow Island off Haiti.[18] It was not until the War was won that he took the political risk of emancipating the bondsmen of loyal slaveholders in the border states; Clay and Webster would have been flattered at his steadfastness as an arch-compromiser. Moreover, he eventually recognized that a stand on behalf of the Negroes would win support for the Union abroad as well as at home. It was necessary, however, to delay the proclamation until a victory had been won, lest it seem the despairing gesture of a lost cause. Antietam, as a victory – if only just – gave him his opportunity. The preliminary proclamation of emancipation was issued after Antietam, and on January 1, 1863, came the definite proclamation itself. Since it applied only to slaves within the Confederacy, it did little except aggravate Southern bitterness; but the conviction – even born of expedience though it was – slowly grew that the conflict was becoming a war to end slavery, and with it Union prestige grew abroad.

The Emancipation Proclamation, in all its qualifications, was at once humanitarian and shrewd. It did not free a single slave on the day it went into effect, since Confederate Southerners did not recognize the validity of proclamations by "foreign" presidents, and loyal Unionist slaveholders were excluded from its terms. But Lincoln put himself and his government on record for emancipation, and in essence doomed slavery in the United States. And he did so without driving border slave states such as Missouri, Kentucky, and Maryland out of the Union, and without destroying the Republican majority in Congress, as some of his advisors feared might happen in the 1862 "off-year" elections, though New York, Pennsylvania, Ohio, Indiana, and Illinois elected Democrats to the House. Most important, Lincoln gave greater meaning to the war for union, and in the Congressional elections the "War Democrats" supported the Republicans. The newspapers were all but unanimous: Greeley's *New York Tribune*, the Chicago Tribune, the *New York Times*, the *Springfield Republican*, the *Philadelphia Press* ("a good deed, at a good time.") However, the Democratic *Chicago Times* struck

[18] Abraham Lincoln, "Address to a Deputation of Negroes," August 14, 1862, in *Collected Works of Abraham Lincoln*, ed. Roy P. Basler (New Brunswick, NJ, Rutgers University Press, 1953), vol. V, pp. 370–5.

a discordant note: "the war is reduced to a contest of subjugation. It has assumed that character that abolitionism has designed from the outset it should assume." For prejudice was never a Southern monopoly. If New England had the best record, cynics could point out that it was the region farthest from the conflict, and from the contacts of white and black. Enthusiasm for abolition was a luxury to be enjoyed — at a distance. Many Northerners had crossed the Ohio, but brought Southern sentiments with them. There were ugly anti-Negro riots in Toledo and Cincinnati in July 1862, when Negroes were employed to replace striking Irish workers. In the 1860 election, girls in Indiana had paraded with Democratic banners: "Fathers, save us from Nigger husbands." Even at a Republican rally in 1860 in Lincoln's own home-town, Springfield, the banners read: "No Negro equality in the North." Even Republican Senator Jacob Howard of Indiana could say: "Canada is very near us, and affords a fine market for wool." In the closing stages of the War a Democratic newspaper in Iowa greeted Congressional approval of the Thirteenth Amendment, which finally abolished slavery, with a bitter blend of sarcasm and racism:

EXCELSIOR, SAMBO!
At last the abolition millennium is about to dawn. The incubus of slavery which weighed down our country for over eighty years, and which was foisted upon us by those slave-driving nabobs, Washington, Jefferson, Jackson, and others of their ilk, is about to be removed, and our disenthralled country, with one huge bound will spring into the fore rank of civilized progress, amid the shouts and songs of the freed, the twang of banjo, the clatter of the "fantastic heel and toe", and "a most palpable odor."

For Frederick Douglass, however, the War was now "invested with sanctity." Anti-slavery had been a part of that War all along, as part of Lincoln's definition of union; but now the President had declared it so. Now the "War for the Union" was also to become a "crusade against slavery." For its part, the South feared a spate of Negro uprisings. Some of the President's supporters in the North doubted his right to issue the Proclamation in his capacity as commander-in-chief. If he was, as commander-in-chief, seeking to suppress not a rebellion of the South but in the South, what would be the position of such a decision after the War was over; would it be binding, and on all? It was more than the "simple" issues of moral right or legal rights. It called for a saint dressed as a Machiavelli, who kept one finger constantly on the nation's pulse. Not the least of Lincoln's skill was that he was patient, and that his taste was

Plate 15 The Battle of Gettysburg.
(The Mansell Collection, London.)

always to take the low road. The Proclamation itself might, as Richard Hofstadter said, have "all the moral grandeur of a bill of lading;" it was done almost by stealth, and was a declaration of intent only; but Karl Marx recognized that, despite the absence of eloquence, "no wrapping himself in the toga of history," the Proclamation was "the most important document of American history since the founding of the Union."[19]

The drastic defeat at Fredericksburg, Virginia, on 13 December 1862, three weeks before emancipation was to apply, deprived the final proclamation of its full effect upon Northern opinion. The decimation of the Army of the Potomac was but another indication that the replacement of McClellan, an able drillmaster for all his caution, and despite his egocentric and Napoleonic personal traits, had been a costly mistake. The quest for a military leader continued.

9 GETTYSBURG

The year 1863 was cheerless in North and South alike. The disaster at Fredericksburg strengthened the belief of thousands that it would be impossible to conquer the South. Burnside lost 12,500 men of his 114,000. As Lee watched the slaughter, he commented: "It is well this is so terrible, or else we might grow fond of it." "Fighting Joe" Hooker, successor to Burnside as commander of the Army of the Potomac, was himself defeated by Lee and Jackson in the battle of Chancellorsville in May 1863, the battle in which Jackson lost his life. The succession of Union defeats led the *Chicago Tribune* to call on Lincoln himself to take command in the field as the only hope of the North. In fact, Chancellorsville was to be the last great Confederate victory in the East.

The turning point of the Civil War came in the first week of July 1863. General Lee decided to invade the North at a time when the morale of his army was high. "Copperhead" (Peace Democrats) agitation was at its height, and the commercial interests of the Northern cities seemed on the verge of panic. Lee's army advanced through Maryland into Pennsylvania, to be halted at Gettysburg, Pennsylvania, by the Army of the Potomac, now under George G.

[19] Richard Hofstadter, *The American Political Tradition* (New York, Knopf, 1957), p. 132; Benjamin Quarles, *Lincoln and the Negro* (New York, Oxford University Press, 1962), p. 131; Leon F. Litvack, *North of Slavery: The Negro in the free states 1790–1860* (Chicago, University of Chicago Press, 1961); *Die Presse*, 12 Oct. 1862.

Meade; and for three days in a hot sun, July 1–3, the battle raged. The artillery duel at Gettysburg was the most sustained of the war. The climax came when George Pickett and 15,000 of Lee's best troops stormed the Federal lines of Cemetery Ridge across one and a quarter miles of open country, only to be mowed down by massive and entrenched rifle-power and artillery fire. At Gettysburg, 75,000 Confederates under Lee opposed 88,000 Unionists; there were over 50,000 casualties. Virginia's "crack" corps, the First Virginia Regiment, which had fought with Washington in the French and Indian War, and again under him at Trenton, Princeton, and Yorktown, lost 80 percent of its men. The failure of Lee's costly attacks marked the end of any hope of outright Southern victory – though the savage hand-to-hand killing of the third day left the Union army victorious but decimated, incapable of giving chase. Meade, a quiet and competent West Pointer, had given the North its first victory since Antietam.

On the very same day, General Pemberton (a Pennsylvanian fighting for the South mainly because his wife was a Virginian) surrendered Vicksburg to General Grant. This achievement was Grant's most brilliant feat in the whole war. It had been a cold and rainy winter, and the river was in flood. The city was perched on a great crest and appeared impregnable. Grant crossed the river into enemy territory, marched 200 miles and won five distinct battles, destroyed arsenals and military storehouses that the South had thought unassailable, and laid siege to the city from the rear: a siege lasting 40 days. The defenders had taken shelter. Seventeen thousand men died there, seeking to capture or to hold the Confederacy's greatest fortress; life on – or, more accurately, below – the Vicksburg Bluff was grim indeed. Its capture was immensely significant. Together with the federal victory at Gettysburg, it saved the Union and forecast the ultimate defeat of the Confederacy. Lee retreated on July 4, and the Union army was unable to press forward a counterattack. When Fort Hudson surrendered five days later, the Union forces controlled the Mississippi, the Confederacy was cut in two, and the precious supplies from Texas and Arkansas were now cut off. So was the supply route for arms, munitions, and medicine, which had been shipped from Europe to Mexican ports to be smuggled into the South. Napoleon III abandoned his efforts to obtain recognition of the independence of the Confederacy. It was now a lost cause. Vicksburg, said General Halleck, was "worth 40 Richmonds." Jefferson Davis soldiered on, but a sadder man – his own home, Brierfield, 20 miles south of Vicksburg, had been sacked.

On November 19, 1863, the cemetery at Gettysburg was dedicated. The Union's greatest orator, Edward Everett, gave a two-hour, now unremembered, address. Lincoln spoke briefly, and was hardly audible. Edward Everett sent a note to the President on the day after the speech was delivered: "I should be glad if I could flatter myself that I came as near to the central idea of the occasion, in two hours, as you did in two minutes." The invitation to the President to speak — extended to him six weeks after Edward Everett had been selected to deliver the principal address — was "an afterthought." The invitation was sent only three weeks before the ceremony was due.

Four score and seven years ago our fathers brought forth on this continent, a new nation, conceived in Liberty, and dedicated to the proposition that all men are created equal.

Now we are engaged in a great civil war, testing whether that nation or any nation so conceived and so dedicated, can long endure. We are met on a great battle-field of that war. We have come to dedicate a portion of that field, as a final resting place for those who here gave their lives that that nation might live. It is altogether fitting and proper that we should do this.

But, in a larger sense, we can not dedicate — we can not consecrate — we can not hallow — this ground. The brave men, living and dead, who struggled here have consecrated it, far above our poor power to add or detract. The world will little note, nor long remember, what we say here, but it can never forget what they did here. It is for us the living, rather, to be dedicated here to the unfinished work which they who fought here have thus far so nobly advanced. It is rather for us to be here dedicated to the great task remaining before us — that from these honored dead we take increased devotion to that cause for which they gave the last full measure of devotion — that we here highly resolve that these dead shall not have died in vain — that this nation, under God, shall have a new birth of freedom — and that government of the people, by the people, for the people, shall not perish from the earth.

10 AIDING THE ENEMY

The Emancipation Proclamation, however liberal its intent, was a war measure, applicable only to slaves of the enemy, the Confederates. Nor was Lincoln liberal on the home front: in 1863 Congress authorized the President to suspend the writ of *habeas corpus* throughout the United States. The purpose of these drastic actions was to crush all opposition to the life-and-death struggle facing the Union. Individuals particularly outspoken against Lincoln's war policy were arbitrarily arrested and tried by court-martial. One of them, a former Congressman from Ohio, Clement Laird Vallandigham, who saw the war as "a bloody and costly failure," was court-martialed, tried for treason, and sentenced to close confinement. Aware that martyrdom would suit his critics, and not aid his cause, Lincoln, always a reluctant and indulgent tyrant — and a shrewd one — mischievously commuted the sentence to banishment to the Confederacy. There too Vallandigham complained of lack of liberty, and Jefferson Davis in turn banished him to the Bahamas. From there he went to Canada, and in Windsor, Ontario, he received the Democratic nomination for governor of Ohio, to lose in 1863 by only 100,000 votes. He was allowed to return to Ohio in June 1864, and he was the keynote speaker at the 1864 Democratic Convention; but he was never again to hold public office.

The line between genuine criticism and aiding the enemy is always a narrow one in wartime, in any society cherishing freedom; and the handling of trouble makers is never easy, in peace as in war. This was especially so in a Mid-West thick with ex-Southerners. Editors of opposition papers who became too critical found their papers suspended and themselves in prison. "Mr Lincoln's War" was being accompanied by the arrests of civilians, deemed to be engaged in "disloyal practices", and their trials by military commissions; the military draft was unpopular, including its undemocratic feature permitting purchase of a substitute; so was the requirement that those subject to conscription should have a pass before they could travel beyond the confines of their home counties. Civil liberties guaranteed in the Constitution were being swept away by "Caesar" Lincoln, the "tyrant." The Peace Democrats or "Copperheads", who included Vallandigham, Congressman Daniel Voorhees, and editor J. J. Bingham, wanted to restore "the Union as it was, and the Constitution as it is." But, as their nickname implied, some of them — unlike the rattlesnake — were suspect as being likely to strike without warning. The Knights of the Golden Circle, with its "temples" and "castles," like the Sons of Liberty — of which Vallandigham was "Supreme Commander" — and the Order of American Knights, were pro-Southern, anti-Republican, genuine constitutionalist, Democratic clubs; but with militant wings, and Southern agents among them. In the case of one Milligan, an Indiana Democrat accused of conspiracy to set free certain Confederate prisoners of war, a military tribunal decreed the death sentence. After the war, in 1866, the Supreme Court annulled that judgment and held that a civilian could not, under the Constitution, be tried by court-martial when regular civil courts were operating "in the proper and unobstructed exercise of their jurisdiction." But that ruling came too late to affect wartime practice; Lincoln, resolved to restore the Union at any price, regretfully saw no alternative to making civil rights subordinate to victory while the battle raged.

In July 1863 the Confederate cavalry leader John Hunt Morgan raided Southern Indiana, and attempted – without success – to organize a Copperhead "Western Confederacy" which would ally with the South. In 1864 an espionage centre was set up in Toronto, with as field operator a young Kentuckian, Thomas H. Hines, a former captain in John Hunt Morgan's cavalry. With the help of mid-western Copperheads and escaped Confederate prisoners then in Canada, Hines plotted a break-away that would put Ohio, Indiana, and Illinois in the Southern Confederacy. The plan included the seizure of such cities as Chicago, the release of thousands of Confederate soldiers from prisoner-of-war camps in the Northwest, and the capture of U. S. S. *Michigan*, the navy's one warship on the Great Lakes. With this, and with impromptu privateers, all of the lake cities from Milwaukee to Buffalo were to be ravaged, Confederate prisoners on Johnson's Island near Sandusky were to be released, armed bands would strike here and there just south of the Canadian border, spreading terror and forcing Washington to detach troops for the war zone, blockade runners converted into warships would seize the Maine coast, New York City would be set in flames, and railroad lines would be cut; all in all, it would be impossible for the North to carry on the war any longer. None of the plans matured. The Copperheads, like the Loyalists 90 years before, talked, but did not perform. Three banks in Vermont were looted. There were frightening, but in the end ineffective, fires in New York hotels – but no conflagration. In the end the plan backfired. When John Wilkes Booth committed his insane act of violence against the President, the Federal government naturally supposed that this was part of the plot; it helped to create in the North a state of mind that hurt Dixie during the reconstruction period. Secretary Stanton's attempt to connect Lincoln's assassination with the Confederate government was given disturbing support by the earlier abortive attempts at sabotage. Yet even these bungled efforts kept the Democratic spirit alive in the Mid-West, curbed the hand of local military commanders, slowed the movement towards abolition, and secured the election to state legislatures, and to Congress, of popular "martyrs" who had suffered military arrest. The Copperhead leaders did not suffer for their views and for their rejection of the Union-Lincoln mystique. War or no War, at least in the Mid-West, this was still a free society.[20]

Claiming nothing but reverence for the Constitution, denying dictatorial ambitions, and acting as commander-in-chief only to save the Union, the weary Lincoln gave two answers to his critics:

First, must I shoot a simple-minded soldier boy who deserts, while I must not touch a hair of a wily agitator who induces him to desert? ... I think that in such a case to silence the agitator and save the boy is not only constitutional, but, withal, a great mercy. Second, was it impossible to lose the nation and yet preserve the Constitution? By general law, life and limb must be protected, yet often a limb must be amputated to save a life; but a life is never wisely given to save a limb.

Lincoln believed that parts of the Constitution might have to be temporarily violated in order to save the Constitution as a whole, and the Union. But Lincoln was a minority President. As the fortunes of war fluctuated, so did his popularity; until the election of 1864 he could not count upon majority support. The uncertainty of civil liberty, the unpopular Draft Acts, the high taxes, the depreciating greenbacks that could be seen as in fact forced loans, the arrest of over 13,000 "suspects" as potential enemies – and a denied appeal to *habeas corpus*, with the suppression of over 300 newspapers for short or long terms, made Lincoln's lot difficult. The Emancipation Proclamation widened the gap between the radical Republicans, who favored it, and the conservatives, who favored evasion. Even the Cabinet was lacking in harmony, as the two chief secretaries led rival factions. There had been heavy Republican losses in the 1862 Congressional elections: no less than six states – New York, Pennsylvania, Ohio, Indiana, Illinois, and Wisconsin – swung from the Republicans to the Democrats. In Ohio two men imprisoned by Lincoln won election to Congress. One result of the 1862 elections had been the freeing of many political prisoners. The Administration's re-election hung upon the slender thread of prompt and decisive military success. However, the Democrats were disunited, split between War Democrats and the regular Democrats, the latter group loyal to the Union but highly critical of Lincoln's conduct of the war. An extreme element in this camp were the "Copperheads," the Northerners who sympathized with the Confederacy and favored peace without victory or terms. In the South,

[20] James D. Horan, *Confederate Agent* (New York, Crown, 1964); Wood Gray, *The Hidden Civil War: The story of the Copperheads* (New York, Viking, 1942).

political division also appeared, as the states' rights doctrine contested the power of the confederate government, or as powerful groups questioned Jefferson Davis's ability.

In the face of such party division, it was difficult to predict the political outcome of the 1864 election. The Republicans assumed the name of the Union party for the election, hoping thereby not only to emphasize their war aim, but also to capture the support of the War Democrats. Lincoln was, of course, re-nominated; and for the vice-presidency Andrew Johnson, a War Democrat of Tennessee, was selected. The platform praised Lincoln's conduct of the war, emphasized a fight to the finish for the Union, and advocated a constitutional amendment abolishing slavery. The Democrats nominated General George B. McClellan, adopted a platform which stood for the preservation of the "Union and the rights of the States unimpaired," called for an early cessation of the War, and denounced the denial of civil liberties – though McClellan, remembering his brave soldiers, denied that the war was a failure, or that peace was more important than Union. In August 1864 Lincoln wrote that "it seems exceedingly probable that this administration will not be re-elected," and other Republican leaders had reached the same conclusion.

In the South – or "at the South," as contemporaries usually put it – Jefferson Davis at least had no problem of re-election: he would, if he and the South survived, serve a single six-year term. But the South remained heterogeneous: upper and lower, tidewater, piedmont, mountain, and river; Vice-President Stephens stayed an ex-Whig at heart; and states' rights remained the reason, especially in Georgia and North Carolina, for opposing centralized authority, for resisting martial law, conscription, and impressment legislation. Only in the last year of the war did separatism weaken: the year when in blunt fact General Sherman's dashing Yankee boys brought the war – for the first time – to the states rights South.

11 GRANT TO COMMAND

As a reward for his services in the West, Grant was promoted to the command of all Union armies between the Alleghanies and the Mississippi north of the Gulf States. But before he left the West he had yet one more triumph. A three-day battle at Chattanooga in November 1863 had resulted in Braxton Bragg's defeat; now Tennessee was secured for the Union. This was one of the most heroic battles of the War. The Union army in Chattanooga had been besieged by Confederate forces commanding the strongly fortified

Missionary Ridge and Lookout Mountain: it was on the first of these that the 4th Kentucky Regiment of the Union army clashed face to face with the 4th Kentucky, CSA. Hooker's men scaled Lookout Mountain on November 24, and Thomas's climbed Missionary Ridge the next day. "By whose orders are those men going up there?" asked Grant. "By their own, I fancy," was the reply. They carried the ridges against all the odds: the second great strategic point in the Confederacy was now in Union hands. With this success, Congress revived a rank unused since George Washington's day — Lieutenant-General of the Armies — and appointed Grant to it, with command of all the armies of the US. For the first time Lincoln could relax; he had a commander — even if a compulsive drunkard, with recurring spells of depression. But as a commander on the field he was successful, and success is the only thing that counts in war. It was part of Lincoln's skill that he knew what not to see.

Grant became the second hero-general of the United States: Jackson was 40 years ahead of him. His capture of Forts Henry and Donelson in Tennessee in February 1862 allowed an invasion of the heartland of the Confederacy. (He was a pipe-smoker, but happened to be enjoying a cigar when Fort Donelson fell; and he was inundated with the gifts of thousands of cheroots. A cigar-smoker he fatally became, for he never found restraint easy. He died of the throat-cancer that this indulgence gave him.)

When called to command in the East, Grant had no doubts about strategy. Between 1861 and the end of 1863, the Army of the Potomac had suffered a combined total of at least 115,000 casualties inflicted by the Army of Northern Virginia. During all that time, and at that terrible cost, it achieved nothing more than holding the *status quo*. In May 1864, when Grant started his campaign, the Federals were barely 35 miles closer to Richmond than they had been in May 1861. Then came Grant. In 45 days he moved more than 75 miles, suffered perhaps 55,000 casualties, and effectively destroyed Lee's army. The price he paid was high; but by paying it he achieved his goal in a fraction of the time his predecessors had spent in paying double that price to achieve nothing. Grant was one of the first to recognize that modern war means attrition and annihilation. Yet there was still no charisma: "a short, round-shouldered man," Richard Henry Dana found him to be, "in a very tarnished ... uniform. ... There was nothing marked in his appearance; he had no gait, no stature, no manner, rough, light-brown whiskers, a blue eye, and rather a scrubby look withal." But he was modest and unselfconscious, and had an almost unique coolness under fire. Grant took command, and Grant won the war. [21]

The superior numbers of the Union army began to tell, and they began to close in on the Confederacy from the north and west. Refusing to see his function as a desk job, Grant was in charge of operations against Lee in Virginia, while Sherman moved into Georgia. Grant hammered his way toward Richmond through the so-called Wilderness at the cost of thousands of men – 9,000 in three hours at Cold Harbor, 60,000 in the four months of campaigning. The gloom caused by these heavy casualties was relieved by Farragut's capture of Mobile Bay in August 1864, by Philip Sheridan's victory over Jubal Early in the Shenandoah valley, and by Sherman's capture of Atlanta, a railroad center, supply center and cannon factory, in September.

Not only had the eleventh-hour victories come, but ultimate victory seemed imminent, for Grant reported that the Confederates had "robbed the cradle and the grave" in their last levy. In the election when the electoral votes were counted, Lincoln and Andrew Johnson the Democrat, his Vice-President to be, had 212 to 21 (New Jersey, Delaware, and Kentucky) for McClellan; but of the 4 million popular votes cast, Lincoln received only 55 percent (2,330,582 against 1,835,985). He almost lost New York; he did lose New Jersey; it was a close-run thing in Pennsylvania. He was helped by the admission of new states – West Virginia, Kansas, and Nevada – and by the soldier vote, some of them given leave to go home to cast their ballots if their states (like Indiana) did not permit voting in the field. To the end Lincoln was the skillful politician – but even so, he was only just the President of the majority. Despite the peace plank in the Democratic platform, McClellan had made it clear that he would continue the war; had he won, Lincoln had planned to help him finish the war before his Inaugural would commit him to peace. Yet, in 1864, as in 1944, in the crises of war, in the confusions of politics, and in all the ambitions of men, democratic elections were held and contested sharply – and fairly. Moreover, the Republican campaign was fought on a platform strongly endorsing a constitutional amendment to end slavery in the United States. On January 31, 1865, the House of Representatives approved the Thirteenth Amendment for ratification by the states. The War was now being fought for the permanent eradication of slavery in the United States.

---

[21] William S. McFeely, *Grant: A biography* (New York, Norton, 1987); Bruce Catton, *Grant Takes Command* (Boston, Little, Brown, 1968).

During the closing months of 1864 Sherman marched from Atlanta through Georgia to the sea, destroying bridges and railroads, livestock and barns, in a path 30 miles or more in width. Owen Lovejoy, the brother of the murdered abolitionist, commented that "if there is no other way to quell the rebellion, we will make a solitude, and call it peace." Atlanta's population was expelled, the town laid waste. Sherman's capture of Savannah in December 1864, and Thomas's defeat of General Hood at Nashville in the same month — the only army totally destroyed on the field in the war — virtually ended Confederate resistance. Virginia's links with the Deep South were broken; the War in the West was won. As Sherman's army marched through Georgia, the flow of refugees reached mammoth proportions. "Every day as we marched on," wrote one of Sherman's generals,

we could see, on each side of our line of march, crowds of these people coming to us through roads and across fields, bringing with them all their earthly goods, and many goods that were not theirs ... They were allowed to follow in the rear of our column, and at times they were almost equal in numbers to the army they were following. [22]

By 1865 the plight of the South was desperate indeed. Desertions were frequent, food was scarce, Federal money was circulating in spite of the prohibition of the Richmond government, and Negroes began to be recruited in the armies. In making the latter proposal, Davis showed rare tact and political skill. He began by asking for an appropriation from Congress to purchase 40,000 black men for noncombatant use by the army. Such requests were normal; the details of the bill, though, were indeed unusual. Davis proposed a "radical alteration in Southern law and custom" by suggesting that the laborers be freed in exchange for their loyal service. Congress gave him the appropriation, but denied any hint of emancipation. The issue was all too plain. Arming the slaves was the last, best hope of Southern victory; but arming the slaves also meant the end of the ante-bellum way of life. Even earlier, in December 1864, the President had sent an emissary to Britain and France to offer emancipation in exchange for recognition. The mission was desperate and fruitless, but it served as an index of how far he would go for the sake of independence.

[22] Henry W. Slocum, "Sherman's March from Savannah to Bentonville," in Clarence Buel and Robert Johnson, *Battles and Leaders of the Civil War*, 4 vols (1887), vol. IV, pp. 688–9.

A delegation headed by Alexander Stephens met Lincoln and Seward at Hampton Roads on February 3, 1865, to discuss terms for the cessation of hostilities. Lincoln insisted on two points: restoration of the Union, and the abolition of slavery. The Southern delegates rejected the offer, calling it a demand for "abject submission."

Sherman's "March to the Sea" was the most spectacular example of the new Northern policy of making war upon the whole South, making no distinction between soldier and civilian. This was what we now know as total war; war was no longer a professional engagement, fought by a mutual code, and until now with a certain chivalry. More than this, a deep-rooted bitterness now permeated both Northerner and Southerner. The bonds of memory to which Lincoln had appealed in his first Inaugural address had been superseded by the recollections of bloody battlefields, of the prisoner camps at Andersonville, Salisbury, Johnson's Island, Point Lockout, and a dozen other places, where both Northern and Southern prisoners died in their tens of thousands, not from ill-treatment but from starvation and neglect. The ugliness into which this now-killing war was deteriorating hit blacks even more than whites. By now Lincoln was using 180,000 black soldiers. The South had replied with savagery: on May 1, 1863, the Confederate Congress authorized Davis to have officers of black units "put to death or be otherwise punished." On April 12, 1864, when the Confederate raider Nathan Bedford Forrest captured Fort Pillow, Tennessee, several dozen of the more than 250 black troops captured had been murdered, along with a score of their white comrades-in-arms. Then on February 1, 1865, Sherman swept into South Carolina putting everything to the torch. Seventeen days later, the as yet largely undamaged capital city of Columbia went up in flames. His men moved north now, plundering as they went. Now only two Confederate states survived.

12 APPOMATTOX

On April 1, the lines protecting Richmond broke, and two days later Federal troops entered the blazing and abandoned capital of the Confederacy. Grant, now with twice his opponents' numbers, hotly pursued the ragged remnants of Lee's once unconquerable Army of Northern Virginia and trapped them at Appomattox Courthouse. There, on April 9, 1865, an immaculately groomed Lee, in a full-dress uniform of gray, with a sword with a jewel-studded hilt, and wearing long gray buckskin gauntlets, surrendered to a casually-garbed Grant – he wore "a blouse of dark-blue flannel, unbuttoned in front," and carried no sword. They met in the parlor of the farmhouse of Wilmer McLean; he had moved there when the farmhouse of his earlier farm had been shelled in 1861 at Bull Run. Ironically, Lee had already freed his slaves, while Grant was still – though only just – a slave-owner. After a few brief words on their old-time army associations, Lee hurried Grant to the terms. They were generous: Lee's army was to lay down its arms, but the officers might retain their side arms, baggage, and private horses. With graciousness appropriate to the occasion and the man, Grant ordered that all men claiming horses or mules be allowed to take them home "for the spring plowing." These terms Lee promptly accepted, and some 28,000 Confederates surrendered. At a suggestion from Lee, Grant ordered that the half-starved army be supplied with provisions. Meanwhile, outside, Union soldiers began firing salutes in celebration but Grant quickly stopped this, saying, "The war is over; the rebels are our countrymen again." Grant said long afterwards that for him there was no exultation, just depression. "I felt like anything rather than rejoicing at the downfall of a foe who had fought so long and so valiantly, and suffered so much for a cause." Returning to his men, Lee, with tear-stained eyes, said, "We have fought through the war together. I have done the best I could for you. My heart is too full to say more." The next day he bade his army farewell and returned to Richmond. His men went home, with their horses, if they had them, since they would need them for the now-late spring plowing – and with their memories of four years of war. Oliver Wendell Holmes served in the War, and, as a young captain, was wounded at Antietam. "In our youth," he wrote later, "our hearts were touched with fire. It was given us to learn at the outset that life is a profound and passionate thing." One of Lee's veterans put it differently. As he threw down his rifle on the pile of surrendered weapons at Appomattox, he said, "Damn me if I ever love another country."[23]

Lee's surrender brought about the collapse of the Confederacy. Lincoln visited the battered capital of the Confederacy, and the advice he gave the military commander was humane; "Let them up easy. Let them up easy." By April 26, Johnston surrendered to Sherman. After four years almost to the day the war was over. On June 17, 1865, after the death of his son Julian at Drewry's Bluff, after the news of the destruction of his Virginia homes, of his

---

[23] Avery O. Craven, *The Coming of the Civil War* (New York, Scribner's, 1942), p. 1.

libraries destroyed and everything of value in furniture broken or stolen, and after he had digested the news from Appomattox, Edmund Ruffin, the distinguished Virginian agriculturist, made this entry in his diary:

I hereby declare my unmitigated hatred to Yankee rule — to all political, social and business connections with the Yankees and to the Yankee race ...

Seating himself erectly in his chair, he propped the butt of his silver-mounted gun against a trunk at his feet, placed the muzzle in his mouth, and, as his son reported in a letter to members of the family, "pulled the trigger with a forked stick."[24]

13   THE END

Whatever Lincoln may have intended the nature of the peace to be, he did not live to shape it. On Good Friday, April 14, 1865, accompanied by his wife, he went to Ford's Theater. John Wilkes Booth was the handsome son of one actor, the great if unbalanced Shakespearean actor Junius Brutus Booth, and the brother of another, Edwin; he was a Washington heartthrob and ladies' man, and a gymnast, a skilled horseman, and a crack shot. He knew, and was known in, the theater and had easy access: he had played Romeo there 18 months before. He entered unseen, reached Lincoln's box and fired a number of shots. He leapt the 12 feet to the stage, his leg breaking as he became entangled in a flag draped over the box. He escaped shouting "Sic semper tyrannis!" Lincoln was carried across 10th Street to a private house, laid on a bed that was too short for him, lingered nine hours, and died the next day. His secretary of state, who was ill after an accident, was knifed in his bed; the life of the Vice-President was spared only by the cowardice of the man deputed to kill him; and General Grant escaped only because he had left town. There was thus evidence of a conspiracy. Panic gripped the streets, and afterwards 8,000 troops were on patrol in the city.

In fact, the assassination was the work of a pathological megalomaniac assisted by a seedy group of half-witted hangers-on — a

---

[24] William R. Taylor, *Cavalier and Yankee* (New York, Doubleday Anchor, 1963), pp. 317–18; Avery O. Craven, *Edmund Ruffin, Southerner* (Baton Rouge, Louisiana State University Press, 1966).

conspiracy so inconsiderable, compared to the other dangers threatening the President, that the security services had heard about it
months before and taken no action. It had been reported by a
fellow-lodger in the Surratt boarding-house on H Street, where
Booth and his associates were open in their plotting — although Mrs
Surratt, a Maryland widow, denied all knowledge of it. There can
have been few more striking examples of the intervention of the
casual, the frivolous, and the mad in human affairs. John Wilkes
Booth was not an obscure maniac, but an actor of considerable
fame and adequate means. He was well known to be a Southerner
in sympathy; and the conspiracy, when he first set it afoot, was
devised as a blow against the enemies of his country. By April 1865,
such a blow was useless; but that did not deter Booth. His real
motive was not patriotism but the gigantic self-advertisement of
an actor gone mad. "When I leave the stage," he said shortly before
his crime, "I shall be the most famous man in America." He expected to be hero-worshipped in the South. The dingy rabble of his
fellow-conspirators, saloon-bar cronies hypnotized by his personality,
could be betrayed and sacrificed as he saw fit. The President's security service was weak. The President usually rode unescorted in
Washington's muddy streets, and at twilight he had often walked
home across the White House grounds from the Telegraph Office,
through a litter of squatters' huts; petitioners wandered through the
Presidential corridors unchecked. On April 14, Lincoln's personal
safety was entrusted to a dead-beat police officer with a bad record,
John Parker, who on the fatal night slipped out for a dram. The
wonder is not that Lincoln died, but that he survived for so long.
Eleven days after the assassination, Booth was surrounded, in a
barn in Caroline County, Virginia, and shot in escaping. "I did it,
sir. I shot John Wilkes Booth," said Sergeant Corbett, a New York
Cavalry trooper. "Why? You were ordered not to." "Providence, sir,
I heard the voice of God." Mrs Surratt and Booth's three companions
were hanged on 7 July 1865. Major Rathbone, the Presidential aide
who had accompanied the President and was in his box, committed
suicide. No action was taken against John Parker, the guard who
was not there. But for Edwin Booth the notoriety drew audiences.
His playing of Hamlet had always been acclaimed. Now it was his
Brutus that drew the largest crowds. One month later the fleeing
Jefferson Davis was captured in disguise in Irwinville, Georgia, and
imprisoned for two years in Fortress Monroe. Lincoln had hoped
that he would escape. He was never brought to trial.

14 A NEW KIND OF CONFLICT

The Civil War was a new kind of conflict: total war. The response
to the calls for men was novel – and noble. Neither side had
experience or training in coping with the size of the volunteer, then
conscript, armies or of provisioning them. The Union, perhaps
because it was more civilian-minded, proved more successful in
applying civilian organizational practices; whatever its difficulties
in finding battlefield leaders, barracks, and hospitals, its quarter-
masters were unsurpassed; and in Richard Current's phrase, "As
usual, God was on the side of the heaviest battalions."[25]

The tactics were new also. The War produced the first un-
orthodox blitzkrieg, when Sherman cut loose from his supply trains
and all the impedimenta of "regular" war to lay waste the land
from Atlanta, Georgia, to the sea, and then northward; dashing
Yankee boys they might be in song, but they acted now as confident and competent poacher-avengers, eating fresh beef and water
melon, driving confiscated horses and mules before them, ripping
up every railroad track within reach – and keeping up a minimum
of 15 miles a day. They were mainly Westerners, and by 1864 seasoned veterans. When Sheridan devastated the Shenandoah valley he
could boast that a crow flying over it "would have to carry his own
provisions." The tactics, in all their horror, like the importance of
railroads and of telegraphic communication, were a discovery made
in the War.[26]

The West Pointers had been trained on Henri Jomini's *Précis
de l'art de guerre*, the text book of the Napoleonic age, which
stressed the importance of the offensive, and belittled the need for
fortifications; the objectives were the capture of enemy territory and
in particular of the enemy capital. Henry Halleck, who became the
North's chief-of-staff in the last year of the War – in essence Grant's
desk-man in Washington – had earned the nickname of "Old Brains"
for his text, *Elements of Military Art and Science*, which, as he
admitted, was little more than a translation of Jomini. There was
another instructor at West Point, Dennis Hart Mahan, who foresaw
the effectiveness of the rifled musket, of field fortifications and of

[25] Richard N. Current, "God and the Strongest Battalion," in David Donald (ed.),
Why the North won the Civil War (Baton Rouge, Louisiana State University Press,
1960), p. 32.
[26] Joseph T. Glatthaar, "The new Civil War history: an overview," *Pennsylvania
Magazine of History and Biography*, 115.3 (July 1991), p. 350.

the limitation of assaults. Defense was to prove as important as attack.

As Lincoln was one of the first to grasp, the West Point theorists saw war as a game for professionals, and minimized politics and ideology; as he saw it, the objective now was the destruction of the enemy army, and of its capacity to make war; and, more than this, to exploit the North's greater resources by applying pressure, even if it meant, as it did, two Union dead for every Confederate: this was the ugly logic of the war experience. "We are not only fighting hostile armies," said Sherman, "but a hostile people, and must make old and young, rich and poor, feel the hard hand of war, as well as the organized armies" ... "War," he said bluntly, "is hell."

In the end the Northern professionals proved more capable of adapting, surviving, and winning than the Southern professionals: and it was a war led mainly by professionals. In 55 of the 60 major battles, both sides were commanded by West Point graduates. It was the dominance of West Pointers (and of VMI – Virginia Military Institute – graduates) in the early years that explains the success of the Army of Northern Virginia at the outset of the War. This dominance of West Pointers in the Northern armies ensured the enmity of the Northern Radical Republicans in Congress and of their Congressional Committee on the Conduct of the War – they resented the professionalism and the inbred qualities of West Point. The Confederacy did not have this experience: their President was proud of being at "the Point." In the South the rivalries and tensions were personal: West Pointers were in general held in respect – though not by Confederate secretary of state turned Georgia general Robert Toombs, who was wounded at Antietam; the Confederacy, he said, "died of West Point."

If Lee and Joseph E. Johnson looked venerable, and were in their fifties, the majority of the generals, like their troops, were young. McClellan was only 34 when called to lead the Army of the Potomac; Stonewall Jackson only 39 when he died in 1863; George Custer, more famous later, became a Union cavalry brigadier-general at the age of 23; the Southern cavalry leader J. E. B. Stuart became a brigadier-general in 1861 at 28, and died aged 31. Fifty-five percent of Confederate generals (235 of 425) were killed or wounded, and 12 of them were wounded on four or more occasions, William Ruffin Cox of North Carolina 11 times. Seventy percent of those Confederates killed or mortally wounded were leading an attack at the time. Half the number of enlisted men were 21 or younger.[27]

---

[27] James I. Robertson, *The Stonewall Brigade* (Baton Rouge, Louisiana State Uni-

The Point was primarily an engineering school, not a center of strategic studies. The most successful of them were the least orthodox, the least distinguished academically, and those who had left the Point for civvy street. In tactics, as in style, total war called for Grants, not McClellans – though both had left the Academy by 1861. Both Grant and Sherman found their first personal as well as their military fulfillments in the War, and in command; they were unusual in resenting the visits of politicians or war correspondents – when Sherman became general-in-chief in postwar Washington he moved his headquarters a thousand miles away to St Louis. Only one of the commanders on either side did not tell it all in an autobiography, or have it told for him – Robert E. Lee, who, on retirement in 1865, became principal of Washington College, a small college in western (not West) Virginia, with 40 students and 4 faculty (now Washington and Lee University), where he, his horse Traveller, and "Stonewall" Jackson lie buried. With equal perversity, a number of the commanders on both sides were not Americans at all. Of the North's 583 general officers, 45 were of foreign birth, and of them 12 were Germans and 12 Irish; of the South's 425 generals, only 9 were foreigners, 5 of them Irish – but Braxton Bragg's chief of ordnance was a Polish colonel, Hypolite Oladowski, and the Texans were led to victory at Sabine Cross Roads in Louisiana by the Count de Polignac – to them, the "Polecat."

The South, accustomed to militia service, the manual of arms, and a profusion of military titles, found recruits easily – at first. The South Carolina planter Wade Hampton organized and equipped at his own expense the Hampton Legion of 1,000 men, in units of infantry, artillery, and cavalry; they started for the front laden with baskets of chicken, ham, and citron tarts. The Lousiana Zouaves wore red fezes, bolero jackets, and scarlet baggy trousers held up by a blue sash. The Union had also felt the impact of the Second Empire: the New York Zouaves (or Duryee Zouaves) also adopted the gaudy uniforms of French North African troops, bought from Brooks Brothers Stores, and for their journey south (and what they expected would be a short war) their packed sandwiches were supplied by Delmonicos. They lost 117 of their 490 at Bull Run, and some of the survivors were at Fredericksburg and Chancellorsville,

versity Press, 1965), p. 243; T. Harry Williams, "The military leadership of North and South", in Donald, *Why the North Won the Civil War*, pp. 23–47; Grady McWhiney, "Who whipped whom," in Irwin Unger, *Essays on the Civil War and Reconstruction* (New York, Holt, Rinehart and Winston, 1970), pp. 308–25.

Seven Days and Antietam. But New York was rich in color; its firemen volunteers became the 11th New York Regiment (The Fire Zouaves), its Irish the 69th Brigade, and its Scots (the Highland Line) the 79th; and the 39th, proudly wearing the feathered headgear of the *bersaglieri* and calling themselves the Garibaldi brigade, were formed by New York Italians – though their colonel was a Hungarian and their surgeon a German.

The War was unique in that the ultimate victor discovered its cause only halfway through the War, and reluctantly; and then found it also had a winning tactic. Emancipation was not only a crusade, but a weapon in the arsenal of total war. The proclamation deprived the Confederacy of a labor force, gave the Union a new source of recruits, and undermined Southern society. Brought in as a war tactic, it gave the struggle a new and a worldwide dimension, and in the end made the Thirteenth Amendment inevitable. [28]

Again, the War was far more thoroughly reported and publicized than any previous war: notably by Matthew Brady, Alexander Gardner, and Tim O'Sullivan as photographers, and – though his pro-Confederate editor Delane did not permit him to stay long after his savage description of the Union panic after the first battle of Bull Run – by William Howard Russell of the London *Times*, and many a local "by-liner."

The Civil War was the great tragic, and the most violent, experience in the history of the United States. Some three and a half million men, white and black, wore uniforms of blue or gray (or did until the dyes ran out), and fought in one or more of the 6,800 separate engagements – now visibly marked as national memorials across the land, from the peninsula of the James River, where two and a half centuries earlier the first palefaces had landed, across Virginia, down to Chattanooga, Atlanta, and Savannah, across to Gettysburg, and to the Vicksburg bluff on the Mississippi. The response in 1861 in the North from militia and volunteers was overwhelming, outrunning the supplies of weapons and shelter – with the not-yet-completed halls of Congress serving as a temporary barracks. As the war developed, in both North and South, state governors offered commissions to any who would raise and equip a regiment or a company. Both sides were remiss in failing to keep regiments up to full strength once they marched off to war; the new regiments, with new and inexperienced officers, went off with inadequate preparation and weapon training for the grim ordeals. 600,000 lost their lives, 1 in 6 of those engaged; 1 in 10 was

---

[28] Joseph T. Glatthaar, "The new Civil War history, an overview," p. 352.

wounded; this was a greater mortality than in World Wars I and II and the Korean conflict combined. It was old-fashioned war, in that a battle would rarely last more than a few hours (though Shiloh lasted two days and Gettysburg three); but in it a regiment, which was usually locally raised, could lose 50 percent or more of its strength. At Gettysburg 1 in every 5 Union soldiers and 1 in every 3 Confederates present was hit, and the 1st Minnesota Regiment lost 82 percent of its men. It was an old-fashioned war, too, in being a war for causes, in which a bishop commanded troops, in which an Episcopal minister (General Pendleton) was Lee's chief of artillery, and generals were in command on the battle-field and led from the front, sword or pistol in hand; in which cavalry played a major role – though less in support of infantry than as scouts and raiders, as J. E. B. Stuart displayed in the Seven Days' battles; in which cousin fought cousin, or in the case of the Crittendens of Kentucky, brother fought brother, and each as a general; and in which pickets fraternized, swapping tobacco for coffee, and the enemy paused in their firing to go out to rescue a wounded man lying between the lines – though not at Cold Harbor in June 1864, in the Wilderness campaign, where 5,000 of Grant's men fell in ten minutes, and Grant refused to ask for a truce to care for the wounded. That day they died where they lay.

The total figures for the dead and the wounded make appalling reading:

	North *23 states*	South *11 states*
Population	22,000,000	5,500,000 whites and 3,500,000 slaves
Enlistments, including blacks[a]	1,556,678	1,082,119
Total deaths[b]	360,222	258,000
Battle deaths	110,070	94,000
Total wounded	275,175	125,000
Total casualties[c]	635,397	383,000

[a] 186,000 black Unionist troops fought in 198 battles (68,000 casualties).

[b] Total for all US wars before 1860: 8,428.

[c] Approximately 40 percent of all forces.

In all, there were 2,400 battles, skirmishes or clashes.

The weapon used was usually a muzzle-loaded musket, sometimes, but not always, rifled. As muzzle-loaders, they could only be fired about three times a minute, or the slaughter would have been even greater. The rifle could kill at a distance of 500 yards or more. It gave immense advantage to defenders. Moreover, members of a regiment knew each other, and had been and were aware of and frank about each other's qualities or lack of them; Lee, as a former superintendent of West Point, knew the habits of mind of many of his ex-students, friend and foe alike. Respect and loyalty had to be won the hard way. Officers could not stay behind as staff wallahs ("yaller dogs" in the South), and there were few rear headquarters. The War was fought between two citizen armies, and the officers who had usually raised the regiments usually led, and led from the front. Morale and discipline depended on their capacity for leadership, not on copybook maxims or long drills on the parade ground. But it was also the first modern war: of total mobilization of resources; in which the telegraph was important, at least from HQ to some commanders in the field; in which railroads permitted relatively speedy troop movements, as at the first Bull Run, in transporting Bragg's army from Tupelo, Mississippi, to Chattanooga via Mobile in 1862, and in transferring James Longstreet's corps from Virginia in time to fight at Chickamauga in 1863 – in which anchored balloons were used for reconnoiter, and in which weapons included repeating rifles (or machine-guns), land mines (then known as torpedoes), and grenades, rockets, flame-throwers, and iron-clad ships. Men went into action according to the tactical doctrines of the previous war – long lines of infantry firing in volleys, smooth and long bayonets – and faced weapons that became standard issue in the next. But West Point and Napoleonic drill patterns held. Men marched or rode horses into battle, and supplies followed in wagons; messages went by couriers on horseback; Stonewall Jackson favored bayonet assaults. At Shiloh the Confederates attacked by corps in four lines across a three mile front – and confusion reigned. In the Wilderness in 1864 both Lee and Grant lost effective control of their armies once the action began. And cavalry – except for scouting and probing – were less important than the handbooks said; and, as a bulwark of defense, artillery firing grape or canister could decimate advancing infantry.

The least chronicled heroes of the War, as in all wars, were those in the Quartermaster's Branch: Josiah Gorgas for the South, heavily dependent on Europe, and Montgomery Meigs for the North, whose staff had grown from 13 in 1861 to 600 by 1865. Meigs had to plan the manufacture of blankets and tents, shoes and uniforms, wagons and ambulances, and ensure their being where they were needed. When Sherman reached Savannah, Meigs as quartermaster-general was present in person and ensured a new outfit for each man in need. The best indexes of the latter's skill were that if Napoleon needed 12 wagonloads of supplies for 1,000 men, McClellan required and received 26 per 1,000 in 1862, and Grant 33 per 1,000 in 1864 (which meant 4,300 wagons moving as he did); Meigs was abetted by a legion of railroad engineers notably Daniel Herman Haupt and Tom Scott as tracklayers and bridgebuilders.

Spies ought to have been less necessary, since much of the ground was familiar, and there was no barrier of language; yet many of the maps were inaccurate and inadequate. But spies there were, notably in Washington drawing-rooms (witness Rose Greenhow and Belle Boyd), and in Richmond's (witness Elizabeth Van Lewis). But to know McClellan's plans all that Lee had to do was to read the Washington newspapers.

Again, if the romance of the lost cause has enhanced the gallantry and the dash of Lee and Jackson, Stuart and Early, Bruce Catton's studies have chronicled the matching gallantry of the conversion of the simple Northern clerks and farm boys who were at the first Bull Run, into the tough and tempered warriors of Gettysburg, Spotsylvania, Virginia in May 1864, and the mountains of Tennessee. The scale of the carnage was utterly shattering – to both sides. So was the scarcity of food and clothing, and – even more – the recurrence of dysentery, diarrhoea ("the Tennessee quick-step"), typhoid, and typhus. More than half of the 600,000 fatalities were the result of disease and infection rather than battle wounds. The chance of surviving a wound was 7 to 1, whereas in Korea in the 1950s it was 50 to 1. Disease killed twice as many Union soldiers as did Confederate weapons. A recurring theme in all soldiers' letters was the dread of falling into the hands of an army doctor. When the war began, there were only a few army hospitals. When it ended there were 350 in the North, 154 in the Confederacy, and no less than 16 in Washington, DC. As for prisoners of war, it is one of the grimmer statistics of the Civil War that as many Americans died in prison camps, North and South, as died – for example – in the Vietnam War. In one year alone, 13,000 died in Andersonville, and they were buried in mass graves.

Because of its impact, and the scale of the carnage, the Civil War altered views of courage. Those who fought in 1861 were astonishingly innocent of war. There was only the conflict with Mexico to call on for experience, and that had hardly been testing. In 1856, Joseph E. Johnston, the future Confederate general, remarked of

the Mexican War to his friend, George B. McClellan, the future
Union general, "there is no comfort like that of going into battle
with the certainty of winning." The common civilian image of what
war was like was of individual heroism on the battlefield. In 1862,
after his first experience of combat, a young private wrote home
that in pictures of battles he had seen," they would all be in line, all
standing in a nice level field fighting, a number of ladies taking care
of the wounded, &c &c but it isent so." In their innocence, North
and South went to war confident that courage alone would see
them through. It was a matter of duty and of honor to demonstrate
courage; God protected those who were courageous and rewarded
them with victory. To line officers, it was courage that was the
cement binding these ill-disciplined armies together. Many an officer
felt (and his men agreed) that the only way to gain respect and
obedience was to exhibit courage on the battlefield. An Ohio colonel
recorded that in the Battle of Perryville he ordered his men to lie
down, while he deliberately remained standing amidst shot and shell
and canister "thick as hail." His regiment was won over, he reported;
"now they are, without exception, my fast friends." But courage
itself was no insurance against fatality. Indeed, it seemed that the
bravest were the first to be killed. One of Sherman's men wondered
if God even knew who among the dead were courageous, and who
were not. [29]

For at least the first two years of the war, as a Confederate
soldier and author, John Easten Cooke, phrased it, there were
"pitched battles once or twice a year," in which the two sides spent
all day killing each other, "and then relapsed into gentlemanly repose and amity." Cooke exaggerated only a little. The Army of the
Potomac, during the two years from Bull Run to Gettysburg, spent
only a total of perhaps a month in pitched battle, however dreadful
those days may have been. But by 1864 warfare was virtually continuous. In Grant's final year-long campaign against Richmond,
his army and Lee's were hardly ever out of killing range of one
another. Sherman's Atlanta campaign was shorter, but also without
halt. As one of Grant's men wrote, it was a case of "living night
and day within the 'valley of the shadow of death' ... We ... learned
more and more to protect ourselves as we advanced, keeping behind trees and displaying ourselves as little as possible." Courage
ceased to be the criterion. It was survival that mattered. Confederate
General John Bell Hood was deprecated as "simply a brave, hard

[29] Gerald E. Linderman, *Embattled Courage; The experience of combat in the
American Civil War* (New York, Free Press, 1987).

fighter" who thought only of attack; his men called him Wooden Head.[30]

If there was a single cause for the Confederate defeat, it was that Davis and Lee, though talking of defense, believed – as Jomini-educated soldiers – that wars are won by attack. Again and again Southern commanders moved to an offensive, hoping that quick successes would bring the North to discuss terms. In 8 of the first 12 major battles of the war the Confederate forces attacked; their losses were 97,000–20,000 more than Union losses in these same engagements. This was less so in and after 1863, for by that time the South had not comparable numbers. Even so, the South still attacked in 3 of the last 10 major campaigns of the war. Lee had not, however, the resources to implement his advances; and, as 1864 revealed, his own special skill was in defense, not attack.

The bravery of the men in the field, and the devotion of the women left behind, was offset in the Confederacy by the opposition to the Richmond government. Newspapers denounced Jefferson Davis as tyrant; so did his Vice-President, who stayed in Georgia. Robert Toombs, the wealthy and turbulent slaveholder from Georgia, gave up the secretaryship of state after four months to serve in the field, notably at Antietam. The governors of the seaboard states resisted the Conscription Acts, the impressment of food, and the control of the militia. Governor Joseph Brown of Georgia threatened to recall from Confederate ranks all sons of Georgia, unless the sovereign rights of the state were left intact. Governor Vance of North Carolina ran his own blockade-running service, in defiance of orders from Richmond, ignored the requests for requisition of produce, and freed military prisoners. Jefferson Davis never had the support that was given to Lincoln by enthusiastic Northern governors like John Andrew of Massachusetts and Oliver Morton of

[30] Bruce Catton, *This Hallowed Ground* (London, Gollancz, 1957), *Mr Lincoln's Army* (Garden City, NY, Doubleday, 1951), *Glory Road: The bloody route from Fredericksburg to Gettysburg* (Garden City, NY, Doubleday, 1952), *A Stillness at Appomattox* (Garden City, NY, Doubleday, 1953), and *Grant Takes Command*; Marcus Cunliffe, *Soldiers and Civilians: The martial spirit in America 1775–1865* (Boston, Little, Brown, 1968); George M. Fredrickson, "Blue Over Gray: Sources of success or failure in the Civil War," in G. M. Fredrickson (ed.), *A Nation Divided* (Minneapolis, Burgess, 1975); Richard Beringer et al., *Why the South Lost the Civil War* (Atlanta, University of Georgia Press, 1986); James M. McPherson, *Battle Cry of Freedom: The Civil War era* (New York, Oxford University Press, 1988); Gerald Linderman, *Embattled Courage: The experience of combat in the American Civil War* (New York, Free Press, 1987); and John B. Walters, "General Sherman and total war," *Journal of Southern History*, 14 (Nov. 1948).

Indiana. The Confederate Congress never gave Davis total authority to suspend the writ of *habeas corpus*. Localism was at once the strength and the weakness of the Confederacy.

15 LINCOLN AND LEE

Lincoln was a surprising choice in 1860; he was totally lacking in executive experience, or in administration – to which he was never reconciled. His slowness to act in 1860–1 was in part because he was not sure *how* to act. Thus far, his had been a small pond to navigate, and his talents seemed appropriate to it – folksy, shrewd, anecdotal, but limited. He had little business acumen, and his shopkeeping had been more notable for his generosity than for his ability to make money. As a soldier he cut a far from dashing figure; a captain in the Black Hawk War, he failed to maintain good discipline among his men, and is remembered chiefly for having saved the life of a friendly Indian who wandered into his camp. Tall, and hollow-cheeked, with grotesquely long arms and legs, who shambled rather than walked, with rustic speech, uncouth manners, and with moods of bar-room humor alternating with deep depression, his Cabinet colleagues could speak of him as "The Ape" or "The Buffoon." "Without mind or manners," said Henry Watterson, "born and bred a rail-splitter ... and a rail-splitter still." Yet it was this world of plain folk that bred a shrewdness that became wisdom, a skill in handling people, however self-important, that brought him quiet confidence, a collection of anecdotes that deflated pomp or anger, a command of prose that was unmatched even by Thomas Jefferson. What was in him the crisis would reveal: to his contemporaries, as to his biographers, it would be an unceasing surprise, and a revelation of rare qualities. When his friend and law partner told him how impressed he had been by Niagara Falls, all he got from Lincoln, it seems, was "The thing that struck me most forcibly ... was, where in the world did all that water come from." He did not tell Herndon that what had really stirred him was that the water had been flowing and falling since long before Columbus, or Christ, or Moses, or Adam.[31]

Lincoln emerged in politics as a Westerner determined to preserve a dis-United Union. He was in the tradition of Jackson and Polk, a believer in a strong executive, and a respecter neither of the states

[31] Elizabeth McKinsey, *Niagara Falls: Icon of the American sublime* (New York, Cambridge, Cambridge University Press, 1985), vol. III, pp. 1–3.

nor of his own Cabinet (Seward was driven to admit that "There is only one vote in the Cabinet and it belongs to him. Executive ability and vigor are rare qualities, but he has them both — he is the best of us"), nor of the courts (as in the Merriman case), nor of Congress, nor even of the prescriptions of the Constitution, if any of them stood in his way. That way had of necessity to be guileful. He had to be capable of facing both ways. "Statesmanship," he said, "is the art of exploiting individual meannesses for the general good." To hold the Border states in line, he had to be ruthless with Fremont, prompt with troops in Maryland, prompt and ruthless in Missouri, prepared to consider the kidnapping of Governor Magoffin in Kentucky. "I hope I have God on my side, but I must have Kentucky."

Lincoln's flexibility and his knowledge of human nature are best exemplified in his treatment of his generals. He recommended aggressive action to McClellan, who was prone to overestimate the enemy and to underestimate his own strength (because, or so Lincoln affected to believe, as a railroad president, McClellan had naturally been anxious to avoid a collision). "I'll hold the general's horse if by so doing he can win the war." But when Burnside was replaced by "Fighting Joe" Hooker, Lincoln's admonitions in January 1863 were for caution:

I have placed you at the head of the Army of the Potomac. Of course I have done this upon what appear to me to be sufficient reasons. And yet I think it best for you to know that there are some things in regard to which I am not quite satisfied with you. I believe you to be a brave and skillful soldier, which, of course, I like. I also believe you do not mix politics with your profession, in which you are right. You have confidence in yourself, which is a valuable, if not an indispensable quality. You are ambitious, which, within reasonable bounds, does good rather than harm. But I think that during Gen. Burnside's command of the Army, you have taken counsel of your ambition, and thwarted him as much as you could, in which you did a great wrong to the country, and to a most meritorious and honorable brother officer. I have heard, in such a way as to believe it, of your recently saying that both the Army and the Government need a Dictator. Of course, it was not *for* this but in spite of it, that I have given you the command. Only those generals who gain successes, can set up dictators. What I now ask of you is military success, and I will risk the dictatorship.[32]

And when General Meade was in command of the Union forces, Lincoln sent him an order to advance, which he said might be torn

[32] Lincoln, *Collected Works*, ed. Basler, vol. VI, pp. 78–9.

up if the action proved successful, and preserved to establish responsibility if it should fail. However, with the appointment of Grant, Lincoln ceased to interfere in military matters. Instead, he stood squarely behind Grant and offered him all the support it was in his power to give.

Lincoln's attitude toward slavery can be seen as typically Republican. In fact, to his natural skills, it should be added that he had lived his life in Kentucky, southern Indiana and downstate Illinois, where opinion on slavery and on the Negro was most divided and where war dissidence was rife. In northern Illinois, he was black, so Stephen Douglas had charged, but in the center mulatto, and in the South lily white; it was true, for it was his chameleon-like adaptability and resilience that were the source of his effectiveness not only as a sectional but as a national leader. He sought to prevent the spread of slavery and to effect a gradual emancipation of the slaves. The war effort was based primarily on the necessity of preserving the Union, not on the issue of slavery. Nevertheless, the question of slavery became increasingly difficult for the North to ignore. In the end, Lincoln concluded that the emancipation of the slaves would have military and diplomatic value, and for that reason the Emancipation Proclamation was issued. Meeting with his cabinet on September 21, four days after the Battle of Antietam, Lincoln told them that the time had come. He read a statement that he had prepared:

That on the first day of January in the year of our Lord, one thousand eight hundred and sixty-three, all persons held as slaves within any state, or designated part of a state, the people whereof shall be in rebellion against the United States, shall be then, henceforward, and forever free, and the executive government of the United States, including the military and naval authority thereof, will recognize and maintain the freedom of such persons, and will do no act or acts to repress such persons, any of them, in any efforts they might make for their actual freedom.

He was not, Lincoln informed the Cabinet, interested in their advice "about the main matter – for that I have determined for myself." He asked only for opinion as to the wisdom of releasing the statement. The Cabinet, after expressing some mild reservations, unanimously agreed with the draft. The Emancipation Proclamation appeared in newspapers the following day. It would have no effect on the status of slaves in the Confederacy until Union troops occupied the enemy's territory, and very little Confederate territory was in Union hands in September 1862. Nor would it have any effect on slaves in the United States. As the London *Spectator* noted, the principle behind the proclamation seemed to be "not that a human being can not justly own another, but that he cannot own him unless he is loyal to the United States." But Lincoln had "irrecovably committed the United States, before the gaze of the whole world, to the early eradication of slavery from those wide regions where it was most deeply rooted.[33] The war had become a revolution. Yet, even then, he acted as politician. He sought not to offend slaveholders within the Union. Emancipation by the federal government of the more than 400,000 slaves in the Border states would have a demoralizing effect on the loyal population of those states. Emancipation for slaves in rebel territories, by contrast, could be defended on the grounds that it would demoralize and weaken the enemy. If enemy they were – for did he not also argue that the seceding states had never left the Union? Moreover, he was using his war powers: he was only going part of the way.

Despite all his reassuring words, the South had no understanding of such dexterity, such intrigue, or of such cajolery – or of such simplicity. They feared that with his election in 1860 they faced a Cromwell with a sword; they had no reason to. He did not want war, nor did he expect the South to want it. "I do not expect the Union to be dissolved," he had said in the "House Divided" speech of 1858. "There will be no war, no violence." And he was made aware of the turmoil each day and all day long in his own home: his wife, from Kentucky, from which his own family hailed, had a brother, three brothers-in-law and three half-brothers fighting for the Confederacy, and three of them were killed; in Washington society she was seen as "two-thirds slavery, and one-third secesh;" when he left the White House to give his first Inaugural address, his wife lay on the floor biting the carpet, in a tantrum. He was casual, tolerant, unconventional, indulgent; she was socially ambitious, extravagant, possessive, jealous, and explosive. "One d is enough for God," said the President, "but the Todds need 2." The early death of two of their four sons, her husband's assassination at her side, and the death in 1871 of their third son, 'Tad' (of whom his father had been especially fond because of his lisp and his speech difficulties), unhinged her mind.

Yet, in a world which had begun to be governed by images, and by the power of newspaper editors, Lincoln was seen in the South as the "black Republican," as dedicated to the abolition of slavery.

---

[33] Allan Nevins, *The Ordeal of the Union*, (New York, Scribner's, 1957), vol. VI, pp. 236–7.

He was not. He was ambitious, but easily depressed, and by nature gloomy – he frequently dreamed of his own death as apocalyptic climax, and of dying in office. He had an almost physical need for laughter, and for escape. He was kind, funny, human – and devious, beyond the capacity of any of his Cabinet colleagues to comprehend. Lincoln had one objective: to save the Union. Beside that, nothing mattered. And he did save it, but only after a long hunt for a ruthless enough commander in Ulysses Grant. To save it, he paid an appalling price: millions of dead, 1 in 5 of those who fought for the South wounded, 1 man killed for every 4 slaves freed, and the South ruined for a generation. He did not fight to free the slaves; he wanted as many of them as possible to be sent back to Africa. He was a complex, compassionate and crafty, infinitely patient, man, telling his tall stories as screens and parables to hide his worries, as he struggled with a problem that none of his predecessors could ever have imagined. He held to his long purpose "like a growing tree," in Edwin Markham's familiar lines, "Held on through blame, and faltered not at praise," and when he went down, he left "a lonesome place against the sky."[34] The simple backwoods lawyer, ill-bred and ill-schooled, became not America's Cromwell but its Bismarck, a man who willed a nation into being. Lincoln's one year of schooling, plus years of reading, had given him one feature that no West Pointer could match: a prose style with a biblical cadence and, in a florid age, of rare simplicity. It showed in the address at Gettysburg, though none who were there, except his fellow-orator Edward Everett, seemed to appreciate it. It emerged again in his Second Inaugural, noted also as an occasion when the President ensured that the Vice-President should not speak, lest his drunkenness mar the occasion. Lincoln reminded his audience that, the war over, a new task lay before them.

With malice toward none, with charity for all, with firmness in the right as God gives us to see the right, let us strive on to finish the work we are in, to bind up the nation's wounds, to care for him who shall have borne the battle and for his widow and his orphan, to do all which may achieve and cherish a just and lasting peace among ourselves and with all nations.

His reward was to be killed in office early in the second term, as he had always feared.

[34] Edwin Markham, "Lincoln, The Man of the People," in Burton E. Stevenson, *Poems of American History* (Boston, Houghton Mifflin, 1922), p. 400.

The risk of assassination walks with every President of the United States. Four Presidents have been killed in office. Almost all recent Presidents have been shot at. On the day he was killed, Lincoln remarked to a bodyguard, William Crook: "Do you know, I believe there are men who want to take my life. And I have no doubt they will do it." The envelope in which he kept assassination-threat letters had 80 in it by March 1865. On the morning of *his* assassination in Dallas on November 22, 1963, John F. Kennedy remarked: "If anybody really wanted to shoot the President of the United States, it would not be a very difficult job – all one has to do is get on a high building some day with a telescopic sight, and there's nothing anybody can do to defend such an attempt."

When he said farewell before the train pulled out of Springfield, in February 1861, Lincoln said that he would not return. He was brought back in a special caisson in a 1,700-mile journey, and mourned all the way.

In Southern eyes, then and since, Lincoln's opponent was not Jefferson Davis, the President of the Confederacy, but Robert E. Lee, the commander of the Army of Northern Virginia. Lee was a much simpler figure than Lincoln, but neither was he the man of marble nor of legend. When he was called from his post in the far South-West in 1861, he was 54. He had no slaves, no sympathy with the institution of slavery, which he thought "a moral and political evil," and no liking for secession. He had spent his life serving the Union and its army. Writing to his son Rooney in January 1861, he had said:

I can anticipate no greater calamity for the country than a dissolution of the union ... I am willing to sacrifice everything but honor for its preservation. ... Secession is nothing but revolution ... If the Union is dissolved and the government disrupted, I shall return to my native state and share the miseries of my people, and save in her defense will draw my sword on none.[35]

On April 18 Lincoln offered him the field command of the US Army, but he declined. After hours of agonizing at Arlington, he resigned from the army, and – unlike his fellow Virginian, General Winfield Scott, under whom he had served in the Mexican War and who stayed with the North, as did Farragut and "Slow-Trot"

---

[35] Douglas Southall Freeman, *Robert E. Lee*, 4 vols (New York, Scribner's, 1934), vol. I, p. 401.

Thomas – he concluded that his only course was to follow the destiny of his state. "You have made the greatest mistake of your life," Winfield Scott said, "but I feared it would be so." Lee's reply was simple: he could not raise his hand "against my relatives, my children, my home." The Lees, says Edmund Wilson, had never really emerged "from the world of the Thirteen Colonies." He gave up Arlington, on its splendid hill above the Potomac (now known as the Custis-Lee mansion) just as, when he was five, his mother was too poor to continue to live at Stratford. He reported in civilian clothes to Richmond, to be offered the command of Virginian forces. He became Jefferson Davis's adviser, with the rank of general, and when Joseph E. Johnston was wounded in June 1862 he assumed command of the Army of Northern Virginia. He brought 32 years' experience and many skills to his new post; he was engineer ("Spades Lee," he was scornfully called when he began fortifying Richmond) as well as cavalryman, as adept in retreat as in planning the invasion of Maryland in 1862 and Pennsylvania in 1863. From his knowledge of his former fellow-students at West Point, he had an uncanny awareness of their temperaments and their likely actions, as he read the minds both of Pope and Hooker. In any telling, his achievement sounds incredible: with inferior numbers and equipment, he created an army as he fought, and for three years repulsed four invasions of his state by forces that were being steadily renewed in numbers and supplies. Until 1861, moreover, he had never commanded in battle, and his real training was as an engineer-officer. Yet he was in the field for 34 months; he fought in the Seven Days' battle that blocked McClellan's threat to Richmond, he routed Pope at Second Bull Run in August 1862, he led at Antietam, he defeated Burnside at Fredericksburg in December 1862 and Hooker at Chancellorsville in May 1863. Though he was defeated at Gettysburg, he blocked Grant in the wilderness campaign in 1864. In all of it, he showed courage, and a superb strategic grasp.[36]

Unlike Lincoln's, Lee's family was distinguished, but he had been abandoned by his colorful but wayward father, "Light-horse Harry" Lee. His mother, Ann Hill Carter of Shirley on the James River, was kin to the hundreds of Carters and their in-laws. His wife, to whom he was a very distant cousin and whose estate Arlington was, was Martha Washington's great-granddaughter; unlike Jefferson Davis's wife, Mary Ann Randolph Custis Lee was a near-permanent invalid, whimsical and temperamental, and she did not enjoy the

[36] Edmund Wilson, *Patriotic Gore: Studies in the literature of the American Civil War* (New York, Oxford University Press, 1962), p. 332.

dull peacetime life of a professional soldier's wife. Lee was strikingly handsome, though not bearded in 1861; he enjoyed the fact that women found him attractive, and he could be flirtatious; to his critics he was "Granny Lee" – in all his commands, he showed a vast and detailed concern with the doings and the welfare of all his lieutenants and their families. He was high-tempered and prone to intense depression. Nor was his career, however competent, especially successful; he owned no land of his own, and this was, for a Virginian of standing, remarkable. But his schooling was thorough, and not only in his perfect record in the West Point class of 1829; he was invariably courteous, uncomplaining, and unselfish, incapable of intrigue (unlike Lincoln), and capable of silence. It was, indeed, his humanity which held him back from crushing the enemy at Fredericksburg, where his cavalry were still intact. His style was gentlemanly, not assertive; the ripostes from others, and their occasional disobedience of orders, he took too easily. When he read criticism of himself in the press, the reply was sardonic but mild: it was a great mistake, he thought, to have allowed "all our worst generals to command armies, and all our best generals to edit the newspapers." Editorial criticism he accepted as part of the game. From him there came no defensive autobiography, no reminiscences in retirement, no re-apportionment of blame, no rebuttals; he was a soldier, not a politician, and took responsibility for all actions where he was called to command. So he remains the riddle unread, the man who

> ... kept his heart a secret to the end
> From all the picklocks of biographers ...
> He was the prop and pillar of a State
> The incarnation of a national dream,
> And when the State fell and the dream dissolved
> He must have lived with bitterness itself.
> But what his sorrow was, and what his joy,
> And how he felt in the expense of strength,
> And how his heart contained its bitterness
> He will not tell us. [37]

The surrender at Appomattox is usually seen as that of a gallant, superbly dressed aristo, the leader of a fallen cause, to the "chunky man from the West," the one-time-disgraced veteran in his old and

---

[37] Stephen Vincent Benet, *John Brown's Body* (London, Oxford University Press, 1945), Book 4; reproduced by kind permission of the estate of Stephen Vincent Benet.

tattered jacket with the stars of his generalship loosely attached to the shoulders. The contrast does not hold. Grant and Lee were old comrades, with much in common and with gossip of the Mexican War to enjoy. Both had fathers they did not trust; both had experienced so much failure that they no longer feared it, and could for that reason be bold in battle, and could ride the storms that came. Both were constantly bedeviled by financial insecurity — Lee's father and Grant's grandfather had both been in debtors' prisons (and Lincoln disowned his father, too). Each had spells of depression — but never in war; each admitted errors; each took all the blame for defeat; each was bewildered about what to do when there was no more war to fight. One, in a triumph in which he was too decent to gloat, and the other in defeat, behaved with dignity, with modesty and with honor.

What gave Lee, Lincoln, and Grant greatness was not foreseeable in 1861: it was the strength of character that the War itself brought out. As Lee rode to Appomattox to surrender, Henry Wise, the former governor of Virginia, put it to him:

Country be damned! There is no country. There has been no country, general, for a year or more. You are the country for these men. They have fought for you. If you demand the sacrifice, there are still thousands of us who will die for you.

Lincoln, Lee, and Grant are now monuments: in Washington, in Lexington, or on Monument Avenue in Richmond, and in New York. The monuments do not portray the contrasts, nor the agonies. At the outset, each had faced an anguish of decision-making. Each has become the symbol and personification of a cause, although in life none of the three was fully committed to any cause. Each preferred patience to passion in solving disputes. Each by nature was lonely and reticent. Here the contrast was not free *vs.* slave nor North *vs.* South, but politician *vs.* soldier. Yet if Lincoln had been only a Machiavelli he would never have gone to war, since the firing of the guns represents the failure of adjustment, of maneuver, of cunning. If Lee had been only, or totally, the soldier, he would have served the Union, not Virginia, and he would have risked more: he rarely followed up success. Indeed, he never used the word "enemy;" for those he opposed he used the words "Those people ...." In the end each transcended his calling; "The only ruler I have is my conscience," said Lincoln. For Lee, there was only Virginia, kin, and kindred. In fact, neither was victorious. It was 25 years before Lee got his monument in Richmond, and 40 before he was seen in the North as a good leader in a bad cause. Lincoln's cause won, but he was martyred in leading it; and the myth-making followed. The reverence accorded Lee was for one who soldiered on, knowing that defeat was inevitable, but who was uncomplaining in meeting it, and afterwards. The North that won the War was not Mr Lincoln's North; the Old South, the dream that never was, died at Appomattox.[38]

16 THE WAR AT SEA AND IN EUROPE

Four days after his call for volunteers, Lincoln declared a federal blockade of the Confederate ports and harbors along a 3,559 mile coastline. It was thus a war of naval blockade as well as of land battles; and a brief summary of the comparative naval resources shows the extent of the disparity. The South had no navy or merchant marine — capital investment had gone into cotton, land, and slaves, not shipbuilding. Of the ten navy yards owned by the United States at the outbreak of war — at Kittery (Maine), Portsmouth (New Hampshire), Charlestown (Massachusetts), Sackett Harbor (New York), Brooklyn (New York), Philadelphia (Pennsylvania), Washington (District of Columbia), Norfolk (Virginia), Pensacola (Florida), and Mare Island (California) — only the Norfolk and Pensacola yards were available to the South. As the Southern states seceded, they managed to seize only a few armed vessels, mostly revenue cutters. A few other ships were purchased in Europe, so that at the first firing of shots in anger, the total Confederate Navy numbered only ten vessels, mounting, in all, 15 guns; in contrast, the North's merchant marine was second in size only to that of Great Britain, and was backed by a long-established and efficient shipbuilding industry.

The United States Naval Register for 1861 listed 90 American warships, but only 42 were in commission; of these only 29 were steam-powered. These were all on their assigned stations, many on far-flung atolls: 12 vessels of 187 guns in the Home Squadron; 3 vessels of 42 guns in the East Indies; 22 vessels of 236 guns in the Pacific. They were manned by some 1,563 officers and 7,600 men — but 322 officers resigned to serve the South. Gideon Welles,

[38] Freeman, *Robert E. Lee*; Virginius Dabney, *Richmond, the Story of a City* (New York, Doubleday, 1976); Thomas L. Connelly, *The Marble Man: Robert E. Lee and his image in American society* (New York, Knopf 1977); Catton, *A Stillness at Appomattox* and *Grant Takes Command*; McFeely, *Grant, a Biography*.

Lincoln's Navy Secretary, at once ordered all warships that were in any degree seaworthy to be put in commission; soon there were 76 vessels, mounting 1783 guns, that flew the Stars and Stripes. But this was only the beginning: Welles purchased 136 more vessels, had them altered for war service, mounted with 518 guns, and put into service; construction of 52 vessels of 256 guns was begun in government and private yards. By December 1861 the United States Navy consisted of 264 vessels, carrying 2,557 guns, manned by 22,000 seamen; its aggregate tonnage was 218,016 tons. By the war's end, by drawing upon the industrial resources and the mechanical skill of the Northern states, Welles had been able to construct 200 new vessels with 1,520 guns — 74 of them iron-clads. And there were 1,242 officers who decided, after making their ethical calculations, to serve the Federal government; among them were men like David Farragut and Samuel DuPont, who were fortunate to have the services of Benjamin Franklin Isherwood as the navy's chief engineer, and Swedish engineer John Ericson as ship-designer extraordinary, the architect of the *Monitor*. The Northern navy had thus grown from 90 vessels in 1861 to 671 in 1865, from 1,563 officers and 760 men to 9,000 officers and 51,000 men, among whom were 7,500 volunteer officers and 42,000 seamen, who had learnt their seafaring in the fisheries and the merchant marine. Throughout the war they had put a 3,500 mile ring-fence around the shores of the Confederate States from the Chesapeake to the Gulf, despite its sand-bars and inlets, protective islands and deltas. They had captured or destroyed 1,504 Southern vessels, warships and blockade-runners of all types, 295 of them steamers. In addition they had cooperated with the Northern armies in every major seaboard operation that the army was able to undertake. Perhaps Seward had been right in his suggested Anaconda strategy of 1861: a naval blockade alone would compel the South to surrender.

Even so, there were not enough ships, and bases for them to use in the South, to make the Unionist blockade totally effective. That being so, in international law the blockade was illegal. Steadily the Union seized a number of bases on the Confederate coast: Hatteras inlet, North Carolina in August 1861, where a landing party of 319 led by Benjamin Franklin Butler lost only one man, and captured 670 prisoners and 35 cannon; Port Royal, South Carolina, in November 1861; Roanoke Island, North Carolina, Norfolk, Virginia, and Fernandina, Florida, in March 1862; Beaufort, North Carolina, in April 1862; St Augustine, Fort Pulaski (to control approaches to Savannah), Key West, Pensacola, Ship Island, and New Orleans, and thus now had repair yards of their own. By the end of 1862 Union forces had occupied practically the entire Atlantic coast of the Confederacy except Wilmington and Charleston, and had crippled Savannah. By 1862 the blockade was highly organized, in four squadrons: the North Atlantic Squadron (Chesapeake Bay to Wilmington), the South Atlantic Squadron (Wilmington to the Bahamas); the East Gulf Squadron (the Bahamas to Pensacola); and the West Gulf Squadron (Pensacola to Matamoros in Mexico). Although chances of capture were only 1 in 10 in 1861, by 1864 they were 1 in 3.[39]

Despite the scale of this 3,500-mile operation, there were still wide gaps in the curtain. Once it had used up its store, Britain needed Southern cotton and tobacco, and Europe needed its sugar, indigo, and naval stores; the Confederacy needed supplies of every kind. So for the South – and for Britain, or for firms like Crenshaw Brothers of Richmond – blockade-running became big, profitable, and adventurous business.

As secretary of the Confederate Navy, Trinidad-born Stephen Mallory of Florida was secretary of a navy that existed only in his mind: there was timber in the South, but it was all in the forests; the iron was in the mines, for the South had never been self-sufficient in iron-making. In the beginning the South's only major foundry was that of the Tredegar Iron Works and Belona Foundry at Richmond. There were only two navy yards, of which the Pensacola Yard was not a construction yard but a repair base and a shelter. But he had an abundance of naval officers, including those who had resigned from Federal service. There was, however, no adequate supply of trained seamen to draw upon in the South, and as late as 1864 there were only 3,674 enlisted men in the Confederate Navy. It never succeeded in creating a sea-going fleet, but used privateers and cruisers to attack Union merchant ships. The Confederacy equipped – in the end – some 30 privateers, for the most part converted from slavers, revenue cutters, pilot-boats, and fishing schooners; all but three of them were small and lightly armed. It had, however, no neutral ports where it could take its prizes. Even so, in the first six months of the war, these highwaymen of the sea (as the New York *Herald* called them on August 10, 1861) captured some 60 Northern vessels. "English bottoms are taking all our trade ... our shipping interest is literally ruined."

Blockade-running – by, overwhelmingly, British ships – became big business; some 600 ships were regularly engaged in it. Goods

[39] Frank L. Owsley, *King Cotton Diplomacy* (Chicago, University of Chicago Press, 1931), ch. 8.

were sent in regular cargo ships to the West Indian ports of Nassau (until it was ravaged by yellow fever), Havana, and also Bermuda, only 600 miles from Wilmington, North Carolina. Munitions and clothing, medicine and luxuries, were transferred to narrow, swift, lead-colored, shallow-draft ships to navigate the shallows and inlets and evade the sand-bars, to be landed at Wilmington, Charleston, or Mobile. In 1863 Charleston's overseas trade was greater than in any prewar year. Their goods, mainly luxury items, of small bulk and high prices, commanded high prices and brought vast profits. The largest and best-known of the blockade-runners was the Confederate-owned, Clyde-built *Robert E. Lee*, which on its return journey could carry out 650 bales of cotton; Lieutenant John Wilkinson of Virginia steered the *Robert E. Lee* through the blockade on 21 occasions in the first nine months of 1863. Cotton was worth five times its prewar value if it reached Britain, and during the war the blockade-runners carried some one-and-a-quarter million bales of cotton. Even more useful than the West Indian ports was neutral Matamoros in Mexico, conveniently across the Rio Grande from Brownsville in Texas: through it came steady supplies of lead, copper, and powder for the Confederacy. Until 1863, blockade-running was private enterprise, and on the whole profitable; but until coordinated, it brought little benefit to the Confederate war effort. The Davis administration continued to argue that cotton diplomacy would bring in foreign allies, and contended that the blockade was, in any case, ineffective. Indeed, Josiah Gorgas, head of the Ordnance Bureau, organized his own blockade-running to meet the needs of the army. In 1863 the War Department acquired some steamers and a controlling interest in others; a Bureau of Foreign Supplies, under the direction of Thomas L. Bayne, was set up to manage the collection and export of cotton – but not until the last year of the war.

The Northern blockade gravely weakened the Confederate war effort, for it prevented the export of Southern produce and the import of necessary manufactures and foodstuffs. In the years 1862–4, only one-tenth of the prewar amount of cotton was exported, and more cotton was shipped overland to the North than to Great Britain. Supplies obtained in this way were not enough, and traders imported luxuries more than necessities – though 600,000 small arms got through. As manufacturing in the Confederacy increased, and some essential industries were taken over by the government, the South still had inadequate quantities of cotton cloth, whiskey, salt, guns, and gunpowder. Gunpowder works were built at Augusta, Georgia, and at Selma, Alabama. Increased domestic manufacturing produced a considerable amount of cotton cloth and leather goods. The war brought a shift in Southern agriculture, too, as cotton production decreased and food production increased. The breakdown of the Southern rail system and the destruction of property by Union armies further aggravated conditions of scarcity.

The Confederacy sought commerce-destroyers as well as blockade-runners. Its agent in Britain, Captain James Bulloch, CSN, bought potential raiders – and built mainly on Merseyside; to do so was of course to forfeit British goodwill, since the British Foreign Enlistment Act of 1819 prohibited the building or equipping of warships for belligerents. The American Minister in London, Charles Francis Adams, sought to convince Foreign Secretary Lord Russell that he ought to detain any suspect vessel being built in Laird's Birkenhead yard. The CSS *Florida* was the first to sail; operating in the Caribbean, it captured or destroyed 37 Northern ships and their cargoes. The second being built, "No. 290" sailed from Birkenhead in July 1862, just before the receipt of Britain's order for her detention; equipped with guns, stores, and crew in the Azores, she became the CSS *Alabama*, Liverpool-crewed (though they only joined her after she left the Mersey) as well as Birkenhead-built; over the next two years she destroyed 62 Unionist vessels, mainly merchantmen and whalers. When in June 1864 she sailed out of Cherbourg harbor, where she had put in for repairs, she went down in the Channel after a duel with the USS *Kearsarge*. And the last of the raiders, the CSS *Shenandoah*, originally a British merchantman, captured and burnt 34 Northern whalers in the Bering Sea and the Arctic Ocean in the last six months of the war. Apart from the subsequent claims of US damages against Britain – Britain paid over $15 million in damages after the war for allowing the ships to escape – and the high insurance rates their activities caused, the direct effect on the outcome of the War seems slight; but by 1865, thanks to their activities, the American merchant marine was in decline, many ships transferred to foreign ownership, and the American whaling fleets were destroyed.

The war at sea, like all major wars, had its technical revolution. To counter the disparity of strength, the Confederates raised the hull of the USS *Merrimac* (re-christened CSS *Virginia*) from the mud of Norfolk navy yard, where she had been scuttled when Virginia seceded; they converted her into an ironclad capable of six knots, and, thus impervious to shot and shell, she did great damage to five Union wooden-hulled craft in Hampton Roads (March 1862), destroying two of them and killing or drowning 257 Northerners for her own losses of only 2 men killed and 8 wounded. Only the launching of a similar Northern ironclad, the USS *Monitor*, variously described as "a cheese-box on a plank" and "a tin can on a shingle," and their inconclusive duel ended Northern fears that their ships would be destroyed *seriatim*, and New York City and Washington bombarded into submission. The *Merrimac* was scuttled when Norfolk was abandoned in May 1862, to Southern dismay; the *Monitor* went down in a gale off Cape Hatteras a few weeks later. But they marked a revolution: as the number of Unionist warships grew — during 1862 it added 163 new warships to its navy of some 420 vessels — a number of them were ironclads.

One factor that gave an edge to Confederate power at sea was the underwater torpedo: the product of experiments first carried out in a portable metal bathtub in a house at 1105 East Clay Street in Richmond, Virginia, where the hydrographer and oceanographer Matthew Fontaine Maury lived. The "Pathfinder of the Seas" was the first superintendent of the United States Naval Observatory, and discoverer of the strong and steady westerlies in the "roaring Forties" south latitude. His invention of the torpedo wrecked many Northern ships. Gideon Welles estimated after the War that the US had lost more vessels by torpedoes than from all other causes. The Confederacy also built primitive submarines — 20 feet long and 5 feet broad, propelled by crews of eight men; they were used six times, once successfully (February 17, 1864), in sinking the USS *Housatonic* in Charleston Harbor but always, as on that occasion, proving to be also self-destructive.

The war at sea involved the Union and the Confederacy in relations with Europe. There opinion was sharply divided concerning the War between the States. Among the governing and opinion-making classes there was some sympathy for the South; and, particularly among shipping interests, there was hostility toward Yankee competition and high tariffs. Both Palmerston and Gladstone foresaw the breakup of the Union. Industrial workers, particularly in Britain, and liberals generally, however, strengthened by the ties with kin and kindred among the emigrants to the Northern (rarely to the Southern) states, favored the Union cause as a battle for working men and for human freedom. It was his spell as the US minister in London that led Charles Francis Adams to appreciate what he called the "moral influence" of American democracy. Not all men were so noble. Thomas Carlyle had little patience with people who were "cutting each other's throats, because one half of them prefer hiring their servants for life, and the other by the hour."[40]

[40] Donaldson Jordan and Edwin J. Pratt, *Europe and the American Civil War* (Boston, Little, Brown, 1931), p. 73.

The believers in Confederate victory, however, miscalculated when they expected that Britain would break the Union naval blockade in order to obtain Southern cotton, and so eventually become an ally of the Confederacy. They withheld much and burned some of their cotton in 1861; only 19,000 bales of cotton were exported as against 650,000 in 1860; in 1861 they were down to 1 per cent. A quarter of Britain's population, they believed, was dependent for its livelihood on the cotton textile industry. Indeed, by December 1862 some 400,000 workers were unemployed in Lancashire's and Cheshire's mills; but they stayed loyal to the anti-slave cause, sustained by charity, and by gifts from the Northern states; of Lancashire's 26 MPs only one, J. T. Hopwood, tried to have the British policy of neutrality changed. In the event, a temporary surplus of cotton in England made it unnecessary to import more during the first months of the War; cotton supplies came in from Egypt, India, and Brazil, and by 1862 the Union blockade was obviously so effective that it could be breached only at a greater risk of war than Britain cared to take. Whatever the vested interest in the Confederacy of cotton merchants, it did not last long; and other merchants and manufacturers were doing well out of the War, in woolens and linens, iron and steel, munitions and shipbuilding, banks and insurance.

The Civil War presented a major but not a new problem in international law. If, as Lincoln contended, he was doing no more than suppress a rebellion in states that were still inside the Union, there was no justification for intervention by a foreign power; all he need do was to announce the closure of the ports of the rebellious states. Instead, he proclaimed a blockade, which involved recognized procedures for neutrals – procedures that had been agreed on by the European powers only five years before, in the Declaration of Paris of 1856. A blockade, it was declared, to be recognized in international law, had to be effective; privateering was banned, and there was to be protection for enemy goods under a neutral flag, and for neutral goods under an enemy flag. But in 1861 the Declaration had not yet been ratified. Indeed, the rights of neutrals on the high seas was, for all Americans, a familiar subject – witness the US efforts at trading as a neutral when Napoleon and Britain in 1805–6 attempted to blockade each other, and in the War of 1812 when Britain had been the maritime trespasser on neutral rights. Now the roles were reversed: the indignant gamekeeper of 1805 and 1812 was a deft poacher from 1861 to 1865, claiming with special irony, that its war was not a war at all, that no "rights of neutrals" arose since it was merely suppressing a domestic rebellion. Indeed, neither the President nor the Supreme Court resolved the question: was this a domestic or a foreign war? To ensure no foreign interference it must be the former. But a blockade was a recognition that there were two belligerents, each of which could raise loans and obtain supplies from abroad, each of which could look for foreign allies (as in 1778). In consequence, in May 1861 Britain, followed by Napoleon III, recognized the belligerent status of the Confederacy, before a battle had been fought. Lincoln's proclamation invoked both "the laws of the United States and ... the law of nations." The Supreme Court in 1863 saw the conflict both as rebellion and as war, as indeed it was.

A diplomatic crisis was precipitated in November 1861 by the action of Captain Charles Wilkes, commanding the USS *San Jacinto*, in removing two Confederate commissioners, James M. Mason and John Slidell, from the English vessel *Trent*, bound for Europe. Mason was bound for Britain, Slidell for France. Had the Union naval captain merely brought the *Trent* into a Northern port, a prize court would probably have found the ship engaged in unneutral actions; the removal of the two agents on the high seas, however, was clearly a violation of international law. Prime Minister Palmerston protested vehemently, but the Prince Consort, just two days before his death, toned down the arrogance of the language; Lincoln tactfully released Mason and Slidell, and their release eased the tension. But the pro-South lobby in Britain, led by William Lindsay of Liverpool, its largest shipbuilder, and Sir William Gregory, was well organized and persistent. Their arguments included criticism of the North's high protective tariff against British goods, and cited sympathy for revolutionary Italy, Greece, Poland, and Hungary, as examples to follow in regard to the South. To build merchantmen and to allow them to sail unarmed was no more reprehensible than the open supply of arms to the North, a trade in which Britain was engaged. Another champion of the South was James Whiteside, representative of the University of Dublin in Parliament, who denied that the North was fighting for the emancipation of the slaves, and pointed out the paradox of the United States government denying to the South the rights of the Declaration. of Independence. *The Times*, the *Morning Post*, the *Manchester Guardian*, all favored the Confederate cause, skillfully fed with comment by the Southern propaganda agent Henry Hotze and his weekly *Index* of news. Darwin as well as Carlyle, Thackeray, and Tennyson, Gladstone and Lord Acton, supported the South. The South had skillful agents in Europe: James D. Bulloch in ship procurement, Colin J. McRae in purchasing. Charles Francis Adams gloomily concluded that "The great body of the aristocracy and the wealthy commercial class are anxious to see the United States go to pieces. ... On the other hand the middle and lower class sympathise with us."

In the summer of 1863 Southern Independence Associations were founded in Manchester, London, and other cities to support the cause and memorialize Parliament to recognize the independence of the Confederacy; and funds were provided by Southern sympathizers, particularly Alexander Collie of Glasgow, who had made immense profits from blockade-running. The leader of the parliamentary group urging recognition was the eccentric John A. Roebuck, MP for Sheffield. The Confederacy had supporters, in other words, in both major parties, but they were not numerous enough to win recognition for the South as an independent state. At a time when British governments were products of coalitions, the balance of power was held by the anti-slavery, pro-Northern group led by John Bright. Cotton mattered in Lancashire. But food mattered to the whole country. And to feed the workers, British imports of Northern wheat increased fivefold between 1861 and 1865. A popular song of the day was: "Old King Cotton's dead and buried, brave young Corn is King." Meanwhile, the trade unions of the Lancashire textile mills, despite the high unemployment of 1862, held firmly to their support for abolitionism. Frederick Douglass as lecturer was immensely popular in Britain.

European sympathy, like British, tended to ebb and flow with the tide of Confederate fortunes. France had traditional ties with the United States, and saw it as a balance to British power; along with distaste for slavery, its textile industry was especially vulnerable to cotton diplomacy. There was the same expectation as in Britain that the War was bound to end in the separation of North and South. The failure of the Union campaign on the Potomac in 1862 increased the possibility of diplomatic recognition being extended to the South, but Lincoln's Emancipation Proclamation was generally approved abroad and strengthened support for the Union. However, the victory at Fredericksburg in December 1862 kept alive the hope that the Confederacy might make good its bid for independence, and it was not until after the Battle of Gettysburg, on July 1–3, 1863, that all possibility of European recognition disappeared. Despite Napoleon III's interest in a joint Anglo-French recognition of the Confederacy, despite Prime Minister Lord Palmerston and Foreign Secretary Lord John Russell's hopes of acting as mediators, Britain stayed neutral – helped by US Minister Charles Francis Adams's skill in stressing that the building of blockade-runners in Liverpool might lead to war, and by the mercenary facts

that Britain was making profits from the war, and that Confederate
warships were generously destroying the American merchant fleet.
Britain stayed neutral, and did well out of it.

> God save me, great John Bull
>   Long keep my pockets full,
>   God save John Bull.
> Ever victorious,
>   Haughty, vainglorious,
> Snobbish censorious
>   God save John Bull.

Napoleon III expressed considerable sympathy for the Confederacy during the early phases of the war, but gave it no substantial
assistance. His interest in the Civil War was less than his interest
in the establishment of the puppet regime of Maximilian in Mexico.
French public opinion was behind him in his sympathy for the
South, but not keen on the Mexican adventure. Napoleon III's
critics – Orléanists, Liberal Catholics, Republicans, socialists, Victor
Hugo and Guizot and the *Revue des Deux Mondes* – lined up with
the North. It was, however, the preoccupation with the Civil War
that allowed French troops to capture Mexico City in 1863, and
to put Maximilian on his throne there in 1864. John Slidell, as
Confederate commissioner, did negotiate a massive loan via the
Erlangers, and won approval for the building of Confederate ships
in Bordeaux and Nantes, but despite cordial relations with Napoleon
III he never got diplomatic recognition. Though Napoleon III was
far less scrupulous than the ministers of Queen Victoria in observing
his obligations as a neutral, he never dared to recognize or aid the
Confederacy unless Britain did so too. Without British seapower,
French intervention was unthinkable.

What is clear is that the attitudes of European governments
were determined almost exclusively by Northern military successes.
The South did not succeed in winning recognition or in having the
blockade broken. Despite the support of *The Times* when the war
began, and despite Gladstone's views, it is clear that the existence
of slavery in the South did not determine the decision-making in
London or in Paris. The governments there stayed lookers-on. Only
Russia showed decisiveness. The Tsar emancipated its serfs during
the Civil War, and he sympathized with the North in its efforts
to destroy Southern slavery. The most backward economy and the
most autocratic of European governments was thus, paradoxically,
the only consistent supporter of the Union. No Emperor of all the

Russias could have sympathy for a secessionist state that might become a model for the Poles to follow. The visits of a Russian fleet to New York and of another to San Francisco in 1863 were seen as gestures of solidarity in the North; they may have been so designed, but the Tsar's primary purpose was to ensure his navy's safety in neutral waters rather than being ice-bound in home bases if the threatened war over Poland's struggle for freedom should occur in Europe. The coincidence of the timing brought Russia and its ruler a rare wave of North American goodwill.

17   THE LEGACY

The Southern historian F. L. Owsley was even more stirred by memories of the 12 years known as Reconstruction (1865–77), when Union troops occupied the conquered South, than by the War itself.

Seldom has there been such a peace as that which followed Appomattox. While Sherman, Sheridan and Grant had allowed their armies to harry and plunder the population of the invaded country all too much, using churches, universities, and state capitols with their archives as stables for horses and mean men, General Grant could pause long enough during the deadly Spotsylvania Courthouse campaign to remove his hat at the house where Stonewall Jackson had died the year before and say, "General Jackson was a gallant soldier and a Christian gentleman." And Grant and Sherman were generous enough to refuse to take the side-arms and horses from the Southern soldiers who surrendered. But after the military surrender at Appomattox there ensued a peace unique in history. There was no generosity. For ten years the South, already ruined by the loss of nearly $2,000,000,000 invested in slaves, with its lands worthless, its cattle and stock gone, its houses burned, was turned over to the three millions of former slaves, some of whom could still remember the taste of human flesh and the bulk of them hardly three generations removed from cannibalism. These half-savage blacks were armed. Their passions were roused against their former masters by savage political leaders like Thaddeus Stevens, who advocated the confiscation of all Southern lands for the benefit of the negroes, and the extermination, if need be, of the Southern white population; and like Charles Sumner, whose chief regret had been that his skin was not black. Not only were the blacks armed; they were upheld and incited by garrisons of Northern soldiers, by Freedmen's Bureau officials, and by Northern ministers of the gospel, and at length they were given the ballot while their former masters were disarmed and, to a large extent, disfranchised. For ten years ex-slaves, led by carpetbaggers and scalawags, continued the pillages of war, combing the South for anything left by the invading armies, levying taxes, selling empires of plantations under the auction hammer, dragooning the Southern population, and visiting upon them the ultimate humiliations.[41]

The results of the War can be reduced to calmer and more accurate prose. The almost 175,000 Confederate veterans remaining in the Southern ranks at the War's end turned homeward to a society demoralized and disorganized by defeat; and lawless bands of marauders, some of them ex-guerrillas (like Quantrill's "boys," who had looted Kansas in the name of the Confederacy, and who included the young Jesse James), many of them simply Southern deserters, were plundering the countryside. More than 258,000 Confederates had died (1 in every 4 of all white males between 20 and 40 years of age), and nearly 101,000 were wounded. One newspaper estimated that about half of all Southern cotton farmers had either met death or been maimed. The University of Virginia (with half the student population of Harvard) had lost over 500 dead against Harvard's 117. On January 1864 two brigades of General Joseph E. Johnston's Army of Tennessee, opposing Sherman's overwhelming strength, had been unable to march farther for want of boots, and unable to halt for sleep because they lacked blankets. The comment of Judah Benjamin, the Confederacy's secretary of state, was that they had probably traded their boots for whiskey. He might not have been merely cynical: the South had introduced prohibition for the duration of the War to ensure that all supplies of alcohol went to hospitals and casualty stations.

Statistics translate the destruction into figures: the total assessed valuation of Southern property according to the 1860 census returns had been almost $4.5 billion, but when the War ended its value barely exceeded $1.5 billion; of the $2.5 billion in valuation losses, about $1.5 billion was accounted for by the abolition of property in slaves; livestock losses between 1860 and 1866 had reduced Southern holdings by well over a third; by 1870 about 18 percent of the tilled soil of 1860 was no longer under cultivation. And billions of dollars of private property had been liquidated without any compensation. But what it meant was homes, factories, warehouses, bridges destroyed, steamboats burned, and wharves rotting

---

[41] F. L. Owsley, in *I'll Take My Stand* (New York, Harper, 1930), pp. 61–3. For a revisionist and more balanced view, see David Donald, *The Politics of Reconstruction 1863–1867* (Baton Rouge, Louisiana State University Press, 1965); Kenneth M. Stampp, *The Era of Reconstruction 1865–77* (New York, Knopf, 1965); and the introduction and documents in Harold Hyman (ed.), *The Radical Republicans and Reconstruction 1861–1870* (Indianapolis, Bobbs-Merrill, 1967).

away; Atlanta, Columbia, and Richmond long rows of blackened chimneys; and mass starvation avoided only by the distribution by the Union Army of millions of rations. And Southern money was worthless. The Confederate Constitution prohibited a protective tariff, but a revenue tariff, imposing rates varying from 5 to 25 percent, was permitted, as were a duty on cotton exports and a direct tax on property (including slaves). The last, however, was to be apportioned among the states according to a population census, which the Confederacy never managed to take. The South had financed the War, as the North had done, in part by loans (including $15 million loan from the Erlanger bank in Paris on the security of its cotton), in part by taxes of various kinds – by income taxes, and license fees on occupations, and in part by issues of paper money which paid no interest, and were not legal tender for private debts. By 1865 the former had been spent and the last was worthless. As inflation mounted, a tax had been imposed on naval stores, tobacco, wool, sugar, and rice, and not least, in 1863, a very unpopular levy in kind of one-tenth of all agricultural products – as difficult to collect as it was to evade, and much of which spoilt for lack of transportation and of storage. As with the North, however, the South relied mainly not on taxes – for which it had neither the manpower nor the machinery for adequate collection, and to which it was not accustomed – but on bond issues, and by a steady proliferation of paper money, unsupported by gold. By the end of the War, the Confederate dollar was worth less than two cents on the dollar in gold – the worst inflation in American history.

She asked me 20 dollars for five dozen eggs and then she said she would take it in "Confederick." Then I would have given her 100 dollars as easily. But if she had taken my offer of yarn: I haggle in yarn for the millionth part of a thread! ... When they ask Confederate money, I never stop to chafer. I give them 20 or 50 dollars cheerfully for anything. [42]

As the war progressed, barter had replaced money; the blockade and the lack of industry drove the South to practice an economy of substitutions: sassafras root tea replacing oriental, honey and molasses for sugar, thorns serving as pins, sea water boiled for salt. Professor Francis Porcher of the Medical College of Charleston produced a 600-page book describing *The Resources of the Southern Fields and Forests*, listing herbs and roots from which drugs and

[42] *Mary Chesnut's Civil War*, Mar. 7, 1864, p. 749.

medicines could be made. Confederate General Nathan Bedford Forrest, whom Sherman thought "the most remarkable man the Civil War produced," said that he entered the War (he was 40) with one and a half million dollars, and came out a beggar.

Certainly the Federal government was no longer "laissez-faire." It was generous with bounties and land grants. It was also greedy, not least in its demand for money; and inexperienced in raising it. Until 1861, the major sources of Federal funds had been the painless customs duties, and income from the sale of public lands; there was no machinery or information for the collection of internal revenue. Add to this the Jeffersonian-Jacksonian distrust of banks; the total divorce of government from the banks as decreed in the Independent Treasury Act of 1846; and, legacy of the panic of 1857, a deficit that had been run by the Federal government for three years in succession. Salmon P. Chase, Lincoln's secretary of the Treasury, originally believed that the war would be over in a matter of months. He placed the main burden of financing the war on bond sales, with Jay Cooke, the Philadelphia banker, acting as his main agent (and doing well out of it). Two billion dollars were raised, and the government obtained three times as much from loans as from all other sources, with the big city banks the principal lenders. When the bonds sold too slowly for the needs of the Union's war machine, however, Congress was forced in 1862 to print some $450 million in paper money — the so-called "greenbacks;" they were legal tender for all debts, public and private. With bills unpaid and soldiers' pay months in arrears, there were four more such paper issues — each of them bitterly opposed by Chase himself. With neither gold nor silver behind them, but only the promise of the government to redeem them, by 1864 a greenback dollar had dropped to 30 cents in value. Not until 1875 were these paper bills made convertible into specie.

The National Banking Act of 1863 allowed the creation of privately owned "national" or state banks, each of which was required to purchase federal bonds to the extent of one-third of its capital stock, and to deposit them with the Treasury; by 1865, 1,500 such institutions were issuing 5,000 different notes, some of which were counterfeit. Since, after 1861, all specie payment was suspended by all the banks, payment from one part of the Union to another was a form of foreign exchange. Southern obligations to Northern merchants were an almost total loss. No longer sure of a short war, in 1862 an income tax was put on the statute books for the first time: 3 percent on incomes from $600 to $10,000, 5 percent on higher income (the latter figure was doubled two years later.) This legislation was an important precedent in American fiscal policy; but its repeal in 1872 left undecided both the ethics and the constitutionality of such progressive taxation. (When in the 1890s it was seen as unconstitutional, an Amendment to "legitimize" it was added to the Constitution.) After passing the Morrill Act in 1861, the Congress of the United States also raised tariff duties several times, and imposed a large number of excise taxes: there were inheritance taxes, stamp taxes on legal transactions, gross receipts taxes, taxes on the transfer of real estate, surcharges on tobacco and liquor, licenses for the professions. But even in 1865 taxes were meeting only about 25 percent of the cost of the war. As did the South, the US fought the War by borrowing and inflation, and borrowing by long-term bonds remained its chief source. Its millions of acres, the resources in them, and confidence in their growing value, then as now, were its real bond.

And if in 1862 only 72,000 immigrants arrived in the US — the smallest number for any year between 1843 and 1932 — nevertheless farmers, supplying Europe as well as armies, entrepreneurs (including bond-sellers), speculators, and war contractors like Colt's had all done well out of the war. A group of key industries developed apace: meat packing, iron products, rail tracks, lumber, clothing, woolens, leather goods, reapers and mowers, flour milling, boots and shoes: and all were abetted by Protection, and by a national banking system. Edward L. Drake had struck oil in northwest Pennsylvania in 1859; by the end of the War petroleum was the sixth largest export of the US. When the gold and silver of the Comstock Lode were discovered in what became the Nevada Territory, also in 1859, there had been another mining boom in the West. As the young and industrious Scots immigrant Andrew Carnegie saw the price of pig-iron climb, he began to raise the capital to finance the building of a blast furnace and a rolling mill in Pittsburgh. When his first dividends came in, he said that he saw capitalism — with or without the Puritan gospel of work — as the goose that laid the golden eggs. Unlike later wars, there was as yet no rationing, no manpower policy, no control of prices, wages, or profits. Small family farms grew apace, or were taken over. The Union stockyards in Chicago were opened in 1865. There was a canning revolution even more than an agricultural revolution: Gail Borden opened his first large condensed-milk plant in New York in 1861.

Thus another revolution had come almost unnoticed: the business of government was now aiding business and the fostering of industrial capitalism; and it did so in the victorious and single nation,

North-east, North-central, Mid-West and Far West, linked after the war was over by the government-sponsored transcontinental railroad, by the telegraph — Western Union now dominating and launching an Atlantic cable in 1866 — and by American Express and its Western subsidiary Wells Fargo. The business of America was big business, including agriculture; it was government-encouraged and now nationwide in extent, from coast to coast. And so — bitter legacy indeed — was the Bureau of Internal Revenue.

During the War, until Federal troops appeared, the slaves, and in particular the privileged house slaves, had generally been loyal; the majority of field hands went on working, perhaps not always realizing that their freedom was an issue until told so by Northern troops. In the last year of the War, however, many of them followed the Northern armies, setting up mobile colonies, and surviving as they could. Many died of disease and starvation; their attitude to property was childlike; and Sherman became vehemently critical of his unwelcome camp-followers. In the course of the war, the South abandoned its *raison d'être*: in March 1865 it agreed to enlist slaves as soldiers: each state was asked for its quota of troops "irrespective of color." If the choice lay between independence and slavery, it would let slavery go — even though as a nation, it had been conceived on a basis of slavery, and dedicated to the conviction that men are not equal in talent or in law. In order to win recognition in Europe, and not for reasons of conviction, it offered emancipation. In other words, it was not fighting to defend or extend slavery, but for the South, for a new nation. Moreover, its economy was transformed. From 1862 almost every Confederate state by law reduced the acreage of cotton and tobacco, or, if Union troops approached, large quantities were burned to prevent it falling into their hands. Cotton production fell from 4,500,000 bales in 1860 to 1,000,000 in 1862, and to 300,000 in 1864: tobacco production, and even the distilling of liquor from corn or other grain, were also curbed.

For at least two years before Appomattox, Lincoln and Congress had been considering the constitutional consequences of victory, including the terms of readmission of the defeated Southern states, and the need for the alleviation of the condition of the Negro after his emancipation. In December 1863, Lincoln outlined a reconstruction program whereby any Southern state government would receive executive recognition as soon as one-tenth of the voters of 1860 in the state took an oath to support the Constitution, and organized a republican form of government. Lest he appear to invade the authority of Congress, he claimed to be acting under the presidential pardoning power; each House would of course retain the decision on seating representation from the Southern states. The plan brought wide respect for Lincoln in the South. He did not, because he could not mention voting rights – that remained a matter for the states; but in March 1864, on the eve of a constitutional convention in Louisiana, he did suggest to Governor Michael Hahn that delegates might consider suffrage for certain blacks – those who had served in the army, paid taxes, or could read and write. The convention did not discuss the proposal.

For the Radical Republicans (Thaddeus Stevens, George Boutwell, and Henry Winter Davis in the House of Representatives, Charles Sumner and Benjamin Wade in the Senate), such terms were in any case much too lenient. Not only did they stress that the re-admission was a matter for Congress, but they sought to ensure that neither politically nor economically would the representatives from the South in Congress be able to shape legislation; the Radicals were determined to block the reappearance there of any who had played any part in leading the Confederate cause. In their Wade-Davis Bill of July 1864, they demanded the raising of the 10 percent to 50, and stipulated that it should be Congress, not the President, who should decide the terms of Southern readmission; Louisiana and Arkansas in 1864 and Tennessee in 1865, reorganized on the Ten Percent Plan, were refused admission by Congress. Lincoln gave the Wade-Davis Bill a pocket veto; their truculent response was a Manifesto accusing Lincoln of "studied outrage on the legislative authority of the people" because of personal ambition, which Horace Greeley unhelpfully published in his *Tribune* in August 1864, three months before the election. Despite Lincoln's handsome victory in November 1864, despite Lee's surrender in April 1865, and despite Lincoln's assassination, there was little sign of peace on Capitol Hill.

Reconstruction took three forms: the presidential, the Congressional, and the Southern. President Andrew Johnson, who had assumed the presidency on Lincoln's death, was even more an example of the log cabin to White House myth than was Lincoln himself, a self-taught yeoman farmer who had served as Congressman and governor, Senator (the only Southerner to serve in the Senate in Lincoln's first term), War Democrat Vice-President and military governor of Tennessee, was nevertheless of limited knowledge – and especially limited knowledge of the North and of Northerners. He had none of Lincoln's skill in handling people. His plan seemed simple and speedy. In the long interval that then obtained between the election of Congress in 1864 and its first session in December 1865, he, like Lincoln, saw the task as falling to the executive anyway. In May 1865 he proposed an amnesty to all Southerners who would take an oath of future loyalty; their property would thus be safe, and they would not be prosecuted for treason. The Southern states would hold conventions to make any necessary changes in their constitutions; but only those who had amnesties, and who qualified under the state laws in operation before secession, could take part in elections for members of these conventions, as voters or as candidates; they thus excluded Negroes. When each state then held elections for Congressmen and Senators and state officials, ex-Confederate leaders and planters reappeared; the newly elected members of the US Congress even included the ex-Vice-President of the Confederacy, Alexander Stephens. And when those elected were disqualified under the terms of the amnesty, the President handed out pardons. Speedy though this might nave been, it was a process that denied any voice to Congress; and to the Radicals in Congress who, in their eyes, had won the War for a cause, the denial of civil rights to the Negro in this process was tantamount to saying that the War had been fought in vain. Plain folk from the South, even when holding high office, seemed as Negrophobe as any planter. When the Congress did meet, the President added fuel to the flames by vetoing, in February 1866, the bill extending the life of the Freedmen's Bureau, which Congress passed over his veto. For its part, Congress passed a series of Reconstruction Acts in March 1867, again over the President's veto, and the Tenure of Office Act denying the President the right to remove federal officials without the consent of the Senate. When Johnson removed Stanton as secretary of war, in defiance of the Act, this was cited as a reason for his impeachment. The War was now being fought on Capitol Hill and between two branches of the federal government, with race riots echoing them in Memphis and New Orleans.

The Congressional view of Reconstruction was disfigured by the bitterness of the Radical campaign against the President. When the impeachment proceedings began in March 1868, the end of his term was but months away; the attempt to remove him was a vindictive political maneuver with undertones of a continuing war: of North *vs.* South, Yankee wealth *vs.* yeoman poverty, Republicans *vs.* Democrats, with a dash of anti-Lincoln and anti-presidency added for good measure. The President, facing charges leveled against him by a committee chaired by Thaddeus Stevens, a humanitarian without humanity, was acquitted by a single vote, since the Senate vote against him (35 Republicans against 19, of whom 7 were Republicans) fell one short of the two-thirds that were needed. In being loyal, the seven sacrificed their careers. In the attack on the President there were two ringleaders. The charges were assembled and presented by Congressman Thaddeus Stevens, the chairman of the Joint Committee of Fifteen which drafted the Fourteenth Amendment – to whom the Southern states were "conquered provinces", "proud traitors" to be stripped of their "bloated estates." Stevens still offers rich pickings to any student of psychohistory. Born in poor circumstances in frontier Vermont, lame with a clubfoot and never physically robust, he became a wealthy lawyer and a rich ironmaster in Gettysburg. Through the war, having been passed over for membership of Lincoln's Cabinet, he played a powerful role in the House of Representatives as chairman of the Committee of Ways and Means, and pushed the cause of emancipation with total dedication: slavery was "a curse, a shame and a crime." "Free every slave – slay every traitor – burn every rebel mansion." He saw the South as an enemy outside the Constitution, an area for total recolonization; he was the antithesis of Lincoln – and of Lee. His policies were rooted in hatred, and were the product of his background: he backed protective tariffs for iron manufacturing, even more so after his Caledonia iron works near Chambersburg were wrecked by Confederate troops in 1863, when vengeance lent further fury to his vitriolic and venomous language. He had a legion of enemies, and he had made them by his assiduous bitterness of spirit; he may have been seen as saint by many Negroes, but to the South and most whites, North and South, he was a sinister ogre. His vengeful temper wrecked whatever nobility of motive he may have had. He never married, and at his death only a nephew and a mulatto housekeeper, believed to be his mistress, were at his bedside. He left his defense on his tombstone in Lancaster:

I repose in this quiet and secluded spot not from any natural preference for solitude, but finding other cemeteries limited by charter rules as to race, I have chosen this that I may illustrate in my death the principles which I advocated through a long life – Equality of Man before his Creator. [43]

The other "opposition" leader was the truculent Senator Benjamin Wade of Ohio, who would, as president *pro tempore* of the Senate,

[43] Fawn M. Brodie, *Thaddeus Stevens: Scourge of the South* (New York, Norton, 1959); David Donald, *Charles Sumner and the Rights of Man* (New York, Knopf, 1970); and for an older view, George Fort Milton, *The Age of Hate* (New York, Coward-McCann, 1930).

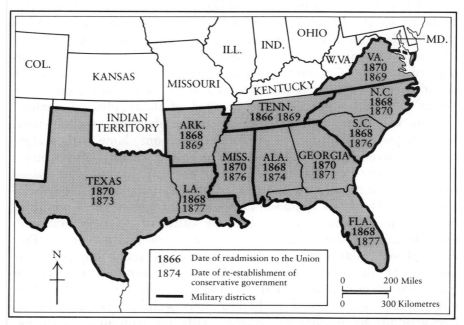

Map 13 Reconstruction. After the War, the South was divided into five military districts and occupying forces installed.

himself have become President to the gleeful and greedy anticipation of his fellow Radicals had the impeachment verdict been guilty. They, and their like, enacted their Reconstruction Acts which among other things divided the South into five military districts under martial law (March 1867), and required the new governments in the South to recognize Negro suffrage. They remained the dominant group in the government of the US to the end of Grant's Administration in 1877, although Stevens died in 1868. They gave legislative form to what is ironically known as Reconstruction, and to the "freeing of the slaves."

However much the Civil War might have been, for Lincoln, a struggle to save the Union, as his presidential oath required of him, slavery was at the center of the legislative executive clash; it was so even more after his death than in his lifetime. For the Radicals in and out of Congress, the emancipation of the slave was indistinguishable from the destruction of the South that had cradled slavery; the farther they were from experience of the war, the more intense their idealism – and their vehemence. Three amendments were added to the Constitution: slavery was formally abolished with emancipation immediate, uncompensated, and universal (Thirteenth

Amendment, ratified December 1865); federal protection and citizenship were extended to the freed Negro: no state was to "deprive any person of life, liberty or property without due process of law," and all persons (except Indians not taxed) should count for representation (Fourteenth Amendment, ratified July 1868); and the Negro was — at least in form — guaranteed basic political rights: that is, the right to vote (Fifteenth Amendment, ratified March 1870). These amendments translated the war-inspired Emancipation Proclamation and the Radicalism of Congress into law, and annulled the Dred Scott decision and the "two-thirds" clause.

Most Southern States rejected the Fifteenth Amendment, but it was declared ratified by Congress. Four million slaves secured their freedom in law, a larger number than were emancipated in all other New World slave societies combined. For the individual ex-slave, there was indeed a new birth of freedom; but, for most of them, since it came *staccato* and without schooling, freedom brought more problems, many more anxieties, and many new experiences of exploitation, than anything they had known in slavery. It brought problems and opportunities to the federal government also. It destroyed the economy of the Old South. But, along with the — almost contemporary (and much smoother) — end of serfdom in Tsarist Russia, slavery was now confined to small strongholds in Spanish and Portuguese America, and to unknown, and still unexplored, areas of Africa and Asia.

For the newly liberated four million blacks, the most important federal Act was that of March 1865 which established the Freedmen's Bureau, designed to help the freedman towards responsible citizenship, and to serve as a relief agency. However benevolent the intention, it was hard for white Southerners, with Northern troops as occupying armies, to see it other than as an instrument of Northern control and corruption, which it became. What was planned by a benevolent Lincoln as an agency of education and welfare became a Northern tool for racketeers. Its agents, for the most part carpetbaggers from the North and "scalawags" (Southerners not disfranchised) who turned Republicans, exploited the South, disfranchised whites who had served the Confederacy, and permitted incompetent and ill-educated blacks to take part in some state governments — to Northern whites' advantage. By the time of its dissolution in 1874, it was little more than a political machine to organize the Negro vote for the Republican Party. Congressional (or "Black") Reconstruction disfranchised 150,000 whites, and registered 700,000 Negro voters — though only in South Carolina, Mississippi, Louisiana, Alabama, and Florida did Negro voters constitute a

majority, and only in South Carolina did they dominate the legislature. Two Negroes served in the US Senate (one of whom, Hiram
Revels, quickly became conservative), and 15 in the House of Representatives. Apart from the vindictiveness of a handful of Radical
Republicans in Congress, who found it good electoral politics to
"wave the bloody shirt," the absence of witch-hunts, war trials,
and executions is a striking feature after the years of carnage. At
least the blood-letting was over. From being, however, an object
for scorn — and for paternal benevolence — the black now became
an object, and a symbol, for Southern fear. The South felt humiliated; it was for a generation desperately poor, its money worthless, its economy in ruins, and its civil government nonexistent. It
was an occupied enemy territory run by soldiers, who were seen as
foreigners — and as blackguards. The South blamed it all on the
blacks, and on the Yankees who exploited them.

Whatever the white attitude toward the black, a rural economy
had its own seasons. Only through the production and sale of
staple crops could the South raise the capital needed to restore basic
facilities. These staples required the utilization of the previously en-
slaved labor force. Some alternative labor system had to be devised.
What was devised was share-cropping. Landlords rented part of
their land to the "cropper" and usually provided living quarters,
food, tools, and seed in return for a share of the crop; frequently,
the return was divided into thirds allocated to land, equipment, and
labor. But launching capital was short, and had to be borrowed.
Farmers who fell into the clutches of merchant creditors by repeated
borrowing on the strength of future crops, found it most difficult
to escape from the system; farm tenantry in general increased in
the South, and the incomes of tenant farmers remained deplorably
low. By 1880, 20 percent of black farmers owned part or all of
the land they farmed; in 1861 none of them had done so. But many
yeomen farmers became share-croppers — and many planters also;
and all were in debt to merchants and bankers, too often Yankees.
The South developed a more diversified economy after the Civil
War, however, but without help from the Northern Radicals, whose
Reconstruction was a dream not of economic recovery but of social
justice — and revenge. It was two decades before cotton and tobacco
·production reached pre-War quantities. By 1900 almost a billion
dollars had been invested in Southern industries; but not until 1900
was Southern property worth what it had been in 1861.

What resulted also were the "black codes" of 1865–6, which
were the response of "a crushed people," the South's own attempt
at Reconstruction, an adaptation to disaster. In the opinion of the

men who formulated them, they were an economic and social necessity. For in much of the Deep South, particularly in Mississippi and Alabama, blacks outnumbered whites, and many blacks chose no form of employment. If the codes were severe in the Deep South, they were mild in Virginia and North Carolina, and nonexistent in Tennessee. The immediate intention was to ensure that black labor was available for agricultural employment, to protect the various states from having to support minors, vagrants, and paupers, and to give the recently emancipated black some legal protection for his or her person and property. But none of them gave Negroes the right to vote, or to rent or lease land outside towns, a provision which effectively circumscribed black economic autonomy. All freedmen had to have evidence of a legal residence or employment by January 1866. Any blacks who left their employer without good cause were to be returned to him, forcibly if necessary. Black children who were without support were apprenticed by the courts, with their former masters usually being given preference. Any freedman who failed to pay his annual one-dollar poll tax to support indigent blacks would be automatically designated a vagrant. Without property, the black was not free. The scale of the situation further buttressed the extreme Radical argument: give white men's land to blacks; and Southerners blamed Radicals and blacks alike.

In defense against military occupation, against scalawag corruption and ill-treatment, and against the attempts to give blacks of little education jobs in government, the Deep South bred the "Mississippi Plan" and the Ku Klux Klan, threatening blacks with violence and intimidation. The Mississippi Plan, a terrorist campaign ("Carry the election peaceably if we can, forcibly if we must") managed to "redeem" Mississippi from Republican control in the elections of 1875. But by that year almost all troops had been withdrawn, and the Upper South was conservative country again.[44] The Klan, first organized in Tennessee in 1866, had only a five-year history as a *mafia*, and was weakened, though not destroyed, by the "Force Acts" of 1870 and 1871, invoking the Fourteenth and Fifteenth Amendments against it. Jim Crow laws were passed, which in some areas enforced a segregation and a color bar far more stringent, and at times more vicious, than anything obtaining before 1861. There were, in the last 20 years of the nineteenth century, over 3,000 recorded cases of lynching.

[44] Vernon L. Wharton, *The Negro in Mississippi 1865–1890* (Chapel Hill, NC, University of North Carolina Press, 1943), esp. ch. 13.

The image of the black as "Sambo" also appeared, and became enshrined in Black and White Minstrel Shows and in the songs of Stephen Foster. Booker Washington, the black university teacher, preached humility and the politics of accommodation and compliance. In the Uncle Remus tales of Joel Chandler Harris (collected in 1881), in Thomas Dixon's *The Clansman* (1905) – turned later into the film, *Birth of a Nation* (1915) – and in Margaret Mitchell's *Gone with the Wind* (1936) and Robert Penn Warren's *All the King's Men* (1946), a Southern legend was born, of the old South seen as mellow and gracious through the bitter salt tears of the grimness of Reconstruction – and transformed by William Faulkner, and by the writers known as the Fugitives in Nashville, into parables of human existence. The literature of the South, in its demagogic politics, its religious fundamentalism, its racialism – that was as effective when tacit as when it was explicit – its easy emotionalism, its attachment to family and kin and *pays*, has the flavor not of the old South, of the chivalry and legitimate worries for his section of John C. Calhoun, or of the War years, but of the much less chivalrous, bitter and anguished years of Reconstruction. And by even more bitter irony, the Jim Crow laws of many Southern states found echoes in the North. Indeed, when the War was over, all but six of the Northern states still denied the vote to their black citizens, and in the immediate postwar years the electorates of several of them reaffirmed their hostility to Negro suffrage. Although the Republican party platform of 1868 demanded Negro suffrage in the South, it left the matter in the North to the individual states. Negrophobia was no Southern monopoly, and the War had not been declared on race prejudice; so that the ban on Negro entry into labor unions, the politics of President Theodore Roosevelt – notably his Anglo-Nordic sympathies – and the domestic views of Southern-bred President Woodrow Wilson revealed that racist ideas were by 1914 no longer a Southern monopoly.

The Supreme Court's ruling in 1896 in *Plessy* vs. *Ferguson* on "separate but equal" facilities, sanctioned a racial segregation in education and in transport that would have been seen as unreal in 1846, and which took another century to overthrow. The price paid for the Civil War was not just the cost in blood and resources, but the century of barrenness and bitterness between 1865 and 1965, a hundred years' war to capture the mind and the conscience of America. It was not Lincoln, but F. D. Roosevelt, who changed the system. It was not until 1941, after astute political pressure from A. Philip Randolph and the National Association for the Advancement of Colored People (NAACP), that the President issued Executive Order No. 8,802, which established complete and equal participation in the defense industry of all workers irrespective of their race, creed, color, or national origin.

The New Reconstruction, as C. Vann Woodward has called it, began. Black and white soldiers still fought in separate units in World War II, but in the years immediately following the war new legislation brought new hope. The poll tax was gradually abolished, the forces integrated, the Fair Employment Practice Commission set up, and in 1954 came the historic Supreme Court decision — reversing its own counsels of 60 years earlier — that segregation of races in education could no longer be regarded as constitutional. Not until 1954, when the Warren Supreme Court decreed that separate educational facilities were in themselves unequal, was real equality conceded — and then it had to be enforced. It took Martin Luther King's 381-day campaign of bus boycotts in 1956 in Montgomery, Alabama, to end the Jim Crow segregation on public buses. It needed marches and demonstrations. In Little Rock, Arkansas, it required federal troops to enforce equality in the schools. It called for the massive nationwide civil rights campaign of the 1960s, and massive federal spending, to end this chapter. It may perhaps have needed also the idea of Black Power and of "Black is Beautiful," the open contempt for the white, the open advocacy not of integration but of separation voluntarily chosen by blacks, before total acceptance of each by the other was possible. Lyndon B. Johnson's Civil Rights Acts — Rooseveltian in their range and spirit — finally enacted the political equality of black and white into law. Nothing, of course, can order it in the hearts and minds of men. Only the power invoked by the Mississippi preacher will do that.

Oh, Lawd, give Thy servant de eye of de eagle and de wisdom of de owl; connect his soul wid de gospel telephone in de central skies; luminate his brow wid de sun of heaben, pisen his mind wid love for de people, turpentine his imagination, grease his lips with possum oil; loosen his tongue wid de sledge hammer of Thy power; 'lectrify his brain wid de lightnin' of de word; put 'petual motion in his ahms; fill him plum full of the dynamite of Thy glory; 'noint him all over wid de kerosene oil of Thy salvation, and set him on fire. Amen.

That is one way. But the years since 1954, and notably since 1963, have done more than did the War between the states or any preacher of the Word to tackle the United States' most difficult political and moral problem.

In crushing the Confederacy, the military force of the Union at last laid the ghost of states' rights, and ended the decades of political debate on that issue. The War determined that the United States *is* rather than the United States *are*. The states remained important, but not supreme. Among the rights they claimed, however, nullification and secession could no longer be numbered. They had been threatened in New England in 1814, and again by Calhoun in 1830; they had been invoked in 1861 ... but never again. Critics, and political parties, in future kept to the advocacy of reform, never again of separation; parties themselves became less voices of distinct regionalisms than agencies of differing views on issues. When the Dominion of Canada was formed in 1867, its founders sought to avoid the states' rights complications of the American constitution by allotting only delegated powers to the provinces, and reserving all other powers to the central government. Power in the United States now lived in Washington. And Washington dominated the continent as well as the nation. Within two years of the end of the War, a Canadian Confederation was born, and Britain withdrew from its responsibility for the defense of Canada; four years later, the Treaty of Washington and the subsequent Geneva arbitration settled the *Alabama* claims and any remaining disagreements with the US. In 1867 Napoleon III withdrew all French troops from Mexico and abandoned the Archduke Maximilian to his fate. And in 1867 Russia agreed to sell Alaska to the US for $7 million. The victory in the Civil War extended the Dominion of the North from the Behring Sea and the Arctic to the Caribbean. Wars always have consequences unforeseen by their authors.

Where, however, in Washington did power live: was it, in today's jargon, downtown (in the White House and its agencies) or on Capitol Hill? The constitution was no guide to the use of federal power in an emergency like 1861. As Lincoln put it starkly, in his first message to Congress in July 1861: "are all the laws, but one, to go unexecuted, and the Government itself go to pieces, lest that one be violated?" In mobilizing manpower and resources to meet the Confederate threat, Lincoln set some important precedents for government action in time of crisis. Before calling Congress in session in July 1861 to give him legal authorization, the President called out the state militia (under a generally forgotten law of 1795); he proclaimed a blockade; he expanded the regular Army and Navy; he spent money without Congressional appropriation; he suspended the writ of *habeas corpus* – a power, prescribed the Constitution, that only Congress could exercise; and he authorized military arrests and trials of individuals not under military jurisdiction.

Congress subsequently approved all his actions except the suspension of *habeas corpus*, but the President continued to withhold the writ whenever he thought it expedient to do so. Nor did an adverse decision by Chief Justice Roger B. Taney, in the case of *Ex parte Merryman*, arising from an arrest in Maryland handed down while Taney was on circuit duty there in the summer of 1861, deter him from his course.

Throughout the war, even with Congress in session, Lincoln continued to exercise wide powers independently of it. He asserted the right to proclaim martial law behind the lines, to arrest people without warrant (some 14,000 suffered in this way), to seize property, to suppress newspapers, to prevent the use of the post office for "treasonable" correspondence, to emancipate slaves, to lay out a plan of reconstruction. No President had ever undertaken such sweeping action in the absence of Congressional authorization. Benjamin R. Curtis, who had been one of the two justices dissenting from the pro-slavery decision in the Dred Scott case, wrote that Lincoln had established "a military despotism." Wendell Phillips, the abolitionist, called him an "unlimited despot." No President before him had exercised such powers; nor would any after his time. But if he was so, he obviously did not become a despot lightly. He was, like Cromwell, the Protector. The nation, as he saw it, faced the most desperate of emergencies; its very survival was at stake. Would the very principles of freedom prevent free government from defending itself? Or, as he later put it, "Was it possible to lose the nation and yet preserve the Constitution?" Where Jefferson, like Locke, saw emergency power as a weapon outside and beyond the Constitution, Lincoln suggested that the crisis itself made it in some sense a constitutional power.

The Constitution, however, could give some guidance. The executive war power was founded first of all, Lincoln believed, in the solemn presidential oath to "preserve, protect, and defend the Constitution of the United States." Here he found justification, or at least consolation, by citing the provision permitting the suspension of *habeas corpus*, "when in Cases of Rebellion or Invasion the public Safety may require it." Lincoln had appointed provisional governors for states as they were won back: Tennessee, Louisiana, North Carolina, Texas, Arkansas. In December 1863 he announced a general policy for the readmission of states as they were detached from the Confederacy: with the exception of military and civilian leaders, he promised amnesty for any Southerner who would take an oath to support the Constitution of the US and the acts of Congress relating to emancipation, as well as the Emancipation Proclamation itself. Moreover, Lincoln came to see the office of commander-in-chief as the locus, if not the source, of the war power. Thus he said; "I think the Constitution invests its commander-in-chief clause with the law of war, in time of war." Thus the Emancipation Proclamation began by invoking "the power in me vested as Commander-in-Chief of the Army and Navy," and ended by justifying the Act as "warranted by the Constitution upon military necessity." He added: "As Commander-in-Chief ... I suppose I have a right to take any measure which may best subdue the enemy." It was a valid argument: the Constitution gave the President not simply the functions of commanding the army and the navy, but the office of commander-in-chief; since the functions were undefined, they could be held to be expansible. But would the Supreme Court accept this extraordinary theory of the war power as being in harmony with the American Constitution? When the seizure of ships by his blockade led to legal claims, a majority of the Court upheld Lincoln's actions. They did so, however, on narrow grounds. The Court simply said that invasion or insurrection created war as a legal fact, which "the President was bound to meet ... in the shape it presented itself, without waiting for Congress to baptize it with a name." The decision was by a 5 to 4 vote. In 1863 it pronounced the War to be both a rebellion and a foreign war. At least the federal government, whether President or Congress was *primus* in it, could no longer be described as a doughnut – a lot of bread and gravy with a hole at the center. The authority of the federal government was the permanent legacy of the War.

Another legacy of the War was the two-party system. Effectively, from 1800 to 1860 the Democratic party, though under changing names, had been in the ascendancy; occasionally in the latter part of this 60-year sway a Whig had won the presidency. In the 70 years after 1860, by contrast, only two Democratic presidents occupied the White House (Grover Cleveland and Woodrow Wilson); the Republicans, the victors of the War, the men who saved the Union and freed the slaves, now held sway. This apparent stability, moreover, rested on a firm geographic base: the South was solidly Democratic; the free white Mid-West farmbelt, plus the Yankee businessmen and the big cities, were reliably Republican, the wearers and the wavers of the bloody shirt. There is, however, oversimplification here. The five presidential elections from 1876 to 1892 were close-run things; in the ten Congressional elections between 1874 and 1892 the Democrats won clear majorities in Congress on eight occasions. And, more than this, the party labels were more often disguises than descriptions – as they always had been. For part of the time the moving force in the Democratic party was William Jennings Bryan's agrarian populism, as much as a memory of the Old South; and the Republican party, while resting for Northern blacks on the continuing magic of the martyr-President, was more than ever that of big business and high tariffs and of the banks than of the family-worked homesteads. If the recurring Democratic vocabulary was still Jeffersonian, the style that of states' rights and small government, both in the Northern cities and in the still-solid South, the Democratic party was the political instrument of white supremacy. In the Louisiana of Huey Long – first governor, then Senator (1931–5) – he could boast that in his democracy every white man was a king and every white lady a queen, but no-one wore a crown – and colored people knew their place.

Not only was federal supremacy over the states achieved, but by an interpretation of the word "person" in the Fourteenth Amendment that came close to a legal quibble, the federal government in fact became the censor of all economic and social experimentation in the states. Property and corporate industry as well as Negroes were "protected," and the tariff against foreign competition went ever higher. The legal "person" protected was seen as small-scale. Business and industry, however, had profited handsomely from the war prosperity, and there was abundance of capital. So mills and factories and corporations, mergers and take-overs flourished, and cities with them. When William Dean Howell's hero, Silas Lapham, in that masterpiece of the rise of the self-made man, returned from the war, he found it "another world." "The day of small things was past, and I don't suppose it will ever come again in this country."[45] Industry outstripped planting, and big business barons replaced the planter in political control. At Appomattox, Lee surrendered to Grant; so did Thomas Jefferson to Alexander Hamilton. Just before his death, Lincoln anticipated this development:

I see in the near future a crisis approaching that unnerves me and causes me to tremble for the safety of my country. As a result of the war, corporations have been enthroned and an era of corruption in high places will follow, and the money power of the country will endeavor to prolong its reign by working upon the prejudices of the people until all wealth is aggregated in a few hands and the Republic is destroyed. I feel at this moment more anxiety for the safety of my country than ever before, even in the midst of war. God grant that my suspicions may prove groundless.[46]

[45] William Dean Howell, *The Rise of Silas Lapham* (1885).
[46] *Collected Works*, ed. Basler, vol. IV, p. 260.

Lincoln's address at Gettysburg expressed his view of the War as a struggle not merely to preserve the Union, but to preserve his idea of democracy as a new type of government for the world. Thirty years later there were other equally gifted Americans who did not like what that democracy they saw had become; Henry Adams, Edward Bellamy, William Jennings Bryan, and Henry James – who became an expatriate out of his dislike of big business, the "Gilded Age," and corruption, of urbanism, nativism, and Jim Crow; and James Russell Lowell, the most intellectual ambassador the US ever sent abroad. Lowell thought Lincoln's government of the people, by the people, for the people, had become a "kakistocracy" – government for the benefit of knaves at the cost of fools. (Though a cynic, not a Lincoln, might add as a gloss on Lowell's bitterness that if Congress did not have some knaves in it, it would not be a representative institution.)

If the Civil War was a war to prevent the further extension of slavery, it was successful. But if that was its sole cause, it was also unnecessary, since, as the census of 1860 revealed, geology made Kansas and Nebraska, and the territories to the north and west of them, unsuited to cotton and to slaves.

If it was a war to free the slaves, as to many in the North, and to the Radicals in Congress it was, and as certainly by 1863 it had become, it was successful. But the freedom enshrined in the amended Constitution was on paper only; as Edmund Burke had said a century before, the laws "go but a little way;" nothing was done to give them economic substance. The South used extra-constitutional methods, fear and terror, to deny the freedom promised; and the Constitution and the courts still find it hard to provide genuinely equal opportunity, and to counter race prejudice.

If the War was – as for many Southerners it was – to defend a new nation, it was unsuccessful. But in fighting so savage and so costly a war, a sense of regional distinctness was born almost as strong as nationalism. Although the present ubiquity of railroad and air communications, of post offices and telecommunications, of main streets and interstate highways, of radio and television, of high-rise public housing, of skyscrapers and chainstores, have all denuded states and regions of distinct identity, the Southernness of Dixie is sharper than the separateness of any other region – because a war was fought for a particular place, and the postwar occupation drove deep the memory of suffering, defeat, and humiliation.

If conclusions are sought from the War designed to help solve contemporary problems – although it is legitimate to query, in

Bolingbroke's phrase, whether history is "a school for statesmen" – they are those grasped not by Jefferson or Madison, the devisers of Constitutions, but by John C. Calhoun, in the heat of the first great debate: how to reconcile the rights of the minority in the Southern states against those of the American majority; and in turn and contemporaneously, how to reconcile the rights of the South's own minority themselves, who happen to be black, against the pressures of the South's own majority, who are white? In his study *The American Civil War*,[47] Peter J. Parish dismisses parallels with the civil war in Nigeria which had been waged just before he was writing, and sees a comparison with Ulster's role in Britain. The emotional intensity that lies behind the religious and historical divide between Catholic and Protestant in Ulster, however, is much less than the differences of race, language, color, and prejudice between black and white in Dixie. Each needs an agency, even an outsider, to exploit it: the IRA in Ulster fighting a terrorist campaign, the Abolitionists in the US in the 1850s. Remove the irritant and the two groups would slowly adapt and adjust, as for long or short periods they did.

Perhaps more apt comparisons could be drawn by looking at all the lands south and east of Vienna. Woodrow Wilson was born in the valley of Virginia five years before the War began, and raised in Georgia and South Carolina in the years of Reconstruction. When as President of the US in 1919 he sought a solution for Europe's repeated wars, he saw imperialism, not poverty, nor race, nor color of the skin, as the cause of the trouble, and not federalism but nationalism as the solution. A member of the large team of pundits shipped to Europe to advise the President in 1919 saw the configuration of European languages, races, and religions all piled on top of each other, paused in his task and asked a still relevant questions "Must every little language have a country all its own?" So too with India, South Africa, Syria, and the Lebanon. Compared to problems like these, the difficulty of 1861 was small. Freedom would probably have come, and, without the costs of war, it could have been accompanied by generous compensation – and by schools. This would have been a preferable solution. Moreover, after every war, however bloody, peace has to be found. To avoid war in the first place requires – as Calhoun knew – endless negotiation and repeated compromises. And living in peace requires that all live with compromise and adjustment – for ever.

[47] Peter J. Parish, *The American Civil War* (London, Eyre Methuen, 1975).

The American Civil War was the first war that never ended. All preceding wars however chronicled in song and legend, did gradually fade as participants died — whatever the tales' told. But the scale and horror of the casualties of the war between the ill-balanced states were enhanced by permanent memory, for this was the first war to be captured on camera — by Matthew Brady and Alexander Gardner and their associates — with "crews" moving from location to location with remarkable dexterity, and thus leaving as souvenir a permanent pictorial record, a reminder of the ugly impact of one section on another. Add the songs, the records of participants in *Battles and Leaders of the Civil War* as they were published in 1887 and later, and the rich literature of Dixie, and it is easy to see assembled the vast archive of a collective memory. For the South, the dregs stay bitter at the bottom of the cup.

One of the best analysts of slavery, Kenneth Stampp, assessed it in *And the War Came*. And the poet Stephen Vincent Benet saw it as the end of a destiny un-manifest and the birth of a new dream.

Yankees went to war animated by the highest ideals of the nineteenth-century middle classes ... But what the Yankees achieved — for their generation at least — was a triumph not of middle-class ideals but of middle-class vices. The most striking products of their crusade were the shoddy aristocracy of the North and the ragged children of the South. Among the masses of Americans there were no victors, only the vanquished.[48]

> Bury the bygone South.
> Bury the minstrel with the honey-mouth,
> Bury the broadsword virtues of the clan,
> Bury the unmachined, the planters' pride.
> The courtesy and the bitter arrogance,
> The pistol-hearted horsemen who could ride
> Like jolly centaurs under the hot stars.
> Bury the whip, bury the branding-bars,
> Bury the unjust thing
> That some tamed into mercy, being wise,
> But could not starve the tiger from its eyes
> Or make it feed where beasts of mercy feed.
> Bury the fiddle-music and the dance
> The sick magnolias of the false romance
> And all the chivalry that went to seed
> Before its ripening.

[48] Kenneth Stampp, *And the War Came: The North and the secession crisis 1860–61* (Baton Rouge, Louisiana State University Press, 1950).

And with these things, bury the purple dream
of America we have not seen,
The tropic empire, seeking the warm sea,
The lost foray of aristocracy
Based not on dollars or initiative
Or any blood for what that blood was worth
But on a certain code, a manner of birth,
A certain manner of knowing how to live
The pastoral rebellion of the earth
Against machines, against the Age of Steam,
The Hamiltonian extremes against the Franklin mean,
The genius of the land
Against the metal hand,
The great, slave-driven bark
Full-carved upon the dark,
With gilded figurehead,
With letters for the crew
And spices for the few,
The passion that is dead,
The pomp we never knew,
Bury this, too. [49]

[49] Benet, *John Brown's Body*, pp. 354–5; reproduced by kind permission of the estate of Stephen Vincent Benet.

L'Envoi

In its first century, American society, like its politics and its industry, was in flux. It was not yet aware of itself as a single entity, nor of being "America." British and French visitors found it crude – and exotic. There could be no inevitability, no certainty, of "progress." It was accustomed to irregular upheavals. Indeed, it began with one easy Revolution, when the British – now an alien – ruling class chose out of loyalty to the king to go into what became permanent exile; the vacuum left behind was filled by (often more talented) locally born men. The period ended in another and more violent upheaval, a shedding of blood until then unparalled in scale, and, again, blood shed by brothers. Wars were recurrent within the century: the War of 1812, a second War of Independence; a war in 1819 along the equally uncertain Florida line; the near-war of 1837 along the debatable Canadian line; a war with Mexico; and innumerable wars with the Indian tribes, resulting in their being driven further and further West. The Indian "clearances" were a matter of deliberate policy – in sharp contrast to the paternalism of the former British superintendents of Indian Affairs; Helen Hunt Jackson's *A Century of Dishonor*, written in 1881, was a massive indictment of Indian policy. And at least one unusual religious group was driven into exile, and sought Elysium in the wilderness. This catalog omits the fact that one-seventh of the population was unfree, and then lived largely segregated lives; many among them tried to run away, and were aided by many more. This was a restless society.

This interpretation might seem to derive from what, in other countries, could be labeled as but aspects of foreign or imperial policy. But, in Edward Countryman's words, "Popular upheaval was central to the revolutionary process." Thus the Stamp Act risings in

1765 and 1766 in Boston, New York, Newport, and Albany, the *Liberty* riot in Boston in 1768, the Battle of Golden Hill in New York and the "Boston Massacre" of 1770, the destruction of the British revenue vessel *Gaspee* in Providence in 1772, and the Boston Tea Party of 1773. Add a domestic thread of disorder: the Hudson valley tenant insurrections, the Regulator uprisings in the Carolinas, the march of the Paxton Boys on Philadelphia before the outbreak of war, Shays' Rebellion in Massachusetts in 1786, and the Whiskey Rebellion in Pennsylvania after it. So frequent was unrest that Lieutenant-Governor Hutchinson of Massachusetts could say that "Mobs, a sort of them, are constitutional."[1] Constitutional advance and social reform, like freedom itself, were marked by turbulence on the streets. Progress did not come smoothly.

Hard on the heels of the second War of Independence came another revolution: the industrial revolution. In the decades after the War of 1812 the output of the small water-powered spinning mills of Rhode Island and southeastern Massachusetts was surpassed by that of the larger factories that integrated spinning and weaving: Waltham ("The City of Precision"), founded in 1813, Lowell on the Merrimack (1822), with its workforce largely recruited from the Puritan country girls from New England farms, then Lawrence in 1847, drawing its labor largely from immigrants in the 1840s and 1850s. As anthracite from Pennsylvania became available, steam-powered integrated mills appeared in Providence, Fall River, and other New England coastal towns. By 1854, 45 percent of the iron made in the United States was being produced by coal-fired furnaces. And a distinctive "American system" of the fabrication and assembling of standardized parts became the main feature in the manufacture of fire-arms, sewing machines, and farming equipment. In the last decade before 1860 Oliver Winchester invented his repeating rifle, William Kelly his process for converting iron into steel, and Edward Drake drilled his first oil well (in Titusville, Pennsylvania). The business of America was becoming invention. One of these inventions – Whitney's cotton "engine" – paradoxically fixed an agrarian pattern on the South. Cotton became its King, and Jefferson's distaste for towns seemed confirmed. Madison foresaw its problems for the South, and Calhoun wrestled unsuccessfully with them. The uniform and widespread character of this fashion for experiment and for industrialization was buttressed by turnpike and

---

[1] Edward Countryman, "Social protest and the revolutionary movement 1765–1776," in Jack P. Greene and J. R. Pole (eds), *The Blackwell's Encyclopedia of the American Revolution* (Oxford, Blackwell, 1991), pp. 184–5.

canal building, by railroads and by steamships. In practical terms, the North and the West were now more closely linked. If most of the South's raw cotton went to British mills, Britain's finished yarn and cloth, its textiles and hardware, came back in return – though mainly via New York and to the profit of Northern shippers; thus to further impose on the South the role of raw material supplier. There were three new and distinct societies here, not one.

Is there a clear pattern here? In recent years and from different hands there have been attempts at a new synthesis that is Anglo-American, but with the politics left out. There is perversity and paradox here. Some distinguished American historians – Bernard Bailyn in *The Peopling of British North America* and, edited with Philip D. Morgan, in *Strangers within the Realm*, David Hackett Fischer in *Albion's Seed*, and D. W. Meinig in *The Shaping of America*[2] – have in the last decade been preoccupied with a quest for synthesis in Anglo-Atlantic relationships seen sharply in geographical-social terms. Despite the central fact that the United States was the product of a long and untidy War of Independence from Britain (just when ties were becoming closer, and when there were a few American-born British citizens prominent in Parliament and in London trade and society), a new synthesis is emerging (or being rediscovered?) of the survival and flourishing in North America of British cultural folkways; the settlement patterns, the land usages, and family organizations were not just of the English but of Scots and Irish, Scotch-Irish and Welsh; there was "a vast Atlantic circuit," in Meinig's words, "a new human network of points and passages binding together four continents, three races and a great diversity of regional parts." The Empire of the North Atlantic is now seen as something richer and more varied than that directed by the Privy Council and its many bureaucracies. Nor did it end in 1783.

Moreover, this new Atlanticism follows another pattern: for the previous two decades many authors have been driven by a quest for social justice; the goal has been less the recording of what is visible in the records, so much as reflecting on what ought to have been there; what is hidden anonymously in statistics, or is believed to have been experienced by those who left no records since they

---

[2] Bernard Bailyn, *The Peopling of British North America* (New York, Knopf, 1986); Bernard Bailyn and Philip D. Morgan (eds), *Strangers within the Realm* (Williamsburg, Institute of Early American History and Culture, 1991); David Hackett Fischer, *Albion's Seed: Four British folkways in America* (New York, Oxford University Press, 1989); D. W. Meinig, *The Shaping of America*, vol. II, *Continental America* (Yale University Press, 1993).

were illiterate, or were denied a role to play. Historians now carry their consciences, and a sense of guilt, as identity cards.

One of the code-words, for our times has been "relevance." Ironically, relevance became in practice a synonym for deliberate selection of those themes hitherto neglected – particularly the accounts of the role of African-Americans and women; and, as a refrain, a stress on the wickedness of any evidence pointing to differences of mental capacity, of industry, or, most heretical of all, of class. Reliance has been put on statistics, on mortality tables, census returns, and shipping records. But no great truths have been unearthed.

In all its abundance, and despite the skill of many non-academic practitioners, biography has had a hard struggle to win acceptance from the historical profession. Even so, that is where history is most fascinating. For whatever pattern historians impose on the chaos of the past, whatever the summaries they devise under labels such as "causes" and "consequences," the story of the past is immensely diverse, rich in contradictions and paradoxes, in moods and fashions, in uncertainty and guesswork – because that is the way people were, and are. Perhaps the most vivid, and the only truly accurate, synthesis is that of the multi-biographical approach: we must people the past.

This approach brings emphases, if not always new discoveries, of its own. Thus, Declarations of Independence or of the Rights of Men are not necessarily accurate maps of a contemporary mood. They are usually presented as manifestos, indeed often little more than Utopian papers drafted by literary-minded and highly-educated self-appointed elites, often totally unrepresentative of their world because of their own discontent with it, happy at proclaiming the wickedness of Man in order to hide their own inadequacies in handling people – Tom Paine, Thomas Young, Sam Adams. Sometimes those charged to be the penmen of Declarations are so because they are less experienced, less realistic, less "hard" men than their colleagues, idealistic and literary-minded, like Jefferson. We note and salute decisiveness, courage, and patience in the war heroes. We note but deplore hesitancy, the too-long balancing of interests, not only in the Loyalists but in Joseph Galloway, John Dickinson, William Franklin. It is usually said of fence-sitters that in the end the barbed wire gets into their souls; they neither make nor write history, but wait until the storm passes. Nor does statesmanship require flamboyance: Madison had none, Ethan Allen too much. But when *demos* was coming, it did not hurt Andrew Jackson; and given the coming of media democracy, speech-writers and salesmen became more important than their products. The facts are harder to master

than a familiar telling assumes. The records show that history is –
to adopt Ralph Waldo Emerson's phrase – the lengthened shadow
thrown by a small number of men. Moreover, at least up to 1861,
it is primarily a story of white men, and told by them. When Indians
or blacks appear as distinct figures, their roles are subsidiary –
scouts, guides, interpreters – or enemies. Again, the size and fecundity
of American families is abundant testament to the work of women,
almost all of them properly married – for, except in Benjamin
Franklin's warm prose, the Polly Bakers of colonial or early national
America had a grim life. The leadership of, like the shaping of,
the new society came from white men, until the 1840s overwhelmingly British; indeed, in the first decades of discovery they were
"Gone to the World's End, but English every one."[3] In language –
if under protest – and in law, in non-established Churches and in
life-style, the United States of America was a republican edition of
the mother-country, a mirror England (or Scotland or Ireland) in
the wilderness. Within the generation after 1865, more in protest
against industrial America than against its pre-Civil War form,
Henry James would lament the price exacted by republicanism and
by political separation from the Old World.

The Constitution was America's unique political institution, just
as cheap and easily available land was its unique social feature. But
the charter was never set in stone; if rarely amended after the Bill of
Rights was added, it was capable of infinitely varied interpretation.
Although the War between the States was a savage expression of
disagreement over whether the Constitution of 1787 constituted a
union of peoples or merely a compact between sovereign states,
both North and South alike accepted one other revolution that was
already transforming the Constitution of 1787. The founding document of 1787 assumed that the President would be a first magistrate,
and no more. Power would rest in the legislature, it was assumed in
1787, as it did – or ought, it was thought – to rest in Westminster;
in, that is, the House of Representatives, since the Senate, then
small, would act, it was expected, only as a council of advisers
to the first magistrate. What had not been foreseen was that the
presidential office itself would grow, and be made great by the good
fortune of the recurring skills of some, perhaps the majority, of its
occupants. When it was held by one less gifted in leadership, or who
lacked the charisma that could be manufactured (as with Jackson,
as early as 1824), the country was in peril – as it was in 1856.
So: planned, daringly, as a republic, the United States had become

---

[3] S. V. Benet, *Western Star* (New York, Farrar and Rinehart, 1943), p. 116.

a presidential but federal state; and, whoever won in 1861–5, it would remain so in South as in North. The office of President would grow in importance as the years passed, enhanced by wars, by crises, by newspapers and by advertisement, later by radio and by television. Equally, all of these forces would remorselessly unify, as did turnpikes and bridges, canals and railroads, so that in 1865, as in 1782, there was a sharper awareness of national unity than before any of the wars began.

The Founding Fathers had not intended, however, that the new country would be ruled in perpetuity by a Cincinnatus, nor by a court of lawyers. The centuries did their own transforming, as Madison had foreseen. The Supreme Court has steadily expanded beyond the limits implied in 1787. At that time the federal structure granted legislative autonomy to the individual states, then 13, now 50 in number. Its federal character, and its extent in providing innumerable opportunities for varieties of political and legal expression, seemed also to ensure the diffusion and the defusion of potentially explosive problems – or so Madison believed. In 1787 only one problem – slavery – was not thus defused, when on this individual states joined their neighbors and produced a too-simple two-sections (two nations?) diversity.

Despite much of the recent debate on the proposed Equal Rights Amendment, on civil rights, and on the "right to privacy," it is worth stressing that nowhere does the Constitution make reference to the Declaration of Independence or to the idea of equality. Moreover, Madison's own notes of the Convention show that the framers had no intention to abolish slavery. Indeed, no less than nine of its clauses specifically protect the institution.

Moreover, there is no inclusion in the Constitution of a requirement for mandatory rotation in office. Presumably, it was taken for granted – as by Washington and by Jefferson, in their emphasis on serving for only two terms as President. "Government is instituted for those who live under it," said Roger Sherman of Connecticut. "It ought therefore to be so constituted as not to be dangerous to their liberties. The more permanency it has the worse if it be a bad government." The absence of rotation in office, of annual elections, and of recall of elected officers, became the major criticisms of the document by the Anti-Federalists in the state debates on ratification.[4]

What was not foreseen in 1787 or in 1865 was that a government of laws would become in practice a government by lawyers.

[4] Max Ferrand (ed.), *The Records of the Federal Convention of 1787* (New Haven, Yale University Press, 1966 edn), vol. I, p. 423.

What was seen as arbiter of last resort would gradually become
itself a third branch of government; what was set up in 1787 to
protect states' rights has become the invader of them. On issues
held to involve a "right to privacy" – abortion, euthanasia, freedom
of expression of opinion, freedom to indulge even in drugs – the
Supreme Court now has power of protection of the individual from
search and seizure, and guarantees against censorship that give it
almost the authority and the legislative power of a third chamber.
Clearly, successive Supreme Courts, whether predominantly liberal
or conservative, have arrogated to themselves near-legislative powers
– especially in "moral" and "personal" issues – that were never
considered "relevant" 200 years before. The Supreme Court is no
more competent to solve the insoluble than are legislatures; but its
verdicts, and not the vote of the people, are the supreme law.

Like the growth of the power and influence of the presidency,
the growth of the power of the Supreme Court was not foreseen in
1787 – or in 1861. Clearly, two conclusions can be safely deduced:
first, rule by one elected man or woman or by nine is infinitely
preferable to a war of brother against brother; and, second, that
in a society now so large, so extensive, and so racially mixed that
clashes if not conflicts are likely to be recurrent, perhaps Supreme
Court justices are more likely than any one else to be able to serve
as today's "enlightened despots."

Does such a conclusion represent a failure of the high hopes of
1776, the end of a vision of a "new" nation conceived in liberty
and dedicated to a proposition? Inevitably so: for in 1776 North
America was agrarian, disunited, and all but exclusively Anglo-
Saxon in its notions of order and of behavior. In 1776 neither the
despotism of a Cincinnatus nor government by nine highly trained
lawyers had been envisaged. To their exhorters in 1776 stirring prose
came easily, the phrases the familiar litany of Protestant dissent
and of republicanism. "We hold these truths ..." wrote Jefferson.
"Only a virtuous people are capable of freedom," wrote Benjamin
Franklin. [5] Samuel Adams's vision of Boston saw it as a Christian
Sparta. The Founding Fathers, however, were neither Utopians nor
dreamers of dreams, but realists, aware that malice and malevolence,
cunning and criminality, perversity, viciousness, and violence were
features of politics and of business – and of human nature – as
much as were benevolence and reason. Madison built his Constitution on a recognition of the pervasiveness not of virtue but of

---

[5] A. H. Smyth (ed.), *The Writing of Benjamin Franklin*, 10 vols (New York,
Macmillan, 1905–7), vol. IX, p. 80.

self-interest, even of selfishness among men. Since men (and women) were not angels, they needed to be governed. Even in a republic, human nature needed curbs as well as spurs. The Founders had at least ensured that their governors were of their own – elaborate and indirect – choosing. Their work, however, had its limitations: by not insisting on regular and binding rotation in office they allowed nepotism and corruption to creep in (and it is still there); they had not anticipated the transformation of democracy into demagogy consequent on the mass hypnosis wrought by newspapers, crowds, and later the media, which play on emotion more than reason; as the decades passed, the scale of riot, rebellion, and racial unrest far exceeded what was already familiar to them as "democratic" protests; law, police forces, rules and regulations – and bureaucracy – were major features of an increasingly urban and racially mixed society.[6] The century from Lexington Green to Appomattox was one of territorial expansion, war, and violence. The lawyer-justices who formed their Court of last resort, however, at least pronounced only when appealed to, and by way of judgment on actual cases of apparent injustice. Their conservatism was a necessary binding cord for a society in turmoil. And their writ ran in the largest republic in human history, stretching from Atlantic to Pacific (and later, beyond), and ensuring a greater measure of freedom there than obtained anywhere else. As a government it was and is far from perfect, but a noble experiment it has remained.

---

[6] On March 4, 1789, the first Speaker of the House, Federick A. C. Muhlenberg, opened the first session of Congress, with no staff. Two hundred years later, House Speaker Jim Wright presided over a session in which there were 48 employees for every member of the House and the Senate. There are also 52 federal regulatory agencies that now employ over 122,000 people. Law-making and regulation are dilatory and time-consuming; and, of course, expensive. They are greedy and remorseless consumers of other people's money: and their numbers grow by what they feed on.

Chronologies

1786

Sept. 11–14   At the Annapolis Convention, delegates from New York, Pennsylvania, New Jersey, Delaware, and Virginia adopted an invitation to the 13 states, written by Alexander Hamilton, to meet in Philadelphia to discuss commercial matters and to draw up provisions necessary to make the government "adequate to the exigencies of the Union."

1787   **The Constitutional Convention.**

May. 25   The convention opened at the Pennsylvania State House. (Independence Hall) in Philadelphia. While all states but Rhode Island took part, only 7 states were represented on the first day. George Washington was chosen to be president.

May 29   The Virginia Plan, composed by James Madison and presented by Edmund Randolph, proposed a new government instead of revising the Article of Confederation:

    (1) It called for a legislature, with a lower house chosen by the people with representation in proportion to free population.

    (2) It proposed a single executive (chosen by the legislature) and a national judiciary.

June 15   The New Jersey Plan, presented by William Paterson, gave the small-state alternative to the Virginia Plan:

    (1) It continued the Articles of Confederation, but granted Congress power to levy duties on imports, to regulate trade, and to "direct the collection" of requisitions from the states.

(2) Congress could name a plural executive and appoint a supreme court.

July 5   The Great Compromise, proposed by Roger Sherman of Connecticut was adopted by the committee of the whole. Representation in the lower house was to be in proportion to population, and in the upper house there was to be an equal vote for each state. Bills to raise money would originate in the lower house. In determining representation, 5 slaves would count the same as 3 free men.

Aug. 6–   The draft constitution was debated.
Sept. 10

Sept. 4   A committee reported in favor of the electoral system for choosing the President.

Sept. 8   A 5-man committee on style and arrangements was appointed, made up of Hamilton, Rufus King, Madison, and Gouverneur Morris, with William Johnson (Connecticut) as chairman. Morris wrote the final draft.

Sept. 17   Each of the 12 state delegations approved the final Constitution. Of the 42 delegates remaining, 39 signed (Elbridge Gerry of Massachusetts and Randolph and George Mason of Virginia refused).

1787–1790   **Ratification of the Constitution.**

1787   During the Confederation Period those favoring a stronger central government were called "nationalists," those for state sovereignty "federalists." During the ratification struggle those who were for the Constitution usurped the name Federalist, leaving those opposed to ratification with the title "Anti-Federalists." In each state a special convention was held to ratify the Constitution.

Oct. 27–   Over 70 essays signed "Publius" in support of the Constitution appeared in New York newspapers. With eight
Apr. 2, 1788   additional essays, they were published in May as *The Federalist Papers*. Written by Hamilton, Madison, and John Jay, *The Federalist Papers* supported a strong yet republican government.

Dec. 7–   The first 5 states ratified the Constitution. Delaware,
Jan. 9, 1788   New Jersey, and Connecticut sought federal protection against New York City and so ratified without a struggle. Georgia needed the help of a strong central government against the Creeks. The Federalists won in Pennsylvania partly because the Philadelphia artisans wanted a strong government.

1788

Feb. 6 — Massachusetts ratified by 187 to 168. Samuel Adams was won over when the convention proposed amendments to the Constitution protecting the rights of the states against a strong federal government.

Mar. 24 — Rhode Island rejected the Constitution through a referendum.

Apr. 28 — Maryland ratified by 63 to 11.

May 23 — South Carolina ratified by 149 to 73.

June 21 — The Constitution came into effect with the ratification of the ninth state New Hampshire, by 57 to 47.

June 25 — Virginia ratified by 89 to 79.

July 26 — New York ratified by 30 to 27.

July — North Carolina rejected the Constitution by 185 to 84.

1789

Nov. 21 — North Carolina ratified by 195 to 77 after the Bill of Rights was proposed by Congress.

1790

May 29 — Rhode Island ratified by a majority of 2.

WASHINGTON AND HAMILTON: ORGANIZING GOVERNMENT
AND ECONOMY, 1789–1796

1789

Feb. 4 — Presidential election: George Washington President, 69 electoral votes (the only man ever elected unanimously); John Adams, vice-president, 34 electoral votes. The two Washington administrations are particularly significant because of the precedents set in both domestic and foreign affairs.

Mar. 4 — First Congress met in New York City but lacked a quorum.

Apr. 6 — Congress organized. Both houses were predominantly Federalist.

Apr. 30 — Washington was inaugurated as President in New York City.

July 4 — Tariff Act, primarily for revenue, levied duties averaging 8 percent.

July 27–
Sept. 2 — Departments of State (Thomas Jefferson, secretary), War (Henry Knox of Massachusetts, secretary), and Treasury (Alexander Hamilton, secretary) were established. Congress gave the President power to remove an appointee without the consent of the Senate.

Aug. 22	Treaty-making: Washington asked the Senate for advice and consent on a treaty with the Creeks. When the Senate delayed, Washington decided henceforth to submit signed treaties and ask only for consent.
Sept. 22	Office of Postmaster General was established.
Sept. 24	Federal Judiciary Act provided for a Supreme Court with a chief justice (John Jay, New York) and five associates. It established 3 circuit courts (two Supreme Court justices per circuit) and 13 district courts. Cases could be appealed from state courts to the Supreme Court. The Act also called for an attorney general (Edmund Randolph, Virginia).
Sept. 25	Bill of Rights was submitted to the states. Ten of the 12 amendments were ratified on December 15, 1791. James Madison led the Bill of Rights movement in the House.

1790

Jan. 14	The first of Hamilton's three reports, the *Report on the Publick Credit* proposed funding the US debt (foreign debt about $12 million; domestic about $44 million) at par value. The US would also assume about $22 million in state debts. Creditors could exchange present securities for new bonds. Hamilton hoped to restore confidence in American credit and give creditors a stake in the government.
Feb. 22	Madison opposed paying the domestic debt at par value because it would benefit speculators who had bought up bonds from the original buyers. Congress rejected his proposal to discriminate in favor of the original buyer. Southerners disliked funding because most securities were held in the North, and assumption of state debts because the Northern states had the largest unpaid debts.
Apr. 12	Madison and others defeated the funding bill in the House.
July 16	Congress voted to put the national capital on the Potomac after Madison secured Southern votes for the funding bill in order to get Hamilton's support for a Southern capital.
Aug. 4	The Funding Act (including the assumption of state debts) was passed. The House vote on assumption was (North) 24–9 in favor and (South) 18–10 against.
Dec. 6	Congress met in Philadelphia, where the capital remained until 1800.

Dec. 13	Hamilton's *Report on the Bank* proposed a Bank of the United States capitalized at $10,000,000 (80 percent private, 20 percent federal), to be the principal depository for federal funds. The Bank's notes would be the nation's principal currency.

1791

Feb. 8	In spite of Madison's opposition the Bank bill passed the House. Northerners voted in favor of the Bank 33–1; Southerners opposed it 19–6.
Feb. 15	Jefferson's *Opinion on the Bank* used strict interpretation of the Constitution to argue that the bank was unconstitutional.
Feb. 23	Hamilton, using loose interpretation, argued that the Bank was justified by the "necessary and proper" clause.
Feb. 25	Washington signed the Bank bill.
Mar. 3	Whiskey Tax passed amid great opposition from the frontier where surplus grain was distilled into whiskey.
Nov. 26	The first Cabinet meeting.
Dec. 5	Hamilton's *Report on Manufactures* urged protective tariffs to encourage manufacturing, bounties to help agriculture, and internal improvements to bind the nation together.

1792

Apr. 5	First Presidential veto (of the apportionment bill) was upheld by Congress.
Apr. 11	In the first Hayburn Case, a US circuit court declared an Act of Congress unconstitutional.
Aug. 21	Resistance to the Whiskey Tax centered in North Carolina and western Pennsylvania. A Pittsburgh convention of farmers threatened to obstruct tax collections.
Dec. 5	Presidential elections: Washington was re-elected with the unanimous vote of 132 electors. Adams was re-elected vice-president with 77 electoral votes. George Clinton (New York), a supporter of Jefferson, received 50 votes as opposition to the Federalists began to arise.

1793

Jan. 23	Congressman William Branch Giles (Virginia) proposed an inquiry into charges of corruption in the Treasury. After Hamilton's defense (Feb. 4 and 13), Giles's resolution to censure Hamilton failed.
Feb. 18	*Chisholm* vs. *Georgia*: Supreme Court decided in favor of two South Carolina citizens who sued Georgia for confiscated property.

1794

Mar. 5   State-rights opposition to the Chisholm decision led Congress to propose the Eleventh Amendment, which provided that a state could not be sued by a citizen of another state in federal courts. It was ratified on January 8, 1798.

July   Whiskey Rebellion in western Pennsylvania. Farmers protested against the Whiskey Tax and against the law requiring those not paying the tax to stand trial in Philadelphia. Congress repealed the trial law in May but too late to prevent the rebellion; the rebels attacked excise officers and forced troops to surrender. A presidential proclamation (Aug. 7) ordered the rebels to return to their homes and called out the militia from four states. In September Washington ordered the suppression of the rebellion and accompanied the troops part of the way. The rebellion evaporated by November as the troops approached.

1796   Land Act (May 18) called for rectangular survey, a minimum price of $2 an acre, and a minimum purchase of 640 acres for land west of the Appalachians.

THE PRESIDENCY OF JOHN ADAMS

1755   Graduated from Harvard University

1765   Wrote Braintree Instructions against the Stamp Act that were adopted in Braintree and in other towns.

1770   Defended British soldiers in the Boston Massacre.

1770–1   Served in General Court (legislature).

1774–5   Served in the Massachusetts Revolutionary Provincial Congress.

1774–5   Published "Novanglus" in Boston *Gazette*.

1774–8   Delegate to First and Second Continental Congresses.

1774–6   Helped draft Declaration of Independence; defended it to the Continental Congress.

1778   Commissioner to France.

1780   Wrote Massachusetts state constitution.

1782–3   Helped negotiate Paris peace treaty with Great Britain.

1785–8   Minister to Great Britain.

1789–96   Vice-President of the US under Washington.

1796–1801	Second President of the US.
Dec. 7, 1796	Presidential election: John Adams, Federalist, was elected President with 71 electoral votes to 68 for Jefferson, Republican. It was the first election conducted even partially on a party basis. Parties, however, were still not organized in every state, and there were no party platforms. Jefferson served as Vice-President.
1798 June–July	The Federalists, fearful of French Revolutionary ideas expressed by editors of Republican newspapers and concerned about the number of foreigners joining the Republican party, passed four Alien and Sedition Acts. The Naturalization Act (June 18) increased the residence requirement for naturalization to 14 years. It was repealed in 1802. The Alien Act (June 25) allowed the President to deport aliens suspected of being dangerous or treasonable. Never enforced, it expired June 25, 1802. The Alien Enemies Act (July 6) allowed deportation or imprisonment of enemy aliens. Since no war was declared, the Act never went into effect. The Sedition Act (July 14) – proposed by Senator James Lloyd (Maryland) and Representative Robert G. Harper (South Carolina) and approved by Adams – provided severe punishments for "false, scandalous, and malicious" statements against the government. It expired March 3, 1801.
July	Matthew Lyon, Republican Congressman from Vermont, made a libelous newspaper statement against President Adams. He was convicted in circuit court and sentenced to four months in jail and a $1,000 fine. Altogether 15 indictments and 10 convictions stemmed from the Sedition Act. Leading the prosecution were secretary of state Timothy Pickering and Justice Samuel Chase.
Nov. 16– Dec. 24	The Alien and Sedition Acts united the Republicans. Jefferson and Madison drew up the Kentucky and Virginia Resolutions, which defended the states' rights theory of government and called the Acts unconstitutional. The Kentucky Resolution (Jefferson) stated that unconstitutional acts of the government were void and that each state could determine its own course. The Virginia Resolution (Madison) simply said that the states could take action.
1799 June 15	New Hampshire passed a Resolution against those of Kentucky and Virginia.

| Nov. 22 | Second Kentucky Resolution (Jefferson) called for a state or states to nullify unconstitutional federal laws. |

1800

May	Federalist caucus nominated John Adams for President and Charles Cotesworth Pinckney for Vice-President. Republican caucus selected Jefferson and Aaron Burr. A schism developed in the Federalist party when Adams dismissed James McHenry, secretary of war, and Timothy Pickering, secretary of state, both Hamilton supporters. John Marshall was named secretary of state.
May 10	Land Act reduced minimum purchase of public land to 360 acres and allowed purchases on credit.
Summer	A two-party system went into operation. States such as Massachusetts and Virginia adopted a state-wide system of voting for presidential electors and thereby encouraged the rise of parties. There were Federalist and Republican parties in each state.
Nov. 17	Congress convened in Washington for the first time. Pierre Charles L'Enfant drew up the plan of the city; the White House and the Capitol were started in 1792–4, burned by the British in 1814, and completed after the War of 1812.
Dec. 3	Presidential election: the states cast their votes for electors at different times during the fall. New York went narrowly for Jefferson. When the Republicans carried South Carolina in December, they won the election. The vote was Jefferson and Burr, 73; Adams, 65; Pinckney, 64; Republicans swept the House 69–36.

1801

Jan. 20	Adams appointed John Marshall as chief justice of the Supreme Court.
Feb. 17	On the 36th ballot to decide between the tied vote for Jefferson and Burr, Hamilton used his influence in the House to turn the election from Burr to Jefferson, who duly became President.
Feb. 27	The Judiciary Act, designed to maintain Federalist control of the courts, reduced the Supreme Court to five justices and created 16 circuit judgeships. Adams made the final "midnight appointments" on March 3, just before leaving office.

PRESIDENTIAL ELECTIONS AND MAJOR EVENTS, 1800–1828

1800	Thomas Jefferson (Democratic Republican) elected over John Adams (Federalist).
1803	*Marbury* vs. *Madison*: John Marshall's Supreme Court declares a law of Congress unconstitutional. Louisiana Purchase.
1804	Thomas Jefferson (Democratic Republican) re-elected over Charles C. Pinckney (Federalist).
1804–6	Lewis and Clark expedition.
1805–7	Mounting seizures of American shipping under British orders in council and Napoleon's decrees.
1807	*Chesapeake–Leopard* affair. Embargo Act.
1808	James Madison (Democratic Republican) elected over Charles C. Pinckney (Federalist).
1809	Non-Intercourse Act replaces Embargo Act.
1810	Macon's Bill No. 2 replaces Non-Intercourse Act.
1811	Re-charter of First Bank of the United States defeated. Power of northwestern Indians broken at Tippecanoe.
1812	James Madison (Democratic Republican) re-elected over DeWitt Clinton (Independent Federalist).
1812–15	War of 1812, and burning of Washington.
1815	Battle of New Orleans.
1814–15	Treaty of Ghent.
1816	James Monroe (Republican) elected over Rufus King (Federalist).
1817	Rush-Bagot Agreement with Great Britain demilitarizes the Great Lakes. General Andrew Jackson invades Spanish Florida.
1818	Convention of 1818 settles outstanding differences with Great Britain.
1819	Adams-Onis Treaty with Spain: US acquires Florida.
1820	James Monroe (Republican) re-elected with only one electoral college vote cast against him. Missouri Compromise.

1823	Monroe Doctrine proclaimed.
1824	John Quincy Adams (Democrat) became President by the decision of the House of Representatives, since no candidate received a majority of the electoral votes (Jackson 99, Adams 84, Crawford 41, Clay 37).
1825	Erie Canal linked the Hudson River (at Albany) to Lake Erie (at Buffalo).
1828	Andrew Jackson (Democrat) defeated John Quincy Adams (National Republican) by 178 electoral college votes to 83 to become President: the first Westerner in the White House.

PRESIDENTIAL ELECTIONS AND MAJOR EVENTS, 1828–1840

1828	Andrew Jackson (Democratic Republican) elected over John Quincy Adams (National Republican).
1830	Jackson vetoes the Maysville Road bill. Indian Removal Act.
	Baltimore & Ohio Railroad begun.
1831	Anti-Masonic party introduced the political convention and party platform.
1832	Tariff of 1832. Remedied the worst abuses of the Tariff of Abominations, but failed to satisfy the South Carolina Nullifiers.
	Jackson vetoes the bill to re-charter the Second Bank of the United States.
	Andrew Jackson (Democratic Republican) re-elected over Henry Clay (National Republican).
	South Carolina nullifies the tariff laws. Bank of US re-charter vetoed.
1833	Compromise Tariff. Gradual reduction of all tariff duties to 20 per cent.
	Force Act. Authorizes president to use military to enforce the laws.
	Jackson transfers the federal deposits from the national bank to selected state-chartered deposit banks.
1836	Jackson issues Specie Circular requiring specie for purchase of federal lands.
	Distribution Act distributing the federal surplus among the states.

Martin Van Buren (Democrat) elected over William Henry Harrison, Daniel Webster, and Hugh Lawson White (all Whigs).

1837   Panic of 1837 forces a general suspension of specie payments and initiates a severe and prolonged economic depression.

Van Buren proposes the independent treasury system.

1838   New York Free Banking Act, a forerunner of general incorporation laws. One of the many efforts by the states to reform and regulate banking.

1840   Independent treasury system finally approved by Congress after three years of debate.

William Henry Harrison (Whig) elected over Martin Van Buren (Democrat), but dies within a month.

John Tyler (Independent Democrat) becomes President, the first Vice-President to succeed.

THE MEXICAN WAR

1830   Over 4,000 Americans lived in Texas. By 1836 Anglo-American settlers outnumbered Mexicans in Texas by 10 to 1.

1832   General Antonio Lopez de Santa Anna seized control of Mexico.

1833   Stephen F. Austin went to Mexico City to demand Texan independence but was refused and jailed.

1835
June 30   Texans seized the garrison at Anahuac.

Oct. 2   Texans defeated Mexican cavalry at the Battle of Gonzalez.

Nov. 3   Convention of settlers at San Felipe voted for local self-government.

1836
Jan.   Santa Anna marched into Texas.

Feb. 23–   Siege of the Alamo mission at San Antonio. Less than 200
Mar. 6   Texans held off 3,000–4,000 Mexicans, but in the end all the Texans were killed, including Jim Bowie and Davy Crockett. "Remember the Alamo" became the Texans' rallying cry.

Mar. 2   Texas declared its independence, and Sam Houston took command of the Texan army.

Apr. 21	Battle of San Jacinto: after retreating eastward, Houston turned and defeated the Mexicans, killing 630.
May 14	Santa Anna signed a treaty (later repudiated) promising Texan Independence with the Rio Grande River as a boundary.
July 1,4	Resolutions in Congress called for the annexation of Texas, but Jackson took no action.
Oct. 22	Sam Houston became the first president of the Republic of Texas. The constitution guaranteed slavery.
1836–50	American and European immigration increased the population of Texas from 30,000 to 212,000.
1837	The US granted recognition to Texas but refused to annex it.
1841	Sam Houston was again elected president of Texas.
1843	Texans broke off annexation discussions and developed close relations with Great Britain, which wanted an independent Texas as a buffer against US expansion. Santa Anna warned that American annexation would lead to war.
1844	
Mar. 6	John C. Calhoun became secretary of state, determined to annex Texas to keep it away from British abolitionists.
Dec. 4	James K. Polk was elected President on a platform calling for the annexation of Texas.
1845	
Feb. 25–8	A joint resolution to annex Texas passed both houses of Congress and was signed by the outgoing President Tyler on March 1.
July 4	Texas ratified the annexation.
Dec. 29	Texas was admitted to the union, with slavery, and the state government was set up Feb. 19, 1846.
Nov. 10	President Polk sent John Slidell to Mexico to offer $30 million in payment for California, New Mexico, and the acceptance of the Rio Grande as the boundary of Texas.
June 15	Polk ordered Gen. Zachary Taylor to a point near the Rio Grande. The area between the Nueces River and the Rio Grande was in dispute because the boundary of the state of Coahuila-Texas had been the Nueces, but Texas had claimed up to the Rio Grande.
July 31	Taylor occupied Corpus Christi, south of the Nueces.
Dec. 16	The Mexican government rejected the Slidell mission.

1846	
May 11	Polk's war message accused Mexico of having "shed American blood on American soil." The Senate and House voted for war 40–2 and 174–14. All antiwar votes were from Northern Whigs. Calhoun and two other Senators abstained. At this time, the American army had only 7,500 men – compared to a Mexican army of 32,000 – but about 100,000 Americans took part in the war before it ended.
	In the battles of Palo Alto and Resaca de la Palma (May 8–9), north of the Rio Grande, Taylor defeated Arista, who retreated south.
May 18	Taylor crossed the Rio Grande. Polk put Taylor in charge of the campaign instead of Commander-in-Chief Winfield Scott partly because Scott was a potential Whig presidential candidate for 1848.
Oct. 8	The battle of Buena Vista near Monterrey. Taylor repulsed Santa Anna, who then withdrew to Mexico City.
1846	The Southwestern campaign of Gen. Stephen W. Kearny began in June when he led 1,700 men west from Fort Leavenworth and captured Santa Fe on August 18. In September an American territorial government was set up in New Mexico.
1847	Scott's assault on Mexico City was the second major campaign.
Apr. 17–18	Scott reached the plateau leading to Mexico City by defeating Santa Anna in battle at the pass of Cerro Gordo. Captains George B. McClellan and Robert E. Lee, later opponents in the Civil War, took part in the battle.
Sept. 8–14	American forces defeated the Mexicans at Molino de Rey and at the hill of Chapultepec and broke through into Mexico City, which they captured.
Oct. 12	Fighting ceased.

HOW THE SOUTH WAS BORN

1808	Slave importation into US became illegal.
1817	American Colonization Society founded to settle Negroes in Africa.
1820	Missouri Compromise; Maine and Missouri became states.
1822	Denmark Vesey rising in Charleston, SC.

1831	First number of William Lloyd Garrison's the *Liberator*. Nat Turner revolt in Virginia: 22 whites killed.
1831–2	Virginia convention voted against emancipation. Beginning of arguments that slavery was a "positive good."
1832	New England Antislavery Society founded by Garrison.
1832–3	Nullification controversy in South Carolina.
1833	American Antislavery Society founded.
1838	John C. Calhoun's Resolutions that Congress not to interfere with slavery passed the Senate.
1840	Fugitive Slave laws in New York and Vermont provided defense attorneys for escaped slaves.
1850	Compromise of 1850; California became a free state. Fugitive Slave Act refused fugitives the right to give evidence or to have trial by jury; New Mexico was admitted into the Union "with or without slavery," as its own constitution prescribed; slave trade in District of Washington abolished.
1852	Publication of Harriet Beecher Stowe's *Uncle Tom's Cabin*.
	Franklin Pierce (Democrat) elected over President Winfield Scott (Whig).
1854	Kansas-Nebraska Act repealed Missouri Compromise; followed by civil war in Kansas (1854–7). Kansas and Nebraska territories organised on principle of squatter sovereignty.
1856	Rise of Republican party. James Buchanan (Democrat) elected over John C. Fremont (Republican) and Millard Fillmore (American).
1857	*Dred Scott* vs. *Sandford*: Roger B. Taney's Supreme Court declared that Congress could not bar slavery from the territories.
	Buchanan failed to force the admission of Kansas to statehood under the pro-slavery Lecompton Constitution.
	Hinton Rowan Helper published *The Impending Crisis of the South*.
	Lincoln–Douglas Debates. In his contest with Abraham Lincoln for Senator from Illinois, Stephen A. Douglas argued, in his "Freeport Doctrine," that slavery cannot survive in a territory without positive supporting legislation.

1859	John Brown's raid on federal arsenal at Harpers Ferry, Virginia, hoping to start a slave rebellion in the South.
1860	Radical Southerners broke up the Democratic party by withdrawing when the Charleston convention refused to endorse their demand for a Congressional slave code.
Nov.	Abraham Lincoln (Republican) elected over Stephen A. Douglas (Northern Democrat), John C. Breckinridge (Southern Democrat), and John Bell (Constitutional Unionist.)

THE WAR BETWEEN THE STATES

1860	
Nov.	Election of Abraham Lincoln as 16th President of the US.
Dec.	Secession of South Carolina.
Feb.	Secession of six states of the Lower South: Texas, Alabama, Louisiana, Mississippi, Georgia, and Florida.
	Formation of the Confederate States of America.
1861	
Mar.	Inauguration of Abraham Lincoln as 16th President.
Apr.	Bombardment of Fort Sumter, a federal fort in Charleston harbor.
	Lincoln called up militia to suppress a civil rebellion.
Apr.–June	Secession of Upper South: Virginia, Tennessee, Arkansas, and North Carolina. Richmond became Confederate capital. In four other slave states (Delaware, Maryland, Kentucky, and Missouri) Unionist sentiments held them loyal, but civil war broke out in Missouri.
	Lincoln proclaimed blockade of the Atlantic coast from South Carolina to Florida.
July 21	First Battle of Bull Run or Manassas: Confederate victory.
1862	
Feb. 16	Gen. U.S. Grant advanced against confederate forts on the Cumberland and Tennessee Rivers, captured Forts Henry and Donelson.
Mar.	*Monitor* vs. *Merrimac*.
Mar.–July	Gen. McClellan's Peninsular campaign: Union forces attempted to seize Richmond, Va.
Apr. 7	Battle of Shiloh: Union forces under Grant and Buell defeated Johnston and Beauregard.

Apr. 26	Union forces under Farragut captured New Orleans.
June	Robert E. Lee appointed commander of Army of Northern Virginia.
	Homestead Act granted free farms of 160 acres to actual settlers.
July	Morrill Land Grant Act gave land grant to the states for agricultural and mechanical colleges; 69 were set up.
July	Pacific Railroad Act: federal subsidies (including 30 million acres) granted for a railroad from Omaha to California.
Aug. 30	Second battle of Bull Run.
Sept.	Battle of Antietam (Sharpsburg). Gen. Robert E. Lee's attempt to invade The North was halted.
Sept. 21	Lincoln announced emancipation of blacks, to be effective Jan. 1863.
Oct.	Grant was appointed Commander, Department of Tennessee.
Nov.	Burnside replaced McClellan.
Dec. 13	Lee defeated Burnside at Fredericksburg, Va.

1863

Jan.	Lincoln's Emancipation Proclamation came into force, declaring free all slaves in Confederate areas.
Feb.	National Bank Act, with a supplementary Act of 1864, established a system of banks issuing a uniform paper currency based on holdings of federal bonds.
May	Lee defeated "Fighting Joe" Hooker at Chancellorsville and advances north through Maryland into Pennsylvania.
July 1–3	Death of "Stonewall" Jackson after battle of Chancellorsville.
	Battle of Gettysburg: turning point of the War. Lee defeated by Union forces under Gen. Meade.
July 3	Surrender by Confederacy of Vicksburg on the Mississippi to Grant cut off Texas, Arkansas, and Louisiana from the rest of the Confederacy. Lee retreated into Virginia.
Nov.	3-day battle at Chattanooga: US victories at Lookout Mountain and Misssionary Ridge in Tennessee.
Dec.	Lincoln announced his "Ten Per Cent Plan" for the easy restoration of the seceded states to the Union; he would recognize any state as legal if ten per cent of the voters of 1860 declared themselves loyal to the union.

1864

Apr.   Gen. Sherman began his march through Georgia; in Sept. captured and destroyed Atlanta.

             Wilderness campaign under Grant to take Richmond.

July   Lincoln vetoed the Wade-Davis bill, containing a harsher Congressional plan for restoration of the seceded states to the Union.

Sept.   Sherman captured Atlanta.

Nov.   Abraham Lincoln (Republican) re-elected over George B. McClellan (Democrat) (212 electoral votes against 21).

             Sherman began march through Georgia from Atlanta. In December he captured Savannah.

1865

Jan. 31 The Thirteenth Amendment abolished slavery throughout the United States (ratified December 1865).

Feb.   Sherman marched through the Carolinas.

Mar.   Lincoln's second Inaugural.

9 Apr. Lee surrendered his army, the Army of Northern Virginia, to Grant at Appomattox Courthouse, Va.

14 Apr. Lincoln assassinated by John Wilkes Booth.

26 Apr. John Wilkes Booth shot in a blazing barn near Bowling Green, Va. Surrender of Johnston to Sherman and of Kirby Smith in trans-Mississippi region brought war formally to an end. President Jefferson Davis captured in Georgia in May.

Nov.   CSS *Shenandoah*, the last of the Southern blockade-runners, surrendered in Liverpool, England.

PRESIDENTS OF THE USA, 1789–1864

1789	George Washington	No party designation
1792	George Washington	No party designation
1796	John Adams	Federalist
1800	Thomas Jefferson	Democratic-Republican
1804	Thomas Jefferson	Democratic-Republican
1808	James Madison	Democratic-Republican
1812	James Madison	Democratic-Republican
1816	James Monroe	Democratic-Republican
1820	James Monroe	Democratic-Republican
1824	John Quincy Adams	Democratic-Republican
1828	Andrew Jackson	Democratic
1832	Andrew Jackson	Democratic
1836	Martin Van Buren	Democratic
1840	William H. Harrison	Whig
1844	James K. Polk	Democratic
1848	Zachary Taylor	Whig
1852	Franklin Pierce	Democratic
1856	James Buchanan	Democratic
1860	Abraham Lincoln	Republican
1864	Abraham Lincoln	Republican

POPULATION OF THE USA, 1790–1860 (in thousands)

1790	3,929
1800	5,297
1810	7,224
1820	9,618
1830	12,901
1840	17,120
1850	23,261
1860	31,513

STATES ADMITTED TO THE UNION

Order of Admission	State	Date of Admission
1	Delaware	December 7, 1787
2	Pennsylvania	December 12, 1787
3	New Jersey	December 18, 1787
4	Georgia	January 2, 1788
5	Connecticut	January 9, 1788
6	Massachusetts	February 6, 1788
7	Maryland	April 28, 1788
8	South Carolina	May 23, 1788
9	New Hampshire	June 21, 1788
10	Virginia	June 25, 1788
11	New York	July 26, 1788
12	North Carolina	November 21, 1789
13	Rhode Island	May 29, 1790
14	Vermont	March 4, 1791
15	Kentucky	June 1, 1792
16	Tennessee	June 1, 1796
17	Ohio	March 1, 1803
18	Louisiana	April 30, 1812
19	Indiana	December 11, 1816
20	Mississippi	December 10, 1817
21	Illinois	December 3, 1818
22	Alabama	December 14, 1819
23	Maine	March 15, 1820
24	Missouri	August 10, 1821
25	Arkansas	June 15, 1836
26	Michigan	January 26, 1837
27	Florida	March 3, 1845
28	Texas	December 29, 1845
29	Iowa	December 28, 1846
30	Wisconsin	May 29, 1848
31	California	September 9, 1850
32	Minnesota	May 11, 1858
33	Oregon	February 14, 1859
34	Kansas	January 29, 1861
35	West Virginia	June 30, 1833
36	Nevada	October 31, 1864
37	Nebraska	March 1, 1867
38	Colorado	August 1, 1876
39	North Dakota	November 2, 1889
40	South Dakota	November 2, 1889
41	Montana	November 8, 1889
42	Washington	November 11, 1889
43	Idaho	July 3, 1890
44	Wyoming	July 10, 1890
45	Utah	January 4, 1896
46	Oklahoma	November 16, 1901
47	New Mexico	January 6, 1912
48	Arizona	February 14, 1912
49	Alaska	January 3, 1959
50	Hawaii	August 21, 1959

Bibliographies

1 WHO SHOULD RULE AT HOME?

There are two valuable anthologies that serve as introduction to the social/ intellectual historiography of the Revolution: Jack P. Greene (ed.), *The Re-Interpretation of the American Revolution, 1763–1789* (New York, Harper and Row, 1968), and Edmund S. Morgan (ed.), *The American Revolution: Two centuries of interpretation* (Englewood Cliffs, NJ, Prentice-Hall, 1965). The most interesting of the radical anthologies are by Alfred Young (ed.), *The American Revolution: Explorations in the history of American radicalism* (DeKalb, Northern Illinois University Press, 1976), and by Erich Angermann et al., *New Wine in Old Skins: A comparative view of socio-political structures and values affecting the American Revolution* (Stuttgart, Klett, 1976).

A number of new studies have now appeared on the Loyalists, largely under the stimulus of the program for Loyalist Studies Publications under the general direction of Professor Robert East in the City University of New York. Andrew Oliver published a new edition of *The Diary of Samuel Curwen* (Cambridge, MA, Belknap Press of Harvard University Press, 1973); and other titles on the Loyalists include William H. Nelson, *The American Tory* (London, Oxford University Press, 1961); Paul H. Smith, *Loyalists and Redcoats: A study in British Revolutionary Policy* (Chapel Hill, NC, Institute of Early American History and Culture [hereafter IEAHC], 1964); Wallace Brown, *The King's Friends* (Providence, RI, Brown University Press, 1965), and his *The Good Americans: The Loyalists in the American Revolution* (New York, Morrow Paperbacks, 1969); Mary Beth Norton, *The British-Americans* (Boston, Little, Brown, 1972); Robert Calhoon, *The Loyalists in Revolutionary America 1760–81* (New York, Harcourt Brace Jovanovich, 1973), his recent collection of essays, *The Loyalist Perception, and Other Essays* (Columbia, University of South Carolina Press, 1989), and his article "The reintegration of the Loyalists and the disaffected," in Jack P. Greene (ed.), *The American Revolution: Its character and limits* (New York, New York University Press, 1978); Carol Berkin, *Jonathan Sewall: Odyssey of an American Loyalist* (New York, Columbia University Press, 1974); Bernard Bailyn, *The Ordeal of Thomas Hutchinson* (Cambridge, MA, Harvard University Press, 1974); Esmond Wright (ed.), *A Tug of Loyalties* (London, Athlone Press, 1974), and *Red White and True Blue* (New York, AMS Press, 1976); Philip Ranlet, *The New York Loyalists* (Knoxville, University of Tennessee Press, 1986); James St G. Walker, *The Black Loyalists: The search for a Promised Land in Nova Scotia and Sierra Leone 1783–1870* (New York, Dalhousie University Press, 1976); Ellen G. Wilson, *The Loyal Blacks* (New York, Putnam's, 1976); and Robert Stansbury Lambert, *South Carolina Loyalists in the American Revolution* (Columbia, University of South Carolina Press, 1987). Loyalist dilemmas have also been described with much sympathy in a number of short sketches: notably Catherine Fennelly, "Governor William Franklin of New Jersey," *William & Mary Quarterly*, 6 (1949), p. 24; and E. M. Baldwin, "Joseph Galloway", *Pennsylvania Magazine of History*, 26 (1902). A definitive reference book is Gregory Palmer (ed.), *Bibliography of Loyalist Source Material in the United States, Canada and the United Kingdom* (Westport, Conn., Meckler Books, 1982).

Recent titles of interest on the role of women are Linda K. Kerber, *Women of the Republic: Intellect and Ideology in Revolutionary America* (Chapel Hill, NC, University of North Carolina Press, 1980); Mary Beth Norton, *Liberty's Daughters: The Revolutionary experience of American women 1750–1800* (Boston, Little, Brown, 1980), and her article, "The evolution of white women's experience in early America," *American Historical Review*, 89 (1984), pp. 593–619. The *Pennsylvania Magazine of History and Biography*, 115.2 (Apr. 1991), is devoted to the theme "Women in the Revolutionary Era."

The freshest writing on the transforming radicalism of the war experience, and on its productive impact on altering a classical ideology into what became today's constitutionalism, is in two studies by Gordon S. Wood, *The Creation of the American Republic 1776–1787* (Chapel Hill, NC, University of North Carolina Press, 1969), and his *The Radicalism of the American Revolution* (New York, Knopf-Borzoi, 1991). Cf. for a more familiar left-wing view Dick Hoerder, *Crowd Action in Revolutionary Massachusetts 1765–1800* (New York, Academic Press, 1977), and two articles of Jesse Lemisch: "Jack Tar in the streets; merchant seamen in the politics of Revolutionary America," *William & Mary Quarterly*, 25 (1968), pp. 371–407, and "The American Revolution from the bottom up," in Barton J. Bernstein (ed.), *Towards a New Past: Dissenting essays in American History* (New York, Pantheon Books for Random House, 1968).

There are two valuable compendia edited in recent years by Jack P. Greene and J. R. Pole, *The Blackwell Encyclopedia of the American Revolution* (Oxford, Blackwell, 1991), and *Colonial British America: Essays in the new history of the early modern era* (Baltimore, Johns Hopkins University Press, 1984).

For a single-volume survey of the research of the last generation, see *In Search of Early America: The William and Mary Quarterly 1943–1993* (Chapel Hill, NC, IEAHC, 1993). It is a collection of 11 of the journal's most valuable articles, plus a fascinating number of postscripts by each contributor, which become pieces of self-analysis and reflection, particularly of the times and the circumstances in which they lived and wrote.

2 MAKING THE GOVERNMENT

There are several invaluable contemporary sources for the making of the Constitution. The essays of Alexander Hamilton, James Madison, and John Jay collected in *The Federalist Papers* (many editions; first published in book form in 1788), written in support of adopting the Constitution, are still an excellent analysis of the problems facing the the new nation. Details of the constitution-making period are given by some of the main protagonists in *The Papers of James Madison*, ed. William T. Hutchinson, William Rachal, Robert Rutland et al., 16 vols to date (vols I-VII, Chicago, Chicago University Press, vols VIII–, Charlottesville, Virginia University Press, 1962–); *The Papers of Alexander Hamilton*, ed. H. C. Syrett, Jacob E. Cooke, et al., 27 vols (New York, Columbia University Press, 1961–87); *The Papers of Thomas Jefferson*, ed. Julian Boyd et al., 22 vols (Princeton, NJ, Princeton University Press, 1950–); Max Farrand, *The Records of the Federal Convention of 1787*, 4 vols (New Haven, Yale University Press, 1911). See also Arthur T. Prescott, *Drafting the Federal Constitution* (Baton Rouge, Louisiana State University Press, 1941), and Irving Brant, *The Bill of Rights: Its origins and meaning* (New York, New American Library, 1967).

Studies of the Confederation and the Constitution have been greatly influenced by the outlook – one might even say the needs – of different generations of Americans. From Charles Beard's attack on the Founding Fathers in the first decades of this century to the present day, no subject in American history has been the scene of bloodier battles. An excellent review of the literature in this area is Jack P. Greene (ed.), *A Bicentennial Bookshelf: Historians analyze the Constitutional era* (Philadelphia, Friends of Independence National Historical Park, 1986). For an anthology of some of the more important articles, see Gordon S. Wood (comp.), *The Confederation and the Constitution: The critical issues* (Boston, Little, Brown, 1973). From the Bicentennial year, see two special issues of journals devoted to the Constitution: *William & Mary Quarterly*, 3rd ser., 44.3 (July 1987): *The Constitution of the United States*; and *Journal of American History*, 74.3 (Dec. 1987); *The Constitution and American Life*, reprinted as David Thelen (ed.), *The Constitution and American Life* (Ithaca, NY, Cornell University Press, 1988). Charles A. Beard's *An Economic Interpretation of*

the Constitution of the United States (New York, Macmillan, 1913; with
new introduction, 1935) has been influential for a generation or more.
See too Richard Beeman, Stephen Botein, and Edward C. Carter II (eds),
*Beyond Confederation: Origins of the Constitution and American National
Identity* (Chapel Hill, NC, University of North Carolina Press, IEAHC,
1987); Richard B. Bernstein and Kym S. Rice, *Are We to Be a Nation?
The making of the Constitution* (Cambridge, MA, Harvard University Press,
1987); Douglass Adair, *Fame and the Founding Fathers: Essays ...*, ed.
Trevor Colbourn (New York, Norton, IEAHC, 1974). Catherine Drinker
Bowen, *Miracle at Philadelphia: The Story of the Constitutional Convention, May to September, 1787* (Boston, Little, Brown, 1966) is a readable narrative of the proceedings in Philadelphia. Other studies are Jackson
Turner Main, *The Antifederalists: Critics of the Constitution, 1781–1788*
(Chapel Hill, NC, University of North Carolina Press, IEAHC, 1961),
and *Political Parties before the Constitution* (Chapel Hill, NC, University
of North Carolina Press, IEAHC, 1973); Robert E. Brown, *Charles Beard
and the Constitution: A critical analysis of "An Economic Interpretation
of the Constitution"* (Princeton, NJ, Princeton University Press, 1956);
David F. Epstein, *The Political Theory of "The Federalist"* (Chicago,
University of Chicago Press, 1984); Forrest McDonald, *Novus Ordo Seclorum: The intellectual origins of the Constitution* (Lawrence, University
Press of Kansas, 1985), and *We the People: The economic origins of the
Constitution* (Chicago, University of Chicago Press, 1958); Ronald Hoffman
and Peter J. Albert (eds), *Sovereign States in an Age of Uncertainty; Per-
spectives on the American Revolution* (Charlottesville, United States Capitol
Historical Society, University Press of Virginia, 1982); Merrill Jensen, *The
New Nation: A History of the United States during the Confederation
1781–1789* (New York, Knopf, 1950); Michael Kammen, *A Machine That
Would Go of Itself: The Constitution in American culture* (New York,
Knopf, 1986).

The two best recent introductions to the politics and ideologies of the
Grand Convention are James H. Hutson, "Riddles of the Federal Constitution Convention," *William & Mary Quarterly*, 44.3 (July 1987), pp.
411–23, and Jack N. Rakove, "The Great Compromise: ideas, interests
and the politics of constitution-making," ibid., pp. 424–57.

Recent scholarship treats both sides of the ratification argument. The
best introduction to the Federalist viewpoint remains in their own words,
edited by Benjamin F. Wright, *The Federalist* (Cambridge, MA, Harvard
University Press, 1961). Garry Wills's *Explaining America: The Federalist*
(Garden City, NY, Doubleday, 1981) provides an interpretation of what
they wrote. Biographies of Federalist writers are also helpful, among them
Jacob Ernest Cooke's *Alexander Hamilton* (New York, Scribner's, 1982);
Forrest McDonald's *Alexander Hamilton: A biography* (New York, Norton,
1979); Broadus Mitchell, *Alexander Hamilton: The national adventure
1788–1804*, 2 vols (New York, Macmillan, 1957–62); Irving Brant's *James
Madison: The nationalist*, 6 vols (Indianapolis, Bobbs-Merrill, 1948–61);

and Ralph Ketcham, *James Madison: A biography* (New York, Macmillan, 1971).

In more recent writing, three interlocking themes – sectionalism, nationalism, and ideology – can be traced. The first is treated by H. James Henderson, *Party Politics in the Continental Congress* (New York, McGraw Hill, 1974), and Joseph L. Davis, *Sectionalism in American Politics 1774–1787* (Madison, University of Wisconsin Press, 1977). Nationalist politics and maneuvers are traced in Jack N. Rakove, *The Beginnings of National Politics* (New York, Knopf, 1979); by Gordon S. Wood in *The Creation of the American Republic 1776–1787* (Chapel Hill, NC, University of North Carolina Press, 1969) and *The Radicalism of the American Revolution* (New York, Knopf, 1991); and by Jack P. Greene, *The Re-Interpretation of the American Revolution 1763–1789* (New York, Harper and Row, 1968); see also Beeman et al., *Beyond Confederation*. The ideology behind the formation of the new republic is also discussed by Wood in the two volumes mentioned above, and by a number of other historians: see, for instance, J. G. A. Pocock, *The Machiavellian Moment: Florentine political thought and the Atlantic tradition* (Princeton, NJ, Princeton University Press, 1975), and idem (ed.) *Three British Revolutions* (Princeton, NJ, Princeton University Press, 1980), particularly for J. M. Murrin, "The Great Inversion, or Court *versus* Country;" Henry F. May, *The Enlightenment in America* (New York, Oxford University Press, 1976); Donald H. Meyer, *The Democratic Enlightenment* (New York, Putnam, 1976); Ralph Ketcham, *From Colony to Country: The Revolution in American thought* (New York, Macmillan, 1975); James H. Hutson, "Country, Court and Constitution: Antifederalism and the historians," *William & Mary Quarterly*, 38 (1981), pp. 337–68; Drew R. McCoy, *The Elusive Republic: Political economy in Jeffersonian America* (Chapel Hill, NC, University of North Carolina Press, 1980); Garry Wills, *Inventing America: Jefferson's Declaration of Independence* (New York, Doubleday, 1978), and Ronald Hemowy's critique of Wills in *William & Mary Quarterly*, 26 (1979), pp. 563–623; Wills, *Explaining America: The Federalist* (New York, Doubleday, 1981); McDonald, *Novus Ordo Seclorum* and Joyce Appleby, *Capitalism and a New Social Order: A republican vision of the 1790s* (New York, New York University Press, 1984).

For John Marshall, see Leonard Baker, *John Marshall: A life in law* (New York, Macmillan, 1974); and Herbert A. Johnson et al. (eds), *The Papers of John Marshall*, 5 vols to date (Chapel Hill, NC, University of North Carolina Press, IEAHC, 1974–). And for Washington, see bibliography to ch. 3, below.

3   FIRST IN WAR, FIRST IN PEACE

For one who is not customarily regarded as an author, Washington left an immense body of writings: John C. Fitzpatrick collected 39 volumes for the Bicentennial Commission in 1931 (Washington DC, US Government Printing Office, 1931–44), and he also edited, in 4 volumes, Washington's very unrevealing *Diaries* (Washington DC, US Government Printing Office, 1925). The University of Virginia is publishing a new edition of *The Papers of George Washington* under the general editorship of Donald Jackson (6 vols for the Diaries), and of William Abbot and Dorothy Twohig (for the Colonial Series, for the Revolutionary War Series, and for the presidency: 70 or more volumes planned). Saxe Commins, *Basic Writings of George Washington* (New York, Random House, 1948) and Saul Padover, *The Washington Papers* (New York, Harper's, 1954) have each produced single-volume collections. Biographies of Washington are legion, from the early hagiography of "Parson" Mason Weems (1800), of John Marshall (1805–7), and of Washington Irving (1855), down to the more critical assessments of the last 40 years. The best, the most detailed, but unhappily an uncompleted study, is Douglas Southall Freeman's *George Washington: A biography*, 6 vols (New York, Scribner's, 1948–53), completed by a seventh volume by John A. Carroll and Mary Wells Ashworth (New York, Scribner's, 1957). All 7 volumes have been abridged by Richard Harwell (New York, Scribner's, 1970). Freeman's volumes are, by any measurement, the best, lovingly detailed, source. There is also a splendid study by James T. Flexner, *George Washington, A Biography*, 4 vols (Boston, Little, Brown, 1965–72), which is a major contribution to American biography, and especially of interest for his discussion of Washington's views on slavery in vol. IV.

Despite the massive resources, George Washington remains a hard man to know. His spare, matter-of-fact, busineeslike diary entries present problems for biographers and others interested in Washington's life and times. The difficulty is not the paucity of his writings but how to master the sheer mass of information – concerning, among other things, army administration, military strategy and tactics, civil–military relations, fashioning the presidency, foreign affairs, and domestic politics – and still keep in focus the man for whom public service was a diversion from the agricultural pursuits of his Mount Vernon community and other wide-ranging interests. There are good recent single-volume studies: J. R. Alden, *George Washington: A biography* (Baton Rouge, Louisiana State University Press, 1984); Ralph Ketcham, *Presidents Above Party: The first American presidency* (Chapel Hill, NC, University of North Carolina Press, 1984); Forrest McDonald, *The Presidency of George Washington* (New York, Norton, 1974); Barry Schwartz, *George Washington: The making of an American symbol* (New York, Free Press, 1987); James M. Smith (ed.), *Washington: A profile* (New York, Hill and Wang, 1969); Esmond Wright, *Washington and the American Revolution* (Harmondsworth, Penguin Books, 1972); John Ferling, *The First Man: A life of George Washington* (Knoxville, University of Tennessee Press, 1988); and Paul Longmore, *The Invention of George Washington* (Berkeley, University of California Press, 1988).

For Washington as a modern-day Cincinnatus, see Garry Wills's 1-volume *Cincinnatus: George Washington and the Enlightenment* (New York, Doubleday, 1984); and for a readable portrait of the man echoing the Roman motif, Marcus Cunliffe, *George Washington, Man and Monument* (London, Collins, 1959). For a survey of his two terms as President, the most incisive recent survey is Forrest McDonald, *The Presidency of George Washington* (New York, Norton, 1974). For an admirable essay review of recent Washington scholarship, see Don Higginbotham in *Pennsylvania Magazine of History and Biography*, 114.3 (July 1990).

4 FEDERALISM, HIGH, LOW AND DEVIOUS

For the origins of the American party system, see Joseph Charles, *The Origins of the American Party System* (New York, Harper Torchbooks, 1956); William N. Chambers, *Political Parties in the New Nation: The American experience 1776–1809* (New York, Oxford University Press, 1963); and Ralph Ketcham, *Presidents above Party* (Chapel Hill, NC, IEAHC, 1984). For the Federalists in power, see John C. Miller, *The Federalist Era* (New York, Harper, 1960); David Hackett Fischer, *The Revolution of American Conservatism* (New York, Harper Torchbooks, 1965); Manning Dauer, *The Adams Federalists* (Baltimore, Johns Hopkins University Press, 1953). For the rise of the Democratic Republicans, see Noble E. Cunningham Jr, *The Jeffersonian Republicans*, vol. I, *The Formation of Party Organization 1789–1801* (Chapel Hill, NC, University of North Carolina Press, 1957).

For John Adams, see *The Diary and Autobiography of John Adams*, ed. L. H. Butterfield, 4 vols (Cambridge, MA, Harvard University Press, 1961) and *The Adams Family Correspondence*, ed. L. H. Butterfield (Cambridge, MA, Harvard University Press, 1961); Lester Cappon (ed.), *The Adams-Jefferson Letters* (Chapel Hill, NC, IEAHC, 1959); Peter Shaw, *The Character of John Adams* (Chapel Hill, NC, IEAHC, 1976); Page Smith, *John Adams*, 2 vols (New York, Doubleday, 1962); Zoltan Haraszti, *John Adams and the Prophets of Progress* (Cambridge, MA, Harvard University Press, 1952; and Stephen G. Kurtz, *The Presidency of John Adams* (Philadelphia, University of Pennsylvania Press, 1957).

There are many books on, and biographies of, both Jefferson and Hamilton; and many varying assessments of each man. For Jefferson, see the bibliography to chapter 5, below. The best studies of Hamilton are by Broadus Mitchell, *Alexander Hamilton: The national adventure 1788–1804* (New York, Macmillan, 1962), and by Jacob E. Cooke, *Alexander Hamilton* (New York, Scribner's, 1982); see also Cooke (ed.), *Alexander Hamilton: A profile* (New York, Hill and Wang, 1967); Gerald Stourzh, *Alexander Hamilton and the Idea of Republican Government* (Stanford, Stanford University Press, 1970); and Forrest McDonald, *Alexander Hamilton: A biography* (New York, Norton, 1979). In *The Conqueror* (New York,

1902), Gertrude Atherton wrote a fictionalized biography of Hamilton which was based on considerable research. On Hamilton's legacy to the US, see Cecilia M. Kenyon, "Alexander Hamilton: Rousseau of the Right," *Political Science Quarterly*, 73.2 (June 1958), pp. 161–78, and Nathan Schachner, "The legacy of Hamilton," *William & Mary Quarterly*, 3rd ser., 3 (Dec. 1946), pp. 720–25. For Hamilton's own writings, see *The Papers of Alexander Hamilton*, ed. H. C. Syrett and Jacob Cooke, 27 vols (New York, Columbia University Press, 1961–87).

For the ambitious, intelligent and ultra-cynical Aaron Burr, see Milton Lomask, *Aaron Burr: The years from Princeton to Vice-President 1756–1805* (New York, Farrar, Straus and Giroux, 1979); and Mary-Jo Kline and Joanne Wood Ryan (eds), *Political Correspondence and Public Papers of Aaron Burr*, 2 vols (Princeton, NJ, Princeton University Press, 1983).

5 THE VIRGINIA DYNASTY

The most detailed account of Jefferson's long life (1743–1826) is in the 6-volume biography by Dumas Malone, with the general title *Jefferson and his Times*, all published by Little, Brown in Boston: *Jefferson the Virginian* (1948); *Jefferson and the Rights of Man* (1951); *Jefferson and the Ordeal of Liberty* (1961); *Jefferson the President: The first term* (1970); *Jefferson the President: The second term* (1974); and *Jefferson, The Sage of Monticello* (1981). It was fortunate for Dumas Malone that he brought his own remarkable longevity, and his own wide experience, to his daunting self-chosen task of being Mr Jefferson's chronicler. As with Douglas Southall Freeman's biography of Washington, Malone's *Jefferson* is an archive, telling the story chronologically and meticulously; for him, biography is history made personal. His 6 volumes – his "journey with Mr Jefferson" he called it – are probably the best and certainly the most sympathetic biography of a President ever written (cf. Merrill D. Peterson, "Dumas Malone": An appreciation," *William & Mary Quarterly*, 45.2 (Apr. 1988), pp. 237–52. For a recent study, see Peter S. Onuf, "The scholar's Jefferson," ibid., 50.4 (Oct. 1993), pp. 671–99.

There are also many good single-volume studies of Jefferson, conspicuously so Merrill D. Peterson, *Thomas Jefferson and the New Nation* (Charlottesville, University of Virginia Press, 1968); the same author's survey of what history made of Jefferson after his death, *The Jefferson Image in the American Mind* (New York, Oxford University Press, 1960); and his *Thomas Jefferson: A profile* (New York, Hill and Wang, 1967. Other important studies of Jefferson are Daniel Boorstin's *The Lost World of Thomas Jefferson* (New York, Holt, 1948); Noble Cunningham, *In Pursuit of Reason: The life of Thomas Jefferson* (Baton Rouge, Louisiana State University Press, 1987); Adrienne Koch, *The Philosophy of Thomas Jefferson* (New York, Columbia University Press, 1943); and her *Jefferson and Madison: The great collaboration* (New York, Knopf, 1950). Marie

Kimball's death prevented the completion of her biography, but her 3 volumes are very readable: *Jefferson: The road to glory, 1743 to 1776* (New York, Coward-McCann, 1943); *Jefferson: War and Peace, 1776 to 1784* (New York, Coward-McCann, 1947); *Jefferson: The scene of Europe 1784–1789* (New York, Coward-McCann, 1950). Buttressing them all are *The Papers of Thomas Jefferson*, ed. Julian Boyd et al. (Princeton, NJ, Princeton University Press, 1950–), planned as a 50-volume collection of all the papers and letters Jefferson wrote – and received.

For the study of the rise of the Jeffersonian Democratic Republicans, see Lance Banning, *The Jeffersonian Persuasion: Evolution of a party ideology* (London, Cornell University Press, 1978); Noble E. Cunningham Jr, *The Jeffersonian Republicans*, 2 vols (Chapel Hill, NC, University of North Carolina Press, 1957 and 1963); George Dangerfield, *The Era of Good Feelings* (New York, Harcourt Brace, 1952); and Joseph Charles, *The Origins of the American Party System* (New York, Harper Torchbooks, 1956). A challenge to all students of Mr Jefferson is Joyce Appleby, *Capitalism and a New Social Order: the Republican Vision of the 1790s* (New York, New York University Press, 1984). Cf. Allan Kulikoff, "A transition to capitalism in rural America," *William & Mary Quarterly*, 46.1 (Jan. 1989), pp. 120–44.

For Madison, the standard life is by Irving Brant, in 6 volumes: *James Madison* (Indianapolis, Bobbs-Merrill, 1948–61), usefully condensed by the same author in his excellent and lively single-volume *Life* (Indianapolis, Bobbs-Merrill, 1970). Compare also Koch, *Jefferson and Madison: The great collaboration*, and Ralph Ketcham's useful and factual 1-volume *James Madison: A biography* (New York, Macmillan, 1971). *The Papers of James Madison*, vols I–VII, ed. William T. Hutchinson and William Rachal, et al. since 1962, were published by the University of Chicago Press, Chicago; from vol. VIII onwards, ed. Robert Rutland and William Pachal, by the University of Virginia Press, Charlottesville. Cf. also Robert Rutland, *James Madison, the Founding Father* (New York, Collier Macmillan, 1987), and Jack N. Rakove, *James Madison and the Creation of the American Republic* (Glenview, IL, Scott Foresman, 1990).

For the War of 1812, Reginald Horsman, *The Causes of the War of 1812* (Philadelphia, University of Philadelphia Press, 1962) is wide-ranging and balanced, and Harry L. Coles, *The War of 1812* (Chicago, University of Chicago Press, 1965), is a clear outline. The best recent study is J. C. A. Stagg, *Mr Madison's War: Politics, diplomacy and warfare in the early American republic 1783–1830* (Princeton, NJ, Princeton University Press, 1983), especially for its first two chapters. See also R. David Edmunds, *Tecumseh and the Quest for Indian Leadership* (Boston, Little, Brown, 1984). For the variety behind its "causes," see Bradford Perkins (ed.) *The Causes of the War of 1812: National honor or national interest?* (New York, Holt, Rinehart and Winston 1962). Still the best summary of the War Hawks is Julius W. Pratt, *The Expansionists of 1812* (New York, Macmillan, 1925); but cf. Robert V. Remini, *Henry Clay, Statesman for the Union.* (New York, Norton, 1992). There are two "popular" and highly readable presentations; Walter Lord, *The Dawn's Early Light* (London, Hamish Hamilton, 1972), and C. S. Forester, *The Naval War of 1812* (London, Landsborough, 1952).

For Monroe see Harry Ammon, *James Monroe: The quest for national identity* (Charlottesville, University of Virginia Press, 1989); and idem, *James Monroe, a Bibliography* (Meckler Books, Westport, Conn., 1991). The still classic study of the Monroe Doctrine is that by Dexter Perkins, *The Monroe Doctrine 1823–26* (Cambridge, MA, Harvard University Press, 1927), supplemented by his son Bradford Perkins's trilogy on Anglo-American relations, *The First Rapprochement* (Berkeley, University of California Press, 1955), *Prologue to War* (Berkeley, University of California Press, 1961), and notably *Castlereagh and Adams: England and the United States 1812–1823* (Berkeley, University of California Press, 1964). Cf. also Samuel Flagg Bemis, *John Quincy Adams and the Foundations of American Foreign Policy* (New York, Knopf, 1949).

6 JACKSONIAN DEMOCRACY

There are three good general surveys of the Jackson years: Marcus Cunliffe, *The Nation Takes Shape: 1797–1837* (Chicago, University of Chicago Press, 1959); Glyndon G. Van Deusen, *The Jacksonian Era 1828–1848* (New York, Harper Collins, 1959), and Edward Pessen, *Jacksonian America: Society, personality and politics*, rev. edn (Homewood, IL, Dorsey Press, 1979); the latter has a valuable 40-page bibliographical essay assessing recent writing, including articles. There are also a number of good interpretative studies of individuals and issues: Marvin Meyers, *The Jacksonian Persuasion, Politics and Belief* (Stanford, Stanford University Press, 1957); Lee Benson, *The Concept of Jacksonian Democracy: New York as a test case* (Princeton, NJ, Princeton University Press, 1961). John W. Ward analyzes the popular conceptions of *Andrew Jackson: Symbol for an age* (New York, Cambridge, Cambridge University Press, 1955); and Douglas T. Miller, in *Jacksonian Aristocracy: Class and democracy in New York, 1830–1860* (New York, Oxford University Press, 1967), argues that the gap between rich and poor was widening during the period. Walter Hugins focuses on New York City in discussing *Jacksonian Democracy and the Working Class* (Stanford, Stanford University Press, 1960); and Richard P. McCormick analyzes and emphasizes the importance of the new party machinery in *The Second American Party System: Party formation in the Jacksonian era* (Chapel Hill, NC, University of North Carolina Press, 1966).

There are three major in-depth and challenging analyses, however. One is A. J. Schlesinger, Jr, *The Age of Jackson* (Boston, Little, Brown, 1945), highly controversial, but valuable in its urban and radical emphasis, and seeing Jacksonian democracy "as a problem not of sections but of classes."

Schlesinger sees Jacksonian Democracy as a movement "to control the power of the capitalistic groups, mainly Eastern, for the benefit of non-capitalist groups, farmers and laboring men, East, West and South." Schlesinger traced the movement to the economic hardships of the 1820s, and he saw the East and the working men as playing the crucial roles in the Jacksonian coalition. The second basic study is Bray Hammond's brilliant *Banks and Politics in America from the Revolution to the Civil War* (Princeton, NJ, Princeton University Press, 1957). The author, a one-time member of the Federal Reserve Board, differed from Schlesinger, and insisted that the real animus of Jacksonian Democracy was not against business, but against the exclusion of new entrepreneurs from business opportunities. Third, and not least, is Charles Sellers, *The Market Revolution: Jacksonian America 1815–1846* (New York, Oxford University Press, 1990) tracing the transformation of an economy based on family subsistence into one geared for the marketplace. As Harry Watson had done earlier, in his *Liberty and Power: The politics of Jacksonian America* (New York, Noonday Press, 1990), Sellers demonstrates how central was the market revolution to the Jacksonian issues, especially to the Bank, and Western expansion.

For Jackson the man, Robert V. Remini's *Life of Andrew Jackson* (New York, Harper, 1988) is a 1-volume summary of the author's 3-volume biography, *Andrew Jackson* (New York, 1981). It is the best account of Jackson's determination to remain in public life after his defeat in the 1824 presidential election, and of his conviction that he could best protect and perpetuate American liberty. In his lectures at Louisiana State University in 1984, published as *The Legacy of Andrew Jackson* (Baton Rouge, Louisiana State University Press, 1988), Remini dealt with some controversial issues, including slavery and the removal of the Indians. A penetrating psychological study is James Curtis's *Andrew Jackson and the Search for Vindication* (Boston, Little, Brown, 1966): he sees a man prompt to see all differences as personal challenges, and ultra-sensitive to slights. With these should be compared Leonard White *The Jacksonians: A study in administrative history 1829–1861* (New York, Macmillan, 1966). Cf. T. P. Abernethy's hostile views in "Andrew Jackson and the rise of Southwestern Democracy," *American Historical Review*, 33 (Oct. 1927), pp. 64–77; *From Frontier to Plantation in Tennessee: A study in frontier democracy* (Chapel Hill, NC, University of North Carolina, 1932); and "Andrew Jackson," *Dictionary of American Biography* (New York, Macmillan, 1981), vol. IX, pp. 526–34. Abernethy's view was that, in the Jackson years, democracy was never applied in politics, but that it was applied in things of the intellect. The uncultured frontier accepted political, but repudiated intellectual, leadership, and made one man's opinion as good as that of any other: "Our civilization has been coarsened and cheapened as a result" (p. 363). See also John Ashworth, The Jacksonian as Leveler", *Journal of American Studies*, 14.3 (1980), pp. 407–22.

There are valuable biographies: Charles M. Wiltse, *John C. Calhoun*, 3 vols (Indianapolis, Bobbs-Merrill, 1951); William N. Chambers, *Old Bullion Benton: Senator from the New West* (Atlantic Monthly Press, 1956); Thomas P. Govan, *Nicholas Biddle: Nationalist and Public Banker* (Chicago, University of Chicago Press, 1959); Robert V. Remini, *Henry Clay, Statesman of the Union* (New York, Norton, 1991); and Glyndon G. Van Deusen, *Thurlow Weed, Wizard of the Lobby* (Boston, Little, Brown, 1947). A first-hand impression of Martin Van Buren can be gained from his *Autobiography* (published in the Annual Report of the American Historical Association, 1918).

The analyses of Jacksonian America by European observers are illuminating. Here the classic is Alexis de Tocqueville, *Democracy in America*, 2 vols (1835–40); but also fascinating are Michael Chevalier, *Society, Manners and Politics in the United States* (1839); Francis J. Grund, *Aristocracy in America* (1839); Harriet Martineau, *Society in America* (1837); and Frances Trollope, *Domestic Manners of the Americans* (1832).

For Manifest Destiny, see A. K. Weinberg, *Manifest Destiny* (Baltimore, Johns Hopkins University Press, 1935); James K. Polk, *Diary of a President 1845–49*, ed. Allan Nevins (London, Longmans, Green, 1952); Charles A. McCoy, *Polk and the Presidency* (Austin, Texas, Haskell, 1960). For the Mexican War, a good survey of the variety of views is in the anthology of Ramon Eduardo Ruiz (ed.), *The Mexican War – Was It Manifest Destiny?* (New York, Holt, 1963); for some good recent studies see Otis Singletary, *The Mexican War* (Chicago, University Press of Chicago, 1960); John S. D. Eisenhower, *So Far from God: The US War with Mexico* (New York, Random House, 1989) and – especially for the popular enthusiasm for the war – Robert W. Johannsen, *To the Halls of the Montezumes and the War with Mexico in the American Imagination* (New York Oxford University Press, 1985). For racialism, see Reginald Horsman, *Race and Manifest Destiny: The Origins of American racial Anglo-Saxonism* (Cambridge, MA, Harvard University Press, 1981); and Marquis James, *The Raven*, a biography of Sam Houston (1962; Austin, University of Texas Press, 1988).

7 THOSE WHO DID NOT BELONG

One of the best guides to the writers of the 1840s and 1850s is Van Wyck Brooks, *The World of Washington Irving*, the cornerstone volume in his epic history of the literature of the US (New York, Dutton, 1944). Compare Carl Van Doren (ed.), *The Cambridge History of American Literature* (London, Cambridge University Press, 1945, and other editions), and, even more valuable, James D. Hart, *The Oxford Companion to American Literature* (New York, Oxford University Press, 1983, 5 edn), a book that took the author (and, as he admits, his family) 45 years to write.

On the utopias, see Mark Holloway, *Heavens On Earth: Utopian communities in America 1680–1880* (New York, Library Publishers, 1951); Arthur Bestor, *Backwoods Utopias* (Philadelphia, University of Pennsylvania Press, 1951); Charles Nordhoff, *The Communistic Societies of the United States* (first published 1875; repr. London, Constable, 1966). For the story of the Mormons, Fawn Brodie's *No Man Knows My History* (London, Eyre and Spottiswoode, 1975) is a shrewd and ironical biography of Joseph Smith; and Stanley Hirshson, *The Lion of the Lord: A biography of the Mormon leader Brigham Young* (London, Dent, 1971), is a vivid, ruthless and bitter portrait. For a corrective see the lifelike sketch of the Mormon leader in Sir Richard Burton's *The City of the Saints*, ed. Fawn Brodie (London, Eyre and Spottiswoode, 1968), recounting the visit of the explorer to Utah in 1860, and his intelligent and sympathetic appraisal of their curious experiences in a wilderness of rock and salt, which they reclaimed, transformed and dedicated to the God they found so strangely.

8 WAS DESTINY MANIFEST? HOW THE WEST WAS WON

The opening up of the West was the work of a succession of explorers with diverse interests – trade and profit, botany and ornithology, geology, curiosity, and even, with Whitman and some of his colleagues, religion – and of military pathfinders, who mapped and described most of the land, culminating with John Wesley Powell's hazardous and comfortless passage along the Colorado River. They were more often illiterate than scholarly. It was, indeed, "respectable" explorers like Pike and Long who created the image of the southwestern "Great American Desert," while John Colter's "Hell" was regarded as a "tall story" until later venturers investigated the Yellowstone region with scientific precision, and found that it did indeed bubble and spout. Bernard De Voto's *Journals of Lewis and Clark* (Boston, Houghton Mufflin, 1953) is the only single-volume edition of the pioneering records of the explorers. Fremont's career has been amply and sympathetically treated by Allan Nevins in his *Frémont: Pathmaker of the West* (New York, Longmans, Green, 1955). For a more recent assessment, see Henry Savage, *Discovering America 1700–1875* (London, Harper and Row, 1980).

For the Indians, the basic handbooks are Harold E. Driver, *Indians of North America* (Chicago, University of Chicago Press, 1961), and the massive detail of the 20-volume collection (gen. ed., William C. Sturtevant), *Handbook of North American Indians* (Smithsonian Institution, Washington, 1979–). John Collier, *The Indians of the Americas* (New York, Mentor Books, 1956), is ultra-sympathetic, written by the Superintendent of the Bureau of Indian Affairs under the New Deal. See also Clark Wissler, *Indians of the United States* (New York, Doubleday, rev. edn, 1966); Roy Harvey Pearce, *The Savages of America* (Baltimore, Johns Hopkins University Press, rev. edn, 1963); and Angie Debo's readable but scholarly

History of the Indians of the United States (Norman, University of Oklahoma Press, 1970) and *And Still the Waters Run* (Princeton, NJ, Princeton University Press, 1940). For a vivid picture of those who led a long, slow and desperate struggle against dispossession and destruction, the Indian leaders, see Alvin M. Josephy, Jr, *The Patriot Chiefs* (New York, Viking Press, 1961) (Hiawatha, King Philip, Pontiac, Tecumseh, Black Hawk, Keokuk, Osceula, Crazy Horse, and Chief Joseph). For the Indian removal, see Ronald N. Satz, *American Indian Policy in the Jacksonian Era* (Lincoln, Neb., University of Nebraska Press, 1975), and for a critical and controversial view, see Michael Paul Rogin, *Fathers and Children: Andrew Jackson and the subjugation of the American Indian* (New York, Transaction Publishers, 1975), and – similarly wide-ranging – Robert V. Remini, *The Legacy of Andrew Jackson: Essays on democracy, Indian removal and slavery* (Baton Rouge, Louisiana State University Press, 1988).

The most vivid picture of the mountain men is in Dale Morgan, *Jedediah Smith and the Opening of the West* (Indianapolis, Bobbs-Merrill, 1953). For the Far West and the frontier, see R. H. Lamar, *The Far South West 1846–1912*, Yale Western Americana series, 12 (New Haven and London, Yale University Press, 1966); "Frederick Jackson Turner", in Marcus Cunliffe and Robin W. E. Winks (eds) *Pastmasters: Some essays on American historians*, pp. 74–109) (New York, Harper and Row, 1969); Frederick Herk, *History of the Westward Movement* (New York, Knopf/ Toronto, Random House, 1978); Francis S. Philbrick, *The Rise of the West 1754–1830*, in The New American Nation series, ed. Henry Steele Commager and Richard B. Morris (New York, Harper and Row, 1965); David M. Potter, *People of Plenty* (Chicago, University of Chicago Press, 1954); F. J. Turner, *The Frontier in American History* (New York, Henry Holt, 1921, and many other editions). See also P. A. M. Taylor, *Expectations Westward: The Mormons and the emigration of their British converts in the nineteenth century* (Edinburgh, Edinburgh University Press, 1965). Norman A. Graebner, *Empire on the Pacific: A study of American continental expansion* (1955), sees mercantile pressures as more important than a sense of manifest destiny.

For the 49-ers, see George R. Stewart, *Committee of Vigilance: Revolution in San Francisco 1851* (Boston, Little, Brown, 1964), and Oscar Lewis, *Sutter's Fort: Gateway to the gold fields* (Englewood Cliffs, NJ, Prentice-Hall, 1966)

In fiction, A. B. Guthrie's three novels – *The Big Sky* (New York, William Sloane, 1947), *The Way West* (New York, William Sloane, 1949), and *These Thousand Hills* (New York, Houghton, 1956), are a superb introduction to the world of the mountain and the cattle men, to life on the Oregon Trail, and to the landscapes of the High Tetons.) "Buffalo Bill" Cody owed much to his writing up by "Ned Buntline." Cody had been a scout – a killer of buffalo, for the US Army and for the workers on the Union Pacific Railroad – a guide, and a rancher before he launched his open-air Wild West show. "Buntline," whose real name was E. Z. C.

Judson, a Philadelphia legal apprentice who ran away to sea, was less orthodox: a turbulent midshipman in the US Navy (resigned), he filled his little leisure by writing (often true and personal) adventure stories and cheap fiction. In 1846 he was lynched in Nashville, Tennessee, while being tried for the murder of a husband with whose wife he was involved, only to be cut down just in time to recover to stand trial but to fail to be indicted. He founded *Ned Buntline's Own* in New York and made it the organ of a rowdy, jingoist, nativist patriotism. He became a founder of the Know-Nothing party, led a mob in the Astor Place Riot in New York City 1840, and another in a riot in St Louis in 1852. In 1862 he enlisted in the 1st New York Mounted Rifles, but was dishonorably discharged in 1864. This did not prevent him describing himself as "Chief of Indian Scouts" and being known thereafter as Colonel Judson. It was as such that in 1869 he met Cody. Cody was thus a man after "Buntline's" own heart, and certainly "Buntline" made Cody the hero of many novels – in all, he is estimated to have written over 400. He persuaded Cody to appear on stage in 1872 in his *The Scouts of the Plains*.

9 THE OLD SOUTH: SLAVERY AND SECESH

The ante-bellum South is probably the best-tilled field in American historical writing. For pictures of the South, and its contrast with the North, see William R. Taylor, *Cavalier and Yankee: The Old South and American national character* (New York, Braziller, 1961; Anchor Books, 1963), and W. J. Cash, *The Mind of the South* (New York, Knopf, Borzoi Books, 1941) – dated, but still valuable. As a South Carolinian turned North Carolinian, Cash wrote as an insider, warm but frank; his death by suicide shortly after publishing his book, and shortly after his marriage, deprived the New South of a distinguished and sympathetic observer of the Old. The militancy that he saw as the product of a frontier agricultural area was brutalized, he held, by the presence of slavery; the Southern aristos were products of "a backcountry grown prosperous;" and the idea of the South was mainly the result of conflict with the Yankee. Among other older sympathetic surveys are Clement Eaton, *The Growth of Southern Civilization 1790–1860* (New York, Harper and Row, 1961), his *History of the Old South* (New York, Macmillan, 1949), and his *History of the Confederacy* (New York, Macmillan, 1954), in which he denies that Southern culture was a product of a small aristocratic elite; it was, he contends, created by all classes of Southern society. The tragedy of the South, in his view, was that it failed to follow the Jacksonian path toward nationalism, but followed, instead, its sectional leaders down the road to secession. It was guilty of "ruinous provincialism and overweening pride;" it was over-romantic and uncritical. Eaton's views are supported by Frank L. Owsley, *Plain Folk of the Old South* (Baton Rouge, Louisiana State University Press 1949). Owsley, himself a Southern agrarian, refused to accept the traditional view of the South as a land of three classes (the planter aristocrat, the poor white, and the slaves), and reinterpreted Southern society on the basis of the preponderant influence of the common folk. Landowning farmers and not plantation owners or poor whites, formed the majority in the Old South. Similarly supportive is Fletcher M. Green, "*Democracy in the Old South*," *Journal of Southern History* (1946). Equally sympathetic to the South are Charles S. Sydnor, *The Development of Southern Sectionalism 1819–1848* (Baton Rouge, Louisiana State University Press, 1948), and Avery Craven, *The Growth of Southern Nationalism 1848–1861* (Baton Rouge, Louisiana State University Press, 1953). Bruce Collins, *White Society in the Ante Bellum South* (London, Longman, 1985), while sharply different, cool and alien in tone, is an attractively-written study.

For pre-World War II students of the Old South, it was not a "section" but a nation, held together by sentiment more than interest, based on what Robert S. Cotterill called a "consciousness of kind" – see his *The Old South* (Glendale, CA, Arthur H. Clark, 1936), p. 143. A very much more detached study of racial attitudes is that of another Southerner, C. Vann Woodward, *American Counterpoint: Slavery and racism in the North-South dialogue* (Boston, Little, Brown, 1971); his *The Burden of Southern History* (Baton Rouge, Louisiana State University Press, 1960) is sophisticated, reflective – and worrying.

Other aspects of ante-bellum culture are probed by Rollin G. Osterweis, *Romanticism and Nationalism in the Old South* (New Haven, Yale University Press, 1949) who, to use Mark Twain's phrase, argues that Southerners read too much of the cloying and saccharine Sir Walter Scott. The "cult of chivalry" which grew out of this literary preoccupation was, according to Osterweis, fully as important in giving color and tone to the Old South as was its Negro slavery or its agrarian economy. T. Harry Williams, *Romance and Realism in Southern Politics* (Athens, University of Georgia Press, 1961) echoed this theme. John Hope Franklin, a leading black historian, in his *The Militant South 1800–1861* (Cambridge, MA, Harvard University Press, 1956), had none of these preoccupations; he searched for the roots of the martial spirit which marked Southern society, noticeable in a glorification of war, in the filibustering expeditions against Latin American neighbors, and in the membership of such organizations as the Knights of the Golden Circle. Franklin sees the roots of this tradition in the Southerner's long career as a frontiersman and Indian fighter, in a social system where personal violence was freely resorted to and the *code duello* commonly accepted, and in the organization and discipline needed to maintain the institution of slavery. As a corrective to this ugly portrait, if on a more down-to-the-good-earth level, are studies of the diversities and realities of the lives and homelands of individual planters, as in James B. Seller's *Slavery in Alabama* (Tuscaloosa, University of Alabama Press, 1950). Weymouth T. Jordan's study of *Hugh Davis and His Alabama Plantation* (Tuscaloosa, University of Alabama Press, 1948) reveals an untypical planter; he was dedicated not only to making a successful money crop (cotton), but also sought to make his establishment self-sustaining by diversification into agriculture and livestock raising; and he kept careful account of his techniques and plantation management. In contrast, Carol Bleser (ed.), *Secret and Sacred: The Diaries of James Henry Hammond, a Southern Slaveholder* (Oxford, Oxford University Press, 1989) provides a self-portrait of a narcissistic and sexually debauched plantation owner. Avery Craven's *Edmund Ruffin, Southerner* (Baton Rouge, Louisiana State University Press, 1966) is a portrait of a much more attractive, if also tragic, figure.

On slavery, the South's "peculiar institution," Ulrich B. Phillips, *Life and Labor in the Old South* (1918, repr. Baton Rouge, Louisiana State University Press, 1967) presents a highly readable, elegant, carefully re-searched but "unreconstructed," and now unfashionable view. In essence, he saw the plantation as a training school for savages. With a labor force of "inert and backward people," the role of the planters was "benevolent in intent and on the whole beneficial in effect;" but by the 1850s, he held, it was ceasing to be profitable. Broadly in agreement are F. L. Olmsted, *The Old South*, first written in 1861 after his tour, republished in 1953, ed. Arthur M. Schlesinger (New York, Knopf); Hinton B. Helper's *The Impending Crisis of the South: How to meet it* (1860); and J. E. Cairnes, *The Slave Power: Its character, career and probable designs* (1862; repr. New York, Harper and Row, 1969). The first rebuttal of Phillips came from Kenneth M. Stampp's *The Peculiar Institution: Slavery in the Ante-Bellum South* (New York, Knopf, 1956), the first of the major post-World War II studies of the institution. He writes a generation (and a world war) later than Phillips. Stampp shows distaste for the institution and for the people who maintained it; he sees the slave system as extremely harsh for the slave and as profitable for the master. In Stampp's view, slavery was a compound of equal parts of selfish paternalism and naked exploita-tion. The institution should be seen through the eyes of the slave as well as through the eyes of the master. See also his article, "Rebels and Sambos: The search for the Negro's personality in slavery," *Journal of Southern History*, 37, (Aug. 1971), pp. 367–92. Stanley Elkins, *Slavery: A Problem in American institutional and intellectual life* (Chicago, University of Chicago Press, 1959), was one of the first attempts to describe (and to penetrate the closed world of) the personality of the slaves. He found the typical slave to be a "Sambo" – "docile and irresponsible, loyal but lazy, humble but chronically given to lying and stealing ... full of infantile silliness," with a "childlike attachment" to his master. Moreover – the point that caught attention – he saw an analogy between the slave plantation and the Nazi concentration camp. Compare the variety of essays in Ann J. Lane (ed.), *The Debate Over Slavery: Stanley Elkins and His Critics* (Urbana, Uni-versity of Illinois Press, 1971), notably Genovese's condemnation of the inadequacy of psychological models in contrast to more orthodox historical research; see also John W. Blassingame, *The Slave Community: Plantation life in the ante-bellum South* (New York, Oxford University Press, 1972); and as evidence that urban life and industry were not incompatible with slavery, note Richard Wade, *Slavery in the Cities* (New York, Oxford University Press, 1964); Robert S. Starobin, *Industrial Slavery in the Old South* (New York, Oxford University Press, 1970); and Ronald T. Takaki, *A Pro-Slavery Crusade: The agitation to re-open the America slave trade* (New York, Free Press, 1971).

Obviously, few slaves left any record, but Frederick Douglass, *Life and Times* (1881), did so: a slave born in Maryland who became an abolitionist lecturer, talked to Lincoln, and later, as elder statesman ("Uncle Tom"?), held office under Presidents Grant, Hayes, and Garfield. He blames all on the South, which came, he says, to hate everything with the prefix "free" – "free soil, free states, free territories, free schools, free speech and freedom generally." There are biographies of him by Philip Foner, *Frederick Douglass* (New York, Citadel Press, 1964), and by William McFeely, *Frederick Douglass (New York, Norton, 1991). A standard history of the black is John Hope Franklin, From Slavery to Freedom* (New York, Knopf, 1947); and the best assessment of the slave traffic is in Philip Curtin, *The African Slave Trade: A census* (Madison, University of Wisconsin Press, 1969). From Professor Curtin's Department of African Studies at the University of Wisconsin and in tribute to him is Paul Lovejoy (ed.), *Africans in Bondage: Studies in slavery and the slave trade* (Madison, University of Wisconsin Press, 1987), a series of essays that is probably the most thorough comparison of Russian serfdom and American slavery. With the work of Curtin and his colleagues, contrast David Eltis, *Economic Growth and the Ending of the Transatlantic Slave Trade* (New York, Oxford University Press, 1987), who contends that, while suppression of the trade was morally correct, it brought economic sacrifice to Britain (by reducing colonial output and trade, and by the costs of the African Squadron). Other significant post-World War II studies include William Jordan, *White over Black: American attitudes toward the Negro 1550–1812* (Chapel Hill, NC, University of North Carolina Press for IEAHC, 1968); David B. Davis, *The Problem of Slavery in Western Culture* (Ithaca, NY, Cornell University Press, 1966), and *The Problem of Slavery in the Age of Revolution 1770–1823* (Ithaca, NY, Cornell University Press, 1975); A. E. Smith, *Colonists in Bondage: White Servitude and Convict Labor in America, 1607–1776* (Chapel Hill, NC, University of North Carolina Press, 1947); and – for the earlier period – Duncan MacLeod's *Slavery, Race and the American Revolution* (Cambridge, Cambridge University Press, 1974); John C. Miller, *The Wolf by the Ears: Thomas Jefferson and Slavery* (New York, Free Press, 1977); Edmund S. Morgan, *American Slavery, American Freedom* (New York, Norton, 1975); C. Duncan Rice, *The Rise and Fall of Black Slavery* (New York, Macmillan, 1975), which does not confine itself to the US, and I. Berlin and G. Hoffman (eds), *Slavery and Freedom in the Age of the American Revolution* (Charlottesville, University of Virginia Press, 1983). But that there were many "Souths" is proved again in John Hebron Moore's *The Emergence of the Cotton Kingdom in the old Southwest: Mississippi 1770–1860* (Baton Rouge, Louisiana State University Press, 1988): the extent of crop diversification and of steam-powered cotton gins, grist mills, cotton presses, and saw mills, and the number of skilled slaves, are all evidence of progress – and profit; the majority of those who profited were farmers, graziers, and lumber workers. Peter H. Woods's article. "I did the best I could for my day," *William & Mary Quarterly*, 25.2 (Apr. 1978), is an excellent guide to the post-1960 revision of black history, and to its bibliography. Of matching quality as a bibliographic survey is the essay by Peter Kolchin in William J. Cooper, Michael F. Holt, and John McCardell (eds) *A Master's Due: Essays in honor of David Herbert Donald* (London, Louisiana State University Press, 1985).

For comparisons with other similar societies, see Robin W. Winks (ed.), *Slavery: A comparative perspective* (New York, New York University Press, 1972); Laura Foner and Eugene D. Genovese (eds), *Slavery in the New World: A reader of comparative history* (Prentice-Hall, Englewood Cliffs, NJ, 1969); and Carl N. Degler, *Neither Black Nor White: Slavery and race relations in Brazil and the United States* (New York, Macmillan, 1971). In Latin America, because of the influence of Roman law and of the Catholic church, slavery was less severe than in the US; the physical conditions "enjoyed" by slaves were, it seems, superior in the US, but manumission in the US was more difficult than anywhere else in the world. In comparison with the widespread Muslim Negro revolts that marked Brazil, especially the Bahia province, in the US only Nat Turner's rising was significant, and that became simple butchery. Probably the most generally accepted view today is that of Kenneth Stampp, that the study of slavery in the US is a study of a harsh but profitable institution. Stampp, rejecting Phillips' paternalism, saw blacks as "only white men with black skins, nothing more, nothing less" (an overstatement that bred its own controversy.) The most recent revisionists see the work of Elkins, Stampp and D. B. Davis as still white-oriented.

On abolition, Dwight L. Dumond's *Antislavery: The crusade for freedom in America* (Ann Arbor, University of Michigan Press, 1961) sees the Civil War in sharply moral terms. For him it was not an accidental confrontation arising from a series of blunders and political failures, but a struggle for human freedom necessitated by the absolute refusal of the slaveholding elite to fulfill the moral imperatives required of them in a society both Christian and free. He sees Garrison as flamboyant, irresponsible and anarchistic – in contrast with Weld and Birney, whom he sees as statesmen. Despite this, they were mobbed, their writings taken from mails and burned, rewards were posted in southern newspapers for their kidnapping "dead or alive" – and newspaper editor Elijah Lovejoy, upholding freedom of the press, was murdered in Illinois. See also Dumond, *A Bibliography of Antislavery in America* (Ann Arbor, University of Michigan Press, 1961), and Merton L. Dillon, "The abolitionists: a decade of historiography 1959–1969," *Journal of Southern History*, 35 (Nov. 1969), pp. 500–22. James Brewer Stewart's biography of *Wendell Phillips: Liberty's hero* (Baton Rouge, Louisiana State University Press, 1986) is a remarkable picture of a Bostonian patrician turned abolitionist – largely, it seems, converted by his marriage – and of his skill as probably the greatest orator of his day. Compare the earlier study of him: Irving Bartlett, *Wendell Phillips: Brahmin Radical* (Boston, Beacon Press, 1961). See also James Brewer Stewart, *Holy Warriors: the abolitionists and American slavery* (1976); Ronald G. Walters, *The Anti-Slavery Appeal: Abolitionism after 1830* (Baltimore, Johns Hopkins University Press, 1976); Jane H. Pease and William H. Pease, *They Who Would be Free: Blacks search for freedom 1830–1861* (New York, Atheneum Publications, 1974), and their documentary collection *The Antislavery Argument*. As counterpoint, Eugene H. Berwanger, *The Frontier against Slavery* (Urbana, University of Illinois Press, 1967), stresses the less liberal anti-expansionism of the West. Compare also Arnold Whitridge, *No Compromise!* (New York, Farrar, Straus, 1960), and "Fanaticism North and South," *Virginia Quarterly Review*, 38 (Summer 1962), pp. 494–509. There are a number of good biographies of abolitionists: John L. Thomas, *The Liberator: William Lloyd Garrison* (Boston, Little, Brown, 1963); Benjamin P. Thomas, *Theodore Weld: Crusader for freedom* (New Brunswick, NJ, Rutgers University Press, 1950); and Betty Fladeland, *James Gillespie Birney: Slaveholder to abolitionist* (Ithaca, NY, Cornell University Press, 1955). See also Larry Gara, *The Liberty Line: The legend of the Underground Railroad* (Lexington, KY, University of Kentucky Press, 1961). For the Anglo-American aspects of abolitionism, see R. J. M. Blackett, *Beating Against the Barriers: Biographical essays in nineteenth-century Afro-American history* (Baton Rouge, Louisiana State University Press, 1986), and Anthony J. Barker, *Captain Charles Stuart, Anglo-American Abolitionist* (Baton Rouge, Louisiana State University Press, 1986).

In a work entitled *And the War Came: The North and the secession crisis, 1860–1861* (Baton Rouge, Louisiana State University Press, 1950), Stampp feels that the war resulted from causes which were basically too deep and too fundamental to lend themselves easily to compromise. The attempted settlements were therefore, he holds, essentially superficial in character; there was no real basis for conciliation as long as the South continued to support and defend the institution of slavery, or as long as the North continued to use its preponderant political power to advance its own interests at the expense of the South. For a study in "cliometrics," claiming to resolve arguments by citing sometimes questionable statistics, see R. W. Fogel and Stanley L. Engerman, *Time on the Cross*, vol. I, *The Economics of American Negro Slavery* (Boston, Little, Brown, 1974) with its methodological supplement. They contend that slavery was efficient and profitable – more indeed than free Northern family farming – and that the slave family was stable and protected by planters. No student should omit a basic older work that throws a new light on slavery and on many other things, and which also sees slavery as profitable: Lewis H. Gray, *History of Agriculture in the Southern United States to 1860*, 2 vols (Washington, Carnegie Institution, 1933); and compare also Alfred H. Conrad and John R. Meyer, *The Economics of Slavery and Other Studies in Econometric History* (Chicago, Aldine, 1964), and their preliminary article in the *Journal of Political Economy*, 66 (1958), pp. 95–130. The unconventional Marxist Eugene Genovese, in his first book, *The Political Economy of Slavery* (New York, Pantheon, 1965), portrayed planters as a paternalistic and precapitalist elite. In his *The world the Slaveholders Made* (New York, Pantheon, 1974), he argued that slaves accepted paternalism, but that to the idea of reciprocal duties they added their own "doctrine of reciprocal rights." The slaves, he argued, carved out for themselves "a breathing space" within a paternalistic system, and in that breathing space they created an autonomous culture, which enabled them not only to survive the experience of enslavement, but to survive it with dignity. Theirs was a twilight world, permanently strung between resignation and rebellion. His is a picture of a warm, affectionate, and complex slave community. He also reinterprets the role played by such misunderstood groups as house servants and black drivers, showing, for example, how the latter often acted not simply as agents of accommodation, but as channels through whom the slaves could express grievances to their masters and exert pressure on overseers. Nor does he believe that the slaves completely relinquished their African religious heritage, and accepted a religion transmitted from their masters. Belief in conjuring, voodoo, and witchcraft existed side by side with Christianity, and, as their songs and hymns testify, the slaves used Christianity to express their own longing for collective deliverance. Like slave culture in general, black religion was neither African nor American: it was truly African-American. When the slave Andy Marion, whose master was a Presbyterian minister, died and left the slave a house and land, Marion exclaimed: "Now dat's what I calls religion." In an essay, "Marxian interpretations of the Slave South," in Barton J. Bernstein (ed.), *Towards a New Past: Dissenting essays in American history* (New York, Pantheon, 1968), p. 117, the North is seen as bourgeois and the South as pre-bourgeois. For an assessment of Genovese's writing, see R. H. King, "Marxism and the Slave South," *American Quarterly*, 29 (1977), pp. 117–31. For a reinforcement of Genovese, see again John Blassingame, *The Slave Community*; Lawrence Levine, *Black Culture and Black Consciousness* (New York, Oxford University Press, 1977); and Leslie H. Owens, *"This Troublesome property": Slave life and culture in the Old South* (New York, Oxford University Press, 1976).

As a survey and summary of the treatment of the ante-bellum South by these various "schools" of historians, see Arthur S. Link and Rembert W. Patrick (eds), *Writing Southern History; Essays in honor of Fletcher M. Green* (Baton Rouge, Louisiana State University Press, 1967), and Peter Parish, *Slavery, History and Historians* (New York, Harper and Row, 1989).

Some influential contemporary commentaries defending and evoking the Old South have now been reprinted: Eric L. McKitrick (ed.) *Slavery Defended: The views of the Old South* (Englewood Cliffs, NJ, Prentice-Hall, 1963), is a collection drawn from the writings of John C. Calhoun, J. D. B. De Bow, George Fitzhugh, Thomas R. Dew, and Edmund Ruffin, including William Grayson's poem "The Hireling and the Slave" and – not least – George Frederick Holmes's scathing review of *Uncle Tom's Cabin*; see too C. Vann Woodward (ed.), George Fitzhugh, *Cannibals Kill! or Slaves Without Masters* (New Haven, Harvard University Press paperback, 4th printing, 1973). For a critical assessment of the pro-slavery arguments, see Eugene Genovese, *"Slavery Ordained of God": The Southern slaveholders' view of biblical history and modern history* (Gettysburg, Gettysburg College, PA, 1985). For an excellent analysis of the evolution of the South's intellectual blockade against "progress," see the study by the North Carolinian Larry E. Tise, *Proslavery: A history of the defense of slavery in America* (Athens, GA, and London, University of Georgia Press, 1987), which in essence replaces the older study of the theme, William S. Jenkins, *Pro-slavery Thought in the Old South* (Chapel Hill, University of North Carolina Press, 1935). Tise examines no fewer than 275 pro-slave writers (overwhelmingly Northern clergymen), and the arguments they used, in a criticism of abolitionism as destructive of the *status quo*.

For sources, see: Willie Lee Rose (ed.) *A Documentary History of Slavery in North America* (New York, Oxford University Press, 1976), and her *Slavery and Freedom*, ed. W. W. Freehling (New York, Oxford University Press, 1982); John W. Blassingame (ed.), *Slave Testimony* (Baton Rouge, Louisiana State University Press, 1977); and Michael Mullin's more stimulating *American Negro Slavery: A documentary history* (Columbia, University of South Carolina Press, 1976). *Slave Narratives*, a folk history of slavery in the United States, was prepared by the Federal Writers Project of the Works Progress Administration between 1936 and 1938, and published in 17 vols by the Library of Congress (Washington DC, 1941); see also George Rawlins, *The American Slave: A composite autobiography*, Series 1, vol. I (Westport, Conn., Greenwood Press, 1972) and Supplement, Series 2 (Westport, Conn., Greenwood Press, 1979).

For the slave trade, see E. Donnan (ed.) *Documents Illustrative of the History of the Slave Trade to America*, 4 vols (Washington, Carnegie Institution of Washington 1930–5). For an admirable single-volume anthology, marshaling the arguments pro and con, see Allen Weinstein and Frank O. Gatell (eds), *American Negro Slavery: A modern reader* (New York, Oxford University Press, 1979); Kenneth M. Stampp (ed.), *The Causes of the Civil War* (Englewood Cliffs, NJ, Prentice-Hall, 1965), which includes many of the more important contemporary views as well as more recent assessments; or, even more briefly, Edwin Rozwenc (ed.), *Slavery as a Cause of the Civil War* (Boston, D. C. Heath, 1949). And for an excellent bibliography in paperback, see David Donald, *The Nation in Crisis 1861–67* (New York, Goldentree Bibliographies, 1969).

10 THE WAR BETWEEN THE STATES

Perhaps no episode in American history suffers more from "presentism" and fashion than the treatment of the Civil War – except slavery itself. Professor James M. McPherson of Princeton dedicated his study of the abolitionists' attempt to achieve equality for the Negro after the Civil War (*The Struggle for Equality: Abolitionists and the Negro in the Civil War and Reconstruction* (Princeton, NJ, Princeton University Press, 1964) "to all those who are working to achieve the abolitionist goal of equal rights for all men." One hundred and thirty years after Appomattox the memories of the Civil War and Emancipation may – only just – be fading, but the issues they raised are still current history in the American Supreme Court, and are living issues for many whites, for all African-Americans, and for the politics of the Third World. It has been so in the five generations since 1851. Five (or more?) distinct patterns of interpretation can be traced.

After the end of the War the conflict was seen either as a rebellion against the sacred principle of majority rule, and even against morality (to the North, the "War of the Rebellion"), or as a war between sovereign states, and thus as a patriotic war of self-defense; the "War Between the States" is still its usual title in the South.

As the emotional heat engendered by War and Reconstruction slowly waned, both sections moved toward a new interpretation. Toward the end of the century, in a period of growing national consciousness, a new group of historians – James Ford Rhodes, Edward Channing, John Bach McMaster, Woodrow Wilson, and Frederick Jackson Turner – saw in the Civil War a tragic interlude in the development of the nation, the inevitable result of a controversy between two sections for the control of the West, and hence of the national government. The result, the preservation of the Union, and the forging not of a federal state but of a nation, they considered a positive good. Southerners as well as Northerners were seen as honorable, if sometimes misguided, men. The balanced perspective was in part the product of the passing of the years, but also of the new professionalism – mainly German-inspired – of university graduate schools in the 1880s and afterwards; men as distinct in backgrounds and interests as Woodrow Wilson and Frederick Jackson Turner were once colleagues at The Johns Hopkins University. By 1914 this nationalist interpretation had practically replaced older moralistic explanations; one could be a Unionist, like Rhodes, or sympathetic with the South, like W. E. Dodd, without impugning treason to one side, aggression to the other, or guilt to either.

The rise of the "new history" after World War I, however, saw a new view. To James Harvey Robinson, Charles A. Beard, and their colleagues, reform was automatically good, and conservatism "a hopeless and wicked anachronism" (James Harvey Robinson, *The New History* (New York,

Macmillan, 1912), p. 265); history must serve as handmaid to reform. To Beard, unlike the Marxist historians, the Civil War was the Second American Revolution: the industrial Northeast defeated the agrarian South and imposed on it and on the unsuspecting West a settlement that ensured the triumph of industrial capitalism. Both slavery and military conflict mattered less than the economic rivalry of North and South. The defeat of the South Beard saw as a defeat for "the people."

The appearance in the South of new problems after World War I, such as tenancy, controversy over the place of the Negro in Southern society, industrialization but low wage-rates, the designation of the South by President Franklin Roosevelt as the "nation's number one economic problem," and the impact of modern scientific and philosophical ideas upon the Southern mind, led to an interruption in the process of reconciliation. Southern historians now began to re-examine "the relationship between the South and the nation," and therefore to re-examine the entire sectional controversy. These historians, led by Charles W. Ramsdell of Texas, U. B. Phillips of Georgia, and Frank L. Owsley, who was born in Alabama, charged that the War had been unnecessary and not worth its cost. It came, they said, from Northern determination to crush the South and drive it from the Union; it came not from a moral crusade but from what Owsley calls the *North's* "egocentric sectionalism." To Ramsdell, the War was caused by the intensity of Northern abolitionism, and by Lincoln's maneuvers to push South Carolina into firing the first shot; Lincoln alone could have averted war. Moreover, Ramsdell argued that the natural limits of slavery had already been reached before 1860; there was no longer justification for sectional controversy over its extension. If the artificial issue of slavery in the territories had not been made a political football, then war could have been avoided. Then why was it not? Ambitious politicians wanted to exploit the issue, average citizens were not adequately informed (for example, about the impracticality of the further extension of slavery), and emotionalism made settlement by compromise difficult.

Owsley and most Southern historians writing pre-1939 were brought up in a section that recalled that it had not only experienced war, but had also endured a decade of postwar occupation by an occupying army that liberated and exploited the Negro. If objectivity was possible, coolness was more difficult. They accepted that with Lincoln's election, conflict was inevitable – see Owsley, "Fundamental cause of the Civil War: egocentric sectionalism," *Journal of Southern History*, 7 (Feb. 1941), pp. 3–19. Benjamin B. Kendrick, Albert B. Moore, and E. M. Coulter joined this attempted "vindication of the South," in part because of a renewed sense of sectional affront and a psychology of self-defense, and, not least, from the influence of Vanderbilt University and its "New Agrarians." The last was marked notably by the publication in 1930 of a manifesto, *I'll Take My Stand* (New York, Harper, 1930), by "Twelve Southerners", among them Robert Penn Warren, Allen Tate, Donald Davidson, and Owsley himself. It was here that he published his essay, "The Irrepressible Conflict," He put the blame firmly on the North, which

defeated the South in war, crushed and humiliated it in peace, and waged against it a war of intellectual and spiritual conquest. In this conquest the North fixed upon the South the stigma of war guilt, of treason, and thereby shook the faith of its people in their way of living and in their philosophy of life. (p. 66)

Another school, the revisionists, reacted in a different way against the nationalist interpretation. Newspaper editors such as George Fort Milton — notably in his biography of Stephen Douglas — Douglas S. Freeman, Gilbert H. Barnes (*The Antislavery Impulse, 1830–1844*, New York, Appleton-Century, 1933), and others presented views of the War which were sharply at variance with earlier interpretations. The War was the product of the emotions born of agitation. Even more important, however, were bitter criticisms of the War that were the result of the hatred which their authors felt for the experience of war itself: in 1917–18 disillusion with its consequences, and irritation and self-analysis in the light of the debate over neutrality legislation in the 1930s. Avery O. Craven, in *The Repressible Conflict 1830–61* (Baton Rouge, Louisiana State University Press, 1939), *The Coming of the Civil War* (New York, Scribner's, 1942), *The Growth of Southern Nationalism, 1848–61* (Baton Rouge, Louisiana State University Press, 1953), and *Civil War in the Making, 1815–1860* (Baton Rouge, Louisiana State University Press, 1959), James G. Randall, and Roy F. Nichols, *The Disruption of American Democracy* (New York, Macmillan, 1948), asserted that the Civil War was not inevitable, that it was caused by the machinations of politicians, by "over-zealous editors" and "pious cranks," and by the emotional excesses and "emotional charges" of fanatics on both sides, without which it could have been avoided. The abolitionists, an "avenging force of puritanism in politics," were to blame. They denied that the War was a moral crusade against slavery, and condemned war as a political instrument. It was a "Repressible Conflict." Concerned with the Question of "cause" and "inevitability," they stressed what Nichols called "hyperemotionalism," and the importance of the Territorial Question, rather than of slavery. A "blundering generation" had transformed an "irrepressible conflict" into a "needless war."

The rise of totalitarianism led to a revision of the revisionists. According to the new version, some struggles do involve moral and ethical principles of such value that war cannot be avoided. Sentimental belief in progress, and in the capacity of rational man to settle problems by patient deliberation, slowly gave way to a gloomier and more "realistic" view; Arthur M. Schlesinger, Jr, Bernard De Voto, Oscar Handlin, and others of this school held that the Civil War was fought over a moral issue and an ideological concept: "The cancer of slavery had to be excised." Moreover, it was impossible in the 1940s and 1950s not to see 1861 in terms of World War II. Further, none of these historians were Southerners, and it was easier for them to see the question in "moral" and theoretical terms, rather than as a problem for solving – or at least for living with. This interpretation has been described as "one more sign of the reappearance in the twentieth century of a South versus non-South sectionalism in the United States." The words are those of Thomas J. Pressly, *Americans Interpret their Civil War* (Princeton, NJ, Princeton University Press, 1954, pp. 307, 308), whose survey of these varied "schools" was an outgrowth of a Harvard doctoral thesis by a scholar born in Tennessee. Pressly sees the causes of this latest interpretation as resting in the Supreme Court decision of 1954, ending segregation in schools, in Martin Luther King's bussing boycotts in Alabama, and in the campaigns of the 1960s for black civil rights. These all revived the questions of "guilt," and of a minority's role as against a majority. The steady advance of white and of black scholarship has also produced its own revisionist histories. These are concerned as much with the economic and social as with the moral aspects of slavery – with divisions inside the "solid South," tensions between the leaders, and with the battles themselves, and those who fought in them. These trends are analyzed and summarized in the five central chapters of Arthur S. Link and Rembert W. Patrick (eds), *Writing Southern History: Essays in historiography in honor of Fletcher M. Green* (Baton Rouge, Louisiana State University Press, 1967). James G. Randall and David Donald have written what is still the standard comprehensive account of *The Civil War and Reconstruction* (Boston, D. C. Heath, rev. edn, 1969). Divergent interpretations of the North's reaction to secession are presented in David M. Potter, *Lincoln and his Party in the Secession Crisis* (New York, Harper, 1950), and Kenneth M. Stampp, *And the War Came: The North and the Secession Crisis 1860–1861* (Baton Rouge, Louisiana State University Press, 1950). Whatever his views on the slavery question, "the price of war," he says, "was too high." The war ended with "the rich richer, and the slaves only half free."

It is now more than 50 years since Jay Monaghan produced his *Lincoln Bibliography* (Springfield, IL, Illinois State Historical Library, 1943–5), a book of 1,079 pages which merely listed the books and articles published on Lincoln up to that date; the best Lincoln scholarship – that of James G. Randall, David Donald, David Potter, and Benjamin Thomas – still lay ahead. Randall's magisterial *Lincoln the President*, 4 vols (New York, Dodd-Mead, 1945–55), was completed by Richard N. Current after the master's death. In it the President appears as dedicated and selfless, a "strange quaint great man," who showed a masterly touch in human relations – and in holding together his own Cabinet and generals. With this new depth of probing, some Lincoln legends disappear: how he grieved over the death of his first and only love, Ann Rutledge, how he once jilted the socially ambitious, vain, and spoilt Mary Todd at the church door, and how she later married him for spite and made their married life into a constant torment. Yarns like these, consisting of varying mixtures of half truth and fiction, were spread abroad after Lincoln's death by his former law partner, William Herndon, and were once widely believed. But modern scholars like Randall and David Donald have now thoroughly exposed Herndon as an amateur psychoanalyst and mythmaker, who often twisted the truth in order to provide spicy entertainment for his readers and auditors, and to vent a personal spite against Mary Lincoln. Ruth Painter Randall, drawing upon the work of her husband and others as well as her own research, has published *Mary Lincoln: Biography of a marriage* (Boston, Little, Brown, 1953), which convincingly sums up the evidence that the Lincolns were a loving and happily married couple. She minimizes the tortured state of mind – and the ultimate insanity – of Mrs Lincoln. See also as comparison David Donald, a former student of Randall's, in a collection of his essays entitled *Lincoln Reconsidered* (New York, Vintage, 1947). Perhaps the most interesting of his interpretations is the argument that the radicals in the Republican party were not a consistent and cohesive faction. Probably the best single volume on Lincoln is *Abraham Lincoln: A biography*, by Benjamin P. Thomas (New York, Knopf, 1952). Another 1-volume biography of merit – despite its folksiness – is Carl Sandburg's *Abraham Lincoln: The prairie years and the war years*, a condensation of his multi-volume study (New York, Harcourt Brace, 1954). Consult also Don E. Fehrenbacher, *The Changing Image of Lincoln in American Historiography* (New York, Oxford University Press, 1968); Benjamin P. Thomas and Harold M. Hyman, *Stanton: The life and times of Lincoln's secretary of war* (New York, Knopf, 1962); Erwin Stanley Bradley, *Simon Cameron, Lincoln's Secretary of War* (Philadelphia, University of Pennsylvania Press, 1966); Glyndon G. Van Deusen, *William Henry Seward* (New York, Oxford University Press, 1967); H. K. Beale (ed.) *Diary of Gideon Welles*, 3 vols (New York, Norton, 1960); and Norman Graebner (ed.), *Politics and the Crisis of 1860* (Urbana, University of Illinois Press, 1961). Some of the "newest" military-political studies include Richard E. Beringer, "A profile of the members of the Confederate Congress", *Journal of Southern History*, 33 (1967), pp. 518–41; and the same author with Thomas B. Alexander, *The Anatomy of the Confederate Congress 1861–1865* (Nashville, Vanderbilt University Press, 1972); see too his more recent volume, R. E. Beringer et al., *Why the South Lost the Civil War* (Athens, University of Georgia Press, 1986).

For the generals, Douglas Southall Freeman's 4-volume life of *Robert E. Lee* (New York, Scribner's, 1934) is outstanding (there is a 1-volume condensation by Richard Harwell, New York, Scribner's, 1961). See also his 3-volume study, *Lee's Lieutenants* (New York, Scribner's, 1942–4). On the Northern side of the lines is a matching and massive, but uncompleted, monument: Kenneth P. Williams, army officer and mathematician turned historian, *Lincoln Finds A General*, 5 vols (New York, Macmillan, 1949–56). From a different viewpoint, Bruce Catton has written the history of the Army of the Potomac in a series of separate books (all Garden City, NY, Doubleday): *Mr Lincoln's Army (1951),*

Glory Road: The bloody route from Fredericksburg to Gettysburg (1952), and the Pulitzer Prize-winning *A Stillness at Appomattox* (1953). This is descriptive rather than critical military history, but Catton's facts are usually accurate, his style forceful and artistic, his ability to convey the sight, sound, and excitement of battle unexcelled. There are two useful collective biographies by Ezra J. Warner: *Generals in Gray: Lives of the Confederate commanders* (Baton Rouge, Louisiana State University Press, 1959), and *Generals in Blue: Lives of the Union commanders* (Baton Rouge, Louisiana State University Press, 1964). There are excellent military studies by T. Harry Williams, especially *Lincoln and his Generals* (New York, Grosset and Dunlop, 1952). There are arresting tactical-psychological interpretations: Grady McWhiney and Perry Jamieson, *Attack and Die: Civil War military tactics and the Southern heritage* (Tuscaloosa, University of Alabama Press, 1982); Herman Hattaway and Archer Jones, *How the North Won* (Urbana, University of Illinois Press, 1983); and Beringer et al., *Why the South Lost the Civil War*. Ulysses Grant's own *Personal Memoirs* (1885–6) has been described by Edmund Wilson as "Nothing less than one of the great American books;" it was written in order to repay debts and when he was dying of cancer. In his telling, the Civil War had two climaxes: Vicksburg, and Lee's surrender at Appomattox. See also William S. McFeely, *Grant, a Biography* (New York, Norton, 1981).

The best – and the kindest – picture of Jefferson Davis is in Rembert W. Patrick, *Jefferson Davis and his Cabinet* (Baton Rouge, Louisiana State University Press, 1944). Hudson Strode's 3-volume biography, *Jefferson Davis* (New York, Harcourt, 1955–64), is as adulatory as it is lavish, portraying him as "the warmest of men" with a "deep humanity." Allan Nevins takes a totally different view of one who was "not a nation-builder." Steven Woodworth offers an admirably objective analysis of Davis's role as commander-in-chief in *Jefferson Davis and his Generals* (Lawrence, University of Kansas Press, 1989). A less kind – and more typical – portrait of Davis as a quarrelsome, meddlesome, and domineering man, is in the Richmond novelist Clifford Dowdey's *Experiment in Rebellion* (Garden City, NY, Doubleday, 1946), his other studies of *Lee* (Boston, Little, Brown, 1965) and of *The Land They Fought For* ((Garden City, NY, Doubleday, 1955) give a kinder picture of a leader and his people – "a people fighting a nation" – defending their agrarian homeland against a modern invading industrial state.

There is another admirable and multi-volume balanced survey of the War, (8 vols, by the time of his death in 1971), in Allan Nevins, *Ordeal of the Union* (New York, Scribner's, 1947–61). Nevins, in what is primarily a political account, sees the South as the enemy of "progress;" but he stresses the part played by "irrational emotion," not least as generated by Kansas-Nebraska's civil war and its abettors outside, and by the inadequacy of the three Presidents who preceded Lincoln. For him, as for Lincoln, slavery could not be compromised away; the institution of slavery was "the greatest wrong, the greatest misery, the greatest curse to white and black alike that America has ever known." A good survey of the South in wartime is Clement Eaton *A History of the Southern Confederacy* (New York, Macmillan, 1954, repr. Collier, 1961), a similarly panoramic view. He ascribes the defeat of the Confederacy not only to steadily increasing Northern strength, the blockade, the shortages, and the transport break-downs, but to the South's mistakes – the failure fully to mobilize its economic resources, its faulty taxation policies, the continuing states' rights attitudes of its own member states, and the weakening morale on the home front. Similarly, to offset the recent emphasis on military history, E. Merton Coulter's *The Confederate States of America 1861–1865* (Baton Rouge, Louisiana State University Press, 1950), vol. III in the *History of the South*, ed. W. H. Stephenson and E. M. Coulter, limits the account of the battles to one chapter, and surveys the social life lived in the South under stress. For the other ranks, the enlisted men, see Bill Wiley, *The Life of Johnny Reb* (Indianapolis, Bobbs-Merrill, 1943) and *The Life of Billy Yank* (Indianapolis, Bobbs-Merrill, 1952). For Chancellorsville, the classic Civil War novel is Stephen Crane's *The Red Badge of Courage* (1895). See also Frank Owsley, *King Cotton Diplomacy* (Chicago, University of Chicago Press, rev. edn, 1958), for the Confederate errors of judgment in withholding cotton from Britain and France. Gerald Linderman, *Embattled Courage: The experience of combat in the American Civil War* (New York, Free Press, 1987) is fresh and moving. Compare also Dudley Taylor Cornish, *The Sable Arm: Negro troops in the Union Army* (London, Longman's, 1956); and Benjamin Quarles, *The Negro in the Civil War* (Boston, Little, Brown, 1952), which challenges the view of the slaves' loyalty to their masters. There are splendid (and weighty) 1-volume surveys and bibliographies, in James M. McPherson, *Battle Cry of Freedom: The Civil War Era* (Oxford, Oxford University Press, 1987), and in Peter J. Parish, *The American Civil War* (London, Eyre Methuen, 1975); and add for vividness the invaluable "I was there" approach of over-90-year-old Henry Steele Commager (ed.), *The Blue and Gray: The story of the Civil War as told by participants*, 2 vols, (Indianapolis, Bobbs-Merrill, 1950; repr. as 1 vol., 1961, Fairfax Press, Va). Edmund Wilson, *Patriotic Gore: Studies in the literature of the American Civil War* (New York, Oxford University Press, 1962), is fascinating, human, and crankily pro-Southern. Bern Anderson, *By Sea and by River: The naval history of the Civil War* (New York, Knopf, 1962), is a competent survey of the crippling impact of the blockade and the South's reply. An invaluable companion reference volume on people and places – as with his matching book on the War of Independence – is Colonel Mark M. Boatner III, *The Civil War Dictionary* (London, Cassell, 1973). For the agony of Reconstruction, see Rembert Wallace Patrick, *The Reconstruction of the Nation* (New York, Oxford University Press, 1967); Avery Craven, *Reconstruction; The ending of the Civil War* (New York, Holt, 1969); Kenneth Stampp and Leon F. Litwack (eds), *Reconstruction: An anthology* of revisionist writings (Baton Rouge, Louisiana State University Press, 1969); and C. Vann Woodward, *The Burden of Southern History* (Baton Rouge, Louisiana State University Press, 1960 and later edns). There is an admirable Civil War bibliography in paperback compiled by David Donald, *The Nation in Crisis 1861–1877* (New York, Appleton-Century-Crofts, Goldentree Bibliographies, 1969). Compare also Joel H. Silbey, "The Civil War synthesis in American political history," *Civil War History*, 10 (1964), pp. 130–140; and Thomas B. Alexander, "The Civil War as institutional fulfillment," *Journal of Southern History*, 47 (1981), pp. 3–32; cf. *idem*, *Sectional Stress and Party Strength: A study of roll-call voting patterns in the US House of Representatives 1836–1860* (Nashville, Vanderbilt University Press, 1967); Joel H. Silbey, *The Shrine of Party: Congressional voting behavior, 1841–1852* (Pittsburgh, University of Pittsburgh Press, 1967); William E. Gienapp, *The Origins of the Republican Party 1852–1856* (New York, Oxford University Press, 1957), and John Niven, *The Coming of the Civil War 1837–1861*, ed. John H. Franklin and A. S. Eisenstadt, with an admirable bibliographical essay (Arlington Heights, Ill., Harlan Davidson, 1990).

Index

Index by Meg Davies